RELIGIOUS PROPAGANDA AND MISSIONARY COMPETITION IN THE NEW TESTAMENT WORLD

SUPPLEMENTS TO
NOVUM TESTAMENTUM

VOLUME LXXIV

Professor Dieter Georgi

RELIGIOUS PROPAGANDA AND MISSIONARY COMPETITION IN THE NEW TESTAMENT WORLD

Essays Honoring Dieter Georgi

EDITED BY

LUKAS BORMANN
KELLY DEL TREDICI
ANGELA STANDHARTINGER

E.J. BRILL
LEIDEN · NEW YORK · KÖLN
1994

The paper in this book meets the guidelines for permanence and durability of the Committee on Production Guidelines for Book Longevity of the Council on Library Resources.

Library of Congress Cataloging-in-Publication Data

Religious propaganda and missionary competition in the New Testament world : essays honoring Dieter Georgi / edited by Lukas Bormann, Kelly Del Tredici, Angela Standhartinger.
p. cm. — (Supplements to Novum Testamentum, ISSN 0167-9732 ; v. 74)
Includes bibliographical references.
ISBN 9004100490
1. Evangelistic work—History—Early church, ca. 30-600. 2. Bible. N.T.—Criticism, interpretation, etc. 3. Bible. N.T.–History of contemporary events. I. Georgi, Dieter. II. Bormann, Lukas. III. Del Tredici, Kelly. IV. Standhartinger, Angela. V. Series.
BR195.E9R45 1994
270.1—dc20 94-9716
CIP

Die Deutsche Bibliothek - CIP-Einheitsaufnahme

Religious propaganda and missionary competition in the New Testament world : essays honoring Dieter Georgi / ed. by Lukas Bormann ... – Leiden ; New York ; Köln : Brill, 1994
(Supplements to Novum Testamentum; Vol. 74)
ISBN 90-04-10049-0
NE: Bormann, Lukas [Hrsg.]; Georgi, Dieter; Festschrift; Novum testamentum / Supplements

ISSN 0167-9732
ISBN 90 04 10049 0

PRINTED IN THE NETHERLANDS

Quid ergo Athenis et Hierosolymis?

CONTENTS

Gospels and Acts

Paul

Early Christian Writings

ACKNOWLEDGEMENTS

Each of the contributors to this volume was invited to taken up the challenge issued in its motto by the Christian apologist and jurist Tertullian: 'What has Athens to do with Jerusalem, what the Academy with the Church, what Christians with Heretics?' (*De Praescriptione Haereticorum* 7.9). His own response entailed a decisive repudiation of any common ground, and the resort to polemics, which at times betray a tendency toward exclusivity and a longing for unequivocal answers, was frequent in the hellenistic marketplace of religious competition. The conviction that this mindset did not always and everywhere prevail, much less correspond to the wider realities of Gentile and Jewish life during the period when the writings of the New Testament were being composed, speaks to the fairness and insight with which Dieter Georgi throughout his teaching career on two continents has explored the vigorous interchange between the hellenistic Greek and Latin-speaking worlds and Judaism. The authors present this Festgabe in gratitude to him on the occasion of his sixty-fifth birthday. May it be a source of joy as well as an incentive to continue the dialogue commenced long ago.

Since this project could not have succeeded without the sustained cooperation and encouragement of others, the editors are especially thankful for the financial support which they received from the Evangelische Kirche in Hessen und Nassau, Harvard University alumnae/i, Enid Schmuch and the members of the Theological Opportunities Program at Harvard Divinity School. To Brill Publishers and its associates, particularly Hans van der Meij, to the Fachbereich Evangelische Theologie at the Johann Wolfgang Goethe-Universität Frankfurt am Main, and to each of the authors, who by means of their written contributions gave generously of their time and ideas, we wish to express our sincere appreciation.

Frankfurt am Main
6 June 1994

Lukas Bormann
Kelly Del Tredici
Angela Standhartinger

ABBREVIATIONS

The abbreviations used in the articles written in English are those found in *Harvard Theological Review* 80 (1987) 243-60.

Abbreviations used in the articles written in German for journals, series and standard reference works are found in Siegfried Schwertner, *Theologische Realenzyklopädie*, Abkürzungsverzeichnis (Berlin/New York: 1994). Ancient sources are abbreviated according to the *Theologisches Wörterbuch zum Neuen Testament*, Abkürzungsverzeichnis (Stuttgart: 1960) or *Lexikon der Alten Welt*, Carl Andresen, H. Erbse, O. Gigon, eds. (Zürich/Stuttgart: 1965) Sp. 3439-64.

THE STUDY OF RELIGION
AND
THE RELIGION OF STUDY

THE STUDY OF RELIGION AND THE RELIGION OF STUDY

Ithamar Gruenwald (Tel Aviv University)

I

Let me introduce my paper with a thesis. It appears that scholars in the field of Religious Studies all too often are doomed to embody academic sadness. Suspected of mixing ecclesiastical interests and considerations with research, they are likely to clothe themselves in defensive robes. This easily can lead to maintaining apologetic positions. But even when this is not the case, the scholars in question may see themselves deprived of the possibility of relishing fully the intellectual stimulation, and even the natural fascination, of their subject-matter. Since by accepted Western standards universities are best off when they define themselves as secular institutions, no form of religious belief is allowed to trespass the premises of their academic ivory-towers. Arguably, when the study of religion is carried out in universities, this self-imposed intellectual restriction should not be ignored. Its absence is likely to be a serious impediment to the academic career of the scholar. My colleague and personal friend, Dieter Georgi, is a scholar whose academic career is sometimes affected by claims against his personal involvement with the various issues of his academic research. To the best of my understanding, that involvement comes from deep cultural, social, intellectual, spiritual and religious concerns. The sixty-fifth birthday of Dieter Georgi is therefore a suitable occasion to reflect upon the subject of the study of religion and the religion of study. This is particularly the case since these reflections will turn in the direction of discussing the various problems which arise from the religious engagement of scholars.

The following will be presented in the form of a philosophical essay and not in the usual form of a fully footnoted article. It is hoped that in so doing the reader will benefit from a less distracted type of reading experience. I hope this will be viewed as an advantage over against the loss of enlightening references and bibliographical data, and that my essay also will be a contribution to the ongoing discussions held in academic circles about the nature, scope, and aims of Religious Studies.

When speaking about personal beliefs and convictions as well as their place in the study of religions, it should be noted that my approach here will be marked by its epistemological nature. I would like to deal with the issues at stake in such a manner that pros and cons will be presented evenly, without prejudice or bias in favor of one view or the other. Generally speaking, when beliefs and convictions become the topic of discussion, distinctions are likely to be made between their religious configurations and all other forms thereof. For one reason or another religions used to occupy, at least in academic circles, a degraded position. It is more common to find people who are reproved for holding religious beliefs and convictions than for maintaining any other type of belief and conviction. From an epistemological point of view so-called "secular" beliefs and convictions should not be viewed as enjoying a higher status than any other category of belief and conviction. Beliefs are beliefs and convictions are convictions no matter where they are anchored and in which direction they aim. They should always be treated as liable to induce prejudice and conceptual distortions.

The separation between "state" and "church" is dogma in most academic institutions which value their name and reputation. This evidently contributes to the creation of a conceit, according to which only religious beliefs should be kept at arm's length. However, as I indicated above, other forms of convictions should not be estimated as enjoying a loftier status than those characterized as religious. God belongs to the church; secular idols are located in the market-place. What really matters, however, is not their respective locations, but the way in which they are viewed in people's minds. In other words, we are interested in basic human attitudes, not in the respective objects of those attitudes. If idols *are* worshiped in the market-place, then what matters is the fact that they *are* worshipped, not the fact that they are idols and not gods. To repeat, beliefs are beliefs and convictions are convictions, no matter where and how they are maintained and enacted. A religious person, though, would find it hard to accept this phenomenological observation with its relativizing overtones. For him or her, any kind of belief that is not basically a religious one is no belief at all. It is either superstition or redundant information.

One conclusion that can to be drawn from this line of argumentation is that neither God nor any kind of idols should be admitted into academia. If God, or idols, are allowed into academia, the risks are unavoidable: Academic decisions are likely to become dictates of gods and postulates of idols. However, it is a question of a different order when one inquires what the attitude and the academic practice should be, if Gods and idols become the object of scientific, that is, critical research? The purpose of Religious Studies is to describe, analyze, compare and systematically categorize forms of religious life, practices and beliefs. God cannot be excluded from all of that. What are the qualifications required for the study of such a subject-matter? What research methods should be applied, and what kind of systematization proposed? Naturally, one may argue that what Religious Studies can offer is at best the perceptive study of the various types of documentation relating to a certain religion, including God and God's celestial retinue. When that is undertaken on a large scale, we call it Comparative Religions. But when documentation becomes the center of research, then the study of religions is likely to be narrowed down to forms of religious expression or literature, and not to religions as such.

To put it in slightly different terms, if in the study of philosophy, for instance, we practice the art of philosophizing, then by analogy, in the study of religions we should aim, among other things, at training students to "religionize," that is, to practice some kind of religious life. If the analogy is made with biology instead of philosophy, then a complication arises there too, for the biologist applies certain tools and research methods *to* the object of his or her research. Only seldom is biology a theoretical science. Now, when we turn to the study of religions, can we carry out our research on the material at hand in the same manner as the biologists? Here the answer must be negative. In the study of religions scholars work mainly with documents. "Documents" here mean any kind of report produced within the framework of a given religion. That report in most cases represents a substitute for the "real thing." The "real thing," that is, religious practice and experience, is not encountered in the document itself. Yet another area of research may be taken as a point of comparison: Art Studies. In this instance one could argue that one studies art without necessarily learning to paint, act, play an instrument, or dance. If this is the case, then, we have reached an ideal point of comparison: Religious Studies, like Art Studies, teach *about* the subject-matter and not the "art" itself.

Where, then, is religion itself taught? In seminaries, Yeshivoth (Jewish institutions for the study of the Torah), and similar religious institutions. In this respect we come close to the notion of art schools where the *practice* of the specific arts is taught and learned. Religious Studies, however, instruct mainly *about* religions, not religion itself. This certainly is a conclusion that many an academic institution which maintains a faculty of Religious Studies would accept as a matter of self-evident and approved policy and practice. However, as we shall see, it is a position that has its flaws as well, particularly when and where academic excellence is the subject of the discourse.

II

The real problem, then, which the student of Religious Studies has to face is: How, and by whom can God, and the language referring to God, be studied? One who considers oneself to be close to that God, or who even shares the spiritual presuppositions that give access to God and to everything that derives from that God, may be well-suited for the task. Of course, one should not forget one's basic scholarly obligations: to study the subject-matter with as objective and as unbiased an orientation as possible. The issue becomes a more complicated one when the student does not share those presuppositions. Access to the subject-matter is indirect and, despite all goodwill and the best of intentions, one is very likely to lack the necessary means of getting at the inner meaning of the "texts" which one studies. For it should be pointed out that in the case of religious language what may appear as simple, almost everyday, parlance is actually a loaded sequence of signs, the nature of which has to be deciphered like any other code. Religious language is created within a framework, the understanding of which requires technical expertise and knowledgeable handling. What even complicates matters in this respect is the fact that, phenomenologically speaking, there is a variety of religious "languages." Verbal expression is not necessarily the only form of religious expression. Icons, symbols, cult and worship (including, for that matter, prayers and prayer gestures or postures) are all forms of religious "language". The less verbal the form of expression is, the more difficult it becomes for an outsider to decipher its contents and meaning. Theoretically speaking, insiders have better access to inside information than do outsiders. Nevertheless, insiders who do not possess the necessary tools and means of interpreting information may be as blind as any outsider in the face of an encoded communication. To be an insider in the full sense of the term does not imply merely a sense of social belonging, but also an acute sensitivity in relation to the so-called "inner-grammar" of the texts in question. By "inner-grammar" I mean the various components that make a statement what it purports to be. What I have in mind is the inner mechanism, or dynamics, that contribute to making a text into a coherent statement in the eyes of the intended, or implied audience. An intended audience is supposed to be the one that is not only the "reader" but the actual "user" of the text. That audience brings practical understanding as well technical expertise to the reading of the text. An outsider lacks all of this and in that respect may display some degree of deficiency in trying to comprehend fully the messages conveyed by the text.

It stands to reason that such comprehending experience is only partially accessible to those considering themselves to be outsiders. Let me give an example: So-called "outsiders," who visit a synagogue (or for that matter a church or a mosque), can relate lengthy stories about their experiences there. These experiences hardly reflect any kind of religious elevation; rather, what the visitors experience is an intense sense of frustration at their own ignorance and inability to participate in the service. It is indeed difficult for such persons to follow the details of any service, if not previously initiated into the technicalities of the ongoing procedures. Religious practice is a densely coded "language." In this sense it is a "text." It requires a technical "dictionary" to "read" and "understand." In most cases, then, it is previous experience that provides one with the necessary informative orientation. That experience usually is gained by active participation and persistent intellectual curiosity. But even the regular practitioner who lacks the necessary background may prove useless when asked for some kind of insider-information. In other words, outsiders who intend to study the religious practices of a particular religion delude themselves, if they assume that they can unaided equip themselves adequately for that task by simply reading or listening to reports about those practices. Reading and asking questions about the subject under investigation can carry the interested person only half-way through one's research. In fulfilling one's desire to know and understand, one always is wisely advised to seek assistance from people who are knowledgeable by virtue of their previous initiation. This can spare the unpleasant moments of misinformed speculations which appear to the insider as sheer ignorance.

In any event, the study of religion cannot be carried out by people who only have acquired a research-method and even a considerable amount of reading experience. It requires more than that. A certain kind of initiation into the technical aspects seems to be indispensable for any study of the inner core of the religious experience. This must be a self-evident conclusion held to be valid by anyone who observes the complexity of the various forms of religious experience. What I am suggesting here is not new to those who follow or even participate in debates held among scholars engaged in the study of religions. These debates have become rather intensive ones in the last twenty or thirty years. What I believe to be different now from what used to be in the past is the general atmosphere in which these debates are conducted. Formerly, much that was tantamount to apologetics accompanied the arguments brought to bear on the course such debates were taking. Even when more hostile and provocative tones were audible, the basic undercurrent was that of apologetics. This is no longer the case. It should be noticed, though, that apologetics was not the exclusive prerogative of those representing the so-called religious side. Apologetics quite often is spread evenly among all participants in the debating transactions.

What I have suggested here is not altogether new in either argument or substance. However, when I deem it necessary to come back to territories already visited before, I do so because the force of the argument has not yet succeeded in opening all the necessary research-doors. There are still people who are not fully convinced and consequently too many published studies that reflect basic misunderstandings of the subject-matter.

Such sweeping generalizations may sound rather arrogant. However, it should not be taken as an expression of intellectual conceit when I point out that many studies published in the area of Religious Studies could do much better if only the information they provide did not come or pass through secondary channels. Many of these studies deal with the world of religion as if it were a literary, philosophical, psychological or sociological issue or phenomenon. The question, then, is: To what extent can such studies rightfully claim admittance into the academic halls of Religious Studies, or do they in reality occupy a marginal status there?

Admittedly, this is a question that many colleagues would consider an illegitimate one to raise. It can be argued rightfully that such questions should not be posed by a serious scholar because they indeed can induce the impression that they advocate academic triumphalism. In order to avoid that, one may argue that everything that deals with the wide range of religious phenomena by definition belongs to the realm of Religious Studies regardless of the method applied, the point of view taken, and the area of research selected. There is more than merely formal justification for such a claim. The way is open for a completely new concept in the organization of Religious Studies. In many cases Religious Studies are a mere conglomerate of areas of study and multiple disciplines that all aim at contributing in their respective ways to the knowledge of the world of religions. In other words, Religious Studies are encouraged to become a multi- or cross-disciplinary enterprise.

But a conglomerate is not a coherent discipline. Coherency in our case is achieved by creating a new core of orientation in which religion is studied *qua* religion. There is much to say in favor of such a concept. It takes full cognizance of the multifaceted aspects of the various areas of knowledge that are the objects of academic research, but it also sees the unifying factors beyond the dissmilar interests and orientation. One of the new ways of looking at the phenomenological world comes from the realization that one discipline of studies suffices for only a rather narrow aspect of a certain phenomenon. And if the phenomena at hand are complex ones, it follows logically that they merit a kind of approach and methodology which take into consideration the collaboration of a variety of approaches. Thus, as in the past, individual research disciplines will continue to be developed for the sake of the specific material which they study. But in addition to that, several disciplines will be joined together for the sake of studying complex phenomena. Religious Studies would become one of the first areas of research in which that kind of multidisciplinary approach is applied.

Nevertheless, the question remains an open one, namely, how is the core of religious experience studied, and not merely the structure of its documentary manifestations? Here I believe my argument concerning the need to have first-hand experience with religious forms of life makes its strongest claim. It does not matter so much from what kind of religion that experience originates. What matters most is the fact that this experience is viewed as relevant, in fact indispensable, for the study of religion in general. That which makes the difference between one person and another in regard to the study of religious experience, however, is the question whether that experience is taken as a model for *enhancing* or even *creating* the same kind of experience, or whether it is taken as a comparative example for *understanding* similar kinds of experience. Naturally, the scholar of Religious Studies aims for the second objective. In short, the question as to how religion as such is to be approached in a manner that satisfies academic standards and requirements is still one that demands some kind of epistemological clarification. Needless to say, the question here relates to academic excellence and integrity and not to ecclesiastical convictions.

For those who require a reminder, I repeat here that, although God, or the various ways of conceptualizing the divine essence, cannot be excluded from the academic study of religion, God should not become part of the academic discussion. In other words, we scholars should not wait for God to nod either in assent or dissent to what we do. In this respect I advocate the need to maintain as strictly as possible the separation between "church" and "state" in academe. No ecclesiastical concerns should be allowed to interfere with our research, and no learned ecclesiastical considerations should be permitted to enter our teaching engagements.

It may be argued that scholars should avoid taking part in ecclesiastical debates or discussions altogether. At least they should be careful not to mix ecclesiastical considerations with their scholarly enterprises. What the Church or the Synagogue do with the outcome of academic research is of no direct concern to the academic scholar, although the latter should give expression to his or her concerns when the Church or the Synagogue abuse the results of academic research and manipulate it for anti-democratic purposes. And when s/he speaks up in Church or Synagogue, s/he should do so as private persons only. It is likewise in the interest of Church and Synagogue that the separation between them and the academic world be strictly maintained.

It should be noted, though, that the student of religion is in no worse position than any other scholar. For an eye is always kept on the student of microbiology, lest thoughts of misusing the outcome of his laboratory work in genetics enter his mind. Psychology can be applied so as to develop techniques of brainwashing. Economics can be manipulated against the needy and the poor ones; and, if "adequately" propelled, political science likewise can be formulated so as to justify any despotic regime. Obviously, all this can come to pass when no adequate controls are applied responsibly. What they are in each case need not be discussed here. I simply want to caution how universal the ills of scientific research can be, and to reiterate that religion is no alarming exception to the rule.

III

The systematic study of religion can take two different turns: Theology and Religious Studies. Theology I would characterize as the more creative of the two. In its own eyes theology is as systematic as any science can be. It sets its own, logical, rules of development; and given its own premisses it can display a consistent methodology. Theology, as opposed to Religious Studies, allows a view of religion from within. The paticipants in its formulation are people whose objective is to present the contents of their own religion in a manner that is conducive to faith and practice ("Liturgy"). Theological deliberations are carried out within the framework of a community of believers and primarily for their own benefit. Academic students of religion may avail themselves of the material discussed and presented in theological circles, but, as indicated already above, they should not take part in the theological discussions themselves. This evidently is a first prerequisite to be considered by any scholar who wishes to uphold on academic premises the separation between "state" and "church."

On the other hand, we find those who study religion from the outside. They bring into the discussion points of view based on notions that do not necessarily derive from and reflect the religion under discussion. These students do not endeavor to contribute to the beliefs and convictions of the people whose religion they study. The observational point of view in the study of religion is generally epitomized by critical methods of research. These methods, in turn, are backed up by comparative study and considerations. Although academics and theologians often view each other with suspicion and disrespect, the substantive divisions between them need not be as deep and extensive as is sometimes believed to be the case. I shall say more on this point later on.

What needs be said at this juncture is that in many instances the academic study of religion is marred by self-conceited presuppositions that are not far from being a "religion" or "theology" themselves. This is particularly so when secular presuppositions force their way into the arena and engage in a display of power that is not as conducive to knowledge as one would wish. In this respect, it has to be conceded that the secular approach to the study of religion is not as a matter of epistemological principle better off than any other, for that matter religious, approach. Indeed, academics often are tempted to believe that the research methods they employ can rescue them from drowning in the waters of theological conceit. Provide them with a critical research method and they will feel girded with a life-jacket that also can be used when the danger of losing critical consciousness draws near. However, matters are not all as simple as that. It should be noted that scholarly fashions or theories have a number of structural and phenomenological features in common with theological doctrines. For any steadfast conviction, whether academic or theological, is – epistemologically and sociologically speaking – as binding and unbending as any other such conviction.

Of course, the respective sources of information as well as the research methods applied make a clear and substantial difference in every respect. To risk an *ad absurdum* example, 2 and 2 make 4, whether by the decree of God or by logical mathematical reckoning. Indeed, some of us may think that there is no God who can speak to human beings, and that any form of relating to God is based on self-conceit and false premisses. In other words, according to such a preliminary assumption the study of religion is the study of the products of mental delusions. If that is the case, then the study of religion becomes the study of the pathology of the human mind. Obviously, this is a conclusion to which almost all scholars in the area of Religious Studies would be unwilling to subscribe.

But this is not the central point which I would like to make here. What I consider of utmost importance in the present context is the question whether religious engagement is of any use and academic benefit in the study of religion, or only conducive to judgmental aberrations. As in everything one does, intentions make the tones into music. And in this respect any kind of academic stubbornness can have as distorting an effect as any theological presupposition. Religious engagement, as such, can affect for good or ill the way a certain religion or religious phenomenon is studied. It can provide the scholar with the necessary means of approaching the subject-matter in a fashion that helps elucidate the phenomenon under investigation. Yet it also can distort the vision and deflect the mind from the real issues of the subject. All this sounds simple and almost commonplace, hardly requiring further comment.

However, there is still one question that was raised already above, but not adequately treated then: How can people who are not among the original audience approach, and even intellectually share, material that derives from sources and cultural presuppositions utterly alien to them? The question is underlined when those people openly declare their reluctance to participate even momentarily, and for the sake of the argument, in the intellectual or cultural experience which they make the subject of their study and research. At face value this is a typical hermeneutical question. But there is more to it than merely that. Within the framework of its basic presuppositions every religious text assumes the sharing of belief. Actually, this is the case with all texts that give expression to theological, ideological and philosophical positions. There are many writings which do not assert such claims; but religious texts *do* make very specific claims. Religious writings are targeted in terms of their audience. Something tantamount to missionary work has to be accomplished when those writings and the ideas contained in them are presented to an unintended audience. In this respect the full realization of the message contained in those writings and ideas places greater demands on the reader than do texts and ideas that have no specific audience in mind. Non-specificity on the part of an audience means that it is not presupposed that the audience in question shares the mental positions applied in composing the texts under consideration.

I have already mentioned above the fact that every branch of knowledge actually requires some kind of intellectual initiation into its technical and cognitive presuppositions. One cannot become fully proficient in any branch of knowledge, unless its cognitive and "philosophical" groundwork is fully accepted. If one is disinclined to accept the cognitive truth of biology, chemistry or physics, respectively, one should choose a different occupation. What matters here is not this or that particular theory, but the overall acceptance of adequacy of those fields of knowledge as modes of cognition in their own right. One cannot study biology without accepting its basic "philosophy." This relates not only to the basic methodological and informational aspects of the subject, but also to the very truth implied by its data. When the basic laws of heredity and the system of genetics are not taken for granted, the whole scholarly activity of the biologist is significantly impaired. In other words, every science is sustained by, and anchored in, a certain Weltanschauung. The analogy with religion needs no special elaboration. In sum, if people who are engaged in academic research wish to avoid the pitfalls of disorientation characteristic of those who are intruders from the outside, they have to concede a certain degree of personal involvement with the cognitive presuppositions of the respective research fields.

All this may sound logical and to a great extent convincing and practicable. However, as everybody acquainted with the basic situation in the area of Religious Studies knows, matters there are quite different from what one may expect, particularly if the foregoing considerations are taken for granted, not to mention consciously accepted. Why is that so? One possible answer is that the contents of religion are believed to be divinely inspired. That is, it is neither a fact of nature, nor is it – at least in the eyes of the believers – a product of the human mind as such. The source of religion is in God. In other words, it involves information that cannot be verified under normal human conditions. As a matter of cognitive fact the contents of religion can be realized only in a state of mind that is ontologically different from any other one known to regular human experience. Verification of religious data that relate to revelation cannot be carried out in any man-made laboratory. Nor can they be assessed experientially by the ordinary modes of cogitation. Do these facts disqualify students of religion from carrying out their research-projects in the regular academic way, that is, under critically observed conditions? If the answer to this question is negative, then the terms of reference for the study of religions (as opposed to the study of their various forms of documentation) have to be established in the clearest way possible. The study of religion, as distinct from theology, does not deal with the truth of revelation which is the ultimate basis and content of religion. Nor does it aim at proving true or false the various components of religion. What it deals with is the contents of religion as perceived and lived by people who consider revelation to be a very basic fact of life. In order to study religion in a serious and responsible manner, one has to engage in that endeavor with as much empathy as possible. Since religion is concerned with such extraordinary experiences and phenomena, the more empathy that can be brought into the study of religion the better.

When speaking of empathy, it should be noted that it is not tantamount to religious belief itself. Empathy does not mean the sharing of every detail of the beliefs that are studied academically. It begins with what T.S. Elliot has called the temporary suspension of disbelief. But it also goes beyond this. In order to study prophecy as a cognitive phenomenon one need not be a prophet oneself. But to study prophecy one has to be positively inclined to treat the prophetic experience and its various forms of expression as something that human beings can genuinely experience without exposing themselves to intellectual fraud and cognitive deceit. We scholars of religion do not have to take the same experiential paths which the prophets themselves took. Neither do we have to follow them in their divinatory seizures, nor be involved in their moral injunctions. But we do have to be as sincere in our thinking as we can, so as not to give the impression that we regard the prophetic experience as fantasy and intellectual humbug. If prophecy is treated as a manifestation of the sick mind, then its study belongs to the area of psychopathology and not to Religious Studies. It is absolutely legitimate to study prophecy in a psychological framework; but we should not delude ourselves into thinking that this is what Religious Studies are expected to do primarily.

One still may argue that psychology is a major tool in the hands of the researcher in Religious Studies. The same argument also may be advanced in the cases of sociology, anthropology, and even, to take an extreme example, economics. These sciences certainly provide very important tools in the hands of scholars who wish to assess all forms of human behavior. Moreover, they are respected sciences in modern academe. But one should not be tempted into thinking that these, and other, sciences should be applied with aim in mind of upgrading Religious Studies from an inferior state of mere speculation to a loftier place of an academic occupation. Religious Studies are an academic field in their own right. They do not depend on any prior processes of academic "upgrading" by methodologically linking them to other disciplines. Some may think that Religious Studies still have a long way to go before reaching the kind of academic status enjoyed by other disciplines and sciences. Whatever one's opinion in the matter, one thing must be clear: those who demonstrate their intellectual concern for Religious Studies should avoid aiding and abetting their own foes. In other words, no concession should be made in face of other academic disciplines. Scholars in the area of Religious Studies still have much to learn. There is always a need to define and redefine the academic agenda and issues in the modern study of religions. There is also the need to improve the research methods at our disposal. However, all this does not mean that we are theologians in disguise. Quite the opposite seems to be true. Some proficient theologians actually are well-qualified scholars.

IV

I want to sum up in the following manner some of the major points made in the previous pages: Any form of ideological attachment, whether it moves in the direction of belief or counter to it, has structural affinities with theological positions. Naturally, one also can maintain the opposite position, namely, that theology has structural affinities with any form of ideological attachment. When viewed from that relativizing angle, there is nothing particularly "holy" in theological positions as such. One may hold fast to any kind of belief as strongly as one wishes, and one may be as lax in maintaining, and in holding to, one's own theological positions as one considers fitting and adequate. Since in the present study I am concerned mostly with cognitive positions, it does not so much matter in my view whether the "belief" in question is of a religious or secular nature. Typologically speaking, mental positions do not change significantly in their basic structure and nature whether applied in this direction or in that. Here the renowned notion of "political theology" as developed by Carl Schmitt readily suggests itself to the observer's mind, as also the more recently developed supplementary notion of "theological politics" suggested by Jan Assmann.[1] Dialectical thinking always is a provocative course to take, particularly when one of its savory results is a relativization of one-sided and dogmatic positions.

Another course explored in the previous pages was the one that led to the hypothesis that in the study of religions the personal experience and involvement of the scholar with religious matters and the suspension of disbelief are likely to reap good fruits, thereby significantly contributing to academic excellence in the area of Religious Studies. On yet another intellectual level, the distancing of oneself from the impact of one's life-experiences and basic convictions is a good tactic which needs be employed by all those who cannot restrain their intense reactions vis-à-vis the subject-matter. But enlightened scholars, who are conscious of the damage that can be done if uncontrolled passions are permitted to interfere with one's studies, can be trusted to apply critical judgment to their personal world-view and inclinations.

When I here speak of the personal engagement of the scholar and the positive bearing it may have on the study of religion, I insist on this: theological dogma as such should not be confused with the personal experience of the scholar in matters that relate to maintaining theologically dogmatic positions. For it is one thing to assume a dogmatic stance and

---

[1] See, J. Assmann, *Politische Theologie zwischen Aegypten und Israel*, Carl Friedrich von Siemens Stiftung – Themen LII, 1992.

another to bring one's own experience with such positions into one's research activity. As much as they contribute to the formulation of attitudes expressive of religious self-identity and self-image, theological positions as such are divisive factors, enhancing prejudice and disrespect for the other. And yet, speaking from my particular point of view, religious experience with such positions need not necessarily be equal to maintaining or propagating them. Hence, scholars' experience with such positions and their awareness of their varied functions should not be condemned universally as pejoratively-defined factors in academic research. On the contrary, such experiences, apart from being conducive to academic performance, can be applied positively to build protective fences around dogmatic conceit and intellectual prejudice!

When speaking of the personal engagement of the scholar with the subject of his or her academic work, I would like to add here that, if that engagement facilitates access to the multi-layered aspects of the material studied and opens additional channels of realizable information, then that which to one scholar appears to be an impediment to scholarly performance may be in the eyes of another a handy instrument for perfecting scholarly skills. Universal agreement in the academy is a rare behavioral species, particularly when positions relating to principle research-attitudes are the subject of the discussion. In this respect what is said here chiefly aims at cognitively clarifying a problem, not at pointing in any one definitive direction. The various options at stake were weighed one against the other as objectively as possible. If I spoke more emphatically in favor of one view over against the other, this was done because I considered that view to be the less-represented one in academic circles. Our discourse here is not divorced from the discussion of academic habits and fashions. I consider that discussion to be as integrally related to research as the research methods themselves. The spiritual principles that sustain research are the ones that create our initial interest in the subject-matter. They define the modes in which questions are asked, and to a large extent they direct our discoveries and our scholarly way of treating them.

V

Finally, let me give one brief example in which this line of argumentation was followed by another scholar. In his comments on *The Rule of Saint Benedict*, the French Benedictine monk and scholar, Adalbert de Vogüè, says:

> "The fact that the author of this commentary feels himself personally engaged in regard to the text studied, and that in his commentary he thinks of other monks in the same situation, this fact may inspire fears for the scientific quality of his work. Let the reader judge if such conditions have harmed the objectivity. For ourselves, on the contrary, we feel the benefit of a personal relation to that object that incites us to scrutinize *with more energy and penetration* (emphasis added). It is not a handicap for the interpreter but a piece of good fortune that he belongs to an institution which claims the *Rule* today as well as yesterday, and which gives a certain experience, limited but real, of observing it."[2]

Such a strongly worded statement may sound apologetic in tone to some. However, it should be pointed out that such a scholar, who is personally involved with the subject-matter of his study and is even concerned with its practical application (=religious life and monastic practice), only intensifies the care with which he handles his texts. For some he may be too preoccupied with matters relating to the practical application of the contents of the book. But, in our case we may well ask, what is the *Rule* if not a book that advocates a certain lifestyle and monastic practice? Too much is at stake for such a scholar. His obligations towards a community of believers evidently place him in a situation where no sophisticated quibbling can rescue him from the criticism of possibly more knowledgeable and experienced persons. In short, the risks of slipping into the snare of redundant formulations are too great for a person who wishes to preserve not only his academic integrity but also his ecclesiastical authority and credibility in the eyes of a community whose concerns he is expected to meet in a respectful manner.

Scholars do not work in a spiritual vacuum. Their minds are full of notions deriving from their life-experiences and

---

[2] *The Rule of Saint Benedict: A Doctrinal and Spiritual Commentary* (Cistercian Studies Series 54; Kalamazoo, MI.: Cistercian Publications, 1983) 4.

academic training. For many years it was almost a doctrinal fashion in academe not to admit to others one's own religious convictions and philosophy of life. Of course, there are institutions in which one's religious affiliations are of no concern to anybody. Needless to say, problems arise only when there is a substantial change in that situation. In most of the academic institutions with which I am familiar, academic freedom is respected. In other, though more rare, instances, the borderlines between academic toleration and dogmatic intolerance are not so carefully maintained.

I am primarily concerned with the quality of research done by scholars who consider their worldview and life-experience to be directly connected to and relevant for their research. If they are fortunate, they are hired for their academic positions by institutions that sanction academic freedom. This is the case even in such institutions that only latently would admit their ecclesiastical or denominational affiliations. Many universities in Europe and the United States clearly would define themselves as secular institutions, even when financially supported by a given church organization. Religious Studies very often are supported by the respective churches or one of their denominations. Although the authority of the church cannot force itself openly on the academy by means of arbitrary decrees, the general agenda of a School of Religion, Divinity School, and Department of Religious Studies frequently is such that their own Christian character is not lost on a basically secular, or even anti-religious, campus.

Any scholar working in such an atmosphere readily would declare that academic freedom permits many species of birds to flock, and thrive, together. Nonetheless, as I indicated above, serious problems may arise, and they evidently do so when scholars enter their respective university faculties without altering their priorities – particularly when these concern convictions and beliefs. These beliefs and convictions need not necessarily be of a religious character. They may well be nonreligious or even anti-religious ones. However, as we have seen, there are good reasons to argue that some experience with religious life and belief can only be advantageous and fruitful for scholarly work undertaken in Religious Studies. Academic excellence is not always achieved where and when the spirit of agnosticism is allowed (or required) to prevail. On the contrary, sometimes a gifted scholar in Religious Studies is someone who is an experienced person of religion.

I hope that in the foregoing pages justice has been done to a rather prickly subject and honor bestowed on a dear friend. There is still much that needs be said, and in some respects the discussion has just begun. For those who consider that discussion to be over before it even commenced, I offer a word of apology: If they regard what they do as being marked by academic excellence already, I regret having aroused ghosts that are more easily mastered when asleep than awake.

DIE BEDEUTUNG DER GNOSTISCHEN NAG-HAMMADI TEXTE FÜR DIE NEUTESTAMENTLICHE WISSENSCHAFT[1]

James M. Robinson (Claremont Graduate School)

Mit der Publikation der Nag-Hammadi Codices trat als unausweichlich eine von der neutestamentlichen Wissenschaft bisher weitgehend vernachlässigte Frage in den Vordergrund, nämlich die nach der Bedeutung der nicht im Neuen Testament enthaltenen und daher "apokryph" genannten Evangelien, Apostelgeschichten, Episteln und Apokalypsen für die neutestamentliche Wissenschaft. Die neutestamentlichen Apokryphen selbst waren der Forschung jederzeit zugänglich (z. B. mit den Editionen von Hennecke-Schneemelcher), doch schien ihnen so wenig Bedeutung zuzukommen, daß sie, abgesehen von eher beiläufigen Verweisen auf ihre bloße Existenz, weitgehend ignoriert werden konnten. Da jedoch mit den Nag-Hammadi Texten nun eine ganze Palette von bis dahin verdrängten und vertuschten frühchristlichen Traditionen ans Licht der Öffentlichkeit kam, ist es nicht länger möglich, diesen Teil der Anfänge des Christentums – eine Art "linken Flügel" – weiterhin auszugrenzen. Vielmehr wird zunehmend deutlich, daß sich uns hier eine neue Dimension unserer Disziplin eröffnet hat. Im französischsprachigen Bereich wurde, angeführt von François Bovon (Genf, jetzt Harvard), dementsprechend erneut das Schwergewicht auf die Erforschung der neutestamentlichen Apokryphen gelegt; ebenso im amerikanischen Bereich, angeführt von Helmut Köster (Harvard). In der deutschsprachigen neutestamentlichen Wissenschaft scheint es dagegen einen nicht geringen Nachholbedarf zu geben, vor allem seit mit der Auflösung des Berliner Arbeitskreises für koptisch-gnostische Schriften die Erforschung der Nag-Hammadi Texte merkbar nachgelassen hat.

Wie sehr das neue Quellenmaterial einfach übergangen wird, ist vielleicht am deutlichsten im Falle des Thomasevangeliums (Nag-Hammadi Codex II,2). Eine solche "Fehlanzeige" kann selbstverständlich schon von der Natur der

[1] Leicht revidierte, für ein breiteres Publikum bestimmte Gastvorlesung, gehalten am 17.6.1993 im Uhlhorn-Konvikt der Universität Göttingen, und am 22.6.1993 an der Universität Bamberg.

Sache her nicht einfach anhand einer Bibliographie nachgewiesen werden, da es natürlich leichter ist Zitierungen aufzuzählen, als die unzitierten Möglichkeiten zu verzeichnen. Wenn jedoch Sprüche kanonischer Evangelien untersucht werden, bleiben Parallelstellen solcher Sprüche im Thomasevangelium oft unerwähnt. Dieses Vorgehen basiert nicht zuletzt auf Wolfgang Schrages wohlbekannter Monographie,[2] in der er für die Abhängigkeit des Thomasevangeliums von den kanonischen Evangelien argumentiert.[3] Weniger oft wird dagegen sein Beitrag in der Haenchen-Festschrift[4] herangezogen, wo er aufzeigt, daß der koptische Text des Thomasevangeliums aus dem 4. Jahrhundert eine größere Nähe zu den neutestamentlichen Parallelen aufweist, als die früheren griechischen Oxyrhynchusfragmente. Damit wird die alternative Hypothese nahegelegt, nach der die koptische Kopie aus dem 4. Jahrhundert, auf der unsere modernen Übersetzungen und wissenschaftlichen Untersuchungen beruhen, weniger von dem kanonischen Text ausging, als ihm vielmehr erst sekundär angeglichen wurde.

Die amerikanische Diskussion wurde dagegen vor allem durch die Dissertationen von John Sieber[5] und Stephen J.

---

[2] Schrage, W.: *Das Verhältnis des Thomasevangeliums zur synoptischen Tradition und zu den koptischen Bibelübersetzungen. Zugleich ein Beitrag zur gnostischen Synoptikerdeutung*, Berlin 1964 (BZNW 29). Wie wenig sich andererseits die heutige neutestamentliche Forschung noch ernsthaft mit dem Thomasevangelium und also mit dem Buch von Schrage auseinandersetzt zeigt sich darin, daß die weitgehend plagiatistische Wiederholung seiner Thesen in der 1988/89 Münchner Dissertation von Michael Fieger, *Das Thomasevangelium: Einleitung, Kommentar und Systematik*, München 1991 (NTA NF 22), so lange unbemerkt bleiben konnte.

[3] Die Reaktion der amerikanischen Forschung auf Schrages Position läßt sich vielleicht am ehesten mit John Dominic Crossan (*Four Other Gospels: Shadows on the Contours of Canon*, Minneapolis, Chicago, New York, 1985) illustrieren: "One example may ... suffice. The first beatitude in Luke 6:20b has 'Blessed are the poor in spirit, for theirs is the kingdom of heaven.' Scholars had long considered that 'in spirit' was a personal, redactional addition by Matthew himself. Now in *Gos. Thom.* 54 we have, 'Blessed are the poor, for yours is the Kingdom of Heaven.' Precisely what is missing is the proposed editorial addition of Matthew. But what if one objects that *Thomas* has simply copied Luke here? That will not work. One would have at least to argue that *Thomas* ... took ... the second person 'yours' from Luke, and ... returned to Matthew for the final 'Kingdom of Heaven.' It might be simpler to suggest that Thomas was mentally unstable."

[4] Schrage, W.: "Evangelienzitate in den Oxyrhynchus-Logien und im koptischen Thomas-Evangelium." In: *Apophoreta, Festschrift für Ernst Haenchen zu seinem siebzigsten Geburtstag am 10. Dezember 1964*, Berlin 1964 (BZNW 30) S. 251-268.

[5] Sieber, J.: *A Redactional Analysis of the Synoptic Gospels with regard to the*

Patterson[6] bestimmt. Beide halten das Thomasevangelium für im wesentlichen unabhängig von den kanonischen Evangelien. Das Bemühen, die sich damit auftuende Kluft[7] zwischen den divergierenden wissenschaftlichen Traditionen beiderseits des Atlantik zu überbrücken, dürfte in einer Festschrift zu Ehren von Dieter Georgi aus Harvard und Frankfurt angemessen sein.

Abgesehen von kanonischen Gründen scheinen vor allem zwei eher marginale Sachverhalte die Rezeption besonders der Nag-Hammadi Texte zu erschweren. Einmal macht die Tatsache, daß es sich größtenteils um gnostische Texte handelt, ihre Hineinnahme in die neutestamentliche Disziplin nicht gerade leichter. Doch wie die Dinge nun einmal liegen, hätte jeder unterdrückte Zweig des frühen Christentums, der lediglich durch einen zufälligen Textfund ans Tageslicht käme, den Hang zu dem, was wir traditionellerweise "häre-

---

Question of the Sources of the Gospel According to Thomas. Claremont 1965.

[6] Patterson, St.J.: *The Gospel of Thomas within the Development of Early Christianity.* Claremont 1988. Published as *The Gospel of Thomas and Jesus.* Sonoma, CA, 1993.

[7] Diese Kluft kann vielleicht am besten in Form von Anekdoten von SNTS Tagungen illustriert werden: Ich war gebeten worden, auf der Baseler Tagung 1984 die offizielle Antwort auf den Beitrag von Nikolaus Walter über Paulus und die urchristliche Tradition zu geben. So warf ich das Problem auf, daß in Walters Beitrag nur Jesussprüche aus den kanonischen Evangelien in Betracht gezogen wurden. Aber Paulus stützte sich nicht auf die kanonischen Evangelien, sondern auf mündliche Traditionen, die dann nicht nur in kanonischen Evangelien ihren Niederschlag fanden, sondern auch in solchen nichtkanonischen Texten wie dem Thomasevangelium. Um ein Beispiel gebeten, nannte ich I Kor 2,9 und Logion 17 des Thomasevangeliums. Als Antwort bekam ich zu hören, daß Paulus diese Tradition nicht als einen Jesusspruch, sondern lediglich mithilfe der Zitationsformel "wie geschrieben steht" einführte. Ich wies darauf hin, daß in dem Beitrag ein ganzer Abschnitt paulinischen Bezugnahmen auf kanonische Jesussprüche, die von Paulus nicht Jesus zugeschrieben wurden, gewidmet ist. Daraufhin wurde eingeräumt, daß solch ein Spruch wie Logion 17 der Vollständigkeit halber tatsächlich hätte einbegriffen werden sollen. Bei der nachfolgenden Publizierung des Beitrags ("Paulus und die urchristliche Jesustradition." *NTS 31* (1985) S.498-522) wurde jedoch dieser Spruch (trotz etlicher anderer Revisionen), zusammen mit dem ganzen Thomasevangelium, schlicht und einfach stillschweigend übergangen. – Bei der SNTS-Tagung 1991, in Bethel bei Bielefeld, gab es im Seminar über die Vorsynoptischen Traditionen die etwas zögernde Übereinkunft, daß auf der Tagung in Chicago, 1993, das Seminar sich auf solche gegenwärtigen Schwerpunkte in Amerika wie das Spruchevangelium Q und das Thomasevangelium konzentrieren könnte. Tatsächlich aber enthielt das Programm des Seminars dann nur Beiträge zur Passionsgeschichte, wo weder Q noch Thomas relevant sind.

tisch" nennen würden. Seit Walter Bauer ist zwar das ganze Konzept "Rechtgläubigkeit/Ketzerei" als stichhaltige historische Unterscheidung in Frage gestellt worden, aber für den Bereich der neutestamentlichen Disziplin hatte das bisher nicht viel zu besagen, da alles "Häretische" ohnehin weitgehend ausradiert war. Ohne historische Quellen gibt es keine Geschichte! Nun aber gibt es Quellen; also sollte es auch Geschichte geben!

Die andere Tatsache, daß nämlich die Nag-Hammadi Texte in einer so bizarren Sprache wie dem Koptischen (statt auf Griechisch) erhalten sind, macht sie umso schwerer annehmbar, als von Forschern generell erwartet wird, daß sie die Sprache ihrer jeweiligen Quellen beherrschen. Die Nag-Hammadi Texte als neutestamentliche Quellen anzusehen, würde in diesem Falle also die Kompetenz einer neuen Fremdsprache erfordern, und das in einer Zeit, in der es ohnehin schon eine Sprachenkrise gibt, da die klassischen Sprachen längst nicht mehr so total beherrscht werden, wie in früheren Generationen. Bedenken solcher Art sollten jedoch nicht die offene Diskussion darüber verhindern, welcher Stellenwert den Nag-Hammadi Codices innerhalb der neutestamentlichen Wissenschaft zukommt, eine Diskussion, die dieser Beitrag fördern möchte.

1. Das Thomasevangelium und die kanonischen Evangelien

Das koptische Thomasevangelium ist nach wie vor die am besten bekannte Schrift aus dem Nag-Hammadi Fund von 1945. Drei griechische Fragmente dieses Evangeliums waren ja schon gegen Ende des 19. Jahrhunderts bei Oxyrhynchus entdeckt worden und hatten zu erstaunlichen Publikationen geführt. Viele unserer gegenwärtigen Einsichten, die ja auf vollständigem Zugang zur koptischen Übersetzung dieses Textes aus Nag Hammadi beruhen, waren schon damals vorhanden. Doch das Interesse an den wenigen Fragmenten versiegte bald wieder, und die weitere Entwicklung der Bibelwissenschaft blieb von diesen Erkenntnissen fast völlig unberührt. Sie schienen weder theologische Implikationen zu haben noch irgendwelche Konsequenzen nach sich zu ziehen. Mit Nag-Hammadi wurde jedoch eine neue Runde eingeläutet; diesmal wird hoffentlich auch der Ausgang ein anderer sein!

In der Auseinandersetzung um das Thomasevangelium aus Nag-Hammadi ging es bisher in erster Linie um die Frage, ob ihm überhaupt eine grössere Bedeutung zukomme. Abgesprochen wird ihm diese mit der Behauptung, das Thomasevangelium habe unserem Wissen über Jesus und den mit ihm verbundenen Traditionen nichts Neues hinzuzufügen, da es von den kanonischen Evangelien abhängig sei. Vertreter dieser Richtung verweisen auf die Spätdatierung, um 140 herum, die man dem Text in den neuziger Jahren des vorigen Jahrhunderts zusprach, als die griechischen Fragmente publiziert wurden. Diejenigen dagegen, die dem Thomasevangelium eine herausragende Bedeutung zubilligen, halten den Text für wesentlich unabhängig von den kanonischen Evangelien und sehen in der Spätdatierung einen tendenziösen Versuch, die Bedeutung des Textes herunterzuspielen. Sie vertreten die Ansicht, daß dieses Evangelium wenigstens chronologisch genauso "apostolisch" sein könnte wie die kanonischen Evangelien. Nur unter dieser zweiten Voraussetzung wäre das Thomasevangelium wirklich für die neutestamentliche Forschung relevant, denn wir hätten mit diesem Text dann tatsächlich neue, außerkanonische Informationen über Jesus und Jesustraditionen von beträchtlicher Anzahl und Bedeutung vor uns liegen.

Die Frage der Abhängigkeit des Thomasevangeliums von den kanonischen Evangelien muß also geklärt werden. Unter seinen 114 Sprüchen (um die konventionelle Zählung beizubehalten) sind viele, die das Neue Testament nicht kennt, und die deshalb nicht von den kanonischen Evangelien abhängig sein können. Einige von ihnen scheinen in der Tat spätere Bildungen zu sein. Doch viele derjenigen Sprüche, die keine Parallelen in den kanonischen Evangelien haben, zeigen zumindest keine stärkeren Markmale einer relativ späten Entstehung als vergleichbare Sprüche in den kanonischen Evangelien selbst.

Eine weitere Beobachtung dürfte vielleicht von noch entscheidenderer Bedeutung im Hinblick auf die Abhängigkeitsfrage sein: Gleichnisse mit Parallelen in kanonischen Evangelien enthalten nämlich in einigen Fällen im Thomasevangelium weniger tendenziöse Formulierungen als diejenigen in den kanonischen Evangelien. Das ist kaum dadurch zu erklären, daß der Schreiber des Thomasevangeliums nach kritischer Sichtung die späteren, tendenziösen Zusätze der kanonischen Evangelien selbst entfernt hätte. Man sollte bei einem Evangelisten der frühen Kirche – wie dem Verfasser des Thomasevangeliums – nicht einen ebensolchen Antrieb zu kritischer Reflexion voraussetzen, wie bei modernen Wissenschaftlern, die durch Entfernen von sekundären Ausformungen die früheste Gestalt eines Jesusspruches zu rekonstruieren suchen. Vielmehr darf man wohl schlußfolgern, daß der Verfasser des Thomasevangeliums Zugang zu geschriebenen oder mündlich überlieferten Quellen hatte, die unabhängig von den kanonischen Evangelien und in einigen Fällen sogar älter als diese waren.

Ein weiteres Argument, das die Annahme einer Abhängigkeit des Thomasevangeliums von den kanonischen Evangelien unwahrscheinlich macht, ist die Tatsache, daß es so viel kanonisches Material eben gerade nicht enthält. Der Verfasser müßte schon ziemlich verrückt gewesen sein, wenn er so viel ihm schriftlich vorliegendes, zweckdienliches Gut einfach weggelassen hätte. An dieser Stelle wird normalerweise bewußt oder unbewußt die These der Irrationalität der Gnosis ins Spiel gebracht. In Wahrheit aber ist im Thomasevangelium kaum Gnostisches zu finden. Auf jeden Fall ist der gnostische Einfluß nicht stark genug, um die Gnosis als hermeneutischen Schlüssel zu verwenden. Inhalt und Auslassungen des Thomasevangeliums damit erklären zu wollen, daß es sich um eine gnostisierende Bearbeitung der kanonischen Evangelien handele, erinnert an den ähnlichen Versuch, das Johannesevangelium als "vergeistigtes" Evangelium zu deklarieren, um seine Andersartigkeit einer tendenziösen Bearbeitung der synoptischen Evangelien zuschreiben zu können.

Um das Thomasevangelium als Bearbeitung der kanonischen Evangelien verständlich zu machen, müßte man zunächst eine radikale Streichung durch den Verfasser voraussetzen, mit der er praktisch den gesamten erzählenden Rahmen der kanonischen Evangelien ausschied, angefangen mit den Kindheitserzählungen (in zwei der kanonischen Evangelien), über die Wundergeschichten und die Leidenserzählungen, bis hin zum Auferstehungsbericht und den Begegnungen mit dem Auferstandenen (in drei der kanonischen Evangelien). Da die Gnosis ihre Soteriologie nicht auf die Heilstaten Christi gründet, sondern auf seine Offenbarung der gnostischen Wahrheit, wurde global argumentiert, daß die Verfasser gnostischer Evangelien sich für berechtigt hielten, die narrativen Zusammenhänge der kanonischen Evangelien in massiver, tendenziöser Weise zu streichen. Andere Nag-Hammadi Texte aber zeigen uns jetzt, daß die gnostische Praxis anders aussah. Man übernahm durchaus narrativen Stoff, von Geburt (TestVer, NHC IX, 45,6-22), über Taufe (TestVer, NHC IX, 30,18-31,5) bis zum Tod (2LogSeth, NHC VII, 55,9-56,19; ApcPt, NHC VII, 81,3-83,15), den man gnostisch umdeutete und ihn so überlieferungswürdig machte. Erscheinungen des Auferstandenen sind bei weitem die beliebteste Gattung christlicher Gnosis; diese aber enthält das Thomasevangelium gerade nicht. Sein Text ist einfach nicht zu erklären als ein Resultat gnostischer Reduktion.

Die Abhängigkeitsthese läßt sich auch hinsichtlich der Reihenfolge der Sprüche schwerlich durchhalten, ebensowenig wie hinsichtlich der Wortwahl und der Wortfolge innerhalb der einzelnen Sprüche. Sich einen Verfasser vorzustellen, der den kanonischen Evangelien Sprüche entnimmt und sie in der Art zusammensetzt, wie sie im Thomasevangelium erscheinen, fällt in der Tat nicht leicht. Es läßt sich keine überzeugende Begründung dafür beibringen, warum er die ursprüngliche Abfolge der Sprüche, wie sie sich in den kanonischen Evangelien findet, total durcheinandergebracht haben soll, wo sie doch dort oft einen grösseren Sinnzusammenhang bilden, wie etwa die rhetorischen Einheiten, die wir Bergpredigt (Mt 5-7) oder Feldrede (Lk 6,20-49) nennen, um ihnen dann eine Ordnung zu geben, deren Sinn bis heute noch niemand durchschaut hat. Ebensowenig konnte bisher einsichtig gemacht werden, warum der Verfasser des Thomasevangeliums die Einzelsprüche der kanonischen Evangelien auf eine so sinnlose Weise umschrieb, indem er nämlich das eine Wort aus *einem* kanonischen Evangelium entliehen haben soll, das nächste aus einem *anderen*, um schließlich die syntaktische Wortfolge einem *dritten* zu entnehmen.

Im Allgemeinen kann man Abhängigkeit von kanonischen Evangelien am leichtesten dann deutlich machen, wenn sich in einem Spruch eindeutig die Sprache des Verfassers eines der kanonischen Evangelien nachweisen läßt. Würde in unserem Falle dieselbe redaktionelle Sprache auch im Thomasevangelium auftauchen, könnte man in der Tat von einem Einfluß der kanonischen Evangelien auf das Thomasevangelium sprechen. Allem Anschein nach gibt es auch solche Stellen, doch nur erstaunlich wenige – so wenige, daß man zunächst nach einer plausibleren Erklärung für ihre Existenz suchen sollte, als sich sofort für eine mit so vielen Unwahrscheinlichkeiten belastete Theorie auszusprechen.

Alle Handschriften kanonischer Evangelien verraten sichtbaren Einfluß der anderen kanonischen Evangelien, denn den jeweiligen Abschreibern der Evangelien war der Wortlaut der anderen Evangelien selbstverständlich bekannt, entweder vom Lesen oder vom Hörensagen, vielleicht sogar vom eigenen, früheren Abschreiben. Keine noch erhaltene Handschrift ist frei von solchen Einflüssen. Nur dadurch, daß der uns heute vorliegende griechische Text des Neuen Testaments, auf dem alle unsere modernen Übersetzungen basieren, dank textkritischer Rekonstruktionen weitgehend wieder von den Verunreinigungen befreit ist, sind wir uns dieser Tatsache der Beeinflussung kaum mehr bewußt.

Auch das Thomasevangelium blieb nicht verschont von Beeinflussungen, denen alle frühchristlichen Evangelien unterlagen. Ursprünglich wurde es auf Griechisch geschrieben. Der griechische Text wurde dann wiederholt abgeschrieben, wie die drei uns bekannten griechischen Textfragmente aus dem dritten Jahrhundert belegen. Danach wurde er ins Koptische übersetzt. Auch im Koptischen wurde er wiederholt kopiert, bis der Abschreiber von Nag-Hammadi Codex II in der Mitte des vierten Jahrhunderts die uns vorliegende Kopie anfertigte. In diesem langen Prozeß des wiederholten Abschreibens, Übersetzens und wieder Kopierens, sind unausweichlich Korruptionen in den Text eingeflossen. Dies kann auch schon teilweise durch einen Vergleich des koptischen mit den Fragmenten des griechischen Textes belegt werden. Keiner der drei griechischen Texte liegt der koptischen Übersetzung zugrunde; diese setzt den Wortlaut einer vierten, verlorengegangenen griechischen Textform voraus. So kann man selbstverständlich voraussetzen, daß der koptische Text aus dem vierten Jahrhundert – über den wir immer sprechen, wenn wir über das Thomasevangelium reden – eine beträchtliche Anzahl von Textkorruptionen enthält, die von einer Beeinflussung der Abschreiber durch die kanonischen Evangelien herrühren. Diese Evangelien waren ja alle im Ägypten der damaligen Zeit sehr wohl bekannt, wie wir durch die relativ große Anzahl von Fragmenten kanonischer Evangelien wissen, die im trockenen ägyptischen Wüstensand bis heute überlebt haben, wie auch von den vielen Zitaten und Anspielungen in frühchristlichen Schriften aus Ägypten. Deshalb ist das Vorhandensein solcher Verunreinigungen in der späteren koptischen Version kein überzeugendes Argument dafür, daß auch die ursprüngliche Komposition des Evangeliums die kanonischen Evangelien voraussetzt. Mit derselben Logik müßte man dann auch die Abfassung *jedes* kanonischen Evangeliums in Abhängigkeit von jedem anderen kanonischen Evangelium behaupten, da ja jede Evangelien*kopie* jeweils die anderen Evangelien voraussetzt. Die Absurdität dieser Logik ist ziemlich offensichtlich.

Datierungsprobleme gibt es besonders im Hinblick auf Spruchsammlungen, da sie weniger in sich geschlossen sind als andere literarische Gattungen. Eine Erzählung braucht zur Schlüssigkeit von Ursache und Wirkung bestimmte Elemente, deren Abwesenheit sofort vermißt werden würde, genauso wie ein fehlendes Argument in einer zwingenden philosophischen oder theologischen Gedankenkette. In einer lose zusammengestellten Abfolge von Sprüchen aber, in der jeder einzelne Spruch eine Aussage für sich darstellt und sich nicht auf Vorhergehendes oder Nachfolgendes bezieht, ist es dagegen relativ einfach, hier und da einen neuen Spruch einzufügen, der bewahrungswürdig erscheint, oder immer wieder einmal einen Spruch zu streichen, dessen Überlieferungswert abgenommen hatte. Vergleicht man die griechischen Fragmente des Thomasevangeliums mit dem späteren koptischen Text, kann man feststellen, daß dies tatsächlich geschehen ist. Der griechische Text (P. Oxy. 1) vereint die koptischen Sprüche 30a und 77b, bzw. trennt der koptische Text eine ursprüngliche Einheit. In jedem Falle blieb die Umstellung solange unbemerkt, bis der koptische Text entdeckt wurde. Der Schluß von Spruch 3 des griechischen Textes (P. Oxy. 654), "wer sich selbst kennt, wird dies entdecken," fehlt im Koptischen; umgekehrt fehlt in demselben griechischen Text (P. Oxy. 654) der im Koptischen vorhandene Schluss von Spruch 6, "und nichts Verborgenes wird überdauern ohne enthüllt zu werden." Auf jeden Fall ist es unsachgemäß, von einem Einzelspruch oder Spruchteil, der eine späte Interpolation darstellen könnte, auf eine späte Abfassungszeit des ursprünglichen Evangeliums zu schließen. Selbst wenn an einigen Stellen des Thomasevangeliums nicht mit Sicherheit auszumachen ist, ob sich ein bestimmter Spruch vom kanonischen Text herleitet, oder ursprünglich unabhängig war, wie das eindeutig bei Sprüchen ohne kanonische Parallelen der Fall ist, sollten die wenigen redaktionellen Spuren kanonischen Textgutes im Thomasevangelium jedenfalls nicht dafür herhalten, das ganze Evangelium für irrelevant zu erklären und aus der neutestsamentlichen Forschung zu verbannen.

2. Kanonische und apokryphe Evangelien

Die Diskussion um das Thomasevangelium ist Teil der umfassenderen Debatte über die Bedeutung der neutestamentlichen Apokryphen. Kanonizität blieb ausschließlich apostolischen Dokumenten vorbehalten. Texte, die gemessen an späterer orthodoxer Glaubensüberzeugung und -praxis für pseudo-apostolisch gehalten wurden, wurden schon allein aufgrund dieser Klassifizierung als aus späterer Zeit stammend angesehen. Das der Unterscheidung von kanonischen und apokryphen Evangelien zugrundeliegende Kriterium der Apostolizität wird heute jedoch grundlegend in Frage gestellt. Hat man die paulinische Definition im Auge, dann ist ein Apostel jemand, dem der Auferstandene erschienen ist (Gal 1,1.11f). Der Apostolizität wäre damit kein zeitliches Ende gesetzt. Verschiedenartige, ja widersprüchliche "apostolische" Lehren konnten diesen Anspruch erheben. Begrenzt man dagegen getreu der späteren orthodoxen Sichtweise, deren Repräsentant Lukas ist, die Zeitspanne der Auferstehungserscheinungen auf 40 Tage (Act 1,3), wird den gnostischen Gruppen, die von Erscheinungen noch nach Jahren sprechen (etwa bis auf 550 Tage, EpJac, NHC I, 2,19f), der Wind aus den Segeln genommen. Allerdings bringt die lukanische zeitliche Begrenzung ja auch Paulus selbst in eine schwierige Position. Darüber hinaus definiert Lukas einen Apostel als jemanden, der mit Jesus seit den Tagen des Johannes des Täufers zusammen war (Act 1,21f). Das reduziert die Liste der potentiellen Apostel ganz beträchtlich (Johannes wurde nach Lk 3,20 gefangen genommen, ehe Jesus seine ersten Jünger berufen hatte!). Die lukanische Definition schließt auch alle kanonischen Evangelisten aus.

Wie die ursprünglich anonymen kanonischen Evangelien,

wurden wohl auch die meisten frühen apokryphen Evangelien erst sekundär zu Pseudepigraphen. Dem Thomas*evangelium* wurde allem Anschein nach der am Ende unserer koptischen Kopie erscheinende Titel erst nachträglich angefügt. Der Text selbst versteht sich offenbar als "Geheime Worte, die Jesus sprach und Judas Didymus Thomas neiderschrieb," wie sein Incipit ausweist. Möglicherweise aber ist sogar die Assoziation mit Thomas sekundär. Sie widerspiegelt den hohen Rang, den Thomas in Logion 13 einnimmt, doch wird in Logion 12 die höchste Position Jakob zugesprochen. Auf jeden Fall trifft der Verweis des Incipits auf geheime *Worte* den Inhalt viel besser, denn der Text selbst verwendet nie das Wort *Evangelium*, sondern spricht wiederholt von *Worten* Jesu. Die kanonischen Evangelien hatten sich ja selbst auch nicht als Evangelien im gattungsgeschichtlichen Sinne bezeichnet. Lukas versteht sein Werk als "Erzählung" (Lk 1,1), Matthäus nennt das seine einfach "Buch" (Mt 1,1). Mk 1,1 bezeichnet lediglich seine Botschaft im engeren Sinne als *Evangelium.*

Auch bezüglich der Datierung der Texte ist die ursprüngliche Gleichsetzung von Kanonizität mit Apostolizität nicht länger zu halten. Wenn mit apostolisch die Zeit gemeint ist, in der die unmittelbaren Anhänger Jesu aktiv waren, dann gehören die kanonischen Evangelien, die alle im letzten Drittel des ersten Jahrhunderts verfaßt wurden, kaum dazu. Die Legende des betagten "Lieblingsjüngers" aus Joh 21 (der ja anonym bleibt) als Verfasser des Johannesevangeliums gibt kaum eine sichere Basis zur Berechnung der Lebensspanne im Ersten Jahrhundert. Wenn wir Kanonizität tatsächlich auf die apostolische Periode beschränken würden, blieben von den siebenundzwanzig Büchern des Neuen Testaments lediglich die authentischen paulischen Briefe übrig (verfaßt von jemandem, der noch nicht einmal als Augenzeuge betrachtet werden kann!). Hinzu kämen noch das Spruchevangelium Q und wohl die Semeiaquelle. So gesehen stünde das Thomasevangelium viel eher auf einer gattungsgeschichtlichen Ebene mit dem Spruchevangelium Q als die kanonischen Evangelien.

Unter dem Verdikt der Apostolizität kommen also die kanonischen Evangelien in denselben Verdacht der Zweitrangigkeit, mit dem ursprünglich die anderen Evangelien als apokryph deklassifiziert wurden. Eine klare, rein objektive Unterscheidung zwischen dem, was als kanonisch und was als nicht-kanonisch anzusehen ist, ist demnach nicht mehr gegeben. Natürlich gelten für uns auch weiterhin die Bücher als kanonisch, die von der frühen Kirche als solche klassifiziert wurden. Die historische Rolle, die der Kanon gespielt hat, läßt sich nicht rückgängig machen, auch wenn die zugrundeliegenden Kriterien unhaltbar geworden sind. Im Hinblick auf die neutestamentliche Forschung sollten diese Kriterien jedenfalls nicht länger ins Spiel gebracht werden.

3. Unterschiedliche Interpretationen der frühen Jesustraditionen

Die hier am Beispiel von Textdokumenten dargelegte Situation reflektiert natürlich eine hinter ihnen stehende kirchengeschichtliche Wirklichkeit. Wie die deutero-paulinischen Briefe und die Apostelgeschichte Paulus interpretierten, um ihn der Theologie einer späteren Zeit anzupassen, ebenso interpretierte das Johannesevangelium die Semeiaquelle, und interpretierten die Evangelien des Matthäus und Lukas das Spruchevangelium Q, indem sie es in Erzählung umsetzten. Es ist nicht verwunderlich, wenn die interpretierten älteren Texte *selbst* nicht weiter tradiert wurden, weil die Kirche natürlich die verbesserten Interpretationen bevorzugte, die ihre eigene aktualisierte Theologie reflektierten.

Dasselbe geschah mit alten Formeln, die wir in paulinischen Texten eingebettet finden; sie wurden im Taufbekenntnis der römischen Gemeinde des zweiten Jahrhunderts aktualisiert. Heute kennen wir sie als das "apostolische Glaubensbekenntnis." Die alten Formeln wurden nicht mehr verwendet und sind heute nur noch durch die Zitierungen bei Paulus bekannt. So ist das "apostolische Glaubensbekenntnis" ein Text, den die ursprünglichen Apostel Jesu, seine direkten Jünger, nie gekannt hatten. Diese ursprünglichen Apostel, die die Jesussprüche aus der Erinnerung zusammentrugen und so das Spruchevangelium Q formten, ebenso wie sie aus der Erinnerung an Jesu Wundertaten die Zeichenquelle formten, hätten sich gewiß verraten gefühlt, wenn sie gewußt hätten, daß das sogenannte *apostolische* Glaubensbekenntnis gerade das auslassen würde, was sie als so überlieferungswürdig angesehen hatten. Man beachte nur die ins Auge stechenden Auslassungen: "Geboren von der Jungfrau Maria, ... , . . . , gelitten unter Pontius Pilatus, gekreuzigt, gestorben und begraben."

Was wir heute als Orthodoxie kennen, steht – historisch betrachtet – keineswegs in kontinuierlicher Linie zu den Taten und Lehren Jesu und seiner Jünger, sondern ist lediglich die Selbstbezeichnung derjenigen, die sich später mit ihrem eigenen Anliegen durchsetzen konnten.

Umgekehrt sind diejenigen, die in diesem Kampf der verschiedenen Interpretationen auf der Strecke blieben, heute als Häretiker bekannt. Diese herabsetzende Bezeichnung könnte angemessen scheinen, wo alten Traditionen Interpretationen gegeben werden, die sie ursprünglich gar nicht hatten. Tatsächlich wurden so die Traditionen aktualisiert – aber dasselbe taten letztlich auch die "Orthodoxen." Deshalb sind – in einer rein beschreibenden, historischen Schau – Orthodoxie und Häresie in den ersten Jahrhunderten gleichsam parallele Phänomene, nämlich miteinander rivalisierende Aktualisierungen von alten Traditionen, die sie ursprünglich teilten und von denen ausgehend sie sich mit unterschiedlichen Interpretationen weiterentwickelten.

Ein Beispiel für diese Entwicklung ist die Häresie des "Adoptianismus," die teilweise auf der Taufe Jesu basiert, wie sie in der Tradition der "westlichen" Lesart von Lk 3,22 überliefert wurde. Hier zitiert die Himmelsstimme Ps 2,7: "Heute habe ich dich gezeugt." So konnte argumentiert werden, daß der ausschließlich menschliche Jesus erst im Nachhinein durch Adoption bei seiner Taufe zu göttlichem Status erhoben wurde. In der Tat hat die älteste Tradition die Zeit Johannes' des Täufers als den Beginn des Evangeliums angesehen. Die ältesten und voneinander unabhängigsten kanonischen Evangelien, Markus und Johannes, setzen mit Johannes dem Täufer ein (Mk 1,4.11; Joh 1,6-8.15.19.36), ebenso wie das Spruchevangelium Q (Q 3,7-9.16f.21f) und wohl auch die Semeiaquelle (falls die Stellen über den Täufer im ersten Kapitel des Johannesevangeliums aus dieser Quelle stammen). Dasselbe gilt für einige Sprüche, von denen man annimmt, daß sie auf Jesus selbst zurückgehen, denn auch sie beziehen sich auf die Zeit des Täufers als den Wendepunkt: Er sei der Größte unter den vom Weibe Geborenen; nach ihm bricht die Gottesherrschaft mit Gewalt herein (Q 7,28a; 16,16). Ein weiteres Indiz für diese Tradition ist die lukanische Aposteldefinition, nach der als Nachfolger für Judas Ischariot nur jemand in Frage kam, der seit den Tagen des Täufers mit Jesus zusammen war (Acta 1,21f).

Schon die kanonischen Evangelien empfanden offenbar als Problem, daß alles mit Johannes dem Täufer begonnen hatte, und besonders, daß Jesus durch seine Taufe als "rite de passage" Mitglied der Täuferbewegung geworden war. Im Matthäusevangelium (3,14-15) muß der Täufer deshalb gegen eine solch unangemessene Prozedur protestieren; Jesus muß Johannes erst überreden, ihn zu taufen. Das Lukasevangelium (3,20-22) löste das Problem, indem es Jesus erst nach der Gefangennahme des Täufers getauft sein ließ, während im Johannesevangelium (1,32-34) Jesus nur mit Geist direkt vom Himmel getauft wird; Jesu Wassertaufe durch die Hand des Johannes wird hier überhaupt nicht mehr erwähnt. Neu am Adoptianismus ist eigentlich nur die Vorstellung, daß Gott Jesus bei der Taufe gezeugt oder adoptiert hat. Diese nachgezogene Vergöttlichung des (dreißigjährigen) Menschen Jesu war es, was dann als Häresie bezeichnet wurde. Matthäus und Lukas halfen sich mit der Vorschaltung einer vergöttlichenden Geburtsgeschichte, die bei Markus, Q, und der Semeiaquelle (wie auch bei Paulus) noch fehlt. Matthäus, Lukas und das apostolische Glaubensbekenntnis hatten mit der Vorstellung von der Jungfrauengeburt ebenfalls auf eine völlig neue Weise zu erklären versucht, daß Jesus Gottes Sohn sei, – doch diese neue Idee wurde dann als orthodox angesehen. Warum aber sollte die eine Ansicht eher "rechte Lehre" sein als die andere, – abgesehen von der Tatsache, daß wir Nachfahren der Seite sind, die gewonnen hat? Die Apokalypse des Petrus aus Nag Hammadi (NHC VII, 74,15-22) verwendet die Bezeichnung "häretisch" gerade für die andere Seite, für unsere "Orthodoxie".

Der sich in der Interpretation der Traditionen von Jesus in den verschiedenen kanonischen und nichtkanonischen Texten widerspiegelnde Streit der Geister zog sich durch die gesamte frühchristliche Theologie. Wir begegnen ihm selbstverständlich auch im breiten Raum der paulinischen Überlieferung. Sakramentale Einheit mit dem auferstandenen Jesus bei der Taufe bedeutete für einige, daß sie selbst *schon jetzt* auferstanden seien. Dieses Verständnis wurde sowohl von Paulus (Phil 3,11f; vgl. I Kor 4,8), als auch von einer deuteropaulinischen Schrift (II Tim 2, 18) als häretisch verworfen. Aber eine Schrift aus Nag-Hammadi (Über die Auferstehung, NHC I), die sich auf Paulus als *dem* Apostel par excellence beruft (NHC I, 45,25), gibt wiederum dem Konzept der "schon geschehenen Auferstehung" der Gläubigen eine sinnvolle christliche Interpretation (NHC I, 49,15-16).

Sicherlich kann man solche Debatten nicht danach entscheiden, wer die traditionelle, in diesem Falle paulinische, Sprache beibehält, denn gerade auf dem nachweisbaren Maß, mit dem die deutero-paulinischen Briefe im Kanon von paulinischer Sprache abweichen, basiert ja das Argument, daß sie nicht von Paulus selbst geschrieben wurden. Und Paulus selbst benutzt so gut wie nie die Sprache Jesu. Man muß hinter die Sprache zurückgehen, sich durch die Sprache hindurcharbeiten, bis man zum inhaltlichen Kern der Aussage vorstößt und sie in ihrer vorgegebenen Situation begreift. Dieselbe Sprache drückt in unterschiedlichen Situationen Unterschiedliches aus und kann so mitunter das Gegenteil von dem zum Zuge bringen, was ursprünglich intendiert war. Die "Orthodoxen" haben damals wie heute oft nicht verstanden, daß sich hinter veralteter Sprache eine Zeitbombe verbergen kann. Sie mögen sich sehr wohl nur darum als orthodox verstanden haben, weil sie der traditionellen Sprache verhaftet waren. Die Gegenseite könnte aber die Sprache so weit modifiziert haben, daß sie die ursprüngliche Bedeutung viel eher bewahrte, und könnte so unberechtigerweise als "häretisch" gebrandmarkt worden sein. Natürlich gab es daneben auch sinnentstellende Veränderungen, aber eine Entscheidung, ob und wann dies der Fall war, liegt nicht allein auf der sprachlichen Ebene.

Sprachliche Modifizierungen im Bemühen um Aussagekontinuitat ist überall im Neuen Testament da belegt, wo ein Text eindeutig einen anderen kopiert: Matthäus und Lukas kopierten und änderten Markus; der Epheserbrief kopierte und änderte den Kolosserbrief; der zweite Petrusbrief kopierte und änderte den Judasbrief. Die Sprache ist nirgends dieselbe, aber man darf annehmen, daß mithilfe der sprachlichen Veränderungen gerade bewahrt werden sollte, was ursprünglich gemeint war. Vor allem deshalb wurde Veraltetes interpretiert, aktualisiert, ausgeglichen oder angeglichen, wie immer es die neue Situation erforderte.

Theologisch betrachtet ist der sensibelste Punkt dieses hermeneutischen Prozesses der Übergang von Jesus und seinen unmittelbaren galiläischen Nachfolgern zur heidenchristlichen Kirche, deren Erben wir sind. Für diesen Übergang sind das Thomasevangelium von Nag-Hammadi und das Spruchevangelium Q die Schlüsseltexte, da sie einen unmittelbareren Zugang zu dem vermitteln, was Jesus zu sagen hatte. Aber sie belegen auch, wie diese Tradition sich in zwei zunehmend sich voneinander unterscheidende Strömungen gabelte, deren eine sich in gnostischer Richtung zur "Häresie," und deren andere sich in apokalyptischer Richtung zur "Orthodoxie" hinentwickelte.

Betrachtet man die älteren Schichten der Spruchtradition, spürt man die Spannung zwischen dieser und der paulinischen Überlieferung. Die Spruchtradition kritisiert diejenigen, die Jesus den Herrn nennen, aber nicht tun, was er sagt (Q 6,46), während Paulus denen Erlösung verheißt, die Jesus mit ihren Lippen als den Herrn bekennen und im Herzen glauben, daß Gott ihn von den Toten auferweckt hat (Röm 10,9). Im Thomasevangelium und im Spruchevangelium wird dagegen die Auferstehung überhaupt nicht erwähnt. In der Tat war die paulinische Missionspraxis sehr verschieden von den Missionsinstruktionen des Spruchevangeliums (Q 10,2-12). Paulus gibt das sogar selbst zu, wenn er seine Praxis der des Petrus und der anderen Apostel gegenüberstellt (I Kor 9,1-18). Ergebnis der Konfrontation in Antiochien scheint die endgültige Trennung der Missionspraxis des Paulus von der desjenigen christlichen Zweiges gewesen zu sein, für den Petrus und der Jesusbruder Jakobus eintraten (Gal 2,9), obgleich Paulus durch seine Kollekte für die Armen in Jerusalem (Gal 2,10) versuchte, den Anschein von Ökumene zu wahren (die Missionsanweisungen des Spruchevangeliums Q untersagten allerdings gerade das Mitführen von Geld! [Q 10,4]).

Der Kernpunkt der Botschaft Jesu scheint am besten bewahrt in der Einsetzungsrede, mit der das Spruchevangelium (Q 6,20-49) Jesus vorstellt. Nicht grundlos beginnt es mit einer Segnung der Armen (Q 6,20) und bezieht sich später noch einmal auf diese Predigt zurück mit der Bemerkung, "die Armen evangelisieren (Q 7,22)." Der Begriff "die Armen" wurde anscheinend zu einer sehr frühen Selbstbezeichnung der nicht-paulinischen Jesusanhänger, die in Gebrauch war, bevor der Terminus "Christen" im paulinischen Bereich eingeführt wurde (nach Acta 11,26 zuerst in Antiochia). Der Name "die Armen" überlebte dann allerdings lediglich in seinem semitischen Äquivalent: die Ebioniten – später als Häresie erwähnt. Das häretische Ebionitenevangelium ist – abgesehen von einigen Fragmenten – leider nicht erhalten.

Die traditionelle christliche Annahme, daß Jesus wirklich so war, wie wir ihn aus den kanonischen Evangelien kennen, ist heute nicht mehr zu vertreten. Ebenso unhaltbar ist die Vorstellung, daß seine Jünger ihn und seine Botschaft durchweg in gleicher Weise verstanden hätten, wie dies das apostolische Glaubensbekenntnis suggeriert, und daß demnach das orthodoxe Christentum durch die Jahrhunderte hindurch auch das glaubte und bewahrte, was er lehrte und lebte. Diese Konstruktion ist weder in der hier übertriebenen Simplifizierung tragbar, noch in den viel subtileren und weiterentwickelten Varianten, in denen sie in unserem christlichen Bewußtsein weiter fortbesteht. Viele würden es vorziehen, sich hier von dem gesamten komplizierten Problem zu distanzieren. Aber für diejenigen, die die Anfänge ihrer eigenen religiösen Tradition und die Person, die diese Tradition zu ihrem Gott erhoben hat, verstehen wollen, gibt es keinen anderen Weg als den des möglichst vorurteilslosen kritischen Studiums all der historischen Quellen, die uns heute noch oder wieder zugänglich sind. An diesem Punkt fordern gerade die Codices von Nag-Hammadi, wie auch die wenigen anderen überkommenen außerbiblischen Literaturquellen, volle Aufmerksamkeit.

Schlussbetrachtung

Mit den Nag-Hammadi Texten wird in einem Maße und in einer Weise wie niemals zuvor der Zugang eröffnet zu einem ganzen Zweig innerhalb der Anfänge des Christentums, der sich nicht durchgesetzt hatte und nicht kanonisiert wurde. Die Gnosis, die sich in den meisten dieser Texte wiederspiegelt, ist ein besonders herausragendes Beispiel solch einer rivalisierenden Richtung, die schließlich unterlag, deren Literatur vernichtet und deren Anhängerschaft ausgerottet wurde, als das römische Imperium die christliche Religion als Staatsreligion übernahm. Anders als im römischen Reich, wo sie als bekämpfte Häresie bald vollständig ausgelöscht wurde, konnte sie sich außerhalb des römisch-christlichen Einflußbereichs, besonders in der Gegend des Persischen Golfs, aber auch weit darüber hinaus, weiterentwickeln: als Manichäismus, der über die Seidenstraße bis nach China gelangte und erst ein Jahrtausend später ausgerottet wurde, und als Mandäertum, das bis heute in der Gegend von Basra im Irak weiterlebte (wie weit es den Golfkrieg überlebt hat, ist unklar).

Schon von daher ist es überaus wichtig, mit Hilfe der Nag-Hammadi Texte Zugang aus erster Hand zu dieser anderen Hauptentwicklung des frühen Christentums zu haben. Der Fund hat schon jetzt gezeigt, wie einseitig unsere traditionellen Ansichten und historischen Darstellungen der Anfänge des Christentums bisher waren. Ein Umschreiben der Geschichte, im Blick auf die gnostische Seite dieser Anfänge, ist bereits in vollem Gange. Bisher war die Gnosis ja nur bekannt durch verzerrte Auszüge in anti-gnostischen Schriften orthodoxer Ketzerbestreiter, die die Gnosis lächerlich machen und widerlegen wollten. Jetzt aber stellt sich heraus, daß die Gnosis durchaus verdient ernst genommen zu werden. Wir hätten dies schon vor langer Zeit erkennen sollen, da wir ja schließlich wußten, daß eine Reihe bedeutender christlicher Denker der ersten Jahrhunderte, von Valentin bis Augustin, Gnostiker waren.

Die Gnosis bot damals für das menschliche Dilemma tatsächlich eine grundsätzliche Erklärung und Lösung an, die uns Respekt und Bewunderung abverlangt, ob man sie nun für sich selbst akzeptiert oder nicht. Gnostische Mythologie ist zunächst schwer zu entschlüsseln, aber genauso geht es Außenstehenden, nicht aus unserem Kulturkreis stammenden, mit unserer orthodoxen Mythologie. Die Gnosis erreichte in der Form des Manichäismus den Rang einer Weltreligion. Sie ist so eine der vier Weltreligionen, die ihren Ursprung im östlichen Mittelmeerraum nahmen: das Judentum, mit seiner Torah und seinem Talmud; das Christentum, mit seinem Alten und Neuen Testament; der Islam, mit seinem Koran; und die Gnosis, heute fast nur repräsentiert durch die Bibliothek von Nag Hammadi und die schwer zu entziffernden, bisher weitgehend unveröffentlichten manichäischen Codices von Medinet Madi aus dem südlichen Ende der Fayyum-Oase in Ägypten. Tatsächlich war es der Gnostiker Mani, der absichtlich in unser Bewußtsein hob, was diese Weltreligionen *auch* verbindet: Sie sind allesamt Buchreligionen. Das "Buch" der Gnosis ist als solches nicht mehr erhalten, doch es kann und muß Stück für Stück wiedergewonnen werden aus dem trockenen Sand Ägyptens und anderswo. Ein überaus wichtiger Teil in diesem Wiedergewinnungsprozeß ist der Fund von Nag-Hammadi, der einzige, zu dem wir heute leichten Zugang haben.

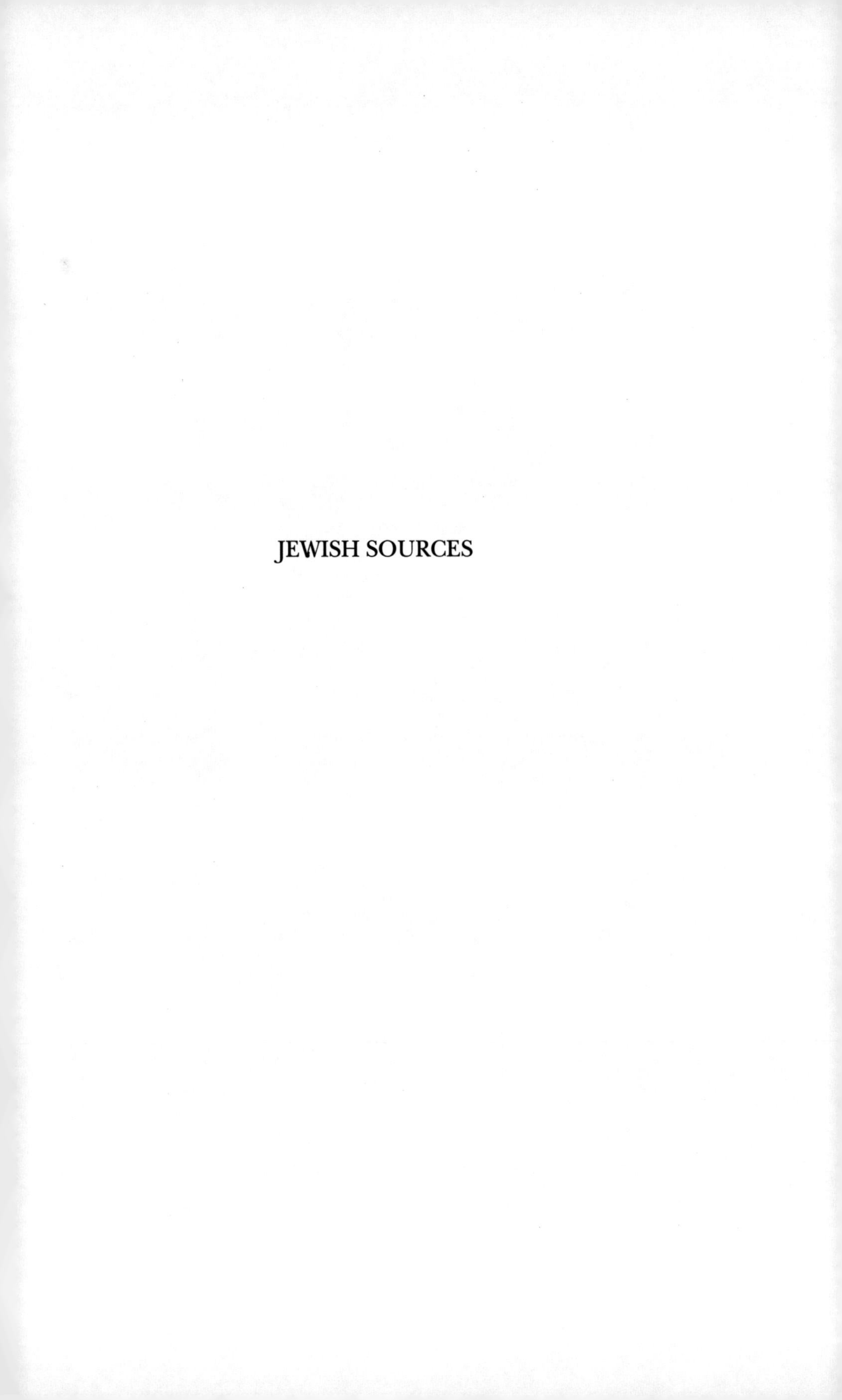

JEWISH SOURCES

JES 52,13: DIE "ERHÖHUNG" DES "GOTTES-KNECHTES"

Klaus Baltzer (München)

So unübersehbar die Literatur zu Jes 52,13-53,12, dem IV. Gottes-Knecht-Text, ist, so hat doch der erste Vers des Textes nicht die Aufmerksamkeit bekommen, die er verdient. 52,13 kann übersetzt werden:

> "Siehe, es wird 'glückselig'[1] sein mein Knecht!
> Er wird aufsteigen
> und emporgetragen werden
> und sehr hoch sein."

Nun ist es keine Frage, daß es im Text um eine außergewöhnliche Ehrung des "Knechtes" geht. So hat es schon die LXX verstanden, wenn sie von "ehren, verherrlichen" (δοξασθήσεται σφόδρα) spricht. Ihr folgen viele Übersetzungen und Kommentare. "Erhöhung" des "Knechtes" wird im übertragenen Sinn verwendet. Sie folgt auf Leiden und Erniedrigung.[2]

Im Folgenden soll gezeigt werden, daß die Aussagen des Verses zunächst viel direkter räumlich zu verstehen sind. Es soll versucht werden, die traditionsgeschichtlichen Zusammenhänge des Textes zu rekonstruieren. Daraus könnten sich Hinweise ergeben, wer mit dem "Gottes-Knecht" hier gemeint ist.

V.13 ist relativ selbständig.[3] Vor allem ist der Vers von v.14-15 zu unterscheiden, denn dort wird weitere Handlung angesagt. Mit "siehe" (הִנֵּה) wird ein deutliches Signal gesetzt. Es beginnt etwas Neues. Wie in 42,1 wird der "Gottes-Knecht" vorgestellt, und das heißt: Er wird sichtbar. Da hier wie in 52,14-15 und 53,11b-12 Gott selbst spricht ("mein Knecht"), liegt die Annahme nahe, daß die ganze Szene im himmlischen Bereich spielt. Das Ziel der "Erhöhung" ist, daß der "Knecht" zu seinem "Herren" kommt. Die Frage nach dem Ausgangs-

---

[1] Zur Übersetzung s.u.

[2] S. C. Westermann, *Das Buch Jesaja. Kap. 40-66* (ATD 19; Göttingen: Vandenhoeck & Ruprecht, [5]1986), S.206-209.

[3] S. W. Richter, *Untersuchungen zur Valenz althebräischer Verben, 2. GBH, ᶜMQ. QSR II* (ATS 25, St. Ottilien: EOS, 1986), S.18-20. Zum vorliegenden v.13 stellt er fest: "Er weist auch syntaktisch nicht über sich hinaus."

punkt läßt sich schwieriger beantworten. Da der "Knecht" ein Mensch ist, kann angenommen werden, daß er aus dem irdischen Bereich kommt. Jedenfalls muß der Abstand zwischen Himmel und Erde überwunden werden. Dies vollzieht sich nach v.13b in drei Stadien: Aufsteigen, Getragenwerden, Sehr-Hoch-Sein.

"Er wird aufsteigen" (יָרוּם). Eindeutig ist die aktive Form der Handlung. Der "Knecht" tut, was sein "Herr" ansagt. Aus diesem Zusammenhang gewinnt das Imperfektum einen jussivischen Ton: "Er soll aufsteigen". Meist wird dies gleich übertragen verstanden, so wenn H.-P. Stähli zur Stelle feststellt: "Positiv ergibt sich die Bedeutung *q.* '(emporsteigen =) zu Ehren kommen' Jes 52,13 ...)".[4] Aber das räumlich-geographische Verständnis der Wurzel רום ist auch möglich, wenn z.B. das Partizip für das Hochsein von Bergen (Deut 12,2; Jes 2,14) und Hügeln (Ez 6,13; 20,28; 34,6) verwendet wird. Vor allem gilt dies vom Substantiv. Dazu schreibt Stähli[5]: "*mārōm* 'Höhe' (vor allem poetisch verwendet) bezeichnet zunächst konkret die Höhe der Berge (2 Kön 19,23 = Jes 37,24a; Jer 31,12; Ez 17,23; 34,14 – hier dürfte nach Zimmerli, BK XIII, 457, die Vorstellung des mythischen Götterberges im Hintergrunde stehen ...)".

So kann zunächst angenommen werden, daß der "Knecht" auf eine Anhöhe, einen Berg, emporsteigen soll. Allerdings besteht die Schwierigkeit, daß nach dem Zusammenhang des IV. Gottes-Knecht-Textes in Jes 53,8-9 der "Knecht" gestorben und begraben ist. Geschieht das "Aufsteigen" zu seinen Lebzeiten, vor seinem Tode oder erst nach seinem Tode – steigt er also aus der Unterwelt auf?

"Und er wird emporgetragen werden" (וְנִשָּׂא). Diese Handlung schließt sich unmittelbar an das Emporsteigen an. Die *nif^cal*-Form des Verbes ist passivisch zu verstehen. Mit dem "Knecht" geschieht etwas. Es wird nicht ausgeführt, auf welche Weise der Raum zwischen Himmel und Erde überwunden wird. Henoch und Elia sind Beispiele für Entrückung, aber auch an Ezechiel ist zu denken, der durch die Hand Gottes vom Geist ergriffen zwischen Erde und Himmel nach Jerusalem getragen wird (וַתִּשָּׂא אֹתִי רוּחַ Ez 8,3; 11,1; vgl. Ez

[4] S. H.-P. Stähli, Art. "רום *rūm* hoch sein", *THAT II* (1979) Sp. 753-761 bes. Sp.757.
[5] *A.a.O.*, Sp.757.

37,1; 40,1). Anzunehmen ist aber, daß der Auftrag zu tragen im vorliegenden Text an himmlische Wesen geht.[6]

"Und er wird sehr hoch sein" (וְגָבַהּ מְאֹד). Mit dieser dritten Etappe ist das Ziel der "Erhöhung" erreicht. Nach Deuterojesaja sind die Himmel "hoch über der Erde" (כִּי־גָבְהוּ שָׁמַיִם מֵאָרֶץ Jes 55,9; vgl. Ps 103,11), und Jahwe thront über dem "Kreis der Erde" עַל־חוּג הָאָרֶץ 40,22), womit möglicherweise der – unbewegte – scheinbare Drehpunkt der Erdachse am Himmel gemeint ist. Wenn Jahwe nach Ps 113,5 "in der Höhe thront" (הַמַּגְבִּיהִי לָשָׁבֶת; vgl. Jes 6,1), so ist der "Knecht" jetzt im himmlischen Bereich angekommen. Dort findet die folgende Szene statt. In ihr wird der "Knecht" in einem Prozeß rehabilitiert. Das ist die höchste Ehrung, die ihm zuteil werden kann. Sie wird schon im ersten Satz unseres Textes angesagt: "'Glückselig' wird sein mein Knecht" (52,13a). Dies ist aber noch einmal am Schluß unserer Überlegungen zu bedenken.

Eine Schwierigkeit im Verständnis von Jes 52,13 liegt in der Knappheit der Aussage. Der Text ist eine Art "Kurzformel". Für die damalige Zeit müssen die weiteren Umstände, vor allem die Elemente des vorauszusetzenden Weltbildes bekannt gewesen sein. Sonst ist die Kurzformel nicht sinnvoll. Für unser heutiges Verständnis ist zunächst die Rekonstruktion des traditionsgeschichtlichen Zusammenhangs erforderlich. Aufschlußreich ist der Vergleich mit Texten, die ebenfalls eine "Erhöhung" zum Gegenstand haben.[7]

Hier ist in Gemeinsamkeiten und Unterschieden ein Text aus der sog. *Assumptio Mosis* von Interesse.[8] Ihrer Form nach ist

---

[6] S. auch Sach 5,9.

[7] S. hierzu bes. George W.E. Nickelsburg, *Resurrection, Immortality, and Eternal Life in Intertestamental Judaism* (HTS 26; Cambridge: Harvard University Press, 1972).

[8] Übersetzung nach Egon Brandenburger, *Himmelfahrt Moses* (JSHRZ V/2 – Apokalypsen; Gütersloh: Gütersloher Verlagshaus, Gerd Mohn, 1976), S. 57-84, besonders S.77. Lateinischer Text: Carl Clemen, Die Himmelfahrt des Mose, in: Hans Lietzmann, *Kleine Texte 10* (Bonn, 1924). Text und Kommentar, in E.-M. Laperrousaz, *Le Testament De Moise* (Semitica 19; Paris, 1970). Der Text der *Assumptio* ist lateinisch in einem Palimpsest erhalten. Wahrscheinlich war er ursprünglich griechisch geschrieben, möglich ist aber auch eine hebräische oder aramäische Grundlage. E. Brandenburger nimmt eine Abfassung "nur wenig nach 6 n.Chr. an", andere wie Laperrousaz eine etwas spätere Zeit. Der Text ist in Teilen schlecht erhalten. Er ist als Ganzes ein Fragment. Auf die literarkritischen Probleme kann hier nicht eingegangen werden.

die *Assumptio* ein Testament. In einer Abschiedsrede wendet sich Mose an Josua, seinen Nachfolger. Es ist ein Rückblick auf die Geschichte Israels und eine Prophetie der Zukunft bis zum endlichen Gericht. Im folgenden Textabschnitt ist die Ansage des Gerichtes mit der Ansage der "Erhöhung" verbunden. Beide Elemente sind aber noch gut in ihrer Selbständigkeit erkennbar. Ich meine, daß in X,8ff ursprünglich Mose eine Prophetie über sein Ende und seine Zukunft gibt. Es ist eigentlich an ihn ergangenes Gotteswort ("Dann wirst *du* glücklich sein ..."), das er hier Josua überliefert.

X 7-10: 7 "Denn der höchste Gott, der allein ewig ist, wird sich erheben,
und er wird offen hervortreten, um die Heiden zu strafen,
und alle ihre Götzenbilder wird er vernichten.
8 Dann *wirst du glücklich sein,* – Israel,
und du wirst auf die Nacken und Flügel des Adlers *hinaufsteigen,*
und sie (die Flügel) werden sich füllen.[9]
9 Und Gott wird *dich erhöhen,*
und er wird *dir festen Sitz am Sternenhimmel verschaffen,*
am Ort ihrer Wohnung.
10 Und du wirst von oben herabblicken ..."

Die wichtigsten Stichworte, die Jes 52,13 entsprechen, sind auch in der lateinischen Fassung erkennbar: "Glücklich sein" (*Tunc felix eris*). Die drei Stadien der "Erhöhung" sind: 1. "Hinaufsteigen" (*ascendes*). "Hinaufsteigen" ist hier das Besteigen eines Adlers als Vehikel der Fortbewegung von der Erde zum Himmel. 2. Eindeutig ist aber, daß es um eine "Himmelfahrt" geht (*et altavit te deus*). 3. Das "Sehr-hoch-sein" von Jes 52,13 ist in der *Assumptio* der "feste Sitz am Sternenhimmel" (*et faciet te herere caelo stellarum ...*). Zu registrieren ist, daß im Text der *Assumptio* ein Singular ("du wirst ...") kollektiv verstanden wird, indem das "Du" auf "Israel" (8a) bezogen ist – ein Problem, das von Deuterojesaja her wohl vertraut ist. Vor allem aber ist in der *Assumptio* deutlich, daß der "Erhöhte" ursprünglich Mose ist. Noch genauer läßt sich sagen, daß der

[9] Hervorhebungen vom Verfasser. E. Brandenburger übersetzt in 8c: "und so werden sie ihr Ende haben". Er versteht die Aussage als Teil der Gerichtsankündigung. M.E. ist *et inplebuntur* auf die Flügel zu beziehen. Sie werden sich wie Segel im Wind füllen, bevor der Adler auffliegt. K.E. Georges, *Ausführliches Lateinisch-Deutsches Handwörterbuch,* 2. Bd. (Hannover u. Leipzig: Hahnsche Buchhandlung, 8. verbesserte und vermehrte Auflage 1918) Sp. 103, verweist auf Celsus: "*flatus vela implet*" sowie Plinius.

Text auf Deut 34, der Erzählung vom Tod des Mose beruht. In X,12 spricht Mose mit Josua "von [meinem] Tode, [meiner] Aufnahme" (*a morte receptione*[*m*])[10]. M.E. bezieht sich dies doch auf die Aufnahme des Mose in den himmlischen Bereich. Auffallend ist, daß die *Assumptio* "Erhöhung" und "Grabtradition" verbindet. Im folgenden Kap. XI der *Assumptio* wird die Frage des Grabes Mose diskutiert. Darin zeigt sich ebenfalls, daß der Text Interpretation von Deut 34 ist.

Die *Assumptio* legt weiterhin Deut 34 und damit die Mosetradition aus, wenn sie Josua sagen läßt:

> XI 5-6.8: 5 "Welcher Ort wird dich aufnehmen?" (*quis locus recipit ... te*)
> 6 "Oder welches Denkmal wird dein Grab bezeichnen ... ?" (*aut quod erit monumentum sepulturae*)

Die Antwort ist:

> 8 "Die ganze Welt ist dein Grab" (*omnis orbis terrarum sepulcrum est tuum*).

Wenn der Text Assumptio X-XI Auslegung von Deut 34 und Auseinandersetzung mit der Mosetradition ist, läßt sich zurückfragen, ob das gleiche nicht schon von Jes 52,13-53,12 gilt. Ist der namenlose Gottesknecht Mose?

Im Folgenden sollen die drei Texte Deut 34, Jes 52-53 und Assumptio X-XI zunächst im Hinblick auf die Topen "Erhöhung" und "Grab" noch einmal verglichen werden.

Nach Deut 34,1 steigt Mose (וַיַּעַל מֹשֶׁה) "von den Steppen Moabs hinauf zum Berg Nebo, auf den Gipfel des Pisga gegenüber Jericho ..." Das geschieht auf Anordnung Jahwes nach Deut 32,48-52. In Jes 52,13 sagt Jahwe das "Aufsteigen" seines Knechtes an. Dieser wird selbst aktiv. Mit der Wurzel רום kann auch, wie oben gezeigt, eine konkrete Anhöhe, ein Berg, bezeichnet werden. Insofern sind Deuteronomium und Deuterojesaja näher beieinander als die *Assumptio*, wenn sie mit "Hinaufsteigen" das Besteigen des "Adlers" verbindet.[11]

Nach Deut 34,3-5 stirbt Mose vor dem Betreten des gelobten

---

[10] Zum Text s. E. Brandenburger, *a.a.O.*, S.77f Anm. 12a.

[11] Möglicherweise ist dieses Motiv wiederum in der *Assumptio* eine Aufnahme von Deut 32,11 aus dem sog. Lied des Mose. – In der Literatur ist die Erwähnung des Adlers als Hinweis auf die Weltmacht Rom verstanden worden. Aber im vorliegenden Text ist der Adler nicht negativ gesehen (siehe dagegen IV. Esra 11-12). Ein Bezug zur zeitgenössischen Situation der römischen Herrschaft könnte in der Erhöhung auf Adlers

Landes. Sein Tod geschieht auf dem Nebo: "Und es starb dort Mose, der Knecht Jahwes (מֹשֶׁה עֶבֶד־יהוה), im Lande Moab." Bei dem Vergleich mit Deuterojesaja ist natürlich auffallend, daß gerade hier im Deuteronomium Mose noch einmal ausdrücklich als Gottes-Knecht bezeichnet wird.

In Jes 52-53 bleibt offen, wo der "Knecht" stirbt. Auf die erste Etappe des Aufstiegs folgt unmittelbar die zweite: "Er wird emporgetragen werden" (Jes 52,13). In 53,9 wird der Tod des Knechtes benannt: "In der Tat, abgeschnitten ist er vom Land der Lebenden" (נִגְזַר מֵאֶרֶץ חַיִּים). Aber es läßt sich erwägen, ob damit nicht auch Deut 34,4 umschrieben wird:

> "Und Jahwe sprach zu ihm: Dies ist das Land, von dem ich Abraham, Isaak und Jakob geschworen habe: Deinen Nachkommen (לְזַרְעֲךָ) will ich es geben. Ich habe es dich mit Augen schauen lassen, aber dort hinein wirst du nicht kommen".

In der *Assumptio* ist die Abfolge verändert, weil die "Erhöhung" als Vorhersage eingeführt wird.

Deut 34,6.8 erinnern an Begräbnis und Grab des Mose:

> "Und 'er begrub ihn' im Tal im Lande Moab, gegenüber von Beth Peor; aber niemand kennt sein Grab bis auf den heutigen Tag".

Der Deuteronomium-Text ist im Hinblick auf das Begräbnis des Mose in der Textüberlieferung nicht eindeutig[12]. Der massoretische Text hat in v.6 וַיִּקְבֹּר אֹתוֹ. Das ist zu übersetzen: "Und er begrub ihn", d.h. Jahwe selbst begrub Mose. Aber an dieser direkten Aussage ist immer wieder Anstoß genommen worden.[13] Schon die LXX hat: "Sie begruben ihn ..." (και

Flügeln trotzdem vorliegen. Zur römischen Kaiser-Ideologie gehört seit Augustus der Adler, der in der Apotheose den vergöttlichten Kaiser in die Lüfte trägt. Vor allem auf Münzen wird dieser Akt dargestellt (s. z.B. den Katalog der Ausstellung *"Spätantike und frühes Christentum"*, Liebighaus, Frankfurt a.M., 1983, Nr. 243, 244, 246 und 248 und Text S. 170 und 260f). Das Motiv geht auf Alexander und die Darstellung im Alexanderroman zurück (s. *Alex.* III 35,5). In der Auseinandersetzung mit der römischen Kaiser-Ideologie beansprucht die *Assumptio* den Adler für die Erhöhung des Mose.

[12] Zum Begriff der 'Uneindeutigkeit' s. Helmut Utzschneider, "Das hermeneutische Problem der Uneindeutigkeit biblischer Texte – dargestellt an Text und Rezeption der Erzählung von Jakob am Jabbok (Gen 32,23-33)", *EvTh 28* (1988), S.182-198.

[13] S. G. von Rad, *Das fünfte Buch Mose*, Deuteronomium (ATD 8; Göttingen: Vandenhoek & Ruprecht, 1983[4]), S.150: "Da Mose nicht ganz ohne

ἔθαψαν αὐτόν entspricht einem hebr. וַיִּקְבְּרוּ), nur daß auch so offenbleibt, wer mit dem "*sie* begruben" gemeint ist, zumal wenn "kein Mensch (אִישׁ) sein Grab kennt bis auf den heutigen Tag" (Deut 34,6b).

Jes 53,9 erwähnt Begräbnis und Grab des "Gottes-Knechtes". Bei dem Vergleich mit Deut 34,6 ist auffallend, daß an der gleichen Stelle eine Textschwierigkeit vorliegt. Der massoretische Text liest: "Und er gab (ihm) bei Übeltätern sein Grab" (וַיִּתֵּן אֶת־רְשָׁעִים קִבְרוֹ). So ist wieder Jahwe der Handelnde.[14] Diesmal hat 1QJes[a] den Plural: "Sie gaben (ויתנו) ... sein Grab".[15] Die "Uneindeutigkeit" der beiden Texte ist die gleiche, sie forderte die spätere Auslegung heraus, wie schon Targum und Midrasch erkennen lassen. Das "Grab bei Übeltätern" im Deuterojesaja-Text, findet seine Erklärung, wenn die Stichworte von Deut 34,6 "im Lande Moab, gegenüber Beth Peor" berücksichtigt werden und der Hintergrund von Num 25,1-5 dazugenommen wird[16]. Schwieriger ist der zweite Teil von v.9a zu verstehen: "Und bei einem Reichen seine Grabstätte" (בְּמֹתָיו[17]). Ich vermute, daß hier ein zeitgeschichtlicher Bezug vorliegt. Wenn ein Zusammenhang Deuterojesajas mit der Neukonstitution Zion/Jerusalems durch Nehemia besteht, ließe sich "ein Reicher" (עָשִׁיר) auf "Tobia, den ammonitischen Knecht" (Neh 2,10.19; 3,35) beziehen. Das Gebiet von Moab/Beth Peor gehörte zur persischen Zeit wahrscheinlich zu Ammon[18]. Tobia war einer der wichtigsten Gegner Nehemias (s. Neh 13,4-9).[19]

Begleitung den Berg bestiegen haben wird, liegt es näher in v.6 zu übersetzen 'man begrub ihn' (Jahwe war im vorausgehenden Satz ja auch nicht Subjekt)."

[14] Aufgrund des Konsonantenbestandes könnte auch ein Passiv gelesen werden: "Es wurde gegeben" (וַיֻּתַּן).

[15] Eine unbestimmte Übersetzung "man gab ihm ... sein Grab" ist auch möglich.

[16] Vgl. Deut 4,3; Ps 106,28 und vor allem Hos 9,10: "... sie wurden so abscheulich wie der, den sie liebten".

[17] Mit LXX (τοῦ θανάτου αὐτοῦ) wird eine Korrektur in "seinem Tod" (בְּמוֹתוֹ) vorgeschlagen.

[18] S. A. Alt, "Judas Nachbarn zur Zeit Nehemias," in: ders., *Kleine Schriften II*, München ^{4}1978, S.338-345, bes. S.341f.

[19] Zu diesem Zeitansatz vgl. K. Baltzer, "Liberation from Debt Slavery after the Exile in Second Isaiah and Nehemia," in: *Ancient Israelite Religion*. Essays in Honor of Frank Moore Cross; hg. von P.D. Hanson, P.D. Miller and S.D. McBride (Philadelphia: Fortress Press, 1987) S.474-484; ders. "Moses Servant of God and the Servants: Text and Tradition in the Prayer of

Die Aufnahme der Grabtradition des "Gottes-Knechtes" Mose könnte ein Indiz für tieferliegende Auseinandersetzungen über theologische Konzepte und Legitimationsfragen sein. Ist der genaue Ort des Grabes Mose nicht bekannt (Deut 34,6), liegt das Grab für den "Gottes-Knecht" bei "Übeltätern" (Jes 53,9), dann ist eine kultische Verehrung des Grabes nicht möglich. Grabkult hängt aber in der Antike eng mit Heroenkult und Stadtkönigtum zusammen. Rüdiger Bartelmus hat die Bedeutung des Heroen-Konzeptes für Juda und das davidische Königtum nachgewiesen.[20] Die Probleme sind, wie die Traditionsgeschichte zeigt, aktuell geblieben. Deuterojesaja "demokratisiert" die Davids-Verheißung (Jes 55,3). Aber es kann für ihn auch keinen Ersatz-Kult am Grabe des "Gottes-Knechtes" geben. Zugleich würde damit aber auch ein Anspruch der Tobiaden im Ostjordanland auf Mose und die Verehrung seines Grabes abgelehnt. Was bleibt, ist der "Gottes-Knecht" Mose, der durch seine Erkenntnis viele gerecht macht.

Für die *Assumptio* ist, wie gezeigt, die ganze Welt das Grab des Mose. Es ist Auslegung von Deut 34,6 "und niemand kennt sein Grab bis auf den heutigen Tag". Die "Uneindeutigkeit" des Deuteronomium-Textes wird damit aufgehoben in die höhere Abstraktion der "ganzen Welt".

In den genannten Punkten: Aufstieg, Tod, Begräbnis, Grab ist die Nähe zwischen Deut 34 und Jes 52-53 signifikant. Deut 34 kennt (noch) keine Erhöhung des Mose über die irdische Sphäre hinaus. Die "Erhöhung verbindet wiederum Deuterojesaja mit der *Assumptio.* Die beiden Texte können sich ein Stück weit gegenseitig erklären. In der Entwicklung der Tradition vom Ende des "Gottes-Knechtes" Mose steht Deuterojesaja zwischen Deuteronomium und *Assumptio.*

Bei Deuterojesaja spielt die gesamte Gerichtsszene im himmlischen Bereich. In ihr wird die Biographie des "Knech-

---

Nehemiah (Neh 1:5-11)," in: *The Future of Early Christianity.* Helmut Koester FS, hg. von Birger A. Pearson with A.T. Kraabel, G.W.E. Nickelsburg, N.R. Peterson (Minneapolis: Augsburg Fortress Press, 1991) S.121-130.

[20] S. R. Bartelmus, *Heroentum in Israel und seiner Umwelt. Eine traditionsgeschichtliche Untersuchung zu Gen 6,1-4 und verwandte Texte im Alten Testament und der altorientalischen Literatur* (AThANT 65; Zürich: TVZ, 1979).

tes"[21] kontrovers vorgetragen. In 53,11 wird bestätigt, was schon in 52,13 von Jahwe über den "Knecht" gesagt wurde: "Der Gerechte, mein Knecht". Dieses Urteil ermöglicht eine neue Existenz. "Nach der Mühsal"[22] seines Lebens "soll er Licht sehen"[23], d.h. er wird der göttlichen Gegenwart gewürdigt. Diese Existenz – soviel läßt der Text erkennen – ist mit "Sättigung" und "Erkenntnis" verbunden.

Nach der *Assumptio* ist das Ziel der "Erhöhung" "der Himmel der Sterne, Ort ihrer Wohnungen" (Assumptio X,9: "*coelo stellarum, loco habitationis eorum*"[24]). Dort wird der "Erhöhte" "bleiben" (*herere*). Das ist im Sinne von Jes 52,13 "sehr hoch". Wahrscheinlich ist mit verschiedenen "Himmeln" zu rechnen.[25] Der "Himmel der Sterne" könnte mit dem "Kreis der Sterne" von Assumptio X,5 (*orbis stellarum*) verbunden werden. Es ist eine Sphäre, die noch über Sonne und Mond liegt. Deutlich ist, daß hier räumliche Vorstellungen und ein entwickelteres Bild von der Welt vorliegen.

Die himmlische Existenz des "Erhöhten" wird in der *Assumptio* angesagt mit: "Dann wirst du glücklich sein ..." (*Tunc felix eris* ...). Nach dem lateinischen Verständnis bedeutet "*felix*": "glücklich, beglückt, vom Glück begünstigt, von glücklichem Erfolg, gesegnet, freudebereitend".[26]

Beim Vergleich der Texte aus der *Assumptio* und aus Deuterojesaja ist auffallend, daß auch Jes 52,13 mit einer vergleichbaren Aussage über das Glücklich-Sein des "Knechtes" beginnt. Im Hebräischen hat שׂכל (*śkl*) verschiedene Nuancen: Es bedeutet im *hif* ᶜ*il* nach *HAL*: "1. verstehen, einsehen ... 2.

---

[21] Dies geschieht unter Aufnahme der Mose-Traditionen des Pentateuch. S. dazu meinen im Erscheinen begriffenen Deutero-Jesaja-Kommentar in der Reihe "Hermeneia", Augsburg Fortress Press, Minneapolis.

[22] S. W.A.M. Beuken, Jesaja deel II B (De Prediking van het Oude Testament; Nijkerk: Callenbach, 1983) S.231 z.St.; vgl. Hen 92,3-4. S. auch Dieter Georgi, *Weisheit Salomos* (JSHRZ III/4); M.J. Suggs, "Wisdom of Solomon 2:10-5: A Homiliy Based on the Fourth Servant Song", *JBL* 76 (1957) S. 26-33 und Udo Schwenk-Bressler, *Sapientia Salomonis als ein Beispiel frühjüdischer Textauslegung* (Beiträge zur Erforschung des Alten Testaments und des antiken Judentums, Bd. 32; Frankfurt a.M.: Peter Lang, 1993).

[23] So mit IQJes^{ab}; vgl. LXX, ferner Hen 92,3-4.

[24] Wahrscheinlich ist *earum* statt *eorum* zu lesen.

[25] Vgl. 1 Kön 8,27.

[26] K.E. Georges, *a.a.O.*, s.v.

Einsicht haben ... 3. einsichtig, klug machen ... 4. Erfolg, Gelingen haben."[27] Es ist ein Terminus weisheitlicher Sprache. Solche "'Einsicht' [ist] in unterschiedlicher Weise von Gott abhängig oder auf ihn bezogen".[28] Gleiches ließe sich von "Gelingen" sagen. Mose spricht nach Deut 29,8 und 32,9 von Einsicht und Gelingen. In seiner Erhöhung erfährt der "Gottes-Knecht" endgültige "Einsicht" und dauerndes "Gelingen". Ich möchte daher יַשְׂכִּיל (*jaśkîl*) im Kontext von Jes 52-53 mit "glückselig" wiedergeben. Der "Knecht" wird unter die Einsichtigen aufgenommen, wobei "einsichtig" immer den doppelten Sinn von "einsichtig sein" und "einsichtig machen" behält. Von den Einsichtigen (הַמַּשְׂכִּילִים) heißt es in Dan 12,3:

> "Und die Einsichtigen werden scheinen wie die Helligkeit des Firmaments und die, die viele zur Gerechtigkeit führen, wie die Sterne für immer."

Jes 52,13 ist ein Beispiel wie Schriftauslegung bereits innerhalb des Alten Testamentes stattfindet. In diesem Fall ist es Auslegung von Deut 34. Das läßt annehmen, daß der Deuteronomium-Text für die Zeit Deuterojesajas eine eigene Dignität hat. Auslegung ist hier nicht einfache Wiederholung der Texte, sondern eine lebendige Auseinandersetzung mit der Tradition. In einer Art Rückkoppelungsprozeß ist mit Hilfe der Texte eine Verständigung gerade auch mit der jeweiligen Gegenwart möglich. Einzelne Elemente der Tradition können weiterentwickelt werden, relativ späte Texte lassen Konsistenz und Veränderungen erkennen. Das ist besonders signifikant in der Auseinandersetzung mit dem Weltbild der jeweiligen Zeit. Neue Erkenntnisse werden aufgenommen und verändert. Deuterojesaja hat ein differenzierteres Weltbild als etwa die Priesterschrift. In Gen 1 ist der Himmel die "Feste" (רָקִיעַ). Bei Deuterojesaja werden die Himmel "ausgespannt" (נטה) wie ein Zelt, während die Erde "festgemacht" (רקע) ist (Jes 42,5). Die Tradition lebt in der Auseinandersetzung. Das lassen bereits die Mose-Erzählungen im Pentateuch erkennen. Nähe und Abstand des Mose gegenüber seinem Gott sowie seine Stellung zwischen Gott

---

[27] Vgl. *HAL* (Hebräisches und Aramäisches Lexikon zum AT, hg. v. L. Koehler u. W. Baumgartner, IV ([3]1990) Leiden: Brill, 1990), Sp. 1238-1239; s. auch M. Saebø, Art. "שׂכל *škl* hi. einsichtig sein," *THAT II* (1979) Sp.824-828.

[28] M. Saebø, *ebenda*, Sp. 825.

und den Menschen werden immer wieder neu bestimmt. Wenn Ex 2,1-2 erklärt: "Ein Mann aus dem Hause Levi ging hin und nahm 'eine Frau aus dem Hause Levi'[29] und die Frau wurde schwanger und gebar einen Sohn ...", dann ist mit dieser Notiz eine göttliche Geburt des Mose ausgeschlossen. Wenn nach Deut 34 kein Mensch das Grab des Mose kennt, so ist ein Heroen-Kult nicht möglich. Für Deuterojesaja ist "Mose" der Gottesknecht, seine Tora (42,4)[30] ist es, die er den Menschen im Auftrag seines Herrn gebracht hat. Wenn Deuterojesaja in einem Werk, in dem ein wichtiges Thema der "Exodus" ist, den Namen des Mose nicht nennt, so ist das möglicherweise wieder zu erklären als eine Auslegung von Ex 32,32, wo Mose anbietet, daß sein Name getilgt werde wegen der Sünde Israels (vgl. Jes 48,19). Der Name Jahwe ist der Name, der allein bleibt (Jes 55,13)!

Die *Assumptio* macht deutlich, wie über eine lange Zeit die Auslegung von Deut 34 fortgesetzt worden ist. Es wäre wert, die weitere Auslegung von Deut 34 und Jes 52-53 in der jüdischen[31] und christlichen Tradition[32] zu vergleichen. Der Text vom "Gottes-Knecht" hat seine Aktualität bis heute behalten.[33]

---

[29] S. die Kommentare z.St., bes. B.S. Childs, *The Book of Exodus* (OTL; Philadelphia: Westminster Press, 1974) und W.H. Schmidt, *Exodus 1-6* (BK II/1; Neukirchen: Neukirchener Verlag, 1988).

[30] S.bes. Neh 10,30: "... zu wandeln in dem Gesetz Gottes (בְּתוֹרַת הָאֱלֹהִים), das er gegeben hat durch die Hand des Mose, den Knecht Gottes" (עֶבֶד־הָאֱלֹהִים); vgl. auch Jos 8,31; 23,6; 1 Kön 2,3; 2 Kön 14,6; 23,25; Mal 3,22; Dan 9,11.13; Esr 3,2; 7,6; Neh 8,1; 2 Chr 23,18; 30,16.

[31] S. dazu besonders Moritz Rosenfeld, *Der Midrasch Deuteronomium Rabba über den Tod des Mose verglichen mit der Assumptio Mosis*, Diss. Bern, Berlin 1899.

Zum Midrasch über den Tod des Mose (פטירת משה; Jellinek 1.122) s. die Literatur bei E.-M. Laperrousaz, *a.a.O.*, S.26-28. Vgl. auch Pseudo-Philo, *Lib Ant Bibl* bes. 19,16, der, wie G. Vermes gezeigt hat, eine besondere Nähe zum Mosebild des Deuteronomiums wie auch zu Deuterojesaja aufweist, G. Vermes, "Die Gestalt des Mose an der Wende der beiden Testamente", in: H. Cazelles u.a., *Moses* (Düsseldorf: Patmos-Verlag, 1963), S.61-93 bes. 86.93.

[32] Hier wäre die Rolle der "Gottes-Knecht" – und Mose-Tradition für die Entwicklung der Christologie noch einmal zu diskutieren. An die Kurzformel von Jes 52,13 mit dem "sehr erhöhen" (וְגָבַהּ מְאֹד) erinnert Phil 2,9 (ὑπερύψωσεν), s. ferner Eph 1,20 (ἐν τοῖς ἐπουρανίοις ὑπεράνω); Hebr 1,3 (ἐν ὑψηλοῖς); 7,26 (ὑψηλότερος τῶν οὐρανῶν). In Act 2,33 wird von Jesus gesagt, daß er durch die rechte Hand Gottes erhöht ist (ὑψωθείς). Dies wird ausgeführt, wenn der erste Märtyrer Stephanus dann die Identität des irdischen Jesus mit dem in den Himmel erhöhten bezeugt: "Er aber, voll

heiligen Geistes, sah auf zum Himmel und sah die Herrlichkeit Gottes (δόξαν θεοῦ) und Jesus stehen zur Rechten Gottes" (Act 7,55).

[33] Dieter Georgi, in Freundschaft und in Erinnerung an die gemeinsame Bemühung um das Verständnis biblischer Texte.

Für die Hilfe bei der Fertigstellung des Manuskripts danke ich Peter Kocher, Anemone Körner und Peter Marincović.

THE SIBYL AND THE POTTER: POLITICAL PROPAGANDA IN PTOLEMAIC EGYPT

John J. Collins
(University of Chicago, Chicago, Illinois)

Much of the literature of the Hellenistic Jewish Diaspora is generally held to have been written with propagandistic or apologetic intent. This is especially true of literature with Gentile pseudonyms (the Sibyl, Aristeas) or composed in traditional Greek forms (the tragedy of Ezekiel, the epic of Philo).[1] It is unnecessary to prolong the debate as to whether the primary audience of this material was Jewish or Gentile.[2] Propaganda typically bolsters the security of the propagandist group by addressing the world around it, whether or not that world is prepared to listen. The Jews of the Hellenistic Diaspora were first of all working out their own identity as people who were Jewish by religion and Greek by culture. There is ample evidence that they welcomed the affirmation of Gentiles who embraced Jewish religious practices in various degrees.[3]

Much of the propaganda of Hellenistic Judaism is religious in nature. It proclaims the one God, denounces idolatry and certain sexual offences, and argues that some apparently irrational Jewish practices (such as the dietary observances) admit of a spiritual, allegorical interpretation.[4] The Sibylline Oracles certainly participate in this religious propaganda. Long passages are devoted to outlining true religious observance.[5] But the Sibyllines differ from most of the Diaspora

---

[1] See e.g. E. Schürer, *The History of the Jewish People in the Age of Jesus Christ (175 B.C.-A.D. 135)* (rev. and ed. G. Vermes, F. Millar and M. Goodman; Edinburgh: Clark, 1986) 617-18. See also the remarks of Dieter Georgi, *The Opponents of Paul in Second Corinthians* (Philadelphia: Fortress, 1986) 83-51. It is a pleasure to offer this essay to Dieter Georgi, who was a reader on my dissertation committee and contributed much to my education in Hellenistic Judaism.

[2] V. Tcherikover, "Jewish Apologetic Literature Reconsidered," *Eos* 48 (1956) 169-93.

[3] L.H. Feldman, *Jew and Gentile in the Ancient World* (Princeton: Princeton University Press, 1993) 288-382.

[4] J.J. Collins, *Between Athens and Jerusalem: Jewish Identity in the Hellenistic Diaspora* (New York: Crossroad, 1983) 137-74.

[5] E.g., Sib Or 3:8-45; 218-64; 545-600; 715-31; 762-66. I use the Greek text of J. Geffcken throughout; the English translations are my own (from Charlesworth *OTP*).

literature insofar as their propaganda also possesses an overt political element. The twelve books of Oracles represent a long tradition over several hundred years, and the political emphases vary in the different books and even within individual books.[6] Here we shall focus on the fountainhead of the tradition, in Egyptian Judaism in the Hellenistic period.

The First Jewish Sibyl

Sibylline oracles were a ready medium for propaganda.[7] The author does not speak in his/her own voice, but conceals his/her identity under the pseudonym of the Sibyl. The choice of this pseudonym offered several advantages to a Jewish author of the second century BCE. She was a figure of great antiquity, known throughout the Hellenistic world. The Sibyl apparently had originated in Asia Minor, but Sibylline oracles were extant in Italy by the late sixth century BCE.[8] Sibyls and Sibylline oracles multiplied in the Hellenistic period, so that Varro, the Roman antiquarian, could list ten Sibyls (none of them Jewish) in the first century BCE.[9] In view of this proliferation it is not surprising that Jews should claim a Sibyl too. She offered a medium that was analogous to Hebrew prophecy insofar as it allowed extended discourses, unlike the circumscribed responses of the oracular shrines. Like the Hebrew prophets, the Sibyl relied on assertion backed by a claim of inspiration rather than argument. Propaganda is most effective when it appears to state what is the case rather than invite rational thought. Sibylline oracles also allowed considerable flexibility in their contents. The form required Homeric hexameters, and so presupposed a certain level of Greek

[6] J.J. Collins, "The Development of the Sibylline Tradition," *ANRW* II.20.1 (1987) 421-59; D.S. Potter, *Prophecy and History in the Crisis of the Roman Empire: A Historical Commentary on the Thirteenth Sibylline Oracle* (Oxford: Clarendon Press, 1990).

[7] See the discussion of propagandistic techniques, with reference to Egyptian oracles, by A.B. Lloyd, "Nationalist Propaganda in Ptolemaic Egypt," *Historia* 31 (1982) 33-55.

[8] H.W. Parke, *Sibyls and Sibylline Prophecy in Classical Antiquity* (ed. B.C. McGing; London and New York: Routledge, 1988) 51-99.

[9] Lactantius, *Divinae Institutiones* 1.6.8-12. Varro did not mention either a Jewish or a Babylonian Sibyl. Pausanias is the first pagan author to mention a Jewish Sibyl, named Sabbe, and he says that others call her Babylonian or Egyptian (Potter, *Prophecy and History*, 107).

education, but otherwise consisted of predictions that "when certain conditions obtain, something will happen."[10] Repetition is endemic to the genre, as the loosely-structured collections go over the same ground time and again, thereby implanting it ever deeper in the consciousness of the reader or listener. The credibility of the Sibyl is enhanced by frequent "prediction" of things that have already happened, a device made possible by the supposed antiquity of the Sibyl.

The third book of Sibylline Oracles is a loosely- structured accumulation of oracles, which grew by addition and insertion over a period of a century and a half.[11] Some passages, such as Sib Or 3:46-92, clearly date to the Roman era (after the battle of Actium in 31 BCE). There is general agreement, however, that the nucleus of the book (vss. 97-294; 545-808) dates from the mid-second century BCE. The key to the dating lies in three references to the "seventh king" of the Greek dynasty, who must be identified either as Ptolemy VI Philometor (180-164 and 163-145 BCE, if Alexander the Great is counted as the first king), or his short-lived successor Ptolemy VII Neos Philopator (145-44 BCE).[12]

If there is a central theme in these oracles, it is the call to the Greek world to honor the Most High God and offer sacrifices in his temple (vss. 624-34; 716-18). The sibyllist is unabashed in praise of the Jewish people and their way of life (218-64; 702-13), and regularly justifies predictions of doom with moral condemnation (185-86 on Roman pederasty; 601-07 on idolatry). The exhortations, however, are framed by political prophecies. A long oracle on world kingdoms in vss. 162-95 concludes with a denunciation of Rome, which will "fill everything with evils," especially for aggression against Macedonia, which was divided by Rome after the battle of Pydna in 168 BCE and annexed in 147 BCE as a Roman province. Then, we are told, in the:

---

[10] Potter, *Prophecy and History*, 104.

[11] J.J. Collins, *The Sibylline Oracles of Egyptian Judaism* (SBLDS 13; Missoula: Scholars Press, 1974) 24-33; idem, "The Sibylline Oracles," *OTP* 1.354-61.

[12] The thesis of V. Nikiprowetzky, *La Troisième Sibylle* (Paris: Mouton, 1970) 215, that the seventh king was Cleopatra VII, has found no followers. Nikiprowetzky was led to this position by his desire to preserve the unity of the book.

> "seventh reign, when a king of Egypt, who will be of the Greeks by race, will rule . . .the people of the great God will again be strong."

Some scholars have seen here an allusion to the Maccabean revolt, which took place during the reign of Philometor.[13] If so, this is the only acknowledgement of the Maccabees in the book, and it is a faint one. It is more likely that the rise of the people of God is a real prophecy, as yet unfulfilled.

This passage does not explicitly state that the seventh king of Egypt will be responsible for the rise of the people of God, but the fact that they rise in his reign invites that inference. The other references to the seventh king are also elliptic. In vs. 318 we find that Egypt will be torn by civil strife in the reign of the seventh king, but then will rest. There was civil war between Philometor and his brother, Euergetes II Physcon, and again briefly between Physcon and Philometor's widow, Cleopatra II.[14] In vss. 608-9 we read that God will punish all people for idolatry "whenever the young seventh king of Egypt rules his own land, numbered from the line of the Greeks." The following verses go on to predict that "a great king will come from Asia" and overthrow the kingdom of Egypt. Antiochus IV Epiphanes conducted a successful invasion of Egypt in 170-69 BCE, at a time when Philometor was still a youth and under the tutelage of advisors.[15] Whether the Sibylline reference is an allusion to this historical event is questionable inasmuch as there is no hint of Antiochus Epiphanes' disastrous second invasion, when he was humiliated by the Romans. It is more likely that historical reminiscences were incorporated into genuine predictions of future upheavals.

None of these passages provides a clear picture of the role of the seventh king. There is, however, one passage that ascribes a more active role to the king. Vss. 652-6 predict:

> "then God will send a king from the sun, who will stop the entire earth from evil war, killing some, imposing oaths of loyalty on others; and he will not do all these things by his private plans but in obedience to the noble teachings of the great God."

---

[13] So A. Momigliano, "La Portata Storica dei Vaticini sul Settimo Re nel Terzo Libro degli Oracoli Sibillini," in *Forma Futuri: Studi in Onore del Cardinale Michele Pellegrino* (Turin: Erasmo, 1975) 1081.

[14] P.M. Fraser, *Ptolemaic Alexandria* (Oxford: Clarendon Press, 1972) I. 119-21.

[15] Mørkholm, *Antiochus IV of Syria* (Copenhagen: Gyldendal, 1966) 64-87.

The identity of this "king from the sun" is the key to the political propaganda of the Sibyl. Many scholars have assumed that the reference is to a Jewish messiah and translated it as "from the east" by analogy with Isa 41:25 (LXX), where the phrase is "from the rising of the sun."[16] But "from the sun" does not mean "from the east," and in any case the Jewish messiah was not expected to come from the east. I argued in my dissertation twenty years ago that the phrase must be understood against the background of Egyptian mythology, where the king was understood as the son of the sun-god Re.[17] A precise parallel is found in the *Potter's Oracle*, a nearly contemporary piece of Egyptian nationalist propaganda in oracular form.[18] The fact that both the Sibyl and the Potter focus their expectations on a "king from the sun" invites a comparison between Jewish and Egyptian political propaganda in the Ptolemaic era.

The Potter's Oracle

The *Potter's Oracle* stands in a tradition of native Egyptian propaganda, exemplified in such works as the *Oracle of the Lamb to Bocchoris* and the *Demotic Chronicle.*[19] It survives in three fragmentary papyri from the second and third centuries CE,[20] but it must date from the Hellenistic era since it is directed against the Greeks, not the Romans. Like the Sibylline Oracles, this oracle is attributed to a legendary figure, a potter in the reign of King Amenhotep,[21] who acts as the incarnation of the creator god Khnum. This potter goes to the island of Helios-Re, where he proceeds to make pottery. The inhabitants,

[16] So Nikiprowetzky, *La Troisième Sibylle*, 133; Momigliano, "La Portata Storica," 1081.

[17] Collins, *The Sibylline Oracles of Egyptian Judaism*, 40-44.

[18] The parallel was noted by E. Norden, *Die Geburt des Kindes* (Leipzig: Teubner, 1924) 55 n. 2, 147. See also J. Gwyn Griffiths, "Apocalyptic in the Hellenistic Era," in *Apocalypticism in the Hellenistic World and in the Near East* (ed. D. Hellholm; Tubingen: Mohr, 1983) 290.

[19] Gwyn Griffiths, "Apocalyptic in the Hellenistic Era," 273-93; Lloyd, "Nationalist Propaganda in Ptolemaic Egypt," 33-55; F. Dunand, "L'Oracle du Potier et la formation de l'apocalyptique en Égypte," in *L'Apocalyptique* (ed. F. Raphael; Paris: Geuthner, 1977) 39-67.

[20] See the edition of the text by L. Koenen, "Die Prophezeiungen des 'Töpfers'," *ZPE* 2 (1968) 178-209.

[21] There were four pharoahs of this name in the eighteenth dynasty (approximately 1550-1300 BCE).

however, smash the pottery and drag the prophet before the king. The potter then interprets this action as a prophetic sign:

> "Just as the pottery has been destroyed, so Egypt and, finally, the city of the followers of the evil god Typhon-Seth [i.e., Alexandria] will be destroyed."

Thereupon

> "Egypt will prosper, when the king from the sun, who is benign for fifty five years, comes, the giver of good things, sent by the great goddess Isi s, so that those who survive will pray that those who have already died may rise to share in the good things."[22]

The potter was buried in Heliopolis, the city of the sun.

Ludwig Koenen argued that the papyrus fragments P_2 and P_3 of the *Potter's Oracle* represent two recensions of the oracle which may be dated soon after 129 BCE and 116 BCE respectively.[23] Their dating depends on a quotation from the *Oracle of the Lamb to Bocchoris*, another Egyptian nationalist prophecy which dates from the Persian period, i.e., prior to Alexander.[24] The quotation from the *Oracle of the Lamb* in the *Potter's Oracle* says that the true king is not the king of two years, but the one who will reign for fifty-five years. (The reference to fifty-five years is missing in P_2). Koenen argued that the king of two years was Harsiesis, who led an abortive revolt in 130-129 BCE, and that the ideal of fifty-five years in the quotation in the *Potter's Oracle* was devised to reject any claim on behalf of Ptolemy VIII Euergetes, who reigned for fifty-four years. Subsequent publication of the *Oracle of the Lamb*, however, showed that both numbers were already present in the older version of the oracle.[25] At most, the *Potter's Oracle* may have applied the older prophecy from the *Oracle of the Lamb* to Harsiesis and Euergetes, but the passage itself cannot have been composed to fit those situations. Already in his edition Koenen had argued that the quotation from the *Oracle of the Lamb* was an interpolation into the *Potter's Oracle*, and in another essay he argued that a prophecy of the same

[22] L. Koenen, "The Prophecies of a Potter. A Prophecy of World Renewal Becomes an Apocalypse," *Proceedings of the Twelfth International Congress of Papyrology* (D.H. Samuel, ed.; Toronto: University of Toronto Press, 1970) 249.

[23] Koenen, "Die Prophezeiungen," 186-93.

[24] Griffiths, "Apocalyptic in the Hellenistic Era," 285-87.

[25] Koenen, "A Supplementary Note on the Date of the Oracle of The Potter," *ZPE* 54 (1984) 9-13.

kind as the *Potter's Oracle* was known to Callimachus, who made use of it in his Hymn to Delos.[26] The *Potter's Oracle*, then, was a fluid tradition, which was updated repeatedly in light of historical events. The use of the present participle κτιζομένην (P_2 col. 1, line 29; P_3 col. 2, line 51) with reference to Alexandria suggests that a stratum of the oracle dates from the beginning of the Hellenistic period.[27] However, the *Potter's Oracle* also refers to a king who will come down from Syria and will be hated by all (P_2 col.1, line 16; P_3 col. 1, line 30). Antiochus Epiphanes was the first Syrian king to invade Egypt, and the *Potter's Oracle* presumably had this precedent in mind. It was still being copied in the third century CE.

If the *Potter's Oracle* evolved gradually over several centuries, as has been suggested, then it is quite possible that the Jewish sibyllist was familiar with it at some stage of its development, and borrowed from it the expression "king from the sun" for the anticipated deliverer. Inevitably, the expression takes on a different meaning in a Jewish context. The Sibyl certainly was not prophesying a restoration of native Egyptian kingship. The old Pharaonic ideology, however, was not the exclusive property of Egyptian nationalists in the Ptolemaic period. The Ptolemies themselves laid claim to the old Pharaonic titles.[28] These titles were translated into Greek under Ptolemy IV Philopator and were applied in abundance to Ptolemy V Epiphanes on the Rosetta Stone. Both these kings were called "son of the Sun."[29] The Ptolemy also is called "son of Re" in the texts inscribed at the temple of Edfu and identified as Horus.[30] The Ptolemies supported the Egyptian priesthood and in return were recognized as the living Horus, even though the sincerity of the honor may be doubted.[31] A "king from the sun," then, was not necessarily a native Egyptian king. The title could be applied equally well to "a king of Egypt from

[26] L. Koenen, "Die Adaptation ägyptischer Königsideologie am Ptolemäerhof," in *Egypt and the Hellenistic World* (ed. W. Peremans; Studia Hellenistica 27; Leuven: Leuven University Press, 1983) 184.

[27] Griffiths, "Apocalyptic in the Hellenistic Era," 289-90.

[28] See especially Koenen, "Die Adaptation ägyptischer Königsideologie," 152-70.

[29] Ibid., 155.

[30] Griffiths, "Apocalyptic in the Hellenistic Era," 289.

[31] See the remarks of H.W. Fairman, *The Triumph of Horus: An Ancient Egyptian Sacred Drama* (Berkeley: University of California Press, 1974) 33.

the line of the Greeks." In view of the importance attached to the reign of the seventh king in Sib Or 3, it is very probable that the king expected by the Sibyl was a benevolent Ptolemy.

In fact, Ptolemy VI Philometor's benevolence to the Jews is well known. It was he who gave Onias IV land to build his temple at Leontopolis, quite near Heliopolis where the potter supposedly was buried. Josephus claims that Ptolemy Philometer set Onias and Dositheus over all his army,[32] and, even if we allow for some exaggeration, it is clear that Onias enjoyed high rank.[33] The Jewish philosopher Aristobulus was allegedly the teacher of Philometor.[34] It is understandable, then, that some Diaspora Jews, especially those who had fled from Jerusalem with Onias on the eve of the Maccabean revolt, would look to the Ptolemaic king as their potential savior.

The *Potter's Oracle* and the Sibylline Oracle, then, put forward rival claims as to who was the true "king from the sun." For the Egyptian oracle it was a native king who would overthrow the Greeks; for the Jewish Sibyl it was the Ptolemaic king in whose reign Jerusalem would be restored.[35]

Horus and Seth

Besides the obvious difference in their ultimate goals, there are other differences between the Potter and the Sibyl. The *Potter's Oracle*, no less than the Sibylline Oracle, champions the restoration of a particular cult. The divine statues will be restored to Egypt. The Potter lacks, however, the moral exhortation of the Sibyl. The characteristically Jewish concerns

[32] *Ap* 2.49.

[33] A. Kasher, *The Jews in Hellenistic and Roman Egypt* (Tübingen: Mohr, 1985) 8.

[34] 2 Macc 1:10.

[35] In view of the consistent montheism of the Sibyl, the title must be taken as honorific. There are, however, a number of documents dating from the second century BCE in which the contracting parties and witnesses are Jewish, and which refer to the Ptolemies as gods (*CPJ* 1.23, 24). Note also the existence of a syncretistic prayer, in Aramaic but in Demotic script, which calls for help on the Egyptian God Horus side by side with the God of Israel. See C.F. Nims and R.C. Steiner, "A Paganized Version of Psalm 20:2-6 from the Aramaic Text in Demotic Script," *JAOS* 103 (1983) 261-74. Evidence for Jewish veneration of Helios comes mainly from the land of Israel, where the sun is depicted on several synagogue floors in the second to the fourth centuries. See Feldman, *Jew and Gentile*, 67, 483.

about homosexuality and idolatry have no reflection in the Egyptian work. The most striking distinction, however, concerns the different ways in which the political situation is symbolized.

The *Potter's Oracle* evokes Egyptian myth not only in the phrase "king from the sun," but also in its labelling of the Alexandrian Greeks as "Typhonians." The Typhonians are the followers of Seth, the adversary of Horus. According to the myth, Seth revolts against Osiris and kills him.[36] The new king, Horus, takes revenge on Seth for his father. Every Egyptian king is Horus; all the enemies of Egypt are followers of Seth. The *Potter's Oracle* envisages the future after the pattern of the myth.

The Ptolemaic rulers, who laid claim to the Egyptian mythology, also were identified with Horus. Callimachus, in his Hymn to Delos, applies the myth of Horus (Apollo) and Seth (Ares) to the victory of Ptolemy II Philadelphus over the Gauls ("the Titans of a later day," vs. 174) in 275 BCE.[37] The Gauls are said to wear ζωστῆρας ἀναιδέας, just as the Greeks in the *Potter's Oracle* are said to be ζωνοφόροι, "girdle wearers." The victory of Ptolemy IV Philopator over Antiochus III at Raphia in 217 BCE was commemorated in a decree which boasted that the Ptolemy slew his enemies as Horus, son of Isis, had slain his foes.[38] The Rosetta Stone proclaims Ptolemy V Epiphanes to be "a god from a god and goddess just as Horus, the son of Isis and Osiris, the defender of his father Osiris."[39] The victory of Horus over Seth was portrayed on the walls of the temple at Edfu, and the Ptolemy was identified as Horus.[40] The myth could be applied in different ways by opposing factions. One

---

[36] See J.G. Griffiths, *The Conflict of Horus and Seth from Egyptian and Classic Sources* (Liverpool: Liverpool University Press, 1960); H. te Velde, *Seth, God of Confusion: A Study of his Role in Egyptian Mythology and Religion* (Leiden: Brill, 1967).

[37] Koenen, "Die Adaptation ägyptischer Königsideologie am Ptolemäerhof," 174-90.

[38] H.J. Thissen, *Studien zum Raphiadekret* (Beitrage zur klassischen Philogie 23; Meisenheim am Glan: Hain, 1966) 7.

[39] S.M. Burstein, *The Hellenistic Age from the Battle of Ipsos to the Death of Cleopatra VII* (Cambridge: Cambridge University Press, 1985), 132; C. Onasch, "Zur Königsideologie der Ptolemäer in den Dekreten von Kanopus und Memphis (Rosettana)," *Archiv fur Papyrus-Forschung* 24/25 (1976) 137-55.

[40] Fairman, *The Triumph of Horus*, passim.

of the native Egyptian rebels under Ptolemy VII Euergetes (Physcon) was named Harsiesis (Horus, son of Isis). In Ptolemaic propaganda, evidenced in a papyrus fragment, he was called ὁ θεοῖσιν ἐχθρός, "the enemy of the gods."[41]

The myth of Horus and Seth lent itself to political propaganda because it provided ready-made labels for heroes and villains. One of the simplest forms of propaganda consists of identifying an individual or group as a focal point of communal hatred.[42] Callimachus identified the Gauls as latter-day Titans. The *Potter's Oracle* identified the Alexandrians as Typhonians. Remarkably, however, no such enemy is identified in the earliest stratum of the *Third Sibylline Oracle.* The "king from the sun" plays the role of Horus, but no one is cast in the role of Seth.[43]

The difference between the Sibyl and the Potter in this respect can be understood readily enough in view of their different relationships to the Ptolemaic rulers. *The Potter's Oracle* is a revolutionary document, aiming at the overthrow of the Greeks. The Jewish oracle, if it was written under Ptolemy VI Philometor, is addressed to a ruler who was well-disposed. While there were various factions in Egypt in the mid-second century, the Sibyl does not wish to antagonize any of them unduly. There is no reflection here of the strained relations between the Jews and Euergetes II Physcon,[44] and no sweeping condemnation of the native Egyptians.[45] The Sibyl's denunciations of idolatry might be offensive to many in Egypt, but no political group is dismissed as an irredeemable enemy.

More surprising, however, is the failure to denounce the

---

[41] L. Koenen, "THEOSIN ECHTHROS: Ein Einheimischer Gegenkönig in Aegypten (132/1)," *Chronique d'Egypte* 34 (1959) 103-119.

[42] Lloyd, "Nationalist Propaganda," 34, citing J.A.C. Brown, *Techniques of Persuasion* (Harmondsworth: Penguin, 1963) 28.

[43] The Sibyl envisages an eschatological assault on the Temple after the manner of Psalm 2, but the adversaries are identified in general terms as "the kings of the peoples" (3:663).

[44] Josephus, *Ap* 2.53-55; V. Tcherikover, *Hellenistic Civilization and the Jews* (New York: Atheneum, 1970) 282; Fraser, *Ptolemaic Alexandria* I.121.

[45] Contrast in this regard the treatment of the Egyptians in Wisdom 15-19, which reflects the hostile relations of the first century CE. On the date of Wisdom I must agree with D. Winston, *The Wisdom of Solomon* (AB 43; Garden City, New York: Doubleday, 1979) 20-25, against D. Georgi, *Weisheit Salomos* (JSHRZ 3/4; Gütersloh: Mohn, 1980) 395-96.

Seleucids, the common enemy of Judaism and Ptolemaic Egypt in the time of Philometor. We have noted already that Antiochus IV Epiphanes had invaded Egypt in the time of Philometor, and may be the prototype of the "king from Syria, who will be hated by all" in the *Potter's Oracle.* We have also noted a possible reminiscence of this invasion in Sib Or 3:611-15, which tells how "a great king will come from Asia" and overthrow the kingdom of Egypt. But the Sibyl's attitude towards this figure is not at all clear. He is certainly not portrayed as an incarnation of Seth, nor is there is any mention of Antiochus' downfall or of his persecution of the Jews.

The Sibyl's silence on Antiochus Epiphanes stands in sharp contrast to the portrayal of the king in the nearly contemporary Book of Daniel, where the Gentile kingdoms are beasts that rise from the chaotic sea, and Antiochus Epiphanes is an upstart horn on the fourth beast. The imagery of Daniel is drawn from Canaanite myth, filtered through a long history of Israelite usage.[46] In the present context, however, it is worth noting that some scholars have argued that Daniel's vision should be understood against the backdrop of the myth of Horus and Seth.[47] There is in any case a basic structural similarity between the various combat myths of the eastern Mediterranean world and the Near East.[48] A positive god of life, fertility or order (Baal, Marduk, Horus) does battle with a negative deity of disorder and chaos (Yamm, Tiamat, Seth). The imagery of all of these myths was equally applicable to political propaganda, and the biblical tradition was not reticent in using mythological labels for political adversaries.[49] If the Sibyl had shared Daniel's feelings about Antiochus

---

[46] For full discussion see the commentary on Daniel 7 in J.J. Collins and A.Y. Collins, *Daniel* (Hermeneia; Minneapolis: Fortress, 1993).

[47] J.W. van Henten, "Antiochus IV as a Typhonic Figure in Daniel 7," in *The Book of Daniel in the Light of Recent Findings: Colloquium Biblicum Lovaniense 1991* (ed. A.S. van der Woude; Leuven: Leuven University Press, 1993) 223-43, building on the suggestion of J.C.H. Lebram, "König Antiochus im Buch Daniel," *VT* 25 (1975) 737-72.

[48] J. Fontenrose, *Python: A Study of Delphic Myth and Its Origin* (Berkeley: University of California Press, 1959).

[49] See J. Day, *God's conflict with the dragon and the sea: Echoes of a Canaanite myth in the Old Testament* (Cambridge: Cambridge University Press, 1985).

Epiphanes, it would not have been difficult to portray him as a Typhonian figure.[50]

The Sibyl and the Maccabees

We touch here on the controverted question of the Sibyl's attitude towards the Maccabean revolt. We have noted the possible allusion in Sib Or 3:194: "then the people of the great God will again be strong." Even if this were read as a reference to the revolt, it is a faint endorsement. I suggested in my dissertation that the sibyllist was a supporter of Onias IV, the exiled High Priest who enjoyed high rank under Ptolemy VI Philometor.[51] This hypothesis might explain the Sibyl's detachment from the cause of the Maccabees, who, from a Zadokite point of view, usurped the High Priesthood. There is certainly hope in the *Third Sibylline Oracle* for a full restoration of the Jerusalem temple and nothing to indicate that the restoration under the Maccabees was satisfactory. The lack of outrage against Antiochus Epiphanes might be explained if the Sibyl wrote in the later years of Ptolemy VI Philometor, when Antiochus Epiphanes was dead and the Syrians no longer controlled Judea.

In any case, the earliest Jewish Sibylline Oracles are remarkably irenic and positive, when viewed in the context of the contemporary Egyptian propaganda and of Jewish apocalypses such as Daniel. They bear witness to an era of Jewish success in Egypt, when it was possible to envision a glorious restoration of the Jerusalem temple under Ptolemaic patronage.

Epilogue

The positive relations between Jew and Gentile reflected in the *Third Sibylline Oracle* contrast sharply with the kind of propaganda we find in a later stage of the tradition, reflected in the *Fifth Sibylline Oracle* from the early second century CE. By then relations between Jews and Egyptians had deteriorated to

---

[50] Van Henten, "Antiochus IV," 242, argues that "it is likely that in Alexandrian circles Antiochus IV was ridiculed and associated with the typhonic," but the argument is *a priori* and lacks supporting evidence.

[51] Collins, *The Sibylline Oracles*, 52-53.

the point where the Jews were portrayed as the Typhonians in Egyptian propaganda.[52] A fragmentary papyrus from the time of the Jewish revolt under Trajan (115-117 CE) urges its readers to "attack the Jews," who are characterized as "lawbreakers once cast out from Egypt by the wrath of Isis."[53] The text warns that Jews will inhabit the land, or city, of Helios.[54] It also warns Egyptians not to let their city become desolate, presumably with reference to Memphis. The Jewish Sibyl, on the other hand, foretells the destruction of Memphis without compunction: "Mighty Memphis, who formerly boasted most to wretched mortals, you will weep in dire straits and disastrous fate."[55] She also predicts the destruction of Isis and Sarapis. The Sibyl does not make use of the myth of Horus and Seth, but the fifth book is full of scathing denunciations of enemies, targeting Rome even more than Egypt. When the Fifth Sibyl looks for deliverance, the hope is no longer for a "king from the sun" but for a "man from heaven" (256, 414). The book ends on a note of despair, with the extinction of all the stars. In fact, the conflict of propaganda among Jews, Greeks, and Egyptians in Roman Egypt, which had raged throughout the Roman era and is reflected only belatedly in the Sibylline Oracles,[56] ended in the virtual extinction of Egyptian Judaism after the failure of the revolt in 117 CE.

---

[52] See David Frankfurter, "Lest Egypt's City be Deserted: Religion and Ideology in the Egyptian Response to the Jewish Revolt (116-117 C.E.)," *JJS* 43 (1992) 203-20.

[53] *CPJ* 520, V. Tcherikover, A. Fuks, M. Stern and D.M. Lewis, *Corpus Papyrorum Judaicarum* (Cambridge: Harvard University Press, 1964) 3.119-21. Frankfurter, "Lest Egypt's City be Deserted," 208, also refers to an unpublished fragment from Oxyrhynchus.

[54] The readings of the two fragments differ at this point.

[55] Sib Or 5:63-65; cf. 180-81.

[56] See J.G. Gager, *The Origins of Antisemitism* (New York: Oxford, 1983), 43-66; Feldman, *Jew and Gentile in the Ancient World*, 84-176.

IMMIGRANTS, EXILES, EXPATRIATES, AND MISSIONARIES

A. Thomas Kraabel
(Luther College, Decorah, Iowa)

I

This essay has a triple theme: the *missionary* activity in antiquity to which this volume's sub-title refers, the *diaspora* in which that activity usually occurred, and the *expatriates* who linked the one to the other. By chance I took up its final editing in Kowloon, in a hotel room looking out across the bay to Hong Kong. In these streets were signs of more immigrants, more diasporas, and – I suspect – more missionaries. Long discussions after a Lutheran worship service for English-speaking expatriates brought vividly to life again the conflicting forces within the diaspora-dweller: the wish to maintain one's particularity in an "alien" culture, and – over against that – the desire to learn, live in, and become part of a world where much of one's life, relationships, and friendships now are centered.

Hong Kong's British immigration already had begun when China ceded the island to Great Britain in perpetuity in 1841. Later, that area knew other, very different diasporas: waves of refugee Chinese after the overthrow of the Manchu Empire in the early part of this century, more in the 1930's ahead of the invading Japanese, and yet again in the early 1950's with the fall of Shanghai. Add to that the "boat people" who began to arrive from Viet Nam in the late 1970's.[1]

In another part of Asia, Japan, there is a significant U.S. diaspora, likewise arriving in several stages: the prisoners-of-war brought in as virtual hostages in the latter part of World War II, then the occupation forces under a victorious General Douglas MacArthur, and finally today's diplomats and entrepreneurs, drawn by the economic and political potential of this Asian giant. While all ages have their diasporas, clearly not all diasporas are the same. One may be created when subjects

[1] J. Fairbanks, *China: A New History* (Cambridge MA/London: Harvard University Press, 1992).

are brought to a new country by force, another if people are expelled from their homeland by hatred and violence, another as immigrants are drawn magnetically to some other nation's power.

Nor do immigrants and other expatriates view unambiguously the homeland they have left once they arrive at their new location. From Marcus Lee Hansen's studies of American immigration comes Hansen's Law: "What the son wishes to forget the grandson wishes to remember." Hansen found that those of the second generation, the first born on American soil, wanted to put the Old Country behind them and become full participants in the New Land. But their children, the third generation, more quickly came to feel at home; with a different view of the past, they developed a new interest in family beginnings and Homeland traditions. Although Hansen's specialty was Scandinavian immigration, his "law" did not attract wide attention until it was applied[2] to the situation of American Jews. The sentiments it describes surely were present also in some Jewish immigrants in antiquity.

In some cases the ambivalence or "dissonance" is even more intense within a single generation or individual. Christian clergy in Asia serving expatriates from the U.S. may manifest a conservative theology and a confrontational preaching style in their concern for demarcating their faith unmistakably within an overwhelmingly non-Christian majority population. At the same time they and their congregants are engaged in sincere efforts to understand the country in which they now live, and to learn its language and customs, viewpoints and philosophy. Some members of the majority population become colleagues, even close friends. Expatriates join local service and fraternal organizations, and ally themselves with groups concerned with social issues of their adopted community. Most strive diligently to understand the people of their host country, and a few will devote themselves to helping the locals understand them and

---

[2] By Nathan N. Glazer, who caused it to be reprinted in *Commentary* in 1952; then Will Herberg coined the term "Hansen's Law" and made broad use of the idea in his *Protestant-Catholic-Jew* (Garden City: Doubleday, 1955). See P. Gleason, "Hansen, Herberg, and American Religion," in P. Kivisto and D. Blanck, eds., *American Immigrants and Their Generations: Studies and Commentaries on the Hansen Thesis after Fifty Years* (Urbana and Chicago: University of Illinois Press, 1990) 85-103, a reference which I owe to J.R. Christianson.

the homeland from which they came. In antiquity, too, people found themselves part of a diaspora for any one of a number of reasons, and responded to it in a variety of ways. Some had been coerced, others volunteered. Some had clear goals, others were driven by circumstance. Over time ties to the Homeland and its traditions may have been preserved or severed or retrieved.

II

"Immigration" is the usual term for the arrival of the people who make up diasporas. Immigrants – or refugees, or displaced persons – are an enormous concern at present both for the United States and for Germany. What we know about them, and what we think about this contemporary issue, may help provide a more complete understanding of the Jews of antiquity in their Mediterranean diaspora,[3] of their literature and their other artifacts.

For that ancient Diaspora I will use an Anatolian site, Sardis in Lydia, as a point of reference because I know it best. Its most familiar monument was begun perhaps by the end of the second century CE. The largest synagogue ever excavated anywhere, it was the last and grandest of at least four controlled by a Jewish community.[4] The first Jews to have known Sardis were refugees from the Babylonian destruction of Jerusalem in 587 BCE; they are mentioned by the Hebrew Scriptures in Obadiah 20, where Sardis is called by its Semitic name, Sepharad.[5] The archaeologist who discovered the building, George Hanfmann, has argued that the permanent community was begun by Jewish prisoners freed from captivity by

[3] Most recently on this theme, W.C. van Unnik, *Das Selbstverständnis des jüdischen Diaspora in des hellenistchen-römischen Zeit,* edited by P.W. van der Horst (Arbeiten zur Geschichte des antiken Judentums und des Urchristentums 17; Leiden: Brill, 1993).

[4] For details see G.M.A. Hanfmann et al., *Sardis from Prehistoric to Roman Times: Results of the Archaeological Exploration of Sardis 1958-1975* (Cambridge MA: Harvard University Press, 1983) and relevant articles in J. Andrew Overman and Robert MacLennan, eds., *Diaspora Jews and Judaism: Essays in Honor of, and in Dialogue with, A. Thomas Kraabel* (South Florida Studies in the History of Judaism 41; Atlanta: Scholars Press, 1992).

[5] C. Hemer, *The Book of Acts in the Setting of Hellenistic History* (WUNT 49; Tübingen: Mohr-Siebeck, 1989) 134-36.

Cyrus of Persia in about 538 BCE. It was probably in continuous existence from that time.[6]

If Hanfmann's hypothesis is correct, Jews had lived in Sardis for over 500 years when the earliest Christian missionaries reached the city. That has important implications for the extent of their integration into the life of the gentile city. Consider more recent immigration: the mainland Chinese who have come to North America or the citizens of Turkey who have entered Germany in the last half-century. What if they had been among us not for fifty years but ten times that long? Imagine a Turkish community in Germany with a continuous history since the time of Luther, or Chinese "immigrants" who had been a part of the North American population since Columbus. Their place in our society certainly would be a different one than in fact it is now.

Or apply another part of the Sardis analogy. Imagine that the Chinese "immigrants" arriving in the U.S. Middle West came not from mainland China directly, but only after several generations of transition, in another part of their diaspora, in Hawaii perhaps, or California. At the beginning of the Common Era, something like that was true for at least some of the Sardis Jews: the Seleucid ruler Antiochus III had brought their ancestors to Lydia in the late third century BCE not from the Holy Land directly, but from Babylonia and Mesopotamia.[7] Centuries separated them from the experience of life in the Israelite homeland. In fact, their last migration was from one part of their diaspora to another.

Josephus' writings help to bring this "expatriate" community to life. His reports make clear their allegiance to their traditions. He records that they faithfully transmitted the annual tax of a half-shekel per capita to support the Temple in Jerusalem (*Ant.* 16.171), and that they were concerned for a proper food supply for themselves because they wished to keep the laws of *Kashrut* (*Ant.* 14.259-261).

By the first century BCE these Jews were an influential group in the gentile city: some of their rights were confirmed by an

---

[6] In "Jews and Lydians at Babylon and Sardis," a manuscript I am preparing for publication.

[7] A. Thomas Kraabel, "Impact of the Discovery of the Sardis Synagogue," in Hanfmann, *Sardis*, 179, reprinted in Overman/MacLennan 270-71.

official of Rome itself, others by the Sardis city council. They also controlled their own *topos* or meeting place, either a designated space in a public building or perhaps an entire building, provided by the city (*Ant.* 14.260). In this *topos* religious ceremonies were carried out and decisions made on community issues, religious and non-religious. The Jews described by Josephus enjoyed considerable autonomy.[8]

The power and status of this immigrant community resulted not only from its persistence though centuries of Sardis history. They are also due to the fact that these Jews happened to be present at two major turning points of the city's existence. The arrival of the first Jews probably coincided with the beginning of the Persian control of Sardis, resulting from the capture of the city by Cyrus in 547 BCE. Three centuries later Jewish residents participated in a complete reorganization and rebuilding of the city which took place after its destruction by Antiochus III in 213 BCE. Thus they were present not only at the beginning of Persian Sardis, but also at the revisioning and reconstruction which created a new, hellenistic city.[9]

The large synagogue building now partially restored on the Lydian plain does not provide direct evidence for the first century. But it was preceded by at least three other buildings or spaces which Jews oversaw in the city. The earliest is referred to in Josephus *Ant.* 14.235, a Roman decree of the mid-first century BCE stating that, "from the earliest times," the Jews in Sardis have had their own courts and "a place of their own" (τόπος ἴδιος). The second, referred to above, is a later *topos* mentioned in a decree of the city preserved in *Ant.* 14.260. If we assume that it in turn was destroyed along with much of the rest of the central city in the severe earthquake of 17 CE, the third building would be whatever space the Jews used as a replacement until the present structure was available. One of the four had an installation that was clearly public: an inscription (*CIJ* no. 751) listing city fountains mentions the

---

[8] Details in Kraabel, "Impact," 179 = Overman/MacLennan 271.

[9] The well-documented early history of this community makes it difficult to accept the conclusions of Helga Botermann, "Die Synagoge von Sardes: Eine Synagoge aus dem 4. Jahrhundert?" *ZNW* 81 (1990) 103-21, or those of Marianne Bonz in "The Jewish Community of Ancient Sardis: A Reassessment of Its Rise to Prominence," *HSCP* 93 (1990) 343-59, and in "Differing Approaches to Religious Benefaction: The Late Third-Century Acquisition of the Sardis Synagogue,"*HTR* 86 (1993) 139–54.

"fountain of the synagogue," municipally licensed and open to all.[10]

Having lived among their gentile neighbors for centuries, generations of Jews had become a respected segment of the Sardis population and a permanent part of the city's political and economic life. As in Germany or the U.S. today, local economics and politics as well as the city's institutions of education[11] played an important role in integrating each generation of these immigrants and their descendants into Sardis society. At the same time, as the last synagogue would vividly demonstrate, these Jews never lost their hold on their own traditions and identities.

The "dissonance"[12] experienced by the diaspora-dweller becomes manageable over time. As with today's expatriates, the heritage of the Old Country and the culture of the New Land drew closer together. The Jewish artifacts recovered by the Sardis excavators bear witness to such a creative and benign juxtaposition of the heritage of Judaism and the urban life and culture of the gentile world under the Roman Empire.[13]

III

The third side of my theme is the missionary activity of this volume's sub-title as it might apply to Sardis. A synagogue community well-established and integrated, and yet self-consciously Jewish, must have given pause to any missionary entering the city, who intended to target local Jews in particular or who sought to pass off a new religion as a better version of Judaism. The writings of Melito, bishop of Sardis at

---

[10] Kraabel, "Impact," 184 = Overman/MacLennan 280.

[11] See my "*Pronoia* at Sardis," forthcoming in *The Jewish Diaspora in the Hellenistic and Roman Periods*, edited by B. Isaac and A. Oppenheimer (*Te'uda*, The Chaim Rosenberg School of Jewish Studies Research Series, vol. 11; Tel Aviv, 1994). For the use of the term *pronoia* at approximately the same time but in a far different sense by Synesius of Cyrene, see A. Cameron and J. Long, *Barbarians and Politics at the Court of Arcadius* (The Transformation of the Classical Heritage 19; Berkeley and Los Angeles: University of California Press, 1993), chapters 5-7, 9.

[12] On the term in this context, see J. Collins, *Between Athens and Jerusalem* (New York: Crossroad, 1983) 8-10.

[13] A collection and critical review of a number of my writings on Sardis Jews are now available in Overman/MacLennan.

the end of the second century, indicate how formidable the synagogue community appeared to that small Christian group established by missionaries who first had come to Sardis at about the time of Paul.[14]

But those were Christian missionaries. What about a mission to Gentiles by Jews? After half a millennium in Lydia, can these settled Jews be seen as parallel in any sense at all to Paul and his itinerant Christian colleagues? The Sardis Jews came as immigrants and subsequently lived in a diaspora. Most scholars, Jews as well as Gentiles, have assumed that *immigrant* Jews in the Greco-Roman *diaspora* must have been concerned with missionary work, with bringing Gentiles into their synagogues, and transforming them into sympathizers and even converts. Dieter Georgi's words would find wide acceptance: "there existed among the Jews a widespread missionary awareness and a corresponding missionary activity."[15] Shaye Cohen has called this "a standard, perhaps the standard, scholarly view."[16] He sees the treatment of the Jewish mission in Georgi's famous second chapter, "Missionary Activity in New Testament Times,"[17] as "[t]he fullest recent statement" of that position.[18] Scot McKnight finds "Georgi's monograph and the revision of Schürer" to be the only substantial studies of the topic in this generation.[19] The drought is apparently over, however. Monographs on the subject are promised by Martin Goodman and

[14] On Melito, see articles by Kraabel and by MacLennan in Overman/MacLennan, and also S. Wilson, "Passover, Easter, and Anti-Judaism: Melito of Sardis and Others," in J. Neusner and E. Frerichs, eds., *"To See Ourselves As Others See Us": Christians, Jews, "Others" in Late Antiquity* (Chico CA: Scholars Press, 1985) 337-55.

[15] *The Opponents of Paul in Second Corinthians: A Study of Religious Propaganda in Late Antiquity* (Philadelphia: Fortress, 1986) 175.

[16] S. Cohen, "Was Judaism in Antiquity a Missionary Religion?," in *Jewish Assimilation, Acculturation and Accommodation: Past Traditions Current Issues and Future Prospects*, ed. M. Mor (Lanham/New York/London: University Press of America, 1992) 17.

[17] The chapter is pages 83-228 of *The Opponents.*

[18] S. Cohen, "Adolf Harnack's 'The Mission and Expansion of Judaism': Christianity Succeeds Where Judaism Fails," in *The Future of Early Christianity: Essays in Honor of Helmut Koester*, eds. Birger A. Pearson, A. Thomas Kraabel, George W.E. Nickelsburg and Norman R. Peterson (Minneapolis: Fortress, 1991) 166, note 14. For similar sentiments, see Cohen's "Was Judaism?," 17, note 4: " . . . the fullest modern expression of this view." The chapter is pages 83-228 of *The Opponents.*

[19] S. McKnight, *A Light Among the Gentiles: Jewish Missionary Activity in the Second Temple Period* (Minneapolis: Fortress, 1991) 4.

Amy-Jill Levine, in addition to McKnight's which appeared in 1991. Louis Feldman's massive new work contains several chapters representing the majority position.[20] Further studies are promised by Cohen as well; they can be expected to develop further the position summarized by him in 1991 as follows:

> "[A] new consensus is beginning to emerge according to which the Greek Jewish literature of antiquity was not propaganda directed to outsiders, [and] diaspora Judaism was not a missionary religion..."[21]

From his study of the rabbinic literature Goodman has concluded that:

> "it was extremely unusual for any Jew in the first century CE to view the encouragement of Gentiles to convert to Judaism as a praiseworthy act...In the diaspora Jews were not much concerned whether particular outsiders joined them or not."[22]

My position for Sardis is similar, but I arrived at it differently. The evidence these scholars used for the Diaspora is chiefly textual. However, no literature produced by Sardis Jews is extant. It was rather on the basis of their synagogue, indeed because of my work within that building, that I concluded that the people who controlled it and expressed themselves in its architecture, iconography, and inscriptions did not fit the conventional image of Diaspora Judaism. For the same reason,

---

[20] L. Feldman, *Jew and Gentile in the Ancient World: Attitudes and Interactions from Alexander to Justinian* (Princeton: Princeton University Press, 1993) – I have not seen this volume, but Professor Feldman has provided me with a preliminary manuscript, for which courtesy I am most grateful. See also his "Jewish Proselytism," in *Eusebius, Christianity, and Judaism*, edited by Harold W. Attridge and Gohei Hata (Studia Post-Biblica 42; Leiden: Brill, 1992) 372-408; his "Proselytes and 'Sympathizers' in the Light of the New Inscriptions from Aphrodisias," *REJ* 148 (1989) 265-305; "Was Judaism a Missionary Religion in Ancient Times?" in Mor, *Jewish Assimilation*, 24-37; and his "Palestinian and Diaspora Judaism in the First Century," in H. Shanks, ed., *Christianity and Rabbinic Judaism: A Parallel History of Their Origins and Early Development* (Washington, DC: Biblical Archaeology Society, 1992) 30-36.

[21] Cohen, "Harnack," 166.

[22] "Proselytising in Rabbinic Judaism," *JJS* 40 (1989) 176-77; Goodman elaborates further in "Jewish Proselytizing in the First Century," in *The Jews among Pagans and Christians in the Roman Empire*, eds. J. Lieu, J. North and T. Rajak (London/New York: Routledge, 1992) 53-78.

I could not see masses of God-fearers in that building either.[23] Curious Gentiles? Surely. Business associates, political allies, neighbors or friends of one Jew or another who were not Jews themselves? Why not? But the semi-converts of the handbooks? Unlikely!

To use the modern analogy one last time: suppose again that immigrant communities in Germany and the United States today had been among us for a full five centuries, since the time of Luther and Columbus, and had maintained a recognizable Turkish or Chinese identity. Would there not have been considerable economic, social and political accommodation to the host country nevertheless? They would know the local language, indeed it might be their only language by this time. They surely would have many friends, colleagues, and supporters – even benefactors on occasion – outside of their own communities. They would have any of a number of reasons for full interaction with the host population. But one of the least of those reasons now would be that members of the majority population were interested in adopting the teachings of Confucius or in conversion to Islam. Turks do not come to Germany or the Chinese to North America today principally as missionaries. Even in the highly unlikely circumstance that they had arrived centuries ago (in the hypothesis which begins this paragraph) with that intent, is it reasonable to surmise that missionizing would have continued to be their goal? If not, why should we presume that intention of such as the Sardis Jews five centuries after the first arrivals from Jerusalem, and three centuries after a larger group made the move from Babylonia and Mesopotamia?[24]

---

[23] Feldman suggests that its "huge size...was necessary to accommodate" the large numbers of God-fearers it attracted, in "Proselytes and 'Sympathizers'," 279. On God-fearers generally, see the relevant articles in Overman/MacLennan, and Murphy-O'Connor, "Lots of God-Fearers? *Theosebeis* in the Aphrodisias Inscription," *RB* 99 (1992) 418-24, cited further below.

[24] The assumption of an extensive mission carried out by Diaspora Jews exists in part because of the influence of handbooks like TDNT and the examples of great scholars of the past, Harnack, for instance. Here is one illustration chosen almost at random: "Nichts ist sicherer, als daß die Juden in dem Römerreiche als ein besonderes Volk gegenüber allen anderen Völkern unterschieden wurden. Ihre bildlose Gottesverehrung und ihre Ablehnung des Staatskultus sowie ihre Exklusivität hoben sie als einzigartig aus allen Nationen heraus," in Adolf von Harnack, *Die Mission und Ausbreitung des Christentums in den ersten drei Jahrhunderten* (4th ed.; Leipzig: J.C. Hinrichs, 1924; reprinted Wiesbaden: VMA-Verlag, 1984) 281.

Furthermore, the influx of Gentiles to Judaism, the expected result of such a mission, was often an apocalyptic expectation: the Ingathering, an event of the Endtime.[25] But it is difficult to conceive of such a theology becoming dominant at Sardis; this was no Qumran! Indeed, it is hard to find two ancient Jewish communities less likely to be in agreement in their views of the gentile world and their place within it than the rude conventicle on the shore of an inhospitable Dead Sea and the Greek-speaking Sardians who endured, persisted, and finally flourished in a cosmopolitan metropolis under Achaemenid, then Seleucid, and eventually Roman control.

IV

New evidence from Aphrodisias carries the argument a step further. Sardis has become the parade example of an ancient synagogue open to visitors who were not Jews. It was located at one of the busiest intersections of the Roman city. Its huge size was bound to attract attention. When its doors were open the entire interior would have been clearly visible from the street outside.[26] In this building (or one of its predecessors) a "fountain of the synagogue," municipally licensed, was accessible to all.[27] But to what purpose was it so accessible? Simple neighborliness and good citizenship are the most plausible reasons. Jerome Murphy-O'Connor's interpretation of the much-cited Aphrodisias inscription of the same period furnishes a cogent parallel from the gentile side. He understands the building from which that inscription came to be "a soup kitchen for the benefit of the poor and vagrants...It met a social need to which it would have been perfectly natural for Gentiles with a sense of civic duty to subscribe because it

[25] A theme which several recent studies have taken up anew; see Paula Fredriksen, "Judaism, the Circumcision of Gentiles, and Apocalyptic Hope: Another Look at Galatians 1 and 2," *JTS* 42 (1991) 532-64; and T. Donaldson, "Proselytes or 'Righteous Gentiles'? The Status of Gentiles in Eschatological Pilgrimage Patterns of Thought," *Journal for the Study of the Pseudepigrapha* 7 (1990) 3-27.

[26] Kraabel, "Impact," 184 = Overman/MacLennan 280.

[27] See *CIJ* no. 751 on page 76 and my note 10 above. The evidence suggests that such openness was not unusual; see the use of this idea in Georgi, *The Opponents*, 83-92, together with the references to the Sardis synagogue on 371-75.

benefited the city and not merely the Jewish community."[28] Why could not the Jews of Aphrodisias have been as open and civic-minded as – on this reading – their gentile neighbors were? And the Sardis Jews likewise?

Murphy-O'Connor continues:

> "From this perspective, to call the non-Jewish subscribers [at Aphrodisias] *theosebeis* would merely be a gracious compliment to their moral character without implying that they belonged in any sense to the local synagogue. [The usual interpretation, of course, is that these *theosebeis* were God-fearers in the sense of the Acts of the Apostles.] The city councilors [listed in the inscription] may have been interested only in the Jewish vote! Or they may have wanted merely to ensure that a Jewish proletariat was looked after before it could become troublesome."[29]

Would it be surprising to find similar attitudes among the Jewish leadership in that city? Or in the even older Jewish community of Sardis?

Not that the majority view of modern scholars about the Jewish evidence both from Aphrodisias and from Sardis, namely, that any interested or well-disposed Gentiles were "seekers" and had a religious interest in Judaism, did not have its ancient analog. Jews and non-Jews, for different reasons, noticed the presence of Gentiles in the synagogues of the Roman Empire. This familiarity and openness surely disturbed some of them. They attributed to this a religious motivation and gave the visitors a religious designation. To rabbinic Jews, less at home in the Diaspora, this helped to explain the proximity of the non-Jews to the synagogue community. They called them *yire'ei shamayim*, "fearers of Heaven,"[30] or *hasidei 'umoth ha-'olam*, "the pious ones of the nations of the world."[31] And from the Christian side Luke made them into "God-fearers," skillfully utilizing them in the plot of Acts. But the evidence from Sardis and Aphrodisias, as sketched above, suggests that there often were less religious and more plausible reasons for Gentiles in the Roman Empire to interact with Jews.

---

[28] Murphy-O'Connor, "God-Fearers?," 422.

[29] See the previous note.

[30] Schürer, *History* 3.162-172 provides the texts.

[31] Most recently on "righteous Gentiles," see Donaldson, "Proselytes or 'Righteous Gentiles'?"

V

In summary, with regard to the Diaspora and its Jewish expatriates, the following positions are becoming increasingly plausible:

Most of the Greco-Jewish literature turns out to have been composed not only *by* Jews but *for* them. This position is typified by Goodman and McKnight, and by Cohen, who summarizes:

> "[I]n recent years scholarship has tended to see Greco-Jewish literature as oriented primarily to Jews and as serving the needs of the Jewish community. Even its apologetic function was intended to persuade not Gentiles but Jews, to show them that loyalty to Judaism did not necessarily mean a denial of their ambient culture...[Further,] if Greek Jewish literature was missionary in character and designed for a pagan audience, it failed miserably. Pagans did not read Jewish literature."[32]

Synagogue architecture, epigraphy and iconography, all the work of Jews or done to their specifications, express one way to be true to the ancestral traditions and simultaneously to be acceptable, and accepted, inhabitants of their largely gentile Diaspora home as well as participants in its culture. I have drawn this conclusion for Sardis chiefly on the basis of the data from its last synagogue, but I would extrapolate it to New Testament times as well. And though Sardis is the best attested example, it was not unique. The art and architecture of the Dura synagogue offer additional examples of immense creativity on the part of Diaspora Jews, in a setting distant from Sardis and with far different results as to the appearance of the building.[33]

The God-fearers, once thought of as persons on the verge of converting to Judaism, in many cases have proved to be "friends of the local Jews" for economic and/or political reasons, or they were motivated by pure neighborliness; witness Murphy-O'Connor for Aphrodisias.

[32] S. Cohen, "Was Judaism?," 17. See his notes 6-8 for greater detail.

[33] On Diaspora synagogues generally, see my "The Diaspora Synagogue," ANRW 2.19.1 (1979) 477-510.

VI

What further generalizations develop from these conclusions? There are several:

The Jews of the Greco-Roman Diaspora look more like the immigrants of today, aspiring to participate in the life of their adopted locations. At the very least they were resigned to making the best of the situation, since the Homeland – for whatever reason – was now closed to them. Members of long-established communities such as the one at Sardis would be much more integrated into city life thanks to the centuries their ancestors had devoted to the common life there.

The Jewish texts written in or translated into Greek, the products of genuine theological and literary creativity (even genius) on the part of these Jews, indicate how hellenized Jews *in general* may have viewed the world. These texts are to be seen now as more typical of Diaspora Jewish thought. Furthermore, the same authors should be given credit for their skill in wielding the common language of the world around them and for their motivation as they interpreted and transmitted the wisdom of their own national traditions, revisioning the host culture around them[34] for the edification of new generations of Diaspora Jews. (It is not only twentieth-century teachers, parents and grandparents who strive to ensure that their most cherished beliefs and practices endure in their posterity.)

With regard to the Jewishness of early Christianity, many classicists and ancient historians would agree with the way Wayne Meeks reads the Christian evidence: "by the end of the first century, and much earlier than that in the Pauline groups, the Christian movement was socially independent of the Jewish communities in the cities of the empire."[35] One of the arguments for this position is that the movement made up of the followers of Jesus, and subsequently of the followers of

[34] In *Allegorical Readers and Cultural Revision in Ancient Alexandria* (Berkeley/Los Angeles/Oxford: University of California Press, 1992), D. Dawson sees Philo using allegorical interpretation not to read the Torah in the light of Greek philosophy but to capture Hellenism, the host culture of Alexandria, for the Jewish community. See my review in *Religious Studies Review* 20 (1994) 54.

[35] W. Meeks, "Breaking Away: Three Separate New Testament Pictures of Christianity's Separation from the Jewish Communities," in Neusner/Frerichs 114.

those first leaders, was much less "Jewish" in thought and expression, in philosophy or theology in each succeeding decade during those earliest generations.

But appearances may have been deceptive. This phenomenon of "declining Jewishness" need not have been merely the result of demographics, that is, of the movement of increasing numbers of non-Jews into the new religion. More Jews than we think might have converted in the Diaspora; after all, Christianity was the most aggressive missionary movement the Greco-Roman world had known, and there is no disputing the presence of large numbers of Jews in its earliest membership in the Holy Land. That circumstance, in turn, well may have worked to attract other Jews as the new religion moved into the Diaspora. But these Diaspora converts would have expressed themselves in language – concepts, images, ideas, forms – which we traditionally saw as "gentile" but now understand to have been used by Greek-speaking Jews commonly among themselves. This would have been particularly true of those Jews recruited in the most established, most intellectually "hellenized" Diaspora synagogue communities. They would have expressed and interpreted Christianity in ways similar to those employed in Greco-Jewish literature. Our mistake may have been that, in studying the writings of these Diaspora converts from Judaism to Christianity, we found them too little "Jewish" in the traditional sense, assumed (incorrectly) that the authors must have been Gentiles, and drew correspondingly false demographic conclusions.

VII

What are the implications for some of the themes and concerns of this *Festschrift*, if we call for a revision in the view that "there existed among the Jews a widespread missionary awareness and a corresponding missionary activity"? – to quote Dieter Georgi's words a second time.

First of all, an extensive Jewish mission is not required as an explanation for the influence of Greco-Jewish literature on early Christian thought and preaching. All that is necessary would be that some Jews who converted to Christianity had been acquainted with the style and argumentation of the Greco-Jewish literature. If we accept that that literature was written *by* Jews and in the first instance *for* Jews, that is not at all unlikely.

Second, without a Jewish mission it will be necessary to find another explanation for the early, energetic and pervasive mission of the new religion. Is it one of the *nova* of Christianity which derive from the message of Jesus himself? His first followers would have been less bold and surely less visionary, when one considers the embryonic Jesus-movement under the aspect of Palestinian Judaism. Paul's activity surely expanded that movement just as surely it predated his entry into the Christian community. It had its genesis somewhere in those very few years between Jesus and Paul.

Later, in Luke's generations, the gentile mission had become – or remained – so controversial as to require justification. That is what Luke provides. And that is why he peopled the middle half of Acts with God-fearers, giving them a visibility and substance (as well as, I fear, a permanence) which far exceeded what the historical evidence would justify. Since the gentile mission was still a theological issue for some Christians, Luke offered the God-fearers as a precedent, allowing him to say in effect, "What we are doing as a missionary movement is precisely what occurs among the Jews of our time, save that we are doing it more effectively."

(The literary usefulness of the God-fearers idea is demonstrated by the way in which it has been employed ever since. Some modern scholars have emulated Luke's ingenuity as they draw detailed pictures of them. Gerd Theissen, for instance, creates a social location for the God-fearers; he sees them as Gentiles of a higher social status, supporters of the Diaspora Jewish communities. Standing "between differing cultural realms," they possessed "an independence with reference to their native traditions and religion...Seen in this light [he continues], the conflict between Christianity and Judaism is easier to understand: the Christian mission was luring away the very Gentiles who were Judaism's patrons."[36] Surely this goes well beyond the available evidence.)

---

[36] G. Theissen, *The Social Setting of Pauline Christianity* (Philadelphia: Fortress, 1982) 103-04; cf. 102-04 with notes.

VIII

The first and most important thing I learned from Dieter Georgi was to pay careful attention always to methodological, cultural and linguistic contexts, one's own as well as those of the person, text or artifact to be understood.[37] A similar concern is coming to characterize the humanities generally, as "attempts to secure firm epistemological foundations for knowledge have given way to a recognition of the ways notions of meaning and truth are functions of the linguistic worlds in which we live."[38] Thus scholars differ in defining the people and communities responsible for and expressing themselves in Greco-Jewish literature, art, and architecture, in part because we begin with different assumptions about our subjects.

In characterizing the ways in which the Hellenistic period and our own resemble each other and differ perhaps from the age in which many of our own "epistemological foundations" were laid, my colleague Wilfred Bunge writes:

> "For many in our world religion is little more than acculturation...Conversion is then not a matter of radical reorientation of one's life, but a kind of conforming to the generalized worldview of another group. Worldview is often not even very sharply defined. It may be no more than a kind of attraction to a set of customs, a way of existing socially in a community...Clearly differentiations among religious communities and between secular and religious loyalties are quite different now from even a generation ago."[39]

While I cannot speak for Germany, this is surely evident in the "habits of the heart" of Americans dwelling in or moving among the "lifestyle enclaves" of today.[40] For the contemporaries of Luther or even of Harnack, in contrast, confessional boundaries were marked clearly and well guarded; their sym-

---

[37] See most recently his "The Interest in Life of Jesus Theology as a Paradigm for the Social History of Biblical Criticism," *HTR* 85 (1992) 51-83, which may be productively compared with chapter 5, on "ecclesiastical historiography," in A. Momigliano, *The Classical Foundations of Modern Historiography* (Sather Classical Lectures, 54. Berkeley: University of California Press, 1990).

[38] Dawson, *Allegorical Readers*, 238.

[39] Excerpt from a letter (private correspondence) which I received from the author.

[40] R.N. Bellah et al., *Habits of the Heart: Individualism and Commitment in American Life* (Berkeley/Los Angeles/Oxford: University of California Press, 1985).

bolic maps showed expansive areas of black and white, few checkerboards, even fewer gray areas – how could one's methodology not reflect that?

With regard to the evidence for ancient Judaism more specifically, recent research by Jacob Neusner suggests still another reason for scholarly disagreement, namely, the multiformity of the data themselves. Drawing on his long acquaintance with the work of Erwin Goodenough, Neusner distinguishes between propositional and symbolic discourse in the "public and official evidence" of ancient Judaism. In this he includes, as *literary evidence*, "the implicit message of canonical and normative writings;" and as *artistic evidence*, "what synagogue communities accepted as the tacit message of [their]...symbols."[41]

Symbolic discourse includes both verbal and iconic expressions. It is Neusner's hunch that symbolic, not propositional discourse, is primary in post-biblical Judaism. I would agree. However, he concludes:

> "in the aggregate, symbolic discourse represented in one medium bears one set of symbols...and symbolic discourse in another medium appeals to a quite different set of symbols altogether...[The resulting image is of] two Judaisms, one of them represented by the symbolic discourse in verbal form of the rabbinic Midrash-compilations, the other by symbolic discourse in iconic form represented by the synagogue ornamentation."[42]

Thus, for ancient Judaism it is not only that 1) scholars' presuppositions differ, or that 2) those who study texts and those who begin with objects and artifacts arrive at divergent conclusions because they start with different methods. Either one of these might be expected. Neusner's point is that 3) for ancient Judaism the primary data themselves tell conflicting stories. There are, in fact, *many* Judaisms represented in the evidence from antiquity and no ideal "Judaism out there" to provide an infallible "reality-test."

Or perhaps it is something as simple as a new vantage point which prompts the revisioning of familiar data. A modern example will clarify the point. In his recent monograph *The*

---

[41] "The Two Vocabularies of Symbolic Discourse in Ancient Judaism," in Overman/MacLennan 80. Extensive amplification in his *Symbolism and Theology in Early Judaism* (Minneapolis: Fortress, 1991).

[42] "Two Vocabularies," 93.

Creators, historian Daniel Boorstin relates the story of the West's "heroes of the imagination," the most creative people in "all the arts." In this good-sized book theologians seldom appear. While Augustine and the Gautama Buddha each receive a few pages, it is Philo of Alexandria who is given the most attention.[43] Although I had been reading Philo off and on for almost forty years, seeing him chiefly through Erwin Goodenough's eyes,[44] the context which Boorstin offered was a new one. The book begins with prehistory. Subsequent chapters take up the most familiar original artists, from Bach and Boswell to Chaucer and Kafka, to Wagner and Virginia Woolf. In Boorstin's judgment Philo deserves a place among them as a "hero of the imagination." In Boorstin's narrative Philo was not someone who tentatively aimed his work outward, offering an *apologia* directed toward an alien world, but rather a creative synthesizer concerned for the most part with his own community.[45] The richness of the Sardis artifacts and (in a different way) the Dura paintings suggests what that world was like. The manifold creativity of the eastern Mediterranean Diaspora, when seen in its independence – witness Dura, Alexandria, Sardis – and not as an "aspect," "heir," or "predecessor" of something else, is truly astonishing. It deserves a great deal more credit than it routinely receives.

Diaspora existence sometimes fosters great achievements, produces *nova* of a most impressive and enduring kind. If we acknowledge that, there are important implications, not only for our teaching and research, but for all who are immigrants, exiles, or expatriates or who live among them in modern times.

---

[43] Boorstin, *The Creators: A History of Heroes of the Imagination* (New York: Random House, 1992) 46-55.

[44] On Goodenough and Georgi, see A. Thomas Kraabel, ed., *Goodenough on the Beginnings of Christianity* (Brown Judaic Studies 212; Atlanta: Scholars Press, 1990) 126, and Georgi, *The Opponents*, 368-371.

[45] See the guides to Philo offered in Schürer, *History* 3.809-89, and Peder Borgen, "Philo of Alexandria: A Critical and Synthetical Survey of Research Since World War II," ANRW 2.21.1 (1984) 98-154; also C. Roetzel, "*Oikoumene* and the Limits of Pluralism in Alexandrian Judaism and Paul," in Overman/MacLennan 163-82.

"UM ZU SEHEN DIE TÖCHTER DES LANDES" DIE PERSPEKTIVE DINAS IN DER JÜDISCH-HELLENISTISCHEN DISKUSSION UM GEN 34

Angela Standhartinger (Universität Frankfurt a.M.)

Der hier zu ehrende Jubilar hat in seinem grundlegenden Werk "Die Gegner des Paulus im 2. Korintherbrief" ein facettenreiches Bild der jüdisch-hellenistischen Mission gezeichnet. Schon 1964 wies er auf die wichtige Rolle von Frauen in dieser Missionsbewegung hin, sowohl auf der Seite der Missionarinnen als auch auf der Seite der von der jüdischen Mission Begeisterten.[1] Im folgenden soll am Beispiel der Dinageschichte, Gen 34, untersucht werden, ob und in welcher Weise diese Beteiligung von Frauen in den theologischen Äußerungen des hellenistischen Judentums einen Niederschlag findet.

Mehr als neun verschiedene Auslegungen von Gen 34 sind in der jüdisch-hellenistischen Literatur erhalten geblieben. Dinas Geschichte wurde neu erzählt, interpretiert und diskutiert. In welcher Weise stellen die jüdisch-hellenistischen Auslegungen Dina dar? Bringen sie Dinas eigene Perspektive auf die Handlung zur Sprache oder wird Dina hier verschwiegen?

Die Geschichte von Leas und Jakobs einziger Tochter, Gen 34,1-31, ist eine Geschichte der Gewalt gegen Frauen. Dina, die "ausgeht, um die Töchter des Landes zu sehen", wird zum Objekt der sie umgebenden Männer und zum Opfer der von ihnen ausgehenden Gewalt. Obgleich die Figur Dina Dreh- und Angelpunkt der Geschichte ist, wird nicht erzählt, was Dina während und nach der Gewalttat sieht, denkt und sagt. Der Auslegerin begegnen eine Reihe von ungeklärten Fragen, wenn sie Dina ins Zentrum ihrer Interpretation von Gen 34 stellt. Ich werde daher zunächst (1.) Gen 34 aus der Perspektive Dinas lesen, d.h. ich werde die Anfragen sammeln, die entstehen, wenn Dinas Sehen, Denken und Handeln im

[1] Dieter Georgi, *Die Gegner des Paulus im 2. Korintherbrief. Studien zur religösen Propaganda in der Spätantike* (WMANT 11), Neukirchen-Vluyn 1964, 100 Anm. 5; 101-104; 105-107; 109f; 116; 121; 130f Anm. 3.

Zentrum der Interpretation des Textes stehen. Im zweiten Teil (2.) werde ich die Darstellung Dinas in den jüdisch-hellenistischen Auslegungen von Gen 34 untersuchen. Nehmen die jüdisch-hellenistischen Bearbeitungen die Anfragen aus der Perspektive Dinas in ihrer Darstellung der Geschichte auf? Welche Probleme stehen in den jeweiligen Auslegungen im Vordergrund und in welcher Weise werden sie gelöst? Im letzten Teil (3.) werde ich eine Kontroverse innerhalb der jüdisch-hellenistischen Literatur um Gen 34 und die Darstellung Dinas aufdecken, in der sich Spuren exegetischer und theologischer Arbeit von Frauen vermuten lassen.

1. Gen 34 aus der Perspektive Dinas

Dina ins Zentrum der Auslegung von Gen 34,1-31 zu stellen, ihr Schicksal, ihr Erleben und ihre Perspektive zum Mittelpunkt der Untersuchung zu machen, führt zu zahlreichen offenen Fragen.[2] Der Text beginnt verheißungsvoll:

> "Aber Dina, die Tochter Leas, die sie dem Jakob geboren hatte, ging aus, um die Töchter der Gegend zu betrachten" (34,1).[3]

Eine Frau, als Tochter einer Frau näher bestimmt, geht aus eigener Veranlassung hinaus, motiviert durch ihr Interesse an anderen Frauen. Doch im weiteren Verlauf der Geschichte stellt sich heraus, daß dies die einzige Handlung Dinas bleibt, die vom Erzähler berichtet wird. Die, die sich in der Gesellschaft von Frauen gefahrlos bewegte, wurde von einem Mann, Sichem, gesehen, der sie "nahm" (λαβών/וַיִּקַּח), "mit ihr schlief" und "sie erniedrigte" (ἐταπείνωσεν/וַיְעַנֶּהָ) (34,2). Dina wird zum Opfer einer Gewalttat. Damit könnte die Geschichte als Darstellung patriarchaler Verhältnisse bereits zu Ende sein. Doch es kommt zu einer überraschenden Wendung:

---

[2] Das Folgende ist eine Auswahl meiner Anfragen an die Geschichte. Vgl. aber auch: Johanna Hooysma, Die Vergewaltigung Dinas. Auslegung von Gen. 33,18-34,31, *Texte und Kontexte* 30 (1986), 26-46 und Danna Nolan Fewell und David M. Gunn, Tipping the Balance: Sternberg's Reader and the Rape of Dinah, *JBL* 110 (1991), 193-221.

[3] Ich lege die LXX zugrunde, da die meisten der im folgenden verhandelten Auslegungen die Gen vermutlich in dieser Fassung gelesen haben. 34,1 M: "um die Töchter des Landes zu sehen."

> "Und er (Sichem) achtete auf die Seele Dinas, der Tochter Jakobs, und liebte die Jungfrau und sprach gemäß der Gesinnung der Jungfrau mit ihr" (34,3).[4]

Aber was sagte er zu ihr, und wie reagierte sie? Empfand sie dies als erneute Bedrängung durch Sichem? Gab sie seinem Drängen aus Angst vor einer ansonsten zerstörten Zukunft nach, oder fand sie selbst Gefallen an ihm? Diese Fragen bleiben unbeantwortet.[5] Stattdessen wird berichtet, daß Sichem, bei den (seiner Meinung nach) zuständigen Männern um Dina bittet (34,4-12). Er ist bereit, alle Forderungen Jakobs und seiner Söhne zu erfüllen (34,12.20-24). Jakob und seine Söhne interpretieren den "Vorfall" jedoch von einer ganz anderen Seite. Aus ihrer Sicht hat Sichem Dina verunreinigt (ἐμίανεν/טִמֵּא).[6] Die Verunreinigung wurde in ihren Augen jedoch nicht durch die gewaltsame Erniedrigung verursacht, sondern liegt im Beischlaf an sich:

> "Unter den Söhnen Jakobs war große Trauer, denn eine Schande machte er in Israel, als er mit der Tochter Jakobs schlief, und so soll es nicht sein"(34,7).

Entweder stand es für sie außer Frage, daß Dina nicht freiwillig mit Sichem geschlafen hat, oder aber es war für ihr Urteil irrelevant. Als die soeben beschnittenen Sichemiter durch Schmerzen geschwächt waren, gingen Simeon und Levi auf sichere Weise nach Sichem hinein, "töteten alles Männliche und nahmen (ἔλαβον/וַיִּקְחוּ) Dina aus dem Haus Sichems und gingen hinaus" (34,26). Dina wird in der Geschichte zweimal "genommen", einmal von Sichem (34,2) und einmal von ihren Brüdern (34,26, vgl. auch die Drohung 34,17). Weil die Sichemiter (Plural) Dina verunreinigten (34,28), plünderten die Söhne Jakobs die Stadt und machten die Sichemiterinnen zu Kriegsgefangenen (34,29), was für Frauen in der Antike zumeist bedeutete, ihre sexuelle Integrität zu

[4] 34,3 M: "Und er hängte seine Seele an Dina, die Tochter Jakobs, und liebte das Mädchen und redete zu dem Herzen des Mädchens."

[5] Vgl. Fewell und Gunn, a.a.O. (Anm. 2), 196: "... the last expression – 'to speak to the heart of' (34,3 M) – may move us beyond the account of Shechem's affections to those of Dinah. It appears to function as a perlocutionary expression, that is, on describing a speech act that produces consequential effects one the feelings, thoughts, or actions of its hearers".

[6] 34,5. Vgl. auch Gen 34,13.27. Sowohl in der LXX (ab 34,13) als auch in der Massora (34,27) sind letztlich alle Sichemiter Subjekt der an Dina geschehenen Verunreinigung.

verlieren.[7] Die Söhne Jakobs gehen in einer anderen Weise mit den Fremden um als Dina. Statt freundlich zu den Sichemiterinnen hinauszugehen, "um sie zu betrachten", vernichten sie die Stadt und versklaven ihre Bewohnerinnen. Von Jakob zur Rechenschaft gezogen, antworteten sie: "Aber gebrauchten sie unsere Schwester nicht als eine Hure?" (34,31). Mit diesem Satz endet die Erzählung in der Genesis. Dina wird lediglich noch in Gen 46,15 als Tochter Leas unter den nach Ägypten Ziehenden aufgezählt. Anders als bei ihren Brüdern wird von ihren Nachkommen nichts berichtet.

2. Die jüdisch-hellenistische Diskussion um Gen 34

Gen 34 wird von Demetrius, Theodotus, Philo und Josephus sowie im Jub, Jdt, TestLev, JosAs, LibAnt, TestHiob und IV Mkk aufgenommen und interpretiert. Diese besonders häufige Aufnahme einer biblischen Geschichte erklären einige Forscher mit dem Hinweis auf die Eroberung Samarias durch den Hasmonäer Johannes Hyrcanus 128 v. Chr. und vermuten, daß in diesem Zusammenhang Gen 34 durch die Gleichsetzung von Samaria mit Sichem zur "Magna Charta jüdischer Gewalttätigkeit gegen die Sichemiter wurde".[8] In neueren Untersuchungen ist jedoch zu Recht darauf hingewiesen worden, daß diese Texte keineswegs auf antisamaritanische Polemik zu reduzieren sind, sondern einen eigenen theologischen Beitrag liefern.[9] James Kugel hat an der Auslegung von Gen 34 im TestLev die hier zu Grunde liegenden exegetischen Fragen und Traditionen exemplarisch aufgezeigt.[10] Es scheinen also noch weitere Motive für die häufige Bearbeitung der Dinageschichte vorzuliegen. Eines dieser allerdings bisher kaum beachteten Motive ist das Interesse an der Figur Dinas, die in

[7] Vgl. z.B. Dtn 21,10-14. Vgl. auch David Schaps, The Women of Greece in Wartime, *CP* 77 (1982), 193-213.

[8] Hans Gerhard Kippenberg, *Garizim und Synagoge* (RVV 30), Berlin 1971, 90. Zustimmend u.a. John J. Collins, The Epic of Theodotus and the Hellenism of the Hasmoneans, *HThR* 73 (1980), 91-104.

[9] Reinhard Pummer (Genesis 34 in Jewish Writings of the Hellenistic and Roman Periods, *HThR* 75 (1982), 177-188) nennt z.B. als Motive für die häufige Aufnahme der Geschichte "the whitewashing of the fathers, the emphasis on the zeal for God, and the justification of a ruse"(188). Vgl. auch ders., Antisamaritanische Polemik in jüdischen Schriften aus der intertestamentarischen Zeit, *BZ* 26 (1982), 224-242.

[10] James Kugel, The Story of Dinah in the Testament of Levi, *HThR* 85 (1992), 1-34.

den jüdisch-hellenistischen Auslegungen von Gen 34 in unterschiedlicher Weise dargestellt wird. Im folgenden werde ich die unterschiedlichen Schwerpunkte in der Darstellung Dinas aufzeigen.

2.1 *Eine Tochter aus gutem Hause (Theodotus und Josephus)*

Unter dem Namen *Theodotus*[11] ist ein im Stil Homers verfasstes Städteepos auf Sichem erhalten geblieben. Die Abfassung eines Epos auf Sichem hat dazu geführt, daß Theodotus für einen Samaritaner gehalten wurde.[12] Dagegen ist zu Recht eingewendet worden, daß die hier an den Sichemitern geäußerte Kritik[13] und die deutlich spürbare apologetische Tendenz des Epos als Abfassungszweck die Verherrlichung der jüdischen Gemeinschaft nahelegen.[14]

Theodotus erzählt Gen 34 als Teil der Stadtgeschichte Sichems. Nach einer Beschreibung der geographischen Lage (Frgm. 1, Eus. praep.ev. 9.22.1) referiert er kurz die Vorgeschichte der Jakobsfamilie (Frgm. 3, Eus. praep.ev. 9.22.3). Hier zeigt sich bereits eine Besonderheit des Theodotus: die Hervorhebung Dinas. Von den Kindern Jakobs heißt es Frgm. 3,17-19, Eus. praep.ev. 9.22.3:

> "Es wurden ihm elf Söhne geboren, mächtig begabt mit Verstand (νόῳ πεπνυμένοι αἰνῶς), und ein Mädchen, Dina, von sehr schönem Aussehen, mit wohlansehnlicher Gestalt und

---

[11] Das Werk des Theodotus ist aus den Exzerpten des Alexander Polyhistor (1. Jh. v. Chr.) bekannt, dessen Werk Euseb zum Teil in seiner *praeperatio evangelica* aufbewahrt hat. Theodotus muß daher im 2. Jh. v. Chr. geschrieben haben. Eine genauere Datierung hängt von der Einschätzung seines Werkes und dessen Bezug auf die politischen Wirren zwischen Juda und Samarien im 2. Jh. v. Chr. ab (s.u.). Im folgenden wird der Text des Theodotus nach der Ausgabe von Carl. R. Holladay, *Fragments from Hellenistic Jewish Authors 2* (Texts and Translations 30), Atlanta, Georgia 1989, 51-204 zitiert.

[12] So Jakob Freudenthal, *Alexander Polyhistor und die von ihm erhaltenen Reste judäischer und samaritanischer Geschichtswerke* (Hellenistische Studien 1f), Breslau 1874-75, 99-101 u.a. Neuerdings u.a. Doron Mendels, The Land of Israel as a Political Concept in Hasmonean Literature, (Texte und Studien zum Antiken Judentum 15) Tübingen 1987, besonders 110-116.

[13] Vgl. Kippenberg, a.a.O (Anm.8), 83f, Collins, a.a.O. (Anm 8), besonders 92-95, und zum Ganzen Holladay, a.a.O (Anm 11), 60-68.

[14] Ob man Theodotus für einen Samaritaner hält oder nicht, seine Aufnahme von Gen 34 gehört nicht nur in Bezug auf die Darstellung Simeons und Levis, sondern auch in Bezug auf die Darstellung Dinas zu dem im folgenden aufgeführten Traditionskreis der Auslegungsgeschichte von Gen 34.

tadellosem Gemüt (καὶ κούρη Δείνα περικαλλὲς ἔχουσα εἶδος, ἐπίστρεπτον δὲ δέμας καὶ ἀμύμονα θυμόν)"[15].

Die Attribute sind geschlechtsspezifisch ausgewählt: für die Söhne Verständigkeit, für die Tochter Schönheit und Tadellosigkeit. Gleiches läßt sich auch im weiteren Verlauf des Textes beobachten, der allerdings, soweit er von Dina handelt, nur als Referat des Polyhistor erhalten ist.[16] Hier heißt es:

> "Und Jakob selbst habe den Acker bebaut, seine Söhne aber – elf an der Zahl – seien Hirten gewesen, die Tochter Dina hingegen und die Frauen hätten Wollarbeit getan" (Frgm. 4,4-7, Eus. praep.ev. 9,22.4).

Der erste Teil dieser Darstellung läßt sich als Auslegung von Gen 33,19 und 34,5 auffassen, wo von Jakob erzählt wird, er habe einen Acker gekauft, während seine Söhne (sein) Vieh weideten. Der zweite Teil erklärt sich aus antiken Vorstellungen von geschlechtsspezifischer Arbeitsteilung und entstammt den zeitgenössischen Vorstellungen von einer "guten Hausfrau und Tochter".[17] Gen 34,1 gibt Theodotus folgendermaßen wieder:

> "Und Dina, die eine Jungfrau war, sei nach Sichem gegangen, als ein Volksfest stattfand und habe die Stadt Sichem betrachten wollen." (Frgm. 4,7-9, Eus. praep.ev. 9,22.4)

Anders als die Genesisvorlage nennt er als Anlaß für Dinas Hinausgehen ein Volksfest (πανήγυρις)[18]. Möglicherweise steht dahinter die Auffassung, daß eine (freigeborene) Tochter bzw. Frau das Haus nur anläßlich eines öffentlichen Festes zu

---

[15] Die meisten dieser Formulierungen finden sich auch bei Homer (Il. 24,377: πέπνυσαί τε νόῳ; Il. 5,389; Od. 11,281: περικαλλής für Frauen; Il. 24,376 οἷος δὴ σὺ δέμας καὶ εἶδος ἀγητός: Il 24,376 u.ö.; ἀμύμων für untadelige Frauen Il. 6,374; 9,128.270; 14,444; 19,245; 23,263; Od. 4,4; 15,15; u.ö.).

[16] Die Referate des Polyhistor machen im Gegensatz zu den metrischen Fragmenten des Gedichtes kaum von der homerischen Sprache Gebrauch. Vgl. Francis T. Fallon, Theodotus, in James H. Charlesworth (Hg.), *The Old Testament Pseudepigrapha 2*, Garden City, New York 1985, 785-793 (785).

[17] Vgl. Xen. oik. VII,6f; Pseudo-Aristot. oik. 43b.26-44a.5; Bryson III 75.80 (Plessner) u.ö., sowie das auf römischen Grabinschriften häufig ausgesprochene Lob auf Frauen: '*donum servavit, lanam fecit*'. Zu den Wollarbeiten als spezifische Frauenarbeit vgl. auch Wilhelm Kroll, Art. Lana, *PRE* 12,1 (1925), 594-617.

[18] Ein Panegyris ist ein Fest, zu dem Menschen von nah und fern zusammenströmen. In hellenistischer Zeit bezeichnet Panegyris vor allem Götterfeste. Vgl. Ludwig Ziehen, Art. Panegyris, *PRE* 18,3 (1949), 581-583.

Ehren der Götter zu verlassen habe.[19] Auch das Interesse Dinas ist hier ein anderes. Statt wie in Gen 34 die Töchter des Landes zu betrachten, betrachtet Dina bei Theodotus die Stadt. Der nächste Satz beschreibt die Handlungen Sichems:

> "Aber als sie Sichem, der Sohn Hemors, sah, habe er sie begehrt, und indem er sie für sich selbst raubte, habe er mit ihr geschlafen und sie geschändet."(Frgm. 4,10f, Eus. praep.ev. 9.22.4)

Theodotus verstärkt im Gegenüber zu Gen 34,2 die Beschreibung der Vergewaltigung, indem er λαβών mit ἁρπάσαντα sowie ἐταπείνωσεν αὐτήν durch φθεῖραι αὐτήν wiedergibt. φθείρειν heißt eigentlich "verderben, zugrunderichten", kann aber auch "schänden" (besonders von Jungfrauen) bedeuten.[20] Dabei schwingt sicher erstere Bedeutung mit, denn einer geschändeten Frau ist nicht nur ihre Jungfräulichkeit zugrundegerichtet worden, sondern sie hat auch ihren Wert für die sie umgebende Gesellschaft verloren.[21] Den schwer zu interpretierenden Satz über das Gespräch zwischen Sichem und Dina (Gen 34,3) läßt Theodotus aus.

Angesichts der ausführlichen einleitenden Bemerkungen über Dina verwundert es, daß sie im folgenden nur noch dreimal indirekt erwähnt wird.[22] In Frgm. 4,12f (Eus. praep.ev. 9.22.5) erbitten Sichem und Hemor sie (αὐτήν) von Jakob zur

---

[19] Vgl. z.B. Theokr. eid. 15; Chariton I.1,4. Phintys, περὶ γυναικὸς σωφροσύνας 154,1-6 (Thesleff).

[20] Vgl. Dion Chr. 11,153; Plut. mor. 712C; Strab. 6.1.6; Lukian. Kataplus 26; Artem. 5,17; Demosth. 45,79 u.ö. Vgl. auch Günther Harter, Art. φθείρω κτλ., *ThWNT* 9 (1973), 94-106. In Eheverträgen heißt es u.a. unter den negativen Pflichten der Frau oft μηδὲ φθείρειν τὸν οἶκον μήδ' ἄλλῳ ἀνδρὶ συνεῖναι (nicht das Haus zu schänden (zugrunde zu richten?), nicht mit einem anderen Mann zu verkehren) (vgl. z.B. P.Berol. 1050,22f; 1051,30; 1052,27; 1098,37; 1101,16). Zur Terminologie und Bewertung von Vergewaltigungen in der griechischen Gesetzgebung vgl. Susan Guettel Cole, Greek Sanctions against Sexual Assault, *CP* 79 (1984), 97-113.

[21] Dion. Hal. 2,25,6f z.B. behauptet, Romulus hätte für Frauen, die geschändet wurden, sowie für weintrinkende Frauen die Todesstrafe vorgesehen. Ähnlich ist wohl auch der Traum, den Artem. 5,17 anführt, zu deuten: Ein Mann träumt, er habe seinen Schlüssel verloren, und als er aufwacht, findet er seine Tochter geschändet.

[22] Vgl. dagegen Gen 34. Hier handelt Dina zwar abgesehen von 34,1 ebenfalls nicht mehr, in vielen der 30 folgenden Verse ist sie aber als Objekt bzw. als Anlaß präsent. Sieben bzw. neun Mal wird ihr Name genannt (34,1.3.5.13.25f; LXX auch 34,15.17); dreimal heißt sie Tochter Jakobs (34.3.7.19 vgl. auch 34,5). Zweimal erscheint sie als Schwester Simeons und Levis (34,14.25), dreimal als Schwester aller Söhne Jakobs

Ehegemeinschaft. Als ein Motiv für das Eingreifen Simeons heißt es: "weil er die Mißhandlung (τὴν ὕβριν) an seiner Schwester nicht auf bürgerliche Weise tragen wollte"[23], und am Schluß des Referats berichtet Polyhistor von den Söhnen Jakobs:

> "sie hätten ihre Schwester befreit (ἀναρρυσαμένους)[24] und mit den Gefangenen (μετὰ τῶν αἰχμαλώτων) in die väterliche Ansiedlung gebracht" (Frgm. 8,20f, Eus. praep.ev. 9.22.10).

Durch diese Formulierung umgeht Theodotus die interpretatorische Schwierigkeit der Genesisvorlage, in der Dina sowohl von Sichem als auch von Simeon und Levi genommen wird (Gen 34,2.26).[25] Über ihr weiteres Schicksal schweigen die erhaltenen Fragmente des Epos. Theodotus ist nur an der "ungeschändeten" Dina interessiert. Sie aber ist eine vorbildliche israelitische Tochter.

Anders als in der Genesisvorlage ist für Theodotus die Schändung Dinas nur ein Auslöser, nicht aber der Grund für die Vernichtung der Sichemiter. Die Ursache für das Eingreifen Simeons und Levis ist ein Orakelspruch Gottes an Simeon, in dem ihm bedeutet wird, Gott werde den Nachkommen Abrahams zehn Völker geben. Durch diesen Orakelspruch kann er Levi von seinem Plan überzeugen (Frgm. 6, 8,6-(9,)14, Eus. praep.ev. 9.22.8f). Als Grund für die Vernichtung wird die Gottlosigkeit der Sichemiter genannt, die schlechte Menschen bei sich beherbergen, das Stadtrecht mißachten und sich um unheilvolle Dinge sorgen (Frgm. 7,1-7, Eus. praep.ev. 9.22.9b). Die Vernichtung der Sichemiter

(34,13.27.31). Einmal werden Jakob und seine Söhne als "ihr Vater und ihre Brüder" bestimmt (34,11). Die LXX nennt sie zusätzlich zweimal παρθένος (34,3), einmal παιδίσκη (34,4) einmal παῖς (34,12). In M heißt sie dreimal Mädchen (34,3.13) יַלְדָּה (34,4), wobei Sichem selbst ebenfalls נַעַר (Jüngling 34,19 LXX: νεανίσκος) heißt.

[23] Frgm. 6.8,5f (Eus. praep.ev. 9.22.8) τὴν ὕβριν τῆς ἀδελφῆς μὴ βουληθέντα πολιτικῆς ἐνεγκεῖν. Nikolaus Walter, *Fragmente jüdisch-hellenistischer Epik: Philon, Theodotos* (JSHRZ IV/3), Gütersloh 1983, 154-171, übersetzt (Frgm. 5,8): "war nicht gewillt, die Vergewaltigung seiner Schwester mit diplomatischer Höflichkeit hinzunehmen".

[24] ἀναρρύω: "befreien" auch Anthologia Graeca 6.300 (Leonidas von Tarent); LXX Ps 33,5 (Aquilla); Iambl. vita Pyth. 7,33. Vgl. auch Holladay, a.a.O. (Anm. 11), 203f (Anm. 149).

[25] Bei Theodotus sind alle Brüder Befreier und die Aktion ist Teil der Plünderung der Stadt, wogegen in Gen 34 Dina zunächst von Simeon und Levi "genommen" wird, bevor die Brüder die Stadt plündern.

wurde von Gott selbst wegen ihrer Mißachtung des Stadtrechts beschlossen. Die Schändung Dinas ist lediglich Auslöser einer verdienten Bestrafung.[26]

Josephus (Ant I.337-341) erzählt Gen 34 ca. 250 Jahre später noch ansprechender für römisch-hellenistische Ohren. Bei ihm fehlt die Beschneidungsforderung. Auch Josephus berichtet, warum Dina nach Sichem geht:

> "Und als die Sichemiter einen Festtag begingen, ging Dina, Jakobs einzige Tochter, hinaus zur Stadt, um sich den Schmuck der einheimischen Frauen anzusehen" (Ant I.337).[27]

Dina will hier also ebenfalls nicht die Frauen selbst betrachten, sondern ihren Schmuck. Die Tat faßt Josephus mit den Worten zusammen:

> "Als sie aber Sichem, der Sohn des Königs Hemor, sah, schändete er sie durch Raub (φθείρει δι' ἁρπαγῆς), und in den Zustand der Liebe versetzt bat er seinen Vater flehentlich, ihm das Mädchen zur Heirat zu geben" (Ant.I.337).[28]

---

[26] In den erhaltenen Fragmenten des Epos fehlt auch der Tadel Jakobs. Es spricht einiges dafür, daß er ganz ausgelassen war. Jakob führt hier die Verhandlungen mit Sichem und Hemor alleine (vgl. Frgm. 4,4-5,6, Eus. praep.ev. 9.22.5-7). Simeon muß also von Jakobs Absichten nichts wissen. Ein Tadel Jakobs gegenüber Simeon (und Levi) wäre ein Tadel gegen die Offenbarung Gottes. Ob Simeon und Levi über die Bewohner der Stadt siegten, weil diese von den Schmerzen der (hier von Jakob allein) geforderten Beschneidung (Frgm. 4,19-5,6, Eus. praep.ev. 9.22.5-7) geschwächt waren, bleibt ebenfalls offen. Eine weitere Besonderheit des Theodotus ist die Heraushebung Simeons als den führenden Bruder (vgl. auch Jdt 9,2-4), die im Gegensatz zur (erwartungsgemäßen) Heraushebung Levis in Jub 30 und TestLev 5-7,3 steht.

[27] Das Festmotiv gehört, wie Martin Braun, *Griechischer Roman und hellenistische Geschichtsschreibung* (FSRKA 6), Frankfurt a.M. 1934, gezeigt hat, "zu den konstanten Größen der hellenistischen Liebeserzählung"(51). Josephus benutzt es auch bei seiner romanhaften Ausgestaltung von Gen 39,7-20 (Ant II.45.47) und in der Samsonerzählung (Ant V.286). Die Erwähnung des Festes sowie die Schilderung der Schändung hat einige Forscher zu der Annahme geführt, daß Josephus "sich bei seiner Nacherzählung von Gen 34... auf Theodotus gestützt hat bzw. das gleiche Material wie er benutzt hat" (Kippenberg, a.a.O. (Anm. 8), 56 Anm. 123). Diese Annahme ist jedoch beim Vergleich mit den folgenden Bearbeitungen nicht zwingend. Besonders Fallon, a.a.O. (Anm. 16) und Kugel, a.a.O. (Anm. 10) haben die Nähe Theodotus' zu TestLev, aber auch zu Jub und Jdt herausgearbeitet (s.u.). Die Gemeinsamkeit von Josephus und Theodotus beschränkt sich vornehmlich auf diese ersten beiden Sätze. Im Gegensatz zu z.B. Jub (vgl. Jub 30,2: "und sie raubten Dina.") nehmen diese beiden Auslegungen Gen 34,1 und Dinas eigenständiges Hinausgehen auf.

[28] Die Interpretation der Tat als Schändung wird nicht nur in Ant I.339 φθορὰν τῆν ἀδελφῆς wieder aufgenommen, sondern auch durch ἁρπάγη

Wie Theodotus betont Josephus die Schändung und unterschlägt Gen 34,3, auch wenn hier die Liebe Sichems, wie in der Genesisvorlage, nach der Tat entsteht. Jakob und die meisten seiner Söhne sind ratlos, was sie angesichts der Bitte des würdevollen Hemors, Dina mit seinem Sohn entsprechend des Gesetzes zu verheiraten, machen sollen (Ant I.338f). Lediglich Simeon und Levi, die Brüder, die von der gleichen Mutter wie das Mädchen geboren wurden,[29] ergreifen die Initiative und überwältigen die Stadt während eines Festes, verschonen nur die Frauen[30] und bringen (ἐπανάγουσι) ihre Schwester zurück.[31] Josephus ändert also ebenso wie Theodotus den Text von Gen 34,26. Er betont durch die Formulierungen "einzige Tochter Jakobs"[32] und "die von der selben Mutter geborenen Brüder" den engen Zusammenhalt der Jakobsfamilie. Seine Darstellung legt die Vermutung nahe, daß Simeon und Levi, vielleicht durch die gemeinsame Mutter mit ihrer Schwester besonders verbunden, im Interesse Dinas handeln, im Gegensatz zu den anderen Söhnen Jakobs, die aus politischer Opportunität klein beigeben. Allerdings verschwinden die dazugehörigen Frauen bzw. Mütter gegen den Genesistext aus der Erzählung des Josephus. Wie Theodotus ist auch Josephus vor allem an der "ungeschändeten" Dina interessiert. Die Darstellung Dinas ist allein auf das Bild einer guten Tochter aus einer vorbildlichen Familie zentriert.

---

verstärkt. Damit steht das Verhalten Sichems im Gegensatz zu der Gesetzgebung Moses, von der es Ap II.200 heißt: "Heiraten aber, gebietet er, darf man nicht, indem man auf die Mitgift achtet, noch durch gewaltsame Entführungen (βιαίοις ἁρπαγαῖς), noch indem man durch List oder Täuschung überredet, sondern indem man bei dem Herrn, der (die Frau) gibt, oder bei verwandten Angehörigen um sie wirbt".

[29] ὁμομήτριοι τῆς κόρης ἀδελφοὶ (Ant I.339). Dina wird bei Josephus zweimal mit Namen genannt (Ant I.337f); zweimal heißt sie Schwester, einmal Tochter und zweimal Mädchen (κόρη). Möglicherweise versucht Josephus, ein später von Augustin (*Questiones in Genesis* 107) bezeugtes Textproblem der LXX zu umgehen. Die LXX spricht in Gen 34,3 von παρθένος, also zu einem Zeitpunkt, an dem sie bereits von Sichem "erniedrigt" wurde.

[30] Ant I.340 φείδονται δὲ τῶν γυναικῶν. Als Zeichen besonderer Grausamkeit führt Josephus das Gegenteil auf, z.B. in Ant VI.260; XVI.263.

[31] Bei den 70 Personen, die nach Ant II.176-183 (vgl. Gen 46,8-27) mit Jakob nach Ägypten ziehen, ist Dina dabei. Ihr weiteres Schicksal bleibt wie in der Genesis ungeklärt.

[32] Durch diese Formulierung fällt Lea, die Gen. 34,1 (und LXX 34,14) genannt wird, heraus.

2.2 *Die Verunreinigung der Gemeinschaft (Testamtent Levi und Jubiläenbuch)*

Das griechische *Testament Levi* geht ausdrücklich der Frage nach, warum ausgerechnet Levi die Rache an den Sichemitern durchführt.[33] Es scheinen im TestLev mehrere Traditionen ineinander verwoben zu sein. Z.B. wird Levis Alter bei der Tat TestLev 2,2 mit 20 Jahren,[34] aber TestLev 12,5 mit 18 Jahren[35] angegeben. TestLev 5,1-7 erzählt eine Vision, in der Levi die Segnungen des Priestertums erhält (5,2). Der Bittengel Israels gibt ihm Schild und Schwert mit der Aufforderung: "Nimm Rache an Sichem für Dina"(5,3).[36] Es folgt ein rückblickender summarischer Bericht von der Vernichtung der Söhne Hemors (5,4).[37] TestLev 6,1-9 erzählt Gen 34 ein zweites Mal ausführlicher.[38] Zwar heißt es hier einleitend: "denn ich war voll Eifer wegen des Greuels, den sie an meiner Schwester[39] verübt hatten" (6,3)[40], jedoch werden anschließend eine Reihe anderer Gründe für ihre Vernichtung aufgezählt. 1. Das Urteil Gottes "war zum Bösem gegen Sichem" (6,8); 2. die Sichemiter wollten bereits an Sara tun, was "sie unserer Schwester Dina (an)taten" (6,8);[41] 3. sie verfolgten Abraham, weil er ein Frem-

[33] Die in Qumran erhaltenen Fragmente des aramäischen TestLev (L 6,21-31) nennen Juda als den Bruder, der die Initiative ergreift. Vgl. Klaus Beyer, *Die aramäischen Texte vom Toten Meer*, Göttingen 1984, 195.

[34] So auch Demetrius Frgm. 2,9 (Eus. praep.ev. 9.21.9).

[35] So auch das aramäische Fragment des TestLev (L 42,16) und das Cambridge-Fragment 78.

[36] Die Mss. α,d,A ergänzen: deine Schwester. Vgl. auch 2,2.

[37] "Und ich vernichtete in jener Zeit die Söhne Hemors, wie es geschrieben ist auf den Tafeln der Väter." Die Mss.-Familie α und ein Teil der armenischen Überlieferung liest "Tafeln des Himmels".

[38] In 6,1 findet Levi erneut ein Schild (ἀσπίς) (5,3: ὅπλον).

[39] Die Mss.-Familie β und ein Teil der armenischen Überlieferung lesen allerdings: "Ich war voll Eifer wegen des Greuels, den sie in Israel machten" (vgl. auch Gen 34,7).

[40] Die Textüberlieferung läßt unklar, ob Levi die Beschneidung veranlaßt oder ablehnt. In 6,3 heißt es: "Ich beriet mit meinem Vater und mit Ruben, meinem Bruder, damit er den Söhnen Hemors sage, daß sie (nicht) beschnitten werden sollten. Zwar ist das "nicht" nur in einer Ms. (c) bezeugt, jedoch hat Kugel, a.a.O. (Anm. 10), 6-12, überzeugende Argumente für dessen Ursprünglichkeit angeführt.

[41] Gedacht ist an Gen 20, die sogenannte Gefährdung der Ahnfrau. (Vgl. auch Gen 12,10-20 und nach der Tradition der α-Mss.-Familie, die Rebekka hinzufügt, auch Gen 26,1-14.) In der Genesis wird kein Zusammenhang zwischen Sichemitern und 'Gefährdung der Ahnfrau' erwähnt.

der war, und traten seine Herden nieder (6,9);[42] 4. sie mißhandelten seinen Knecht (6,9); 5. so machten sie es mit allen Fremden und raubten mit Gewalt die fremden Frauen (6,10).[43] Wie bei Theodotus ist auch hier die Vernichtung von Gott selbst beschlossen (vgl. auch 6,11; 7,1). Levi ist (nur) Ausführender des Urteils. Das Schicksal Dinas gerät in diesen apologetischen Ausführungen[44] Levis völlig aus dem Blick bzw. verschwindet hinter den Formulierungen "Rache für Dina" (2,1; 5,3) bzw. "Greuel" (6,3). Lediglich am Ende der Darstellung in 7,3 heißt es: "Denn sie (die Sichemiter) machten eine Torheit in Israel, als sie unsere Schwester verunreinigten (μιᾶναι)". Das Stichwort "verunreinigen" nimmt TestLev aus Gen 34,5.13.27 auf. Das ursprünglich dem kultischen Zusammenhang entstammende Wort wird in der Bibel nur selten in Bezug auf den (illegitimen) geschlechtlichen Umgang von Frauen verwendet.[45] Verunreinigte Menschen sind nicht kultfähig und müssen sich von der Gemeinschaft fernhalten.[46] Das weitere Schicksal Dinas bleibt im TestLev offen.

Das *Jubiläenbuch*[47] verbindet ebenfalls Levis Erwählung zum Priestertum (30,18-20) sowie eine ausführliche Paränese gegen Mischehen und Unreinheit (30,7-18.20f) mit der Erzählung von Gen 34. Anders als im TestLev wird die Vernichtung der

---

[42] Kugel, a.a.O. (Anm. 10), 21f versteht dies als Auslegung von Gen 13,7f in Verbindung mit Gen 34,30.

[43] Die Mss.-Familie α-bdeg lesen: "ihre Frauen".

[44] Auffällig ist, daß TestLev den Zorn Jakobs über die Vernichtung der soeben Beschnittenen ausdrücklich erzählt und Jakobs Segen Gen 49,6f erwähnt (6,6). Levi sündigt, weil er gegen das Wissen Jakobs gehandelt hat (6,7) (vgl. Josephus Ant I.340f). Die weitere Deutung wird durch die unterschiedliche Überlieferung erschwert. Die meisten Mss. lesen: "Und ich wurde krank an jenem Tag", die Mss. b,c: "Und er wurde krank...". Im Zusammenhang der TestXII deutet diese Formulierung auf eine große Sünde hin (vgl. TestRub 1,8; TestSim 2,12; 4,1; TestGad 4,9). Die Gesamtdarstellung Gen 34 TestLev scheint mir eine Apologie des einem Priester nicht angemessenen Vorgehens Levis zu sein und läßt auf diesbezügliche Angriffe schließen.

[45] Vgl. Num 5,13f; Dtn 24,4; Jer 3,1 (ohne M) beschreiben die Unreinheit einer Frau für einen Mann. Hi 31,11 (ohne M); Ez 18,6.11.15; 22,11; 23,17 ermahnen, eine Frau nicht zu verunreinigen. Vgl. auch TestLev 14,6 (nur ß). Im grHen werden die Himmelssöhne von den Menschentöchtern verunreinigt (7,1; 9,8; 10,11; 12,4; 15,3f).

[46] Vgl. u.a. G. André, Art. טָמֵא, *ThWAT* Bd.3 (1982), 352-366.

[47] Ich übernehme den Text in der Übersetzung von Klaus Berger, *Das Buch der Jubiläen* (JSHRZ II/3), Gütersloh 1981. Zur Auslegung von Gen 34 in Jub 30 vgl. auch: John C. Endres, *Biblical Interpretation in the Book of Jubilees*, Washington, DC 1987, 120-154.

Sichemiter ohne Problematisierungen positiv bewertet und führt dazu, daß Levi "als Freund und Gerechter auf den Tafeln des Himmels" aufgeschrieben ist (30,20).[48] Die eigentliche Erzählung Gen 34 ist in Jub stark gekürzt und umrahmt die Ermahnung (30,2-4.24f).[49] Die Beschneidungsforderung an die Sichemiter fehlt.[50] Von Dina wird lediglich berichtet, daß sie im Alter von 12 Jahren[51] geraubt und verunreinigt wird (30,2).[52] Das Wort "verunreinigen", die lateinische Fassung von Jub liest *polluo*, bleibt das Leitwort des ganzen Kapitels.[53] Die Vernichtung der Sichemiter wurde im Himmel angeordnet, weil sie Dina verunreinigten (30,4-6). Ebenso sollen alle Israeliten, die Israel verunreinigen, die ihre Töchter oder Schwestern Heiden geben[54] bzw. sich mit heidnischen Frauen

[48] Simeons Anteil an der Tat wird lediglich in 30,4 kurz erwähnt. Der in der Genesis (34,30) erzählte Tadel Jakobs fehlt (angedeutet Jub 30,25). Statt des Segens Jakobs (Gen 49), der Simeon und Levi ausnimmt, erzählt Jub vom Segen Isaaks für Levi und Juda (31,8-25.31f). Gen 49 wird auf einen einzigen Vers (Jub 45,14) reduziert.

[49] Die Verhandlungen mit den Sichemitern fehlen, wie Endres, a.a.O. (Anm. 47) gesehen hat, vermutlich, um Jakob vom Verdacht zu befreien, er habe erwogen, seine Tochter den Heiden zu geben. Die Genesiserzählung bzw. deren Auslegungen werden allerdings einige Male exegetisch ausgewertet (vgl. 30,6.12.17.23).

[50] Andeutungen finden sich in 30,3 (vgl. Gen 34,13) und 30,12 (vgl. Gen 34,14).

[51] Die Angabe soll wohl die Geschlechtsreife und Jungfräulichkeit Dinas zum Ausdruck bringen. Nach der Chronologie des Jub ist Dina allerdings erst neun Jahre alt, geboren am 7.7. im sechsten Jahr der vierten Jahrwoche (28,23) (als Zwillingsschwester Sebulons) und geraubt am 1.1. des vierten Jahres der sechsten Jahrwoche (30,1). Vgl. auch Endres, a.a.O. (Anm. 47), 125-127. Die Darstellung Dinas als Kind bzw. gerade zur Geschlechtsreife gelangtes Mädchen unterstreicht ihre Passivität im Gegensatz zur Genesis.

[52] Endres, a.a.O. (Anm. 47), 124, meint, die Auslassung von 'Dinas Hinausgehen' zeige, daß der oder die AutorIn "implicitly attested to her innocence". Zwar trifft es zu, daß zahlreiche spätere Autoren Dina selbst die Schuld an ihrem Schicksal zusprechen (so gemäßigt auch Endres selbst: "... she was vulnerable because she had gone out..."(123)), jedoch vermeiden alle erhaltenen und hier verhandelten jüdisch-hellenistischen Bearbeitungen von Gen 34 diese Auslegung. Die extreme Kürzung der Genesiserzählung entspricht an diesem Punkt m.E. dem fehlenden Interesse an der Figur Dinas, die hier eben kein "ancestral hero" (Endres, ebd., 124) ist, sondern deren Leben wie das jeder Frau, die von einem Nicht-Israeliten vergewaltigt wird oder einen solchen freiwillig heiratet, nach der Meinung des Jub verwirkt ist.

[53] Jub 30,2-10.15f.22 insgesamt 17 Mal, davon in der lateinischen Überlieferung 11 Mal *polluo/pollutio*.

[54] Jub interpretiert dies durch "seinen Samen dem Moloch geben"

einlassen, gesteinigt werden (30,7.9-16). "Und auch die Frau sollen sie verbrennen mit Feuer, denn sie hat verunreinigt den Namen des Hauses ihres Vaters" (30,7).[55] Eine "Ehebrecherin" und "Unreinheit" zerstört die Heiligkeit Israels (30,8 vgl. auch 30,15f). Obgleich die Tat an Dina als "Raub" bezeichnet wird (30,2), geht die weitere Auslegung nur von ihrer Verunreinigung aus. Innerhalb der Paränese legt sich sogar die Vermutung nahe, daß Dina selbst die Verunreinigung Israels aktiv herbeiführt. Dinas Geschichte ist, wie die Bilhas (vgl. Jub 33,1-20)[56] und Thamars (vgl. Jub 41)[57], lediglich Anlaß zu einer grundsätzlichen Ermahnung über Unreinheit und Heiligkeit (30,20f). Zwar wird Dina im Gegensatz zur angedrohten Strafe nicht verbrannt, sondern aus dem Haus Sichems ins Haus Jakobs zurückgeführt,[58] aber sie stirbt, wie Bilha, zur Zeit des Verkaufs Josephs an die Ismaeliten (Jub 34,15).

TestLev und Jub reduzieren die Darstellung der Figur Dinas auf ein Minimum. Im TestLev ist ihr Schicksal, wie bereits bei Theodotus, lediglich Auslöser, nicht aber Grund für die Ver-

(30,10). Die Strafe stammt aus Lev 18,21; 20,2-4. Mit dieser Auslegung stand der Autor oder die Autorin des Jub offenbar nicht allein. In Meg 4,9, vgl. auch bMeg 25a, wird diese Auslegung ausdrücklich verboten.

[55] Jub weitet das Priestergesetz Lev 21,9 auf alle Israelitinnen und Israeliten aus. Vgl. auch Endres, a.a.O. (Anm. 47), 137-147.

[56] Die Erzählung von Rubens Blutschande ist im Gegensatz zu Gen 35,21 stark ausgebaut (vgl. auch TestRub, besonders 3,11-15). Auch hier ist die Unreinheit, die Ruben durch seine Tat Bilha zufügt, Anlaß zu einer ausführlichen Paränese nicht nur über Inzestverbote (vgl. 33,7-12.19), sondern, mit ähnlichen Formulierungen wie in Jub 30 (vgl. besonders 30,11-17.20f mit 33,13-20), über Unreinheit überhaupt. Das Problem der Nichtbestrafung Rubens wird in Jub 33,15-17 thematisiert und mit der noch nicht vollständigen Offenbarung des Gesetzes zu dieser Zeit begründet.

[57] Auch an diese Erzählung schließt Jub eine Paränese über Unreinheit an (41,25-28), die wiederum Verbrennung angedroht (vgl. auch 40,20). Juda entgeht seiner Strafe, weil seine zwei Söhne nicht mit Thamar gelegen haben (41,27). Thamar bleibt offenbar weiterhin ehelos (40,20). Über ihr weiteres Schicksal wird nichts gesagt.

[58] Die lateinische Überlieferung liest "*eiecerunt*" (sie haben sie herausgeworfen/vertrieben, 30,25). Damit könnte eine Tradition aufgenommen sein, nach der Dina (vielleicht in Interpretation von Gen 34,3) nicht freiwillig in das Haus Jakobs zurückkehren wollte. Vgl. BerR 80,11: "Und sie nahmen die Dina (Gen 34,26). Daraus zieht R. Judan den Schluß, daß sie dieselbe zerrten und hinausführten. R. Hun(i)a(h). sagt: Diejenige, welche einmal von einem Unbeschnittenen beschlafen worden ist, trennt sich nicht mehr von ihm. Nach R. Huna sprach sie nämlich: Wohin soll ich mit meiner Schande gehen? (II Sam 13,13), bis ihr Simeon schwor, sie zu heiraten" (übers. August Wünsche, *Der Midrasch Bemidbar Rabba*, Leipzig 1885).

nichtung der Sichemiter. Jub rückt an die Stelle der Geschichte von der Vergewaltigung der Dina eine Paränese über Unreinheit. Dieses im Gegensatz zur biblischen Vorlage auffallende Verschweigen Dinas ist jedoch, besonders im Vergleich zu den folgenden Auslegungen, ein wichtiger Befund.

2.3 *Das Schicksal Dinas (Demetrius, Liber Antiquitatum Biblicarum und Philo)*

Demetrius[59] gibt in seiner Darstellung der Jakobsgeschichte jeweils das genaue Alter der Beteiligten an. Nach ihm sind Dina und Joseph, also die Kinder Jakobs, die sexuellen Übergriffen unterworfen sind, genau gleich alt (Frgm. 2,5.8, Eus. preap.ev. 9.21.5.9).[60] Die einzige Ausschmückung in seiner stark gekürzten Fassung von Gen 34 (Frgm. 2,9, Eus. preap.ev. 9.21.9.) ist die Altersangabe Dinas mit 16 Jahren und 4 Monaten.[61] Dina ist hier also im Gegensatz zu Jub bereits eine Frau und hat dementsprechend Handlungs- und Entscheidungsmöglichkeiten. Wie Theodotus und Josephus spricht Demetrius davon, daß Dina "geschändet" (φθαρῆναι) wurde. Jedoch ist bei ihm im Gegensatz zu Theodotus und TestLev die "Schändung" Dinas der einzige Anlaß zur Vernichtung der Sichemiter. Dina kommt im Alter von 39 Jahren mit ihrem Vater und ihren Brüdern nach Ägypten (Frgm. 2,17, Eus. prap.ev. 9.21.17).[62] Im Gegensatz zu Jub lebt Dina nach Demetrius dort weiter.[63]

Das *Liber Antiquitatum Biblicarum*[64] zeigt in seiner ebenfalls

---

[59] Die Schrift des Demetrius ist ebenfalls hauptsächlich durch das Werk des Alexander Polyhistor und dessen Aufnahme bei Euseb bekannt. Nach Nikolaus Walter, *Fragmente jüdisch-hellenistischer Exegeten, Aristobulos, Demetrios, Aristeas* (JSHRZ III/2), Gütersloh 1975, 280-292 hat Demetrius in den letzten beiden Jahrzehnten des 3. Jh. v. Chr. gewirkt und ist somit die älteste der hier verhandelten Auslegungen von Gen 34.

[60] Vgl. Gen 39,7-20. Nach Jub 28,23f sind Dina und Sebulon Zwillingsgeschwister und 3 Monate jünger als Joseph.

[61] Joseph wird nach Demetrius im Alter von 17 Jahren verkauft (Frgm. 2,11, Eus. praep.ev. 9.21.11).

[62] Demetrius zählt nur die Kinder Jakobs, nicht aber deren Söhne und Töchter (vgl. Gen 46,7-27) mit den jeweiligen Altersangaben auf.

[63] Demetrius nennt übrigens von der ganzen in griechisch erhaltenen jüdisch-hellenistischen Literatur den Namen "Dina" am häufigsten, nämlich 5 mal. (Frgm. 2,5.8f(3x).17, Eus. praep.ev. 9.21.5.8f(3x).17).

[64] Zum Text vgl. Daniel J. Harrington, *Pseudo-Philon, Les Antiquités*

verhältnismäßig kurzen Darstellung von Gen 34 ein deutliches Interesse an Dinas Schicksal. Sie ist neben der Schwiegertochter Thamar das einzige von den Kindern Jakobs, dem genauere Beachtung geschenkt wird.[65] Es heißt:

> "Und Jakob wohnte im Lande Kanaan, und Sichem, der Sohn Hemors, des Horiters, raubte Dina, seine Tochter, und erniedrigte sie (*humilavit*)" (LibAnt 8,7).

Mit *humilavit* nimmt LibAnt als einzige der bisher verhandelten Auslegungen den terminus technicus der LXX für Vergewaltigung, nämlich ταπεινοῦσθαι, auf.[66] Die gesamte weitere Geschichte wird, wie bei Demetrius, in einen einzigen Satz zusammengefaßt (8,7b). Statt der Ausschmückung der Erzählung durch die Taten Simeons und Levis berichtet LibAnt 8,8, daß Hiob Dina zur Frau nimmt und sie 6 Töchter und 14 Söhne bekommt.[67] Auch wenn Betsy Halpern-Amaru mit Recht herausstellt, daß diese Darstellung "with his (Pseudo-Philos) emphasis on maternal roles" übereinstimmt[68], darf nicht übersehen werden, daß LibAnt diese Details vermutlich nicht erfunden hat, sondern in dem Bericht von der Heirat Dinas und Hiobs eine in der rabbinischen Literatur weit verbreite Tradition aufnimmt, die u.a. auch das TestHiob (1,6) kennt.[69] Dina geht in LibAnt samt ihren Nachkommen mit ihrem Vater und ihren Brüdern nach Ägypten (8,11).

Bibliques 1, Paris 1976. Der lateinische Text geht auf eine griechische Vorlage zurück, diese wiederum auf ein hebräisches Original. Die Bibelzitate des Pentateuch sind aus der LXX entnommen. Vgl. Harrington, The Biblical Text of Pseudo-Philo's Liber Aniquitatum Biblicarum, *CBQ* 33 (1971), 1-17.

[65] Vgl. auch Betsy Halpern-Amaru, Portraits of Women in Pseudo-Philo's Biblical Antiquities, in: Amy-Jill Levine (Hg.), *"Women Like This", New Perspectives on Jewish Women in the Greco-Roman World*, Atlanta, Georgia 1991, 83-106, besonders 91.

[66] Gen 34,2; Deut 22,24.29; Ri 19,24; 20,5; II Sam 13,12.14.22.32 Ez 22,10f. Die LXX nimmt nur Ez 16,52 φθείρειν für "Unzucht" auf.

[67] Zweimal drei Töchter und sieben Söhne (vgl. Hi 1,2 und 42,13). Auch die Namen der Söhne werden im Gegensatz zum biblischen Buch Hi, das nur die Namen der später geborenen Töchter kennt, benannt. Allerdings heißen die Töchter hier anders als Hi 42,14 (vgl. auch TestHiob 1,3; 46,5-52,4).

[68] Halpern-Amaru, a.a.O (Anm. 65), 91.

[69] Im TestHiob ist Dina die zweite Frau Hiobs, nachdem die erste stirbt. Dina wird ebenfalls Hiobs Frau nach bBB 15b; THiob 2,9; BerR 19,12; 57,4; 76.9; 80,4 u.ö. Nach BerR 80, heiratet sie Simeon. (vgl. auch Louis Ginsberg, *The Legends of the Jews*, Philadelphia 1909-1928, 2, 37f, 5, 336 Anm 96 u.ö.

Philo bezieht sich in seinem allegorischen Kommentar an zwei Stellen auf die Dinageschichte. In Mut 193f sucht er am Beispiel Sichems, dem "Abkömmling des Unverstands", nachzuweisen, daß der Schlechte zwar das Gute hervorragend erklärt, aber das Schimpfliche tut:[70]

> "Die Weissagungen sagen 'er redete gemäß der Gesinnung der Jungfrau', nachdem Sichem sie vorher erniedrigt hatte (ταπεινώσας). Ist nicht mit Überlegung gesagt, "er redete nach der Gesinnung der Jungfrau", fast zur Offenbarung dessen, der das Gegenteil, von dem, was er sagte, tat?"(Mut 194)

Philo nimmt somit als einziger der hier verhandelten Ausleger von Gen 34 den V.3 auf, um das widersprüchliche Handeln des Unvernünftigen zu demaskieren. Dina, die immer jungfräuliche, deren Namen Philo hier als das "unbestechliche Urteil" deutet, läßt sich von der "Schönheit der Rede" nicht beeinflussen (Mut 194f).

In Migr 223-225 führt Philo Gen 34 erneut an, um auf die Notwendigkeit mühevoller Erziehung hinzuweisen. In seiner Zusammenfassung lautet die Geschichte:

> "Denn Sichem, (...) der Unverstand pflegt und in Scham- und Maßlosigkeit aufgewachsen ist, erkühnte sich, der Erzfrevler, die Urteilskraft des Gedankens (Dina vgl. Migr 223) zu beflecken (μιαίνειν) und zu schänden (φθείρειν) (...), wenn nicht rascher die Freunde und Anhänger des Verstandes, Simon und Levi, ungefährdet in das Haus, nachdem sie sich gesichert hatten, eingedrungen wären und die getötet hätten, die unvermindert sich den Mühen der Lust, der Leidenschaft und der Unbeschnittenheit hingaben. Denn infolge eines Schriftverses: 'Nicht soll eine Hure unter den Töchtern Israels', des Schauenden, 'sein' (Dtn 23,18) rissen sie die jungfräuliche Seele heraus, in der Hoffnung, verborgen zu bleiben."[71]

Hier ist implizit die Antwort der Brüder auf Jakobs Vorwurf aus Gen 34,31 aufgenommen. Das Schicksal Dinas scheint lediglich aus der Sicht Simeons und Levis betrachtet zu sein. Im folgenden nimmt allerdings Philos Auslegung eine unverhoffte Wendung:

---

[70] "Hemor ist nämlich sein Vater, der übersetzt Esel heißt" (Mut 193). Diese Deutung findet Philo bereits im Text, vgl. Gen 34,28.

[71] Migr 224, Übers. Posner, in: Leopold Cohn u.a. (Hg.) *Philo von Alexandria. Die Werke in deutscher Übersetzung* 5, Berlin 1962 (2). ἀπεριτμήτῳ πόνῳ spielt m.E. deutlich auf Gen 34,24f an.

> "Denn nicht mangelt es an Helfern den widerrechtlich Behandelten, sondern wenn es auch einige glauben, so mögen sie es nur glauben, werden aber bald durch die Tatsachen des Irrtums überführt werden. Denn wahrlich, es gibt, ja es gibt die Feindin des Schlechten, die unerweichliche, unerbittliche Helferin der Mißhandelten, die Gerechtigkeit, die die Scharen der Schänder der Tugend stürzt; sind diese aber erst gefallen, so kehrt die Seele, die geschändet zu sein schien, wieder zur jungfräulichen Reinheit zurück; sie schien es ja nur, betone ich, denn wirklich entehrt war sie nie."[72]

Anders als die anderen bisher aufgeführten Auslegungen von Gen 34 deutet Philo die Situation der Frau an, die hinter der Erzählung Dinas steht. Im Bewußtsein, daß nach der Meinung (nicht allein) seiner Zeitgenossen eine Vergewaltigung für eine Frau nicht nur den Verlust körperlicher Integrität, sondern auch ihres Wertes für die Gemeinschaft bedeutet (vgl. Jub 30, TestLev 7,3), spricht er an dieser Stelle den Frauen eine Helferin zu und negiert die Folgen der "vermeintlichen" Schändung.[73] Sicherlich handelt es sich hier um eine Allegorie. Philo selbst kann kaum als Vorkämpfer für Frauenemanzipation in der Antike in Anspruch genommen werden.[74] Frauen bzw. das Weibliche, mit Ausnahme der Jungfrauen, stehen bei ihm für die Sinnlichkeit und damit für das Uneigentliche.[75] Einige seiner Allegorien zeigen jedoch Frauen als Lehrerinnen und Führerinnen der Weisen.[76] Auch wenn Philo selbst diesen Widerspruch an zahlreichen Stellen aufzuheben sucht, indem er jene Frauen vermännlicht bzw.

---

[72] Migr 225, Übers. Posner, ebd.

[73] Die Auslegung bleibt allerdings ambivalent, da sie Gefahr läuft, das Leiden der Frauen zu ignorieren. Philo, für den Apathie ein Ideal ist, kann diese Dimension kaum einholen.

[74] Judith Romney Wegner, Philo's Portrayal of Women – Hebraic or Hellenic? in: Amy-Jill Levine, *"Women Like This"*, a.a.O. (Anm. 65), 41-66.

[75] Vgl. Richard A. Baer, *Philos's Use of the Categories Male and Female*, Leiden 1970, passim und Dorothy Sly, *Philos's Perception of Women* (Brown Judaic Studies 209) Atlanta 1990, passim. Für Sly ist Dina in Philos Darstellung daher auch keine Person, sondern "entirely an allegorical interpretation, in which Dina represents a particular virtue of the soul, judgement" (174). Jedoch übersieht Sly, daß Philo im Gegensatz zu vielen anderen jüdisch-hellenistischen Auslegungen der Geschichte, Dinas Zukunft in den Blick nimmt. Eine Weiterentwicklung seiner Antwort auf Vergewaltigungen von Frauen findet sich in dem frauengeschichtlich interessanten gnostischen Text 'die Hypostase der Archonten' (NHC II 89,19-31).

[76] Vgl. z.B. Abr 99; Leg All 82; Post 146-152; Det 115-118.

ihre (unweibliche) Jungfräulichkeit betont,[77] darf vermutet werden, daß er hier Traditionen übernimmt, deren Tendenz sich gerade nicht mit seinem Frauenbild in Einklang bringen läßt.[78] Es ist nicht auszuschließen, daß in Philos Werken einige der theologischen Gedanken allegorisch geschulter Frauen, wie der von Philo selbst gerühmten Therapeutinnen, verborgen sind.[79]

Demetrius, Philo und LibAnt stellen Dinas Zukunft in den Vordergrund ihrer Auslegungen von Gen 34. Dinas Schicksal nimmt breiten Raum in diesen Darstellungen der Geschichte ein. Damit nehmen sie Anfragen an diese Geschichte aus der Perspektive Dinas auf.

2.4 *Neuerzählungen der Dinageschichte (Judith und Joseph und Aseneth)*

Der Anfang des Gebetes *Judiths*, mit dem sie die Rettung ihrer Heimatstadt Betulias beginnt, enthält ebenfalls eine Erzählung der Dinageschichte. In Jdt 9,2-4 heißt es:

> "Herr, Gott meines Vaters Simeon, dem du ein Schwert in die Hand zur Rache an den Fremden gegeben hast, die den Schoß der Jungfrau zerstörten[80] zur Verunreinigung (μίασμα) und die Schenkel entblößen[81] zur Schande (αἰσχύνην) und den Schoß entweihten (ἐβεβήλωσαν) zur Schmach (ὄνειδος). Du sagtest nämlich: "Nicht soll es so sein"(Gen 34,7) und sie taten (es). (9,3) Deswegen gabst du ihre Herrscher zum Mord und ihr Lager, das sich ihres Betruges (ἀπάτην)[82] schämte, (aber selbst) betrogen wurde zum Blut, und erschlugst die Sklaven bei den

[77] Vgl. z.b. Fug 50-52.128; Ebr 59-64, Quest in Ex 1,8 und Cher 49-52.

[78] Einen Aufweis, wie und in welchem Maß sich Philo auf (allegorische) Traditionen stützt, hat Burton L. Mack, Weisheit und Allegorie bei Philo von Alexandrien, Untersuchungen zum Traktat De Congressu eruditionis, *Studia Philonica* 5 (1978), 57-105, geführt. Vgl. auch zum Ganzen: Dieter Georgi, Frau Weisheit oder das Recht auf Freiheit als schöpferische Kraft, in: Leonore Siegele-Wenschkewitz (Hg.), *Verdrängte Vergangenheit, die uns bedrängt. Feministische Theologie in der Verantwortung für die Geschichte*, München 1988, 243-276, besonders 248-253.

[79] Vgl. besonders VitCont 28f.

[80] Zur Übersetzung von λύω vgl. Carey A. Moore, *Judith* (The Anchor Bible 40B) Garden City, New York 1985, 191. Erich Zenger, *Das Buch Judit* (JSHRZ Bd.I/6), Gütersloh 1981, konjeziert statt τὴν μήτραν, τὴν μίτραν: "... die den Gürtel der Jungfrau lösten...".

[81] γυμνόω in der LXX nur noch Jdt 9,1 (Judith entblößt sich zum Gebet) und Gen 9,21 (Blöße Noahs).

[82] ἀπάτη gehört zu den Leitworten der Schrift (vgl. Zenger, a.a.O, (Anm. 80), 433f).

> Fürsten und die Fürsten auf ihren Thronen. (9,4) Und du hast ihre Frauen zur Plünderung und ihre Töchter in die Kriegsgefangenschaft gegeben und ihre Beute zur Verteilung unter die von Dir geliebten Söhne, die deinen Eifer eiferten und die Schändung ihres Blutes verabscheuten und Dich zur Hilfe anriefen. Gott, mein Gott, höre auf mich, die Witwe."

Deutlicher noch als bei Theodotus und TestLev ist hier Gott der eigentlich Handelnde bei der Vernichtung der Sichemiter. Die direkte Rede der Brüder Gen 34,7 "... so soll es nicht sein" wird als Gotteswort interpretiert und Gott, der in Gen 34 an keiner (anderen) Stelle eingreift oder spricht, als explizit mithandelnd gedacht. In der Interpretation Judiths steht Gott eindeutig auf der Seite der vergewaltigten Tochter Israels und tritt dafür ein, daß diese Tat (auch) für die Täter nicht folgenlos bleibt. Neben der Nichtbeachtung Levis liegt m.E. eine weitere Besonderheit dieser Nacherzählung von Gen 34 in der starken Reflexion auf die beteiligten Frauen. Nicht nur Dinas Erleben der Gewalttat und deren Folgen nehmen einen breiten Platz ein (9,2), sondern auch die Kriegsgefangenschaft der Sichemiterinnen wird benannt (9,4), ein Schicksal, das die Jerusalemerinnen für sich selbst befürchten (4,12; 16,4).[83] Das führt zur Frage, warum sich Judith zu Beginn ihrer Rettungstat überhaupt auf Gen 34 beruft. Zum einen überbietet sie die Tat ihres Stammvaters Simeon.[84] So wie er die Rache an den Fremden übt (9,2), soll sie Rache an den Feinden Betulias üben (8,35).[85] Die Jungfrau Dina steht für Betulia[86] bzw. das

[83] Vgl. 9,4: καὶ ἔδωκας γυναῖκας αὐτῶν εἰς προνομὴν καὶ θυγατέρας αὐτῶν εἰς αἰχμαλωσίαν ... mit 4,12: μὴ δοῦναι εἰς διαρπαγὴν τὰ νήπια αὐτῶν καὶ τὰς γυναῖκας εἰς προνομὴν... und Gen 34,29. Vgl. auch Jdt 8,21f. Knapp ein Drittel des Textes Jdt 9,2-4 bezieht sich auf das Schicksal der beteiligten Frauen, was im Vergleich zu Gen 34 und den jüdisch-hellenistischen Aufnahmen der Geschichte bemerkenswert ist. Im Vergleich zu anderen biblischen (und nicht-kanonischen) Schriften wird in Jdt die Beteiligung von Frauen an den Ereignissen bzw. deren Auswirkungen auf sie häufig benannt. Vgl. z.B. 4,10-12; 6,16; 7,14. 22f 27.32; 14,12f. 16,4.9.

[84] Simeon bekam ein Schwert, mit dem Gott "... die Sklaven bei den Fürsten und die Fürsten auf ihren Thronen..." schlug. Judith bittet: "Schlage den Sklaven bei dem Herrscher und den Herrscher bei seinem Diener, durch den Betrug/die Verführung (ἀπάτης) meiner Lippen" (9,10).

[85] vgl. auch 9,9f; 13,5.

[86] בְּתוּלָה die Stadt Judiths heißt auf hebräisch: "Jungfrau". Vgl. Amy-Jill Levine, Sacrifice and Salvation: Otherness and Domestication in the Book of Judith, in: James C. VanderKam (Hg.), *"No One Spoke Ill of Her." Essays on Judith, Atlanta,* Georgia 1992, 17-30, 18.

Heiligtum (τὰ ἅγια), das in Gefahr steht, der Entweihung und Schändung anheimgegeben zu werden.[87] Die Sichemiter, als betrogene Betrüger (9,3),[88] stehen für den Assyrer Holofernes, der betrügen will (12,16), aber selbst betrogen wird (13,16).[89] Zum anderen geht Judith aber wie Dina aus der Stadt heraus (ἐξῆλθεν 10,10 (10,6.9) vgl. Gen 34,1), jedoch kann Holofernes an ihr keine Sünde "zur Verunreinigung und Schande" tun.[90] Die Geschichte erhält ein neues 'happy end'. Weder Judith noch das Heiligtum/Dina werden verunreinigt, der Aggressor ist getötet, die Feinde fliehen und das ganze Volk kann sich an die Plünderung machen (15,6f.11 vgl. Gen 34,27-29). In ähnlicher Weise, wie Jdt die Geschichte Deborahs und Jaels (Jdc 4f), Mirjams (Ex 15) und andere biblische Erzählungen aufnimmt und als Modell benutzt,[91] arbeitet dieses Buch auch mit Gen 34. Indem Judith sowohl die Rolle Simeons als auch die Rolle Dinas in Gen 34 einnimmt, kann sie Dina jedoch aus ihrer Passivität befreien, in die der größte Teil der Genesiserzählung Leas Tochter drängt.

Auch *Joseph und Aseneth* 22-29[92] nimmt die Dinageschichte

---

[87] Vgl. 4,12: μὴ δοῦναι (...) τὰ ἅγια εἰς βεβήλωσιν καὶ ὀνειδισμόν. Vgl. auch 8,21f; 9,8; (1,14).

[88] Es ist viel gerätselt worden, auf was sich die Formulierung ἔδωκας (...) τὴν στρωμνὴν αὐτῶν, ἣ ᾐδέσατο τὴν ἀπάτην αὐτῶν, ἀπατηθεῖσαν εἰς αἷμα (9,3) bezieht (vgl. z.B. Zenger a.a.O. (Anm. 80), 493 Anm. 3). M.E. widerspricht aber der Plural des αὐτῶν nicht der Deutung auf die Vergewaltigung Dinas, da eine Reihe anderer Auslegungen von Gen 34 den Sichemitern eine kollektive Schuld zusprechen (vgl. z.B. Jub 30,2 u.ö.; TestLev 6,3.8; 7,3). Diese Deutung wird durch die Formulierung Gen 34,27 M טִמְּאוּ, Gen 34,13.27 LXX ἐμίαναν unterstützt. ἀπατηθεῖσαν nimmt m.E. Gen 34,13: בְּמִרְמָה/μετὰ δόλου auf und spielt somit auf die Beschneidung an.

[89] Vgl. auch 9,10.13; 14,18; 16,8.

[90] καὶ οὐκ ἐποίησεν ἁμάρτημα μετ' ἐμοῦ εἰς μίασμα καὶ αἰσχύνην (13,16).

[91] Vgl. u.a. Toni Craven, Tradition and Convention in the Book of Judith, *Semeia* 28 (1983), 49-61 und Sidnie Ann White, In the Steps of Jael and Deborah: Judith as Heroine, in: James C. VanderKam (Hg.), *"No One Spoke Ill of Her"*, a.a.O. (Anm. 86), 5-16.

[92] Im folgenden lege ich die Textrekonstruktion von Marc Philonenko, *Joseph et Aséneth. Introduction, Texte critque, traduction et notes* (SPB 13), Leiden 1968 und damit die kürzeste der erhaltenen Textfamilien zugrunde. Die Beschränkung auf eine Textrekonstruktion geschieht hier zum einen aus Platz-, zum andern aus inhaltlichen Gründen. Die verschiedenen Textfassungen JosAs unterscheiden sich nicht nur ganz erheblich im Umfang, sondern sie enthalten auch unterschiedliche theologische Tendenzen und stellen ein jeweils eigenes Frauenbild dar. Zur Begründung dieser These, sowie zur spezifischen Bearbeitung der

auf und erzählt sie erneut mit neuen Personen und verändertem Ausgang.[93] Der Sohn des Pharao sieht Aseneth, die Frau Josephs (Gen 41,45), und begehrt sie (JosAs 23,1f). Um sie in seine Gewalt zu bringen, sucht er unter den Brüdern Josephs nach Bundesgenossen. Zunächst ruft er Simeon und Levi und beginnt seine Rede mit folgenden Worten:

> "Ich weiß, daß ihr mächtige Männer seid, mehr als alle Menschen auf der Erde, und mit euren Rechten ist die Stadt der Sichemiter unterjocht worden und mit euren zwei Schwertern habt ihr 30000 kämpfende Männer erschlagen."(23,3)

Der Sohn des Pharaos, der Simeon und Levi für die Unterjochung Sichems hier rühmt, ist allerdings der Antiheld der Geschichte, dessen Pläne auf lächerliche Weise scheitern werden.[94] Wenn er die ungeheuer grausame Vernichtungstat (30000 Männer) rühmt,[95] klingt Kritik am Vergeltungs-

---

Dinageschichte in der längeren Textrekonstruktion von Christoph Burchard (vgl. u.a. *Joseph und Aseneth* (JSHRZ II/4) Gütersloh 1983) vgl. meine Dissertation *"Der Beitrag von 'Joseph und Aseneth' zur Diskussion um das Frauenbild in jüdisch-hellenistischer Zeit"*, sowie bereits Ross S. Kraemer, *Her Share of the Blessing*, New York, Oxford 1992, 110-113.230.

[93] Seit Beginn der Erforschung von JosAs ist die Aufnahme von Gen 34 in JosAs 22-29 aufgefallen. Einige Forscher sehen darin die Aufnahme einer rabbinischen Legende, nach der Aseneth die Tochter Dinas und Sichems ist, die als illegitimes Kind ausgesetzt wurde und in das Haus des Pentephres als Pflegetochter gelangt (vgl. besonders Victor Aptowitzer, Asenath, the Wife of Joseph. A Haggadic Literar-Historical Study, *HUCA* 1, 1924, 239-306 und neuerdings George W. E. Nickelsburg, Stories of Biblical and Early Post-Biblical Times, in: Michael E. Stone (Hg.), *Jewish Writings of the Second Temple Period*, Assen-Philadelphia, Pa. 1984, 65-71.86). Jedoch ist diese rabbinische Legende erst relativ spät bezeugt und konkurriert z.B. mit einer Legende, nach der Aseneth die Tochter der Frau des Potiphar (Gen 39) ist. Matthias Delcor (Un roman d'amour d'origine thérapeute: Le Livre de Joseph et Aséneth, *Bulletin de Littérature Ecclésiastique* 63 (1962) 3-37) und Christoph Burchard (*Untersuchungen zu Joseph und Aseneth. Überlieferung-Ortsbestimmung* (WUNT 8) Tübingen 1965, 96-99) haben jedoch überzeugend gezeigt, daß der Großteil des Textes JosAs der Bekanntschaft oder Verarbeitung dieser Dinalegende widerspricht. Joseph nennt Aseneth zwar 7,10 seine Schwester, aber erst nachdem ihm versichert wurde, daß sie eine Jungfrau sei wie er selbst. Zudem lehnt er ihren Kuß 8,5f ab, weil sie eine "fremde Frau" sei. Wenn JosAs, wie ich im folgenden zu zeigen versuche, ein eigenständiger Beitrag zur Diskussion um Gen 34 ist, kann auch ohne Hinzuziehung der "Aseneth-Tochter-Dina-Legende" erklärt werden, warum in JosAs 22-29 diese Geschichte in den Mittelpunkt gestellt wird.

[94] Er kann z.B. seinen Vater nicht umbringen, weil dieser Schmerzen hat (25,3) und schlafen muß.

[95] Diese Anzahl der getöteten Sichemiter ist sonst m.W. nirgendwo in der jüdisch-hellenistischen Literatur belegt.

gedanken an. Levi und Simeon lehnen sein Ansinnen ab. Seiner Drohung, sie zu töten, begegnen sie ebenfalls mit einem Rekurs auf Gen 34:[96]

> "Hast du diese Schwerter gesehen? Mit ihnen rächte der Herr, Gott, die Mißhandlung (τὴν ὕβριν) an den Söhnen Israels (τῶν υἱῶν 'Ισραήλ), die die Sichemiter machten wegen unserer Schwester Dina, die Sichem, der Sohn Hemors, verunreinigte (ἐμίανε)." (23,13)

Auch hier erscheint die Rache als Tat Gottes. Wie in Gen 34,5.13.27; Jub 30; TestLev 7,3 und Jdt 9,2 wird die Vergewaltigung Dinas als Verunreinigung bezeichnet, gleichzeitig allerdings auch als Mißhandlung (Vergewaltigung, Schädigung)[97] der Söhne Israels. Es bleibt zunächst offen, ob alle Kinder Israels oder nur die Jakobssöhne gemeint sind. Das Schicksal der Frau, das hier nur in seinen Auswirkungen und im Nebensatz bedacht wird, bekommt aber für die an Gen 34 erinnerten Leserinnen und Leser JosAs' im Fortgang der Erzählung neue Dimensionen. Der Sohn des Pharaos findet in den Söhnen der Mägde Silpa und Bilha Verbündete für seinen Plan, Aseneth zu rauben (JosAs 24).[98] In der spannenden Schilderung der Schlacht zwischen dem Sohn des Pharaos, den Mägdesöhnen und den Leuten Aseneths werden zunächst die 650 Männer Aseneths getötet (26,5). Sie selbst wird jedoch aus den Händen des Pharaos durch ein Wunder Benjamins gerettet (27,1-5), der den Sohn des Pharaos verwundet (vgl. I Sam 17). Vor dem zweiten Angriff durch die Söhne der Mägde schützt sie ein Gotteswunder, das die gegen Aseneth ausgestreckten Schwerter zu Asche werden läßt (27,8). Gott, der in der Erzählung Gen 34 abwesend scheint, schützt Aseneth

---

[96] Als der Sohn des Pharaos sein Schwert zieht, will ihn Simeon sogleich töten. Levi hält ihn jedoch ab mit den Worten: "Es ziemt sich nicht für einen gottesfürchtigen Mann, Böses mit Bösem seinem Nächsten zu vergelten." (23,9). Im nächsten Satz führt der Erzähler den Sohn des Pharao als Levis Nächsten ein (23,10).

[97] ὕβρις κτλ. kann Vergewaltigung (von Frauen) bedeuten. Vgl. Theodotus Frgm. 6,8,5, Eus. praep.ev 9.22.8) (hier die Tat an Dina); Pseudo-Phokylides 189; Philo Spec 3,76.78; Virt 113 u.ö. Zur Bedeutungsbreite vgl. Georg Bertram, Art. ὕβρις κτλ., *ThWNT* 8 (1969), 295-307.

[98] Diesmal u.a. mit dem Argument: "Siehe, ich weiß, daß ihr starke Männer seid und nicht wie Frauen sterben werdet, sondern männlich handelt und euren Feinden vergeltet" (24,7 vgl. auch 25,8). Gerade diese hier so gerühmten Brüder müssen ironischerweise später bei Aseneth um Erbarmen flehen (28,2).

vor der ihr bevorstehenden Vergewaltigung (vgl. Jdt 9,2). Die Mägdesöhne flehen nun bei Aseneth um Erbarmen und um Schutz vor der Rache ihrer Brüder. Sie antwortet ihnen:

> "Seid getrost und fürchtet euch nicht, denn eure Brüder sind gottesfürchtige Männer und vergelten nicht Böses mit Bösem irgendeinem Menschen"[99].

Nachdem sie die Mägdesöhne in ein Versteck geschickt hat, setzt sie ihre Schonung gegenüber den Söhnen Leas durch (28,10f). Simeon ist jedoch mit diesem Vorgehen zunächst nicht einverstanden. Aseneth hält ihm entgegen: "Keineswegs, Bruder, wirst du Böses mit Bösem deinem Nächsten vergelten, denn der Herr rächt diese Mißhandlung" (28,14).

Die Formulierung τὴν ὕβριν ταύτην (diese Mißhandlung) bezieht sich dabei sowohl auf die Mißhandlung Aseneths (vgl. 28,3) als auch auf Vergeltung überhaupt. Vergeltung gegenüber dem Aggressor, dem Sohn des Pharao, als Nächstem (vgl. 23,10) oder überhaupt gegenüber jedem Menschen (vgl. 28,4) ist nicht mehr die Sache des gottesfürchtigen Mannes. Die Vergebung wirkt über die Grenzen des Volkes Israel hinaus (vgl. auch 29,3). Aseneth nimmt hier Dinas Interesse an den Töchtern des Landes und den fremden Frauen auf und formuliert ein theologisches Konzept vom Umgang mit Fremden.

So rettet Aseneth nicht nur die Söhne der Mägde vor dem Zorn ihrer Brüder, wie der Erzähler bzw. die Erzählerin abschließend feststellt (28,16), sondern sie bringt auch eine neue Ethik zum Ausdruck, die statt grausamer Vergeltung (30000 Männer) allgemeine Vergebung lehrt. Das ethische Problem, das Gen 34 den jüdisch-hellenistischen Auslegungen stellt, nämlich wie die Vernichtung einer ganzen Stadt durch Simeon und Levi gerechtfertigt werden kann, wird hier auf eine originelle Weise gelöst. Nach Aseneths Rettungstat kann es keine Vergeltung unter Menschen mehr geben; nach ihrer Lehre ist Vergeltung gegen Gottes Willen.

3. Die Perspektive Dinas in der jüdisch-hellenistischen Literatur

Die vorangegangenen Untersuchungen haben gezeigt, daß die Aufnahme von Gen 34 in der jüdisch-hellenistischen Literatur

---

[99] 28,4. Aseneth verallgemeinert mit τινι ἀνθρώπῳ Levis Formulierung aus 23,9: "Es ziemt sich nicht für einen gottesfürchtigen Mann, Böses mit Bösem seinem Nächsten (τῷ πλησίον αὐτοῦ) zu vergelten."

in sehr unterschiedlicher Weise geschieht. Theodotus und Josephus beschreiben Dina als "gute Tochter aus vorbildlichem Hause", sind jedoch beide an der "geschändeten" Dina nicht mehr interessiert. TestLev und Jub verschweigen sie fast völlig. Dagegen stellen Demetrius, LibAnt, Philo, Jdt und JosAs in je spezifischer Weise gerade ihre Zukunft und ihr Erleben ins Zentrum ihrer Bearbeitung dieser Geschichte.

Eine Reihe von exegetischen und ethischen Problemen mit dieser Geschichte werden hinter den hier vorgestellten Bearbeitungen sichtbar. Als problematisch wird fast immer die hinterhältige Vernichtung der Sichemiter durch Simeon und/ oder Levi, den Priester und Hüter des Gesetzes, empfunden.[100] Daher lassen Josephus, Jub, LibAnt, Demetrius (und JosAs) die Beschneidungsforderung aus. Philo und Jdt reduzieren sie auf Andeutungen und Theodotus läßt ihre Durchführung offen.

Für einige Ausleger scheint die "Schändung" bzw. "Verunreinigung" Dinas als Begründung für das Vorgehen der Brüder nicht auszureichen. Theodotus und TestLev (und Jub) führen eine Reihe weiterer Missetaten der Sichemiter auf. Dagegen steht für andere Ausleger das Schicksal Dinas nicht nur im Mittelpunkt der Begründung für das Vorgehen der Brüder, sondern im Zentrum ihrer Bearbeitungen von Gen 34 überhaupt. LibAnt, TestHiob, Demetrius und Philo nehmen vor allem Dinas Zukunft, ihre Heirat und ihren Einzug nach Ägypten in den Blick. Jdt und JosAs erzählen die Geschichte mit glücklichem Ausgang neu.

Auch in der Darstellung der Tat Sichems selbst lassen sich unterschiedliche Gewichtungen feststellen. Lediglich LibAnt und Philo nehmen die Formulierung "und erniedrigte sie" aus Gen 34,2 auf. Die anderen Ausleger sprechen entweder mit Gen 34,5.13.27 von "verunreinigen", oder von "schänden" bzw. "mißhandeln". Als geschändete Frau, deren Jungfräulichkeit zerstört wurde, findet Dina bei Theodotus und Josephus kaum weitere Beachtung. Die Vernichtung der Verunreiniger begründet in TestLev und Jub Levis Erwählung zum Priestertum. Als Verunreinigte hat Dina nach Jub in Israel, Gottes Heiligtum, keinen Platz mehr. Sie stirbt vor dem Einzug nach Ägypten. Dagegen setzt für Philo die Helferin der

[100] Vgl. auch die deutliche Kritik IV Mkk 2,19.

Mißhandelten, die Gerechtigkeit, die geschändete Seele in ihren ursprünglichen Zustand zurück. In den Neuerzählungen Jdt und JosAs können sich die Frauen erfolgreich gegen die Vergewaltigung bzw. Mißhandlung wehren.

Ein weiteres Thema dieser Bearbeitungen ist die Frage nach Gott. Gott scheint in Gen 34 abwesend zu sein. Für Theodotus und TestLev legitimiert eine Vision oder ein Orakel Gottes die Vernichtung der Sichemiter. Aber nicht Dinas Schicksal veranlaßt Gott zu seinem Eingreifen, sondern eine Reihe anderer schwerwiegender Vergehen der Sichemiter. Für Theodotus und TestLev ist Gott an Dinas Erleben völlig uninteressiert. Anders führt in JosAs und Jdt Gott selbst die Rache aus. Jdt interpretiert Gen 34,7b als Gotteswort. Das Interesse dieser Neuerzählungen gilt aber vor allem den Frauen als Opfern der Vergewaltigung. Gott läßt eine weitere Vergewaltigung von Frauen (Israels) nicht zu. Gott greift ein, hilft ihnen, sich gegenüber ihren Angreifern zu verteidigen. Jdt und JosAs versuchen eine theologische Antwort auf Gewalt gegen Frauen zu geben. Damit werden eine Reihe Anfragen aus der Perspektive Dinas aufgenommen. Es scheint, daß ihre Perspektive Jdt und JosAs dazu führte, die biblische Vorlage nicht unkommentiert zu belassen, sondern neu zu erzählen.

Während jedoch Gott in Jdt nur an den Töchtern Israels interessiert ist und für die Vernichtung der Vergewaltiger eintritt, durchbricht Aseneth in JosAs den Vergeltungskreislauf und lehrt Vergebung gegenüber allen Menschen. Die innerhalb des hellenistischen Judentums virulente Kritik an der Rache an den Sichemitern wird so von Aseneth aufgenommen und in Richtung auf eine über die Grenzen des eigenen Volkes wirkende Vergebung weiterentwickelt.

Die unterschiedliche Darstellung Dinas zeigt, daß diese Figur diskutiert wurde.[101] Einige der Anfragen an Gen 34 aus der Perspektive Dinas werden in den jüdisch-hellenistischen

---

[101] Nicht alle Auslegungen von Gen 34 sind als "whitewashing" (Pummer, a.a.O., Anm. 9) der Patriarchen zu verstehen. Vielmehr wird z.T. harsche Kritik am Vorgehen Simeons und Levis geübt (IV Mkk 2,19), und es zeigen sich Spannungen, wenn Theodotus und Jdt Simeon hervorheben, TestLev und Jub dagegen allein den Priester Levi ins Zentrum stellen. In JosAs wird ebenfalls leichte Kritik an Simeon geübt, aber auch Levi erscheint hier anders als in Jub und TestLev nicht als Priester, sondern als Prophet. In JosAs ist Aseneth seine ebenbürtige Partnerin.

Auslegungen aufgenommen und beantwortet. Andere sind durch die hier vorgenommenen neuen Darstellungen gelöst. In keiner der Auslegungen wird Dina sowohl von Sichem als auch von ihren Brüdern "genommen". Alle Auslegungen ändern mindestens an einer Stelle diesbezüglich den Text.[102] Außer Philo nimmt keine andere Interpretation Gen 34,3 auf. Dina steht somit implizit auf der Seite der Brüder. Die Frage, ob sie freiwillig in das Haus ihres Vaters zurückkehrt, stellen jedoch diese Auslegungen (noch) nicht.[103]

Im Gegensatz zu späteren Interpretationen der Geschichte spricht aber auch keine der erhaltenen jüdisch-hellenistischen Dina explizit die Schuld an ihrem Unglück zu.[104] Allerdings nehmen von den hier besprochenen Auslegungen nur Theodotus und Josephus den Satz von Dinas eigenständigem Herausgehen (Gen 34,1) auf. Beide Ausleger verändern jedoch das Objekt von Dinas Sehen. Anstelle der Töchter des Landes betrachtet sie bei Theodotus die Stadt. Damit verfolgt Dina hier nicht (mehr) ihr eigenes politisches Konzept vom Umgang mit den fremden Frauen. Bei Josephus schaut sie den Schmuck der Frauen des Landes an, was an geschlechtsspezifische Zuschreibungen erinnert. Durch diese neuen Objekte wird die kritische Schärfe der Vorlage abschwächt.

Die häufige und unterschiedliche Aufnahme von Gen 34 deckt eine Kontroverse um die Dinageschichte auf. Wenn dabei die einen vor allem an Dinas Vergangenheit, die andern aber an ihrer Zukunft interessiert sind, die einen Dina

---

102 Vgl. Theodotus: "raubte"/"befreiten", Josephus: "schändete durch Raub"/"zurückführen", Jub: "raubte"/"führten", LibAnt: "raubte"/"nahmen".

103 Vgl. aber BerR 80,11, s.o. Anm. 58.

104 Anders jedoch spätere Auslegungen z.B. BerR 80,1, wo von einem Streit zwischen Rabbi (Judah dem Patriarchen) und Rabbi Jose von Maon berichtet wird, in dem letzterer behauptet: "Wenn die Kuh stößt, so schlägt die Tochter (das Kalb) aus; wenn die Mutter buhlt, so ist auch die Tochter ausschweifend. (Rabbi entgegnet ihm: ')Wenn dem so ist, so hat auch unsere Mutter Lea gebuhlt('?) Er sprach zu ihnen: 'Und Lea ging heraus ihm entgegen' (Gen 30,16), das will sagen: sie ging aus wie eine Buhlerin geputzt, darum ging auch ihre Tochter Dina heraus." (übers. Wünsche, a.a.O.(Anm. 58).) Vgl. auch Ginsberg, *Legends of the Jews* 1, 66 und 395-396 und 5, 89, a.a.O. (Anm 69) und 313-314 Anm 285. Christliche Ausleger stehen hier ebenfalls nicht nach. Vgl. z.B. Hier. *epistulae* 22,25; 107,6 (4.Jh) oder die Auslegung von Gen 34,1 des niederländisch-calvinistischen Theologen Abraham Kuyper (19.Jh) (vgl. Spiegelungen, *Texte und Kontexte* 30 (1986), 47f) oder auch Gerhard von Rads Auslegung von Gen 34,1 in: *Das erste Buch Mose. Genesis* (ATD 2/4), Göttingen 1976, 269.

verschweigen, während die anderen Dinas Schicksal zum Zentrum der Geschichte machen und Gewalt gegen Frauen als ein theologisches Problem begreifen, wird eine Diskussion um Frauenbilder sichtbar. An welchen Stellen und mit welchen Positionen Jüdinnen und von der jüdischen Mission begeisterte Frauen diskutierten, kann man nur vermuten. Die kontroverse Diskussion macht aber deutlich, daß die Frauen der jüdisch-hellenistischen Gemeinden nicht sprachlos geblieben sind.

UMSTRITTENER AUFERSTEHUNGSGLAUBE

Gerhard Barth (Kirchliche Hochschule Wuppertal)

Flavius Josephus erklärt in seiner Schrift gegen Apion (II,218), daß alle Juden den festen Glauben haben, Gott werde ihnen bei der Äonenwende ein neues, besseres Leben geben, wenn sie das Gesetz halten und, wenn nötig, selbst dafür zu sterben bereit seien. Dazu beruft er sich auf die Zusage Gottes, die Verheißung des Gesetzgebers und das Zeugnis des eigenen Gewissens. Zwar nimmt er an anderer Stelle[1] die Sadduzäer ausdrücklich von einem solchen Glauben an ein Leben jenseits des Todes aus. Hier dagegen erklärt er pauschal, daß bei den Juden jeder[2] diese Überzeugung habe, was – unter Berücksichtigung der Aussage über die Sadduzäer – bedeutet, daß nach seiner Meinung, von den Sadduzäern abgesehen, alle Juden eine Art von "Auferstehungsglauben"[3] teilen.

Diese pauschale Aussage des Josephus hat die neutestamentliche Forschung weithin bestimmt. So nimmt Albrecht Oepke zwar Sadduzäer und Samaritaner davon aus, erklärt aber: "Das ganze Spätjudentum hat die Auferstehungshoffnung als festen, notwendigen Bestandteil seines Glaubens", und auch Rudolf Bultmann spricht generell von der "traditionellen jüdisch-christlichen Lehre von der Auferstehung der Toten"[4].

Daß diese verbreitete Annahme eines – wie auch immer

---

[1] Jos. Bell. II,165; Ant. XVIII,16.

[2] αὐτὸς ἕκαστος...πεπίστευκεν.

[3] "Auferstehungsglaube" wird im Folgenden nicht im strengen Sinn als Glaube an eine "leibliche" Auferweckung am Jüngsten Tag gebraucht, sondern im weiteren Sinn als Glaube an ein Leben jenseits des Todes oder an ein ewiges Leben. Daß sich hier zwischen Dan 12,2; II Makk 7,9. 14; Weish 3,4; 6,18f; IV Mkk 14,6; IV Esra 7,31ff und etwa Schemone Esre 2 durchaus unterschiedliche Begriffe und Vorstellungen finden, ist bekannt. Vgl. auch Hans C.C.Cavallin, Leben nach dem Tode im Spätjudentum und frühen Christentum, I. Spätjudentum, *ANRW II, Bd. 19,1* (1979) S.240-345. Im Folgenden wird aber generell nach einer Hoffnung jenseits der Todesgrenze gefragt, ohne die verschiedenen Ausprägungen gesondert zu untersuchen.

[4] A.Oepke, *ThWNT 1* (1933) S.370; R.Bultmann, *Theologie des Neuen Testaments,* [9]1984, S.347; vgl. weiter E. Lohse, Art. Auferstehung, IV Im Judentum, *RGG 1* ([3]1957), S.694; G.Kegel, *Auferstehung Jesu – Auferstehung der Toten,* 1970, S.99.

gearteten – generellen Auferstehungsglaubens im Judentum korrekturbedürftig ist, hat Hans C.C.Cavallin betont.[5] Seinen diesbezüglichen Beobachtungen soll hier weiter nachgegangen werden. Cavallin bezieht sich zunächst auf eine unveröffentlichte Oxforder Dissertation von A.J.Berefold 1971: "A.J.Berefold has examined most of the Jewish documents of the period under consideration with the question whether they speak about life after death. In many cases the answer was negative". Als Bücher, die keinerlei Jenseitshoffnung kennen, nennt Cavallin Jesus Sirach, Judith, Tobit, Baruch, Aristeasbrief, das 1. und das 3. Makkabäerbuch, 3.Esra, Paralipomena Jeremiae, Assumptio Mosis und das Martyrium Jesajae. Natürlich kann solches Schweigen zuweilen auch zufällig oder durch die andersartige Thematik bedingt sein. Aber bei einigen Schriften, deren Inhalt durchaus dazu hätte Anlaß bieten können, ist dieses Schweigen doch bezeichnend. Das gilt etwa von Büchern, die von Verfolgung und Martyrium handeln, wie 1. und 3.Makkabäerbuch und Martyrium Jesajae. Auf den Siraciden soll noch gesondert eingegangen werden.

Höchst unklar ist der Befund in den Qumran-Schriften. Das positive Zeugnis des Josephus[6] wird von den Qumran-Texten nicht bestätigt[7]. Cavallin kommt zu dem Ergebnis:

> "Of all passages in the Qumran scrolls (including CD) which may testify to a belief in the resurrection of the dead or life after death in generall, only one text, or possibly two, proved to represent a sure supporting testimony. The rest was found to be most doubtful as statements supporting after-life. Assertions of the eternal life of the elect ... are not so rare, but nothing is said about their death".[8]

Positiver urteilt Kurt Schubert[9], der in den Texten eine Auferstehung der Toten mit neuer Leiblichkeit vorausgesetzt sieht, dafür aber keine Belege aus den eigentlichen Qumran-Schriften bringt, sondern sich auf Henoch und die Apokalyptik beruft. Nun wurden zwar in den Qumran-Höhlen

---

[5] H.C.C.Cavallin, *Life after Death. Paul's Argment for the Resurrection of the Dead in 1 Cor 15*, Part I: An Enquiry into the Jewish Background, Lund 1974; das folgende Zitat S.193.

[6] Jos. Bell. II,163; Ant. XVIII, 18.

[7] Zu beachten sind vor allen 1QS 4,6-8. 12-14. 18f; 1QH 4,21f; 6,29f. 34f; 7,30f; Cavallin untersucht darüber hinaus 1QS 11,7-9; 1QSb 3,4-6; 1QH 8,31; 11,10-14; 4QAmram.; 4QpsDa 38-40; 4Q 181.

[8] *A.a.O.*, S.65.

[9] J.Maier / K.Schubert, *Die Qumran-Essener*, München 1973, S.94ff.

auch Henochfragmente gefunden. Aber deren Aussagekraft ist in dieser Frage doch kaum größer als die der unzähligen Fragmente alttestamentlicher Schriften, die gleichfalls gefunden wurden. Dagegen erklärt Günter Stemberger: "Auferstehungsvorstellung nicht eindeutig nachzuweisen".[10] Qumran kennt zwar die Naherwartung und die Hoffnung auf eine endzeitliche Überwindung der Mächte der Finsternis, aber dies ist – wie 1QM zeigt – ein primär diesseitiges Geschehen. Daher läßt man die Qumran-Schriften bei unsrer Frage am besten außer Betracht.

I

Für die spätere jüdische Orthodoxie gilt der Auferstehungsglaube als festes Dogma. Sanh 10,1: "Ganz Israel hat Anteil an der zukünftigen Welt. Und dies sind die, welche keinen Anteil an der zukünftigen Welt haben: Wer sagt: es gibt keine Auferstehung der Toten nach der Torah"[11]. Das ist aber eine Lehre, die sich erst in der Zeit nach der Tempelzerstörung (70 n.Chr.), als sich der Pharisäismus als Orthodoxie herauskristallisierte, allmählich durchsetzte. Und selbst hier zeigt die Formulierung, daß dieser Glaube nicht unbestritten war. Wie umstritten ein Glaube an Auferstehung oder ewiges Leben war, zeigen mehrere Texte aus spätisraelitisch-frühjüdischer Zeit.

Bekanntlich gehört Kohelet mit seiner rein auf das Diesseits gerichteten Heilserwartung ganz in den Rahmen dessen, was sich auch sonst im Alten Testament über die Haltung gegenüber Tod und Scheol[12] findet: "Ein lebender Hund ist besser als ein toter Löwe. Und: Die Lebenden erkennen, daß sie sterben werden; die Toten aber erkennen überhaupt nichts mehr. Sie erhalten auch keine Belohnung mehr; denn die Erinnerung an sie ist in Vergessenheit versunken ... Auf ewig haben sie keinen Anteil mehr an allem, was unter der Sonne

---

[10] G. Stemberger, Art. Auferstehung I/2 Judentum, *TRE 4* (1979) S.445. Vgl. auch den zwar schon etwas älteren, aber unfassenden Bericht von H.Braun, *Qumran und das Neue Testament*, II, Tübingen 1966, S.266-272.

[11] אֵין תְּחִיַּת־הַמֵּתִים מִן הַתּוֹרָה

[12] Vgl. Ps 6,6; 30,10; 88,11-13; 115,17; Jes 38,18; Hi 14,7. 10. 12; Koh 9,10; dazu und zu der erst spät auftauchenden Auferstehungshoffnung in Jes 25,8; 26,19; Dan 12,2. 13 Otto Kaiser u. Eduard Lohse, *Tod und Leben*, 1977 (Kohlhammer Tb Biblische Konfrontationen).

getan wurde" (Koh 9,4f). Selten beachtet wird aber, daß derselbe Verfasser offensichtlich von der Hoffnung auf ein ewiges Leben gehört hat, sie in seiner Skepsis aber ablehnt. In 3,18-21 stellt er fest, daß es dem Menschen nicht besser gehe als dem Vieh. Beide haben ein und dasselbe Geschick.

> "Wie diese sterben, so sterben jene. Beide haben ein und denselben Atem. Einen Vorteil des Menschen gegenüber dem Tier gibt es da nicht. Beide sind Windhauch. Beide gehen an einen und denselben Ort. Beide sind aus Staub entstanden, beide kehren zum Staub zurück. Wer weiß, ob der Atem (רוּחַ LXX πνεῦμα) des einzelnen Menschen wirklich nach oben steigt, während der Atem der Tiere ins Erdreich hinabsinkt?"

(Koh 3,19-21). Vor allem der letzte Satz ist bezeichnend. Kohelet polemisiert hier gegen die Behauptung, die *ruach* des Menschen steige im Tode nach oben auf im Unterschied zu der der Tiere, die nach unten sinkt. Er "greift damit eine Anschauung an, die wohl aus der hellenistischen Welt ins Judentum eingedrungen war und dort den ersten Ansätzen zu einer Hoffnung auf ein ewiges Leben Raum gegeben hatte ... Sowohl bei Euripides wie in griechischen Grabgedichten erscheint mehrfach die Vorstellung, daß die menschliche Seele nach dem Tode zu ihrer himmlischen Wohnstätte, dem αἰθήρ, dem Sitz der Götter aufsteige..."[13]. Kohelet dagegen polemisiert gegen diese Anschauung – und die ambivalente Bedeutung von *ruach* als "Atem" wie "Geist" gibt ihm dazu die Möglichkeit – : woher will man das wissen, daß die *ruach* des Menschen ein anderes Schicksal habe als die des Viehs? Daß er gegen diesen Gedanken polemisiert, zeigt, daß er ihn aus seiner Umgebung, und das heißt doch wohl aus seiner israelitischen Umgebung, gekannt hat.[14]

Polemik gegen eine Jenseitshoffnung in Israel findet sich

---

[13] Martin Hengel, *Judentum und Hellenismus*, Tübingen ²1973, S.228; ebenso Kaiser, *a.a.O.*, S.68; N.Lohfink, *Kohelet*, Würzburg ²1980, S.35; A.Lauha, *Kohelet*, Neukirchen 1978, S.77. Lauha weist darauf hin, daß die Masoreten durch ihre Vokalisation den Sinn abänderten."Zur Zeit der Masoreten empfand man einen derartigen Zweifel an der Unsterblichkeit des Menschen als ketzerisch und deutete darum nur mit Hilfe der Vokalisation die Aussage um":"Wer kennt des Menschen Atem, der nach oben steigt, und den Atem des Viehs, der zur Erde hinunterfährt".

[14] Die diesbezügliche Unterscheidung zwischen Mensch und Tier wird später in Rabbinat geradezu zum Beweis für die Möglichkeit der Totenerweckung gebraucht: eine Totenbeschwörung durch Zauberei sei nur bei Menschen, aber nicht bei Tieren möglich; Midr. Ps 19 bei *Bill. I*, S.897.

auch bei Jesus Sirach. Gemeinhin achtet man nur auf die Negativhaltung im Blick auf den Tod, die der oben erwähnten Haltung in vielen Psalmen[15] entspricht: Im Totenreich gibt es kein Gotteslob, keine berechtigten Unterschiede, daran zu denken bringt nur Bitterkeit (Sir 17,27f; 41,1.4). Aber diese Einstellung ist bei Sirach noch stärker radikalisiert: "Alles, was aus dem Nichts kommt, wird zum Nichts zurückkehren" (Sir 41,10). Das erinnert an den Nihilismus einiger hellenistischer Grabepigramme: "Ach, ich kam aus dem Nichts und werde ein Nichts sein wie früher".[16] Darüber hinaus aber findet sich an zwei Stellen eine ausdrückliche Polemik gegen Jenseitshoffnungen. Sir 14,16: "Gib dem Bruder und gib und verwöhne dich selbst, denn es ist nicht möglich, in der Unterwelt Wonne zu suchen". Die Aufforderung der 1. Zeile, die Freuden des irdischen Lebens zu genießen[17], wird in der 2. Zeile damit begründet, daß es in der Unterwelt nicht möglich ist "Wonne zu suchen". Dabei wird nicht nur einfach bestritten, daß es dergleichen in der Unterwelt gibt, sondern es wird von einem "Suchen" nach jenseitigen Wonnen gesprochen. Der Verfasser kennt also Leute, die nach dergleichen im Jenseits "suchen", und dem tritt er entgegen. Noch deutlicher wird das in 14,12, wenn man mit Georg Sauer dem hebräischen Text folgt:[18]

> "Denke daran, daß im Totenreich keine Wonne herrscht, und daß der Tod nicht zögert, und was in Bezug auf die Unterwelt festgesetz ist, ist dir nicht mitgeteilt".

Die erste Zeile bestreitet wieder, daß es im Jenseits besser sein könnte, die zweite erinnert an die Ungewißheit der Todesstunde, worauf die dritte Zeile sagt, daß uns der in Bezug auf die Scheol geltende חוק (=Maß, Verpflichtung, Gesetz, Ordnung, bestimmte Zeit) nicht mitgeteilt ist. In der Septuaginta fehlt die erste Zeile, sodaß man den für die Unterwelt geltenden חוק auf die zweite Zeile, auf die Todesstunde beziehen muß. Aber die längere, hebräische Fassung dürfte ursprünglicher sein. Die Auslassung der ersten Zeile

---

[15] Oben Anm. 12.

[16] *Anthologia Graeca*, Griech.-Deutsch ed. H.Beckby, München ^{2}1965, VII, 339; vgl. X, 118 und VII, 524.

[17] Vgl. Koh 9,7-10.

[18] Georg Sauer, *Jesus Sirach*, Gütersloh 1981 (JSHRZ III) S.481ff; *Sepher ben Sira* (The Book of Ben Sira), Text, Concordance and an Analysis of the Vocabulary, Jerusalem 1973.

erklärt sich am besten aus einer späteren Zeit, in der solches Bezweifeln der Jenseitshoffnung als anstößig erschien. Dann besagt die dritte Zeile aber nicht nur, daß uns der für die Todesstunde geltende Termin unbekannt ist, sondern generell, daß uns über die im Jenseits geltende Ordnung nichts bekannt ist. Bestritten wird, daß man überhaupt über das, was nach dem Tode kommt, etwas wissen könne. Die Kritik der Jenseitshoffnung ist hier am grundsätzlichsten ausgedrückt: Über das, was nach dem Tode kommt, ist uns nichts mitgeteilt, kann man nichts wissen.

Auf die andere Seite dieser Auseinandersetzung treten wir bei der Weisheit Salomos. Hier wird durchgehend eine Jenseitshoffnung vertreten, die deutlich hellenistisch geprägt ist, wie die Bezeichnung des Hoffnungsgutes als Unsterblichkeit und Unvergänglichkeit[19] und die Unterscheidung von Leib und Seele zeigen: "Der Gerechten Seelen sind in Gottes Hand".[20] Diese Begrifflichkeit ist hier das Gewand, in der sich die gut alttestamentliche Hoffnung auf Gottes Gerechtigkeit ausdrückt. Aber diese Hoffnung auf ein ewiges Leben ist nicht unangefochten. In der Beispielerzählung vom Geschick des Gerechten 1,16-2,22 + 5,1-14 werden die gottlosen Verfolger des Gerechten gerade dadurch charakterisiert, daß sie jede Hoffnung auf ein Leben nach dem Tod bestreiten: Der Tod bringt für den leidenden Gerechten keine Heilung (2,1); wie der Mensch durch Zufall (2,2)[21] entstanden ist, so vergeht er mit dem Tod wieder, sein Leben verflüchtigt sich "wie Spuren einer Wolke"(2,4); sein Geist (πνεῦμα) wird mit dem Tod nicht zu Gott zurückkehren, sondern wird sich "wie dünne Luft auflösen"(2,3). Darum der massive Aufruf, die irdischen Güter zu genießen (2,6-9), denn *dies* ist unser Teil (μέρις) und unser Los (κλῆρος)! Wenn so betont davon gesprochen wird, daß nur das Genießen irdischer Freuden unser "Teil" und "Los" sei, dann muß man nicht nur an Ps 73,26 denken, wo der Beter bekennt, daß nur Jahwe selbst sein "Teil" (μέρις) sei, sondern vor allem an Weish 5,5, wo bei der endlichen Restitution des

[19] ἀθανασία 3,4; 4,1; 8,13. 17; 15,3; ἀφθαρσία 2,23; 6,18f.

[20] 3,1ff; der Gegensatz Leib / Seele besonders deutlich 9,15. Zur Jenseitshoffnung vgl. weiter 3,7f; 4,7; 5,15; 6,18f; 1,13; 2,23; 8,13. 17.

[21] 2,2: αὐτοσχεδίως "aus dem Stegreif"; Georgi: "durch Zufall". Ich folge weithin der Übersetzung von Dieter Georgi, *Weisheit Salomos*, Gütersloh 1980 (JSHRZ III).

leidenden Gerechten die Gottlosen bekennen müssen, daß er "sein Los (κλῆρος) unter den Heiligen hat". Angesichts dessen besagt 2,9, daß es für die Gerechten kein himmliches Los bei Gott geben soll, sondern daß das Los des Menschen eben nur in irdischen Freuden gesucht werden könne. So jedenfalls sehen und propagieren es die Feinde des Gerechten. Die Hoffnung auf ewiges Leben ist also keineswegs unangefochten. Und wenn die Frommen sich hier bedrängt und verfolgt fühlen, dann bedeutet das doch, daß ihre Gegner eine relativ große und mächtige Gruppe sein müssen und nicht bloß eine Quantité negligeable.

Auch in den Mahnreden des äthiopischen Henochbuches stehen die leidenden Gerechten und die Sünder gegenüber, und die Sünder verfolgen und peinigen nicht nur die Gerechten (95,7; 100,7), sondern sie verspotten auch deren Hoffnung auf ein Leben nach dem Tod. Wenn die Gerechten sterben, sagen sie:

> "Wie wir sterben, sterben die Gerechten, und welchen Nutzen hatten sie von ihren Werken? Siehe, sie sterben wie wir in Kummer und Finsternis, und welchen Vorzug haben sie uns gegenüber? Von nun an sind wir ihnen gleich. Und wie werden sie sich erheben, und was werden sie in Ewigkeit sehen? Denn siehe, sie sind gestorben, und von nun an bis in Ewigkeit werden sie das Licht nicht sehen"

(102,6-8).[22] Deshalb müssen die Gerechten in ihrer Hoffnung auf ein ewiges Leben und ewigen Lohn bestärkt werden (103,1-4). Wieder sieht sich die kleine Gruppe der Gerechten einer offenbar großen Gruppe von "Sündern" gegenüber, die deren Hoffnung auf ein Leben nach dem Tod nicht teilen, sondern mit den bekannten Argumenten[23] verspotten. Daß bei diesen Sündern nicht an Heiden, sondern an Israeliten zu denken ist, zeigt sich an dem Vorwurf, daß sie (Gottes) ewiges Gesetz übertreten (99,2).

Daß die Lehre von der Auferstehung der Toten noch lange umstritten war, zeigt auch 2.Makk 12,43-45. Zuvor wird berichtet, daß bei der Einholung der in der Schlacht (12,33-37) gefallenen Juden an deren Leichen Amulette heidnischer

---

[22] Übersetzung von Sieghart Uhlig, *Das äthiopische Henochbuch*, Gütersloh 1984 (JSHRZ V).

[23] vgl. äthHen 103,5 mit Weish 2,6-9; Koh 9,7ff; Sir 14,14. 16 und äthHen 102,6-8 mit Weish 2,1-4; Koh 3,19-21.

Götzen gefunden wurden. Daraufhin veranstaltete Judas eine Sammlung für die Darbringung eines Sündopfers in Jerusalem.

> "Er tat daran gut und klug, denn er dachte an die Auferstehung. Hätte er nicht erwartet, daß die Gefallenen auferstehen werden, wäre es nämlich überflüssig und sinnlos gewesen, für die Toten zu beten. Auch hielt er sich den herrlichen Lohn vor Augen, der für die hinterlegt ist, die in Frömmigkeit sterben. Ein heiliger und frommer Gedanke! Darum ließ er die Toten entsühnen, damit sie von der Sünde befreit werden"

(12,43c-45). Günter Stemberger[24] rechnet an dieser Stelle mit der Einarbeitung von Glossen. "Während eine Randglosse sagt, für Tote zu beten sei sinnlos, kommentiert ein anderer Leser, Sündopfer für Tote seien gut. Ein Kopist hat beide Glossen harmonisierend in den Text einbezogen". In der Tat stört die breite Reflexion über Sinn oder Unsinn von Sündopfern für Tote 12,43c-45 in dem sonst knappen Bericht über die kriegerischen Unternehmungen des Judas, sodaß die Annahme von Glossen und deren spätere Einarbeitung naheliegt. Aber selbst ohne die Annahme einer Einarbeitung von Glossen zeigt der Text mit seiner breiten Reflexion, daß der Glaube an die Auferstehung der Toten umstritten war.

Schließlich wird der Zweifel an einem ewigen Leben nach dem Tod auch im Testament Hiobs zum Ausdruck gebracht. Hiobs Freunde wollen die Trümmer des Hauses wegräumen, unter denen dessen Kinder begraben liegen. Da sagt Hiob:

> "Müht euch nicht vergeblich ab. Ihr werdet meine Kinder nicht finden, denn sie sind aufgenommen worden in den Himmel von ihrem Schöpfer, dem König. Da antworteten sie (sc. die Freunde) mir: Wer würde nicht wieder sagen: Du bist von Sinnen und irre! wenn du sagst: Meine Kinder wurden in den Himmel aufgenommen. Darum sage uns die Wahrheit"

(39,12-13).[25] Daraufhin betet Hiob und heißt sie nach Osten zu blicken. "Und sie sahen meine Kinder bekränzt (stehen) vor der Herrlichkeit des Himmlischen"(40,3). Erst diese durch Hiob erbetene Vision überwindet ihren Zweifel gegenüber dem Glauben an das ewige Leben. Das ist offenbar die Grundhaltung des Volkes: An Auferstehung oder ewiges Leben kann

[24] G.Stemberger, Art. Auferstehung I/2, *TRE 4* (1979) S.445.

[25] Übersetzung von Berndt Schaller, *Das Testament Hiobs*, Gütersloh 1979 (JSHRZ III).

man nur glauben auf Grund außerordentlicher Visionen oder anderer Zeichen. Auch Hiobs Frau kommt erst auf Grund dieser Vision zum Glauben an ein ewiges Leben.

II

Obwohl für die tannaitischen Rabbinen der Glaube an die Auferstehung der Toten ein fester Lehrsatz ist, bleibt dieser Glaube im Judentum doch weiter umstritten. Das zeigt der Zusatz, der im Mischnatraktat Sanh 10,1 zu dem Bekenntnis, daß ganz Israel Anteil an der zukünftigen Welt habe, hinzugefügt wird: Diejenigen haben keinen Anteil, die behaupten, daß die Auferstehung der Toten nicht aus der Torah zu entnehmen sei. Diese Behauptung kann nicht nur von ein paar wenigen Außenseitern gemacht worden sein, sonst wäre ein Zusatz zu dieser zentralen Aussage kaum nötig gewesen. Geändert aber hat sich gegenüber den früheren Texten, daß das Gewicht nun auf die schriftgemäße Begründung des Auferstehungsglaubens fällt. Zwar begegnen in bSanh 91a auch Argumente zur Möglichkeit der Totenauferstehung, aber die Begründung aus der Schrift steht eindeutig im Vordergrund, wobei der Torah (=Pentateuch) höheres Gewicht als den Propheten und Hagiographen zukommt. Zwar erklärte R.Gamaliel (um 90), die Auferstehung der Toten sei "aus dem Gesetzbuch, aus den Propheten und aus den Hagiographen" zu entnehmen (bSanh 90b),[26] aber in der Gemara die sich im babylonischen Talmud an die Mischnastelle Sanh 10,1 anschließt, steht doch die Begründung der Auferstehung aus dem Gesetzbuch im Vordergrund. Die weit umfangreicheren Propheten und Hagiographen werden neunmal herangezogen (Jos 8,3o; Jes 4,3; 26,19; 52,8(zweimal); Ps 84,5; Cant 7,10; Dan 12,2.13), der Pentateuch aber zehnmal (Ex 6,4; 15,1; Num 15,31; 18,28; Dtn 4,4; 11,9; 31,16(dreimal); 33,6).

Es lohnt sich, diese exegetische Beweisführung in bSanh 90b-92b näher anzusehen. Als Gegner, die die Totenauferstehung bestreiten und Schriftbeweise verlangen, werden

---

[26] Ich halte mich im Folgenden weithin an die Übersetzung von Lazarus Goldschmidt, *Der Babylonische Talmud,* Bd.7, Haag 1933. Nur an zwei Stellen, die ich gesondert nenne, ist seine Übersetzung ungenau oder irrig (Druckfehler?).

genannt: die Sadduzäer, die Samaritaner, Römer und Häretiker. Die Nennung der "Römer" (einmal der "Kaiser" bSanh 91a) ist offensichtlich fiktiv. Römer würden in der Diskussion mit einem Juden kaum nach Schriftbeweisen für den Auferstehungsglauben gefragt haben (schon eher nach Vernunftgründen, wie 91a), und schon gar nicht dagegen Einwände auf Grund der hebräischen Grammatik erhoben haben (90b gegen R.Jehošua ben Hananja). Der Römer figuriert hier für den Auferstehungsleugner überhaupt.

Daß die Sadduzäer die Totenauferstehung bestritten, ist aus Josephus Bell II,165; Ant XVIII,16 und Mk 12,18; Act 23,8 bekannt. Daß auch die Samaritaner die Auferstehung leugneten, wird hier (bSanh 90b) und an einigen anderen rabbinischen Stellen[27] ausgesprochen; es entspricht dem, daß sie auch nur den Pentateuch als heilige Schrift anerkannten.

Fraglich ist, wer mit dem Häretiker (מינא zweimal) gemeint ist. Sadduzäer können es nicht sein, da diese eigens genannt werden. Auch Judenchristen dürften damit kaum gemeint sein, da diese gleichfalls sonst eigens genannt werden[28] und kaum als Bezweifler des Auferstehungsglaubens gegolten haben dürften. Es muß sich also um Angehörige anderer jüdischer Gruppen oder Richtungen handeln. Von der Existenz solcher Gruppen berichten kirchliche Schriftsteller, wenn sie auch nicht mehr als die Namen zu nennen wissen.[29]

---

[27] Vgl. *Bill. I,* S.551f. Doch ist diese Aussage etwas pauschal; daß sie wohl nicht von allen Samaritanern galt, zeigt Reinhard Pummer, Einführung in den Stand der Samaritanerforschung, in: F.Dexinger u. R.Pummer, *Die Samaritaner,* Darmstadt (WdF) 1992, S.42. Im übrigen ist zu beachten, daß Samaritaner nicht nur in der Landschaft Samaria lebten, sondern daß es eine umfangreiche samaritanische Diaspora gab (vgl. H.G.Kippenberg, Die Synagoge, ebd. S.331-360), sodaß Kontakte und Auseinandersetzungen mit ihnen weit häufiger gewesen sein dürften.

[28] Vgl. die 12. Benediktion im Schemone Esre: הַנֹּצְרִים neben הַמִּינִים, ferner *Bill. I,* S.1053, und *Bill. II,* S.66.

[29] Justin (Dial. 80,4) nennt neben Christen, die die Auferstehung leugnen, weil die Seele gleich beim Tod in den Himmel aufgenommen würde, und die man gar nicht als Christen bezeichnen sollte, auch jüdische Gruppen, die gar keine richtigen Juden seien: die Sadduzäer oder die verwandten Sekten der Genisten, Meristen, Galiläer, Hellenianer, Pharisäer-Baptisten (andere Lesart: Pharisäer und Baptisten). Aber ob von diesen Gruppen auch die Auferstehungsleugnung gelten soll, ist zumindest fraglich. Hegesipp nennt (bei Euseb HE IV 22,7) die Essäer, Galiläer, Hemerobaptisten, Masbotheer, Samaritaner, Sadduzäer, Pharisäer. Vgl. auch F.Dexinger, Art. Judentum, *TRE 17* (1988) S.341f.

Doch nun zu den genannten Schriftbeweisen für die Auferstehung. Natürlich werden die beiden einzigen wirklich eindeutigen, wenngleich späten, Stellen Jes 26,19 und Dan 12,2. 13 genannt. Aber selbst gegen die Aussage von Jes 26,19 "deine Toten werden leben, meine Leichen werden auferstehen", wird ein möglicher Einwand genannt (bSanh 90b):"aber vielleicht (sind hier) die Toten, die Ezechiel belebt hat (gemeint)".

Insgesamt viermal wird ein hebr. Imperfekt als Futur gedeutet. So zu Ex 15,1: "R.Meir (um 150) sagte ... es heißt: damals *wird* Mose mit den Israeliten folgendes Lied dem Herrn singen (אָז יָשִׁיר); es heißt nicht *sang*, sondern *wird singen;* hier ist also die Auferstehung der Toten in der Gesetzeslehre angedeutet". In gleicher Weise wird Jos 8,30 (יִבְנֶה = wird bauen) und Jes 52,8 (יְרַנֵּנוּ = sie werden jauchzen) gedeutet, und schließlich auch Ps 84,5: "es heißt nicht: sie priesen dich, sondern: sie werden dich preisen (יְהַלְלוּךָ)''. Zu dieser Deutung von Jos 8,30 wird wieder ein Einwand erhoben: "Es heißt ja aber auch: Damals wird Šelomoh dem Kemoš, dem Scheusal der Moabiter, eine Anhöhe errichten; ist etwa auch hier zu erklären, er *werde* errichten!?"[30]. Es wird also dagegen eingewandt, daß an anderer Stelle das Imperfekt Vergangenheitsbedeutung habe, was dann auch für die strittige Stelle gelten kann.

An drei weiteren Stellen werden Repräsentanten einer Gruppe oder eines Volkes als Individuen gefaßt. So bSanh 90b:

> "Wo ist die Auferstehung der Toten in der Gesetzeslehre angedeutet? Es heißt: Ich habe mit ihnen (sc. Abraham, Isaak und Jakob) sogar ein Abkommen getroffen, daß ich ihnen das Land Kenaan geben werde; es heißt nicht euch, sondern ihnen".

In gleicher Weise wird die Erzväterzusage von Dtn 11,9 durch R. Gamaliel gedeutet. Und R.Johanan (3.Jh.) entnimmt aus der Weisung von Num 18,28, daß die Abgaben dem Priester Aaron übergeben werden sollen, der zur Zeit der Landnahme

---

[30] Übersetzung Goldschmidt. Gemeint ist: Hier ist das gleiche Imperfekt als Vergangenheit gemeint. Die Fortsetzung: "vielmehr die Schrift rechnet es ihm an, als hätte er sie errichtet", ist schwer verständlich. Die Vergangenheitsbedeutung ist damit ja zugegeben, nur wird Salomo ein Stück weit in Schutz genommen. Soll dies eine dritte Diskussionsstimme sein?

ja gar nicht mehr lebte, daß sich dies auf die zukünftige Welt beziehen müsse, in der Aaron wieder leben und die Abgaben von Israel empfangen werde.

Bezeichnend ist, wie R.Gamaliel, R.Jehošua ben Hananja und R.Šimon ben Johaj die Auferstehung mit Dtn 31,16 begründen. Moderne Übersetzungen haben hier:

> "Siehe, du wirst dich (bald) zu deinen Vätern legen; aber dieses Volk wird aufstehen (וְקָם) und wird den fremden Göttern des Landes ... nachhuren".

Die Rabbinen aber beziehen das וְקָם zu dem vorangehenden Satzteil: "Du wirst dich (bald) zu deinen Vätern legen und aufstehen". Gegen diese Deutung erhoben die Sadduzäer Einspruch: "Jene entgegneten ihm: Vielleicht (lese man) und aufstehen wird dieses Volk und nachhuren". Sie zogen also, wie es dem Kontext entspricht, das וְקָם zum folgenden Satzteil. R.Jehošua ben Hananja muß diesen Einspruch auch anerkennen. Da ihm eine doppelte Frage, die nach der Totenerweckung und nach Gottes Vorherwissen gestellt war, antwortet er: "Die Hälfte (der beiden Fragen) habt ihr ja jedenfalls, daß er nämlich weiß, was geschehen wird".[31]

Eine ähnlich gewagte Deutung findet sich zu Num 15,31. R.Elieser ben R.Jose (um 150) sagte:

> "...ihr (sc. Samaritaner) sagt, die Auferstehung der Toten sei nicht in der Gesetzeslehre angedeutet; es heißt ja: Vertilgt, ja vertilgt soll diese Seele werden, ihre Sünde haftet an ihr. Vertilgt, ja vertilgt auf dieser Welt; ihre Sünde haftet an ihr,-wann?- wahrscheinlich doch in der zukünftigen Welt".

Hier wird also der Parallelismus membrorum dazu benutzt, die zweite Aussage auf die zukünftige Welt zu deuten. R.Papa meinte sogar, aus dem Infinitivus absolutus "vertilgt, ja vertilgt" die Auferstehung entnehmen zu können, da in der Doppelung des Verbs die jetzige und die zukünftige Welt angedeutet seien. Dazu wird auch die Autorität R.Aqibas angerufen: "Vertilgt, ja vertilgt; vertilgt auf dieser Welt; ja vertilgt in der zukünftigen Welt". Diese Deutung wird dann aber doch zurückgewiesen: "Die Gesetzeslehre bedient sich der gewöhnlichen Redeweise der Menschen". Außerdem

[31] In den vorangehenden Zeilen liegt bei Goldschmidt ein sinnentstellender Fehler (Druckfehler?) vor: Der Einwand der Gegner "aufstehen wird dieses Volk" wird fälschlich auch dem R. Jehošua zugeschrieben.

werde schon im vorangehenden Satz (Num 15,30) von der Vertilgung des Menschen gesprochen, und bei konsequenter Anwendung solcher Deutung müsse man dann ja auf drei Welten kommen. Die Stelle zeigt, wie man aus den kleinsten Besonderheiten eines Textes eine Andeutung der Totenauferstehung zu entnehmen suchte, entweder aus der Doppelung des Verbs beim Infinitivus absolutus, oder aus dem Parallelismus membrorum. Sie zeigt zugleich die Einwände, die gegen solche Deutungen erhoben wurden.

Eine ähnlich problematische Argumentation samt nachfolgender Zurückweisung findet sich zu Cant 7,10 (bSanh 90b). Daneben kann aber auch ein doppelter Schriftsinn postuliert werden. Das Wort von Dtn 4,4 "Ihr aber, die ihr an dem Herrn, eurem Gott, festhieltet, seid allesamt heute am Leben", habe einen einfachen zeitgeschichtlichen Sinn und beziehe sich daneben zugleich auf die zukünftige Welt.[32]

Die Betrachtung dieser "Schriftbeweise" zeigt, wie außerordentlich schwer es dem Rabbinat fiel, die Lehre von der Totenauferstehung aus der Schrift und vor allem aus dem Pentateuch zu begründen, oder doch wenigstens angedeutet zu finden. Zu den meisten Beweisgründen finden sich auch noch Gegenargumente, die schwer zu entkräften waren. Von einer allgemeinen Selbstverständlichkeit des Auferstehungsglaubens wird man daher auch in tannaitischer Zeit nicht reden können.

III

Daß die Hoffnung auf eine Auferstehung der Toten und/oder ein ewiges Leben in der für den Neutestamentler relevanten Zeit der beiden ersten Jahrhunderte n.Chr. keineswegs jüdisches Allgemeingut war, bezeugen auch die jüdischen Grabepigramme. Es soll hier nicht eine erneute Untersuchung der Grabepigramme vorgelegt werden; es genügt zunächst, die Untersuchungen von Ulrich Fischer und Pieter W. van der Horst[33] zu beachten.

---

[32] Die Übersetzung von Billerbeck (*Bill. I,* S.893) ist hier wesentlich genauer als die Goldschmidts, der den schwierigen Mittelteil des Satzes einfach ausläßt.

[33] Ulrich Fischer, *Eschatologie und Jenseitserwartung im hellenistischen Diasporajudentum,* Berlin 1978, S.215-254, untersuchte mehr als 750

Fischer kommt zu den Ergebnis, daß aufallend wenige Inschriften eine postmortale Hoffnung, sei es als Auferstehung der Toten, ewiges Leben oder Versetzung in den Bereich der Sterne, bezeugen. Selbst bei solchen Epigrammen, die einen Friedenswunsch für den Verstorbenen ausdrücken und die gut ein Viertel der untersuchten Texte ausmachen, ist nicht deutlich, ob mit diesem "Frieden" ein seliges Leben im Jenseits gemeint ist. Nur bei den wenigen Friedenswünschen, bei denen sich der Zusatz μετὰ τῶν ὁσίων, *cum justis* oder אם צדיקים findet,[34] ist dies einigermaßen sicher als ein ewiges Leben zu deuten. Da sich aber mit dem Friedensgruß anderwärts auch Jenseitspessimismus verbinden kann,[35] besagt der einfache Friedenswunsch noch nichts über eine Jenseitshoffnung; er braucht nicht über das hinaus zu gehen, was in Gen 15,15 und Jer 34,5 damit verbunden ist, wenn von Abraham oder Jeremia gesagt wird, daß sie "in Frieden" sterben bzw. ruhen werden. Deutlicher drückt sich eine Jenseitserwartung in den Fluchformeln aus, mit denen mögliche Grabschänder bedacht werden: Gottes kommendes Gericht wird sie treffen.

Fischer meint, daß dieses dürftige Ergebnis zwar auch damit zusammenhängen könne, daß nur wenige Juden sich eine umfangreiche Grabinschrift leisten konnten, oder "daß die Verwendung bestimmter sepulkraler Formeln für individuelle Glaubensaussagen wenig Raum ließ. Der Hauptgrund für das weitgehende Fehlen irgendwelcher Auferstehungsaussagen auf den jüdischen Sepulkralinschriften aber dürfte darin zu sehen sein, daß der Auferstehungsglaube bei den Juden der westlichen Diaspora kaum eine Rolle spielte".[36] Durch den Vergleich mit den ca. 200 von Schwabe/Lifshitz herausgegebenen Grabinschriften aus dem palästinischen Beth She'arim, die wesentlich häufiger eine Auferstehungshoffnung bekunden, sieht er sein Ergebnis nur bestätigt. Fischer meint, diesen Unterschied damit erklären zu können, daß die in Beth

---

jüdische Grabinschriften der westlichen Diaspora. P.W.van der Horst, *Ancient Jewish Epitaphs. An introductory survey of a millenium of Jewish funerary epigraphy*, Kampen 1991, berichtet über die Auswertung von etwa 2000 jüdischen Grabinschriften.

[34] Fischer, *a.a.O.*, S.219f; van der Horst, *a.a.O.*, S.116f.

[35] Fischer, *a.a.O.*, S.222ff.

[36] Fischer, *a.a.O.*, S.236.

She'arim Begrabenen zumeist aus der östlichen Diaspora stammten. Aber eine andere Erklärung, liegt näher. Nach Lifshitz[37] stammen diese Gräber aus den 3. und 4.Jh. n.Chr., also aus einer Zeit, in der sich der Auferstehungsglaube der jüdischen Orthodoxie im palästinischen Judentum schon weit stärker durchgesetzt hatte.

Das negative Ergebnis von Fischer wird von P.W. van der Horst weithin bestätigt."Most of our epitaphs yield disappointingly little information concerning the ideas of either survivors or the deceased about life after death"[38] Er betont zwar, daß das argumentum e silentio hier besonders gefährlich sei. Aus dem Schweigen vieler Grabinschriften könne man noch nicht schließen, daß alle ihre Besitzer keinerlei Jenseitshoffnung hegten. Das ist sicher richtig; vor Prozentzahlen muß man sich auf jeden Fall hüten. Angesichts aber der Tatsache, daß sich auch Jenseitspessimismus auf jüdischen Grabinschriften findet,[39] ist die geringe Zahl von positiven Hoffnungsaussagen doch aufschlußreich. Auch van der Horst muß als Ergebnis feststellen:"it cannot be stated on the basis of our evidence that belief in the bodily resurrection... was an undisputed dogma among Jews in the imperial period"[40].

IV

Trifft es zu, daß der Glaube an eine Auferstehung der Toten oder ewiges Leben in neutestamentlicher Zeit keineswegs allgemein-jüdische Überzeugung, sondern auch im Judentum umstritten war, dann hat das auch Konsequenzen für neutestamentliche Texte. Da ist vor allem das Streitgespräch über die sogenannte "Sadduzäerfrage" zu nennen.[41] Mit seiner zeitlos-gelehrten Diskussion über Berechtigung oder Unmöglichkeit des Auferstehungsglaubens paßt es schlecht in die Verkündigung Jesu, die ganz von der andrängenden Nähe der hereinbrechenden Gottesherrschaft bestimmt ist. Man wird

---

[37] B.Lifshitz, Beiträge zur palästinischen Epigraphik, *ZDPV 78* (1962) S.78.

[38] Van der Horst, *a.a.O.*, S.114.

[39] Vgl. Fischer, *a.a.O.*, S.222ff, van der Horst, *a.a.O.*, S.121.

[40] Van der Horst, *a.a.O.*, S. 126.

[41] Mit der Sadduzäerfrage befaßte sich neuerlich die umfangreiche Mongraphie von O. Schwankl, *Die Sadduzäerfrage (Mk 12,18-27 parr)*, 1987 (BBB 66); vgl. auch E.Reinmuth, *ThLZ 113* (1988) S.593.

dieses Streitgespräch daher der palästinischen Gemeinde zuzuordnen haben. Und da die zur Jerusalemer Führungsschicht gehörenden Sadduzäer[42] kaum die üblichen Diskussionspartner der frühen Christengemeinde gewesen sein dürften, geht man wohl nicht fehl in der Annahme, daß es vor allem auch die Auseinandersetzung mit anderen ähnlichen Bestreitern des Auferstehungsglaubens war, die zu seiner Entstehung und Tradierung führte. Die Sadduzäer wurden deshalb als die Gesprächspartner genannt, weil sie eben die bekanntesten und prominentesten Vertreter dieser Negativhaltung waren. Da diese Bestreitung aber auch von vielen anderen im jüdischen Volk geteilt wurde, war eine einsichtige Begründung der Auferstehungshoffnung für Judenchristen eine drängende Notwendigkeit. Unser Ergebnis könnte auch für das Verständnis der lukanischen Theologie von Bedeutung sein. Lukas kann zuweilen den Inhalt christlicher Verkündigung auf "Jesus und die Auferstehung"(Act 4,2; 17,18) reduzieren. Zwar kann er zu dieser zentralen Hoffnung auch auf die Spannung zwischen Pharisäern und Sadduzäern sich berufen (Act 23,6), aber dies besagt noch nicht, daß er damit nur im Gegensatz zu den Sadduzäern stünde. Es ist vielmehr ein allgmeiner und weltweiter Gegensatz, der auch nicht nur die heidnischen Griechen (Act 17,18), sondern wohl auch weite Teile des jüdischen Volkes umfaßt. Es ist eine in der Welt umstrittene und angefochtene Botschaft.[43] Es genügt nicht, sie einfach aus der Umwelt zu übernehmen. Sie muß begründet werden.

---

[42] Vgl. Meyer, Σαδδουκαῖος, *ThWNT* 7 (1964) S.44f.

[43] Daß das allgemeine Umstrittensein des Auferstehungsglaubens auch in die Argumentation des Apostels Paulus in 1.Kor 15,19 und 30-32 hineinspielt, habe ich in dem Beitrag "Zur Frage der in 1.Korinther 15 bekämpften Auferstehungsleugnung", *ZNW 83* (1992) S.187-201, zu zeigen versucht.

THE JESUS-MOVEMENT IN THE LIGHT OF PAGAN SOURCES

TABLE FELLOWSHIP AND THE HISTORICAL JESUS

Dennis E. Smith
(Phillips Graduate Seminary, Enid, Oklahoma)

Table fellowship with Jesus was obviously a historical reality in Jesus' own day. But did Jesus use table fellowship as a mode of proclamation? A large number of scholars say he did, though they often disagree on how this was done and what message was communicated. Too often such conclusions have been drawn on the basis of inadequate data and untested presuppositions about the structure and social function of ancient meals. It is the goal of the present study to examine this issue in the light of a more comprehensive model of the ancient banquet both as a social institution and as a literary motif.[1]

The model I will be utilizing for this study is that of the banquet in the Greco-Roman world.[2] I have developed a comprehensive description of that model in its various aspects in a larger study which I now am completing for publication by Fortress Press entitled: *From Symposium to Eucharist: The Banquet in the Early Christian World.* I shall be utilizing results of that study in this paper.

---

[1] An earlier version of this work appeared as "The Historical Jesus at Table," *Society of Biblical Literature 1989 Seminar Papers* (David J. Lull, ed.; Decatur, GA: Scholars Press, 1989) 466-86.

[2] My initial research on the form of the ancient meal and its relation to the interpretation of the New Testament was undertaken for my doctoral dissertation at Harvard Divinity School ("Social Obligation in the Context of Communal Meals: A Study of the Christian Meal in 1 Corinthians in Comparison with Graeco-Roman Communal Meals" [Th.D. dissertation, Harvard University, 1980]). The advisor for that thesis in its latter stages was Dieter Georgi. It was he who encouraged me to follow my instincts and develop my argument in what at the time was a new, uncharted direction, one I have since come to identify as a type of social history analysis. Such open-ended creativity and freshness always have characterized the work of Dieter Georgi and are the legacy he has passed on to his students. I am pleased to salute him with a new phase of my research on the banquet and the New Testament.

I. A Review of Scholarship on the Historical Jesus.[3]

A review of recent research on this subject must begin with Norman Perrin, whose *Rediscovering the Teaching of Jesus* remains an authoritative resource. His judgment on this issue has been used widely by subsequent authors, at times in the same form and sometimes in a modified form. He proposed the authenticity of the tradition that Jesus offered table fellowship to "outcasts," or "tax collectors and sinners," as recorded especially in Matt 11:16-19 ("Look, a glutton and a drunkard, a friend of tax collectors and sinners!" [NRSV]). Furthermore, Jesus' table fellowship utilized the symbolism of the messianic banquet as defined in Matt 8:11: "I tell you, many will come from east and west and will eat with Abraham and Isaac and Jacob in the kingdom of heaven" (= Luke 13:28-29). Both of these texts Perrin judged to be "indubitably authentic."[4] His basic argument for authenticity in both cases was along the lines of the classic criterion of dissimilarity, that is, that these texts represent perspectives more appropriate to Jesus' setting than to that of the early church.[5]

According to his interpretation, therefore, "a regular table fellowship" would have been held by Jesus and his followers which would have included "Jews who had made themselves as Gentiles," Perrin's interpretation of the meaning of "tax collectors and sinners." By employing the symbolism of the kingdom, especially as exemplified by the messianic banquet imagery which symbolized the anticipated final kingdom, Jesus' action in effect served "to welcome those people back into the community."[6]

According to Perrin this reconstruction is seen as authentic because it explains how Jesus came to die: his actions defiled the boundaries of the community and thus functioned as an act of such offensiveness to Jewish sensibilities that Jewish

---

[3] For a recent critical review of historical Jesus research, see Dieter Georgi, "The Interest in Life of Jesus Theology as a Paradigm for the Social History of Biblical Criticism," *HTR* 85 (1992) 51-83.

[4] *Rediscovering the Teaching of Jesus* (New York: Harper & Row, 1967) 102-08.

[5] Ibid., 119-21, 161-64. Actually, Perrin's analysis is much more detailed than my cryptic summary suggests, but for the sake of brevity I would emphasize dissimilarity as the cornerstone of much of his argumentation.

[6] Ibid., 103.

leaders called for his death. It also accounts for how the early Christian community came to practice a communal meal together, a practice that came into existence so early that it must have been a continuation of the practice of Jesus himself.[7]

Subsequent scholarship has persisted along these same lines. Thus, for example, the idea that Jesus offered the kingdom to outcasts by means of his table fellowship figures prominently, with some variation and elaboration, in the recent studies of James Breech, E.P. Sanders, Richard Horsley, Marcus Borg, John Dominic Crossan, and Bruce Chilton.[8] This is not to say that they all arrive at the same place; on the contrary, their reconstructions of the historical Jesus differ on significant points. Yet they all agree in giving prominence to the table fellowship theme. Indeed, for many scholars the theme of table fellowship with outcasts is primary and essential to any valid reconstruction of the historical Jesus. Crossan, for example, states emphatically:

---

[7] Ibid., 102-08.

[8] See James Breech, *The Silence of Jesus: The Authentic Voice of the Historical Man* (Philadelphia: Fortress, 1983) 22-64; E. P. Sanders, *Jesus and Judaism* (Philadelphia: Fortress, 1985) 174-211, 271-73; Richard Horsley, *Jesus and the Spiral of Violence: Popular Jewish Resistance in Roman Palestine* (New York: Harper & Row, 1987) 178-80; Marcus Borg, *Conflict, Holiness and Politics in the Teachings of Jesus* (Studies in the Bible and Early Christianity 5; New York and Toronto: Edwin Mellen, 1984) 78-121; Idem, *Jesus: A New Vision* (New York: Harper & Row, 1987) 101-02, 131-33; John Dominic Crossan, *The Historical Jesus: The Life of a Mediterranean Jewish Peasant* (San Francisco: Harper Collins, 1991) 260-64, 332-53; Bruce Chilton, *The Temple of Jesus: His Sacrificial Program Within a Cultural History of Sacrifice* (University Park, PA: Pennsylvania State University Press, 1992) 137-54. To be sure, I have truncated severely the detailed and distinct arguments of these scholars by grouping them together in this manner, but it is only to underscore the point that they all place significant emphasis on the table fellowship motif, although they may interpret it differently. Some of their divergent arguments will be referenced later in this paper. Others who emphasize the table fellowship theme as part of the historical Jesus data are Günther Bornkamm, *Jesus of Nazareth* (New York: Harper & Row, 1960) 80-81; Joachim Jeremias, *The Parables of Jesus* (6th ed.; London: SCM, 1963) 227; idem, *New Testament Theology: The Proclamation of Jesus* (New York: Charles Scribner's, 1971) 115-16; Geza Vermes, *Jesus the Jew: A Historian's Reading of the Gospels* (London: William Collins, 1973) 224; Morton Smith, *Jesus the Magician* (San Francisco: Harper & Row, 1978) 122-23, 152; Martin Hengel, *The Charismatic Leader and his Followers* (New York: Crossroad, 1981) 67; Elizabeth Schüssler Fiorenza, *In Memory of Her: A Feminist Theological Reconstruction of Christian Origins* (New York: Crossroad, 1983) 119-21, 126-30. The list could go on. There are a few sceptics; see, e.g., William O. Walker, "Jesus and the Tax Collectors," *JBL* 97 (1978) 221-38; and Burton L. Mack, *A Myth of Innocence: Mark and Christian Origins* (Philadelphia: Fortress, 1988) 80-83.

> "My wager is that magic and meal or miracle and table . . . is the heart of Jesus' program. . . . If that is incorrect, this book will have to be redone."[9]

The question that needs to be posed is whether the picture of Jesus utilizing table fellowship with a symbolic meaning as integral to his teaching program can be plausibly reconstructed as a real event in first-century Palestine. There is no doubt that it is a powerful image on the literary level. But the issue is whether it could function in the same way on the historical level in the time of Jesus.

The meals of Jesus mentioned in the gospels tend to be occasions at which the most formal of social conventions are practiced. These include such external features as reclining[10] and such ideological features as the idea that table fellowship creates social bonds among the diners. Such motifs derive from Greco-Roman meal customs as associated especially with the archetype of the formal meal, the banquet. The Greco-Roman banquet was a social institution that was practiced in its broad details throughout the Mediterranean world. It is the form utilized in Judaism of this period as well as in earliest Christianity.[11]

What we know about the Greco-Roman banquet derives especially from literary data. Literary documents tend to employ the banquet as a motif with characteristics deriving from such models as the literary form of the symposium or the idealization of the hero at table in folklore and literature. Inasmuch as the gospels are literary presentations of the Jesus

---

[9] *The Historical Jesus*, 304.

[10] In all of the formal meals at which Jesus is present as described in the gospels, when a posture is mentioned it is one of reclining. Jeremias argued that this meant that the gospels refer only to unusually festive meals (*The Eucharistic Words of Jesus* [3rd ed.; New York: Scribners, 1966] 48-49). Rather, the gospel accounts are to be understood as presenting Jesus at table in a setting corresponding to the conventions of Greco-Roman formal meals in general as they were practiced and represented in classical and hellenistic literature.

[11] For example, redarding the Passover meal in second-temple Judaism S. Safrai says: "Hellenistic customs affected the actual course of the meal, which resembled to some extent the symposium of the Greeks: it was eaten in a reclining position, and was the setting for important discourses on a set theme" (S. Safrai and M. Stern, eds., *The Jewish People in the First Century, Vol. 2: Historical Geography, Political History, Social, Cultural and Religious Life and Institutions* [CRINT; ; Philadelphia: Fortress, 1976] 809-10). Safrai especially relies on the study of S. Stein, "The Influence of Symposia Literature on the Literary Form of the Pesah Haggadah," *JJS* 8 (1957) 13-44.

story, they too are subject to the use of such motifs. That means that their use of table fellowship themes has clear literary precedence which may override historical considerations. These factors complicate our evaluation of this data.

II. The New Testament Evidence

There are four categories of meals with Jesus either alluded to or described in the data: 1) meals with Pharisees, 2) miraculous feedings, 3) meals with "tax collectors and sinners," and 4) meals with disciples. Of these, only three and four offer a high degree of historical probability. References to meals with Pharisees are found only in the Gospel of Luke and clearly are redactional.[12] The miraculous feeding stories present their own problems for interpretation as miracles and should be analyzed separately under that rubric. It is the meals with his disciples and meals with tax collectors and sinners that are the prime candidates for table fellowship as a part of Jesus' proclamation.

II.A. Meals with Disciples: General References

That Jesus had meals with his disciples, and that they subsequently looked back on them as full of meaning, is quite likely. But are any of the stories in the gospels candidates for historical events? And, if so, are they examples of the use of table fellowship as a mode of proclamation?

There are isolated references in the gospels in which seemingly incidental events take place at meals. In these instances the meal provides the setting for the event, but the meal symbolism is secondary to the overall theme. Thus, even if these references were judged to be historical, the meals themselves do not carry the symbolic weight requisite in order to be judged parabolic actions of Jesus. The most important example is the story of the anointing of Jesus at a meal which occurs in various forms in the gospels (Matt 26:6-13 = Mark 14:3-9 = Luke 7:36-50 = John 12:1-8). This text most likely

[12] Luke 7:36-50, 11:37-54, 14:1-24. See my article "Table Fellowship as a Literary Motif in the Gospel of Luke," *JBL* 106 (1987) 613-38, for further elaboration on this point.

originated as a redaction by Mark.[13] Another text is the story of Martha and Mary at a meal setting which is encountered only in Luke 10:38-42 and is best understood as another instance of Luke's extensive use of the literary motif of table fellowship.[14]

References to meal symbolism also may be found in the sayings of Jesus. Such sayings could have originated in a meal setting, such as in the "table talk" of Jesus, but there is not sufficient evidence to affirm this. At the very least, these references show the pervasiveness of meal symbolism as a motif in folklore and literature. One need not assume that they refer to actual meals of Jesus.[15]

There are various other meal references in the gospels in which the primary motif is Jesus' opposition to certain interpretations of Jewish dietary laws.[16] Such a debate could only take place in a context dominated by Pharisaic viewpoints, since these are not issues endemic to Judaism as a whole. Indeed, it was the Pharisees who had interpreted the purity laws, including the dietary laws, as applying to daily life within the community. For the majority of Jews they applied only to the temple. Non-Pharisees followed the purity laws when they were involved with ritual at the temple; otherwise the laws did not apply to their daily lives.[17]

---

[13] See especially Werner H. Kelber, "Conclusion: From Passion Narrative to Gospel," *The Passion in Mark: Studies on Mark 14-16*, in Werner H. Kelber, ed. (Philadelphia: Fortress, 1976) 153-80, especially 173.

[14] Dennis E. Smith, "Table Fellowship as a Literary Motif in the Gospel of Luke," especially 622, 633.

[15] Examples, listed according to title and number in John Dominic Crossan, *Sayings Parallels: A Workbook for the Jesus Tradition* (Philadelphia: Fortress, 1986) (hereafter abbreviated *SP*), are as follows: 1) The Feast (*SP* 12, 365 [Matt. 22:2-13 = Luke 14:16-23 = *Gos. Thom.* 64:1]); 2) Blessed the Hungry (SP 39, 3 [Matt. 5:6 = Luke 6:21a = *Gos. Thom.* 69:2]); 3) Salting the Salt (*SP* 44; see also 212, 213 [Matt. 5:13 = Mark 9:50 = Luke 14:34-35]); 4) Patches and Wineskins (*SP* 98; see also 212 [Matt. 9:16-17 = Mark 2:21-22 = Luke 5:36b-38 = *Gos. Thom.* 47:4]); 5) Leader as Servant (*SP* 172, 447 [Matt. 20:25b-28 = Matt. 23:11 = Mark 9:35b = Mark 10:42b-45 = Luke 9:48b = Luke 22:25-27 = John 13:14]); 6) Patriarchs and Gentiles (*SP* 94 [Matt. 8:11-12 = Luke 13:28-29]).

[16] Some examples of these texts are as follows: 1) Unwashed Hands (*SP* 437 [Matt. 15:1-9 = Mark 7:1-13]), 2) What Goes In (*SP* 147 [Matt. 15:11 = Mark 7:15 = *Gos. Thom.* 14:3]), 3) Leaven of Pharisees (*SP* 152 [Matt. 16:6, 11b = Mark 8:15b = Luke 12:1b]), 4) Inside and Outside (*SP* 187 [Matt. 23:25-26 = Luke 11:39-41 = *Gos. Thom.* 89]).

[17] See Jacob Neusner, *The Idea of Purity in Ancient Judaism* (SJLA 1; Leiden: E.J. Brill, 1973) 64-71.

If Jesus was debating dietary laws, as the texts surveyed above suggest, he therefore would have been debating with the Pharisees. This is, of course, what the tradition states. However, when we place these debates within the context of Judaism of the first century, we discover that they do not represent the social stance which they appear to represent. For by separating himself from the viewpoints of the Pharisees, Jesus would simply be identifying with the masses in "ordinary" Judaism as opposed to the sect that was Pharisaism.[18] This would not at all indicate, therefore, that Jesus and his followers were taking a separatist or sectarian position in Judaism. And it certainly would not imply that they formed a separate table fellowship community.

This tradition does develop a distinctive sectarian direction later in the early Christian community, however. This can be seen in the gospels whereby the trajectory of Jesus' critique of dietary laws results in the interpretation: "Thus he declared all foods clean" (Mark 7:19). This perspective is clearly one that derives from a time in which the early Christian community is developing its self-consciousness as a sectarian group within the social world of Judaism.

Thus, even if the references to debates of Jesus with Pharisees over purity laws were historical, they would not imply that Jesus and his followers formed separate meal communities. Rather, that idea is to be associated with the development of a distinctive community consciousness, a phenomenon not to be found in the lifetime of Jesus but only after his death. It was at that time that the Christian communal meal and its ideology began to develop. And consistent with that development was the interpretation of the Jesus tradition to represent a sectarian point of view in regard to dietary laws.

II.B. The Last Supper

The most highly elaborated description of a formal meal of Jesus with his disciples is that of the Last Supper. This

[18] On the Pharisees as a minority movement in first century Judaism, see Morton Smith, "Palestinian Judaism in the First Century," *Essays in Greco-Roman and Related Talmudic Literature*, in Henry A. Fischel, ed. (New York: KTAV, 1977) 183-97; Jacob Neusner, *From Politics to Piety: The Emergence of Pharisaic Judaism* (Englewood Cliffs, NJ: Prentice-Hall, 1973) 64-96; Sanders, *Jesus and Judaism*, 190-93.

tradition is attested in 1 Cor 11:23-25 and in Mark, which then was used as a source by Matthew and Luke.

The earliest text is in 1 Corinthians, a text whose form is that of an etiological legend.[19] Mark has taken this tradition and incorporated it into his narrative.[20] Mark's passion narrative, however, has been shown in recent research to be largely a creation of the gospel writer.[21] Thus neither the text of 1 Corinthians nor that of Mark possess a form that is demonstrably historical. Nevertheless, one could inquire whether the core data in these texts might be considered historical.

Those who support the historicity of the tradition in Mark tend to emphasize that Jesus celebrated a Passover meal with his disciples as his last meal and that reminiscences of that meal are contained in our Last Supper account.[22] Closer analysis has shown, however, that there is very little relationship to a passover meal in the Last Supper text at all other than the introductory reference (Mark 14:12-16), and that is clearly Mark's creation.[23] Accordingly, even if Jesus did celebrate a Passover meal with his disciples as his final meal, we possess no clear reminiscence of such a meal in the description now available to us.

A historical reconstruction based on the Pauline text might point to the reference to these events taking place "on the night when he was arrested" [παρεδίδετο; NRSV translates "betrayed"] (1 Cor 11:23).[24] Thus the pre-Pauline tradition referred to this as Jesus' last meal and placed it in relation to

---

[19] See Mack, *A Myth of Innocence*, 116-20.

[20] Ibid., 299.

[21] See Vernon Robbins, "Last Meal: Preparation, Betrayal, and Absence (Mark 14:12-25)," *The Passion in Mark: Studies on Mark 14-16*, in Werner H. Kelber, ed. (Philadelphia: Fortress, 1976) 21-40; Robert M. Fowler, *Loaves and Fishes: The Function of the Feeding Stories in the Gospel of Mark* (SBLDS 54; Chico, CA: Scholars Press, 1981); Philip Sellew, "The Last Supper Discourse in Luke 22:21-38," *Forum* 3,3 (September, 1987) 70-95; John L. White, "The Way of the Cross: Was there a Pre-Markan Passion Narrative?" *Forum* 3,2 (June, 1987) 35-49; Idem., "Beware of Leavened Bread: Markan Imagery in the Last Supper," *Forum* 3,4 (December, 1987) 49-63.

[22] See Jeremias, *The Eucharistic Words of Jesus.*

[23] See, e.g., Eduard Schweizer, *The Lord's Supper according to the New Testament* (FBBS 18; Philadelphia: Fortress, 1967) 29-32; Robbins, "Last Meal: Preparation, Betrayal, and Absence," 22-28.

[24] Another possible translation is "given up," with God understood as the one who "gave him up" as in Rom 8:32.

an assumed historical sequence of events. On the other hand, it should be noted that the so-called "eucharistic words" of Jesus in all forms in which we have them, both in 1 Corinthians and in Mark, are primarily concerned to interpret the death of Jesus. It seems highly unlikely that such traditions represent Jesus' self-understanding during his own lifetime. Rather, they most likely represent a retrojection back into Jesus' time of an interpretation that originated in the early church. Accordingly, whatever might be proposed as the historical core of a meal or meals of Jesus with his disciples, it cannot have centered on an interpretation of Jesus' death. Consequently the Last Supper traditions do not provide adequate data to reconstruct a historical meal of Jesus with his disciples. Perhaps the last word on this subject has been stated by Crossan:

> "Obviously, in such a situation, Jesus and those closest to him would have had a last supper, that is, a meal that later and in retrospect was recognized as having been their last one together . . . . I do not presume any distinctive meal known beforehand, designated specifically, or ritually programmed as final and forever."[25]

II.C. Meals with "Tax Collectors and Sinners"

These references all represent criticisms against Jesus and his followers. There are two basic versions of this data: 1) a description of a meal of Jesus at the home of a tax collector, and 2) a tradition in which meal-practices play a part in a larger argument in which Jesus is being contrasted with John the Baptist. The first tradition appears in its earliest form in Mark, the second in "Q."

Both texts are defined as types of the *chreia* form. This form has been given extensive analysis and definition in recent research on the gospel tradition.[26] The *chreia* was a form of

---

[25] *The Historical Jesus,* 361.

[26] See especially Ronald F. Hock and Edward N. O'Neil, *The Chreia in Ancient Rhetoric, vol 1: The Progymnasmata* (SBLTT 27; Atlanta: Scholars Press, 1986). An excellent brief discussion of the *chreia* with an annotated bibliography is found in Vernon Robbins, "The Chreia," in David E. Aune, ed.; *Greco-Roman Literature and the New Testament: Selected Forms and Genres* (SBLSBS 21; Atlanta: Scholars Press, 1988) 1-23. See also the helpful review of scholarship on this form in Mack, *A Myth of Innocence,* 172-78.

rhetoric that is described in ancient literature and was taught in the schools. It is related to the form known as the pronouncement story. It is defined as:

> "a saying or act that is well-aimed or apt, expressed concisely, attributed to a person, and regarded as useful for living."[27]

Particularly important in the definition for our study is that a *chreia* normally was employed to characterize a famous person or hero.[28] *Chreiai* were used extensively therefore in the philosophical tradition to characterize famous philosophers.

These traditional usages provide us with a further definition of the *chreia* form. At least two types can be singled out as widely used, the Stoic *chreia* and the Cynic *chreia*. The Stoic *chreia* is characterized by its emphasis on moral teaching. The Cynic *chreia*:

> "distinguishes itself by the odd, extreme, and often even burlesque action (or basic situation or final statement) of the central Sage-Hero that becomes the basis for a demonstration of Cynic ideals and values."[29]

Recent studies have concluded that the *chreiai* in the Jesus tradition tend to be of the Cynic type.[30] This is also true for the examples studied here.

II.C.1. Defining a Chreia *in Mark*

Mark's description of a meal of Jesus at the home of a tax collector has been identified as a *chreia* of the Cynic type. The text is as follows:

> "And as he sat at dinner [Greek: κατακεῖσθαι; "reclined"] in Levi's house, many tax collectors and sinners were also sitting with [Greek: συνανέκειντο; "reclining with"] Jesus and his disciples – for there were many who followed him. When the scribes

[27] Robbins, "The Chreia," 2.

[28] See especially Henry A. Fischel, "Studies in Cynicism and the Ancient Near East," in Jacob Neusner, ed., *Religions in Antiquity: Studies in Honor of Erwin Ramsdell Goodenough* (Studies in the History of Religions 14; Leiden: E.J. Brill, 1968) 372-411, especially 374.

[29] Ibid., 373. See also Mack, *A Myth of Innocence*, 179-82.

[30] John S. Kloppenborg, *The Formation of Q: Trajectories in Ancient Wisdom Collections* (Studies in Antiquity and Christianity; Philadelphia: Fortress, 1987) 322-25; Mack, A Myth of Innocence, 182-92; see also idem, "The Kingdom That Didn't Come: A Social History of the Q Tradents," in *SBLASP 1988* David J. Lull, ed. (Atlanta: Scholars Press, 1988) 608-35; Ron Cameron, "'What Have You Come Out to See?' Characterizations of John and Jesus in the Gospels," *Semeia* 49 (1990) 35-69.

> of the Pharisees saw that he was eating with sinners and tax collectors, they said to his disciples, 'Why does he eat with tax collectors and sinners?' When Jesus heard this, he said to them, 'Those who are well have no need of a physician, but those who are sick; I have come to call not the righteous but sinners'" (Mark 2:15-17/Matt 9:10-13/Luke 5:29-32 [*SP* # 97]).

The basic, core *chreia* is reconstructed by Burton Mack as follows:

> "When asked why he ate with tax collectors and sinners, Jesus replied, 'Those who are well have no need of a physician, but those who are ill.'"[31]

The logic of the text takes on a Cynic cast because it represents a counterargument to the implied conventional logic of the objection. Furthermore, the saying about a physician is a conventional one, and is especially congenial to the Cynic tradition where a comparison of the philosopher with a physician was widely used.[32] The core *chreia* has then been elaborated with data that relates it to its context in Mark, especially by identifying the setting as the home of the tax collector whom Jesus has called to follow him and by identifying Jesus' detractors as "scribes of the Pharisees."

The text in its present form, therefore, represents a creation by Mark to coordinate with his own literary aims, both in terms of context and themes.[33] Moreover, the form that the description takes has an air of unreality about it. It is difficult to imagine how Pharisees can be present in the dining room

---

[31] *A Myth of Innocence*, 183.

[32] See especially Diogenes Epistles 38.4: "I did not dine with everyone but only with those in need of therapy" (in Abraham J. Malherbe, ed., *The Cynic Epistles: A Study Edition* [SBLSBS 12; Missoula: Scholars Press, 1977] 163; quoted in Leif E. Vaage, "Q: The Ethos and Ethics of an Itinerant Intelligence" [Ph.D. dissertation, Claremont Graduate School, 1987] 379). For other examples, see also Malherbe, "Self-Definition among Epicureans and Cynics," in Ben F. Meyer and E. P. Sanders, eds., *Jewish and Christian Self-Definition, vol. 3: Self-Definition in the Greco-Roman World* (Philadelphia: Fortress, 1982) 53; Mack, *A Myth of Innocence*, 183-84, especially 184, n. 8.

[33] Bultmann (*The History of the Synoptic Tradition* [2nd ed.; New York: Harper & Row, 1968] 47-48) confidently asserts about this text: "the artificiality of the composition is clear as day." He notes especially how artificially the story involves the disciples. In this respect it is parallel to other stories in the tradition whose function is to defend the conduct of the disciples. Thus it is ultimately the church rather than Jesus that is on trial; the text, therefore, would originate in the early church.

such that they can observe and comment without themselves being participants.[34] Such a feature cannot be made to fit conventional dining customs and settings, but obviously presents no problems to a narrator who is imagining a story world.

Another discordant historical note is presented by the phrase, "I have come to call not the righteous but sinners." This saying represents an elaboration on the physician saying but has an independent relation to the meal setting as well. The word "call" (καλέω) is used here as a pun; the same term is the ordinary term meaning "invite" to a meal.[35] According to this saying Jesus is not the guest but the host, the one who invites to the meal. Although this presents insurmountable difficulties if the text is taken to be historical, it works quite well on the literary level, where irony can have its full sway. Here, whereas the character Levi the tax collector thinks he is the host who has invited Jesus, the reader perceives Jesus as the one who extends the invitation and his invitation is to that which the meal merely symbolizes. Furthermore, the theme of calling is inherent to the context of Mark, where the meal is connected with a "call" story.[36] Thus the meal symbolizes redemption and calling to discipleship, a symbolism that works quite well in the literary context but is difficult to reconstruct in a historical setting. The meal description presented in this instance, therefore, represents a literary idealization rather than a recalling of an actual event.

When taken out of its context in Mark and reduced to its basic form, as is the case in Mack's reconstruction quoted above, the text as *chreia* does not present a description of a specific meal but rather presents a characterization of Jesus. The assumption behind the *chreia* is that Jesus routinely dined with "tax collectors and sinners," that this somehow was indicative of his overall character, and, furthermore, that it was inherently an unconventional thing to do.

---

[34] Ibid., 18, n. 3; 66; See also Walker, "Jesus and the Tax Collectors," 233.

[35] See, e.g., Bultmann, *History of the Synoptic Tradition*, 163; Karl Ludwig Schmidt, "καλέω, κτλ," TDNT 3 (1965) 488-89.

[36] According to Vernon Robbins (*Jesus the Teacher: A Socio-Rhetorical Interpretation of Mark* [Philadelphia: Fortress, 1984], especially p. 109), the calling of the disciples in Mark is part of a larger theme in the Gospel as a whole, in which the writer utilizes classic literary motifs of the day to present Jesus as a teacher who calls and instructs his disciples.

The logic behind the assumption that Jesus was engaging in an unconventional act by dining with such individuals appears to relate to traditional Jewish dietary laws and to the assumption that Jesus would be transgressing those laws in some manner by eating with such people.[37] But the logic of the text on the literary level is difficult to reconstruct on the historical level.

The status of the dietary laws in the time of Jesus has been discussed already above. The point is that Jesus would not have been perceived to be making a statement such as this text assumes merely by dining with questionable individuals. Rather, he would simply have been making the statement that he was not a Pharisee. On the other hand, it may not be dietary laws *per se* that lie behind this characterization of "tax collectors and sinners," and it is difficult to account for these individuals as being clearly in the unclean category.[38] In any case, in the text before us, the reconstructed basic *chreia*, these terms already are functioning symbolically, for the text assumes that they represent an aspect of the teaching program of Jesus. How they derived their symbolic meaning predates this *chreia* and will be considered below.

The text goes on to compare dining with Jesus with being healed by a physician. This is at best a subtle symbol, inasmuch as it assumes that this apparent "parabolic action" of Jesus can be perceived as part of his teaching program. As the discussion below will point out, however, such an interpretation is difficult to reconstruct on the level of social reality, although it works effectively on a literary level. Since the *chreia* in its basic form represents an attempt to typify the teaching of Jesus by utilizing a popular proverb about a physician, it has the form of a text created in a community that is idealizing its hero.

Thus the tradition represented in this text in both its elaborated form as found in Mark and in its basic *chreia* form can be seen to have had its origin in the early church. There is one aspect of this tradition that deserves further investigation, however. Since both Mark and "Q" have independent versions of the motif that Jesus characteristically dined with "tax col-

[37] So Mack, *A Myth of Innocence*, 183.
[38] See Sanders, *Jesus and Judaism*, 174-211.

lectors and sinners," the motif clearly took shape in the tradition at a very early stage. In order to trace it further I shall now look at the form it takes in "Q."

II.C.2. Jesus Contrasted with John the Baptist

The "Q" saying about Jesus' eating habits occurs in the larger context of an elaborated *chreia* in which Jesus is being contrasted with John the Baptist. The larger block of texts of which this text is a part includes "Q" (Luke) 7:1-10, 18-23, 24-26, 16:16, and 31-35. These texts all contrast John and Jesus with "this generation."[39] Our passage in its immediate context is as follows:

> "To what then will I compare the people of this generation, and what are they like? They are like children sitting in the market place and calling to one another, "We played the flute for you, and you did not dance; we wailed, and you did not weep." For John the Baptist has come eating no bread and drinking no wine, and you say, "He has a demon"; the Son of Man has come eating and drinking, and you say, "Look, a glutton and a drunkard, a friend of tax collectors and sinners!" Nevertheless, wisdom is vindicated by all her children. (Luke 7:31-35 = Matt 11:16-19)."

John Kloppenborg has defined three layers in the compositional history of "Q." The earliest layer consists of wisdom speeches, the second represents the introduction of sayings "which adopted a critical and polemical stance with respect to Israel."[40] This text is located at the second or Q2 layer. It is part of a larger group of texts concerned with the theme of judgment and opposition to "this generation." Likewise characteristic of the stage represented by this text is the fact that Jesus and John are included together rather than portrayed as rivals. Thus they are pictured here as allies against "this generation," as two types of "children" of wisdom.[41]

In terms of textual history it seems apparent that the parable in Luke 7:32 is independent of the saying in verses 33-34, which have been attached as an explanation for the parable. Thus verses 33-34 represent an independent saying.[42]

---

[39] See Kloppenborg, *The Formation of Q*, 107-17.

[40] Ibid., 317.

[41] Ibid., 110-12; see also Arland Jacobson, "Wisdom Christology in Q" (Ph.D. dissertation, Claremont Graduate School, 1978) 84-91; Cameron, "'What Have You Come Out to See?'"

[42] See Kloppenborg, *The Formation of Q*, 111.

Furthermore, the primary contrast here is between "fasting" and "feasting." Since the corollary added to the description of Jesus, that he is a "friend of tax collectors and sinners," has no parallel referent in the descriptive phrase referring to John, it is secondary and must have been added at a later point.[43] Indeed, it has the potential to have existed as an independent tradition since table fellowship is a traditional motif for expressing the idea of friendship.[44]

A social history connected with this text in its larger context in "Q" has been proposed by Burton Mack.[45] He defines the group represented by Kloppenborg's Q1 level of tradition as taking a critical stance to society and to the norms of social roles and rankings, yet not proposing a radical break with the social order such as would be represented by a sectarian mentality. Their mode of discourse, the wisdom saying, was consistent with that view, particularly when located within the context of a Cynic perspective in which society is critiqued but not with a view toward radical revision of its structures.[46] Mack understands this perspective to represent that of the earliest Christian group which can be identified on the basis of the "Q" data. Furthermore, he finds this definition to be closest to the perspective that is most likely to be attributed to the historical Jesus.[47]

Our text derives from Q2, however, and as such is to be connected with a subsequent development in the history of the "Q" community. At this stage, a disruption within the social order of their world has taken place; indeed, they evidently have suffered rejection. This text and others of this level in the tradition present a literary record of that social history by preserving the community's attempts to rationalize and explain its experience. Accordingly, the text assumes a rejection has already occurred; a distinction is drawn already

---

[43] Also noted by Jacobson, "Wisdom Christology in Q," 86-87, and Wendy J. Cotter, C.S.J., "The Parable of the Children in the Market-Place, Q (Lk) 7:31-35: An Examination of the Parable's Image and Significance," *NovT* 29 [1987]) 303, n. 58.

[44] See, for example, Plutarch's reference to "the friend-making character of the table" (*Quaes. conv.* 612D). This is a standard motif in banquet literature.

[45] See his "The Kingdom That Didn't Come."

[46] Ibid., 613-16, 621-23.

[47] Ibid., 633-34. See also idem, *A Myth of Innocence*, 67-69, 73-74.

between "this generation" and the Jesus community. Indeed, the line is now so strictly drawn that judgment is pronounced on the detractors, a classical mode of legitimizing discourse in an apocalyptic community. Thus a changing social situation serves as a catalyst for a change in the mode of discourse in "Q" from wisdom to apocalyptic.[48]

Mack's reconstruction provides a basis for an ingenious explanation of the intriguing contrast of Jesus and John proposed here. The presentation of Jesus and John on the same side as opponents of "this generation," yet also as representives of contrasting forms of messages, functions as a means for correlating the two forms of discourse in "Q." Jesus as one who "feasts" represents here the wisdom figure, John as one who "fasts" the prophetic, apocalyptic figure. The juxtaposition of two modes of discourse within one social world is thus legitimized.[49]

Especially important in Mack's reconstruction, however, is his proposal that "social formation" or sectarian identity is not to be found until the Q2 level of the tradition. Indeed, as he reads the data the history represented in "Q" provides the best explanation for the history of the Jesus movement in general. That is to say, the earliest occurrence of what can be called a sectarian identity of a Christian group within Judaism is to be located neither at the level of the historical Jesus nor at the level of the earliest identifiable group within the Jesus movement. That sectarian identity only develops in the context of conflict in the later history of the movement.[50] And, it should be added, it is only when that sectarian identity has developed that the meal can function as it does here as a boundary marker setting off one group from another.

There are two basic meal motifs present in this text: feasting *versus* fasting and dining with "tax collectors and sinners." As has been already indicated, textual analysis suggests that these originate as separate motifs. As Mack suggests, the feasting *versus* fasting symbolism is best interpreted as a referent for another idea, in this instance as a cipher for the inclusion of wisdom and apocalyptic modes of discourse and lifestyles within the same community. It can hardly serve, however, as a pro-

[48] See idem, "The Kingdom That Didn't Come," 616-17, 620, 624-26.
[49] Ibid., 630.
[50] Ibid., 626.

file of the community meal nor as a critique of the dining customs of "this generation." Thus up to 34b, the meal data is employed in a strictly symbolic sense without any logical reference to actual meal customs within the community.

It is 34c that refers the meal symbolism to some implicit aspect of actual meal practices. Being a "friend of tax collectors and sinners" by means of undiscriminating table fellowship serves to define the self identity of the community over against "this generation."

Mack assumes that the social world indicated by the idea that dining with "tax collectors and sinners" is somehow scandalous is that of Pharisaic Judaism. This text, then, would have originated in an early Christian community that was tied closely to Pharisaic Judaism and somehow had been ostracized by that group. Mack proposes that the "Q" community existed as "house groups" in the context of a synagogue dominated by Pharisaic teachings. Some sort of tension would have developed in their recent history, which led to their being ejected from that community and, in effect, rejected by their social world. This reconstruction would provide a context to explain the development of the various anti-Pharisaic teachings in "Q."[51]

Many of these anti-Pharisaic texts involved questions regarding dietary laws as is appropriate to the Pharisaic tradition. Such disagreements evidently would develop in the larger context of a conflict over rules of table fellowship. Such a conflict implies the existence of some sort of community meal, although it is difficult to determine whether it would be in the Jewish community as a whole or limited to the Christian groups (as "house groups") or in both.[52] The ejection of the Q2 group from the community was connected with a charge

---

[51] Ibid., 624-25.

[52] Neusner (*The Idea of Purity in Ancient Judaism*, 66-67; see also his, *From Politics to Piety: The Emergence of Pharisaic Judaism* [Englewood Cliffs, NJ: Prentice-Hall, 1973] 87-89) has emphasized the point that while the Pharisees' preoccupation with dietary laws meant that table fellowship took on a special significance for them, it did not mean that they gathered for meals as a group or celebrated "ritual" meals comparable to the Christian Lord's Supper. He is surely correct that there were no special rituals which characterized their meals, but this does not rule out the possibility that there may have been communal meals among some groups of Pharisees. See also Borg, *Conflict, Holiness & Politics in the Teachings of Jesus*, 80-81, who argues that for the Pharisees the table had come to symbolize "the cultural dynamic of holiness."

that it had become tainted somehow by practicing table customs that were not discriminating enough. In our text the phrase "tax collectors and sinners" is made to serve a symbolic function to represent in a general manner this critique. The text provides a rationale for the developing identity that has been defined by this community conflict by means of a story that connects Jesus with apparently "impure" dining companions. In the context, the phrase "tax collectors and sinners" functions as a generic term for scandalous companions and thus functions symbolically rather than referring to specific figures in the community. That is to say, one need not posit the existence of "tax collectors" in the early Christian community in order to understand the invective involved in the use of this phrase.

This text, therefore, is best understood as developing out of a social context within the early Christian community, one in which the conflict and social separation inherent in the text make sense. Nevertheless, it might be proposed that the separate themes, dining with tax collectors and sinners and feasting *versus* fasting, be considered as independent and potentially authentic Jesus traditions.

III. Analyzing the Earliest Motifs

To this point I have analyzed the specific texts that are the most likely to represent table fellowship practices of the historical Jesus. I have presented arguments in each case that the social context and social world represented by these texts is most likely that of the early church. However, it is also appropriate to look beyond the texts and ask if the motifs they utilize could be construed as historical. The best candidates for this inquiry are the two motifs, dining with tax collectors and sinners and feasting *versus* fasting.

III.A. Dining with "Tax Collectors and Sinners"

In its basic meaning this tradition is concerned with the regular practice of dining with people who are beneath one's own social status. In favor of this tradition as being historical is its consistency with other references from the most probable historical core that Jesus favored the less fortunate in the world (see, e.g., "Blessed are the poor"), although it should be pointed out that "tax collectors" hardly could be considered "less fortunate." Rather, what is most scandalous about tax collectors can be said to be their exploitation of the poor. It is usually argued, therefore, that what is in common in the mix of "tax collectors," "sinners," and "poor" is their supposed social location on the fringes of Jewish society.[53] But it should be noted that Jesus is not said to dine with the "poor." The symbolism connected with the meal is not that of a charity dinner.

In order to understand how this tradition functions, the elements that make it up must be isolated and analyzed separately. The basic motif, that Jesus is criticized for dining with unacceptable individuals, assumes that all of the parties involved – Jesus, his critics, the "tax collectors and sinners" – share the same social world in significant details. For example, they must share the same view of dietary laws and of the position of Jesus within the social world. The motif only succeeds if all of the parties involved assume that a person like Jesus would not be expected to dine with such individuals.

First, let us consider the definition of the term "tax collectors and sinners." Attempts to provide a historically based definition for these characters that fits the story have proved problematic. In regard to "tax collectors" discussion has revolved around identifying who they were and what their offense was such that table fellowship with them would be scandalous. Distinctions have been drawn between tax collectors and toll collectors, and the suggestion made that in the time of the gospels only the latter could be found in Palestine.[54] As to their offense, it has been argued that they were hated because of their status as "quislings," those who had consorted with the enemy, and because theirs was considered to be an occupation characterized by dishonesty. The scandal in dining with them could have involved ritual purity since they would be "Jews who had made themselves as Gentiles [by becoming quislings]," or, alternatively, it could have been a

[53] See, e.g., Jeremias, *New Testament Theology*, 109-13. Horsley, *Jesus and the Spiral of Violence*, 212-17, proposes that the reference to tax collectors is strictly slanderous; thus, while the accusation is historical, what it states (i.e. that Jesus dined with tax collectors) is not.

[54] See Jeremias, *New Testament Theology*, 110; Donahue, "Tax Collectors and Sinners," 39-61.

moral question, since they were dishonest people.[55]

"Sinners" have been widely assumed to be the impure and thus roughly equivalent with the '*amme ha arets* with whom the Pharisees presumably could not eat. Thus virtually every non-Pharisee could be included under this term.[56] Recently, however, E.P. Sanders has proposed an important qualification of the meaning of this term. He argues that it cannot refer to the ritually impure but only to "the wicked . . . those who sinned wilfully and heinously and who did not repent."[57] Purity laws, on the other hand, had very little to do with normal table fellowship, but affected only access to the temple. The sole group for whom purity laws did affect table fellowship were the *haverim*, a group which Sanders distinguishes from the larger group of Pharisees. He points out that they would have been a minority group in first century Palestine and not at all sufficiently influential to set the standards for acceptability in Jewish society at large. This means that if Jesus dined with the impure it would only identify him as a non-*haver*; it would not constitute an offense to Jewish sensibilities.[58]

Sanders goes on to conclude, nonetheless, that Jesus' act consisted not in welcoming the impure into the kingdom, but rather in welcoming the "wicked" into his community. By offering his kingdom to them without first requiring repentance he was engaging in an act contrary to Jewish tradition and therefore scandalous.[59] Such, then, is Sanders interpretation of the table fellowship texts:

> "His eating with tax collectors and sinners has, probably correctly, been seen as a proleptic indication that they would be included in the kingdom: the meal looks forward to the "messianic banquet," when many would come from east and west and dine with the patriarchs (Matt 8:11)."[60]

Sanders, however, has limited his interpretive options by committing himself to this tradition as being historical. Since

---

[55] Quisling: Perrin, *Rediscovering the Teaching of Jesus*, 93-94. Dishonesty: Jeremias, *New Testament Theology*, 110-111; Donahue, "Tax Collectors and Sinners," 59.

[56] As suggested in Jeremias, *New Testament Theology*, 109-13, especially 112.

[57] *Jesus and Judaism*, 177.

[58] Ibid., 182-99.

[59] Ibid., 203-08.

[60] Ibid., 208.

"tax collectors and sinners" must be equated with specific individuals in Jesus' time, he is compelled to propose a situation in which Jesus might be accused of associating with such people. This prompts him to suggest the dubious scenario that Jesus was offering "his" kingdom to the unrepentant and that this was viewed as opprobrious. What Sanders has failed to recognize is the inherent character of this tradition as a literary motif.

In the basic form of the tradition, the category "tax collectors and sinners" must be construed from the outset as symbolic and as representative of a type, for the motif that Jesus associates/dines with them is taken to represent a pattern for him and not a one-time individual activity. Accordingly the identity of the group so designated is not based so much on the actual as on the symbolic value of the terms. That is to say, at the earliest level of the tradition "tax collector and sinner" belong together and operate as symbolic terms to define social position through the use of a set of apparently traditional terms of slander.[61]

The story also assumes that those designated by the term "tax collectors and sinners" must be desirous of the table fellowship from which they are excluded. But why would tax collectors feel excluded if *haverim* or Pharisees refused to dine with them?[62] After all, the Pharisees themselves represented a sectarian position within Judaism. This points up the problem

---

[61] See, e.g., Jeremias, *Jerusalem in the Time of Jesus* (Philadelphia: Fortress, 1969) 303-12, who includes "tax collectors" in a list of "despised trades" culled from the Mishnah. What these references indicate is that the term "tax collector" had become synonymous with other categories of despised persons. In the New Testament it has taken on the overtones of a generic term in such expressions as "tax collectors and prostitutes" (Matt 21:31) and particularly in the "church order" text of Matt 18:17: "If the offender refuses to listen even to the church, let such a one be to you as a Gentile and a tax collector." James D. G. Dunn has made a similar point in regard to the term "sinner" in our texts. In opposition to Sanders he argues that the term does not refer to a specific group in the social setting of first-century Palestine, but rather is a term of opprobrium used most often in a sectarian context, referring to those outside of one's own group ("Pharisees, Sinners, and Jesus," in Jacob Neusner et al., eds., *The Social World of Formative Christianity and Judaism: Essays in Tribute to Howard Clark Kee* [Philadelphia: Fortress, 1988] 276-80, especially 278). Thus, neither actual tax collectors nor actual sinners are being singled out specifically in the phrase "tax collectors and sinners." Rather, it is a term of slander used to define the boundaries between one's own group and outsiders.

[62] Pointed out by Sanders, *Jesus and Judaism*, 193, 202-03.

in correlating the presuppositions inherent in the motif with historical reality.

One indication of the literary, or oral narrative, character of the motif is its basic nature as an example of irony. That Jesus dines with "tax collectors and sinners" functions as a criticism of him and is understood to be a true statement. But to the "reader" or "listener" it would convey a different meaning than that which Jesus' critics in the story are applying to it. In truth, the motif assumes, Jesus does characteristically dine with what appear to be unsavory individuals; yet these are in fact the types of individuals of which the kingdom is composed. Seen from this perspective, this motif would not be scandalous at the earliest level of its occurrence in this form. It always would have represented a characterization of the companions of Jesus with which the church could identify.

A further assumption of the story is that table fellowship with Jesus effectively breaks down barriers that exist in the social world. Thus the story requires that Jesus be recognized by all parties involved, even his critics, as more than an average teacher, that he symbolize somehow in his person the presence of the "kingdom." A prevalent explanation, and one that is consistent with the gospel tradition, is that Jesus somehow made table fellowship with him take on the aura of a messianic banquet. There are numerous problems with this interpretation. Among other things it requires that Jesus be in charge of the meal so that its form and structure be attributable to him. While it is quite possible that Jesus did host meals,[63] the gospel texts make no such distinction. No matter who might ostensibly host a meal, if Jesus is present the gathering takes on overtones of a messianic banquet. Thus the motif does not rely on historical data.

A additional question in regard to the Jesus material is this: how can a messianic banquet be envisioned in real life? Note that such a meal requires the presence of a messiah, a "real" messiah who has full access to heavenly blessings, not a messianic pretender or someone in process of becoming a messiah. I do not find it plausible that the historical Jesus could have added that dimension to a meal merely by virtue of

[63] Note, however, that this would be unlikely if he was an itinerant, as Crossan, *The Historical Jesus*, 345-48, especially emphasizes.

his presence. Indeed, I find it highly unlikely that any historical figure could celebrate such a meal centered around his or her own person. The messianic banquet is in its essence a mythological meal, a meal that takes place on a divine level with the participation of divine characters.[64] It functions well as a literary idealization of the apocalyptic consummation. There may even have been real communal meals that ritualized the presence of mythological forces or beings (the so-called "proleptic" messianic banquet).[65] But there can be no messianic banquet with Jesus until Jesus has become a mythological character. Note, however, that this process has already begun in the "Q" text when it is stated, "The Son of Man has come eating and drinking..." (Luke 7:34 = Matt 11:19).

In my opinion it is only in a narrative context that all of the conditions necessary to make this motif operable could be present. Accordingly, this tradition would originate in the form of a *chreia* functioning to characterize the self-consciousness of the early Christian community. It cannot succeed if placed in a real, historical context. It only works when presented in a literary context in which the presuppositions of the situation and characters can be carefully controlled. The prior motif, which in fact may be an historical one, is that of Jesus preaching against the norms of social stratification in his society. Early Christian preachers then exemplified that idea by creating a *chreia* which utilized the stock motifs of the hero at table and the generic opprobrious term, "tax collectors and sinners."

III.B. Feasting versus *Fasting*

In favor of the historicity of this motif are the various classic arguments that have been proposed in past studies to the effect that this is a case of dissimilarity. Perrin's conclusion is typical:

---

[64] See my review of the evidence in "The Messianic Banquet Reconsidered," in Birger A. Pearson, ed., *The Future of Early Christianity: Essays in Honor of Helmut Koester*, Minneapolis: Fortress, 1991, 64-73.

[65] The communal meal at Qumran is most often proposed as an example of such a banquet, but see my reservations in "The Messianic Banquet Reconsidered," 71.

> "The designation of Jesus as 'a glutton and a drunkard' belongs to the polemics of the controversy surrounding Jesus' earthly ministry during his lifetime, rather than to the circumstances of the controversies between the early Church and Judaism."[66]

What is not always emphasized, however, is the full meaning of the motif. That is, the primary motif includes the contrast of feasting with fasting as well as the contrast of Jesus with John the Baptist. Note, for example, that feasting in itself is not a revolutionary act; as indicated here, it only becomes a symbolic act when proposed in contrast to fasting. Furthermore, note that both fasting and feasting are constituent parts of Jewish piety. Thus to choose such actions does not necessarily set one apart from the group as a whole.

If this is to be taken as a historical reference to the ministry of Jesus, then it must not be separated from the connection with the John the Baptist tradition. In fact, there may be a historical core here, designating Jesus as one who was known to have considered but rejected the monastic lifestyle of John. In the earliest form of the text, however, it presupposes a literary context. For here the lifestyles of Jesus and John are taken as wholes and placed side-by-side as two parts of a single message. Thus the text presents a characterization of Jesus and John in the form of a retrospect, one that confidently can sum up what Jesus and John were all about and how they were in the end not highly successful in their missions to Israel.[67] The context for the formation of this motif, therefore, would most likely be the early church. While it may represent a reminiscence of an authentic characteristic of the historical Jesus, it only takes on the symbolism of a characterization of his ministry in the form that originates in the early church.

III.C. The Motif of the Hero at Table

According to the analysis presented up to this point, the earliest meal texts in the Jesus tradition are *chreiai* which present idealizations of Jesus by means of traditional meal motifs. When we examine these materials more closely, we can detect

---

[66] *Rediscovering the Teaching of Jesus,* 120.

[67] The function of the original *chreia* as presenting a characterization of John and Jesus is nicely stated by Cameron, "'What Have You Come Out to See?'" 54, 60.

a pattern. By and large the type of characterization of the hero represented in these texts is roughly parallel to the one we encounter in Cynic traditions. What many of these early texts have in common is a characterization of Jesus as one who parodied the institutions of society as a means of proclaiming his message, a message, therefore, that had a Cynic style to it.[68] Furthermore, the motifs present here are also commonplace in Cynic tradition, such as the motif of the "hedonistic" Cynic or the use of the meal motif as a means of characterizing the Cynic hero.[69]

Thus the proposal that the early Jesus-tradition is related to Cynic themes and motifs provides the best explanation for the context in which the table fellowship texts developed. This need not suggest that Jesus was himself a Cynic or identified with Cynic traditions. But it does suggest that certain early Christian communities utilized Cynic traditions to characterize and idealize Jesus as a hero. It also means that there need be no other explanation for the development of these traditions than this. While authentic data may be utilized in the development of these *chreiai*, it is not necessary to propose any authenticity to the meal traditions in order to explain these data. Indeed, when it is noted that the meal data are utilized as a motif to characterize a particular aspect of Jesus' ministry, what emerges as prior and more important is not, perhaps, the motif itself but the characteristic that is illustrated thereby.

III.D. The Motif of "Open Commensality"

John Dominic Crossan has introduced a new motif into the discussion of table fellowship and the historical Jesus. He centers his argument on the text in which the disciples are sent out in a manner in direct contrast to that of the Cynics. Whereas the Cynics carry a staff, bag, and food, the disciples are to carry none of these.[70] But the most important point is

[68] On the Cynic worldview and its relation to the early Jesus-movement, see especially Burton L. Mack, *The Lost Gospel: The Book of Q and Christian Origins* (San Francisco: Harper Collins, 1993) 111-30.

[69] See especially Cameron, "'What Have You Come Out to See?'."

[70] Nevertheless, Crossan concludes: "The general background for the dress and equipment codes [of Jesus and his disciples] is the counter-cultural Cynic life-style" (*The Historical Jesus*, 338; see also 72-88); compare Mack, *The Lost Gospel*, 129.

that they are to carry no food: "Take nothing for your journey, no staff, nor bag, nor bread, nor money; and do not have two tunics" (*SP* 103 [Mark 6:8-9 = Luke 9:3; see also Matt. 10:10]). When they arrived at a house, they were to "eat what is set before you; cure the sick who are there" (Luke 10:8-9 = *Gos. Thom.* 14:2) "for laborers deserve their food" (Matt. 10:10). In contrast to the Cynic insistence on self sufficiency the disciples of Jesus would be insisting on social dependency.[71] Crossan combines this with the idea that Jesus was a peasant who was proposing a revolutionary social program. His program was characterized by social egalitarianism. The symbolic means for achieving this goal was by offering "open commensality" through his mission command. That is, when the disciples entered into a village and were to eat whatever was set before them, they were participating in a revolutionary act that was meant to change society because they were participating symbolically in a table that had no boundaries.[72]

Crossan's reference to the theme of social egalitarianism in the original preaching of Jesus, such as in the parable of the Great Feast, is a strong point.[73] But when he links it to an actual symbolic meal, particularly a meal in which the ones receiving the benefits are the ones acting as hosts, his thesis begins to lose contact with historical probability and to take on the form of literary idealization. First, in order that open commensality – which Crossan defines as social egalitarianism at the table- – could be experienced, there must be significant social stratification involved. Yet Crossan envisions Jesus and his hearers as all being part of the peasant class. Though he and his disciples would come as "magicians" who "share a miracle" they remain part of the same peasant class.[74] The strongest evidence for the open commensality theme in the Jesus tradition is the theme that Jesus dined with tax collectors and sinners. Yet, this theme only works best if Jesus is not of the same social class with tax collectors and sinners. If all parties involved, including Jesus, are peasants, then the motif fails, for

[71] See Crossan, *The Historical Jesus*, 339. Compare Mack's (*The Lost Gospel*, 129) interpretation of this same text: "Behavior is spelled out in terms of conventional rules of hospitality: Eat what they provide; do not offend the host by accepting another's hospitality and going on to another house."

[72] See Crossan, *The Historical Jesus*, 341-44.

[73] See especially ibid., 260-64.

[74] Ibid., 304-10, 341.

there is no experience of social stratification at table.[75]

Consequently, while Crossan has made a strong argument for a theme of social egalitarianism in the preaching of Jesus, I think he has weakened his case by making Jesus into a peasant. Furthermore, his view that Jesus had a "social program" to offer social egalitarianism to all by means of sharing open commensality at the table, a program which was initiated by Jesus and his disciples arriving on the scene as itinerants without food – this makes for a wonderful folktale but becomes difficult to picture in actual practice.

IV. Conclusions

This study has found that none of the texts in which Jesus teaches by means of his table customs can be unambiguously affirmed as historical. Neither can it be affirmed that the cumulative effect of all these references implies a historical core because one can explain the development of all these traditions merely by reference to existing oral and literary motifs. It is not necessary in order to explain these texts to posit that Jesus made use of meals in his overall teaching program.

On the other hand, it must be admitted that all of the characteristics of meals utilized in these texts are historically and socially valid. It *is* the case that meals defined community boundaries and, particularly in certain Jewish and Christian literary traditions, carried implications of the messianic kingdom. These factors are part of the function of meals among various social groups in the ancient world and were adopted into the myth and ritual of the early Christian communities. Accordingly, these texts certainly represent social reality. The question is where that social reality is to be located.

My argument is that what is being identified as the historical

[75] Note that one of Crossan's crucial texts for the social egalitarian commensality of Jesus, that of the parable of the Great Feast, is one in which social stratification plays a central role, in as much as the one who invites those of the streets to the feast is a person of means who possesses a home and servants (*SP* 12 [Matt. 22:2-13 = Luke 14:16b-23 = *Gos. Thom.* 64:1]). Crossan does not reference this feature in his reconstruction, however. See *The Historical Jesus*, 261-62.

Jesus at table is more likely to be the idealized characterization of Jesus at table produced in and by the early Christian community. The social realities of such meals are still being correctly assessed, but the one who presents parabolic messages by means of meal practices is more likely to be the idealized Jesus than the historical one. And the social realities defined by these meals, in which table fellowship is equated with a new community self-consciousness, are more likely those of an already developing early Christian community than those of the motley crowds who came to hear Jesus teach.

On the other hand, it is likely that there is some consistency between these traditions and the historical figure of Jesus. It is quite likely, for example, that Jesus was known to have chosen a lifestyle different from the monastic style of John and that Jesus' lifestyle was understood to be consistent with the tenor of his teachings as a whole. Consequently, since the ministry of Jesus was seen early on to function in tandem with that of John, Jesus' positive attitude toward attending banquets easily could have been interpreted as an intentional expression of a parabolic message.

In the context of Jesus' ministry as we might reasonably imagine it, such actions would not likely be able to convey the offering of "his kingdom" to those with whom he dined, for then he would have to be one who actually hosted all of the banquets he attended. That would make him much more of a stationary figure, namely, a homeowner, than we normally picture him to be. Rather, the meaning conveyed by Jesus' partaking of banquets would be that of one who, in contrast to John, existed in the urban world and affirmed that world.[76] Indeed, it is not too big a leap to see Jesus' preference for urban living developing into the idea that he preferred the company of persons of dubious character. Out of this context at some point the label "glutton and drunkard, friend [table-companion] of tax collectors and sinners" readily could have developed. But it is a characterization that does not derive from any specific use by Jesus of table fellowship as a mode of proclamation.

---

[76] Against Crossan, *The Historical Jesus*, 340: "Jesus, however, is establishing a rural rather than an urban mission."

PANTA KOINA: THE FEEDING STORIES IN THE LIGHT OF ECONOMIC DATA AND SOCIAL PRACTICE[1]

Richard I. Pervo
(Seabury-Western Theological Seminary, Evanston, Illinois)

Dieter Georgi has continually raised provocative questions about the interface between ideological formulations and their social and economic contexts. The following, essentially descriptive, essay would honor him by probing aspects of the miraculous feeding stories of the gospel tradition.[2]

Food Fights

I begin, however, not with feeding miracles of the usual sort but with food fights. In the bourgeois tradition (with the general support of Greco-Roman antiquity) it is presumed that fighting at and about meals is indecorous. On this point the New Testament is ambiguous.

1. Corinth according to Paul (1 Cor 11:17-34)

In 1 Cor 11:20-21 Paul, who here, as often, aligns himself with that aspect of conventional morality that treasures decorum, writes: "When you come together,[3] it is not really to eat the Lord's supper (κυριακὸν δεῖπνον). For when the time comes to eat, each of you goes ahead with your own supper (ἴδιον δεῖπνον), and one goes hungry and another becomes drunk."[4]

---

[1] For those who worked with him at Harvard, Dieter Georgi was a difficult and extraordinary teacher: extraordinary because of his respect for his students, difficult for the same reason. With his fertile, creative, and informed intelligence he always kept us off balance by leaping across apparently unfathomable chasms and pointing to dimensions we never had seen. This essay appeared in preliminary form in a paper read at the Midwest Regional meeting of the Society of Biblical Literature, Evanston, Illinois, 11 January 1989. I am most grateful to Robert Jewett for his assistance.

[2] These include, in particular, Mark 6:32-44 parr., John 6:1-15, Mark 8:1-10 parr., Luke 24:13-35, John 2:1-11; 21:1-14, and *Acts of John* 93.

[3] Note the frequency of συνέρχομαι in 1 Cor 11-14: 11:17, 18, 20, 33, 34, and 14:23.

[4] Unless otherwise indicated, English translations follow the *New Revised Standard Version*.

This presents a conflict, as modern scholarship has recognized, particularly since the work of J. Weiss and H. von Soden,[5] between two spheres, the sacramental and the social. The conflict is one of the earliest known instances of that enduring tension between the eschatological/utopian/sacramental realm and the life of believers in human societies. Among its many dimensions are the questions of whether the Christian community is to find its model in an ideal (or conventional) *polis* or an ideal (or conventional) *oikos*, or in some manifestation that rejects both. The first two positions find support in the pauline (and deutero-pauline) literature; the third underlies at least some strands of the Gospel tradition, especially "Q." Since the ancient intellectual tradition tended to envision the *oikos* as a microcosm of the *polis*, and the latter as a microcosm of the *cosmos*, confusion was inevitable.[6]

1 Cor 11-14 illustrates this confusion profusely. If 1 Cor 12:12-27 is the most famous pauline example of the *polis*-model, with its image of the church as a body,[7] 1 Cor 11 treats the boundaries between (private) home and house-church.[8] Is the eucharist a "community meal" with (naturally for antiquity) religious elements, a family gathering with equally natural

---

[5] Johannes Weiss, *The History of Primitive Christianity* (trans. Frederick Grant *et al.*; New York: Wilson-Erickson, 1937) 2, 648-89, and Hans von Soden, "Sacrament und Ethik bei Paulus," which first appeared in 1931 in the Rudolf Otto *Festschrift*, but is more conveniently available in his *Urchristentum und Geschichte* (Tübingen: Mohr-Siebeck, 1951) 239-75, and Karl H. Rengstorf, ed., *Das Paulusbild in der neueren deutschen Forschung* (Darmstadt: Wissenschaftliche Buchgesellschaft, 1964) 338-79.

[6] Plato (*Respublica*) is an early representative, but see Aristotle *Pol.* 1, 125A 7.9, for another view. A relevant example is the discussion by Plutarch's Seven Sages of the governance of states, households, and the universe (*Sept. Sap. Conv.* 6-21 = Plutarch *Moralia* 150F-164D).

[7] See the various commentaries, for example Hans Conzelmann, *1 Corinthians: A Commentary on the First Epistle to the Corinthians* (trans. ed. George W. MacRae, S.J.; *Hermeneia*; Philadelphia: Fortress, 1975 [= *Der erste Brief an die Korinther. MeyerK.* 11 (Göttingen: Vandenhoeck & Ruprecht, 1969)]) 211, as well as Robert Grant, *Early Christianity and Society* (San Francisco: Harper & Row, 1977) 36-37 and 170.

[8] 1 Cor 11:2-16 evidences a similar clash of boundaries. From one perspective the assembly could be described as an intimate domestic situation in which people could "let their hair down." Paul appeals to public standards regarding the hair-styles of women (and men). Note also his appeal to impressions upon "outsiders" in 14:23-24. Chs. 5-8 deal with other boundary difficulties, in particular those between church and world, summarized sarcastically in 5:10.

religious elements, or a *symposium* of social equals to which others are invited "after dinner"[9] for a (sacral) "snack"? Stated theologically, is the eucharist to be a kind of heavenly banquet in the here and now or an essentially "symbolic" meal not intended to alleviate hunger? Those among the οὐ πολλοί who were wise, powerful, and well-born would have tended to offer an answer at variance from the response of the more numerous[10] "poor."

Paul's own account of the "Institution Narrative" (1 Cor 11:23-26) lacks references to both οἱ πολλοί and a heavenly banquet.[11] Unity and sharing (κοινωνία) emerge through transcendence of, rather than through abolition of, social differences. The apostle does not aspire to convince the "strong" to abandon their social lives and ideals so much as not to flaunt them in the presence of their "weaker" sisters and brothers. In response to the question of "meat offered to idols" (1 Cor 8; 10:23-11:1) Paul's argument goes all the way around Robin Hood's barn before concluding, in effect, that it is often acceptable to be "strong" so long as there are no "weak" present. This attitude would stimulate those of the appropriate social levels to keep their participation in *symposia* separate from life in the church.

As 1 Cor 10:1-22 indicates, however, the question is more difficult when the cultic character of a meal more nearly approaches that which Christians of a later time would call a "sacrament." 1 Cor 11:17-34 deals with such a meal. Paul's fundamental tool for management of this conflict is social differentiation: the "haves" are to do their banqueting at home.[12] G. Theissen[13] has emphasized that the behavioral differences

---

[9] 1 Cor 11:25.

[10] Note ὑπὲρ πολλῶν in Mark 14:24.

[11] 1 Cor 11:26 limits the celebration of the eucharist to the present age, in obvious contrast with Luke 22:16-18. It is "an institution for the age of the church from the resurrection of Christ to his parousia," Conzelmann, *1 Corinthians,* 202.

[12] 1 Cor 11:22a can be answered affirmatively only by some. The final τοὺς μὴ ἔχοντας; usually is translated as "those who have nothing." In the context one might supply οἰκίας as object. 11:34a would sound equally insensitive to those who could not control the quantity or quality of their meals. For the point of view see the comment of Augustus, according to Quintilian 6.3.63, who, when disturbed by the sight of *equites* drinking at the games, said: *Ego, si prandere volo, domum eo.*

[13] Gerd Theissen "Social Integration and Sacramental Activity: An Analysis of 1 Cor 11:17-34," in *The Social Setting of Pauline Christianity* (trans.

relate to social distinctions. Those hungry were poor; the rich were drunk. Even under the most luxurious circumstances conceivable – a free-standing villa with a dining-room that would recline at most two, possibly three, dozen on couches – the less privileged would be compelled to sit[14] about on the floor or in the *atrium* space, like clients attending their betters.[15] Paul thus seeks to reduce social tensions in the assembly by allocating their more blatant manifestations to private contexts. He does not, for example, issue a forthright call for more equitable distribution – in this context.[16]

1 Cor 11:21b contrasts the hungry not with the sated but with those who are drunk. One may (with an eye to 1 Cor. 10: 1-22 and across a vast social gap) presume that the problem is

ed. John H. Schütz; Philadelphia: Fortress, 1982) 145-74 (= "Soziale Integration und sakramentales Handeln: Eine Analyse von 1 Cor 11,17-34," *NovTest* 16 [1974] 179-206).

[14] Sitting at dinner was a mark of social inferiority. Jerome Carcopino, *Daily Life in Ancient Rome* (trans. Earnest O. Lorimer; New York: Bantam, 1971) 302: says "[The Romans]...considered the reclining position indispensable to their physical comfort, but also a mark of elegance and of social distinction." One feature of "the good old days" was the posture of women at dinner: seated at their husbands' feet (Val. Max. 2.1.2). When they were promoted to the *triclinia*, children sat on stools before their parents (Suetonius *Claud.* 32, cf. Tacitus *Ann.* 13.16) as did, of course, slaves, except on holidays (Columella *De Re rust.* 11.10). In response to the victory of Julius Caesar the younger Cato vowed to eat seated so long as the tyrant ruled (Plutarch *Cato Minor* 56). If Gauls and the like also ate seated (for refs. see Carcopino, n.121, 365), that was no more than one might expect of unenlightened yokels, and sitting to eat was one of the hardships of travelers forced to resort to taverns (Martial 5.70, supported by wall-paintings from Pompeii).

[15] Relatively few first-century believers would have had access to free-standing villas. As far as houses are concerned, Mark 2:1-2, which depicts a crowd pressing around an open door, is probably more like the norm. In the large cities tenements of the *insula*-type were the likely sites of most assemblies. At Corinth, however, some believers did have houses, even if these were not elegant villas. Plutarch discusses the problem of space in *Quest. Conv.* 5.5, 678C.

[16] Gal 6:6, which deals with the support of community leaders, is quite forthright. Theissen (*Social Setting*, 164) observes that "It would be much more consistent with the idea of community to demand that this 'private meal' be shared." He regards the solution he finds as a manifestation of "patriarchalism modified by love" (Liebespatriarchalismus). Peter Lampe, in an important article ("Das korinthische Herrenmahl im Schnittpunkt hellenistisch-romischer Mahlpraxis und paulinischer Theologia Crucis [1Kor 11,17-34]," *ZNW* 82 [1990-91] 183-213, 204) argues, against Theissen, that Paul does wish a nourishing meal to be served. If that is Paul's wish, his directions are not explicit.

sacrilege, but Paul, who is not unwilling to condemn such actions vigorously,[17] does not so label it. The fact is that some lack a decent meal while others have enjoyed the experience of a *symposium.*

Symposia

The description of the worship assembly at Corinth in 1 Cor 11-14 would strike ancients as an account of an unruly *symposium,* as recent research has demonstrated.[18] Since all formal meals, "pagan" no less than Jewish,[19] included religious elements, one should not seek strict delineations between sacred and secular banquets. The basic procedure is summarized easily: first they ate and then they drank. The dinner proper (*cena*/δεῖπνον[20]), which began with a "grace" invoking the gods, and included a relatively small company, was followed by a transition, during which the tables were removed, ointment and garlands might be distributed, after which, following libations and a hymn, there was drinking and entertainment, including music, conversation, the reading of a new or familiar work, and various "desserts." The latter, *secundae mensae*/ δευτέραι τράπεζαι constituted the *symposium* proper. After dinner additional guests might appear, including those of a lower social standing. Like Paul, the ancient authorities discussed

[17] Cf. 1 Cor 5-6.

[18] See Dennis E. Smith, "Social Obligation in the Context of Communal Meals: A Study of the Christian Meal in 1 Corinthians in Comparison with Graeco-Roman Communal Meals" (Diss., Harvard University, 1980); David Aune, "*Septem Sapientium Convivium* (*Moralia* 146B-164D)" in Hans Dieter Betz, ed., *Plutarch's Ethical Writings and Early Christian Literature* (*SCHNT* 4; Leiden: E.J. Brill, 1978) 51-105, esp. 74-78; and Lampe, "Das korinthische Herrenmahl," esp. 185-203. Primary sources include not only the classical *symposia* of Plato and Xenophon but also Plutarch's *Quest. Conv., Sept. Sap. Conv.*; Athenaeus's *Deipnosophistae*, and Aulus Gellius *Noctes Atticae.* Comparison exists on two levels, both legitimate, but in need of distinction: A) the "Symposium" as a *literary* form, in which the banquet establishes a framework for a dialogue, and B) the social practice of dinner parties (at which, for instance, too much philosophy was seen as a bit of a bore. See Dio of Prusa *Or.* 10.27.2-3, Lucian *De Parasito* 51, and Plutarch, *Quest. Conv.* 1.1.; 2.10-11).

[19] The Passover *Seder* constitutes the best modern survival of a Greco-Roman *symposium.* New Testament scholars give little notice to the rules for Christian *symposia* set forth in Hippolytus *Apostolic Tradition,* chs. 23-33 (Botte).

[20] Paul's term thus implies a full meal.

guest-lists, menu, manners, and suitable types of entertainment and conversation. They, like Paul, could dread the possibility of disorder.[21]

Comic writers have served up a rich menu of unruly *symposia* to assist exegetes of 1 Corinthians. Trimalchio's banquet[22] is but the most famous arrangement. The *Symposium* of Lucian, which describes a chaotic wedding reception rent by strife among αἱρέσεις (cf. 1 Cor 11:19), may provide the most interesting parallels. His wayward philosophers, who do not practice what they preach, engage in many forms of intellectual and sexual excess while exhibiting greed and boorishness. They fight about seating arrangements,[23] engage in simultaneous and exhibitionistic performances,[24] and disagree about the distribution of portions.[25] When, in due course, the lamp is knocked over, the polemic takes on familiar tones. Acts 23:1-6 portrays such a brawl between factions, who happen to be Jewish. Christians settle their disputes in admirable fashion.[26] Philo gives another view by contrasting the observance of Yom Kippur with pagan *symposia.*[27] Other instructive tales of dinner parties done or gone wrong include Horace *Sat.* 2.8 and Juvenal *Sat.* 5.[28]

The New Testament has some unruly *symposia* of its own, in particular the various accounts of the "Last Supper" and the great counter-Messianic banquet held by "King" Herod to celebrate his birth (Mark 6:17-29). The entertainment for that gathering of the elite[29] included a "dancing girl" of royal

---

[21] Paul summarizes his program in 1 Cor 14:40. For congenial sentiment in antiquity see Aune, *Septem Sapientium Convivium,* 73. Plutarch provides a sound summary of opinion: "...if ignorance and lack of culture keep company with wine, not even that famous golden lamp of Athena could make the party refined and orderly...the outcome of undisciplined chatter and frivolity, when it reaches the extreme of intemperance, is violence and drunken behavior – an outcome wholly inconsistent with culture and refinement." (*Quest. Conv.* 8, 716D-E [trans. Earnest L. Minar *et al.*; LCL 9; Cambridge: Harvard University Press, 1969] 109.)

[22] Petronius *Satyricon* 26-78.

[23] 9; cf. Luke 14:7-14.

[24] Cf. 1 Cor 12-14.

[25] 42-43.

[26] Most notably in Acts 15. On Acts 6:1-7 see pages 170-71 below.

[27] *Spec. Leg.* 2.193.

[28] There is general agreement that the later Greek and Latin authors depend upon Hellenistic (and earlier) antecedents.

[29] Mark 6:21.

blood.[30] The most notable dessert (δευτέραι τραπέζει) offering was the head of John the Baptist on a proper platter. Trimalchio's banquet is an upper-class send-up of the manners of the *nouveaux riches.* Herod's banquet is a lower-class parody of the manners of *les Aristos.* Because of its obvious ties with the Passion of Jesus and links to the surrounding material, the passage makes an important statement about meals.[31]

Private or Dominical Meal?

In 1 Cor 11:17-34, Paul contrasts two types or understandings of the meal (δεῖπνον): κυριακόν and ἴδιον, private *versus* dominical. How is κυριακόν to be understood? A more customary opposition pits ἴδιον against κοινόν, the personal or private *versus* that which is common or shared, or, in political terms, private *versus* public, the personal sphere in contrast with the realm of the social group, including the *polis* or *res publica.* The term under discussion in 1 Corinthians is an activity also called κοινωνία, sharing, communion. My thesis is that one understanding of κυριακόν in early Christianity linked it to κοινόν. To separate food (*et al.*) from personal use (ἴδιον) and transform it into dominical use was also to make it available to the community, κοινόν.

For support I appeal both to the governmental sphere, where the contrast between ἴδιος and κυριακός is explicit,[32] as

---

[30] Mark 6:22 is a piece of scandalous "lower-class" gossip about the behavior of the gentry, such as fills the tabloids of today. When Fortunata, the wife of Trimalchio, is induced to perform a *cordax* (*Satyricon* 52), the true characters of host and hostess come to light. Dancers at *symposia* were not of the aristocracy. In the empire Spanish dancers were much admired (Martial 5.78, 26-28; Juvenal *Sat.* 11. 162-164, probably dependent upon Martial. Both assure prospective guests that *their* dinners will not include such dancers). People like the younger Pliny disapproved of such entertainment (*Epist.* 9.17). See also Louis Ginsberg, *Legends of the Jews* (7 vols.; New York: Jewish Publication Society, 1928) 6. 455, nn. 31-35.

[31] The Feeding of the Five Thousand follows, then conversation about the loaf, purity regulations, and the encounter with the Syro-Phoenician woman, which uses imagery evocative of the feeding (Mark 7:27-28, note τράπεζα). Note also the associations with "Jairus' Daughter," a κοράσιον like the daughter of Herodias (Mark 5:41; 6:22), who is to be fed (Mark 5:43).

[32] See Adolf Deissmann, *Bible Studies* (trans. Andrew Grieve; Edinburgh: T & T Clark, 1901) 217-18 (= *Neue Bibelstudien* 44), who cites *OGIS* 669 (= *CIG* 4957.18) of T. Julius Alexander (Egypt 68 CE), and the following papyri: *Berlinische griechische Urkunden* 1. 15-16 (Egypt III CE), *Berlinische grie-*

well as to Acts 2:42-47, which contains a famous description of early Christian utopian life.[33] This passage affirms that all the believers devoted themselves eagerly to "κοινωνία, the breaking of bread, and the prayers." Does the text intend to denote three activities or one? The sequel includes signs and wonders, miracles, in short. One of the more noteworthy miracles was the refusal to regard anything as ἴδιον but hold all in common. The faithful liquidated their holdings and placed the proceeds at the apostles' feet for distribution. In this account the vexing tension between ἴδιον and κοινόν is wondrously resolved through the power of the κύριος. Between these circumstances and early Christian life at Corinth there is some tension. It also appears that the solution to economic inequity described in Acts is at variance with the proposals advanced by Paul.

2. *Jerusalem according to Luke (Acts 6:1-7)*

The aggrieved group here is the "Hellenist Widows." Distribution is once more the problem. The author envisions two groups (the intended constituency of which remains disputed) that had evidently contributed money to a common fund. Members of one of these groups evidently claimed that they were not receiving a fair share of the proceeds. The text does not speak of an antiseptic cash dole, but actual daily meals, concretely depicted: διακονεῖν τραπέζαις (vv. 1-2).[34] Acts 2:46 (καθ' ἡμέραν...κλῶντές τε κατ' οἶκον ἄρτον, μετελάμβανον τροφῆς ἐν ἀγαλλιάσει καὶ ἀφελότητι καρδίας) aptly confounds efforts to make nice distinctions between sacrament and nourishment. The complainants are marginal: poor, female, lacking male

chische Urkunden 266.17-18 (216-217 CE), and the following inscriptions from imperial Asia Minor: *CIG* 3919 (Hierapolis), *CIG* 3953 (Phyrgia), *CIG* 2842 (Aphrodisias), and *CIG* 3490 (Thyatira). In his *Light from the Ancient East* (trans Lionel R.M. Strachan; New York: Harper and Brothers, 1927) 357-58, Deissmann provides further discussion and a photograph of *OGIS* 669. *LSJM* add *CIG* 2827 (Aphrodisias), *SEG* 2.567 (Caria), both of the imperial era, and *POxy*. 474.41, (Egypt, II CE).

[33] For further discussion of utopian ideals, see pages 175-78 below. A summary of the affinities between Acts 2 and 4 and ancient utopias may be found in Richard Pervo *Profit with Delight* (Philadelphia: Fortress, 1987) 69-70.

[34] To read this as an avoidance of socially demeaning action by the "apostles" is misleading. See Luke 17:7-10. τράπεζα has a religious function in formal meals. Cf. Plutarch *Sept. Sap. Conv.* 158C (= *Moralia*, and cf. Mark 7:28; 11:15; 1 Cor 10:21).

protection, and (presumably) representatives of a linguistic/ ethnic minority. This is by no means the last time that ancient Christian leaders would have to manage conflict related to widows,[35] nor would the subject of distribution cease to be an issue.[36]

These two disputes, one apparently sacramental, the other usually deemed to reflect the breakdown of a welfare system,[37] are introduced as reminders that those who recorded, heard, and recited the feeding stories (which, if not known in Corinth in the 50's were certainly familiar to the readers of Acts) also were liable to be engaged in fights over food. The first (in narrative sequence) "apostles" who sought to evade responsibility for "waiting on tables" were the disciples who urged their impractical master to cut short his preaching mission so that his listeners could be dispatched to buy dinner. They appear experienced enough at the business to provide an estimate of the cost of such a meal.[38] Who is likely to be responsible for a story in which leaders, who are made to appear blind or dull, advance the hackneyed argument "We'd like to help you, but the expense would be too great"? The

---

[35] Bonnie Bowman Thurston, *The Widows: A Women's Ministry in the Early Church* (Fortress: Minneapolis, 1989), assembles somewhat uncritically (see ATR 73 [1991] 332-33) a collection of evidence mainly from "orthodox" sources. Robert M. Price, "*The Widow Traditions in Luke-Acts: A Feminist-Critical Scrutiny*" (Diss., Drew University, 1993) 313-19, considers a variety of texts. See also Richard Pervo "Aseneth and Her Sisters: Women in Jewish Narrative and in the Greek Novels," in Amy-Jill Levine, ed. "*Women like This": New Perspectives on Jewish Women in the Greco-Roman World* (Atlanta: Scholars Press, 1991) 155-160. Acts 9:36-43 includes the story of Tabitha, a relatively well-to-do single woman, who enabled a number of widows to achieve economic security. 2 Tim 5:3-16, which discusses support for widows from common funds, stands in temporal and spatial proximity to Luke-Acts and shows that criteria for eligibility was a contemporary problem. It is possible that Luke has retrojected this into the past, recast in terms of an incipient Jewish-gentile rift, to introduce the ministry of the Seven. (See Dieter Georgi, *The Opponents of Paul in Second Corinthians* [Philadelphia: Fortress, 1986] 27-32, 168).

[36] The problems of distribution from a common purse are widespread: John 13:29; 2 Thess 3:10; Polycarp *Phil.* 11; and *The Shepherd of Hermas* (*Similitude* 9.26.2), which has some unkind things to say about those responsible for distribution (In both Acts and *Hermas* the verb is διακονεῖν.)

[37] This "failure" has been manna from heaven to opponents of socialism, communism, and welfare states.

[38] The Feeding of the Five Thousand (Mark 6:36-37). In John 6:7 Philip is the sole accountant.

viewpoint is certainly not that of leaders struggling with limited funds.

Those who regard strife during dinner as rather "unchristian" would do well not to read the Gospels. "Meals in Mark are nearly always controversial affairs"[39] – to which one may add Matthew through Revelation. Specifically marcan examples in support of this assertion begin in chapter 2 (vv. 15-17, 18-19, 23-28) and continue through through the Last Supper (14:17-25). Karris' list of references to food and eating in Luke fills two pages.[40] Matters in contention include who gets to eat, with whom one eats, what, how much, and in which state of purity.[41] The feeding stories were not recited in circumstances very far-removed from such disputes. I wish to shed some light upon them by means of reference to ancient utopian notions and to actual social practice, with the object of viewing these stories as utopian/eschatological/sacramental presentations of the civic/communal meal as it ought to be, under the presidency of the great κύριος.

FEEDING STORIES: PRELIMINARY REMARKS ON FORM AND FUNCTION

The feeding stories were once included with other so-called "Nature Miracles."[42] For the purpose of classification this term is of limited value. "Nature" also plays a role in the physiological dimension of healings, for example, and antiquity did

[39] Robert M. Fowler, *Loaves and Fishes: The Function of the Feeding Stories in the Gospel of Mark* (SBLDS 54; Chico, CA: 1981) 132.

[40] Robert J. Karris, *Luke: Artist and Theologian* (New York: Paulist, 1985) 49-51.

[41] Purity issues have economic implications. "Beggars cannot be choosers" (including begging missionaries, Luke 10:8, *Gos. Thom.* 14). Moreover, maintenance of ritual purity was more difficult for the poor, who thereby could be excluded from invitations as "unclean." *Kosher* food, for example, could be more expensive. The "unclean" might only hope to compete with animals for crumbs falling from the masters' tables (Mark 7:28). The prohibition of εἰδωλόθυτα (Acts 15:29, 21:25; Rev 2:14, 20; *Didache* 6:3, Justin, *Dial.* 34.8-35.1; Irenaeus *Adv. Haer.* 1.6,3; 24,5; 26,3; 28,2) cut against rich and poor in different ways. As Theissen noted ("The Strong and the Weak in Corinth," in *Social Setting* 125-28 [= Die Starken und Schwachen, *EvTh* 35 (1975) 155-72]), many of the urban poor experienced meat mainly in connection with public (i.e., religious) holidays. This prohibition, therefore, would largely eliminate meat from their diets. For the more well-off the ban would place limits upon their social lives.

[42] This is the category of Rudolf Bultmann, *The History of the Synoptic Tradition* (trans. J. Marsh; New York: Harper & Row, 1968) 215-18.

not possess a uniform notion of "nature" (or "laws of nature") to set over against "miracle."[43] Theissen prefers the term "Gift Miracles." He relates the feeding stories to material culture rather than to nature.[44] I believe that his classification represents an illuminating advance. By focusing upon the "presenting problem," i.e., shortage of food, Theissen's category opens the path to exploration of social contexts.

The connection between these stories and the eucharist generally is recognized – or at least viewed as probable enough to require refutation.[45] Researchers are, in fact, increasingly inclined to regard all NT references to eating in the light of their possible implications for sacramental doctrine and practice, and *vice-versa.* I presume that a connection does exist and seek to explore the meaning of the eucharist in the light of the feeding stories rather than view them in tension with a *theologia crucis.*[46]

Following Theissen, I concentrate upon the role of the feeding and related stories as means for *legitimation and motivation in conflict situations.* Miracles are, so to speak, a particular requirement for "new gods," missionary deities freshly proclaimed, who often accredit themselves and gain renown by performing services that established gods may seem to neglect. Miracle stories reflect the shattering of old boundaries and the creation of new realms. They are phenomena accompanying the advent of a new religious perspective. Miracles enlarge, as it were, the *pomerium* of the heavenly city. Thus the dissolution of the barrier between Jews and gentiles in Acts 10-11 emerges among visions and spiritual manifestations, for it is no less a miracle in lucan terms (and pauline, for that matter) than would be the healing of an incapacitated individual or the exorcism of an obnoxious demon.

---

[43] On the subject see Mikeal Parsons and Richard Pervo, *Rethinking the Unity of Luke and Acts* (Minneapolis: Fortress, 1993) 94-101.

[44] Gerd Theissen, *The Miracle Stories of the Early Christian Tradition* (trans. John Riches; Philadelphia: Fortress, 1983) 45, 52, 55-56, 67, 103-106.

[45] Note in particular the presence in the feeding stories of the characteristic "four-fold" action of taking, blessing, breaking and sharing, which gives shape to the eucharist. Those who reject a connection between the feeding accounts and the eucharist tend to view the eucharistic theologies of Mark and Paul as normative.

[46] The approach taken here does not deny the presence of such a tension.

"Rule Miracles,"[47] extraordinary phenomena that shatter an existing principle or establish a new law, make explicit one function of miracle in conflict management.[48] To state it in another way: miracles may be one means by which God communicates or ratifies rule changes, so to speak.[49] Miracle is, among other things, a powerful instrument for the authorization and promulgation of change in religious or social behavior. Focus upon questions raised by science, reason, or "theologies of glory" has its value, but tends to obscure some original functions.

The New Testament miracle stories, not surprisingly, often respond to problems experienced chiefly or more intensely by those of the lower social orders. They actualize the declarations of the Beatitudes, bringing relief to those who are poor, oppressed, hungry, or in mourning. Comparison with the Beatitudes serves to emphasize that these stories nearly always possess some eschatological or utopian element, however tenuous, individualized, or spiritualized this may have become in the history of tradition or interpretation.

The same may be said of sacraments, a correlation important in the present context. Sacraments, which likewise smash old boundaries and create new spheres of existence, challenge social margins and propose utopian solutions to social conflicts. They have therefore been the bases for forging Christian unity and institutionalizing or domesticating conflict. The best-known New Testament examples of the latter are the conflicts around the eucharist in 1 Cor 11:17-34 and the debate about sex roles in 1 Cor 11:2-16 (apparently motivated by a baptismal declaration like that of Gal 3:26-28). These disputes arose from the acute tensions between the eschatological condition bestowed in the sacraments and the social realities of temporal existence.

[47] "Rule Miracles" are another of Theissen's thematic classifications; see his *Miracle Stories* 45, 105-12, 114-16, 118, and 283.

[48] The number of Sabbath healings in this class indicates that the type flourished in a period of tension with Judaism.

[49] On this point emergent Christianity and nascent rabbinic Judaism took opposing positions. The latter is typified in *b. B. Me.* 59b, where the miracles of R. Eliezer are rejected as evidence for his views. See Albert Guttmann, "The Significance of Miracles for Talmudic Judaism," *HUCA* 20 (1947) 363-406.

Utopia

Utopianism is a phenomenon no less complex and elusive of definition than is apocalypticism. If utopias are to be viewed as projections, such as miracles in the critical estimate of Ludwig Feuerbach and the more sympathetic appreciation of Ernst Bloch, utopias certainly are projections with a purpose.[50] Serious utopias, like apocalypses, strive to depict new symbolic universes. Paul Ricoeur's paradigm provides a tool for more precise analysis from both a functionalist and a conflict orientation. Ricoeur posits three types of correlations between ideology and utopia:[51]

1. Only where and when ideology becomes distortion do utopian concepts become fancy, madness, or escape.
2. Where ideology seeks legitimation, utopian concepts lay down a challenge to authority.
3. When ideology involves integration, utopias explore what is possible, with the intention of changing the present order.

Examples of each type can be illustrated in the Hellenistic and Roman eras. The composition of philosophical "Republics" had become a venerable project. Aristophanes already found it a fit subject for parody.[52] The geographical advances of the Hellenistic period stimulated stories of ideal societies discovered in the course of voyages.[53] Lucian in turn found *them* a fit subject for parody.[54] One of the most famous utopian novelists, Euhemerus of Messene, was in the service of Cassander.[55] Euhemerus' (mostly lost) work can be correlated

---

[50] Oscar Wilde: "A map of the world that does not include Utopia is not worth even looking at," according to Moses I. Finley, "Utopianism Ancient and Modern," in Kurt Wolff and Barrington Moore, Jr., eds., The *Critical Spirit* (Boston: Beacon, 1967) 3-20, cited by Finley on page 3.

[51] Paul Ricoeur, *Lectures on Ideology and Utopia* (New York: Columbia University Press, 1986).

[52] *Eccl.*, which terminates with a riot mocking the sexual ideas of utopians rather with than a *hieros gamos.*

[53] See the references in Richard Pervo, *Profit with Delight*, 162-63. The survey of Erwin Rohde, *Der griechische Roman und seine Vorläufer* (Hildesheim: Georg Ohlms, 1974) 167-287 is still valuable. See also John Ferguson, *Utopias of the Classical World* (London: Thames and Hudson, 1975).

[54] See the quotation on pages 179-80 below from Lucian's *Vera Historia.*

[55] Cassander (c. 358-297 BCE) was the founder of a famous New Testament city, Thessalonica, and the fond object of Peripatetic admiration as the executioner of Alexander's mother, widow, and son.

with his master's program[56] and thus ascribed an integrative function.

Rather the same could be said of that hearty stream of imperial propaganda that, in poems,[57] coins,[58] and art,[59] celebrated the return of the Golden Age. Modern estimates take their shape from current evaluations of the period in question and the cynicism of individual critics, who tend to understand efforts of the period from Nerva to Marcus as instances of Ricoeur's third category, while placing in the foremost one the products of the later Empire. Such judgments are not entirely without merit, but there is a need for caution.

By logical contrast much[60] of the utopian literature and thought of nascent Judaism and Christianity belongs to the second category, in which ideology aims at legitimation and utopias exist to challenge the *status quo.* To reiterate, utopias are a type of symbolic universe set up in opposition or contrast to the phenomenal universe. Sharp divisions between "Greco-

---

[56] This is the thesis of Heinrich Dörrie, *Der Königskult des Antiochus von Kommagene im Lichte neuer Inschriften-Funde* (Göttingen: Vandenhoeck & Ruprecht, 1954) 219-23.

[57] For a survey of the theme in Augustan poets alone see Lucien Cerfaux and Jean Tondriau, *Le culte des souverans* (Paris: Desclée, 1957) 332-34. Claudian *In Rufinum* 1.372-387 shows the endurance of the imagery at the end of fourth century.

[58] An outstanding example is the obverse of a Denarius issued under Hadrian, *Coins of the Roman Empire in the British Museum* (London: British Museum Coins Publications Limited, 1976) 3.312 (Plate 52, no. 10); *Roman Imperial Coinage* (London: Spink, 1972) 2.136. The legend begins SAEC AUR. Hadrian is depicted within a golden frame as the spirit of the Golden Age, standing upright, holding a phoenix on a globe. Other examples are illustrated in Jean Beaujeu, *La Religion romaine à l'époque de l'empire,* vol. 1: *La Politique religieuse des antonins* (Paris: Desclee, 1955), Plates 5 and 7. Such legends as FELICITAS TEMP, FELICITAS SAEC are common on imperial coinage from the end of the first century CE, as are symbols like the cornucopia. Popular types include *Annona, Abundantia,* and *Liberalitas. Aequitas,* more or less identical with *Moneta,* who appears with her scales in hand, is another relevant type.

[59] An outstanding portrayal of utopian themes in plastic art is the *Ara Pacis Augustae,* with its scrolls in the form of Golden Age vegetation, swans (Apollo's birds, in effect a reference to Virgil's *Fourth Eclogue*), and reliefs on the front side portraying the primeval glory of Romulus and Remus together with Tellus, who exudes the fertility of the Golden Age.

[60] Much is not all. The utopian aspects of Luke-Acts seek to integrate "church" with Empire and to reform both. Philo's various utopian descriptions of Jewish life, such as *Praem. Poen.* 101-103, 168; *Congr.* 173; *Vit. Mos.* 2.267; and his portrait of the Therapeutae (*De Vit. Contemp.*) have a kindred objective. In a similar vein is the utopian description of Jerusalem in *Ep. Arist.* 83-120.

Roman" utopias and (mostly) "Jewish" or "Oriental" apocalypses obscure much of their overlapping content and function. Whether these texts describe the past, the present, or the future – whether they are heavenly, mythical, or earthly – is not the primary means for categorization. Comparisons among apocalyptic descriptions of the "true" *cosmos* and utopias of various kinds reveal a number of shared visions and images.

Without Money and Without Price

One consistent feature of ancient utopias, whether Greek, Roman, Jewish, or other "Oriental," was the continual availability of food – food fresh and obtained without toil, nourishment both abundant and ubiquitous. The theme forms an *inclusio* in the Christian Bible, for it is one quality shared by both the rustic precincts of Eden and the urban splendor of the heavenly Jerusalem. Descriptions of meat and drink, without money and without price,[61] may be found in the humble scribblings of oppressed peasants as well as in the learned poetry of Virgil and Horace, the dialogues of Plato, and the propaganda of rulers. The following examples attempt to illustrate the range and depth of this theme and the desires to which it attests:

Homer *Odyssey*

> "[The Cyclops]...neither plow
> nor sow by hand, nor till the ground, though grain –
> wild wheat and barley – grows untended,
> and wine-grapes in clusters, ripen in heaven's rain." (9.108-111)[62]

Alcinous' paradise in Phaeacia is

> "an orchard...
> with trees in bloom or weighted down for picking;
> pear trees, pomegranates, brilliant apples,
> luscious figs, and olives ripe and dark.
> Fruit never failed upon these trees: winter
> and summer time they bore, for through the year the breathing Westwind

[61] Isa 55:1.

[62] *Homer: The Odyssey* (trans. Robert Fitzgerald; Garden City, New York: Doubleday, 1963) 148. The Cyclops stand here as an example of "primitive society" unspoiled by the wiles of civilization. For a collection of texts see Arthur O. Lovejoy and George Boas, *Primitivism and Related Ideas in Antiquity* (2 vols.; Baltimore: Johns Hopkins University Press, 1935), vol. 1.

> ripened all in turn
> ...After the vines came rows of vegetables
> of all the kinds that flourish in every season,
> and through the garden plots and orchard ran
> channels from one clear fountain, while another
> gushed through a pipe under the courtyard entrance
> to serve the house and all who came for water.
> These were the gifts of heaven to Alcinous."(7.112-132)[63]

Within the Biblical tradition these features occur most often in descriptions of the wilderness experience and of the future "messianic banquet." The wilderness/exodus tradition has left an obvious imprint upon the Gospel stories of miraculous bread.[64] The motifs remained rooted firmly in prophetic traditions, e.g., Isa 25:6:

> "On this mountain the LORD of hosts will make for all peoples a feast of rich food, a feast of well-aged wines, of rich food filled with marrow, of well-aged wines strained clear."[65]

Nor is food is lacking from announcements of eschatological blessing: Luke 1:53a "He has filled the hungry with good things,"[66] and 6:21a "Blessed are you that hunger now, for you shall be satisfied."[67]

Next I turn to the second of the "Einsiedeln Eclogues," amateurish pieces of imitative Latin poetry written during the early years of Nero, whom the author sagely equates with Apollo (an estimate Nero shared), who is reestablishing the Golden Age:[68]

---

[63] Fitzgerald, 114-15. Note Rev 22:1-2b. Alcinous' kingdom is the opposite of primitive. Rather than enjoy life without labor (Gen 3:17-19; Hesiod *Op.* 109-120), the inhabitants have transformed their world into a paradise through skill.

[64] John 6 connects the Feeding of the Five Thousand to the coming Passover. Among the more obvious motifs are the ἔρημος τόπος, division of the body into companies, and dining on the grass. John 6:15 also speaks of "the Prophet." I say little about these connections because I presume they are well-known.

[65] LXX adds ointment and speaks of εὐφροσύνην (cf. Acts 14:17). Note also Isa 55:1, which provides the governing allusion.

[66] Note the emphasis upon ἀγαθά, i.e., not nourishment of any kind, but food of fine quality.

[67] χορτάζω "eating to satiety," is a regular feature of the feeding stories: Mark 6:42, (cf. 7:27), 8:4, 8 parr., and John 6:26. It is common in the psalter: Pss 81:16, 107:9 (the source of Luke 1:53), 132:15.

[68] See 2.23: *Saturni rediere dies...*

"Now doth earth untilled yield fresh produce from the rich soil, now are the wild waves no longer angry with the unmenaced ship; tigers gnaw their curbs, lions endure the cruel yoke: be gracious, chaste Lucina, thine own Apollo is now King."[69]

This Eclogue, which is roughly contemporaneous with the traditions behind the written Gospels, happens to treat subjects upon which the Gospels also touch: produce,[70] storms at sea,[71] and the behavior of wild beasts.[72] Nature transformed symbolizes the presence of utopia. What Christians claimed for Jesus, this fine bard attributed to Nero.

Revelation 21-22, with its city built of jewels and precious metals,[73] its light superior to that of fickle sun and moon, its river gurgling with the clear water of life, and its tree bearing a different kind of fruit each month – with, in short, a solution to every social problem – is one picture of what it means to "fill the hungry with good things."

Lucian was familiar with such fantasies and deemed them worthy of his ridicule:

"We were taken into the city and to the table[74] of the blessed. The city itself is all of gold and the wall around it of emerald. It has seven gates...the foundations of the city and the ground within its walls are ivory...around the city runs a river of the finest myrrh...it is neither night among them nor yet very bright day, it is always spring...the grape-vines yield twelve vintages a year, bearing every month... Instead of wheat-ears, loaves of bread all baked[75] grow..."[76]

Sibylline Oracles 7.744-746 [At the end of time]

---

[69] 2.35-38, in *Minor Latin Poets* (trans. John W. and Arthur M. Duff; LCL; Cambridge, MA: Harvard University Press, 1935) 335.

[70] Cf. Mark 4:1-9 and Mark 6:30-44.

[71] Cf. Mark 4:35-41 and parallels. Among the numerous pagan parallels for such protection I single out the ships of the Phaeacians, which navigated automatically and without fear of weather (*Od.* 8.557-559).

[72] Cf. Mark 1:13; Ps.-Mark 16:18; Acts 28:6.

[73] The description of Alcinous' paradise cited above is preceded by an account of the marvelous buildings (*Od.* 7.81-102).

[74] ...εἰς τὴν πόλιν... καὶ...συμπόσιον.

[75] Cf. Wis 16:20 ἕτοιμον ἄρτον ἀπ' οὐρανοῦ.

[76] *Vera Historia* 2.11-13, in *Lucian* (trans. Arthur M. Harmon; LCL 1; Cambridge, MA: Harvard University Press, 1913) 313-15. Lucian's parody is of value precisely because it presumes that such descriptions were well-known. On this occasion it does seem appropriate to call attention to one other ancient description of the primitive utopia: Virgil *Georgica* 1:125-132.

> "...the all-bearing earth will give the most excellent unlimited fruit to mortals, of grain, wine, and oil and a delightful drink of sweet honey from heaven..."[77]
>
> There will be a resurrection of the dead and most swift racing of the lame, and the deaf will hear and blind will see, those who cannot speak will speak, and life and wealth will be common to all. The earth will equally belong to all..." (ibid., 8.204-209)[78]

2 Baruch 29.5-8

> "The earth will also yield fruits ten thousandfold. And on one vine will be a thousand branches, and one branch will produce a thousand clusters, and one cluster will produce a thousand grapes, and one grape will produce a cor of wine. And those who are hungry will enjoy themselves and they will, moreover, see marvels every day. For winds will go out in front of me every morning to bring the fragrance of aromatic fruits and clouds at the end of the day to distill the dew of health. And it will happen at that time that the treasury of manna will come down again from on high, and they will eat of it in those years..."[79]

John 2:1-11 would more often be treated among the miraculous feeding stories, were it not a miraculous drinking story.[80] 1 Cor 11:21 once again raises its swirling head. The issue is not simply that wine long has been more of a staple than a rare and dangerous luxury in the Mediterranean diet, but also the presence of a frank appreciation for the pleasures and ecstasy that alcohol may convey.[81] The *maître de* of John 2:10 does not, after all, say:

---

[77] Trans. John J. Collins, in *OTP* 1.378.

[78] Ibid., 423. In the background stands the "Q" passage found at Luke 7:23. This Sibylline interprets πτωχοὶ εὐαγγελίζονται as life and wealth for all. See also *Sib. Or.* 2:29-32 and 3.619-623.

[79] Trans. Albertus F.J. Klijn, in *OTP* 1.630-31. See also Papias fr. 1.2 and *1 Enoch* 10.18-20. Greco-Roman examples of such prodigal quantities of grapes/wine include Ovid *Met.* 1:109-111; Lucian *Saturnalia* 20, *Aetna* 9-16; Horace *Epodes* 16.44; Athenaeus *Deipnosophistae* 269D, and Lucian *Vera Historia* 2.14. For a recent discussion, see Robert Grant, "The Problem of Miraculous Feedings in the Greco-Roman World," Center for Hermeneutical Studies (Colloquy 42; Berkeley, CA, 1982) 2-6.

[80] The Dionysiac parallels to John 2:1-11, which are not without significance for understanding the utopian perspective, are well-known and omitted from this discussion.

[81] Aune, "*Septem Sapientium Convivium*," 93, and Lampe, "*Das korinthische Herrenmahl*," 190, note the discussions of ecstasy induced or aided by wine (and music) in ancient *symposium* literature, and are alert to the relevance of this for 1 Cor 14. See, for example, Plutarch *Sept. Sap. Conv.* 149F-150F and Lucian *Symp.* 3.

> "Everyone serves the good wine first, followed by the inferior wine after some of the less temperate guests have taken a drop or two more than the situation strictly requires."

Such non-utopian economies depend upon a common level of jaded palates. The Baptizer, to be sure, was a teetotaler and abstemious with regard to food. Jesus, whom Christian tradition holds to be his superior, was neither.[82]

To the practically inclined it may seem inappropriate nonetheless that the most elaborate eschatological utopian fantasies extol an abundance of grapes rather than of wheat. As amelioration of a sort, one might introduce the Parable of the Sower (Mark 4:1-9) with its (apparently) remarkable yield, and the leaven of Matt 13:33, which produces enough dough to feed one-hundred persons.[83] Then there is that dreadful *Infancy Gospel of Thomas*[84] 12.1:

> "Again, in the time of sowing the child went out with his father to sow wheat in their land. And as his father sowed, the child Jesus also sowed one corn[85] of wheat. 12.2 And when he had reaped it and threshed it, he brought in a hundred measures; and he called all the poor of the village to the threshing-floor and gave them the wheat, and Joseph took the residue of the wheat. He was eight years old when he worked this miracle."

This "primitive" text, with its naive approach to miracle and disturbing portrait of a small boy brimming with numinous force, has elicited its full and fair share of revulsion. Be that as it may, the uncouth author or underlying tradents display some sage reflection upon the relation of the Parable of the Sower to the feeding stories, as well as upon the christological implications of each. And then there is that most primitive and miraculous of all prospects: care for the poor.
The author of *2 Baruch* proclaims:

> "Those who are hungry will enjoy themselves and they will, moreover, see marvels every day."[86]

Against this notion of a coming utopia stands a rather more durable ancient quotation:

---

[82] See Luke 7:33-34. Luke 7:36-50 illustrates his habits.

[83] For additional consolation one may contemplate the large hauls of fish in Luke 5:1-11 and John 21:1-14.

[84] English translation of Oscar Cullmann, in *NTApoc* 1.447.

[85] According to Cullmann's (ibid.) n. 13, 450, the Slavic tradition softens this to "a bushel of wheat."

[86] 29:6.

> "The people don't give a damn any more. Once they bestowed Legions, the symbols of power, all things, but now they are cautious, playing it safe, and now there are only two things that they ask for, bread and the games."[87]

"Bread and spectacles"[88] or, in the words of *2 Baruch*, "The hungry are enjoying themselves and seeing marvels every day." This proverbial tag,[89] often introduced in criticisms of the welfare state, reflects a snobbish, conservative critique of one utopian program, the provision of free food and entertainment, the Roman realized eschatological equivalent of the messianic banquet. What were the social realities?

Utopia in Its Proper Place[90]

Most food consumed by residents of the Mediterranean world was grown locally. All but the largest cities regularly produced nearly all of their basic food supplies. Imported grain was quite expensive, and most of that was already spoken for. Only Sicily, at times, North Africa, and Egypt generated a substantial and exportable surplus. Supply of food for cities thus constituted a major social problem.[91] Even a poor crop yield could produce acute local suffering. Severe shortages and ruinously high prices were common. The fluctuating price of grain was a

[87] Juvenal *Sat.* 10.78-81, in *The Satires of Juvenal* (trans. Rolf Humphries; Bloomington: Indiana University Press, 1958) 124.

[88] The *De Spectaculis* of Martial, which celebrates the opening of the Flavian amphitheater (the Colosseum), makes generous use of the language of miracle. Like his predecessor the author of the Einsiedeln Eclogues (whose patron Martial despises), Martial can celebrate the calming of wild beasts and unruly waves as an imperial gift (29.7-8, 25). See the recent study of the late John P. Sullivan, *Martial: The Unexpected Classic* (Cambridge: the University Press, 1991) 6-15, 137-45.

[89] See, for example, Jos. *Ant.* 19.16, Dio of Prusa *Or.* 32.1.

[90] Resources for the following survey include Richard Duncan-Jones, *The Economy of the Roman Empire: Quantitative Studies* (Cambridge: The University Press, 1974); Peter Garnsey, *Famine and Food Supply in the Graeco-Roman World: Responses to Risk and Crisis* (Cambridge: The University Press, 1988); A.R. Hands, *Charities and Social Aid in Greece and Rome* (Ithaca, New York: Cornell University Press, 1968); Arthur H.M. Jones, *Cities of the Eastern Roman Provinces* (Oxford: The Clarendon Press, 1971); David Magie, *Roman Rule in Asia Minor* (2 vols.; Princeton: The University Press, 1950); and Paul Veyne, *Le Pain et le cirque* (Paris: Editions du Seuill, 1970).

[91] Garnsey, *Famine*, 16, concludes that "the vast majority of communities of the Mediterranean...were endemically vulnerable to food crisis through a combination of human and natural causes."

leading cause of urban suffering.[92] Even worse – from the viewpoint of the aristocracy – it was a potential incentive to urban unrest.[93]

Nearly every city that had no particular wish to cultivate urban unrest had seen fit, by the Roman period, to establish an office or board to deal with the problem of ensuring an adequate supply supply of grain (and, often, oil) at more or less reasonable prices.[94] With the exception of Rome, this goal was most often achieved, when it was achieved, less through state grants than by recruiting private citizens to exercise benefaction. The wealthy were expected to spend their own money to buy grain and sell it at lower prices.[95] They thus merited the title εὐεργέτης and were voted innumerable statues and other honors.[96]

Other opportunities for largesse existed. Holidays were occasions for public banquets. Many notables left testamentary dispositions to endow municipal banquets on holy days. Citizens thus ate from the table of the god or from the generosity of the benefactor, or both. The picture of a civic holiday that emerges from numerous inscriptions shows residents eating communally out of doors, perhaps arranged by tribes in batches of fifty each one or one hundred, recently bathed (often with donated oil), possibly garlanded, each one thus prepared to enjoy a religious banquet.

There is nothing unusual in the preceding sketch. What I wish to emphasize is that the experience of such *al fresco fêtes* was not something early followers of Christ read about in history books. For early urban Christians, public banquets were

---

[92] Cf. Rev. 6:6 and Magie, *Roman Rule,* 1.581.

[93] For a vivid collection of relevant texts and documents see Napthali Lewis and Meyer Reinhold, eds., *Roman Civilization,* vol.2: *The Empire* (New York: Harper & Row, 1966) 138-42, 336-40. Stopping a bread riot could require the services of a θεῖος ἀνήρ (Philostratus, *Apollonius of Tyana* 1.15).

[94] These officials were called ἀγορανόμοι and σιτῶναι. See Jones, *City* 350; Magie, *Roman Rule,* 1.646; 2. n.41, 1511.

[95] The system did not always work: Garnsey, *Famine,* 257-61.

[96] "Euergitism" is the particular focus of Veyne, *Le Pain.* See also Garnsey, *Famine,* index *s.v.* "euergetism," 298. The patronage of individuals is not germane here, for it involved a smaller and somewhat select network/*familia.* However, it is worth recalling that clients called their patrons *dominus/kyrios* and had many complaints about the system, which led to conversion of the routine in-kind benefit, namely, a meal, to an outright cash dole. Martial is a major source of data for the client's point of view, e.g., 2.18, 3.7, and 3.12. See also Juvenal *Sat.* 5.

a part of their own histories and therefore an element of the *Sitz-im-Leben* of the feeding stories.

In addition to the civic banquets, there were also celebrations by members of clubs, frequently endowed by benefactors. At Lanuvium (Italy) there was established in 136 CE a now famous benevolent society in honor of Diana and Antinous.[97] Caesennius Rufus, a patron of the municipality, endowed it with the interest on 15,000 sesterces. Slaves were eligible for membership in this burial society. About six times a year dinners were held, with an amphora of good wine for each celebrant, bread, and four sardines.

Competitively speaking, civic celebrations and association dinners presented emergent Christianity with a challenge and a threat. Religious clubs offered meals, often subsidized, and cities and temples might, through various benefactors, provide public banquets. However much appreciated and however socially and religiously valuable these celebrations were, they did not relieve the basic problem of procuring adequate food for regular consumption. Such amenities, and the boards of officers appointed to control grain prices, reduced but did not eliminate the chronic problem of food shortage.

Public Charity

In addition to the above, there were various devices to provide aid to dependent children[98] and programs for distributing grain and sometimes other commodities.[99] These schemes were of limited benefit to the urban poor of the Greek East. In the first place, they failed to proliferate. Rome and its emperors may have set good examples, but they found few imitators. In the second place, public welfare in the Roman world rarely included among its recipients the most needy members of the populace.

Rome could indulge in substantial distributions of food, for it reaped the bounty of other provinces. There was little left

[97] *CIL* 14.2112 (= *ILS* 7212).

[98] The *Alimenta.* See Lewis and Reinhold, *Roman Civilization,* 2.344-47; Duncan-Jones, *Economy,* 288-319; and Garnsey, *Famine,* 262, for examples and evaluation. This program was one of several means, including tax privileges, used as an incentive to population growth.

[99] For a summary and evaluation see Garnsey, *Famine,* 263-67.

for ordinary cities to glean. Even at Rome, however, the distribution of food was not, by modern standards, a form of charity, for such tests as existed were based upon status rather than need. In the Mediterranean world as a whole, the higher one was upon the social scale, the more likely one was to benefit from such distributions. When limitations existed, those excluded were the poor rather than the rich. Nor was family size a normal consideration. The vast majority of benefactions, one-time or ongoing, was restricted to (usually male) members of the citizen body. Only rarely did these gifts embrace resident aliens, slaves,[100] children, or women.[101]

Evidence collected by Duncan-Jones from fifty eight inscriptions of Italian provenance relating to multiple distributions in which different segments of the populace receive different amounts, reveals that the town-councilors are always recipients and usually the most privileged.[102] This well-to-do group benefited from all fifty eight. In fourty four cases *augustales* gain special consideration. They, too, were relatively well-off. The ratio of discrimination against ordinary citizens is normally three or four to one and may be as high as fifty to one. These data affirm that eligibility was based upon honor rather than philanthropy, status rather than need.[103] Those who had much had even more given to them. The following examples illustrate the pattern:

IGRR 3.801 (Pisidia, Sillyon, II CE):

> "Menodora gave, on behalf of her son 300,000 silver denarii for the maintenance of children. In her term as gymnasiarch she gave each councilor eighty five denarii, seventy seven to each

---

[100] Charity given to slaves was, of course, a subsidy to their masters, who were spared the cost of feeding them. See Hands, *Charities*, 94.

[101] In the view of Duncan-Jones, women were not normal beneficiaries of these distributions (*Economy*, 143). When included they usually received smaller rates, one-fifth, on the average, of that given to men. There are a few exceptions. This exclusion and discrimination suggest that Mark 6:44 as well as John 6:10 would have been understood as a distribution to five thousand males.

[102] "An Epigraphic Survey of Costs in Roman Italy," *Papers of the British School at Rome*, 33 (1965) 189-306. See also Duncan-Jones, *Economy*, 141-43, 283-87.

[103] Many endowed clubs were bands of friends (usually peers). Bequests for such groups led Polybius (*Hist.* 20.6.1-6) to complain with reference to Boeotia (192 BCE): "Many Boeotians had more feasts provided for them in the month than there were days in it" (20.6). Although he no doubt exaggerates, he does discuss a known practice.

> member of the assembly, three to their wives, nine to other citizens, and three each to freedmen and others. Councilors thus received 9.4 times the sum of ordinary citizens and 28.3 times the amount given to non-citizens (and wives of assemblymen)."

CIL 11.6481 (Central Italy, 125-150 CE): An unknown benefactor provided four-hundred sesterces for decurions, three-hundred for members of the board of six and *augustales*, and two-hundred for ordinary citizens.

CIL 11.3013 (Central Italy, post 120 CE): An unknown benefactor arranged sixteen sesterces for councilors, twelve for augustales, eight for ordinary citizens, and one-half a sestertius for the children of all the above.

It does not appear that the poor were singled out for compensatory treatment. In the vast majority of efforts to reduce the cost of grain and in distributions they would get little. When the poor did receive anything like equality, it would be upon a religious occasion.[104]

An example of the latter form of benefaction may be found in SEG IV 247-261 (Panamara, Lagina II CE). The priests were to give festival banquets for citizens, Romans, resident aliens, and visitors. Invitations were extended by the priests inviting all, free and slave, to the table of the god (Zeus) to share in the κοινὴ εὐφροσύνη.[105]

IG XII.389 (Aigiale, Amorgos [Aegean], I CE) honors Kritolaos and Parmenion who, as *choregoi*, supplied during the feast grain for all residents and, after sacrifice to Apollo and Hera, meat and a feast for two days. *Bulletin de correspondance hellénique* 1891, 184-185, no. 29, speaks of Theophilos and Tryphera who

> "opened the sacred refectory of the god to every class and age and to the out-of-town visitors with the most ready good will and lavish generosity..."[106]

Most of the evidence for Asia Minor comes from the second century. In the first century there was even less to share, and

---

[104] Hands, *Charities*, 88.

[105] Cf. Acts 14:17. Regarding these inscriptions see Magie, *Roman Rule.* 1.587; 2. n.34, 997.

[106] Translation by Hands, *Charities*, 190, whose collection of documents (179-207) is most useful. Note also the texts in Michael M. Austin, *The Hellenistic World from Alexander to the Roman Conquest: A Selection of Ancient Sources in Translation* (Cambridge: The University Press, 1981) 195-201.

distributions were likely to have been even more discriminatory. This means that rank and file Christians, inhabitants but not often citizens of the cities of the Greek East – or of Rome, for that matter – were among those least likely to secure benefits from the general endowments, distributions, and gratuities. In the light of these facts and experiences, I shall offer some social and economic comments on the Feedings of the Five Thousand and the Four Thousand.[107]

Stories That Feed

The immediate context of both primary accounts of the Feeding of the Five Thousand is leadership. Mark 6:34 speaks of πρόβατα μὴ ἔχοντα ποιμένα, John 6:15 of an effort to make Jesus king. "Shepherd," a widespread ancient image for rulers, was applied not only to Jesus but also to early Christian leaders.[108] The following discussion operates with the hypothesis that the "disciples of Jesus" represent for the Christian rank and file examples for their own leaders.

The stories take place in the "desert," ἔρημος, a region marked with both triumph and failure, fear and promise.[109] There, away from towns and cities with their restrictions and prejudices, it may be possible to construct a new society and establish a genuinely equitable system of sharing and distribution.

Both of the chief feeding stories[110] do not open with a request for a miracle but with a disavowal by the disciples of their responsibility to provide food.[111] They employ economic

[107] Since this survey is not an exegesis of a particular pericope or a reconstruction of some single source, it accumulates data from the various accounts.

[108] This is particularly true of the verb ποιμαίνειν, which has the connotation "nourish": 1 Cor 9:7; Luke 17:7; Acts 20:28; 1 Peter 5; John 21:16. Jude 12, with its reference to ἀγάπαι, may indict those who feed themselves at community meals while neglecting others. Ποιμαίνειν became the operative verb for the consecration of bishops: Hippolytus *Trad. Ap.* 3.4; Serapion *Euch.* 28.2.

[109] See, for example, Rudolph Kittel, ἔρημος, *TDNT* 2: 657-60; Walter Radl, ed., ἐρημία, *Exegetical Dictionary of the New Testament* 2: 51.

[110] Mark 6:32-44, 8:1-10. The Feeding of the Five Thousand is also narrated in John 6:1-15.

[111] The repetition of this doubt in Mark 8:4, after the previous experience, does suggest that the disciples are not very interested in the provision of food.

language (ἀγοράζω[112]) and can stipulate a specific sum, two hundred denarii,[113] enough to sustain sixty seven families for three working days. Some food, loaves and fishes, is available; precisely, in fact, what members of the burial society at Lanuvium consumed at their festivities.

The company is ordered to recline.[114] This is the position in which the gentry eat, as well as the proper attitude for banquets and festivals. It is thus a socially marked posture.[115] The people sit in συμπόσια.[116] Mark and the other evangelists do not depict a casual evening snack; the setting is festive with crowds disposed as for a holiday meal. Paul's description of the situation at Corinth, where a *symposium* was the privilege of a few and nibbles the fare of the many, stands in notable contrast to these arrangements.

The groupings of fifty and one-hundred may reflect the military organization of the Exodus, but they also parallel the means by which rations were distributed and the populace arranged for civic festivals.[117] Eating on the grass certainly does evoke the miraculous feeding in the wilderness. The Greco-Roman world would knew outdoor meals as part of the heroic tradition[118] and as one of the amenities of the Isles of the Blessed.[119]

(Δια)δίδωμι, etc.,[120] is a term used in for civic and other distributions. Luke 18:22 and Acts 4:35 provide pointed New Testament examples of this connotation. The wealthy are to sell their possessions and distribute the proceeds according to

---

[112] Mark 6:36; John 6:5.

[113] Mark 6:37; John 6:7.

[114] Mark 6:39; 8:6; John 6:10.

[115] See n.14 above.

[116] Mark 6:39 (twice).

[117] For example the Samian law on grain distribution (*Dittenberger Syll.* 976.54-58 II BCE), which provides for monthly distribution by *chiliastys*, a tribal sub-division. A fragment from the histories of Posidonius preserved in Athenaeus *Deipnosophistae* 4, 153B, describes the practice of Heracleon of Beroea, who entertained his soldiers in groups of one thousand as they reclined on the grass.

[118] Virgil *Aen.* 5.101-102: *ordine...fusique per herbam* (of a ritual meal); Apollonius Rhodius, *Arg.* 1.450ff.

[119] Virgil *Aen.* 6.656-657; Lucian *Vera Historia* 2.14. Tibullus 2.5.95, 98-99, depicts a harvest festival in similar terms: *Tunc operata deo pubes discumbet in herba...at sibi quisque dapes et festas extruet alte/caespitibus mensas caespitibusque torum.* (*Caespes* = "grassy.")

[120] Mark 6:41; John 6:11.

need (rather than, for example, status). Luke 11:22 is also of interest. Feeding the hungry is one means for dividing up the booty of the "strong."[121] Μερίζω[122] raises the question of portions. Since *symposia* were celebrations of friendship and meals intended as instruments for building community, the ancients discussed at great length the questions about how food was to be gathered, apportioned, and served. Equity (ἰσότης, *aequitas*) is the *Leitmotif*, but the means for achieving equity were debated, and the discussion illuminates the opposition between ἴδιον and κοινὸν δεῖπνον.[123] Xenophon reports the following about Socrates and his disciples:

> "Whenever some of the members of a dining club brought more meat than others (τῶν συνιόντων ἐπὶ δεῖπνον οἱ μὲν μικρὸν ὄψον), Socrates would tell the waiter either to put the small contribution into the common stock (κοινὸν τιθέναι) or to portion it out equally among the diners (ἢ διανέμειν ἑκάστω τὸ μέρος). So the high batteners felt obliged not only to take their share of the pool, but to pool their own supplies in return; and so they put their own supplies into the common stock (ἐτίθεσαν οὖν καὶ τὸ εἁυτῶν εἰς τὸ κοινόν). And since they thus got no more than those who brought little with them, they gave up spending much on meat. 2. He observed on one occasion that one of the company at dinner had ceased to take bread, and ate the meat by itself...4. The young man, guessing that these remarks of Socrates applied to him, did not stop eating his meat, but took some bread with it. When Socrates observed this, he cried: 'Watch the fellow, you who are near him, and see whether he treats the bread as his meat or the meat as his bread.' 5. On another occasion he noticed one of the company at dinner tasting several dishes with each bite of bread..."[124]

The theological or sacramental significance of the fish[125] is also a matter for debate, but its social meaning is clear

[121] Compare the categories of "strong" and "weak" in 1 Corinthians.

[122] Mark 6:41.

[123] Lampe, "Das korinthische Herrenmahl," 188-206, illustrates the issue with extensive discussion and citations.

[124] Xen. *Mem.* 3.14 (trans. Earnest C. Marchant; LCL; New York: Putnam's Sons, 1923), 259. Other important texts include Plutarch *Quest. Conv.* 2.10, 642F-644D, and Aulus Gellius *Noct. Att.* 7.13.1-3. The meager communal meals of the Spartans were intended to obliterate social barriers and forge unity. For similar sharing among Cretans see Athenaeus *Deipnosophistae* 4, 143A-B, E. Plato's republic, as is well known, envisioned similar arrangements (*Resp.* 7, 45A-48C).

[125] Mark 6:41; John 6:8-11; cf. Luke 24:42; John 21:9-13.

enough: fish and bread make a true meal.[126] χορτάζω, which refers to full stomachs, and not to a symbolic bite of ritual food, underlines this understanding.[127] Further evidence of ample supplies and sated diners comes from the quantity of left-overs, which are gathered in baskets. Baskets were used for begging,[128] shopping, transporting food for "pot-luck" diners,[129] and for removing "left-overs" provided by hosts. *Apophoreta* were often gathered in napkins.[130] When baskets were required, the host had been particularly generous.[131] Problems arose when guests appropriated food intended for others.[132] In charitable use *kuppah* ("basket") designated the weekly distribution to needy Jews.[133]

The introduction to the Feeding of the Four Thousand[134] mentions to a fast of three days' duration. The practice of not eating may refer not only to the lack of food or money, a common enough state of affairs, or to piety;[135] one means by which those with limited resources could feed others even poorer than they were deprive themselves for two or three days in order to raise alms. So Hermas[136] and Aristides:

> "And if there is among them any that is poor and needy, and they have no spare food, they fast two or three days in order to supply to the needy their lack of food."[137]

The Acts of John includes this miraculous feeding:

> "Whenever he [Jesus] happened be accept an invitation from a Pharisee, we [disciples] would accompany him. Each of us would

---

[126] Lampe, "Das korinthische Herrenmahl," 204-05.

[127] See n.67 above. Cf. also *Did.* 10.1: μετὰ δὲ τὸ ἐμπλησθῆναι.

[128] Juvenal *Sat.* 3.14 (referring to the Jews).

[129] See the references in Lampe, "Das korinthische Herrenmahl," 195-96.

[130] Petronius *Sat.* 60; Martial 2.37.7, 7.20.13.

[131] As in the extravagant wedding meal described in Athenaeus *Deipnosophistae* 4, 130A.

[132] For example, Lucian *Symp.* 36.

[133] The daily distribution was called *tamchui*, "tray." See George F. Moore, *Judaism in the First Centuries of the Christian Era* (3 vols.; New York: Schocken 1967) 2.176-79.

[134] Mark 8:2.

[135] The *Didache* introduces the topic of fasting at 8:1, preceding the discussion of the eucharist.

[136] In particular, *Similitude* 5.55-56, specifically 56.7. *Barnabas* 3.2 describes charity as the proper form of fasting (with a citation from Isa. 58:6-20).

[137] *Apol.* 15.9, in *ANF Suppl. Vol.* (trans. Donald M. Kay; reprinted Grand Rapids: Eerdmans, 1978) 279.

> receive from the hosts the customary loaf of bread, as would he. After blessing his he would distribute[138] it to us. Each of us would be filled[139] by that small piece. Our own loaves would remain intact – to the astonishment of our hosts."[140]

Since this passage, which echoes the stories of the miraculous feedings, does not introduce a hungry crowd, it is possible to speak of miracles worked "for their own sake" to titillate debased readers. On the other hand, the left-over loaves of those disciples could be placed in baskets and given to the needy.[141]

The survey of these accounts has revealed associations with utopian stories, including the messianic banquet and the wilderness traditions, civic, and sacral celebrations, with resonances of the problems experienced in various public distributions. Behind the miraculous feedings lies the perpetual and desperate effort to obtain food and possess a stomach that does not rumble. Many poor Christians faced with problems of insufficient food would turn, like their compatriots, to their leaders for relief.

Mark 6:30-44 stands, as noted, under the rubric of the compassionate shepherd, the leader who cares for his flock. Juxtaposition of this simile with the disciples' strong and reiterated reluctance justifies the hypothesis that the story models proper leadership. Mark appears to strengthen this with the evidently redactional modification of v. 41: Jesus gives the blessed and broken loaves to the disciples for distribution.[142] As Kelber says, Jesus teaches the disciples how to feed the people.[143] From the perspective of the poor, the collection and equitable distribution of resources was a primary responsibility of their leaders. Similarly, the poor wished to enjoy a *symposium* in which all were equals.

Luke places the feeding immediately after the Mission of

---

[138] διεμέριζεν.

[139] ἐχορτάζετο.

[140] 93.4-11 (my translation).

[141] The frequentative imperfects imply habitual practice. Eucharistic practice provides both a model of and empowerment for self-deprivation in the service of others.

[142] This element is absent from the other feeding stories, which portray Jesus as the *minister*, much in the fashion of the Roman coin-types in which the emperor is portrayed as personally distributing largesses.

[143] Werner Kelber, *The Kingdom in Mark* (Philadelphia: Fortress, 1974) 56-57.

the Twelve.[144] Those who gather followers are to feed them. Luke 12:42 provides reinforcement. σιτομέτριον is a technical term within the realm of food distribution.[145] In the language of power: the disciples fail to recognize their authority (ἐξουσία).[146] The poor would have them claim and exercise it.

The balance of this lucan parable (12: 43-47) reinforces the point, as does 17:3-10. The climax comes in 22:14-30, a festal meal in which Christian leaders are compared with other "benefactors" (such as those who give to those who already have much). One of the best ways to earn the prized epithet εὐεργέτης was through the provision of grain at a reduced cost and by underwriting public banquets. The opening chapters of Acts present a vivid account of sharing, with due warnings to those who feign more generosity than they practice. In Acts 6:1-7 the leaders move rapidly to rectify a situation of unequal distribution. 20:31-35 are Luke's last words on the subject. They bring us into that realm where greedy and possibly embezzling officials exist, a situation like that known to the author of the Pastoral Epistles and to Polycarp.[147]

One function of the feeding stories was to hold up to leaders (and the relatively well-off in general) models of care for the poor of their community. In Luke 14:1-24, Jesus's rules for hosts reject the traditional principles of social discrimination and demand invitations for those who are poor, maimed, lame and blind. The disabled were by definition poor, usually beggars with their baskets, and often cultically excluded. The Parable of the Great Supper has more implications for the rich than for the poor, who did not have all that many opportunities to issue invitations.

---

[144] Luke 9:1-17.

[145] See, for example, Garnsey, *Famine* 262-64.

[146] Note the use of ἐξουσία in Mark 6:7 and Luke 9:1, in proximity to the Feeding of the Five Thousand, and frequently in 1 Corinthians (five times in ch. 9).

[147] Polycarp *Phil.* 11 (cited im n.36 above). According to 1 Tim 3:8 greed is an undesirable quality for διάκονοι. Tit 1:7 says the same of ἐπίσκοποι. The allegation that grain prices were up because the rich were hoarding supplies to create artificial scarcity was an all but sure-fire method for stirring up the populace of an imperial city (Tacitus *Ann.* 6.13.1). The Parable of the Rich Fool and the story of Ananias and Sapphira (Luke 12:16-21; Acts 5:1-11) have a different piquancy when read in that context, for hoarding and embezzlement are more than thoughtless actions of the self-centered.

Conclusion

The miraculous feeding stories proclaim the needs and concerns of the poor, in whose interest they acquired their pre-Gospel shape. In their present form these stories still reveal genuine and specific concerns for acquiring adequate food and the desire to realize the eschatological hope of a common meal as a banquet accessible to all. Those with resources should partake and contribute without dissembling or witholding. Leaders are to gather what is available and distribute it upon a regular basis in accordance with need. One purpose of the feeding stories was to legitimate this practice of sharing and motivate the community to continue it in accordance with Jesus' own example.

This utopian dimension forms a stream of nascent sacramental theology. In the eucharist, private possessions (ἴδια) are transformed into τὰ ἅγία τοῖς ἁγίοις,[148] into κυριακά, possessions of the κύριος, to be distributed to all of his servants. The eucharistic action of taking, blessing, breaking, and distributing transforms ἴδια δεῖπνα into κυριακὰ δεῖπνα.[149]

The implicit theology and practice reflected in this rite likewise presented a challenge to the ruling power, for the emperors were also called κύριοι and hailed as shepherds charged with bringing back the Golden Age.[150] Roman distributions were portrayed as utopian fulfillments. For the city of Rome "Give us this bread always"[151] was not a negotiable demand.[152] Imperial patrons responded to that cry with elaborate plans to which they gave personal attention and massive publicity. The concept of the Christian κυριακὸν δεῖπνον posed (and poses) a challenge to any "empire" that claims to have ushered in the millennium or to have brought back the Golden Age.

---

[148] This is the invitation to communion in the Liturgy of St. John Chrysostom, rendered in the American (Anglican) *Book of Common Prayer* as "the gifts of God for the people of God" (e.g., p. 364).

[149] The Offertory, in which the people's gifts of bread, wine, tithes, and offerings are placed upon the altar, continues to express this early sacramental understanding.

[150] Dio of Prusa *Or.* 1-4; Cassius Dio 57.10 (of Tiberius).

[151] John 6:34.

[152] "A hungry people does not listen to reason," according to Seneca *Vit. Brev.* 18.5.

The feeding stories do not characterize Rome as Babylon, but they do establish an opposition between the earthly and heavenly cities. The echoes of these stories have reverberated down through Christian and Western history. If they embarrass people because they are incredible, one might ask: "What is more incredible about them? The miraculous multiplication of loaves, or the social and economic expectations to which they give expression?"

NEUTESTAMENTLICHE WUNDERGESCHICHTEN UND ANTIKE MEDIZIN

Dieter Lührmann (Philipps-Universität Marburg)

I

Zu den schärfsten Kritikern des Judentums und des frühen Christentums gehört der Mediziner Galenos, geb. 129 n.Chr. in Pergamon. Er begann in seiner Heimatstadt als Gladiatorenarzt, wirkte ab 161 bis zu seinem Tod (199) mit nur einer kurzen Unterbrechung in Rom, u.a. als Leibarzt Marc Aurels. In seinem umfangreichen Werk finden sich mehrere polemische Aussagen gegen Juden- wie Christentum. Beiden wirft er vor, Glauben zu fordern, ohne Beweise zu liefern.[1]

Die ausführlichste von ihnen richtet sich dagegen, daß Mose annimmt, alles sei Gott möglich (πάντα γὰρ εἶναι νομίζει τῷ θεῷ δυνατά). Dagegen setzt er unter Berufung auf Platon und die anderen griechischen Philosophen, daß einiges unmöglich sei von Natur aus und daß Gott deshalb gar nicht erst solches versuche, vielmehr aus dem Möglichen das Beste wähle.[2] Das Beispiel, an dem er dies demonstriert, sind die menschlichen Wimpern, deren Länge stets unveränderlich ist.

Zwar richten sich diese Ausführungen allein gegen Mose und seine Anhänger, und in der Tat läßt sich ein solcher Satz, daß bei Gott alles möglich sei, ja breit belegen in alttestamentlichen und jüdischen Texten.[3] Er findet sich aber auch im Neuen Testament zitiert (Mk 10,27 parr.), und es hätte Galenos wohl noch mehr empört, daß nach Mk 9,23 nicht nur Gott, sondern den Glaubenden alles möglich ist.

Galens Kritik trifft also durchaus einen wesentlichen Zug des biblischen Gottesbildes, und er erweist sich zugleich als Erbe der mit Hippokrates (ca. 460-370 v.Chr.) einsetzenden

---

[1] Richard Walzer, *Galen on Jews and Christians*, London 1949.

[2] De usu partium XI 14, zitiert bei Walzer, *Galen on Jews and Christians*, S.12f.

[3] Gen 18,14 Hiob 42,2 Sach 8,6 LXX, Philo, Abr 112.175 u.a.

antiken medizinischen Tradition.[4] Für sie gibt es nicht einen grundsätzlichen Gegensatz von Medizin und Religion, ja nicht einmal von Medizin und Wunder – sie verehrt den Gott Asklepios, und an dessen großen Heiligtümern z.B. in Epidauros ereignen sich die bemerkenswertesten Heilungswunder, in Kos offenbar gleich neben der medizinischen Akademie.

Wohl aber gilt für diese antike Medizin bereits der Grundsatz, daß es keine, aber auch keine Krankheit gebe, die nicht eine natürliche Ursache habe;[5] jedenfalls sei keine Krankheit zurückzuführen auf Götter oder Dämonen. Heilung bedeutet in diesem Sinne mögliche Aufhebung einer Störung der Natur; wichtig ist dabei der präventive Charakter dieser Medizin. Die Diätetik als Einstellung auf eine in jeder Hinsicht angemessene Lebenshaltung ist ihr Kern.

Die Wundergeschichten des Neuen Testaments jedoch nennen, wenn überhaupt, als Ursache von Krankheit Dämonen; ihre Austreibung, der Exorzismus, bringt Heilung. Vom Stand der antiken Medizin ist in ihnen wenig erkennbar, allenfalls eine aggressive Polemik gegen Ärzte, die nichts können, sondern nur Geld machen wollen; Mk 5,26 ist freilich bei Matthäus gestrichen und von Lukas abgemildert worden. Sonst ist die Existenz von Ärzten in dem sprichwortartigen Satz Mk 2,17parr. lediglich vorausgesetzt.

II

In den in großer Zahl vorliegenden Arbeiten zu den neutestamentlichen Wundergeschichten ist der Vergleich mit antiker Medizin fast nie in den Blick gekommen, allenfalls ganz am Rande. Neben den alttestamentlichen Weissagungen hatten die Wunder in der altprotestantischen Dogmatik den Beweis für die Christologie liefern sollen. Seit der Aufklärung wurde beides zum Problem, und bis heute läßt sich ein allgemein

---

[4] Vgl. insbes. Antje Krug, *Heilkunst und Heilkult,* München 1985; Hellmut Flashar (Hg.), *Antike Medizin,* 1971 (WdF 221); Richard Toellner, Art. "Heilkunde/Medizin II", *TRE 14* (1985) S.743-752; Fridolf Kudlien, Art. "Heilkunde", *RAC 14* (1988) S.223-249; eine Sammlung repräsentativer Texte: W. Müri, *Der Arzt im Altertum,* Darmstadt [5]1986.

[5] Hippocr, morb sacr 1: περὶ τῆς ἱερῆς νούσου καλεομένης ὧδε ἔχει. οὐδέν τί μοι δοκεῖ τῶν ἄλλων θειοτέρη εἶναι νούσων οὐδὲ ἱερωτέρη, ἀλλὰ φύσιν μὲν ἔχει καὶ τἆλλα νοσήματα, ὅθεν γίνεται, φύσιν δὲ καὶ αὕτη καὶ πρόφασιν.

akzeptierter Konsens in etwa auf den Nenner bringen: in der Antike waren Wunder bzw. Wunder*geschichten* gang und gäbe, in der Neuzeit gibt es die Medizin.

Da auch die Medizin sich im 19. Jahrhundert von ihren Wurzeln löste und sich als Naturwissenschaft im modernen Sinne neu definierte, geriet auch dort die Erinnerung, daß das Problem des Wunders bereits in der Antike angelegt war, in Vergessenheit. Nur Medizin*historiker* lesen heute noch die alten griechischen und lateinischen Texte, kaum die Mediziner.

Theologen dagegen sind verpflichtet auf Texte aus der Antike, wie auch immer die Wundergeschichten dabei eingebracht werden. Moderne Spielarten sind nach wie vor religions- und formgeschichtliche Vergleiche mit jüdischen und/oder hellenistischen Wundergeschichten. Damit kann mehr oder weniger deutlich verbunden sein die Frage nach der Historizität der Wunder. Sie wird weithin zugestanden für Exorzismen als auch in der Neuzeit noch denkbare "unerklärliche" Heilungen. Verneint wird sie hingegen für alle "Manipulationen" sowie für die spektakulären großen Wunder; der religionsgeschichtliche Vergleich kann dabei apologetische Elemente enthalten, insofern der Verweis auf Parallelen in hellenistischer Literatur eine späte Entstehung beweisen soll. Dieses Bild ergibt sich bei allen Differenzen z.B. aus der Behandlung der Wundergeschichten in den klassischen Werken der Formgeschichte.[6]

Unter redaktionsgeschichtlicher Perspektive hat großen Einfluß gewonnen Dieter Georgis These zum Wunder als Mittel der religiösen Propaganda, die Stilisierung des Wundertäters als θεῖος ἀνήρ.[7] Er hatte sie entwickelt in der Bestimmung der Gegner des Paulus im 2. Korintherbrief. Aufgenommen wurde sie aber vor allem in der Frage der Bedeutung der Wundergeschichten im Markusevangelium als Möglichkeit, die eigene Theologie des Evangelisten zum Teil schroff

---

[6] Vgl. Rudolf Bultmann, *Die Geschichte der synoptischen Tradition*, [3]1957 (FRLANT 29) S.223-260; Martin Dibelius, *Die Formgeschichte des Evangeliums*, Tübingen [3]1959, S.34-100; vgl. insgesamt Alfred Suhl (Hg.), *Der Wunderbegriff im Neuen Testament*, 1980 (WdF 295); der dort (S.338-373) abgedruckte Aufsatz von Rudolf und Martin Hengel, Die Heilungen Jesu und medizinisches Denken, streift die klassische Medizin nur am Rande.

[7] *Die Gegner des Paulus im 2. Korintherbrief*, 1964 (WMANT 11).

abzusetzen von den von ihm durchaus aufgenommenen Geschichten.[8]

Notorisch ist freilich das Problem, vergleichbare Texte in hellenistischer Literatur zu finden, die nicht eine Kenntnis der christlichen Überlieferung voraussetzen; das ist bei den immer wieder zitierten Lukian-Texten ja der Fall. Texte wie Apg 13,6-12, 19,13-17 oder Mk 9,38-41 belegen zwar die Konkurrenz zu anderen, hier jüdischen Wundertätern, nicht aber den Typ des θεῖος ἀνήρ.

Gerd Theißen meint daher, daß der frühchristliche Wunderglaube selbst einer der Katalysatoren spätantiken Wunderglaubens gewesen ist.[9] Seine weithin aufgenommene Analyse arbeitet insbesondere mit dem Instrumentarium der Literatursoziologie und zielt auf die – soziale, religionsgeschichtliche und existenzielle – Funktion der Wunder*geschichten.*

III

Ein solcher kurzer und notwendig verkürzender Überblick über die Forschung zu den neutestamentlichen Wundergeschichten zeigt, daß der Vergleich mit antiker Medizin bisher keine Rolle gespielt hat. Deren Existenz in frühchristlicher Zeit kann aber nicht einfach geleugnet werden.[10] Das im Corpus Hippocraticum gesammelte Material wurde über Generationen weiter überliefert und ergänzt.[11] Bekannt sind Schriften weiterer Mediziner bis hin zu dem eingangs erwähnten Galen. Kontinuität haben auch die Ausbildungsstätten.

Keine Vergleichsmöglichkeit ergibt sich freilich in formgeschichtlicher Hinsicht. Die Krankengeschichten der "Epidemien" beschreiben Symptome und Verläufe von Krankheiten, z.B.:[12]

> "Ähnliches beim Sohn des Anechetos: als er sich im Winter im Bade neben einem Feuer salbte, wurde er heiß und stürzte

---

[8] Vgl. bes. Theodore J. Weeden, *Mark – Traditions in Conflict,* Philadelphia 1971.

[9] *Urchristliche Wundergeschichten,* 1974 (StNT 8) S.273.

[10] So Theißen, *a.a.O., S.267.*

[11] Auswahlausgabe von W.H.S. Jones/E.T. Withington, 4 Bände in *LCL;* Gesamtausgabe: E. Littré, Œuvres complètes d'Hippocrate, 10 Bde, Paris 1839-61.

[12] Epid 7,46, zitiert nach Müri, *Der Arzt im Altertum,* S.269.

> plötzlich unter epileptischen Krämpfen zu Boden. Als die Krämpfe nachließen, blickte er um sich, war aber nicht bei sich selber. Nachdem er zu sich gekommen war, wurde er anderntags früh wieder gepackt: Krämpfe, Schaum, aber nicht viel. Am dritten Tage: schwere Zunge; am vierten an der Zunge Spuren des Anfalls; er stieß an, war nicht imstande zu reden, sondern blieb bei den ersten Silben der Worte stecken; am fünften: Zunge heftig mitgenommen; Krampf trat dazu, und er verlor das Bewußtsein. Als das nachließ, fand die Zunge nur mit Mühe zum normalen Gebrauche zurück. Am sechsten, während er sich aller Speisen enthielt, auch der Krankensuppe und der Getränke: nichts. Er hatte keine Anfälle mehr."

Häufiger enden freilich solche Geschichten so: "Er/sie war tot." Es handelt sich um Fallstudien für den Unterricht, und aus einer Vielzahl solcher einzelner Geschichten lassen sich Regeln ableiten, z.B.:[13]

> "Epilepsie bei Jugendlichen wird vor allem geheilt durch den Wechsel im Alter, in den Jahreszeiten, im Wohnsitz, in der Lebensführung." oder:[14] "Epileptische Anfälle vor dem mannbaren Alter sind der Wandlung zugänglich. Wenn sie nach dem 25. Lebensjahre auftreten, bleiben sie meistens bis zum Tode."

Die behandelnden Ärzte bleiben anonym – solche Texte sind nicht zum Preis eines Wundertäters geschrieben, der Ehrenkodex der hippokratischen Medizin gebietet vielmehr den Rückzug bei aussichtslosen Fällen.

Ungenutzt ist diese Tradition bisher im Blick auf den religionsgeschichtlichen Vergleich mit Wundergeschichten. Der im ersten Teil dieses Aufsatzes zitierte Grundsatz, daß es keine Krankheit gebe, die nicht eine natürliche Ursache habe, steht in der hippokratischen Abhandlung "Über die heilige Krankheit", worunter in etwa die Epilepsie bzw. Anfallskrankheiten verschiedener Art zu verstehen sind.[15]

Diese umfängliche, überaus polemische Schrift stellt sich damit einem in der Antike und darüberhinaus in hohem Grade religiös besetzten Phänomen.[16] Erst an ihr können letzte Grenzen ärztlichen Wissens erreicht werden. Wäre es

---

[13] Aphor 2,45, Müri, *a.a.O.*, S.269.

[14] Aphor 5,7, Müri, *a.a.O.*, S.271.

[15] Text mit Übersetzung bei Müri, *a.a.O.*, S.234-269, ausschnittweise als Beilage 4 in meinem Kommentar: *Das Markusevangelium*, 1987 (HNT 3) S.274-279.

[16] Vgl. E. Lesky, J.H. Waszink, Art. "Epilepsie", *RAC 5* (1962) Sp.819-831.

aber nicht frömmer, jedenfalls hier göttliche Einwirkung zu respektieren? Das jedenfalls behaupten "Zauberer und Sühnepriester und Scharlatane und Marktschreier, Leute, die tun, als ob sie weiß wie fromm wären und mehr wüßten als andere." Sühnungen und Besprechungen bieten sie an, verbieten Bäder und bestimmte Speisen, und wenn das nichts hilft, sind ja die Götter schuld.

Dagegen stellt der Autor dieser Schrift Folgerungen aus den empirischen Beobachtungen wie den oben zitierten und schließt:

> "Wer es versteht, den Patienten durch Diät trocken und feucht, kalt und warm zu machen, der könnte wohl auch diese Krankheit heilen, sofern er den rechten Augenblick und das richtige Maß für die nützlichen Mittel erkennt – und zwar ohne Entsühnungen und ohne Magie."

Im Griechischen steht hier ein Optativ mit ἄν im Hauptsatz, also ein *Potentialis* der Gegenwart, nicht ein Irrealis!

Was diese Schrift "Über die heilige Krankheit" belegt, ist also nicht weniger als die Auseinandersetzung der antiken Medizin mit gleichzeitigen Wundertätern, die alle möglichen Krankheiten zu heilen versprechen. Es ist also kein Wunder, daß Galen sich empört über den Wunderglauben von Juden und Christen!

Literatursoziologisch führen diese Texte in eine in der frühchristlichen Literatur nicht erreichte Welt, die des medizinischen Schulbetriebs. Wäre Lukas der Arzt (Kol 4,14) tatsächlich der Verfasser des dritten Evangeliums und der Apostelgeschichte, spräche das gegen seine medizinische Bildung, aber der Titel war in der Antike durch keine Approbationsordnung geschützt!

Sozialgeschichtlich ergibt sich für die Antike die Frage, welchen Bevölkerungsschichten derartig ausgebildete Ärzte zur Verfügung standen. Das mögen vor allem die Bessergestellten und die Stadtbewohner gewesen sein; von ihrem Selbstverständnis her waren Ärzte aber für alle da. Für alle Schichten aber stellte sich vermutlich die Frage, wer bereit war, eine solche Medizin zu akzeptieren, denn die beschränkte sich auf das Mögliche, verzichtete auf Wunder.

IV

Für die Zeit des frühen Christentums ist also durchaus ein Problembewußtsein für den Umgang mit Krankheit vorauszusetzen. Die neutestamentlichen Wundergeschichten spiegeln ihn auf einem niedrigen Niveau insofern, als die häufige Verwendung von Wörtern wie ξηρός, ξηραίνω die für die antike Medizin grundlegende Lehre von den "Säften" enthält: "verdorrt, vertrocknet". Deren Behebung geschieht aber nicht mit Hilfe von Diätetik, sondern durch Wunder.

Auf der anderen Seite setzt die ebenfalls häufige Verwendung von Wörtern wie καθαρός, καθαρίζω voraus, daß "Reinigung" Heilung bedeutet, auch wenn sie außerhalb des Kultus erfolgen kann. Zumindest viele Krankheiten, wenn auch nicht alle, werden auf Dämonen zurückgeführt, nicht auf klimatische, konstitutionelle und andere Ursachen wie in der Medizin.

Keine Möglichkeit einer Verständigung zwischen beiden Seiten besteht im Blick auf die "heilige Krankheit". Mk 9,14-29 setzt voraus, daß Dämonen hinter ihr stecken, daß ein Exorzismus zum Erfolg führt, für die Jünger dann das Gebet.[17] Hätte Galen diesen speziellen Text gekannt, hätte er seine Kritik in der Tat noch viel grundsätzlicher formulieren können.

Eine letzte Möglichkeit der Verständigung schneidet Joh 5 ab. Für die antike Medizin gab es eine überraschend friedliche Nachbarschaft zu den Heilheiligtümern. Die Heilung des Kranken am Teich Bethesda lebt zumindest in einer Grundschicht davon, daß jemand an einem solchen Ort vergeblich auf Heilung hoffte und nun Jesus ihn heilt.[18]

Das frühe Christentum hat sich auf seine Weise also durchaus mit anderen in der Antike möglichen Weisen des Umgangs mit Krankheit auseinandergesetzt. Gegenüber der antiken Medizin gibt es die bittere Polemik Mk 5,26, gegenüber konkurrierenden Wundertätern die oben genannten Texte, gegenüber Heilheiligtümern Joh 5. Was bleibt, ist ein sozu-

---

[17] Vgl. meine Auslegung, *a.a.O.*, S.159-163; Andreas Lindemann, Jesus und der epileptische Knabe, in: *Medizinisches und Theologisches zur Epilepsie*, 1988 (Bethel-Beiträge 38) S.130-140.

[18] Auf diesen in der Literatur kaum beachteten Zusammenhang hat mich geprächsweise Hans Dieter Betz hingewiesen.

sagen "normaler" Umgang mit Krankheit wie in Jak 5,14: Gebet (vgl. Mk 9,29), Salbung mit dem üblichen Heilmittel Öl (vgl. Mk 6,13). Im Vordergrund aber stehen die Wunder als Überwindung von "unheilbaren" Krankheiten und letzten Gefährdungen bis hin zum Tod. Die antike Medizin gab diesen Bereich auf, Wundergeschichten aber ließen hoffen.

V

In der jüdischen Überlieferung gibt es einen Text, in dem die biblischen Traditionen und die antike Medizin zusammenkommen, Sir 38,1-15:[19]

1 Wende dich an den Arzt entsprechend seiner Aufgabe,
denn auch ihn hat Gott bestimmt.
2 Durch Gott ist der Arzt weise,
und vom König empfängt er Geschenke;
3 die Erkenntnis des Arztes erhöht sein Haupt,
und bei Fürsten hat er Zutritt.
4 Gott läßt aus der Erde Heilmittel hervorgehen,
und ein verständiger Mann soll sie nicht verachten.
5 Wurde nicht vom Holz das Wasser süß,
um jedem Menschen ihre Kraft kundzutun?
6 Und er hat dem Menschen Verstand gegeben,
um sich zu verherrlichen mit ihrer Macht.
7 Mit ihnen bringt der Arzt den Schmerz zur Ruhe
8 – und ebenso fertigt der Salbenmischer Salbe –,
damit sein Werk nicht aufhöre
und Hilfe da sei auf seiner Erde.
9 Mein Sohn, in Krankheit sei nicht unachtsam!
Bete zu Gott, denn er heilt!
10 Fliehe vom Unrecht und vom Ansehen der Person,
und von allen Sünden reinige das Herz!
11 Bringe dar Wohlgeruch und Speisopfer,
und richte Fett zu bis zur Grenze deines Vermögens!
12 Aber auch dem Arzt gib Raum,
und er bleibe nicht fern, denn auch für ihn besteht eine Aufgabe.
13 Denn es gibt Zeit, da ist in seiner Hand Gelingen,
14 denn auch er betet zu Gott,
der ihm gelingen läßt Deutung
und Heilung um der Lebenserhaltung willen.

[19] Vgl. dazu meinen Aufsatz: Aber auch dem Arzt gibt Raum (Sir 38,1-15), *WuD 15* (1979) S.55-78.

15 Wer sündigt vor dem, der ihn geschaffen hat,
der beträgt sich übermütig gegenüber dem Arzt.

Im Gefolge der alttestamentlichen Weisheit kann der Verfasser die ihm bekannte medizinische Tradition integrieren trotz aller ihm ebenfalls bekannten Vorbehalte. Für das alte Israel hatte es ja weder Heilgötter noch Ärzte gegeben; allein der Gott Israels war der, der heilen konnte (Ex 15,26)!

Neu ist deshalb der vorsichtige, aber doch entschlossene Versuch Sirachs (um 180 v.Chr.), die Hinzuziehung eines Arztes zu begründen aus Gottes eigener Schöpfung. Der Enkel des Autors, der diesen Text dann ins Griechische übersetzte, konnte für Alexandrien den Umgang mit Ärzten schon sehr viel selbstverständlicher voraussetzen; er empfiehlt nicht mehr bloß, sich an den Arzt zu wenden, sondern er fordert dazu auf, den Arzt auch gebührend zu ehren.[20]

Philon von Alexandrien wiederum sieht sich veranlaßt, vor allzu selbstverständlichem Umgang mit Ärzten und Arzneimitteln zu warnen.[21] Josephus schließlich fügt völlig anachronistisch Ärzte in seine Wiedergaben alttestamentlicher Texte ein, nicht nur in die Erzählungen, sondern auch in die Gesetzgebung.[22]

Bemerkenswert ist es deshalb schon, daß in der frühchristlichen Literatur bis weit in das 2. Jhdt. hinein jegliche positive Beziehung zur Medizin vermieden wird, obwohl von den Anfängen an deren Kenntnis vorausgesetzt ist. Origenes z.B. referiert in seinem Matthäus-Kommentar (13,6) die Ansicht der Mediziner über die Ursachen der Epilepsie; er selbst will aber lieber dem Evangelium glauben, daß diese Krankheit auf einen Dämon zurückgeht.

Erst allmählich ergeben sich dann auch Möglichkeiten einer christlichen Rezeption der antiken Medizin; eine Rolle spielte dabei u.a. der oben zitierte Sirach-Text, der ja kanonisch war. Ein anderer Weg der Überlieferung lief über die Araber, und auch das spätere Judentum war daran beteiligt, das antike medizinische Wissen in Erinnerung zu halten und zu nutzen. Seit dem späten Mittelalter und der Renaissance kommen

[20] Er wandelt auch v.15 um: "Wer vor seinem Schöpfer sündigt, der soll dem Arzt in die Hände fallen."

[21] Leg all III 177f; sacr 70.

[22] Nach antiqu I 208 konsultierte Abraham Ärzte; in IV 277 fügt Josephus die Erstattung der Arztkosten in Ex 21,18f.20f ein.

dann diese drei Ströme auch wieder zusammen.

Seit der Aufklärung verschärft sich das Problem des Wunders, entsteht aber nicht erst da, sondern ist ein Problem bereits der Antike. Die Wunderkritik gehört zu den Anfängen historischer Interpretation der Bibel. Einen vergessenen historischen Aspekt in Erinnerung zu bringen, war das Ziel dieser knappen Skizze, ihn auszuwerten, stände noch aus. Grundlage dafür wäre ein neues Studium der antiken Quellen, das leitende Interesse ergäbe sich aus der elementaren Erfahrung von Krankheit. "Athen" und "Jerusalem" scheinen hier besonders fern voneinander – kaum aber für Tertullian selber, offenbar ein guter Kenner der antiken Medizin.[23]

---

[23] Vgl. Heinrich Schipperges, Art. "Krankheit IV", *TRE 19* (1990) S.686-689, hier S.688.

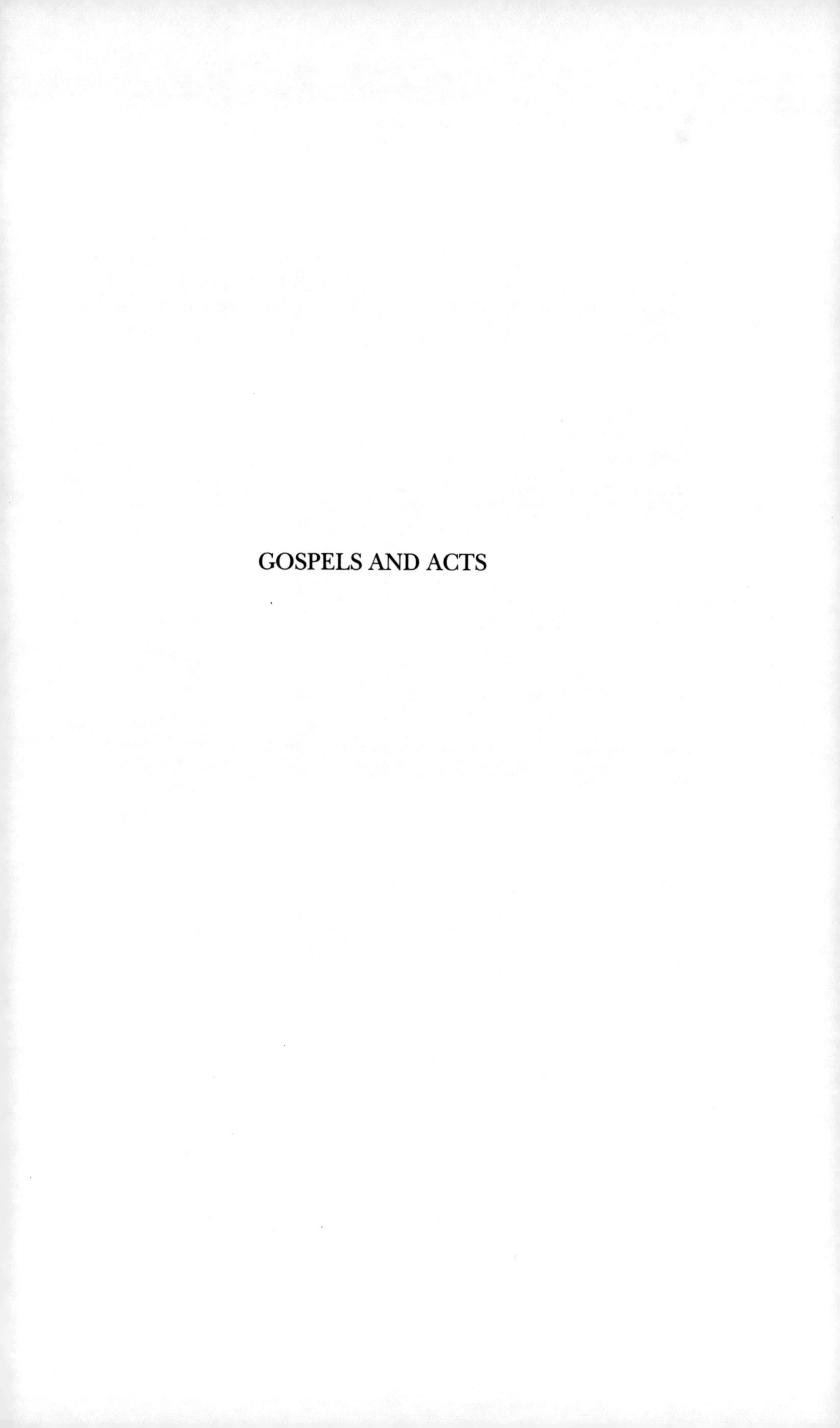

GOSPELS AND ACTS

RULERS, DIVINE MEN, AND WALKING ON THE WATER (MARK 6:45-52)

Adela Yarbro Collins
(University of Chicago, Chicago, Illinois)

It is a pleasure and an honor to present this study to Dieter Georgi, who has contributed so much to our understanding of Jewish, pagan, and Christian missionary activity in the ancient world.[1] My intention in writing this article is to clarify the role of Christology in early Christian propaganda by means of a study of the early tradition-history of one miracle story and its context in the history of religions.[2] I hope to demonstrate that the origin of the story is seen best in the formation of Christian oral tradition within a pluralistic cultural and religious context. Both Jewish and Greek traditions contributed to the formation and adaptation of the story, although the Jewish tradition contributed most to the expression and adaptation of the epiphany theme whereas the Greek was more influential with regard to the motif of walking on water. Finally, the distinction between tradition and redaction sheds light on the Markan understanding and use of the passage.

THE PRE-MARKAN FORM OF THE STORY

Paul Achtemeier has made a persuasive case for the hypothesis that the story about Jesus' walking on the water was the first narrative in a pre-Markan *catena* of miracle stories and that originally it was followed by the healing of the blind man in Bethsaida.[3] He and many others have attempted to reconstruct the pre-Markan form of the narrative itself. It begins with the remark:

---

[1] See especially Dieter Georgi, *Die Gegner des Paulus im 2. Korintherbrief: Studien zur Religiösen Propaganda in der Spätantike* (Neukirchen-Vluyn: Neukirchener Verlag, 1964); ET with an epilogue: idem, *The Opponents of Paul in Second Corinthians* (Philadelphia: Fortress, 1986).

[2] As outlined by Georgi, *The Opponents of Paul in Second Corinthians*, 170-71.

[3] Paul Achtemeier, "Toward the Isolation of Pre-Markan Miracle Catenae," *JBL* 89 (1970) 281-84.

> "And immediately he compelled his disciples to get into the boat and to go ahead (of him) to the other side, to Bethsaida, while he himself dismissed the crowd."[4]

The last clause of this sentence (ἕως αὐτὸς ἀπολύει τὸν ὄχλον) was added by the evangelist to connect this story with the previous one; a great crowd is mentioned in vs 34, and the disciples had suggested dismissing the crowd prematurely in vs 36.[5] This conclusion is supported by the observation that the separation of Jesus from the disciples is doubly motivated: (1) he stayed behind to dismiss the crowd and (2) he wanted to be alone to pray (vs 46). The latter motive is probably original, since the presence of the disciples would not be a problem for the dismissal of the crowd by Jesus.[6] Furthermore, ἀποταξάμενος in vs 46 is more appropriate to leave-taking than to dismissal. It derives from the source and referred originally to Jesus' saying farewell to the disciples (αὐτοῖς). The other compelling case for redactional activity relates to the conclusion of the story, "For they did not understand with regard to the loaves, but their hearts were hardened" (vs 52). The reference to the "loaves" is redactional and represents Mark's attempt to link the story about the walking on the water with the feeding of the 5,000 (6:34-44) in terms of his own conception of the role of the disciples.[7]

Although many suggestions have been made in this regard, there is no compelling evidence of editorial activity in vss 46-51. The remark that the wind abated (καὶ ἐκόπασεν ὁ ἄνεμος; vs 51b) is identical in wording to a statement in the story about the stilling of the storm (4:39c) and thus has been interpreted as an addition by the evangelist in order to assimilate this story to the Stilling of the Storm. But the wind is necessary to motivate Jesus' walk upon the water, as vs 48 makes clear. Vs 51b is thus better construed as an integral part of the pre-Markan story.

---

[4] Mark 6:45; all translations are by the author unless otherwise noted.

[5] Achtemeier, "Toward the Isolation of Pre-Markan Miracle Catenae," 283.

[6] Rudolf Bultmann, *The History of the Synoptic Tradition* (rev. ed.; New York: Harper & Row, 1963) 216.

[7] Achtemeier, "Toward the Isolation of Pre-Markan Miracle Catenae," 282-83.

GENRE AND THEMES IN THE PRE-MARKAN STORY

As is well known Martin Dibelius defined the story of Jesus' walking on the sea as a "tale" (*Novelle*).[8] The function of the tales is to manifest the divine power of the divine wonder-worker; this function gives them the character of epiphanies. He interprets the remark in vs 48 (καὶ ἤθελεν παρελθεῖν αὐτούς; "and he wanted to pass by them") to mean that Jesus did not wish to enter the boat, but rather by walking on the sea to reveal his nature to the disciples.[9] The problem with the latter point is, of course, that the first two parts of that verse imply that Jesus' intention was to assist the disciples in their struggle with the wind ("and when he saw them impeded in their progress, for the wind was against them, ..."; vs 48ab). Dibelius meets this objection by arguing that the underlying story was originally about Jesus' intervening helpfully in a difficulty caused by winds and waves. This story then was extended by the addition of the motif of Jesus' passing by, which transformed it into an epiphany. This particular epiphany, however, was unlike the Gospels and probably arose under some non-Christian influence.[10] Matthew then counteracted this secularization by adding the episode in which Peter walks on the water to Jesus. In that scene, the sea represents the mythological waters of death.[11]

Bultmann classified Mark 6:45-52 as a "nature miracle." He argued that the original motif for the story is the walking on the water, and the storm motif has been added to it (from Mark 4:37-41) as a secondary feature.[12] He argued that the (secondary) introduction has made unintelligible the obviously original comment about Jesus wanting to pass by the disciples. He also argued that the supplementary motivation of vs 50 (for Jesus' speech or for his decision to enter the boat, i.e., that they all saw him and were terrified) conflicts with vs 49 ("Now when they saw him walking on the sea, they thought that he was a ghost, and they cried out"). Bultmann con-

---

[8] Martin Dibelius, *From Tradition to Gospel* (New York: Scribner's Sons, 1935) 71.

[9] Ibid., 94-95.

[10] Ibid., 100.

[11] Ibid., 277.

[12] Bultmann, *The History of the Synoptic Tradition*, 216.

sidered the evidence insufficient to determine whether the addition of the storm motif was effected by Mark or by a pre-Markan editor. Achtemeier's argument that the Stilling of the Storm and the Walking on the Water belonged to two previously independent *catenae* of miracle stories makes it unlikely that a pre-Markan editor conflated the two stories. But the verses involving the storm motif in the Walking on the Water show none of the typical signs of Markan redaction. Bultmann also noted that some had argued that this story was originally an Easter story brought back into the life of Jesus, but concluded that certainty on this point was unobtainable.[13]

Gerd Theissen defined this pericope as a "soteriological epiphany" in his synchronic catalogue of themes.[14] He stated that the typical motifs constituting this theme are the extraordinary visual phenomenon, the φάντασμα; the withdrawal of the god (παρελθεῖν); the word of revelation, "It is I"; and the numinous amazement of the disciples. The main problem with Theissen's definition is the relevance of the motif involving an extraordinary visual phenomenon. The narrator states that *when they saw him walking on the sea,* they thought that he was a ghost (φάντασμα; vs 49). There is no mention of light, of the brightness or whiteness of the clothing of Jesus, or any such visual phenomenon. The point seems to be rather that, since no human being could walk on water, the entity they see doing so must be a ghost. The presence of an extraordinary visual phenomenon is not essential to the genre epiphany,[15] so the definition could stand in spite of this lack. In his diachronic analysis of the narrative, Theissen, following Bultmann and others, concluded that an epiphany on the water may have attracted motifs from a rescue story.[16] He also suggested, on the basis of a comparison of Matthew, Mark and John, that originally there was an appearance story in which Jesus did actually pass by. He did not clarify, however, whether he intended "appearance story" to be synonymous with "epiphany," or

---

[13] Ibid., 230.

[14] Gerd Theissen, *The Miracle Stories of the Early Christian Tradition* (Philadelphia: Fortress, 1983) 97.

[15] Elpidius Pax, *ΕΠΙΦΑΝΕΙΑ: Ein religionsgeschichtlicher Beitrag zur biblischen Theologie* (Münchener Theologische Studien, I. Historische Abteilung 10; Munich: Karl Zink Verlag, 1955) 39.

[16] Theissen, *The Miracle Stories of the Early Christian Tradition,* 186.

whether he was entertaining the possibility that the narrative originated as an account of the appearance of the risen Lord.

The evidence seems to be insufficient to determine whether the story in Mark 6:45-52 was originally an epiphany, to which a storm motif was added, or a rescue story which was transformed into an epiphany. It seems best to say that, once the clearly Markan editorial changes are identified, the pre-Markan story which emerges is a complex one with more than one important theme whose diachronic development cannot be reconstructed. The overall genre may be defined as miracle story or "tale," but it is difficult to say which of its three major themes is dominant. One of these is Jesus' performance of a superhuman or divine deed: walking on the surface of the sea. Another is the assistance afforded by Jesus to the disciples by overcoming the contrary wind. Although this theme is not identical with the theme or motif of the storm, in which the lives of the recipients of the miracle are in danger, it is similar to it and has some of the same connotations. One could say that there is an affinity between this theme and that of the storm.[17] The third theme is the epiphany, which resonates with or has an affinity with the resurrection-appearance story. These three (or five) themes are woven together to create the deceptively simple narrative which the evangelist found in one of his sources.

Context in the History of Religions

Although it seems impossible to reconstruct the literary history of the pre-Markan narrative and to determine an original, "pure" story based on a single theme, it can be said that the most distinctive and characteristic theme of the story is the extraordinary deed of walking on the sea. The source or model of this theme has been debated. One important issue is whether the process was oral or literary. In addition, the question has often been framed in terms of a biblical or Jewish

[17] Theissen, following G. Ortutay, argued that related or similar types exert an attraction on each other and thus create new variants (*The Miracle Stories of the Early Christian Tradition*, 19-20). Theissen suggested that an affinity between epiphanies and rescue miracles was operative in the formation of Mark 6:45-52 (ibid., 185-86).

context versus a Hellenistic or Roman milieu. If the form-critical hypothesis is correct, that miracle stories were created as a means of attracting interest in Jesus and recruiting followers, it is likely that the narrative originated in an oral context. But literary factors probably came into play when such stories were collected and written down, and of course when such collections were incorporated into the Gospel of Mark. The warning against a dichotomy between "Jewish" or "Palestinian" and "Hellenistic" has often been repeated, but seldom heeded. A distinction, if not a dichotomy, is to some degree justified when the texts under discussion were written in Hebrew or Aramaic. But in the analysis of Christian or Jewish texts written in Greek, the interpreter must be sensitive to the possibility of dual influence or even of a confluence or merging of traditions.

The motif of walking on the water may be seen as part of the larger theme of control of the sea. The ability to control the sea is an important element in the portrayal of the God of Israel in both prose and poetry in the Hebrew Bible. For example, in a context alluding to creation, God is described in Job 9:8 as the one who "trampled the back of the sea dragon" (or "trampled the waves of the Sea").[18] This text, like Ps 74:12-17, associates the activity of God as creator with the ancient myth of a combat between the king of the gods and the deity or monster associated with the sea, a theme that is prominent in the Babylonian creation epic, the *enuma elish*, in which Marduk battles Tiamat, and appears also in the mythic texts from Ugarit concerning the storm-god Baal.[19] In Isa 51:9-11 the mythic image first evokes creation, then is applied to the Exodus, and finally reinterpreted as an eschatological motif. All of these texts are poetic.

In the poetry presented as God's first speech from the whirlwind in Job, the confinement of the sea to its allotted place, like laying the foundations of the earth, is one of God's

---

[18] The latter translation is given in the text of the NRSV; the former in a note. Translations from the Hebrew Bible from here onward are from the NRSV.

[19] Two recent studies of this tradition are John Day, *God's Conflict with the Dragon and the Sea: Echoes of a Canaanite Myth in the Old Testament* (University of Cambridge Oriental Publications 35; Cambridge/New York: Cambridge University Press, 1985); Bernard F. Batto, *Slaying the Dragon: Mythmaking in the Biblical Tradition* (Louisville, KY: Westminster/John Knox, 1992).

acts in creation. In this context God asks Job, "Have you entered into the springs of the sea, or walked in the recesses of the deep?"[20] Here the poet speaks of God's activity in anthropomorphic language, but as a deed impossible for a human being to perform. In Ps 77:16, the fear of the waters before God and the trembling of the deep evoke the combat myth and resonate with theophanic poetry. Like Isa 51:10, the psalm then links this creation-motif with the Exodus in vss 19-20, "Your way was through the sea, your path, through the mighty waters; yet your footprints were unseen. You led your people like a flock by the hand of Moses and Aaron." Vs 19 expresses a conviction similar to that of some Greeks of the Hellenistic period who interpreted military victories as epiphanies of Apollo or Zeus: the presence of the deity is affirmed, but in the events and their outcome, not in a visual appearance.[21]

Like Isa 51:9-11, the oracle in Isa 43:16-21 associates the Exodus with eschatological salvation, but here the emphasis is on the future: "Do not remember the former things, or consider the things of old. I am about to do a new thing ... (vss 18-19). The "way in the sea," the "path in the mighty waters" (vs 16) seems to refer here more to the dry ground on which Israel walked through the sea (compare vss 19b-21) and less to the divine presence itself. In contrast, the theophany of Habakkuk 3 is more visually oriented, emphasizing the glory, brightness, and radiance of God (vss 3b-4). The poem is a call for God to be active once again in the present; in this context the Exodus is remembered in language reminiscent of the combat myth: "Was your wrath against River, O Lord? Or your anger against River, or your rage against Sea, when you drove your horses, your chariots to victory?" (vs 8).[22] The image of the Divine Warrior shines through also in the lines, "You trampled the sea with your horses, churning the mighty waters" (vs 15). In a more everyday sense, the power of God over the sea is manifested by the hurling of a great wind upon the sea to punish the reluctant prophet Jonah and the provision of a large sea-creature to swallow him (Jonah 1-2).

---

[20] Job 38:16; in the LXX the word translated "walked" is περιπατεῖν.

[21] Pax, *ΕΠΙΦΑΝΕΙΑ*, 36-37, 39.

[22] The translation is in accordance with the notes in the NRSV; the text has "the rivers" instead of "River" and "the sea" in place of "Sea."

The portrayal of God in the Hebrew Bible is complex in part because, in a monotheistic context, the one and only God had to assume all the characteristics which would have been distributed among a number of deities in a polytheistic context.[23] The one God is creator, savior, and redeemer in all sorts of ways and contexts. In Greek religion the god of the sea was Poseidon. He was the god *of* the sea rather than its mythic opponent. But like the God of Israel, to him was attributed control of the sea. He is portrayed in classical poetry as traveling in his chariot along the surface of the sea. Homer, for example, describes Poseidon's journey to his glorious house in Aigai as follows:

> "[he] climbed up into his chariot and drove it across the waves. And about him the sea beasts came up from their deep places and played in his path, and acknowledged their master, and the sea stood apart before him, rejoicing. The horses winged on delicately, and the bronze axle beneath was not wetted."[24]

The Roman picture of Neptune is similar. Virgil has him say to Venus, when she asks him to keep the remnant of Troy safe, "I have earned this trust, for I have often checked the frenzy and great anger of the sea and sky."[25] The poet describes Neptune's departure after he has reassured the goddess:

> "Upon his azure chariot he lightly glides across the waters' surface. Beneath his thundering axletree the swollen waves of the sea are smoothed, the cloud banks flee the vast sky."[26]

We see then that Jewish, Greek and Roman tradition shared the notion of a deity controlling wind and sea and the image of that deity making a path in the sea.

In both the Jewish and the Greek traditions, the deity is said to grant power over the sea or rivers to certain human

---

[23] See the discussion of the Hebrew Bible in relation to the polytheistic religions of ancient Mesopotamia by Tikva Frymer-Kensky, *In the Wake of the Goddesses: Women, Culture and the Biblical Transformation of Pagan Myth* (New York: Macmillan, 1992).

[24] Homer *Iliad* 13.26-30; the translation cited above is by Richmond Lattimore, *The Iliad of Homer* (Chicago: University of Chicago Press, 1951) 272. For the Greek text, see A.T. Murray, *Homer: The Iliad* (vol. 2; London: Heinemann; Cambridge: Harvard University Press, 1957) 4-5.

[25] Virgil *Aeneid* 5.1057-59; translation cited is by Allen Mandelbaum, *The Aeneid of Virgil* (Toronto & New York: Bantam Books, 1971) 130.

[26] Virgil *Aeneid* 5.1081-85; Mandelbaum, *The Aeneid of Virgil*, 131.

beings.[27] The best known example is, of course, the prose account in Exod 14:21-29, according to which the Lord divided the sea through Moses so that the people of Israel could cross over and escape from the Egyptians. The narrative of Joshua 3:7-4:18 relates how God divided the Jordan River by means of the ark, carried by priests, together with the leadership of Joshua over the people, so that they would know that Joshua was the successor of Moses. The power of Elijah is described in more autonomous terms: he split the Jordan simply by rolling up his mantle and striking the river with it (2 Kings 2:8). Much of Elisha's wonder-working is described autonomously also, but in this case, he struck the river with Elijah's mantle, but also called out, "Where is the Lord, the God of Elijah?" (vs 14). This question, as well as the act which imitates Elijah, is meant to make the point that Elisha is the successor of Elijah as mighty prophet or man of God.

These gifts of divine power over the sea have their analogues in Greek tradition.[28] It was said that Poseidon gave as a gift to the hero Euphemus, who was his son, the ability to travel over the sea unharmed, as over the land (τὴν θάλασσαν ἀπημάντως διαπορεύεσθαι ὡς διὰ γῆς). This tradition is attributed to Asclepiades.[29] If the Asclepiades in question is Asclepiades of Tragilus, the tradition could be as old as the fourth century BCE.[30] If he is Asclepiades of Myrleia in Bithynia, it could be dated to the first century BCE.[31] In any case, a very similar tradition is attested already in the third century BCE by Apollonius of Rhodes. He lists Euphemus of Taenarum, whom Europa bore to Poseidon, among the heroes who went in

[27] In the Wisdom tradition this power is exercised by Wisdom as an aspect of God or as a being intermediate between God and human beings; see Sir 24:5-6, Wis 10:18-19, 14:3.

[28] See the discussion by Barry Blackburn, *Theios Anēr and the Markan Miracle Traditions* (WUNT, 2nd series 40; Tübingen: Mohr-Siebeck, 1991) 145-47.

[29] Greek text from A.B. Drachmann, ed., *Scholia Vetera in Pindari Carmina*, vol. 2: *Scholia in Pythionicas* (Leipzig: B.G. Teubner, 1910; reprinted, Amsterdam: Adolf M. Hakkert, 1967) 106. The same tradition with almost identical wording is cited by Tzetzes (twelfth century) and attributed to Asclepiades in a *scholium* on Lycophron's *Alexandra* 886 (see Eduard Scheer, ed., *Lycophronis Alexandra*, vol. 2: *Scholia continens* [Berlin: Weidmann, 1908] 287).

[30] On Asclepiades of Tragilus, see "Asclepiades (1)," *The Oxford Classical Dictionary* (2nd ed., 1970) 129.

[31] On Asclepiades of Myrleia, see "Asclepiades (4)," ibid.

quest of the Golden Fleece. He characterized this hero as follows:

> "He was wont to skim the swell of the grey sea (κεῖνος ἀνὴρ καὶ πόντου ἐπὶ γλαυκοῖο θέεσκεν οἴδματος), and wetted not his swift feet, but just dipping the tips of his toes was borne on the watery path (οὐδὲ θοοὺς βάπτεν πόδας, ἀλλ' ὅσον ἄκροις ἴχνεσι τεγγόμενος διερῇ πεφόρητο κελεύθῳ)."[32]

In the first or second century CE, a tradition is attested that Orion was Poseidon's son and was granted by his father the power of striding across the sea (διαβαίνειν τὴν θάλασσαν).[33] A work attributed to Eratosthenes states that:

> "Hesiod says that [Orion] was the son of Euryale, the daughter of Minos, and of Poseidon, and that there was given to him as a gift the power of walking upon the waves as though upon land (δοθῆναι δὲ αὐτῷ δωρεὰν ὥστε ἐπὶ τῶν κυμάτων πορεύεσθαι καθάπερ ἐπὶ τῆς γῆς)."[34]

In the third century Porphyry recorded a tradition about Abaris, the Hyperborean and legendary servant or priest of Apollo, who was known as

---

[32] Apollonius Rhodius *The Argonautica* 1.179-84 (text and translation from R.C. Seaton, *Apollonius Rhodius: The Argonautica* [LCL; London: Heinemann; New York: Putnam's Sons, 1930] 14-15). See also Hyginus *Fabulae* 14.15, which lists Euphemus among the Argonauts as "the son of Neptune and Europa, the daughter of Tityus; from Taenarium; he is said to have run on top of water without wetting his feet" (*Euphemus Neptuni et Europes Tityi filiae filius, Taenarius; hic super aquas sicco pede cucurrisse dicitur*; text cited from H.J. Rose, ed., *Hygini Fabulae* [Leiden: Sythoff, 1933] 17). This work probably dates to the second century CE (so C.J. Fordyce, "Hyginus [3]," *Oxford Classical Dictionary* [2nd ed.; 1970] 533-34).

[33] Apollodorus *The Library* 1.4.3 (text and translation from James G. Frazer, *Apollodorus: The Library* [2 vols.; LCL; Cambridge: Harvard University Press; London: Heinemann, 1961] 1. 30-31).

[34] Pseudo-Eratosthenes *Catasterismi* 32 (Greek text cited according to Alexander Olivieri, ed., *Pseudo-Eratosthenis Catasterismi*, vol. 3, fasc. 1 of *Mythographi Graeci* [Leipzig: Teubner, 1897] 37-38; the translation is from Hugh G. Evelyn-White, *Hesiod: The Homeric Hymns and Homerica* [LCL; Cambridge: Harvard University Press; London: Heinemann, rev. ed., 1936] 71; the portion of the Greek text cited is identical to that of Evelyn-White). The latter scholar assigns this fragment to a work entitled *Astronomy* (or *Astrology* as Plutarch called it), but does not necessarily conclude that it was actually written by Hesiod (ibid., xi-xii, xix-xx). The same tradition is also attributed to Hesiod by the scholiast on Nicander's *Theriaca* 15 (see Heinrich Keil, *Scholia in Nicandri Theriaca* p.3, lines 26-28; this work is bound with Otto Schneider, ed., *Nicandrea: Theriaca et Alexipharmaca* [Leipzig: Teubner, 1856]) and by Hyginus *De Astronomia* 2.34 (see Ghislaine Viré, ed., *Hygini De Astronomia* [Stuttgart and Leipzig: Teubner, 1992] 80).

"'air-walking' because, riding on the arrow given him by the Hyperborean Apollo, he crossed rivers and seas and impassible places, somehow walking on the air ...."[35]

Later in the same century or early in the fourth, Iamblichus recorded the same tradition.[36] This tradition may have been known already to Herodotus. In his *History* 4.36, he says:

"Thus far have I spoken of the Hyperboreans, and let it suffice; for I do not tell the story of that Abaris, alleged to be a Hyperborean (τὸν γὰρ περὶ Ἀβάριος λόγον τοῦ λεγομένου εἶναι Ὑπερβορέου οὐ λέγω), who carried the arrow over the whole world, fasting the while (ὡς τὸν οἰστὸν περιέφερε κατὰ πᾶσαν γῆν οὐδὲν σιτεόμενος)."[37]

Here Herodotus seems to hesitate to tell an incredible story, but his mention of the arrow and of Abaris' travels throughout the world indicates that the tradition he knew was similar to the one recorded by Porphyry and Iamblichus.

The traditions about Euphemus and Orion are more precisely parallel to the motif of Jesus' walking on water, but those concerning Abaris are analogous in the implied exception to what came to be called the law of gravity.[38] The more autonomous power of Elijah has its analogue in late traditions about Heracles. Seneca preserves a tradition that, when shipwrecked off the African coast, Hercules "crossed over seas on foot"

---

[35] Porphyry *Life of Pythagoras* 29; for the Greek text see Édouard des Places, *Porphyre: Vie de Pythagore, Lettre à Marcella* (Collection des Universités de France; Paris: Société D'Édition "Les Belles Lettres," 1982) 49. The translation cited above is from Moses Hadas and Morton Smith, *Heroes and Gods: Spiritual Biographies in Antiquity* (Essay Index Reprint Series; Freeport, NY: Books for Libraries Press, 1970) 117. For discussion of the motifs of flying through the air and translation to another place, see Hans Dieter Betz, *Lukian von Samosata und das Neue Testament: Religionsgeschichtliche und Paränetische Parallelen* (Corpus Hellenisticum Novi Testamenti; TU; Berlin: Akademie, 1961) 167-69.

[36] Iamblichus *On the Pythagorean Way of Life* 136; see John Dillon and Jackson Hershbell, *Iamblichus: On the Pythagorean Way of Life: Text, Translation, and Notes* (SBL Texts and Translations 29; Atlanta: Scholars Press, 1991) 156-57.

[37] Text and translation are from A.D. Godley, *Herodotus* (4 vols.; LCL; Cambridge: Harvard University Press; London: Heinemann, 1963) 2. 234-35.

[38] On the relation between miracle-working on the one hand and philosophy and science on the other, see Robert M. Grant, *Miracles and Natural Law in Graeco-Roman and Early Christian Thought* (Amsterdam: North Holland Publishing, 1952).

(*maria superavit pedes*).[39] The emperor Julian wrote in the fourth century in his oration to the Cynic Heracleios, speaking of Heracles:

> "... and then there is his journey over the sea itself in a golden cup, though, by the gods, I do not think it was really a cup, but my belief is that he himself walked on the sea as though it were dry land (βαδίσαι δὲ αὐτὸν ὡς ἐπὶ ξηρᾶς τῆς θαλάττης). For what was impossible to Heracles?"[40]

The Jewish traditions in which a human being is granted power over the sea involve cultural heroes in the broad sense (Moses and Joshua), who later often were described as prophets, as well as the prophets Elijah and Elisha. The Greek and Roman traditions discussed so far involve a hero (Euphemus) and legendary or mythological characters (Orion, Abaris and Heracles). It should be noted that, at least by the fifth century BCE, power over the sea began to be associated with rulers and kings.[41] In book 7.33-57 of his *History*, Herodotus tells the awesome story of the crossing by Xerxes and his army of the Hellespont. Although the crossing was more an achievement of technology than a miracle, mythic elements emerge in the story as well. No sooner was the strait bridged for the first time, than a great storm occurred and destroyed the work. When Xerxes heard the news, he was very angry and commanded

> "that the Hellespont be scourged with three hundred lashes (ἐκέλευσε τριηκοσίας ἐπικέσθαι μάστιγι πληγὰς), and a pair of fetters be thrown into the sea (καὶ κατεῖναι ἐς τὸ πέλαγος πεδέων ζεῦγος)." He "sent branders with the rest to brand the Hellespont (στιγέας ἅμα τούτοισι ἀπέπεμψε στίξοντας τὸν Ἑλλήσποντον)." He "charged them while they scourged to utter words outlandish and presumptuous (ἐνετέλλετο δὲ ὦν ῥαπίζοντας λέγειν βάρβαρά τε καὶ ἀτάσθαλα): 'Thou bitter water,' they should say, 'our master thus punishes thee, because thou didst him wrong albeit he had done thee none. Yea, Xerxes the king will pass

[39] Seneca *Hercules furens* 322-324; text and translation (slightly modified) are from Frank Justus Miller, *Seneca* (10 vols.; LCL; Cambridge: Harvard University Press; London: Heinemann, 1979) 8.28-29.

[40] Julian *Oration* 7.219D; text and translation are from Wilmer Cave Wright, *The Works of the Emperor Julian* (3 vols.; LCL; London: Heinemann; Cambridge: Harvard University Press, 1949) 2.110-11.

[41] See also the discussion in Wendy J. Cotter, "The Markan Sea Miracles: Their History, Formation and Function" (Ph.D. diss., University of St. Michael's College, 1991) 298-322.

over (διαβήσεται) thee, whether thou wilt or no; it is but just that no man offers thee sacrifice, for thou art a turbid and a briny river.' Thus he commanded that the sea should be punished (τήν τε δὴ θάλασσαν ἐνετέλλετο τούτοισι ζημιοῦν), and they who had been overseers of the bridging of the Hellespont should be beheaded."[42]

The second attempt was successful and the eventual crossing required seven days and seven nights:

"There is a tale that, when Xerxes had now crossed the Hellespont, a man of the Hellespont cried, 'O Zeus, why hast thou taken the likeness of a Persian man and changed thy name to Xerxes, leading the whole world with thee to remove Hellas from its place? For that thou mightest have done without these means.'"[43]

A passage from Dio Chrysostom's third discourse on kingship, probably delivered before Trajan in 104 CE, shows that Xerxes' feat had been mythicized further and was well known during the period of Roman rule in the East. Dio sets forth the views of Socrates, using a dialogue form, and has his interrogator say:

"... you know perfectly well that of all men under the sun that man is most powerful and in might no whit inferior to the gods themselves who is able to accomplish the impossible – if it should be his will, to have men walk dryshod over the sea (πεζεύεσθαι μὲν τὴν θάλατταν), ... – or have you not heard that Xerxes, the king of the Persians, ... led his infantry through the sea, riding upon a chariot just like Poseidon in Homer's description? (διὰ δὲ τῆς θάλαττης τὸν πεζὸν στρατὸν ἄγων ἤλαυνεν ἐφ' ἅρματος, ὥσπερ τὸν Ποσειδῶνα φησὶν Ὅμηρος;)"[44]

Although Dio, through a speech attributed to Socrates, rejects this point of view, the text provides evidence that it was held by a sufficient number of people to warrant refutation.

Similar power was attributed to Alexander the Great.[45] Menander, the Attic poet of the New Comedy, wrote toward the end of the fourth century BCE:

---

[42] Herodotus *History* 7.35 (text and translation from A.D. Godley, *Herodotus* [4 vols.; LCL; London: Heinemann; New York: Putnam's Sons, 1922] 3.346-49).

[43] Herodotus *History* 7.56 (Godley, *Herodotus*, 3.370-71).

[44] Dio Chrysostom 3.30-31 (text and translation from J.W. Cohoon, *Dio Chrysostom* [5 vols.; LCL; London: Heinemann; Cambridge: Harvard University Press, 1961] 1.116-19).

[45] See the evidence discussed by Cotter, "The Markan Sea Miracles," 303-9.

> "How very Alexander-like is this forthwith: 'If I require someone's presence, of his own accord he will appear! And if, forsooth, I needs must tread some pathway through the sea, then it will give me footing!' (ὡς Ἀλεξανδρῶδες ἤδη τοῦτο· κἄν ζητῶ τινα, αὐτόματος οὗτος παρέσται· κἄν διελθεῖν δηλαδὴ διὰ θαλάττης δῇ πόρον τιν', οὗτος ἔσται μοι βατός)."[46]

The poet satirizes the attitude, but his target is surely those who are willing to grant such powers to the ruler as well as the ruler himself.[47]

These passages show that the motif of walking on water had become proverbial for the (humanly) impossible and for the arrogance of the ruler aspiring to empire.[48] The motif appears in this form in 2 Maccabees, a Hellenistic Jewish text which dates to the early first century BCE, as a characterization of Antiochus IV Epiphanes:

> "So Antiochus carried off eighteen hundred talents from the temple, and hurried away to Antioch, thinking in his arrogance that he could sail on the land and walk on the sea, because his mind was elated (Ὁ γοῦν Ἀντίοχος ὀκτακόσια πρὸς τοῖς χιλίοις ἀπενεγκάμενος ἐκ τοῦ ἱεροῦ τάλαντα θᾶττον εἰς τὴν Ἀντιόχειαν ἐχωρίσθη οἰόμενος ἀπὸ τῆς ὑπερηφανίας τὴν μὲν γῆν πλωτὴν καὶ τὸ πέλαγος πορευτὸν θέσθαι διὰ τὸν μετεωρισμὸν τῆς καρδίας)."[49]

Although the extraordinary deeds are not actually performed and the expectation of such performance is condemned, the figure of speech expresses proverbial impossibility and implies that human beings who claimed divinity, or to whom divinity was attributed, especially kings, were associated with such feats within the cultural context of this work.

In striking contrast to, and probably in deliberate defiance of, the popularity of the motif as expressive of the proverbially impossible, walking on water appears in magical and related texts as something that the properly trained or instructed person can accomplish. A text included in the magical papyri,

---

[46] Menander frg. 924 K (text and translation from Francis G. Allinson, *Menander: The Principal Fragments* [LCL; Cambridge: Harvard University Press; London: Heinemann, 1964] 532-33). The fragment is classified under "Unidentified Minor Fragments."

[47] Cf. also Lucian *How To Write History* 40.

[48] See further the discussion by Cotter of Roman rulers in the first century CE ("The Markan Sea Miracles," 312-22).

[49] 2 Macc 5:21; the translation is from the NRSV; the Greek text from Alfred Rahlfs, ed., *Septuaginta* (2 vols.; 7th ed.; Stuttgart: Württembergische Bibelanstalt, 1935) 1.1112.

but which may be a fragment of a novel, contains the following statement:

> "... [the sun] will stand still; and should I order the moon, it will come down; and should I wish to delay the day, the night will remain for me; and should we in turn ask for day, the light will not depart; *and should I wish to sail the sea, I do not need a ship*; and should I wish to go through the air, I will be lifted up. It is only an erotic drug that I do not find, not one that can cause, not one that can stop love. For the earth, in fear of the god, does not produce one... (emphasis added)."[50]

The text dates to the second or third century CE.[51] A Jewish text entitled the *Sword of Moses* contains a spell for walking on water.[52] It reads:

> "To walk on the waters of the sea take the wooden helve of an axe, bore a hole through it, pass a red thread through it, and tie it on to thy heel, then repeat the words of the 'Sword,' and then you may go in and out in peace."[53]

The matter-of-fact tone of the spell is noteworthy.

The motif of walking on water also occurs in connection with dreams. It appears in Dio Chrysostom's eleventh discourse, a sophistic argument that Troy was not captured by the Greeks. After giving a list of reported, but improbable events, Dio asks:

> "Does not all this in reality remind one of dreams (ἐνυπνίοις) and wild fiction (ἀπιθάνοις ψεύσμασιν)? In the book *Dreams*

---

[50] PGM XXXIV.1-24; trans. by E.N. O'Neil from Hans Dieter Betz, ed., *The Greek Magical Papyri in Translation* (2nd ed.; Chicago/London: University of Chicago Press, 1992) 267-68. Cf. Apuleius *Metamorphoses* 1.3.

[51] See also PGM I.119-21.

[52] On the character, date, and provenance of this text, see Emil Schürer, *The History of the Jewish People in the Age of Jesus Christ* (rev. ed. by Geza Vermes, Fergus Millar and Martin Goodman; 3 vols.; Edinburgh: T.& T. Clark, 1973-87) 3.1 (1986) 350-52.

[53] Translation from Moses Gaster, *Studies and Texts in Folklore, Magic, Mediaeval Romance, Hebrew Apocrypha and Samaritan Archaeology* (3 vols.; New York: Ktav, 1971) 1. 331. This text is from Codex Oxford 1531,6 (Gaster's *Sword of Moses,* recension B). For the Hebrew text, see ibid., 3. 90. See also the text and translation in Peter Schäfer, ed., *Synopse zur Hekhalot-Literatur* (Texte und Studien zum Antiken Judentum 2; Tübingen: Mohr [Siebeck], 1981) § 609 01531, p. 235 and idem, ed., *Übersetzung der Hekhalot-Literatur IV: §§ 598-985* (Tübingen: Mohr [Siebeck], 1991) § 609 01531, p. 11. There is a related spell in Codex Gaster 178 (Gaster's *Sword of Moses,* recension A) which reads "To walk upon the water without wetting the feet, take a leaden plate and write upon it [name] No. 125 and place it in thy girdle, and then you can walk" (Gaster, *Studies and Texts.* 1. 328; Hebrew text, 3.87).

('Ονείρασιν) by Horus people have such experiences (οἱ ἄνθρωποι τοιαύτας ὄψεις ὁρῶσι), imagining at one time that they are being killed and their bodies stripped of arms and that they rise to their feet again and fight unarmed, at other times imagining they are chasing somebody or holding converse with the gods (τοῖς θεοῖς διαλέγεσθαι) or committing suicide without any cause for the act, and at times, possibly, flying offhand or walking on the sea (καὶ οὕτως, εἰ τύχοι ποτέ, πέτεσθαι καὶ βαδίζειν ἐπὶ τῆς θαλάττης). For this reason one might well call Homer's poetry a kind of dream (ἐνύπνιον), obscure and vague at that (καὶ τοῦτο ἄκριτον καὶ ἀσαφές)."[54]

Here the motif represents, not only that which is humanly impossible, but the wild and unrealistic type of thing that one sometimes dreams. The motif also appears in a serious study of the interpretation of dreams by Artemidorus of Daldis in Lydia, who lived in the second century CE. In his work, Artemidorus divides dreams into two types: the ἐνύπνιον, which indicates a present state of affairs, and the ὄνειρος, which indicates a future state of affairs.[55] In the former, certain experiences such as love, fear, hunger and thirst, cause manifestations in sleep. The latter, however, call the dreamer's attention to a prediction of future events just as the vision (ὅραμα) and the oracular response do (1.2). Only those dreams that are unexpected reveal the future. If the dreamer has been anxiously concerned about something and dreams about it, the dream belongs to the ἐνύπνιον-class and is non-significative (1.6). Artemidorus also divides dreams into the theorematic (direct) and the allegorical (1.2). The meaning of an unexpected and allegorical dream about walking on the sea depends on the gender, legal and social status, and particular circumstances of the dreamer.[56] The most interesting interpretation for our purposes, in light of the association of walking on water with rulers, is the last:

"On the other hand, for all those who earn their living from crowds, for statesmen, and popular leaders, it prophesies ex-

---

[54] Dio Chrysostom 11.129; text and translation from J.W. Cohoon, *Dio Chrysostom*, 1.544-45.

[55] Artemidorus *Oneirocritica* 1.1; for the Greek text, see Roger A. Pack, *Artemidori Daldiani Onirocriticon Libri V* (Leipzig: Teubner, 1963); for an English translation and commentary, see Robert J. White, *The Interpretation of Dreams: Oneirocritica by Artemidorus* (Park Ridge, NJ: Noyes Press, 1975).

[56] Compare the passage on dreams about walking on the sea (3.16) with the theoretical discussions in 1.3, 5, 7-8.

> traordinary gain together with great fame. For the sea also resembles a crowd because of its instability."

This passage reinforces the traditional link of the motif to the ruler and suggests that, in such a context, the deed symbolizes the power of the ruler.[57]

The Significance and Function of the Pre-Markan Story

According to the rationalist and satirist Lucian of Samosata, the ability to walk on water is something invented by the poet or the (bad) philosopher or historian. He writes:

> "In the case of [poetry], liberty is absolute and there is one law – the will of the poet. Inspired and possessed by the Muses as he is, even if he wants to harness winged horses to a chariot, even if he sets others to run over water or the tops of flowers, nobody gets annoyed."[58]

He likewise wrote *A True Story* in which everything

> "is a more or less comical parody of one or another of the poets, historians and philosophers of old, who have written much that smacks of miracles and fables."[59]

One of the topics that he parodies is the notion of a human being walking on water; he presents people who are able to do so because their feet are made of cork.[60]

Apart from the satirical intention and effect, Lucian's point is well taken and may be applied to the early Christians who created the oral form of this narrative. It was an act of *mythopoiesis*, the imaginative construction of an incident in the life of Jesus that was intended to honor him and to win adherents to his cause. Whether the story was originally intended as an account of an actual event (analogous to Artemidorus' theorematic dream) or as a symbolic or allegorical narrative (corresponding to Artemidorus' allegorical dream) is

---

[57] Artemidorus *Oneirocritica* 3.16; translation from White, *The Interpretation of Dreams*, 162. For a different interpretation of this passage, see Cotter, "The Markan Sea Miracles," 336-40.

[58] Lucian *How to Write History* 8; translation is from K. Kilburn, *Lucian* (8 vols.; LCL; Cambridge: Harvard University Press; London: Heinemann, 1959) 6.13. The allusion is to Homer *Iliad* 20.215-29.

[59] Lucian *A True Story* 1.2; translation is from A.M. Harmon, *Lucian* (8 vols.; LCL) 1.249-51.

[60] Lucian *A True Story* 2.4; for discussion, see Betz, *Lukian von Samosata*, 166-67.

impossible to say. It is probable, however, that the story was understood by some tradents and by some in the audience in the former manner and by others in the latter.

It is also likely that the audience included both Jews and Gentiles, and that the tradents included Jesus-believers from both backgrounds. The flexibility of the symbolic narrative (or of the account of an event open to a symbolic or allegorical reading) allowed for various interpretations. Such flexibility implies that members of the audience familiar with Jewish tradition were likely to perceive this story as resonating with the Biblical accounts of the power of God and the delegated power of the Jewish cultural heroes and prophets. The fact that it is God alone in the Hebrew Bible who is said to walk on water and the presence of theophanic elements in the story imply a relatively "high" Christology. This observation has led some to emphasize the Hellenistic analogies to the narrative. But a relatively high Christology is not impossible in Jewish Christianity.[61] On the other hand, the fact that the motif of a human or semi-divine being walking on water is considerably more widespread in Greek and Roman tradition than in Jewish circles makes it likely that members of the audience familiar with such tradition would be inclined to associate the story with instances of it, even if they had been instructed in the Jewish analogies to the story in the Biblical writings or in oral tradition.

The most probable focal point for a fusion of traditions is the messianic character of (or attributed to) Jesus. In certain strands of Judaism, especially those characterized as apocalyptic, the messiah is expected to assume some of the functions normally reserved for God.[62] Such assimilation of the messiah to God would facilitate the attribution to Jesus of God's portrayal as one able to walk upon the sea. As noted above, the power to walk on water frequently was associated in Greek and Roman tradition with rulers, especially those to whom divinity was attributed. This tradition would make the

[61] See Adela Yarbro Collins, "The 'Son of Man' Tradition and the Book of Revelation," *The Messiah: Developments in Earliest Judaism and Christianity* (ed. James H. Charlesworth; Minneapolis: Fortress, 1992) 536-68; Blackburn, *Theios Anēr*, 145-82.

[62] See John J. Collins, "Introduction: History of Interpretation, Jewish," *Daniel* (Hermeneia; Minneapolis: Fortress, 1993); Blackburn, *Theios Anēr*, 171-73.

presentation of Jesus as the messiah (king of Israel or of all creation) intelligible to a Hellenized or Romanized audience. The philosophical discussions about true kingship would prepare such an audience for the attribution of kingship to someone without literal political power.

The likelihood of the messianic significance of this story would be enhanced if the other narratives in the *catena* to which it belonged, as reconstructed by Achtemeier, could be shown to have messianic implications as well. The exploration of this issue must be reserved for another occasion, but the feeding of the four thousand (preserved in Mark 8:1-10) may be understood as a symbolic representation or a foreshadowing of the messianic banquet. Similarly, the healings of the blind man (8:22-26) and the deaf-mute (7:32-37) may be understood messianically if they can be shown to allude to passages of older Scripture which were interpreted messianically.

The Adaptation of the Story by Mark

As noted previously, only two elements in the story can be established with a high degree of probability as Markan redactional elements. The first is the addition of the clause "while he himself dismissed the crowd" (ἕως αὐτὸς ἀπολύει τὸν ὄχλον) at the end of verse 45. This addition serves to link the story of the walking on the water, which was the first in a *catena* of miracle stories adapted by the evangelist, with the narrative about the feeding of the five thousand, the last unit in another *catena*.[63] The second feature is the composition and addition of the conclusion to the story, "For they did not understand with regard to the loaves, but their hearts were hardened" (vs 52). It is likely that this Markan conclusion replaced an acclamation like the one that appears in the parallel in Matthew (14:33): "Truly, you are the Son of God." The acclamation is a typical concluding element in the Christian miracle story which has analogies in the ancient world, especially in Egyptian and Roman tradition.[64] Mark most probably suppressed the acclamation that was in his source, not because he wished

[63] Achtemeier, "Toward the Isolation of Pre-Markan Miracle Catenae," 265-66, 281-91.

[64] See Theissen (who in part follows E. Peterson), *The Miracle Stories of the Early Christian Tradition,* 71-72, 74, 152-73. See also Georgi, *The Opponents of Paul in Second Corinthians,* 170.

to negate the implications of the story for the identity of Jesus, but because he wished to integrate them into his narrative as a whole and thus into a more complex picture of Jesus' identity. Matthew's restoration of the typical acclamation does not undercut the hypothesis of Matthean dependence on Mark. Matthew's redactional change was based either on his knowledge of another form of the story, possibly from oral tradition, which had the acclamation, or upon his own sense of the genre. He restored the typical ending because he wished to reduce in importance the Markan theme of the disciples' lack of understanding.

The reference to the "loaves" in the conclusion, like the addition in vs 45, links this story to the one about the feeding of the five thousand (6:30-44). The disciples fail to understand the significance of the walking on water and the rescue-epiphany because they have previously failed to understand the multiplication of the loaves. Similarly, the remark that their hearts were hardened assimilates them to the opponents of Jesus in 3:5, where the context also involves a miraculous deed (cf. also 8:17).

The story about the stilling of the storm is similar in topic to the one about walking on water and, as noted above, there is verbal similarity as well (compare the remark that the wind abated [καὶ ἐκόπασεν ὁ ἄνεμος] in 4:39c with 6:51b). Yet the former story ends with an acclamation,[65] whereas the latter does not. This state of affairs supports the idea that Mark is not adverse to the propagandistic function of the miracle stories, but subordinates that function in the case of the latter story to the theme of the mystery of Jesus' identity. The choice of the second story for this purpose may be explained by the relation of the story, as Mark found it in his source, to older Scripture.

As noted earlier, the picture of Jesus walking on the sea in Mark 6:48 (περιπατῶν ἐπὶ τῆς θαλάσσης) resonates with the portrayal of God in Job 9:8 as the one who "trampled the back of the sea dragon" (περιπατεῖν ... ἐπὶ θαλάσσης in the LXX).[66]

---

[65] So also Theissen, *The Miracle Stories of the Early Christian Tradition*, 71.

[66] Bultmann (*The History of the Synoptic Tradition*, 230) was correct in doubting that the Job passage could have been the sole model for the creation of the story of Jesus walking on the water, particularly if the latter arose in an oral context. But once the story was written down, and especially when the tradents of the written tradition were educated in older Scripture, as Mark probably was, the influence of such passages was likely to come into play.

Jesus' intention to "pass by" the disciples (παρελθεῖν αὐτούς) in the same verse of Mark resonates with yet another verse of Job in the same context, "Look, he passes by me, and I do not see him; he moves on, but I do not perceive him."[67] Ernst Lohmeyer argued that the term "pass by" (παρελθεῖν) belongs to the motif of the divine epiphany in the Old Testament, more strongly in the LXX than in the MT.[68] But in Job 9:11 the term does not describe God's appearance in an epiphany.[69] In fact, one could argue that this verse in Job is an anti-epiphany; it calls into question the very possibility of such an event: even if God were to pass directly by me (a mere human being), I would not be capable of perceiving or comprehending the divine presence.

As mentioned earlier, Mark 6:45-52 combines the motif of walking on the sea with the epiphany-theme. The hypothesis that Mark associated the motif of Jesus walking on the sea with Job 9:8 as a prototype and the epiphany-theme with Job 9:11 is an attractive one. The negative perspective of the latter verse was congenial to Mark's theme of the lack of understanding on the part of the disciples, so it inspired him to replace the concluding acclamation of the source with the negative conclusion in vs 52:

> "For *they did not understand* (οὐ γὰρ συνῆκαν) with regard to the loaves, but their hearts were hardened" (emphasis added).

If this hypothesis is correct, it implies that Mark, in this context at least, wished to say something about the difficulty of perceiving the divinity of Jesus, rather than engage in polemics against the historical disciples or those who subsequently claimed their authority for their own views and practices.

---

[67] Job 9:11; the MT reads:

הֵן יַעֲבֹר עָלַי וְלֹא אֶרְאֶה
וְיַחֲלֹף וְלֹא־אָבִין לוֹ׃

The LXX reads:

Ἐὰν ὑπερβῇ με, οὐ μὴ ἴδω·
ἐὰν παρέλθῃ με, οὐδ᾽ ὣς ἔγνων.

[68] Ernst Lohmeyer, "Und Jesus ging vorüber," *Nieuw Theologisch Tijdschrift* 23 (1934) 206ff; reprinted in idem, *Urchristliche Mystik: Neutestamentliche Studien* (Darmstadt: Hermann Gentner Verlag, 1956) 57-79. He discussed the appearance of the motif in the LXX of Genesis, Exodus, 2 Kings, 3 Kings, and Daniel. See also John Paul Heil, *Jesus Walking on the Sea: Meaning and Gospel Functions of Matt 14:22-33, Mark 6:45-52 and John 6:15b-21* (AnBib 87; Rome: Biblical Institute Press, 1981) 69-72.

[69] Heil notes this fact (*Jesus Walking on the Sea*, 71, n. 98), but does not draw out its implications for Job or for Mark.

THE AUTHORITY OF THE EXCLUDED: MARK'S CHALLENGE TO A RATIONAL HERMENEUTICS

Michael LaFargue
(University of Massachusetts/Boston, Boston, Massachusetts)

Two important things I learned from Dieter Georgi were, first, concrete historical imagination: always to keep in mind that concrete people in concrete situations wrote the texts that we read, and that reconstructing these concrete settings is crucial to understanding the texts. Secondly, I learned to combine depth of understanding with fairness to diverse viewpoints. I hope this essay in tribute to Dieter Georgi exhibits these qualities, although, of course, the specific ideas I advance here are my own.

My paper proposes an hypothesis about the meaning of Mark's Gospel that depends in turn on an hypothesis about its social setting. I would also like to deal with several problems that this Gospel raises for theoretical hermeneutics, specifically the relation of sociologically-oriented interpretation to theological *Sachkritik.* (Dieter Georgi is the one who pointed out to me that my interests were still "theological," at a time when I thought I had left that behind.) I take as my starting point one of the most far-ranging and stimulating recent studies of Mark, Burton Mack's *A Myth of Innocence: Mark and Christian Origins.*[1]

One great strength of Mack's book is its critique of what I would call the "fideism"[2] of Christian scholars, which prevents them from raising questions at a sufficiently fundamental level, and so prevents them from fully explaining the origins of Christianity. I call "fideist" all those scholarly accounts that implicitly appeal to unquestioned assumptions of a modern Christian audience, that of course Jesus speaks with divine

---

[1] Philadelphia: Fortress, 1988.

[2] Mack does not use the term "fideism"; he does speak of the assumption that Christian origins constitute a "radically new beginning," unique and without analogy in history, *A Myth,* 3-7. The supposed "uniqueness" of Christianity has also been, to be sure, a target of criticism for Dieter Georgi, see "Rudolf Bultmann's *Theology of the New Testament* Revisited," in Edward C. Hobbs ed., *Bultmann, Retrospect and Prospect* (Philadelphia: Fortress, 1985) 85-86.

authority, of course his death is a saving event, of course Jesus-followers were right to follow Jesus and to condemn those who rejected him, and so on. Taking these beliefs for granted means that scholars do not really imagine themselves back into a time before Jesus-followers began to hold them, and attempt to fully account for the origins of these beliefs. Mack shows the way that recent scholarship on Mark is at many points[3] governed by a more explicit fideism, the view that the basis for the Christian faith is so discontinuous with the rest of reality-so "unique" and without analogy-that one cannot describe this basis in terms taken from general human experience. This view manifests itself in the way that interpreters at some point lapse into language that, as Mack says, "marks the point beyond which the scholar chooses not to proceed with the investigation, indeed the point beyond which reasoned argument must cease." This language

> "hold[s] a space for the unimaginable miracle that must have happened prior to all interpretation...[It is a] rhetorical device for evoking the myth of Christian origins without having to explain it."[4]

Fideism thus sets firm limits both to rational explanation and to empathic *Verstehen.*

A second great strength of Mack's book is that he treats the question of Markan origins not as a question of Mark's testimony to a real and historical "Christ-event" that preceded the Gospel but, rather, as a question of how a group in a diaspora synagogue came to imagine the Jesus-story the way they did, as an *imagined story* about their origins. Mack treats Mark's Gospel as essentially "serious fiction,"[5] a narrative using stories set in rural Galilee in the early 30's to dramatize issues of importance to people attached to a Southern Syrian synagogue in the early 70's.[6] Mack's study is outstanding for its sensitive and detailed treatment of Markan narrative art and the way in which Mark's plot and narrative themes are

---

[3] See especially his discussion of scholarship on the parables (*A Myth,* 145-47) and on the crucifixion (ibid. 257, 260, 268).

[4] Ibid. 7.

[5] He emphasizes Markan control of the main elements of his narrative as well as the way Mark uses this control to dramatize issues important to him. This is especially true in Mack's analysis of the passion account, which he thinks is largely a Markan creation.

[6] Ibid. 315.

plausibly related to problems faced by Jesus-followers in conflict with other groups in a diaspora synagogue. I find myself in agreement with very many of Mack's individual analyses of these narrative themes, although I want to offer here a fundamentally different account of the origins of Markan belief.

Mack's Treatment of the Controversy Stories (Mark 2:1-3:6)

Though developed in much complex detail, the core of Mack's thesis about Markan origins[7] can be stated rather simply: The community for which Mark speaks was originally a reform movement within a diaspora synagogue community in Southern Syria. It battled another, Pharisaic reform movement for influence in this community, and lost. Mark makes Jesus' crucifixion at Pharisaic hands central to his Gospel in order to rationalize this defeat; their defeat, like Jesus' crucifixion, was part of "God's plan." This community's current weak status in the world now conflicts with its exalted self-image. Community members compensate for their actual weakness by making highly exaggerated claims for themselves and their Lord, Jesus, and demonizing those who had defeated them. The expression and rationalization of such claims is the main purpose of Mark's Gospel.[8] To put this in terms more blunt than Mack uses: What is most distinctive about the Markan community is not anything substantive that it stands for, but its *chutzpah*, its audacity and skill at creating an authority figure of such monumental proportions to support its own vastly overblown self-image.

The approach by which Mack arrives at this conclusion can be illustrated by considering his discussion of the controversy stories in Mark 2:1-3:6. The chief importance of these stories for Mark's narrative consists in the fact that they provoke the plot of the scribes and Pharisees to have Jesus crucified, and present Mark's claim that this plot results from a refusal to recognize Jesus' "authority" (*exousia*). These stories have to

---

[7] I deal here only with Mack's account of the immediate origin and purpose of the Gospel of Mark, not with his lengthy discussions of other early Christian movements leading up to Mark.

[8] See ibid. 94-96, 124-26, 129, 170, 192-99, 203-07, 244-45, 331, 339, 353-57.

bear a considerable weight because the Jesus/Pharisee conflict they describe turns out to be, as Mack says, "a conflict of apocalyptic proportions,"[9] causing God to destroy the sacred Temple, to disown the leaders formerly entrusted with the Judaic heritage, and to give this heritage to the Jesus-followers.

Mack rightly poses the very fundamental question: On what basis did Mark's community accord to Jesus such immense authority? He then argues that the stories themselves do not provide any basis. Jesus in these stories "violate[s] the basic ground rules of human discourse and dialogue." "There is no point of leverage outside the sayings of Jesus to qualify or sustain the argumentation." "[He] uses assumptions that his questioners did not share or could not have known."[10] Nothing Jesus says or does in these stories could serve a normal-rational reader as a plausible basis for believing that Jesus possesses special authority.

Mack converts this accurate observation into an argument, central to his overall thesis, that Markan Jesus-followers had no basis for the stands they took on issues dramatized in these stories (their inclusion of sinners in table-fellowship; their rejection of strict Sabbath observance and of fasting-customs common to other Jewish groups). It is because they have no basis for these stands that they create this image of their leader Jesus in these stories and, by simple *fiat*, endow him with supreme authority, so that he may in turn authorize their views and practices. Their claims about Jesus' authority are truly extravagant, and stridently asserted, and Mack offers a psychological explanation for this: The extravagance and stridency are a compensatory mechanism, compensating for the group's half-conscious awareness that it had no basis for its distinctive views and practices. Jesus' authority authorizes these, while this authority itself is without any other basis, serving as its own authorization, completely self-referential. Mark becomes the first Christian fideist when this "self-referential oddity [of Jesus' claimed authority] was now transformed into a revelation of the divine."[11]

I have two criticisms of Mack's approach here. First, it gives us a picture of the Markan community that is curiously empty

[9] Ibid. 9.
[10] Ibid. 175-78, 195-99, 203-07.
[11] Ibid. 205.

at its center. Mack makes little attempt to conjecture *why* it was that individual Markan Jesus-followers began to "follow Jesus" in the first place, and what motivated their fierce commitment to their group. He gives us only a very weak picture of what it meant to them to "follow Jesus," beyond their adherence to a group which had egalitarian leanings, included "sinners", did not follow the law-codes of some other Jewish groups, and considered itself followers of Jesus.[12] For Mack, Mark's narrative is purely a propaganda piece; and the themes of this propaganda are *almost completely external* to the real reasons why Markan Jesus-followers are committed to Jesus. This is very odd from a human perspective. Ultimately, the people involved do not appear very plausible concrete human beings, but sociological abstractions: They will blindly believe to be true whatever they would like to be true, whatever contributes to "the construction and maintenance of social structures"[13] to which they are attached and rationalizes the claims they want to make over against other groups. This sociologically motivated picture of the Markan community is humanly speaking rather flat, and seems but a reverse image of Christian fideism. In both cases early Jesus-followers have no explainable basis for their views. For fideists this is a function of unique and unexplainable divine origins. For Mack, it is a function of an enormous and fierce desire for self-legitimation, whose fierceness is only weakly explained by reference to a general sociological axiom that this is just what religious groups do. Mack's picture is not the product of a careful consideration of alternatives. It is the product of a simple omission, neglecting to *consider* whether Mark's Gospel reflects some of the real bases for the beliefs of Markan Jesus-followers, and neglecting to try to reconstruct a thoroughly plausible picture of them as concrete and human beings. This, it seems to me, is what happens often today in biblical studies when the sociology of knowledge serves as a *substitute* for empathic *Verstehen* rather than as an aid to it.[14]

---

[12] Ibid. 318-19.

[13] Mack speaks more exactly of the way that religious phenomena and images "*are intimately related to*" the construction and maintenance of social structures (*A Myth*, 9), a more general formulation with which I would agree. But in his specific explanation of Mark's Gospel the relationship is one in which Mark's narrative and images function simply as external rationalizations serving to bolster status claims Mark's group wants to make.

[14] I have argued this point further in my "Socio-historical Research and

Secondly, Mack's approach is an easy target for the charges that fideists always level against their critics: He subjects Mark's message to rational criteria established independently of the Gospel itself. Doing this guarantees a priori that the Gospel will not fundamentally challenge any of our pre-established notions about what a valid basis for belief might consist in.

I would like to propose a different approach, not only for Mark but for any difficult text[15] from a distant culture. Let us not start by seeing whether the reasons expressly presented in a writing, considered rationally, are sufficient to justify the claims it makes. Rather, let us begin our work with the provisional assumption that the claims made by a text have a plausible substantive basis in something else that the text says. A central interpretive task is to devise some way of *construing* what the text says in a way that would plausibly support the claims that it makes. Often what this means is imaginatively constructing a picture of the kind of human audience – a picture that accords with our knowledge of possible socio-cultural settings in this era – who would naturally have construed the text in this way. Let us imagine the most respectable, but humanly understandable audience possible, who would have been convinced by a given writing.

Such an effort will result, of course, in an hypothesis, rather than in proven results. But I argue that this "hypothesis formation" – the aim of the present writing – is one of the more difficult aspects of interpretation, one that requires and also deserves considerable imaginative effort. It generates "charitable" readings, but not uncritical ones, as I will attempt to show at the end of this essay.

---

the Contextualization of Biblical Theology" (P. Borger, J.S. Frerichs, R. Horsley, and J. Neusner, eds., in *The Social World of Formative Christianity and Judaism: Essays in Honor of Howard Clark Kee* [Philadelphia: Fortress, 1988] 3-12).

[15] Lest I be suspected of an apologetic intent here, I offer as examples my interpretation of two books whose messages differ very greatly from that of Mark, the Gnostic *Acts of Thomas*, and the Chinese Taoist *Tao Te Ching*. See my *Language and Gnosis* (Philadelphia: Fortress, 1985) and *The Tao of the Tao Te Ching* (Albany: State University of New York Press, 1992).

An Alternate Interpretation of the Controversy Stories

As an illustration of this approach, let me propose the following as a plausible audience for the series of controversy stories in Mark 2:1-3:6 – an audience who would have seen in these stories some plausible basis for according Jesus great *exousia.*

Three centuries of Hellenistic and Roman rule had broken down traditional and organic social organization that had previously prevailed in many local communities throughout the Mediterranean world. The "high culture" it tried to replace this with was foreign and alien to many, especially among the poorer classes. This produced a widespread sense of alienation coupled with anomie. Many people were alienated, in the sense that participation in community life was not enough to give their lives meaning; and the forces that ruled over their world at the top of the political spectrum lacked any felt legitimacy, i.e., they were not experienced as representing anything reflecting the felt values of many people.[16] Many were in a condition of anomie, in the sense that there was no well-established set of social norms in terms of which they could define and maintain a stable personal identity and sense of self-worth. Jewish people in Palestine represented only one instance of this widespread condition.

Dieter Georgi has argued, and many others agree,[17] that

---

[16] The widespread attraction of apocalypticism, gnosticism, and Cynic philosophy are among the many indications of this alienation. See for example Hans Jonas' comparison between alienation in the Hellenistic world and in our own (*The Gnostic Religion* [Boston: Beacon, 1958] 320-40), and G. Reale on Cynicism as "a philosophy of the Greek proletariat" (*A History of Ancient Philosophy*, vol. 4: *The Schools of the Imperial Age* [Albany NY: State University of New York Press, 1990] 159). As Hegel said perceptively: "Dadurch, daß es der Zweck des Staates ist, daß ihm die Individuen in ihrem sittlichen Leben aufgeopfert werden, ist die Welt in Trauer versenkt, es is ihr das Herz gebrochen, und es is *aus* mit der Natürlichkeit des Geistes, die zum Gefühle der Unseligkeit gelangt ist." (G.W.F. Hegel, *Werke in zwanzig Bänden, Werke 12, Vorlesungen über die Philosophie der Geschichte* [Frankfurt am Main: Suhrkamp, 1970] 339).

[17] Georgi draws on evidence gathered by Juster and Harnack (See Dieter Georgi, *The Opponents of Paul in Second Corinthians* [Philadelphia: Fortress, 1986] 83-84, and 176-78 notes 2-15). Elias Bickerman agrees (see "The Augustan Empire" in *The Columbia History of the World* [New York: Harper and Row, 1972] 216). Apart from population figures for "Jews" outside of Palestine, a widespread Gentile attraction to Judaism seems a necessary presupposition for the success of early Christian missionaries in the Mediterra-

there were widespread conversions of non-Jews to Judaism in diaspora synagogues outside of Palestine during this period. Judaism was one of the most successful of the "Eastern Religions" that took hold throughout the Roman Empire during this period. What accounts for this? Who were these non-Jews who came to think of Jewish history and tradition as their own history and tradition, to read the Jewish scriptures as their own sacred books, and to accept the Jewish God as the one true God? One likely group would be those described above, the people whom the *Imperium Romanum* left suffering from alienation and anomie. People in this situation needed some alternative social framework, some culture or subculture, within which to define and maintain a stable identity. This framework needed to be something they could personally relate to, something that had some innate appeal to them.

Consider first the attractiveness of law-oriented Judaism in this context. It responds especially well to the problem of anomie. In this respect I think the Black Muslim community in the U.S.[18] provides a helpful analogy. The black community in the United States also suffers greatly from alienation and anomie, stemming from social exclusion and often also from a breakdown in stable socio-cultural structures. The Black "Nation of Islam" has also adopted a foreign "Eastern Religion," and defines itself as the true following of Allah, in specific contrast to the alien and illegitimate, "demonic" American economic and political establishment. But the Nation of Islam also emphasizes rigorous discipline in adhering to very specific codes of discipline covering not only moral decency but regulating everyday matters such as dress and eating. Adherence to this code gives outward expression to a distinctive identity, superior to the masses of non-Muslim Black people still living in a state of social disintegration that lies in the past of many Black Muslims, and superior also to the "illegitimate" dominant American culture.

Consider this as a possibility to account, in a similar fashion,

---

nean world; why else would the earliest Christian documents which we have all emphasize that Christianity is the true heir of the Judaic tradition? And Paul's polemic against "Judaizers" in Romans presupposes not only some leaders wanting to impose Jewish customs on Gentiles, but many Gentiles willing voluntarily to adopt them.

[18] See C. Eric Lincoln, *The Black Muslims in America* (Westport CT: Greenwood, 1982).

for the attractiveness of law-oriented Judaism to people suffering from alienation and anomie in the first- century Mediterranean world. It offers this group a well-defined set of rules and practices which serve as clear external signs of their adherence to an idealistic moral code. Rigorous adherence to these practices gives people a tangible sense of pride in being members of a superior community that sets them apart from others still suffering from social disintegration and anomie, or compromising themselves by attempting to assimilate to an alien and illegitimate political regime.

But there is a price to be paid for this. One of the main costs is that, within the framework which this kind of Judaism offers for defining one's identity, that identity is defined by contrast with other alienated people. These "unclean sinners" are an important part of the symbolically constructed world of law-oriented Judaism; a law-abiding "Jew" is righteous before God precisely because she is not like others ("sinners") who do not adhere to certain codes. Hence one of the important codes she follows is one that externally dramatizes this difference: refusing to eat with those who do not follow the codes.[19] She has to "blame the victims," so to speak: rather than identifying and sympathizing with others who (like herself formerly) are victims of social disintegration, she has to regard many of these as symbolic embodiments of the central evil (i.e., the moral anarchy) over against which she defines the goodness of her own disciplined way.

Another weakness of law-oriented Judaism in this context is that people consciously looking for a "tradition" with which they can identify have a different attitude to tradition than do people whose tradition is an organic part of long-established patterns of community life. Attachment to tradition for the former will always have something of an artificial character which has to be sustained by conscious will, rather than being sustained as an organic part of their social lives. This would be true even of many ethnic Jews living for several generations outside of Palestine.

Suppose we imagine, then, a group of alienated people, among whom are both ethnic Jews and non-Jews, who fre-

[19] See Jacob Neusner, *From Politics to Piety* (Englewood Cliffs NJ: Prentice Hall, 1973) 80, 122.

quent[20] some diaspora synagogue and think of Judaism as their tradition. This synagogue is a voluntary association, sociologically similar to the many private clubs that arose during this period. There is no official authority which dominates the synagogue community and is able to impose its interpretation of Judaism on all.[21] But law-oriented Judaism has some prestige here, both for reasons given above, and because it has some claim to be "traditional" Judaism. Those who emphasize and excel in matters of traditional law are especially admired (some of these may have connections with Palestinian Pharisees).[22]

But some members of this group, attracted as they were to the Judaic heritage, feel the emphasis on Jewish law and custom to be somewhat artificial. They feel that law-orientation involves simply suppressing their own feelings of deep alienation, and their own deep feelings of identification with the excluded unclean "sinners" whom they have been asked to cut out of their circle of friends. These feelings have become emotionally powerful *because* they have been suppressed. Some Jesus-preachers who came to the synagogue awakened and appealed to these previously rejected feelings, and presented the group with a new version of Judaism in which these powerful feelings have a central place. The stories of Jesus/Pharisee conflicts now preserved in Mark 2:1-3:6 convey vivid images that appeal to these suppressed feelings.

Consider, for example, how the story of the healing of the paralytic on the Sabbath (3:1-6) would appear to this audience. The "scribes and Pharisees" in the Gospel represent those who emphasize law-oriented Judaism in this diaspora synagogue. From a normal and realistic point of view, the Pharisee position in the story might appear quite rational: Jesus could easily wait one more day to heal the man, thus

---

[20] It may be best to envision groups loosely connected with a diaspora synagogue, who have sufficient contact to quarrel with each other, but who are not necessarily struggling for control of an organized synagogue community. More recently Mack has expressed reservations about his own characterization of Mark's community as a "synagogue reform movement"; see "A Myth of Innocence at Sea" (*Continuum* 1:2, Winter-Spring 1991) 151.

[21] See Georgi, *The Opponents*, 88.

[22] On this hypothesis the "scribes and Pharisees" in Mark are dramatic representations of law-oriented Jews in the diaspora synagogue community to which Mark belonged. These latter may or may not have called themselves "Pharisees" and have been connected with Pharisees in Palestine.

both meeting the needs of the crippled man and observing the Sabbath. Jesus' angry charge that he is in favor of healing on the Sabbath while the Pharisees are in favor of "killing" on the Sabbath is surely an outrageously gross exaggeration, considered realistically. But for my hypothetical audience these elements of the story would be highly charged with special meanings because they would see the story as a symbolic dramatization awakening deep and strong feelings that were previously suppressed. This audience already feels that Judaic law-orientation denies their feelings of identification with and concern for the unfortunate. This is represented in the story by portraying the law-orientation of the Pharisees as something that "hardens their hearts" against human concern for the plight of the crippled man. The intensity the audience feels around this issue motivates the hyperbole in Jesus' charge that the Pharisees are in favor of "killing" the man. Jesus implicitly asserts by contrast that "saving the life" of an unfortunate person is the *true* way to "keep the Sabbath." This mirrors their feeling that identification with the unfortunate merits a higher place than lawkeeping in the true moral code, and hence ought to be considered central to "true Judaism."

Jesus heals the man by an act that combines law-breaking in a synagogue on the Sabbath, an angry and highly confrontational condemnation of law-oriented Judaism, a show of supernatural power, and a healing from physical distress. Supernatural power is extra-ordinary power, the power that is beyond the ordinary and lifts one out of the ordinary. In the symbolic image presented by the story, the extraordinary healing power joins the powerful feelings of identification with the unfortunate – feelings that, though powerful, also seem to have no place within the ordinary world, and have especially been excluded from the orderly world of law-oriented Judaism. The story of the healing miracle thus attains a special meaning in this context because of these associations, a meaning the same miracle would not have if performed, say, by a Roman priest on behalf of a Roman emperor's son. The physicality of the miracles – relieving the unfortunate of obvious physical distress – would also be important for my hypothetical audience, in that the concerns of those on the bottom rungs of the social ladder are often focused on such immediate physical distress. Thus this story creates a complex image of Jesus in which many elements combine to convey a sense of emotional and ethical power for this particular audience. For this audience there would be no need to invoke an independent belief in Jesus' *exousia* to validate his words and deeds in theses stories. Rather, in this account (in contrast to Mack's account) the words and actions of Jesus evoke a substantive basis for according Jesus an extraordinary *exousia.*

This interpretation illustrates the hermeneutic principle I proposed earlier: that we ought to stretch our imaginations to form an hypothesis in which the claims made by a text are plausibly supported by other things that the text says. This interpretation achieves this without lapsing into the fideist language that Mack rightly decries. Although this account ends up very different from that of Mack, it remains true to his guiding principle, namely, that Mark's stories are to be read as dramatizations of issues important to some group in a diaspora synagogue. It is also in accord with other indirect indications Mark gives of the character of his audience,[23] as well as with our current picture of the situation in diaspora synagogues.[24]

[23] Mark presupposes readers for whom conflicts over Jewish fasting customs (2:18-22), Sabbath-observance (2:23-3:6), table-fellowship (2:15-17), and dietary laws (7:14-23) (i.e., customs familiar in their milieu) are very important; yet who are unfamiliar with some "traditions of the elders" concerning ritual washings observed by "the Pharisees and all the Judeans" (7:3) (actually newer customs introduced by Pharisees and [in Mark's mind] observed by many Jews in Judea). They are interested in Aramaic phrases used by Jesus, but do not understand them (see Mack, *A Myth*, 296 n. 2; H.C. Kee, *The Community of the New Age: Studies in Mark's Gospel* [Philadelphia: Mercer University Press. 1983] 101). They are unfamiliar with the exact geography of Galilee (See Dennis Nineham, *Saint Mark* [Baltimore: Penguin Books, 1963] 40). They reject some Jewish customs and some influential Jewish leaders, but Jewish scriptures and the fate of the Jerusalem Temple are very important to them, and it is very important to them also to claim that they are the true heirs of the Judaic tradition (Mark 12:1-12). They are doing something that provokes others in synagogues to beat them and to accuse them (of being trouble-makers) before governors and kings (13:9; i.e., they are making exclusive claims to the Judaic heritage within synagogue communities and condemning others who disagree, while flaunting their rejection of many customs these others hold dear). I take their expectation of the imminent end of the world (9:1, 13:1-37) as an indication that they were alienated from their social world in general (not only from law-oriented Judaism). This alienation is probably also indicated by their lack of attachment to family life (1:16-20; 3:21, 31-35; 6:1-6; 10:28).

[24] Here I am indebted primarily to Dieter Georgi's *The Opponents,* 83-174; see also Mack, *A Myth*, 94-95, 192-98, 316-31.

Let me now proceed to fill out my hypothesis by dealing with two other major aspects of Mark's Gospel: the Markan Secret, and the idea that the crucifixion was part of God's plan.

The Markan Secret

The above approach to the controversy stories suggests a solution also to at least one important, but puzzling, aspect of the famous "Markan Secret." This is the puzzle that arises if one imagines that the secret that the disciples do not understand must consist in some piece of information. If this information consists in something told to the disciples in the Gospel (for instnace, that Jesus is the Messiah, that the Messiah must suffer), in what sense is there still something important that they do not understand? If this information is not something told to the disciples, then why is it withheld?

The previous discussion suggests that even the controversy stories have a meaning that is in some sense "hidden." The stories are meant to convey Jesus' *exousia*, but only certain readers will feel this *exousia* – the ones whose special life-experiences cause particular aspects of the stories to be highly charged with meaning. Other readers – Pharisee-sympathizers, or the rational readers Mack assumes as normal – will feel no charismatic "power" in the Jesus portrayed here. It is in this sense that the *exousia* of Jesus would be "hidden" from them, and no amount of explicit explanation could un-hide it. They could grasp the surface meaning of the words, "Jesus' *exousia* was greater than that of the scribes," but these words would not "make sense" to them.

In the same way, then, the disciples in the Gospel (representatives of Jesus-followers without understanding) can *hear the words* "This is my beloved Son" (9:7) and "The Son of Man must suffer many things...and be killed" (8:31), but the words do not have the *meaning* for them that they do for Mark. In particular, the idea that the Messiah must suffer does not make sense to them, because they are unreceptive to the solution this part of Mark's story implicitly presents (in the interpretation given below) to the problem of alienation and anomie.

There is nothing particularly unique or mysterious about

the phenomenon I am pointing to here. The general point I am making could be made of most jokes, for example. Every joke has a point, which some listeners might get and others fail to get. This point is not something one can extract from the joke and tell someone instead of telling them the joke. The essential thing the joke-teller is trying to present can only be presented by telling the joke, and it will only be grasped by a listener properly attuned to this joke, i.e., who shares the same "sense of humor" as the joke-teller. Something analogous could be said of many poems and of much serious modern fiction. In order to truly understand some modern fiction, the reader must be able to see the story as a dramatization of certain issues that she herself is able (at least vicariously) to care deeply about.[25]

This explanation accords with Mark's own "reader-reception" theory given in his chapter four. The parable of the sower emphasizes the necessity of being "good ground" for the message of Jesus, and clearly conceives of this as a moral qualification. People who are not "good ground" because of worldly cares, or because of the "shallowness" of their attraction to Jesus, are clearly morally blameworthy. This explains also why Mark casts his "Gospel" (i.e., his preaching) in the form of a story. What he wants to get across can only be gotten across in narrative form. The entire Gospel has the character of a "parable" which some *Jesus-followers* can understand and some cannot. (Jesus-followers who think they understand but really do not are represented by the disciples. Even though the disciples are given *information* about the meaning of Jesus'

[25] For example, at the end of Margaret Atwood's novel, *Surfacing* (London: Virago, 1979), the heroine undergoes a kind of psychotic episode, in which she feels guided by an internal "power," identified in some scenes with the ghosts of her dead parents who appear to her. This power causes her to break off human contact and tells her to destroy mementos of her past "false" life; not to go into any area that is walled or fenced- in; to dig vegetables out of the wet ground with her bare hands and eat them raw; to take off her clothes and sleep in a lair like an animal. The novel leads up to this by presenting the heroine as one whose feelings are greatly at odds with many features of the modern world (cast in a very negative light) but who internalizes social conventions and represses her feelings to the point of self-deception. A reader whose experience of the modern world is similar to that of the heroine will understand her "psychotic episode" as a healing "surfacing" of a much better self. A reader with no comparable experience is likely only to see the heroine inexplicably "going crazy."

parables, they ultimately fail to understand the core of what Mark thinks it is essential to understand.)[26]

I will argue later that this kind of sympathetic reading of Mark does not require us to agree also that he was justified in condemning those whose sensitivities prevented them from understanding the hidden meaning of his Jesus-story. That is, this might be a case of conflicting value-orientations, rather than a case of moral concern *versus* lack of moral concern.

Why Must the Messiah Suffer?

Let me now suggest a way that this kind of explanation could be applied to the question about the centrality of suffering in Mark's Gospel. On what basis does Mark expect his readers to buy the idea that God willed the crucifixion, that Jesus' death saves, and that they themselves must "deny themselves and take up the cross." Familiar acceptance of these ideas in subsequent Christianity places a veil over our eyes here, that we must try to wipe away. In order to reconstruct the original basis for the acceptance of these ideas we must imagine ourselves back into a time before these ideas became familiar, and try to imagine why anyone would first come to believe they were true.

My account begins with a description of a certain kind of personal transformation and "salvation." This experience provides the basis for the Markan belief in the centrality of suffering, as well as for several other beliefs such as the belief that Jesus is a divine Messiah.

First, we can develop further the picture described above of an audience suffering from severe alienation and anomie. Alienation and *anomie* produce a certain split in the way the world is constructed for such people. On the one hand, there are what might be called conventional legitimating structures

[26] Mack also considers the possibility that the Gospel could be internal self-criticism of Markan Jesus-followers themselves, but rejects it because he thinks that the Markan apocalypse is a vindication of all who associate themselves with Mark's community of Jesus-followers, whether or not they understand "following Jesus" in the same sense that Mark does. This apocalyptic element precludes self-criticism within the Markan community (idem, *A Myth,* 337). According to the present interpretation, "the elect" in 13:27 should be given a narrower sense, referring only to those whom Mark would regard as true Jesus-followers.

and categories. One who wants to be "legitimate" as a person, to validate her sense of self-worth, normally does so by showing how her character, actions, or achievements exemplify certain ideals admired in her cultural context. These ideals have a great deal of power as "social facts" (Durkheim), determining what counts as personal success and personal failure. They are inevitably felt by most people as ultimate "authorities," determining what is indeed good and bad, valid and invalid in human beings.

But even in normal times there are ways in which people's actual moral sensitivities are in conflict with conventional legitimating categories: they perceive some "successful" people as not really deserving their success, and *vice-versa* for some "unsuccessful" people. This phenomenon is greatly exacerbated in cases of extreme alienation: The values people feel most strongly about on a personal and instinctive level become polarized over against the legitimating structures and categories which seem authoritative in public life. It is not only that some individuals enjoy unmerited success. The very standards by which success is measured in public life are at odds with the moral sensitivities of alienated people. These sensitivities are themselves "excluded" from the social world.

The social split in Pharisaism between the righteous and the excluded sinners has a counterpart here in the internal struggle between that part of oneself that has internalized the power of conventional legitimating structures, on the one hand, and one's own deepest moral sensitivities, on the other. Some alienated people attempt to repress their own deepest sensitivities and focus on trying to appropriate some socially recognized badges of status and worth.[27] Mark essentially advocates the opposite move, and this in a very radical way. He wants his readers to identify with sensitivities and characteristics in themselves that are excluded from the social world, and to take these as an alternative legitimating norm. He wants his readers to identify with these precisely *as* excluded. Such

[27] See Frantz Fanon's description of the way that, under colonial domination, native populations sometimes become envious and want to imitate the colonizers (*The Wretched of the Earth* [New York: Grove, 1963] 39, 52). Fanon's description of what it feels like to be a colonized people suggests possible helpful analogies to the mentality of Mediterranean communities under Roman rule.

identification would amount to a fundamental psychological transformation, that is, a transformation in the way a person feels the issue of legitimacy and tries to establish a sense of personal worth.[28] It would mean taking one's own powerfully felt instinctive moral passion as a guide, in opposition to external legitimating social structures. This identification would "save" the transformed person. What it saves her from is the acute feeling that alienation and anomie produces, a feeling that "nothing is right." The world is not right, but one's own self is also not right (one feels "sinful"; in Pauline terms, one cannot feel "justified" under these conditions.) Mark instinctively sees that the root of this not-right-ness is the flight from one's powerlessness. "Salvation," the achievement of a sustainable sense of personal rightness, comes about through complete identification with the powerless and excluded part of oneself, *as* powerless and excluded in this world and *permanently* so.

Identifying with what is permanently and by nature excluded from the social world means that one can never "win" in the world: the real social world will never be transformed to such an extent that these excluded sensitivities can themselves become social norms. Such a person "must" suffer in the world, and everything will not come together in a sustainable feeling of rightness unless this destiny is taken on fully and deliberately. (There will not necessarily be physical suffering, of course; and physical suffering when it does come will come as a physical sign of this more fundamental exclusion from the world.) Identifying with what is excluded from the social world also makes it difficult to legitimate one's views "rationally," since rational legitimation usually consists in appealing to some standards of legitimacy well accepted in one's society. (I hope the above account does, however, indicate a different way in which rational legitimation of Mark's views might proceed.)

---

[28] I am drawing here on John Cobb's notion of variations in different peoples' "structure of existence" (see *The Structure of Christian Existence* [New York: Seabury, 1979] 15-20). Cobb intends "existence" here in Karl Jaspers' sense of *Existenz*: not physical existence, but one's personal being as something in need of validation. Different "structures of existence" are different ways in which people conceive of this validation together with the different cultural frameworks within which they try to achieve validity. I have developed this notion further in *Tao and Method* (forthcoming from State University of New York Press), chapter 11.

Mark's ideal reader will not learn these things from the Gospel as ideas or doctrines. She will probably not be conscious of the ideas as I have just sketched them. In the ideal case she will find herself engaged with the story because she will feel the story, deeply but implicitly, as a dramatization of these issues that affect her life so deeply. When she comes to the episodes surrounding the crucifixion she will simply feel a power in the figure of the suffering and crucified Jesus. This is a power that, on my reflective account, derives from the fact that Jesus represents the good-but-excluded part of herself. But in the ideal case she will not herself be reflectively aware of this fact, and so will give it an external-objective rather than a subjective-psychological interpretation. In reading the story she will implicitly identify with Jesus, feel herself transformed by this identification, and so attribute her salvation to the "power" of the Jesus pictured in the story. (This accounts for the extraordinary emphasis placed on the *person* of Jesus in Mark. The fact that Jesus is associated with what is permanently "powerless" in the world also accounts for the often-remarked fact that the Markan resurrection accounts emphasize Jesus' absence rather than his presence as a risen Spirit, as in Paul.)[29]

This psychological transformation will also transform the world (the *Lebenswelt*) in which the transformed person lives, including the divine being whom she assumes rules over this world. The divine is what legitimates, that upon which one ultimately depends for legitimation. The utterly defeated Jesus on the cross is now *the* earthly manifestation and representative of God on earth; this gives the very word "God" a different meaning than it has for those for whom God is the authority standing behind some particular legitimating social structures. It truly "stands God on his head."[30]

A person transformed and saved in this way will perceive a strong intrinsic relationship between suffering and Messiahship. The Messiah "must" be a Defeated One because identification with something defeated in the world is what saves. The Jesus in Mark's story who willingly accepts suffering is

---

[29] See Mack, *A Myth*, 309 n. 7.

[30] In this respect it parallels Paul's thought, pointed out by Dieter Georgi, in *Theocracy in Paul's Praxis and Theology* (Minneapolis: Fortress, 1991) 20-23.

partly a model for the transformed Jesus-follower, who also must identify with the "suffering"-excluded part of herself, for the reason given above (page 245 and note 36). But the fact that the last part of Mark's story is motivated by "God's plan that the Messiah should suffer"[31] also reflects the fact that the Jesus in the story is not entirely a human figure with whom the reader can identify, but in some measure a symbolic image charged with the divine "power" that the reader feels in his identification with suffering. The suffering is partly what "baptizes" the figure (10:38) and *renders* him for the reader a Messiah with divine powers.

This interpretation makes the saving transformation of the reader and the reader's world the basis of all other beliefs in the Gospel. Suffering and defeat are necessary to make Jesus the Messiah, because identification with What Suffers Defeat is what saves. Jesus is a divine "Son of God" because what suffers defeat in the world is the ultimate locus of authority in the world. Those who identify with what suffers defeat are the true inheritors of the Judaic tradition because they are the followers of the one true divine Authority. Thus, although Mark considers personal conversion necessary, this is not to be interpreted individualistically. My assumption, at least, is that members of the Markan community gathered together on the basis of a roughly similar conversion experience shared by most of their number (owing to their similar previous social experience). They also of course *interpreted* their experience in terms that connected them with the historical community of Israel, and that led to important consequences for interactions within their own small community.

Mark and Conversion to the Good

This account has a weakness in that it seems obvious that not just *any* "identification with what suffers defeat" is something good. In showing how various additional features of Mark's Gospel support my account, I want to show also some ways in which Mark's Gospel makes more specific the kind of iden-

---

[31] Mack notes that this "supernatural" idea is necessary to Mark's plot since the Pharisaic persecution-plot cannot motivate Jesus' decision to go to Jerusalem (*A Myth*, 244, 282).

tification involved, in such a way as to point the reader toward identification with something that is truly good. (In my account, this goodness is what makes the personal transformation good[32] and provides a plausible substantive basis why Mark could expect his community to accept what he is trying to convey in his Gospel).

First, this approach can claim simply to be taking seriously Mark's claim that there is a hidden meaning to the Jesus-story he tells, and that failure to understand this hidden meaning is the sign of a moral failure. Put in other words, Mark is suggesting that a pure concern for a certain kind of good is one of the factors that makes one "competent"[33] to understand the meaning of the story he tells. One only understands the story as Mark wants it to be understood if one lets a pure concern for this good shape one's reading.

Turning to specifics, consider first the well-known turn, in the middle of the Gospel, from Jesus/Pharisee conflicts, to increasing criticism of the disciples. On this reading, the Jesus in the first part of the Gospel is the hypostatized spirit of Markan Jesus-followers, defined in opposition to law-oriented Jewish groups in their diaspora-synagogue community. Jesus' successes reflect their claims to stand for something superior to that which these opposing groups represent. This part of the Gospel encourages an "us *versus* them" mentality, in which "we" (Markan Jesus-followers) are better than "they" (law-oriented Jews). Some might easily assume (as Mack appears to assume) that who "we" are and who "they" are is easy to recognize, simply by looking at the people with whom one associates. The critique of the disciples, increasing especially after 8:17, symbolically represents criticism turned in upon the group of Markan Jesus-followers themselves. This criticism is the basis for a division within this group, between what Mark

[32] I am drawing here on a pluralist conception of the good, and on a generalized notion of "conversion to the good" as what validates any valid worldview, that I have developed and explained more fully in "Radically pluralist, thoroughly critical: a new theory of religions," *JAAR* LX/4 (Winter 1992) 693-715 (esp. 702-9) as well as in chapter 11 of my forthcoming *Tao and Method.*

[33] See Jonathan Culler, *Structuralist Poetics: Structuralism, Linguistics, and the Study of Literature* (Ithaca NY: Cornell University Press, 1975) 113-130. I have elaborated on the notion of competence in "Are texts determinate? Derrida, Barth, and the Role of the Biblical Scholar," *HTR* 81:3 (1988) 354-55.

would regard as *true* Jesus-followers, and those who might associate with this group, but whose attitudes and actions show that they have not truly understood and internalized the way of being Mark thinks is the essence of "following Jesus." This critique is motivated by the fact that if one is devoted to something good for its own sake, one will sometimes be willing to sacrifice one's own tangible interests and the tangible interests of one's group[34] for the sake of this good.

Mark's critique is most obvious in the case of the criticism of the disciples' competition over "who is the greatest" (an indirect criticism of those among Markan Jesus-followers who struggle for status within this group.) One whose mind is focused on the dogmatic assertion that "our group is better than their group," will also want to be admired as an exemplary member of "our" group. But if (1) a person thinks that each individual is good *insofar as* she is dedicated to the good for which our group stands, and (2) if what our group stands for is identification with something powerless and excluded, then she would not be anxious to enhance her personal status within the group.

One can also identify something good for its own sake by defining it in relation to other more familiar good and bad traits. Suppose, for example, that a person suffering from anomie identifies "what is excluded" with all of the chaotic and disordered feelings engendered by anomie itself. This would obviously include many impulses that are not good. Such disordered impulses are plausibly represented in Mark by pictures of people "possessed by unclean spirits." This con-

[34] This is perhaps the most crucial methodological point on which I would disagree with Mack, and with many other sociologically-oriented biblical scholars. The latter tend to assume *as a methodological axiom* that groups always do and say only what it is in their tangible interest to do and say (by "tangible interest" I mean such things as group survival and prestige, group status vis-à-vis other groups). The interpreter's task is only to discover the *ways in which* what groups do and say furthers their interests. I tend to agree that the pursuit of group self-interest is indeed most often the dominating force in the stream of changes in world history, but that in general we do not stand to learn a great deal from the study of how individual groups have pursued their interests. Sometimes individuals and groups also propose *ideals* that have an intrinsic worth and goodness – as Mark does in the present hypothesis – and the study of such ideals is a much more worthwhile endeavor. My conception of "the good" is pluralist and contextual, and so understanding ideals requires understanding the relation of these ideals to socio-cultural circumstances.

trasts with the "*holy* spirit" that Jesus brings, a unifying and order-bringing force in peoples' lives. Identification with this excluded but *holy* spirit expresses itself, for example, in the avoidance of "fornication, theft, murder, adultery, avarice, malice, deceit, indecency, envy, slander, pride, folly" (7:21-23); in being faithful to one's marriage-partner (10:2-12); and in loving others as oneself (12:31).

Finally, one could imagine several ways of identifying with What is Defeated in the world that would not be good, and could see the ways in which Mark's picture of Jesus stands in contrast to these. For example, one could envision oneself as the concrete personal embodiment of justice in an unjust world, and could identify one's struggle to gain personal power purely and simply with a struggle for justice. Alternatively, one could withdraw into oneself and disengage from any kind of competitive struggle in the world. One could acquiesce in one's own humiliation, internalizing a low self-image that mirrors one's low status in the world. One could masochistically seek out suffering. One could use suffering as an occasion for self-pity. One could use personal suffering as a way of manipulating the sympathies of others.[35]

By contrast, one outstanding characteristic of Jesus throughout Mark's Gospel is the way he aggressively and confrontationally asserts the authority of the difficult-to-grasp values for which he stands and aggressively condemns the world and its commonly recognized standards of success as devoid of authority. He does this in full awareness that he "must" ultimately lose in these confrontations (standing as he does for something that must by nature remain powerless in the world). He conducts himself with dignity throughout his trial, either making a simple assertion of his otherworldly authority or remaining silent.

Consider, in the light of these observations, the last moment in the crucifixion scene, the climax of Mark's Gospel toward which everything else leads. Just before Jesus dies he cries out, "My God, my God, why have you abandoned me?" Then Mark says, "And the centurion, *seeing how he died*, said, 'This man

---

[35] See the sensitive accounts of the various good and bad attitudes one can take to suffering in Dorothee Soelle's *Suffering* (Philadelphia: Fortress, 1975).

indeed was a Son of God'"(15:34, 39). The centurion's remark suggests that Jesus' final moment was also a final revelation of his divinity, a revelation of his status as the representative of God on earth. This cry is, on the one hand, a sign of human weakness and total defeat. Jesus' acceptance of his suffering destiny wavered in Gethsemane, but he managed to remain committed to it. On Golgotha the physical distress, the humiliation, and the desertion by his followers have pushed him to the extreme where he is no longer able to maintain his own faith that God is with him. His defeat and human weakness penetrate him thoroughly. "Why have you abandoned me?," however, is at the same time an implicit but aggressive protest and assertion of his innocence. Although he feels abandoned by God, he maintains his conviction that he does not deserve to be so abandoned. When taken as a climax of the motifs sketched in the preceding four paragraphs, this picture of the dying Jesus is the perfect imagistic representation of that which, in each human being, is excluded, untainted by any shred of connection with the legitimating structures of the social world, but conscious and assertive of its own rightness. This is the ultimately authoritative, the ultimate revelation of the divine.[36]

I do not offer this hypothesis as a decisive and proven solution to the problem of Mark's meaning – that would require another book. I offer it principally as an illustration of a general *kind* of approach to interpretation that I think remedies the weaknesses both in the fideist approaches Mack criticizes and in the socio-historical approach he pursues.

One way in which this approach differs from fideist approaches is that the interpretation to which it leads provides

[36] One can see here a continuity with a certain strand of exilic and post-exilic Judaism. Many of the psalms are laments spoken by relatively powerless people unjustly oppressed by those more powerful than they, laments in which one can sense a great deal of emotional power in the voice of the sufferer. As the situation of Israel grows more and more hopeless, there is an increasing emphasis on the Suffering Just Man as the *key* example of the person close to God, the most "Beloved by God," the "First-born Son of God" (as in the well-known examples of Wis 2-5, Isa 52:13 – 53:12). In the context of this progressively developing tradition, Mark is the one who turns the final corner: not only is the Suffering Just Man the *favorite* of God. This figure is the key *representative* of God on earth, the one worthy to be Lord of the coming Kingdom of God.

us with a critical norm for deciding *under what interpretation* a given Markan belief might have a valid basis. Partly what is at stake here is the manner of construing what might be called the "implicit epistemological structure" of Markan beliefs: what is based on what? Although it is unlikely that Markan belief is based on *explicit* reasoning; nevertheless, it has some implicit epistemological structure, in the sense that there are some considerations that serve as basic motivations, and other beliefs that are based on these considerations. We take Mark most seriously if we consider Markan origins, not chronologically or causally (what chain of causes led up to his beliefs?), but epistemologically (what in reality is the cognitive basis of his beliefs?).

For example, is the belief in an apocalyptic vindication of Markan Jesus-followers a *basis* for their belief that they are the new chosen people? On what basis, then, do they believe in apocalyptic vindication? Do they believe they are the chosen people simply because they want to believe this? On the above account, this belief has *some* valid basis. In the ideal case, the experience of Markan Jesus-followers was structured in such a way that yielding to the power of the excluded good was perceived as committing themselves to the highest good that appeared in their experience, a good they rightly perceived to be also *one* of the central foci of the Judaic tradition.[37] This is what they expressed by claiming that commitment to this good was the new "will of God," and that being seized by the power of this good was a sign of being "chosen" by the Jewish God. The power of this good is real, but it is something that by nature cannot appear powerful in this world. Its power belongs to another dimension of reality, and this is what is pictured in the apocalyptic image of the utopian Kingdom of God to come.

These Markan beliefs are *partially* justified, *under some interpretations,* by the basis I have proposed for them. One can also see what is not justified by this basis. For example, from my own historicist and pluralist perspective, I would say that the experience of many Pharisaic Jews may simply have been structured differently, and so Mark's claim that they are guilty of a great sin against the one true God would be unjustified.

---

[37] See previous note.

(And if this is true, it is also true that we cannot take for granted the validity of the Markan worldview for Europeans and Americans in the 20th century.)

Some Markan Jesus-followers might have believed that they had become members of the new chosen people merely by associating with the group who thought of themselves as Jesus-followers. This belief is completely unfounded. On the present account the purpose of Mark's criticism of the disciples is precisely to make a distinction within this group, of those who are "true" Jesus-followers and those who merely claim the name. Mark and his audience most probably did think that the kingdom of God was literally coming soon. But perception of the highest good is not good evidence about what is actually going to happen in the future; and so, as a *literal* picture of the future this belief was without any substantive basis.

Something similar could be said about belief in the resurrection. It makes no sense to say that, epistemologically, belief in the resurrection was the basis for the Christian belief that Jesus' crucifixion was not really a defeat. For this, one would have to provide some plausible basis, independent of the rest of the Jesus-story, for believing that the resurrection happened. On the present account, Mark's ideal audience would already feel a divine "power" revealed in the crucifixion story itself. The resurrection, as an image, dramatizes the power they already felt in the crucifixion. That power required some concrete representation, and this is why they would feel that the resurrection "must" be part of the story. (To construe this dramatic/aesthetic "must" as factual evidence for the resurrection would, of course, be a mistake.)

These observations illustrate the way in which an account of the basis for Markan belief can also serve as a critical norm for interpretation. That is, the idea of an implicit epistemological structure provides a more philosophical and pluralist basis for the practice of *Sachkritik*, the critical evaluation of what a text says in the light of our own grasp of the reality of which it speaks[38] (or as I would say, a grasp of the basis-in-reality of the worldview which it proposes or to which it tries to convert us.

---

[38] See Bultmann, "Existentialist Interpretation" (in R. Johnson, *Rudolph Bultmann: Interpreting Faith for the Modern Era* [San Francisco: Collins, 1987] 142-46), James M. Robinson and John B. Cobb Jr. eds., *The New Hermeneutic* [New York: Harper and Row, 1964] 19-39), Hans-Georg Gadamer, *Truth and Method* [New York: Crossroad, 1982] 258-74). The present account is

Thus, it remedies a fundamental weakness of fideist accounts of Christian origins.

I think it also remedies the weakness in Mack's approach. Mack tends, like many current biblical scholars, to assume a dichotomy between theological interpretation and socio-historical interpretation. On this view, theological interpretation construes everything in terms of debates about purely intellectual and personal "theological beliefs," conceived of as timeless truths independent of social and cultural context. Socio-historical interpretation, by contrast, tends to assume as axiomatic that all religious beliefs are really indirect strategies for pursuing (or "rationalizing") group interests. The core of "interpretation" consists in telling the story of the group responsible for a given writing, what their situation was and what their interests were, and how their various beliefs furthered those interests. As often as not the story the social historian tells is a moral tale, taking sides in the struggles between ancient groups and implicitly assigning praise or blame to an author's intentions, according to which side the historian supports. (This is essential in making the story into something from which we can learn, rather than merely something to satisfy antiquarian curiosity.) The side the historian takes is usually governed by his own values and his involvement in modern debates. Mack's unflattering story of Mark's community, for example, is clearly informed by the priority given to values (which I share) of rationality and tolerance among 20th century liberal intellectuals.[39] The historian does not try to see the world as the text's author saw it, but substitutes his (more "objective") picture of the author's situation for the author's picture. The interpreter never directly *confronts* the author as someone whose ideas and values should be taken seriously as potential competitors with the ideas and values of the interpreter.

The approach illustrated above is "theological" in a broadly Tillichian sense.[40] Of course, it does not treat Mark as an intellectual theologian attempting to teach some doctrines

---

more historicist and pluralist than that of the above authors in that it recognizes a plurality of valid bases for religious worldviews. See chapter 11 of my forthcoming *Tao and Method*.

[39] This is made explicit in Mack, *A Myth*, 361-76.

[40] I refer here to Tillich's insistence that "theology" not be defined as the study of a particular set of (Christian) beliefs, but as a general subject-

about the objective structure of otherworldly reality for purely speculative purposes. It does treat Mark as someone who has some very different and interesting views on the topic of what ought to be of ultimate concern, views worthy of our critical engagement and critical comparison with other views that we might have on this subject. These views were shaped by Mark's social experience. And they have directly social consequences, in that commitment to the authority of what is excluded in oneself is intrinsically related to identification with, and an active compassion for, other individuals excluded from social legitimacy.

On the present view the study of Christian origins is best conceived of as an exercise in *Geistesgeschichte* after the manner of the sketches[41] given in Hegel's *Phenomenology*. (Dieter Georgi gave me one of the best clues to understanding his own thinking when he remarked several times offhandedly that he had been much influenced by Hegel.) The most interesting and important aspect of early Christian history does not lie in the moral tales we can tell of concrete struggles between various Jewish and Christian groups. The reconstruction of social setting is important because human consciousness is a thoroughly social reality. The most important object of research into early Christianity is the origins of the dramatic transformation that movement represented in human consciousness, in people's feelings about the relation between external legitimating structures and internal moral passion.

---

matter about which different people have different assumptions (as, for example, astronomy is a general subject-matter about which different astronomers have different theories), and that this subject matter is "what is of ultimate concern" (Tillich, *Systematic Theology* [Chicago: University of Chicago Press, 1951] 1.8-15). I would again push Tillich's principle in a more pluralist direction, in that different cultures and religions have many different "structures of existence" (see my note 28 above), many different valid ways of conceiving of and relating to the question as to what ultimately matters.

[41] I emphasize Hegel's *individual sketches* of transforming moments in the development of Western consciousness because I take as my model the *approach* that he illustrates in these sketches (not their specific content, and certainly not his attempt to fit all them into one grand metaphysical scheme).

CONCLAMATIO UND PROFECTIO: ZUR VERANSCHAULICHUNG NEUTESTAMENTLICHER WUNDERGESCHICHTEN

Willy Schottroff (Universität Frankfurt a.M.)

Die folgenden Ausführungen gelten den Erzählungen von der Auferweckung der Tochter des Jaïrus (Mk 5,21-43 parr.) und ihres männlichen Gegenstückes, des Jünglings von Nain (Lk 7,11-17). Am Beispiel dieser beiden Wundergeschichten soll paradigmatisch gezeigt werden, welchen Beitrag die Auswertung antiker Bilddenkmäler zur Veranschaulichung neutestamentlicher Überlieferungen und zur Klärung ihres sozialgeschichtlichen Hintergrundes zu leisten vermag. Nicht zuletzt soll damit die Notwendigkeit eines sozialgeschichtlichen Bildkommentars zum Neuen Testament unterstrichen werden.

I

Neutestamentliche Wundergeschichten wie die zwei genannten Totenerweckungen und mit ihnen zusammen der weitere Bereich der Heilungswunder, zu denen sie gemeinhin gerechnet werden, darüber hinaus aber ganz allgemein auch die übrigen Arten von Wundererzählungen, die das Neue Testament enthält, waren bislang vor allem Gegenstand form- und religionsgeschichtlicher Analysen.[1] Dabei galt das vorrangige Interesse einerseits dem Stil, der Topik und der Tendenz dieser Erzählungen. Anderseits aber richtete es sich in genauer Erkundung von Übereinstimmung und Differenz auf die Klärung des Verhältnisses, in dem die neutestamentlichen Wunder zur antiken Wunderüberlieferung stehen.

So enthält etwa, um den form- und religionsgeschichtlichen

---

[1] Vgl. M. Dibelius, *Die Formgeschichte des Evangeliums*, Tübingen ^{3}1959, S.66-100 und 165-172; R. Bultmann, *Die Geschichte der synoptischen Tradition* (FRLANT 29), Göttingen ^{4}1958, S.223-260, dazu: *Ergänzungsheft* (bearb. von G. Theißen und P. Vielhauer), Göttingen ^{4}1971, S.77-87; G. Theißen, *Urchristliche Wundergeschichten* (StNT 8), Gütersloh ^{6}1990; neuerdings mit Kritik an der in der vorangehenden formgeschichtlichen Diskussion üblichen Bestimmung der Gattung "Wundererzählung": K. Berger, *Formgeschichte des Neuen Testaments*, Heidelberg 1984, S. 305-318.

Vergleich an den beiden genannten Totenerweckungen zu verdeutlichen, Lk 7,11-17 mit dem Motiv: "Wunder bei der Begegnung unterwegs" einen verbreiteten Zug, der auch in antiken Wundererzählungen vorkommt.[2]

Als Belege kann man dafür auf das epidaurische Heilungswunder B 25[3] und auf die Totenerweckungen verweisen, die Philostrat (in seiner Vita Apollonii IV.45) von Apollonius von Tyana[4] und Apuleius von Madaura (Florida 19) von dem Arzt Asklepiades von Prusa[5] berichten. Das Wunder ereignet sich hier jeweils in aller Öffentlichkeit bei der Begegnung des Wundertäters[6] mit der Bahre. Auf einer Bahre wird in der ersten der zitierten Wundererzählungen eine Kranke vom Asklepiosheiligtum in Epidauros, wo sie vergeblich Heilung gesucht hatte, wieder nach Hause getragen; in den beiden anderen Parallelbeispielen bringt man gerade (vermeintliche) Tote auf der Bahre zur Leichenverbrennung und Bestattung, als der Wundertäter ihnen begegnet.[7] In Lk 7,14 liegt der Tote

---

[2] Vgl. O. Weinreich, *Antike Heilungswunder. Untersuchungen zum Wunderglauben der Griechen und Römer* (RVV VIII/1), Gießen 1909 (Nachdruck: Berlin 1969), S.171-174.

[3] R. Herzog, *Die Wunderheilungen von Epidauros. Ein Beitrag zur Geschichte der Medizin und der Religion* (Ph.S XXII/3), Leipzig 1931, S.18f; vgl. K. Berger/ C. Colpe (Hg.), *Religionsgeschichtliches Textbuch zum Neuen Testament* (Texte zum NT 1), Göttingen-Zürich 1987, S.143 Nr. 237a.

[4] Vgl. K. Berger/C. Colpe (Hg.), *a.a.O.*, S.132 Nr. 220; s. dazu G. Petzke, *Die Traditionen über Apollonius von Tyana und das Neue Testament* (SCHNT 1), Leiden 1970, S.129f, und K. Berger/ C. Colpe (Hg.), *a.a.O.*, S.133f.

[5] Vgl. K. Berger/C. Colpe (Hg.), *a.a.O.*, S.132f Nr. 221; s. auch Plin. nat. VII.124, Cels. II.6.

[6] Daß sich solche Wundertraditionen jedoch nicht nur an *männliche* Thaumaturgen hefteten, sondern daß man der Figur des θεῖος ἀνήρ die der θεία γυνή an die Seite stellen muß, lehren beispielsweise die der Thekla in einer Version des Schlusses der Acta Pauli et Theclae zugeschriebenen Heilungswunder, vgl. R. A. Lipsius [/M. Bonnet] (Hg.), *Acta apostolorum apocrypha I*, Leipzig 1891 [Nachdruck: Darmstadt 1959], S.271, und s. dazu: R. Albrecht, *Das Leben der heiligen Makrina auf dem Hintergrund der Thekla-Traditionen. Studien zu den Ursprüngen des weiblichen Mönchtums im 4. Jahrhundert in Kleinasien* (FKDG 38), Göttingen 1986, S.286-290.

[7] Diesem Motiv ist auch die verschiedentlich den Wunderbericht beschließende, die Realität der Heilung demonstrierende Aussage zuzurechnen, daß der Geheilte sein Bett nimmt und davongeht: Mk 2,11f parr.; Joh 5,8f; Lukian. Philops. 11, vgl. O. Weinreich, *a.a.O.*, S.173f, und s. dazu die Darstellungen dieser Szene in der frühchristlichen Kunst z.B. bei W. F. Volbach, *Elfenbeinarbeiten der Spätantike und des frühen Mittelalters* (Römisch-Germanisches Zentralmuseum zu Mainz. Kataloge vor- und frühgeschichtlicher Altertümer 7), Mainz ^{3}1976, Nr. 152.170.179.182; P. Lopreato, Il

– anders als in diesen Belegen des Topos – allerdings nicht auf einer Bahre (κλίνη) sondern merkwürdigerweise in einem (wohl offen zu denkenden hölzernen Kasten-)Sarg (σορός),[8] obwohl es auch in Palästina üblich war, Tote auf einer Totenbahre zu Grabe zu tragen.[9] Zu den für diese Erzählungen typischen Zügen gehören, wie insbesondere der Vergleich von Lk 7,11-17 mit Philostrat, Vita Apollonii IV.45, lehrt, auch die Betonung der besonderen Schmerzlichkeit eben dieses Todes, der den einzigen Sohn einer Witwe bzw. ein Mädchen aus konsularischer Familie in der Stunde seiner Hochzeit getroffen hat, ferner: die große Menge, die das Trauergeleit bildet, das Anhalten des Leichenzuges und das Niedersetzen der Bahre, der wunderwirkende Gestus der Berührung des Sarges bzw. des Leichnams mit der Hand,[10] die Anrede des Wundertäters an den bzw. die Tote(n) und schließlich die ausdrückliche Feststellung des Erfolgs der Wunderhandlung. Dieser zeigt sich beim Jüngling von Nain daran, daß der Tote sich aufsetzt und zu sprechen beginnt (Lk 7,15). Auch das totgeglaubte Mädchen, von dessen Auferweckung Philostrat berichtet, zeigt durch sein Sprechen an, daß es lebt. Trotz der weitgehenden Übereinstimmung, die in der literarischen Topik zwischen Lk 7,11-17 und seinen hellenistischen

---

miracolo del paralitico su un frammento di orlo di patera in >terra sigillata chiara< C del Museo di Aquileia, *Aquileia Nostra 50* (1979) S.329-340; C. Nauerth, Heilungswunder in der frühchristlichen Kunst, in: *Spätantike und frühes Christentum. Ausstellung im Liebieghaus Museum alter Plastik Frankfurt am Main*, Frankfurt a.M. 1983, S.339-346.

[8] Solche Sarkophage (oder Ossuare?) aus römischer Zeit haben sich in der Wüste Juda erhalten, vgl. N. Avigad, (The Expedition to the Judean Desert, 1961) Expedition A-Nahal David, *IEJ 12* (1962) [S.169-183] S.182f mit Pl. 22A; s. dazu M. Weippert, Art. Sarkophag, Urne, Ossuar, in: *BRL*[2], S.269-276 bes. S.271 (2a). 275 (4b).

[9] Vgl. S. Krauss, *Talmudische Archäologie II*, Leipzig 1911 [Nachdruck: Hildesheim 1966], S.58-60. Lediglich Kinder unter drei Jahren pflegte man im Sarg hinauszutragen, s. *Bill. IV/1*, S.548f. Daß σορός hier "*Bahre*", und nicht "Sarg" bedeute, wie im Gefolge von E. Klostermann (z.St.) häufig behauptet wird, ist ebensowenig zu erhärten wie die Meinung von W. Grundmann (z.St.), die Erwähnung eines Kastensarges sei als solche schon ein Indiz, das die "Formung der Geschichte in hellenistischem Bereich" vermuten lasse (doch vgl. die vorige Anmerkung!).

[10] Zu diesem Gestus vgl. O. Weinreich, *a.a.O.* (s. Anm. 2), S.1-75. Er spielt insbesondere auf bildlichen Darstellungen der Asklepios zugeschriebenen Wunderheilungen eine Rolle: K. Sudhoff, Handanlegung des Heilgottes auf attischen Weihetafeln, *AGM 18* (1926) S.235-250 mit Tf. IX-XII; A. Krug, *Heilkunst und Heilkult. Medizin in der Antike* (Beck's Archäologische Bibliothek), München 1984, S.134-141.

Seitenstücken besteht,[11] ist ein Unterschied, der beide trennt, unübersehbar: In Lk 7,11-17 handelt es sich wie in anderen biblischen Totenerweckungen (vgl. I Reg 17,17-24; II Reg 4,8-37; 13,20f; Mk 5,21-43 parr.; Joh 11,1-45; Act 9,36-42; 20,7-12) im Sinne der Texte um die Belebung eines oder einer wirklich Toten, also um ein echtes Wunder. Dagegen sind es nach Philostrat und Apuleius Scheintote, die zum Leben zurückgebracht werden. Ἀφύπνισε τὴν κόρην τοῦ δοκοῦντος θανάτου – "er erweckte das Mädchen vom scheinbaren Tod", beschreibt Philostrat den Hergang und beschließt seine Schilderung mit Überlegungen zu einer rationalistischen Erklärung des Berichteten. Bei Apuleius schließlich wird der Vorgang der Wiederbelebung eines Scheintoten vollends seines wunderhaften Charakters entkleidet und ganz auf die ärztliche Kunst des Asklepiades zurückgeführt. Kraft ihrer entdeckt dieser Arzt in dem Scheintoten Anzeichen verborgenen Lebens, und mit medizinischen Mitteln gelingt es ihm, den Atem des vermeintlich Toten wiederzubeleben[12] und seine Seele, die sich im Körperinnern versteckt hatte, von dort hervorzulocken.

Topik und Stil antiker Wundererzählungen prägen ebenfalls die in Mk 5,21-43 parr. überlieferte Auferweckung der Tochter des Synagogenvorstehers Jaïrus, in die sich bei allen drei Synoptikern als retardierendes und auf diese Weise das Wunder steigerndes Moment die ursprünglich wohl für sich entstandene und tradierte Heilung der blutflüssigen Frau einschiebt (Mk 5,25-34 parr.).[13] Anders jedoch als die Erzählung von der Auferweckung des Jünglings von Nain besitzt Mk 5,21-43 parr. keine direkte religionsgeschichtliche Parallele.

---

[11] Vgl. als Zeugnis hellenistischen Judentums noch Paral Jerem 7,12b-20; K. Berger/C. Colpe (Hg.), *a.a.O.* (s. Anm. 3), S.133 Nr. 222. – Die relativ seltsamen Totenerweckungen, die die rabbinische Literatur enthält, unterscheiden sich demgegenüber in ihrer Topik nicht unerheblich von den neutestamentlichen und ihren oben angeführten hellenistischen Gegenstücken, vgl. P. Fiebig, *Jüdische Wundergeschichten des neutestamentlichen Zeitalters unter besonderer Berücksichtigung ihres Verhältnisses zum Neuen Testament bearbeitet,* Tübingen 1911, S.36-38; ferner: *Bill. I,* S.560.

[12] Vgl. dazu Diog.Laert. VIII.60f.67, wo die Wiederbelebung einer "Atemlosen" durch Empedokles berichtet wird.

[13] Die Verflechtung dieser beiden Wundergeschichten scheint Mk bereits in der von ihm verarbeiteten Tradition vorgegeben gewesen zu sein, vgl. M. Dibelius, *a.a.O.* (s. Anm. 1), S.220 mit Anm. 1, und R. Bultmann, *a.a.O.* (s. Anm. 1), S.228-230.

Daß sich aber die Totenerweckung hier nicht wie dort unter freiem Himmel und in aller Öffentlichkeit vollzieht, sondern nach Entfernung des Publikums in der Abgeschiedenheit des Hauses, in dem die Tote aufgebahrt ist, verbindet diese Geschichte mit den in I Reg 17,17-24; II Reg 4,8-37 und Act 9,36-42 berichteten Totenerweckungen, die gleichfalls in einer Kammer unter Ausschluß der Öffentlichkeit stattfinden. Auch enthält diese Geschichte noch weitere für den Stil solcher Wundererzählungen typische Züge.[14] Zu ihnen gehört etwa das Motiv, daß den Wundertäter von Seiten des Publikums Zweifel, verächtliche Äußerungen und Spott treffen (Mk 5,40: – καὶ κατεγέλων αὐτοῦ "und sie lachten ihn aus"),[15] ferner: das Handauflegen (Mk 5,28) bzw. das Ergreifen bei der Hand (Mk 5,41) als Wundergestus,[16] der Gebrauch einer wunderwirkenden Formel in fremdsprachiger (aramäischer) Gestalt (ταλιθα κουμ[ι], Mk 5,41)[17], das plötzliche Eintreten des Wunders (εὐθύς "sofort", Mk 5,42) und schließlich die Feststellung des Erfolgs des Wunders: die Tote steht auf und geht umher (Mk 5,42); zum Erweis, daß die Lebenskraft in sie zurückgekehrt ist, läßt der Wundertäter in der lukanischen Version der Geschichte ihr zu essen geben (Lk 8,55).

Hinsichtlich der Tendenz der Wundergeschichten und des in ihnen zum Ausdruck kommenden Interesses vertritt die formgeschichtliche Forschung die Auffassung, daß die Wunder Jesu überliefert und weitererzählt worden seien, weil man in ihnen "Erweise... seiner messianischen Kraft bzw. seiner göttlichen Macht"[18] oder – in hellenistischem Umfeld – Manifestationen seines Charakters als θεῖος ἄνθρωπος bzw. θεῖος ἀνήρ sah.[19] Die Kranken, die in den Heilungswundern von

---

[14] Zum folgenden vgl. die reichhaltige Materialsammlung bei R. Bultmann, *a.a.O.* (s.Anm 1), S.236-241.

[15] Dieser Topos begegnet mehrfach in den Wunderheilungen von Epidauros: R. Herzog, *a.a.O.* (s. Anm. 3), S.8-13.22f (A 3.4.9; B 36). In dem ἴαμα A 3 wird der ungläubige Zweifel an Asklepios' Vermögen zu helfen als ἀπιστεῖν bezeichnet, also als das Gegenteil des von Jesus in Mk 5,36 geforderten: μὴ θοβοῦ, μόνον πίστευε –, "fürchte dich nicht, glaube nur!"

[16] S. oben Anm. 10.

[17] Der Wortlaut dieser Formel ist nicht einhellig überliefert, vgl. Nestle-Aland, *Novum Testamentum Graece*, Stuttgart [26]1979, App. z. St. Eine Zauberformel in "barbarischer Rede" (ῥῆσις βαρβαρική) wird auch bei Lukian. Philops 9 (vgl. 31) erwähnt.

[18] R. Bultmann, *a.a.O.* (s. Anm. 1), S.234.

[19] S. dazu L. Bieler, *ΘΕΙΟΣ ΑΝΗΡ. Das Bild des "göttlichen Menschen" in Spätantike und Frühchristentum I-II*, Wien 1935-1936 (Nachdruck: Darmstadt

ihren Leiden befreit oder vom Tod erweckt werden, erscheinen dabei in einer Optik, die sie zum bloßen Zubehör macht: "der Kranke kommt nur als Objekt der wunderbaren Heilung in Betracht".[20] Und die Funktion der neutestamentlichen Wunder ergibt sich bei dieser Betrachtung aus ihrem doppelten Zweck, nach innen hin den in den frühchristlichen Gemeinden reichlich auftretenden (Mt 10,8; Mk 16,17f u.a.) christlichen Wundertätern Vorbild und Anleitung zu geben"[21] sowie nach außen als "Mittel der Mission" zu wirken und "werbende Kraft" zu entfalten (vgl. dazu z.B. Mt 9,26; Lk 7,16f).[22] Aber bereits der Vergleich mit den Heilungswundern von Epidauros läßt Zweifel aufkommen an dieser Perspektive, die den Blick einseitig auf den (göttlichen) Wundertäter zentriert. Denn der Zweck dieser Sammlung von ἰάματα ("Heilmitteln" oder "Heilungen") des Asklepios war "nicht in erster Linie Propaganda und Reklame nach außen", sie sollte vielmehr zunächst "auf die Pilger, die sich zur Heilung drängen," wirken, ihnen Hoffnung und Mut einflößen und ihren Willen zur Heilung stärken.[23] Deshalb besitzen die Person der Kranken und ihre Leiden in ihnen eigenständige Bedeutung. Auch für die neutestamentlichen Wunderge-

1967); D. L. Tiede, *The Charismatic Figure as Miracle Worker* (SBLDS 1), Missoula, Mont. 1972; W. Schottroff/ H. D. Betz/ A. Grillmeier, Art. Gottmensch I-III, in: *RAC XII* (1983) Sp.155-366; ferner verschiedene Beiträge in dem oben in Anm. 7 genannten Ausstellungskatalog des Liebieghaus Museums (S.161-222). S. auch oben Anm. 6!

[20] R. Bultmann, *a.a.O.* (s. Anm. 1), S.235.

[21] M. Dibelius, *a.a.O.* (S. Anm. 1), S.100.

[22] M.Dibelius, *a.a.O.* (s.Anm.1), S.93. Diesen beiden Aspekten gegenüber hebt K. Berger, *a.a.O.* (s.Anm.1), S.309, vielmehr die Beziehung der Wundererzählungen "zu bestimmten Grundentscheidungen der Geschichte des Urchristentums" als maßgebend für die Erfassung ihrer Funktion hervor, – nämlich ihren Bezug auf "Konflikte, Probleme und legitimationsbedürftige Ansprüche..., die durch charismatische Machterweise exemplarisch geregelt" würden. Für die beiden hier zur Diskussion stehenden Totenerweckungen wird ein solcher Bezug jedoch nicht deutlich.

[23] S. dazu R. Herzog, *a.a.O.* (s. Anm.3), S.46-64 bes. 59-61 (hier auch die Zitate). M. Dibelius, *a.a.O.* (s.Anm. 1), S.166-172, der immerhin die Urberichte der Geheilten auf Weihgaben und Tafeln auf das "Bestreben, dem Gott zu danken und seinen Namen zu erheben", zurückführt und die Verehrung des Heilgottes (bzw. – bei den novellistisch ausgestalteten Erzählungen – auch ">fromme< Mirakelsucht" und Unterhaltungsbedürfnis) als "Sitz im Leben" ansieht, vermutet allerdings als Zweck der einheitlich redigierten Endfassung die "Propaganda des Asklepioskultes"(S.171).

schichten ist primär eine analoge Funktion zu vermuten. Zumindest zeigt allein schon die erneute Musterung der beiden besprochenen Totenerweckungen, daß sie auf der menschlichen Seite mehr und auch andere Züge aufweisen, als angebracht und nötig wären, wenn diese menschliche Seite nur die Aufgabe hätte, die Folie für das Eingreifen des Wundertäters abzugeben, das in der oben gebotenen form- und religionsgeschichtlichen Analyse allein im Vordergrund der Aufmerksamkeit stand. Die Frage nach der menschlichen Seite der Wundererzählungen und ihrer Funktion ist die Frage nach dem Alltag und der Alltagserfahrung, die diese Erzählungen einfangen. Ihre Beantwortung läßt die Einbeziehung antiker Bilddenkmäler mit vergleichbarer Thematik als sinnvoll erscheinen.

II

Wunderdarstellungen sind in der Antike nicht eben häufig. Denn unter den Weihgaben,[24] mit denen die auf wunderhafte Weise von einem Gott Geretteten oder Geheilten dem Retter- oder Heilgott ihren Dank abstatteten, bilden neben den Marmorstelen mit inschriftlichen Schilderungen wiederfahrener Heilungen, wie sie aus dem Asklepieion von Epidauros auf uns gekommen sind,[25] die Weihreliefs, welche die Heilung durch den Gott selbst zeigen, nur eine relativ seltene Kategorie. Häufiger sind Reliefs, auf denen dargestellt ist, wie der

---

[24] Zu der im folgenden zugrundegelegten Klassifizierung dieser Weihgaben s. A. Körte, Bezirk eines Heilgottes, *MDAI.A18* (1893) [S.231-256]236.

[25] Vgl. Paus. II.27.3: "Innerhalb des heiligen Bezirks standen von alters viele Stelen, zu meiner Zeit [d.h. im 2.Jh.n.Chr.] noch sechs. Auf ihnen sind die Namen von Männern und Frauen verzeichnet, die von Asklepios geheilt wurden, und dazu die Krankheit, an der jeder litt, und wie er geheilt wurde. Geschrieben ist das in dorischer Sprache" (Übers.: E. Meyer/F. Eckstein).- Die Inschriften der bei Ausgrabungen in Epidauros gefundenen drei und einer fragmentarischen vierten Stele sind veröffentlicht in *IG IV²1* Nr. 121-124 und wurden bearbeitet von R. Herzog, *a.a.O.* (s. Anm. 3); kritisch zu dieser Bearbeitung (besonders zu derjenigen der Stele *IG IV²1* Nr.123) s. W. Peek, Fünf Wundergeschichten aus dem Asklepieion von Epidauros (1963), in: G. Pfohl (Hg.), *Inschriften der Griechen. Epigraphische Quellen zur Geschichte der antiken Medizin*, Darmstadt 1977, S.66-78.

Geheilte und die Seinen dem Heilgott ihren Dank abstatten,[26] oder Reliefs und Nachbildungen geheilter oder dem Gott zur Heilung anvertrauter Glieder.[27] Von diesen beiden Klassen von Votivgaben, für die etwa das Asklepieion am Südabhang der Akropolis im Athen zahlreiche Beispiele geliefert hat,[28] ist die dritte die verbreitetste und bei weitem am häufigsten belegte. Doch ist ihre Interpretation nicht in jedem Falle eindeutig. So ist bei den sogenannten "Ohrenvotiven"[29] jeweils zu fragen, ob es sich bei den dargestellten Ohren wirklich um die geheilten (oder zu heilenden) Körperorgane handelt und nicht vielmehr um Symbole der Aufmerksamkeit, die man von dem Gott, dem man sie darbrachte, als einem "erhörenden Gott" (θεὸς ἐπήκοος) für die an ihn gerichteten Gebete und Bitten erwartete.[30] Ähnliche Vorbehalte gelten auch für die Interpretation der Abbildungen von Fußabdrücken oder der

---

[26] Vgl. z.B. das Athener Marmorrelief, das an der Spitze eines Zuges von Verehrern eine Frau zeigt, die Asklepios knieend ihren Dank abstattet (J. Leipoldt/ W. Grundmann [Hg.], *Umwelt des Urchristentums III. Bilder zum neutestamentlichen Zeitalter*, Berlin [6]1987, Nr. 24), oder das ebenfalls aus Athen stammende, leider nur fragmentarisch erhaltene Relief der Kasseler Antikensammlung, auf dem dargestellt ist, wie sich der Gott einem vor ihm liegenden Kranken zuwendet (d.h. wohl zugewandt hat), während sich von der entgegengesetzten Seite ein (von dem Geheilten angeführter?) Zug von Angehörigen mit Dankesgaben naht (vgl. A. Krug, *a.a.O.* [s.Anm. 10], S.151 mit Abb. 67; P. Gerke, Heilgötter und Heilkunst in der Antike. Asklepios, Hygieia und Telesphoros, *Kassel kulturell* Nr.12/Dezember 1989, S.34-37 bes. S.36 mit Abb.3).

[27] S. dazu L. Stieda, Über alt-italische Weihgeschenke, *MDAI.R 14* (1899) S.230-243. Ein Beispiel für die Vielzahl derartiger Votivgaben bieten die heute im Museo Oliveriano in Pesaro befindlichen Funde aus dem dortigen heiligen Hein (lucus sacer Pisaurensis), vgl. J. Zicàri, *Guida del Museo Oliveriano di Pesaro*, Pesaro 1969, S.11. Aus Athen stammt ein hier einzuordnendes berühmtes Weihrelief des 4.Jh.v.Chr., das den Heilheros Amynos vor einem riesigen Bein mit einer Krampfader zeigt, das diesem damit zur Heilung anvertraut wurde, vgl. A. Körte, *a.a.O.* (s.Anm. 24), S.235-238; J. Leipoldt/W. Grundmann (Hg.), *a.a.O. III*, Nr. 23; A. Krug, *a.a.O.*, S.148f mit Abb. 65.

[28] Zur Verehrung des Asklepios und anderer Heilgötter in Athen und Attika sowie zu ihren Heiligtümern und den Zeugnissen ihres Kultes hier s. K. Kerényi, *Der göttliche Arzt. Studien über Asklepios und seine Kultstätten*, Darmstadt [3]1975, S.71-73; A. Krug, *a.a.O.*, S.147-159. In diesen beiden Arbeiten finden sich auch Überblicke über die übrigen Kultstätten des Gottes.

[29] Beispiele sind abgebildet bei J. Leipoldt/W. Grundmann (Hg.), *a.a.O. III*, Nr.22 (Athen), und bei A. Krug, *a.a.O.*, S.151 Abb. 68; bzw. P. Gercke, *a.a.O.* (s.Anm.26), S.35f mit Abb. 2 (Kassel).

[30] S. dazu O. Weinreich, ΘΕΟΙ ΕΠΗΚΟΟΙ, *MDAI.A 37* (1912) S.1-68.

in Wallfahrtsheiligtümern häufig begegnenden Votivfüße.[31] Bei ihnen ist jeweils im Einzelfall zu prüfen, ob es sich um geheilte (oder zu heilende) Gliedmaßen oder aber um den Fuß(abdruck) bzw. die Füße oder Fußabdrücke eines zum Wallfahrtsheiligtum des Gottes gekommenen Pilgers handelt, der mit dieser Votivgabe um die heile und unversehrte Rückkehr nach Hause bat. Als weitere Möglichkeit kommt in Betracht, daß die Darstellung des Fußes oder Fußabdruckes des zu Hilfe eilenden Gottes intendiert war. Derartige Votivfüße sind im Kult des Asklepios-Serapis, aber auch anderer Götter belegt.[32] Die erwähnten Weihreliefs, welche die Heilung von Kranken durch Asklepios zeigen, bilden diese freilich in der Regel nicht in der Art der in den Evangelien oder in antiken Wundererzählungen berichteten als durch direktes Eingreifen des Gottes bewirktes Wunder ab: sie zeigen den Kranken vielmehr, wie er im Tempelschlaf die Epiphanie des Gottes erlebt, bei der dieser ihm das Heilmittel oder den Weg zur Heilung offenbart. Das leichte Anrühren des schlafenden Kranken durch den erscheinenden Gott (oder sein heiliges Tier, die Schlange) ist meistens das einzige, was vom Vorgang der Heilung wiedergegeben ist.[33] Totenerweckungen fehlen unter den auf den Weihreliefs aus dem

---

[31] S. dazu M. Guarducci, Le impronte del *Quo vadis* e monumenti affini, figurati ed epigrafici, *RPARA 19* (1942-43) S.305-344.

[32] S. dazu M. Guarducci, *a.a.O.*, S.322-330. Für Palästina vgl. einerseits den heute im Musée du Louvre in Paris befindlichen Votivfuß mit der Inschrift: Πονπηΐα Λουκιλία ἀνέθηκεν "Pompeia Lucilia hat (es als Weihgeschenk) aufgestellt", der ebenso wie die zwei wohl zusammengehörigen Fragmente eines Reliefs, das eine geringelte Schlange und Ähren vor einer Tempelfront zeigte, und weitere Fundgegenstände aus dem Asklepios-Serapis-Heiligutum stammt, das bereits im 1. Jhr.n.Ch. beim Teich Bethesda in Jerusalem bestand, s. dazu A. Duprez, *Jésus et les dieux guérisseurs. A propos de Jean, V* (CRB 12), Paris 1970, S.28-54. 89-95 mit Pl. XVII.3 und XVIII. Andererseits ist auf den Torso eines doppelt lebensgroßen Votivfußes vom Karmel (heute in der Sammlung des Stella-Maris-Klosters in Haifa) hinzuweisen, dessen Plinthe die Inschrift trägt: Διΐ Ἡλιοπολείτῃ Καρμήλῳ | Γ. Ιουλ. Εὐτυχᾶς Κόλ(ων) Καισαρεύς "Dem Zeus Heliopoleites Karmelos G(aius) Jul(ius) Eutychas, Bürger von Caesarea", s. dazu. M. Avi-Yonah, Mont Carmel and the God of Baalbek, *IEJ 2* (1952) S.118-124 mit Pl. 8A/B; K. Galling, Der Gott Karmel und die Ächtung der fremden Götter, in: *Geschichte und Altes Testament* (BHTh 16), Tübingen 1953, [S.105-125] S.110-121; O. Eißfeldt, *Der Gott Karmel* (SDAW.S 1953.1), Berlin 1953, S.15-25 mit Taf. IV.4-5.

[33] Beipiele bei K. Kerényi, *a.a.O.* (s. Anm. 28), S.30 Abb. 17. 33 Abb. 18. 34 Abb. 19, sowie bei A. Krug, *a.a.O.* (s. Anm. 10), S.134-155 mit Abb. 57-61. 67. 70. S. dazu K. Sudhoff, *a.a.O.* (s. oben Anm. 10).

Asklepioskult dargestellten Heilungen völlig, obwohl, wenn auch nicht die Heilungsberichte, so doch die mythologischen Überlieferungen über Asklepios auch Kunde von einer Totenerweckung enthalten.[34]

Wenn man nach Darstellungen von Totenerweckungen sucht, muß man sich den verschiedenen Bereichen der frühchristlichen Kunst zuwenden, in der neben anderen Arten von Wundern auch das Thema der Totenerweckung vielfältig belegt ist.[35] Wie bei anderen Darstellungen von Wundern handelt es sich auch bei den Totenerweckungen jedoch nicht immer um die Wiedergabe von Jesuswundern, sondern daneben auch um solche von Jüngern und Aposteln (Totenerweckungen: Act 9,36-42; 20,7-12; andere Wunder: Act 3,1-11; 5,12-16; 8,5-8; 9,32-35; 19,11f; 28,1-10; vgl. die Summarien: Act 2,43; 4,30; 5,12; 6,8; 14,3). Auch erfolgt die Charakterisierung der Leiden und die Darstellung der Wunder vielfach so chiffreartig und typisierend, daß ein konkreter Bezug auf ganz bestimmte neutestamentliche Wundererzählungen nicht erkennbar wird und offenbar auch nicht intendiert ist.[36] Den einzelnen Bildtypen liegen vielmehr als Bausteine verschiedene, aus dem paganen Bereich stammende Bildformeln und Bildelemente zugrunde, die allein auftreten oder in unter-

[34] Vgl. Pind. Pyth. III.54-58 und s. dazu H. J. Rose, *Griechische Mythologie. Ein Handbuch*, München [2]1961, S.136f mit Anm. 2. Zum Fehlen eindeutiger Darstellungen antiker Erweckungswunder vgl. C. Nauerth, *Vom Tode zum Leben. Die christlichen Totenerweckungen in der spätantiken Kunst*, Theol. Diss. Heidelberg 1978, S.250-258.

[35] Vgl. C. Nauerth, *ebenda*. S. ferner R. Darmstädter, *Die Auferweckung des Lazarus in der altchristlichen und byzantinischen Kunst*, Phil. Diss. Bern 1955, und das reiche Bildmaterial etwa bei W. F. Volbach, *a.a.O.* (s. Anm. 7). S. auch A. Weiser, *Was die Bibel Wunder nennt. Ein Sachbuch zu den Berichten der Evangelien*, Stuttgart 1975, S.122-133 mit den dort gebotenen Abildungen.

[36] Dies gilt, um nur ein Beispiel zu nennen, etwa für die Darstellungen auf den beiden in der Mitte des 19. Jh.s in der Vigna Maccarani auf dem Aventin in Rom gefundenen polychromen Platten mit Heilungswundern von Aposteln: "Die Darstellungen illustrieren ... das lebendige Weiterwirken des Geistes und bringen die bildliche Bezeugung der Heilungswunder, wie sie in den Summarien aufgenommen sind; nicht geht es um eine Herausstellung dieses oder jenes Apostels", E. Dinkler, *Christus und Asklepios. Zum Christustypus der polychromen Platten im Museo Nazionale Romano* (SHAW.PH 1980.2), Heidelberg 1980, S.27. Auch bei Jesuswundern ist ein eindeutiger Bezug auf bestimmte Texte des Neuen Testaments in vielen Fällen nicht gegeben, vgl. C. Nauerth, *a.a.O.* (s. Anm. 7), S.329-346, vor allem aber – auch zum folgenden – die bereits in Anm. 34 angeführte Dissertation dieser Autorin, die sich eingehend mit der Bildtradition und der Bildersprache der frühchristlichen Darstellungen von Totenerweckungen befaßt.

schiedlicher Weise kombiniert werden konnten. Solche Bildformeln, die speziell bei der Darstellung von Totenerweckungen Verwendung fanden, sind z.B. die typischen, immer wiederkehrenden Elemente "Sarkophag", "Wickelleiche", "*Aedicula*" oder auch "nackter Leichnam". Es handelt sich also zunächst nur um die Darstellung der Todesüberwindung als solcher: "Christus (oder etwa auch ein Apostel) erweckt einen Toten". Erst nachträglich, im Zuge der weiteren Entwicklung wurde durch die Hinzufügung spezifischer Beigaben die Möglichkeit geschaffen, daß die Darstellung als Wiedergabe eines bestimmten Textes (z.B. als Wiedergabe der Auferweckung des Lazarus, Joh. 11,1-45) identifiziert werden konnte.[37]

Aber nicht nur die bildnerische Intention und die typisierende Art der Darstellung lassen diese Zeugnisse frühchristlicher Kunst als wenig geeignet erscheinen, zur Illustration der realen Situation beizutragen, welche die neutestamentlichen Totenerweckungen voraussetzen. Vielmehr erscheint die Situation im einzelnen vielfach schon dadurch verfremdet, daß Christus in diesen Wunderdarstellungen in einer dem Neuen Testament ganz unbekannten Weise wiedergegeben ist. So wird er als Wundertäter nicht selten durch die Philosophentracht, in die er gekleidet ist, und die Buchrolle, die er in der Hand hält, zum Philosophen stilisiert. Oder er nimmt, was allerdings umstritten ist, die Physiognomie des bärtigen Heilgottes Asklepios an.[38] Oder aber er wird in der Rolle des Magiers dargestellt, der mit dem Zauberstab, der *virga thaumaturgica*, das Erweckungswunder vollbringt.[39] Auch bringt die Perspektive, in der die Dargestellten in diesem Zusammenhang oft erscheinen: der (oder die) Wundertäter groß, die Geheilten bzw. die Adressaten sonstiger Wundertaten dagegen klein, unübersehbar eine Hierachie in die Bilder, welche die skeptische Frage wecken muß, ob sie der Sichtweise des Neuen Testaments wirklich noch im entfern-

---

[37] So mit C. Nauerth, *a.a.O.* (s. Anm. 34). Vgl. hier besonders S.268-283, wo die Autorin ihre Ergebnisse zusammenfaßt.

[38] So E. Dinkler, *a.a.O.* (s. Anm. 36), S.21-35.37f; doch vgl. dagegen die Besprechung von Dinklers Arbeit durch F. W. Deichmann, *RQ 77* (1982) S.136-138; s. auch D. Stutzinger in: *Spätantike und frühes Christentum. Ausstellung im Liebieghaus Museum alter Plastik Frankfurt am Main*, Frankfurt a.M. 1983, S.607-609.

[39] S. dazu C. Nauerth, *a.a.O.* (s.Anm. 34), S.259-267.

testen angemessen ist (vgl. nur Mk 9,33-35 parr.!). Durch die Konzentration der bildlichen Darstellung auf das Geschehen zwischen dem Wundertäter und dem, an dem sich die Wundertat vollzieht, sowie auf den Erfolg des Wunderhandelns werden schließlich aus dieser alle Züge ausgeblendet, die in den Wundererzählungen zur Charakterisierung der Situation der betroffenen Menschen dienten. So gesehen, erweisen sich die frühchristlichen Darstellungen von Totenerweckungen sogar als ganz ungeeignet zur Illustration des realen Hintergrunds und der sozialen Zusammenhänge, welche die entsprechenden Wundererzählungen des Neuen Testaments reflektieren. Sie haben ihre Bedeutung als Zeugnisse der geistigkulturellen und künstlerischen Bedingungen ihrer Entstehungszeit; als Illustrationen der neutestamentlichen Lebenswelt müssen sie dagegen ausscheiden.

III

In die Lücke, die sich damit für die Veranschaulichung neutestamentlicher Wundergeschichten durch zeitgenössische oder dem Neuen Testament zumindest zeitlich nahestehende Bildwerke auftut, können im Falle der beiden eingangs genannten Totenerweckungen indessen zwei römische Reliefs eintreten, welche zwar nicht das wunderhafte Geschehen als solches, aber die genauen Umstände abbilden, in die die Wunder eingebettet sind: für Mk 5,21-43 parr. die Aufbahrung einer Toten und die Leichenklage (*conclamatio*), für Lk 7,11-17 das Totengeleit (*profectio*), in dem ein Toter zur (Verbrennung und) Bestattung hinausgebracht wird. Dabei handelt es sich einerseits – als Illustration der hinter Mk 5,21-43 stehenden Alltagswirklichkeit – um ein aus zwei Blöcken bestehendes Relief (Abb.1), das sich im Museo Gregoriano Profano im Vatikan befindet (Inv.-Nr. 9999).[40] Zusammen mit anderen hier ausgestellten Reliefs stammt es von dem 1848 südöstlich

[40] Vgl. O. Benndorf/R. Schöne, *Die antiken Bildwerke des lateranischen Museums*, Leipzig 1867, S.221-224 Nr. 348; W. Helbig/ H. Speier (Hg.), *Führer durch die öffentlichen Sammlungen klassischer Altertümer in Rom I. Die Päpstlichen Sammlungen im Vatikan und Lateran*, Tübingen [4]1963, S.775f Nr. 1074; J. M. C. Toynbee, *Death and Burial in the Roman World: Aspects of Greek and Roman Life*, London 1971, S.44f; Th. Klauser, *Die Cathedra im Totenkult der heidnischen und christlichen Antike* (LWQF 21), Münster/W. [3]1979, S.24f.

bb. 1: Darstellung einer *conclamatio* vom Haterier-Grab im Vatikan, Museo Gregoriano Profano (Inv.-Nr. 9999). Photo: Deutsches Archäologisches Institut/Abteilung Rom.

Abb. 2: Darstellung einer *profectio*. L'Aquila. Museo Nazionale d'Abruzzo (Inv.-Nr. 95). Photo: Deutsches Archäologisches Institut/Abteilung

von Rom an der Via Labicana (heute: Via Casilina) unweit von Centocelle ausgegrabenen Haterier-Grab, das, nach den auf ihm abgebildeten Bauten (Inv.-Nr. 9997) und dem auf ihm ebenfalls wiedergegebenen Baukran (Inv.-Nr. 9998) zu schließen, wohl von einem reichen Bauunternehmer der flavischen Zeit errichtet worden ist.[41] Darstellungen dieser Thematik, die den oder die Tote(n), umgeben von trauernden Angehörigen, auf einer κλίνη zeigen, sind auf Sarkophagen öfter belegt.[42] Manchmal beschränkt sich dabei der Reliefschmuck auf die Darstellung der conclamatio; in anderen Fällen ist diese in eine Bilderfolge eingereiht, die den Lebenslauf eines Kindes wiedergibt. Das hier gewählte Beispiel vom Haterier-Grab ist sicherlich nicht nur der monumentalste, sondern auch von seiner Aussagekraft her der eindrücklichste und in seiner Alltäglichkeit der sprechendste Beleg dieses Bildtypus. Auf der anderen Seite läßt sich das in Lk 7,11-17 geschilderte Totengeleit nur mit einem einzigen, thematisch ganz für sich stehenden Relief illustrieren (Abb. 2), das 1879 in den Abruzzen beim Straßenbau zwischen Preturo und S. Vittorino (Amiternum) zum Vorschein kam und sich heute in L'Aquila im Museo Nazionale d'Abruzzo befindet (Inv.-Nr. 95).[43] Inschriften, die an der Fundstelle ebenfalls aufgefunden wurden und paläographisch in die Zeit der ausgehenden Republik oder des Prinzipats des Augustus zu setzen sind,[44] sowie interne Indizien, die das Relief selbst enthält,[45] deuten auf

---

[41] Zu den beiden genannten weiteren Reliefs vom Hateriergrab s. W. Helbig/H. Speier (Hg.), *a.a.O. I*, S.776-780 Nr. 1075f.

[42] Vgl. G. Koch/H. Sichtermann, *Römische Sarkophage* (Handbuch der Archäologie), München 1982, S.107-113 bes. S.112f; R. Amedick, *Die Sarkophage mit Darstellungen aus dem Menschenleben* (Die antiken Sarkophagreliefs I/4), Berlin 1991, S.60-74 bes. S.72ff. Einzelbeipiele u.a.: F. Baratte/C. Metzger, *Musée du Louvre: Catalogue des sarcophages en piere d'époques romaine et paléochrétienne*, Paris 1985, S.33-35 No. 5; S. Walker, *Catalogue of Roman Sarcophagi in the British Museum* (Corpus Signorum Imperii romani. Great Britan II/2), London 1990, S.17f No. 6.

[43] Vgl. Vgl. C. Hülsen, *MDAI.R 5* (1890) S.72f; N. Persichetti, Due rilievi Amiternini, *MDAI.R 23* (1908) S.15-25 mit Tf. IV; L. Franchi, Rilievo con pompa funebre e rilievo con gladiatori al museo dell' Aquila, in: R. Bianchi Bandinelli (Ed.), *Sculture municipali dell'area sabellica tra l'età di Cesare e quella di Nerone* (Studi Miscellanei 10 /1963-64), Rom 1966; S.23-32 mit Tav. V-XII; J. M. C. Toynbee, *a.a.O.* (s. Anm. 40), S.46f.

[44] Vgl. C. Hülsen, *a.a.O.*, S.72.

[45] L. Franchi, *a.a.O.*, S.27-29; verweist auf den mit Mondsichel und Sternen besetzten Baldachin über der Toten, den sie als Symbol für die in der späten Republik unter dem Einfluß des Neupythagoreismus ein-

ein Datum um die Mitte des 1. Jh.s v. Chr.

Es ist freilich die Frage, ob Darstellungen von Leichenbegängnissen im Zentrum der römischen Welt, auch wenn sie nahezu gleichzeitig sind, überhaupt zur Illustration von Schilderungen entsprechender Gebräuche im Osten der Mittelmeerwelt herangezogen werden können. Nur soviel sei hier vorweggenommen, daß der Vergleich diese Möglichkeit bestätigt, weil trotz spezifischer Unterschiede die Grundzüge der Trauerbräuche im wesentlichen gleich sind.[46] Auch haben Ausgrabungsfunde inzwischen grundsätzlich verdeutlicht, daß die hellenistisch-römische Einheitskultur auch in Palästina rasch bis in die Bereiche des Alltagslebens vorgedrungen ist und sie erobert hat.[47] Besonders deutlich geht diese bereits lange vor 70 n.Chr. einsetzende Durchdringung Palästinas durch die hellenistisch-römische Einheitskultur aus den neuen Ausgrabungen in der Jerusalemer Altstadt[48] und im galiläischen Sepphoris[49] hervor.

Die Erzählung von der Auferweckung der Tochter des Synagogenvorstehers Jaïrus (Mk 5,21-43 parr.) zeigt jedenfalls deutliche Berührungen mit dem, was auf dem Relief vom Haterier-Grab dargestellt ist. Das soeben verstorbene zwölf-

---

setzende mystische Sehnsucht nach einem ewigen Weiterleben der Seele im Himmel interpretiert. S. dazu Cic. rep. VI.14 (Somnium Scipionis).

[46] Vgl. dazu S. Krauss, *Talmudische Archäologie II*, Leipzig 1911 (Nachdruck: Hildesheim 1966), S.54-82, auf der einen, J. Marquardt, *Das Privatleben der Römer I*, Leipzig 1886 (Nachdruck: Darmstadt 1975), S.340-385, auf der anderen Seite. Ferner: A. Mau, Art. Bestattung, in: *PRE 5* (1897) Sp.331-359; G. Stählin, Art. κοπετός in: *ThWNT 3* (1938) S.829-851; L. Koep (L. Dürr)/ E. Stommel/ J. Kollwitz, Art. Bestattung, in: *RAC II* (1954) Sp.194-219; O. Nußbaum, Art. Geleit IV. Totengeleit, in: *RAC IX* (1976) Sp.924-939; J. M. C. Toynbee, *a.a.O.* (s. Anm. 40), S.43-61; J. Prieur, *La mort dans l'antiquité romaine*, o.O. 1986, S.11-31.

[47] Vgl. dazu z.B. den Katalog der Ausstellung "*Function und Design in the Talmudic Period*", die das Haaretz Museum Tel Aviv 1978/79 veranstaltete. Die Ausstellung belegte den tiefreichenden kulturellen Einfluß, dem Palästina seit der herodianischen Zeit unterlag, gerade mit alltäglichen Gebrauchsgegenständen wie Küchen- und Tafelgeräten, Lampen, Kosmetikartikeln, aber auch "Burial und Burial Customs" und "Tomb Offerings".

[48] S. dazu N. Avigad, *Discovering Jerusalem*, Nashville, Tennessee 1983, S.81-207; M. Ben-Dov, *In the Shadow of the Temple. The Discovery of Ancient Jerusalem*, New York 1985, S.149-167.

[49] Vgl. nur E. M. Meyers/E. Netzer/C. L. Meyers, Sepphoris – "Ornament of All Galilee", *BA 49* (1986) S.4-19; dies., Artistry in Stone. The Mosaics of Ancient Sepphoris, *BA 50* (1987) S.223-231; dies., *Sepphoris Winona Lake*, Indiana 1992 (mit Bibliographie).

jährige (Lk 8,42) Mädchen, zu dem Jesus (nach der Version von Mk und Lk) trotz der dringenden Bitte seines Vaters nicht mehr rechtzeitig vor Eintritt des Todes gelangt war, weil er durch die ihn umdrängende Menge und die blutflüssige Frau aufgehalten wurde, ist, so hat man die Szene zu verstehen, die alle drei Synoptiker entwerfen, im Hause des Synagogenvorstehers – wohl auf ihrem Sterbebett – aufgebahrt. Die Leiche, so hat man sich weiter vorzustellen, ist, nachdem man der Toten die Augen zugedrückt hat, inzwischen gewaschen, gesalbt und angekleidet worden.[50] Auch hat die Leichenklage bereits eingesetzt, an der sich außer den unmittelbaren Familienangehörigen (Lk 8,51f) auch die Menge der Verwandten und Bekannten (Mt 9,23-25; Mk 5,38f) sowie berufsmäßige Flötenbläser (Mt 9,23:αὐληταί, Vg. *tibicines*) und Klagefrauen (lat. *praeficae*) beteiligten.[51]

Dies ist genau die Szene, die das Relief vom Haterier-Grab vor uns entstehen läßt, wenn hier der Aufwand für das Leichenbegängnis vielleicht auch im Vergleich mit normalen palästinischen Gegebenheiten um einiges prächtiger ist. Dargestellt ist die feierliche Aufbahrung (*collocatio*) einer vornehmen Frau auf einem Totenbett (*lectus funebris*), das wohl im Atrium des Hauses aufgestellt ist. Von dem Haus selbst gewahrt man im Hintergrund das Ziegeldach mit *imbrices* und *tegulae*, d.h. dem römischen Gegenstück zu "Mönch" und "Nonne", ferner, auf der rechten Seite, einen aus Quadern erbauten, vorspringenden Gebäudeflügel, dessen Dach offensichtlich flacher als das des linken Gebäudeflügels ist. Hinter dem Totenbett stehen drei große Vasen, von denen eine verdeckt ist; zwischen ihnen hängen Girlanden aus Blumen und Früchten sowie zwei große Muscheln, in denen sich Jenseitssymbolik aussprechen mag.[52] Vier große Fackeln sowie zwei große figürliche Lampen auf pflanzengestaltigen Kandelabern umstehen das Totenbett und erinnern an die ältere Zeit, in der in Rom Begräbnisse noch bei Nacht stattfanden.[53] Vor dem Bett sind auf der Erde zwei niedrige, kelchförmige Räuchergeräte (*acerrae* bzw. *thymiateria*) aufgestellt, aus denen

[50] S. dazu S. Krauss, *a.a.O.* (s. Anm. 46) II, S.55-60.

[51] Vgl. *Bill. I*, S.521-523.

[52] S. dazu J. M. C. Toynbee, *a.a.O.* (s. Anm. 40), S.44f.

[53] Vgl. J. Marquardt, *a.a.O.* (s. Anm. 46), S.343-345; J. Gagé, Art. Fackel (Kerze), in: *RAC VII* (1969) [Sp.154-217] Sp.164-166. Die Fackeln wurden später beibehalten, als die Totenbegängnisse am Tage stattfanden.

Flammen hochschlagen.[54] Die im Vergleich mit den übrigen Figuren, die auf dem Relief wiedergegeben sind, überlebensgroß erscheinende Tote liegt auf einem Prunkbett mit gedrechselten Füßen, das auf einem Podest oder erhöhten Unterbau steht und mit zwei quergestreiften Matratzen und einem Kopfkissen versehen ist. Die über das Kopfkissen herabhängende, doppelt gelegte und mit Fransen versehene Binde ist wohl als Kopftuch (*ricinum*) oder Schweißtuch (*orarium, sudarium*, bzw. *mappa*) zu deuten.[55] Die Tote, die mit zwei Blumenkränzen bekränzt ist und, wie es scheint, von einem hinter dem Bett stehenden Leichensalber (*pollinctor*), vermutlich einem Sklaven des professionellen Leichenbesorgers (*libitinarius*), gerade einen dritten umgelegt bekommt,[56] ist in eine dünne, langärmelige Tunica und in ein Obergewand gekleidet, das offenbar in der Höhe der Hüften um die Beine geschlagen ist.[57] An der linken Hand trägt sie Ringe.[58] Zur ihren Füßen, die wohl der Eingangstür zugewandt zu denken sind,[59] liegt ein Stapel von drei Schreibtafeln (*pugillares*), – wohl das Testament der Toten.

Doch nicht nur die feierliche Aufbahrung der Toten ist auf dem Relief wiedergegeben, sondern auch die Totenklage (*conclamatio*), die wie in Mk 5,38f parr. bereits begonnen hat, ist in die Darstellung einbezogen. Die beiden links vom Leichensalber hinter dem Totenbett stehenden Frauen, die das Haar gelöst haben und sich die Brust schlagen,[60] sind

---

[54] Vgl. K. Wigand, Thymiateria, *BoJ 122* (1912) [S.1-97] S.78.

[55] Die erste Möglichkeit erwägen O. Benndorf/R. Schöne, *a.a.O.* (s. Anm. 40), S.222, die zweite E. Simon in: W. Helbig/H. Speier (Hg.), *a.a.O.* (s. Anm. 40) I, S.776.

[56] Daß die Tote hier "gegen die römische Sitte" bekränzt sei, wie O. Benndorf/R. Schöne, *ebenda*, behaupten, wird man im Blick auf Dion. Hal. XI.39 bestreiten müssen. Auch Lukian. de luctu 11, der die Vorbereitung des Leichnams für die Aufbahrung genau beschreibt, setzt voraus, daß dieser "mit den Blumen, die die Jahreszeit mit sich bringt, bekränzt" wird.

[57] Vgl. O. Benndorf/R. Schöne, *ebenda*. Das Zwölftafelgesetz beschränkte in Anlehnung an Solons Gesetzgebung (vgl. Plut. Sol. 21) den Aufwand für Tote auf "drei Kopftücher (*ricinium*), eine purpurne Tunica (*tunicula purpurae*)", Cic. leg. II.59.

[58] Vgl. dazu Prop IV.7.9 und s. A. Böhme, *Schmuck der römischen Frau* (Kleine Schriften zur Kenntnis der römischen Besatzungsgeschichte Südwestdeutschlands 11), Stuttgart 1974, S.16-18.

[59] Vgl. Pers. III. 103-106, bes. 105: "die starren Beine nach der Türe streckend" (Übers: O. Weinreich), s. auch Plin. nat. VII.46.

[60] Zu diesen beiden Trauergesten s. Petron. 111.2. – Lukian. de luctu 12 nennt in seiner Schilderung der Totenklage weitere Trauerriten: "Nun

sicher als gemietete Klagefrauen (*praeficae*) zu verstehen. Ihnen möchte man die Frau in der Haartracht der flavischen Zeit[61] zuordnen, die links des Totenbetts auf einem Säulenstumpf sitzt und die Klageweisen auf einer Doppelflöte[62] begleitet. Schwer zu deuten sind dagegen die hinter ihr stehende verschleierte Frau, die mit gefalteten Händen (– einem Trauergestus –)[63] zum Totenbett emporblickt, und die je zwei Männer und Frauen, die – ebenfalls mit Trauergebärden[64] – vor einem vom Totenbett herabhängenden, den Unterbau verdeckenden Vorhang langsam nach rechts schreiten. Handelt es sich bei ihnen um Angehörige: die Familie der Toten,[65] – oder hat man zumindest bei den vier vor dem Totenbett Einherschreitenden an die Dienerschaft zu denken: "zwei Sklaven und zwischen ihnen ein Mädchen mit langem Haar und eine Alte, wohl die Amme"?[66] Um testamentarisch

---

geht das Geheul und Gewinsel der Weiber an, alle Anwesenden fangen auf einmal an zu weinen, schlagen sich auf die Brust, raufen sich die Haare aus dem Kopfe und zerritzen sich die Wangen; an vielen Orten ist überdies noch der Gebrauch, seine Kleider zu zerreißen und Asche aufs Haupt zu streuen" (Übersetzung: C. M. Wieland). Vgl. hier auch 19. – Doch verbot nach dem Vorbild von Solons Gesetzgebung (vgl. Plut. Sol. 21) das römische Zwölftafelgesetz das Zerkratzen der Wangen und das Anstimmen von Klagegeschrei und beschränkte die Zahl der Musikanten auf 10 Flötenspieler, s. Cic. leg. II.59. 64 und vgl. R. Düll, *Das Zwölftafelgesetz* (Tusculum Bücherei) München ^{4}1971, S.58f.

[61] Vgl. H. Blanck, *Einführung in das Privatleben der Griechen und Römer* (Die Altertumswissenschaft), Darmstadt 1976, S.74 Abb. 17C.76: "Unter den flavischen Kaisern beginnt dann die bis in die Regierung des Traian dauernde auffallende Haarmode mit hohen, fast virtuosen diademförmigen Lockenaufbauten über der Stirn, die ohne Zuhilfenahme von Toupets wohl kaum zu erzielen waren".

[62] Zur Doppelflöte (griech. αὐλός, lat. *tibiae*) s. F. Behn, *Musikleben im Altertum und frühen Mittelalter*, Stuttgart 1954, S.96-104; H. Besseler/M. Schneider (Hg.), *Musikgeschichte in Bildern II/5. Musik des Altertums. Etrurien und Rom*, Leipzig 1964, S.52f. Zur ihrer Verwendung bei Leichenbegängnissen s. O. Nußbaum, *a.a.O.* (s. Anm 46) IX, S.932.

[63] Vgl. Apul. met. III.1.2 ("mit übergeschlagenen Beinen und die Hände mit verschlungenen Fingern über dem Knie gefaltet, so saß ich ... zusammengekauert auf dem Bettgestell und vergoß Tränenströme", Übers.: R. Helm); Amm XXIX.2.15 ("entblößten Hauptes und barfuß, ... mit gefalteten Händen", Übers.: W. Seyfarth). S. dazu Th. Klauser, *a.a.O.* (s. Anm. 40), S.24.

[64] Alle vier schlagen sich an die Brust und scheinen das Totenbett zu umkreisen.

[65] So O. Benndorf/R. Schöne, *a.a.O.* (s. Anm. 40), S.222; T. Klauser, *ebd.*

[66] So E. Simon in : W. Helbig/H. Speier (Hg.), *a.a.O.* (s. Anm. 40) I, S.776.

freigelassene Sklavinnen handelt es sich jedoch eindeutig bei den drei rechts des Totenbetts in einer Ebene hintereinander auf niedrigen Korbstühlen oder -hockern hingekauerten Frauen, die zum Zeichen ihrer Trauer das rechte Knie mit den Händen umfassen.[67] Ihr Haar ist aufgelöst. Darüber tragen sie als Symbol ihrer erlangten Freiheit den pilleus, eine runde, festanliegende Filzmütze.[68] Von rechts kommt ein bartloser, gebeugter Mann herzu, der in seinen vorgestreckten Händen etwas herbeiträgt. Bis auf wenige Einzelheiten, zu denen etwa die mit dem *pilleus* bekleideten Freigelassenen gehören, kann man sich die ganze hier abgebildete Szene auch in der Welt des Neuen Testaments vorstellen und sie als Illustration der in der Wundererzählung Mk 5,21-43 parr. vorausgesetzten Situation betrachten.

Trotz ihrer vielleicht etwas größeren Fremdartigkeit gilt ein vergleichbares Urteil aber auch für die genannte Reliefdarstellung eines Leichenzugs (*profectio* bzw. *pompa funebris*) im Verhältnis zu Lk 7,11-17. Die Angaben zur vorausgesetzten Situation und zu den Begleitumständen des Wunders sind in der Erzählung von der Auferweckung des Jünglings von Nain allerdings denkbar knapp: wir erfahren nur, daß die Szene außerhalb der Stadt Nain in der Nähe des Stadttors spielt, daß es sich bei dem Toten um den einzigen Sohn einer Witwe handelt[69] und daß eine große Menge Menschen (ὄχλος πολύς, V.11) dem Toten das Trauergeleit gibt.[70] Auf die Besonderheit, daß die Träger den Toten hier im (offenen) Sarg, nicht auf der Bahre transportieren, ist schon hingewiesen worden.[71] Es ist gerade die Knappheit der die Situation charakterisie-

---

[67] Zu diesem Gestus vgl. T. Klauser, *a.a.O.* (s. Anm. 40) S.24f. Die Sitzgelegenheiten, auf die sich diese freigelassenen Sklavinnen kauern, unterscheiden sich deutlich von den üblichen, mit Lehnen versehenen römischen Korbsesseln, in denen vornehme Frauen zu sitzen pflegten; sie ähneln eher umgestülpten Weidekörben, wie sie vielfältig Verwendung fanden, s. W. Gaitzsch, *Antike Korb- und Seilerwaren* (Schriften des Limesmuseums Aalen 38), Stuttgart 1986, bes. S.19-21. 63f (Abb. 26 und 27). 87.

[68] Vgl. App. Mithr. 2; Cod.Iust. VII.6.5; s. auch Liv. XXXVIII.55.2 und Pers. III.106.

[69] Dieser Zug der Erzählung berührt sich mit I Reg 17,17-24 (II Reg 4,8-37) und ist vielleicht von dort her beeinflußt.

[70] Die Bestattung der Toten, zu der auch die Teilnahme am Totengeleit gehört, war eines der jüdischen Liebeswerke, s. dazu aus der oben in Anm. 46 genannten Literatur vor allem die Arbeit von S. Krauss, *a.a.O. II*, S.54-82, und vgl. damit das bei *Bill. IV/1*, S.578-592 zusammengestellte Material.

[71] S. oben S. 258f.

renden Angaben in Lk 7,11-17, die das Relief gewissermaßen als Ergänzung des Textes und als Hilfe zur Ausfüllung der in der Schilderung des Leichenzugs verbleibenden Lücken geeignet macht: erst aufgrund des Reliefs gewinnt die in Lk 7,11-17 vorausgesetzte Szene an Anschaulichkeit.

Der Trauerzug, der sich auf dem Relief nach rechts bewegt, wird eröffnet von einer Gruppe von Bläsern, die in zwei Registern übereinander angeordnet sind, in Wirklichkeit jedoch auf einer Ebene hinter- bzw. nebeneinander zu denken sind. Die vier Musikanten auf dem unteren Register blasen die schon vom Relief des Haterier-Grabes her bekannte Doppelflöte.[72] Doch war diese, wie das obere Register unserer Reliefdarstellung zeigt und wie auch aus literarischen Zeugnissen hervorgeht, keineswegs das einzige Instrument, das bei Leichenbegängnissen Verwendung fand.[73] Von den drei auf den oberen Register dargestellten Musikern sind die beiden letzten unzweifelhaft Hornbläser (*cornicines*). Ihr Instrument ist "das kreisförmig gewundene Horn (*cornu*) mit dem hölzernen Quergriff", das von einer Reihe bildlicher Darstellungen her bekannt ist und von dem in Pompeji zwei unversehrte Exemplare gefunden worden sind.[74] Dagegen macht die Identifizierung des Instruments des Musikers, der den beiden Hornbläsern auf dem oberen Register vorausgeht, Schwierigkeiten. Handelt es sich bei ihm um einen Trompeter (*tubicen*)?[75] Doch eine Tuba besitzt "ein gerades, konisch erweitertes Rohr aus Bronze oder Eisen" mit abnehmbarem Mundstück,[76] während das elegant geschwungene Instrument, das auf dem Relief abgebildet ist, seiner Form nach am ehesten als Zinken (*lituus*) anzusprechen wäre,[77] wenn nicht durch eine Bemerkung bei Aulus Gellius (Gell. XX.2.1) der

---

[72] S. oben S.275.

[73] Das Geschmetter der Trompete (*tuba*) erwähnen z.B. Hor. sat. I.6.44; Prop. II.7.12; Pers. III.103, den Klang des Horns (*cornu*) ebenfalls Hor. sat. I.6.44, ferner u.a. Sen. apocol. 12,1 und Petron. 78,5f; s. dazu O. Nußbaum, *a.a.O.* (s. Anm. 46) IX, S.932f.

[74] F. Behn, *a.a.O.* (s. Anm. 62), S.139f sowie die Abb. 147 und 175-177. S. auch L. Franchi, *a.a.O.* (s. Anm. 43), S.25.

[75] So C. Hülsen, *a.a.O.* (s. Anm. 43), S.72f; J. M. C. Toynbee, *a.a.O.* (s. Anm. 40), S.47.

[76] F. Behn, *a.a.O.* (s. Anm. 62), S.136f mit Abb. 172 und 174.

[77] Vgl. F. Behn, *a.a.O.*, S.137-139 mit Abb. 173. Als *liticen* deuten den Musiker H. Besseler/M. Schneider (Hg.), *a.a.O.* (s. Anm. 62) II/5, S.54 mit Abb. 25; L. Franchi, *a.a.O.* (s. Anm. 43), S.25, und O. Nußbaum, *a.a.O.* (s. Anm. 46) IX, S.933.

Gedanke nahegelegt würde, daß hier eine spezielle Art der Tuba wiedergegeben sein könnte, die den *siticines* eigen war, die bei den Leichenbestattungen musizierten.[78] Den Hornbläsern folgen auf dem oberen Register der Reliefdarstellung zwei Klagefrauen mit aufgelösten Haaren. Sie wenden sich der Bahre mit dem Toten zu. Während sich die zweite die Haare rauft, hat die erste von ihnen pathetisch die Arme erhoben (oder klatscht in die Hände?)[79] und trägt aller Wahrscheinlichkeit nach ein Leichenlied (*nenia*) mit dem Lob des Toten vor,[80] wenn ihr Gestus nicht einfach nur als Trauergestus zu deuten ist.[81]

Im Zentrum der Darstellung steht die von acht Männern, wohl den Söhnen, Verwandten und Erben des Verstorbenen auf den Schultern getragene Bahre (*feretrum*) mit dem Toten.[82] Ihr geht, wie vor allem bei den großen und öffentlichen Trauerzügen üblich, ein Ordner des Leichenbegängnisses (*dissignator*), hier jedoch bei einem privaten Begräbnis (*funus privatum*) vermutlich ein Angestellter des Begräb-

---

[78] So N. Persichetti, *a.a.O.* (s. Anm. 43), S.16f.

[79] L. Franchi, *a.a.O.* (s. Anm. 46), S.26, deutet die erhobenen Arme als "un gesto patetico e declamatorio". Rhythmisches Zusammenschlagen der Hände bzw. Händeklatschen ist für die jüdische Totenklage belegt, vgl. S. Krauss, *a.a.O.* (s. Anm. 46) II, S.65-68, und *Bill. I,* S.521f; es wird hier nicht nur von den Klagefrauen, sondern – neben dem Aufstampfen mit den Füßen – auch von den Männern geübt, *Bill. IV/1,* S.582.584.

[80] Zu den *neniae,* d.h. den von den Klagefrauen gesungenen Lobliedern auf den Verstorbenen s. J. Marquardt, *a.a.O.* (s. Anm. 46) I, S.352; O. Nußbaum, *a.a.O.* (s. Anm. 46) IX, S.933. Auch im Judentum wurde von den Klagefrauen jedesmal eine Totenklage mit dem Lob des Verstorbenen angestimmt, wenn der Leichenzug anhielt und die Totenbahre abgesetzt wurde, s. S. Krauss, *a.a.O. II,* S.64f; *Bill. I,* S.521f. Von solchen kurzen Klagerufen und Klageliedern ist im Judentum die eigentliche Trauer- oder Leichenrede, die beim Grab gehalten wurde, in Rom die bei öffentlichen Bestattungen (*funus publicum*) von einem vom Senat beauftragten amtlichen Redner auf der Rostra des Forums gehaltene *laudatio funebris* zu unterscheiden, vgl. Polyb. VI.53f und s. dazu einerseits S. Krauss, *a.a.O. II,* S.68f; *Bill. IV.1,* S.583.585-590, andererseits J. Marquardt, *a.a.O. I,* S.357-360.

[81] So O. Nußbaum, *ebd.*

[82] Zu den Trägern der Totenbahre s. J. Marquardt, *a.a.O.* (s. Anm. 46) I, S.355; O. Nußbaum, *a.a.O.* (s. Anm. 46) IX, S.936. Belege für Söhne: Vell. I.11.7; Plin. nat. VII.146; für die Söhne und andere Verwandte: Cic. Tusc. I.85; für die Erben: Hor. sat. II.5.85f. Neben den Genannten kommen als Träger auch die testamentarisch freigelassenen, an ihrem *pilleus* (s. oben S.276) kenntlichen Sklaven in Betracht (Pers. III. 106), sind jedoch auf dem Relief nicht abgebildet. Für das Judentum s. S. Krauss, *a.a.O.* (s. Anm. 46) II, S.64; *Bill. IV/1,* S.590.

nisunternehmers, voran und dirigiert den Zug.[83] Auf der Bahre steht das Prunkbett mit gedrechselten Beinen, auf dem sich zwei Matratzen und zwei Kissen befinden. Auf ihnen liegt der Tote, in eine kurzärmelige Tunika und eine Toga gekleidet, auf seiner linken Seite lang hingestreckt und den bekränzten Kopf auf den linken Arm gestützt, während er einen langen Stab, wohl das Zeichen seiner Kommandogewalt, in der rechten Hand hält. Den auf vier Löwenfüßen stehenden, kastenähnlichen Gegenstand, den man unter dem Prunkbett gewahrt, könnte man als eine Art Schemel und als Symbol irgendeines (vielleicht munizipalen) Amtes, das der Verstorbene innehatte, betrachten.[84] Aber es ist wahrscheinlicher, daß es sich in Wirklichkeit um den Sarg (*capulus*) mit den sterblichen Überresten des Verstorbenen handelt[85] und daß dessen Platz auf dem Prunkbett beim Leichenbegängnis stellvertretend ein Schauspieler eingenommen hat.[86] Das mit Sternen und einer Mondsichel dekorierte, wandteppichartige Gebilde, das hinter dem Prunkbett aufragt, ist wohl als Baldachin, der sich über dem Toten erhebt, zu interpretieren.[87] Auf ihm liegt eine Art Helm, wohl das Zeichen eines militärischen Ranges, den der Verstorbene als städtischer Magistrat in der Miliz innehatte.[88]

Die Personen, die der Bahre folgen, sind auf drei Ebenen angeordnet. Sie befinden sich aber in Wirklichkeit auf einer Ebene neben – oder hintereinander. Die drei weiblichen Personen mit aufgelösten Haaren auf der obersten Ebene, die der Totenbahre am nächsten sind, sind wohl die Ehefrau des Toten und, ihr zur Seite, ihre beiden Töchter, die sich an die Kleider der Mutter anklammern. Auf einer etwas höher angebrachten Linie folgen ebenfalls mit gelöstem Haar und

---

[83] S. dazu J. Marquardt, *a.a.O.*, S.351.

[84] So. C. Hülsen, *a.a.O.* (s. Anm. 43), S.73.

[85] So L. Franchi, *a.a.O.* (s. Anm. 43), S.27. Der Tote selbst läge dann also ebenso im Sarg, wie es beim Jüngling von Nain vorausgesetzt ist, s. oben S.258f.

[86] So L. Franchi, *ebenda*; O. Nußbaum, *a.a.O.* (s. Anm. 46) IX, 935. Diese Substitution ist vor allem bei den großen *funera publica* (oder *indictiva*) geübt worden, weniger bei den *funera privata*, s. A. Mau, *a.a.O.* (s. Anm 46) V, S.351. Auch wurde der Tote zuweilen "durch ein plastisches Portraitbild (*effigies*), d.h. eine bekleidete Holzfigur mit Wachsslarve" repräsentiert, s. J. Marquardt, *a.a.O.* (s. Anm. 46) I, S.354.

[87] So schon N. Persichetti, *a.a.O.* (s. Anm. 43), S.18.

[88] So N. Persichetti, *ebd.*; vgl. J. M. C. Toynbee, *a.a.O.* (s. Anm. 40), S.46.

weinend, drei Frauen, Verwandte, Bekannte oder auch Sklavinnen des Toten.[89] Unter (d.h. wohl hinter) ihnen schreiten zwei weitere weibliche Gestalten, vielleicht Sklavinnen, von denen die rechte einen Gegenstand in ihrer Linken trägt, den man für einen Speer mit glatter Spitze, also für ein weiteres Symbol des militärischen Ranges des Verstorbenen, halten könnte,[90] der jedoch wohl eher einen Fächer oder eine Fackel darstellt.[91] Den Leichenzug beschließt ein kleiner Sklave, der einen Palmzweig über die linke Schulter gelegt hat und in der rechten Hand einen kleinen Eimer oder Kessel trägt, vermutlich ein Salbgefäß, um den Leichnam zu besprengen, oder ein Gefäß für Libationen oder auch einen Kessel mit Weihrauch.[92] In der Art dieses Leichenzuges, wenn auch nicht mit allen seinen Einzelheiten, muß man sich das Trauergeleit des Jünglings von Nain vorstellen.

IV

Die Betrachtung von bildlichen Darstellungen wie den beiden hier behandelten eröffnet eine neue Perspektive für das Verständnis neutestamentlicher Wundererzählungen wie z.B. der beiden genannten Totenerweckungen. Sie zieht den Blick ab von dem großen Wundertäter, der in der herrschenden Interpretation so gut wie ausschließlich im Mittelpunkt steht, und lenkt die Aufmerksamkeit hin auf die beteiligten Menschen und auf ihre Realität. Ihre Leiden und ihr in den Texten so deutlich zum Ausdruck kommender Schmerz, aber auch ihre Möglichkeiten mit ihrem Leiden und ihrem Schmerz umzugehen, werden bei dieser Betrachtung, die sich in erster Linie den betroffenen Menschen zuwendet, erkennbar. Der hier vorgeschlagene Zugang zu neutestamentlichen Überlieferungen möchte zunächst einmal dazu beitragen, daß

---

[89] Die Identifizierung der ersten Dreiergruppe kann für ziemlich eindeutig gelten, die der zweiten ist unsicher, vgl. die in Anm. 43 genannte Literatur.

[90] So N. Persichetti, *ebd.*

[91] So L. Franchi, *a.a.O.* (s. Anm. 43), S.26. C. Hülsen, *a.a.O.* (s. Anm. 43), S.73, sprach von einem schwer bestimmbaren Gegenstand, der die Form eines Blattes oder Fächers habe.

[92] N. Persichetti, *a.a.O.*, S.18, hält diesen Sklaven für den Leichensalber (*pollinctor*, s. oben S.274). Ihm folgt der Sache nach L. Franchi, *ebd.* Für die beiden anderen Deutungsmöglichkeiten vgl. O. Nußbaum, *a.a.O.* (s. Anm. 46), S.934.

die in diesen eingefangene Alltagswirklichkeit, ihre menschliche Seite also, in stärkerem Maße als bisher Berücksichtigung findet und ernst genommen wird. Mit diesem Perspektivenwechsel, der die Menschen und ihre in den Wundergeschichten eingefangene Realität ins Zentrum stellt, verändern aber auch diese Erzählungen selbst ihren Charakter. Aus Zeugnissen der religiösen Auseinandersetzung und Dokumenten missionarischer Propaganda wozu sie im Laufe der Zeit sicher auch gebraucht und mißbraucht worden sind, werden sie wieder zu dem, was sie ursprünglich einmal waren: zu Zeugnissen menschlicher Hoffnung und menschlichen Glaubens an die göttliche Heilkraft, die sich in der Begegnung mit Jesus und in der solidarischen Gegenseitigkeit der Gemeinde den Einzelnen in Krankheit und sogar Tod ebenso erschloß, wie in der gemeinsamen Praxis der Nachfolge auch alle andere Not wie Hunger, Nacktheit und Obdachlosigkeit – nicht weniger wunderbar – ihre Überwindung fand (vgl. Mt 11,5 par. in Aufnahme von Jes 35,5f und 61,1). Diese Sicht der neutestamentlichen Wunder, speziell der Heilungswunder, bedeutet nicht einen Rückfall in ein fundamentalistisches Wahrhabenwollen der uns uns überlieferten Wunderberichte, wohl aber ein anderes Ernstnehmen der Erfahrungen der frühesten Gemeinden. Sie setzt zudem eine andere, den Texten angemessere, ganzheitliche Auffassung von Not, Krankheit, Tod und Heilung voraus, als sie der heutigen Schulmedizin und überhaupt dem modern-aufgeklärten Wirklichkeitsverständnis eigen ist. Auf sie sollte sich die theologische Wissenschaft als auf ihre eigenste Sache neu besinnen.

DIE VERRECHTLICHUNG DER FRÜHESTEN CHRISTLICHEN ÜBERLIEFERUNG IM LUKANISCHEN SCHRIFTTUM

Lukas Bormann (Universität Frankfurt am Main)

I Methode und Begriff

Die Bedeutung, die der Verfasser des Doppelwerkes ad Theophilum rechtlichen Fragen zumißt, hat schon lange die Aufmerksamkeit der neutestamentlichen und althistorischen Wissenschaften auf sich gezogen. Dabei unterscheiden sich die Fragestellungen, die an die Texte herangetragen werden, in der in ihnen vorausgesetzten Einschätzung der Historizität der lukanischen Berichte und ihrer Quellen. Konnte noch Theodor Mommsen in seinem Aufsatz über "die Rechtsverhältnisse des Apostels Paulus" nahezu alle in der lukanischen Apostelgeschichte angesprochenen rechtlichen Sachverhalte ohne größere Schwierigkeiten in den Horizont römischen Rechtes einordnen,[1] erwachsen gegenüber dieser Sicht zunehmend Bedenken. Es werden inzwischen nicht nur einige rechtliche Details der lukanischen Darstellung in Zweifel gezogen, sondern auch die für den Aufbau und den Geschehensablauf des zweiten, des paulinischen Teiles der Apostelgeschichte wesentlichen rechtlichen Konstruktionen, das römische und tarsische Bürgerrecht des Paulus und seine Appellation an den Kaiser, in Frage gestellt.[2]

Vor diesem Hintergrund stellen sich Fragen an den Verfasser des Lukasevangeliums und der Apostelgeschichte, der hier Lukas genannt werden soll. Beruhen seine Darstellungen rechtlicher Sachverhalte auf einer durch seine Quellen vermittelten Kenntnis dieser Vorgänge in der Frühzeit der

[1] Theodor Mommsen, Die Rechtsverhältnisse des Apostels Paulus, *ZNW* 2 (1902) S.81-96.

[2] Peter Garnsey, The LEX IULIA and appeal under the empire, *JRS* 56 (1966) S.167-189; ders., The criminal iurisdiction of governors, *JRS* 58 (1968) S.51-59; T.D.Barnes, Legislation against the Christians, *JRS* 58 (1968) S.32-50; Wolfgang Stegemann, Zwei sozialgeschichtliche Anfragen an unser Paulusbild, *EvErz* 37 (1985) S.480-490; ders., War der Apostel Paulus römischer Bürger?, *ZNW* 78 (1987) S.200-229.

Kirche? Verdanken sie sich seiner Fähigkeit, die ihm bekannt gewordenen Ereignisse juristisch zu rekonstruieren? Oder haben wir es hier mit einer Tendenz im lukanischen Schrifttum zu tun, die ihre Ursache nicht in den rechtlichen Implikationen der von Lukas aus der Geschichte des frühesten Christentums berichteten Ereignisse hat, sondern in dem Interesse des Verfassers, diese Ereignisse nachträglich in juristische Kontexte einzuordnen? Wenn diese letztgenannte Frage positiv beantwortet werden muß, schließt sich daran eine weitere an: welche Intentionen verfolgt der Verfasser mit dieser Art des Umganges mit der Tradition?

Um auf diese Fragen Antworten zu finden, muß der Charakter der zu ihrer Beantwortung heranzuziehenden Quellen vergegenwärtig werden. Die neueren Arbeiten zur Apostelgeschichte betonen, daß Acta im Gesamt des lukanischen Doppelwerkes zu verstehen sei.[3] Wer sich über die theologische Konzeption und den Abfassungszweck äußern möchte, sollte seine Argumente am Ganzen des lukanischen Doppelwerkes gewonnen haben. Nun ist aber deutlich, daß die beiden Werke durchaus unterschiedlichen Charakter haben, der in ihrem jeweiligen Gegenstand begründet ist, im einen Fall das Auftreten des Kyrios Jesus Christus, dessen Märtyrertod und seine in den Schriften prophezeite Auferweckung, im anderen Fall die Entstehung der Jesusanhängerschaft und deren Ausbreitung bis nach Rom.[4] Mit der letztgenannten Thematik ist eine enorme schriftstellerische Herausforderung verbunden. Der Verfasser des Lukasevangeliums konnte sich auf das Markusevangelium, Q und auf Sondergut stützen. Er war auch durchaus bereit, sich von diesen und möglicherweise noch anderen Quellen im Aufbau und bei der Konzeption seines

[3] Gerhard Schneider, *Die Apostelgeschichte*, 2 Bde., Freiburg-Basel-Wien, 1980 u. 1982 (HThK 5) S.143-5; Ferdinand Hahn, Der gegenwärtige Stand der Erforschung der Apostelgeschichte, *ThRev* 82 (1986) Sp.177-190, hier Sp.183; Rudolf Pesch, *Die Apostelgeschichte*, 2 Bde., Neukirchen-Vluyn 1986 (EKK 5) S.29-34. Für die Belege aus dem angelsächsischen Raum s. Mikael C. Parsons and Richard I. Pervo, *Rethinking the Unity of Luke and Acts*, Minneapolis: Fortress 1993, S.1-7.

[4] Jürgen Roloff, *Die Apostelgeschichte* , Göttingen 1981 (NTD 5); ders., Die Paulus-Drastellung des Lukas, *EvTh* 39 (1979) S.510-531, hier S.526f. Kritik bei Eckhard Plümacher, Acta-Forschung 1974-1982, *ThR NF* 48 (1983) S.1-56 und *ThR NF* 49 (1984) S.105-169, hier S.19f. Wie wenig paulinisch diese Perspektive von Acta ist, zeigt Arthur J. Dewey, "Εἰς τὴν Σπανίαν: The Future and Paul," s. S.322 in diesem Band.

Evangeliums leiten zu lassen, wie er selbst in seinem Proömium Lk 1,1-4 andeutet. Die Apostelgeschichte hingegen forderte eine eigenständige Gestaltung des disparaten Stoffes unterschiedlichster Herkunft (mündliche Tradition und schriftliche Quellen mit zum Teil lokaler Überlieferungsgeschichte).[5]

Beobachtungen am Lukasevangelium haben bei der Herausarbeitung der Eigenart der lukanischen Tendenz aus methodischen Gründen besonderes Gewicht. Nur hier sind durch die synoptischen Seitenreferenten Vergleichsmöglichkeiten gegeben. Wir haben an diesen Stellen von den Quellen, mit denen Lukas arbeitet, eine recht deutliche Vorstellung. Anders ist die Lage in Acta. Dort müßte zunächst eine Rekonstruktion der lukanischen Quellen unternommen werden, die mit einer Vielzahl von hypothetischen Schlüssen belastet bliebe.[6]

Welche Texte des Lukasevangeliums geben uns Auskunft über die möglicherweise verrechtlichende Tendenz ihres Verfassers? Die Themen, die die Gattung des Evangeliums vorgibt, bieten sich nur zum Teil für eine Anreicherung mit juristischen Details an. Deswegen erstaunt es nicht, daß nur an wenige Texte des Lukasevangeliums die Frage nach einer verrechtlichenden Bearbeitung gestellt werden kann. Es handelt sich um die lukanische Passionsgeschichte und zwei ursprünglich apokalyptisch orientierte Texte, Lk 12,11f und 21,12-19, die von Verfolgung und Bewährung der Jesusanhänger sprechen. Nun ist aber auch die Quellenlage in der lukanischen Passionsgeschichte umstritten. Folgt Lukas hier noch seiner Markusvorlage und ergänzt er sie nur um Einzeltraditionen oder verdankt sich die ganze Erzählung von Kreuz und Auferstehung einer Sonderquelle?[7] Deswegen soll der erste Schritt in Richtung auf eine Beantwortung der gestellten Fragen mit Hilfe der Diskussion von Lk 12,11f und

---

[5] Hahn, *a.a.O.*, Sp.182.

[6] Daran ändern auch die neueren Versuche zur Scheidung von Redaktion und Tradition in der Apostelgeschichte nichts: Gerd Lüdemann, *Das frühe Christentum nach den Traditionen der Apostelgeschichte: ein Kommentar*, Göttingen 1987; M.-E. Boismard und A.Lamouille, *Analyses littéraires*, Paris 1990 (EtB Nouvelle Série 14); dazu Justin Taylor, The making of Acts: a new account, *RB* 1990 (97) S.504-524.

[7] Diskussion und Literatur bei Werner Georg Kümmel, *Einleitung in das Neue Testament*, Heidelberg [20]1980, S.103-5.

21,12-19 erfolgen. Dort sind die von Lukas bearbeiteten Quellen am sichersten zu fassen. Läßt sich an diesen Texten erkennen, wie Lukas mit seinem Material umgeht und welche Intentionen er damit verfolgt, ist damit auch ein Schlüssel zum Verständnis der Abschnitte gewonnen, in denen die Quellenlage unsicherer ist.[8]

Die folgenden Überlegungen schlagen damit eine andere Richtung ein als die Arbeit von Wolfgang Stegemann, *Zwischen Synagoge und Obrigkeit*.[9] Stegemann konzentriert sich ganz auf die redaktionelle Ebene der lukanischen Schriften. Er interpretiert die dort behandelten rechtlichen Fragen als Probleme der konkreten Lebenswelt lukanischer Christen. Sein Versuch, von der "erzählten Welt zweier antiker Schriften auf die Welt ihres Autors und die besonderen Erfahrungen seiner christlichen Zeitgenossen"[10] zu schließen, ist allerdings nicht unproblematisch, verdanken sich diese Schriften doch deutlich einem Verfasser, der sich ausdrücklich als eine Schriftstellerpersönlichkeit, wenn nicht gar als ein Historiker,[11] vorstellt, dem es um die Darstellung vergangener Ereignisse für die Leser der Gegenwart geht. Auf diesem Hintergrund erscheinen eine Reihe von Schlußfolgerungen Stegemanns auf die historische Situation der lukanischen Christen und ihrer Umwelt recht gewagt.[12]

---

[8] Vgl. zum Methodischen die Überlegungen von Willem Cornelis van Unnik, *Flavius Josephus als historischer Schriftsteller*, Heidelberg 1978, S.60.

[9] Wolfgang Stegemann, *Zwischen Synagoge und Obrigkeit: Zur historischen Situation der lukanischen Christen*, Göttingen 1991 (FRLANT 152).

[10] *Ebd.*, S.7.

[11] Vgl. Eckhard Plümacher, Die Missionsreden der Apostelgeschichte und Dionys von Halikarnass, *NTS* 39 (1993) S.161-177. Plümacher zieht die in der neutestamentlichen Wissenschaft zu wenig beachtete Schrift des Dionysios von Halikarnass, *Antiquitates Romanae*, zur Profilierung der Eigenart des lukanischen Werkes heran.

[12] Stegemann (*Zwischen Synagoge und Obrigkeit*) schließt nicht nur von der von ihm erhobenen Intention des lukanischen Werkes auf "lukanische Christen" zurück, sondern sogar auf die außergemeindliche historische Situation ("Welt"), in der sich diese Gruppen befunden haben sollen. Wenn aber Lukas in seinen Schriften z.B. die Synagogen als Institutionen darstellt, die disziplinarische Gewalt nur über Judenchristen haben, ist der Schluß auf die tatsächliche Kenntnis des Lukas gerade bei diesem Autor gewagt, der offensichtlich an entscheidenden Stellen schweigt (z.B. Tod bzw. weiteres Schicksal des Paulus, oder aber auch über die von Paulus II Kor 11,24 erwähnten Synagogenstrafen u.a., vgl. Martin Hengel, *Zur urchristlichen Geschichtsschreibung*, Stuttgart 1979, S.37). Stegemann geht schon zu weit, wenn er scheinbar zurückhaltend schreibt, "Lukas kennt...".

Demgegenüber verstehen sich die nachfolgenden Überlegungen als Beitrag zum Verständnis einer schriftstellerischen Tendenz des Verfassers des Lukasevangeliums und der Apostelgeschichte. Sie befassen sich mit einer Linie innerhalb des lukanischen Doppelwerkes, deren Wahrnehmung der Diskussion um den umstrittenen Abfassungszweck der Apostelgeschichte neue Impulse geben kann.[13]

Zuvor soll aber noch genauer definiert werden, was hier unter Verrechtlichung zu verstehen ist. Der Begriff ist kein Begriff historischer Forschung, sondern ist erst in der modernen Gesellschaftstheorie dieses Jahrhunderts eingeführt worden.[14] Er meint dort die Ausdehnung und Verdichtung des Rechtes in Lebensbereiche, die zuvor nicht oder nicht so detailliert rechtlich geregelt waren,[15] und gewinnt eine kritische Spitze gegen die Verrechtlichung von Lebensbereichen, die um ihrer Funktionsfähigkeit willen auf nicht rechtlich einholbare Verständigungs- und Integrationsprozesse angewiesen sind, z.B. Familie, Schule oder die politische Willensbildung, die durch Verrechtlichung berechenbarer wird, aber auch notwendige Handlungsspielräume verliert.

In dem Zusammenhang, der uns hier beschäftigt, wird der Begriff ganz unsoziologisch verstanden. Er meint hier die Tendenz eines Autors, Überlieferungen mit rechtlichen Details anzureichern, Vorgänge innerhalb juristischer Kategorien zu interpretieren und juristische Problemstellungen in den Erzählablauf zu integrieren, ohne daß das durch die benutzten

---

Er verläßt den Bereich einer tragbaren Hypothese völlig, wenn er dieses "Lukas kennt..." unkritisch in historische Sachverhalte übersetzt. So z.B. ebd., S.106 und 111f. Aus dem lukanischen Werk können Schlüsse auf historische Tatbestände oder Ereignisse nur unter äußerst kritischer Rekonstruktion, insbesondere der Scheidung von Redaktion und Tradition, und im Vergleich mit den den jeweiligen Sachverhalten nahestehenden außerbiblischen Quellen gezogen werden.

[13] Die Unterscheidung von *einem* Hauptzweck und mehreren "Nebenzweck(en)" (Pesch, *a.a.O.*, S.29) entspricht dem vielschichtigen lukanischen Schrifttum weniger als eine differenzierende, aber nicht hierarchisierende Diskussion der in ihm verfolgten Absichten.

[14] Jürgen Habermas, *Theorie des kommunikativen Handelns.* II, Frankfurt ³1985, S.522-547; *Verrechtlichung*, hg.v. Rüdiger Voigt, Königstein/Ts. 1980; *Gegentendenzen zur Verrechtlichung*, hg.v. ders., Opladen 1983 (Jahrbuch für Rechtssoziologie und Rechtstheorie 9). Der Begriff dient sowohl der Rechtswissenschaft als auch der Politikwissenschaft zur Beschreibung eines für den bürgerlichen Rechts- und Sozialstaates systemtypischen Vorganges.

[15] Rüdiger Voigt, Verrechtlichung in Staat und Gesellschaft, in: *Verrechtlichung*, S.16-18.

Quellen vorgegeben ist.[16] Der Begriff Verrechtlichung soll einen bestimmten Umgang einer Autorin oder eines Autors mit dem jeweiligen Gegenstand seiner literarischen Bemühungen, sei es eine mündliche oder schriftliche Quelle oder ein literarisches Thema im weitesten Sinne, charakterisieren. Von der *Tendenz* der Verrechtlichung ist die mit ihr verbundene *Intention* zu unterscheiden. Um einer Klärung dieses im Falle des lukanischen Schrifttums komplexen Phänomens näher zu kommen, ohne sich mit dem Schlagwort von dem "apologetischen Interesse" zufrieden zu geben, soll im Schlußteil der traditions- und sozialgeschichtliche Hintergrund der Verrechtlichungstendenz im jüdisch-hellenistischen Schrifttum und der römisch-hellenistischen Welt angedeutet werden. Es kann gezeigt werden, daß sich in der literarischen Tendenz der Verrechtlichung eine historische Entwicklung spiegelt: die mit der Ausbreitung der römischen Herrschaft über den Mittelmeerraum einhergehende Ausweitung des römischen Rechtes.

II Das Trostwort Lk 12,11f

In Lk 12,11f und in der lukanischen Apokalypse 21,5-36 wird die in Mk 13 vorgegebene Thematik des Vernichtungsgerichtes[17] aufgegriffen und neu interpretiert. Lk 12,11f ist die lukanische Fassung eines Logions aus Q, dessen ursprüngliche Form durch einen kritischen Vergleich mit der Mt-Fassung (Mt 10,19) rekonstruiert werden kann.[18] Mit ihm schließt eine

[16] Der Begriff Verrechtlichung steht damit neben den für die Interpretation der lukanischen Konzeption bedeutsam gewordenen Begriffen "Historisierung" (z.B. Hans Conzelmann, *Die Mitte der Zeit: Studien zur Theologie des Lukas,* Tübingen ^{4}1962 (BeHTh 17) S.88; S.158 u.ö.) und "Enteschatologisierung".

[17] Egon Brandenburger, Art. Gericht Gottes III NT, *TRE* 12 (1984) S.469-483, hier S.479; ders., *Markus 13 und die Apokalyptik,* Göttingen 1984 (FRLANT 134) S.144.

[18] Das Argument für die Herkunft aus Q und gegen eine Herleitung aus Mk 13,11 ist die Übereinstimmung zwischen Mt 10,19 und Lk 12,11 in den Wörtern πῶς ἤ τί gegen Mk 13,11 nur τί. Eduard Schweizer (*Das Evangelium nach Lukas,* Göttingen 1982 [NTD 3] S.134) hält Mt 10,19 für der Q-Fassung näherstehend als die Lukasversion. Dagegen sieht Heinz Schürmann (Zur Traditions- und Redaktionsgeschichte von Mt 10,23, *BZ NF* 3 [1959] S.82-88, hier S.83) in Lk 12,11f die ursprüngliche Fassung von Q. Seine Argumentation belegt aber nur die Herkunft von Lk 12,11/ Mt10,19 aus Q (ebd., Anm.10). Die Priorität von Lk 12,11f ist damit nicht

frühe Sammlung zum Thema "Furcht und Bekenntnis" ab.[19] Daneben hat das Logion Lk 12,11/Mt 10,19 auch im Rahmen eines paränetischen Einschubs Eingang in die markinische Apokalypse gefunden (Mk 13,11).[20] Die Doppelüberlieferung führt dazu, daß Lukas das Logion in zwei Varianten mitteilt, einmal auf Q basierend in Lk 12.11f, das andere Mal, stärker an der Mk-Fassung und ihrem Kontext orientiert, in Lk 21,14f.[21] Mt dagegen bringt nur die Q-Fassung ausführlich (Mt 10,19), während er Mk 13,9-12 in Mt 24,9a knapp zusammenfaßt.

Lukas verknüpft in Lk 12,11f das Logion der Spruchquelle mit Teilen von Mk 13,9, die aber umgearbeitet werden.[22] Er ersetzt das ihm stilistisch zu primitiv erscheinende λαλεῖν an beiden Stellen mit εἰπεῖν, läßt es dabei aber nicht bewenden, sondern ergänzt die markinische Formulierung (τί λαλήσητε) bemerkenswerterweise mit dem juristische Konnotationen tragenden ἀπολογεῖσθαι (τί ἀπολογήσησθε ἢ τί εἴπητε). Dieses Wort ist ebenso in die Parallele Lk 21,14 eingewandert. Es kommt nur an diesen beiden Stellen in den synoptischen Evangelien vor, wird aber in der Apostelgeschichte sechsmal verwendet. ἀπολογεῖσθαι benennt einen Vorgang, der nicht mehr nur "be-

---

bewiesen und aufgrund der lukanischen Wortwahl ganz unwahrscheinlich. So auch Ulrich Kellermann, Art. ἀπολογέομαι, ἀπολογία, *EWNT*² 1 (1992) Sp.329f. Am besten folgt man Siegfried Schulz (*Q: Die Spruchquelle des Evangelisten*, Zürich 1972, S. 442-4), der beide Fassungen unter literarkritischen Gesichtspunkten untersucht und die matthäischen wie die lukanischen Elemente benennt. Ihm folgen John S. Kloppenborg, *Q-Parallels: Synopsis, critical notes and concordance*, Sonoma: Polebridge Press 1988, S.126f; Friedrich Wilhelm Horn, Judentum und Christentum in der Logienquelle, *EvTh* 51 (1991) S.344-364, hier S.351. Stegemann dagegen (*a.a.O.* S.77f) meint, Lk 12,11f sei "nach dem Vorbild von Mk 13,11 (Lk 21,14f) von Lukas selbst formuliert worden".

[19] Horn, *a.a.O.*, S.351. Vgl. *ebd.*, S.345 zu den verschiedenen Phasen der Entstehung von Q.

[20] Brandenburger, *Markus 13 und die Apokalyptik*, S.75 und S.147-161.

[21] Paul Hoffmann (*Studien zur Theologie der Logienquelle*, ³1982 [NTA NF 8] S.269) merkt zu Lk 12,11f und 21,14f an: "Wenn Lukas aus der Markusvorlage und aus Q ähnliche Sprüche in sein Evangelium aufnimmt, so variiert er häufig die Formulierung oder tauscht einzelne Wendungen unter ihnen aus, um eine wörtliche Übereinstimmung bei der Wiederholung zu vermeiden."

[22] Schulz (*a.a.O.*, S.442f) sieht mit Wernle (*Die synoptische Frage*, S.85) in den ἀρχαὶ καὶ ἐξουσίαι eine lukanische Einfügung, die die Gerichtsszene auf heidnische Gerichte ausdehnt, hält aber die Nennung von Instanzen schon für in Q ursprünglich. Vgl. Gerhard Schneider, *Das Evangelium nach Lukas*, Gütersloh 1977 (ÖTK 3/1+2) S.280.

kennen" meint, sondern "verteidigen", und zwar ein Verteidigen, das einen Freispruch vor Gericht bzw. in einer als forensisch interpretierten Situation erwirken kann.[23] Lukas bemüht sich also nicht nur um "gewähltes Griechisch"[24], sondern verändert auch die Aussage.[25]

Mk 13,9-11 nennt als Orte der der Endzeit vorausgehenden Verfolgungen und Prozesse die Synhedrien und Synagogen. Lukas sieht sich dadurch zu juristischen Präzisierungen herausgefordert. Er läßt den Plural συνέδρια bei Mk (Mk 13,9) und wahrscheinlich in Q (Mt 10,17) aus, denn nach seiner Vorstellung gab es nur ein Synhedrion, nämlich das Jerusalemer.[26] Lukas fügt stattdessen καὶ τὰς ἀρχὰς καὶ τὰς ἐξουσίας ein, eine "der profanen Verwaltungssprache zugehörige(n) Wendung".[27] Strobel hat gezeigt, daß der Hintergrund dieser Formulierung nicht in Engel- oder Dämonenspekulationen zu suchen ist, sondern daß es sich um einen Sammelbegriff für die verschiedenen Formen von Behörden in der lateinisch-griechischen Welt handelt.[28] Die so entstan-

---

[23] Vgl. die übrigen Stellen im lukanischen Schrifttum von ἀπολογεῖσθαι und ἀπολογία: vor dem δῆμος (Act 19,33; 22,1), vor iuristischen Instanzen (Act 24,10; 25,8.16; 26,1.2.24.), aber auch der Gebrauch bei Paulus selbst, der durchweg prozessuale Kontexte assoziiert, die mit Freispruch oder Verurteilung rechnen: weltliches Gericht (Phil 1.7 und 16), göttliches Gericht (Röm 2,15) und Gemeindekonflikt (I Kor 9,3; II Kor 7,11 und 12,19). Dazu auch Ernst Lohmeyer, *Die Briefe an die Philipper, an die Kolosser und an Philemon*, Göttingen 1954 (KEK IX) S.24, Anm.2; Heinrich Schlier, Art. βέβαιος, *ThWNT* 1 (1933) S.600-603, hier S.603; Kellermann, a.a.O.; Stegemann (*Zwischen Synagoge und Obrigkeit*, S.84) meint auch, daß Lukas mit der Möglichkeit des Freispruches rechnet.

[24] Joachim Jeremias, *Die Sprache des Lukasevangeliums*, Göttingen 1980 (KEK Sonderband) S.214.

[25] Conzelmann, *a.a.O.*, S.132: "Das Auftauchen der Worte ἀπολογεῖν, ἀπολογία erweist sich durchweg als Hinweis des Verfassers auf den Zweck seines Berichtes." Conzelmann sieht diesen Zweck in der politischen Apologetik.

[26] Lk 22,66; Act 4,15; 5,21.27.34.41; 6,12.15; 22,30; 23,1.6.15.20.28; 24,20. Etwas anders urteilen Eduard Lohse, Art. συνέδριον, *ThWNT* 7 (1964) S.858-869, hier S.865; und August Strobel, Zum Verständnis von Rm 13, *ZNW* 47 (1956) S.67-93, hier S.73. Lukas schweige von den Synhedrien als den Lokalgerichten, "da ein Heidenchrist im allgemeinen mit diesem Begriff keine konkrete, sachgemäße Vorstellung verbinden konnte."

[27] Strobel, *a.a.O.*, S.75. Schon vor ihm ähnlich Gerhard Delling, Art. ἄρχω, *ThWNT* 1 (1933) S.476-488, hier S.481; Werner Förster, Art. ἐξουσία, *ThWNT* 2 (1935) S.559-572, hier S.562. Ihnen folgt auch Wolfgang Schrage, Art. συναγωγή, *ThWNT* 7 (1964) S.798-850, hier S.832. Zurückhaltender Schulz, a.a.O., S.443, Anm. 291.

[28] Stegemann (*a.a.O.*, S.83f) versucht den Begriff noch enger zu fassen

dene dreigliedrige Bezeichnung der Orte, zu denen die Jüngerinnen und Jünger geschleppt werden, hat durchaus ihre juristische Logik. Die Synagogen regelten die religiösen und die damit verbundenen nach heutigem Verständnis eher profanrechtlich verstandenen Konflikte innerhalb der jüdischen Gemeinschaft selbst.[29] Die höhere Gerichtsbarkeit und die Konflikte, die über die Synagogengemeinschaft hinausgingen, waren den jeweiligen Behörden vorbehalten.[30] Damit ist für die Auslassung der Synhedrien, den palästinischen Lokalgerichten, ein zusätzlicher Grund denkbar. Lk zeichnet in Lk 12,11f den Instanzenweg für Rechtsstreitigkeiten außerhalb Palästinas nach, der über die Synagogen zu den

---

und sieht mit ihm nur "städtische Beamte" bezeichnet. Diese Präzisierung wäre zwar hilfreich, aber die dafür bemühten Belege (Philo, *LegGai* 71 und Platon, *Alk* I 135a-b) vermögen nicht zu überzeugen. Die Stelle bei Philo meint keinen Geringeren als den Caesar Gaius Caligula und dessen Schwiegervater M. Iunius Silanus, der aus einer der vornehmsten Familien Roms stammte, Konsul des Jahres 15 n.Chr. war, später Prokonsul, und das Vorrecht der ersten Stimme im Senat hatte. Vgl. Art. M. Iunius Silanus, *PRE* 19 (1918) Sp. 1097f. Die als Volksmeinung wiedergegbene Sentenz geht auf eine altrömische Anekdote zurück, in der ein Konsul im Mittelpunkt steht (Livius XXIV, 44,9-10; Aulus Gellius II, 2,13; vgl. Philo von Alexandrien, *Die Werke in deutscher Übersetzung*, hg.v. Leopold Cohn u.a., Bd. VII, Göttingen 1964, S.193, Anm. 3). Im übrigen greift die Unterscheidung zwischen "städtischen Beamten" und "römischen Oberbeamten" überhaupt nicht, denn natürlich waren auch die Provinzialbeamten, insoweit sie senatorische Magistrate wahrnahmen, Beamte der Stadt Rom (Max Kaser, *Römische Rechtsgeschichte*, Göttingen [2]1986, S.93-5 u. 117-9). Ähnliche Einwände sind gegen den Beleg aus dem ersten Dialog des Sokrates mit Alkibiades, dessen Echtheit umstritten ist, geltend zu machen. Natürlich kann Sokrates nur von der Polis und deren Amtsinhabern sprechen, weil für ihn das einzige zu diskutierende politische System die Polis ist. Dies dann zu einem Gegensatz zwischen "städtischen Beamten" und "Oberbeamte(n)" auszubauen, geht in die falsche Richtung.

[29] Jos *Ant* XIV 117f. Wolfgang Schrage, *a.a.O.*, S.824f; Harald Hegermann, The Diaspora in the Hellenistic age, *The Cambridge History of Judaism*, Bd. 2, Cambridge 1989, S.115-166, hier S.151-154; Alfredo M. Rabello, The Legal Condition of the Jews in the Roman Empire, *ANRW* II,13 (1980) S.662-762, hier S.719-724 und 731-733; E. Mary Smallwood, *The Jews under Roman Rule From Pompey to Diocletian*, Leiden 1976 (SJLA XX) S.133-138, hier 133: "...they (Diaspora synagogues) were responsible for the organization and administration of all aspects of the life of the community and not for a single aspect, religious worship, alone"; S.Applebaum, The Legal Status of the Jewish Communities in the Diaspora, *The Jewish People in the First Century*, 2 Bde, hg. v. S. Safrai and M. Stern, Assen [2]1974, S.420-463. Ders., The Organization of the Jewish Communities in the Diaspora, *a.a.O.*, S. 464-503.

[30] Natürlich können die jeweiligen lokalen Verhältnisse im Detail erheblich differieren.

weltlichen Behörden in ihren verschiedenen Erscheinungsformen führt.[31] In diesem Zusammenhang wären die Synhedrien fehl am Platze.

Die Jüngerrede Lk 12,1-12 schließt mit einem der Tradition entnommenen Trostwort. Der Trost besteht nicht mehr allein in der Hoffnung auf den Beistand Gottes bei der bekennenden Bewährung in Verfolgungen, die das Bestehen im Endgericht garantiert, sondern verweist auf die pragmatischen Chancen einer geistgewirkten Verteidigung[32] vor den weltlichen Behörden der römisch-griechischen Welt. Der apokalyptische Horizont der Mk und Mt Parallele ist damit stark abgeschwächt, wenn nicht ganz aufgegeben. Der Akzent der Überlieferung verschiebt sich von der apokalyptischen Dramatik der letzten Tage zu einer juristischen Szene, die den prozessualen Rahmen konkretisiert. Kommt es dem eschatologisch orientierten Spruch in Mt 10,19 wesentlich auf das Bestehen der dem endzeitlichen Gericht vorausgehenden und

[31] Hier kompliziert Stegemann (*a.a.O.*, S.77-80) die Sachlage unnötig. Er bestreitet zwar nicht, daß die Synagogengemeinschaft eine beschränkte Iurisduktion hatte, die lokal variieren konnte, behauptet aber, daß dies nach Ansicht des Lukas nicht zutreffe, der an keiner Stelle von einer forensischen Funktion der Synagoge spreche. Es entspricht der lukanischen Intention, die Konflikte zwischen der frühen paulinischen Mission und den örtlichen Gemeinschaften von Juden nicht mehr in der Kompetenz der Synagogengemeinschaften anzusiedeln, sondern sie der jeweiligen kommunalen Obrigkeit, mit besonderer Vorliebe aber der römischen Provinzialverwaltung zuzuweisen. Die Synagogalstrafe (II Kor 11,24), die Steinigung (II Kor 11,25) und andere mit der jüdischen Gemeinschaft als Gegenüber gedachte Rechtskonflikte des Paulus (II Kor 11,26) zeigen, daß dies nicht mit der Realität der paulinischen Mission übereinstimmt. Lukas beschreibt in Lk 12,11 den Instanzenweg, den er aber – das könnte die Intention der Darstellungen in Acta sein – ablehnt. Die Konflikte zwischen Juden und Jesusanhängern sind nach seiner Ansicht innerhalb der Synagoge nicht mehr zu klären, sondern müssen vor die nächsthöhere Behörde gebracht werden. Jos *Bell* II 289f zeigt, wie sehr die Synagogengemeinschaft mit der Frage ringt, ob sie mit ihrem Anliegen überhaupt vor eine nächsthöhere Instanz treten soll. Es ist viel naheliegender, von der lukanischen Darstellung auf eine lukanische Intention zu schließen als auf die historische Realität lukanischer Christen.

[32] Geist und heiliger Geist können bei Lukas ganz pragmatische Funktionen wahrnehmen. Lk 12,11f ist falsch interpretiert, wenn man das Wirken des heiligen Geistes so versteht, daß die Jüngerinnen und Jünger zum "Werkzeug Gottes" und "Sprachrohr des Heiligen Geistes" würden. So Rudolf Laufen, *Die Doppelüberlieferungen der Logienquelle und des Markusevangeliums*, Königstein/Ts. – Bonn 1980 (BBB 54), S. 159f. Das sieht auch Stegemann, *a.a.O.*, S.84-90.

zu ihm in enger Beziehung stehenden Verfolgungen an und behält er deswegen den von Mk 13,9-13 vorgegebenen Kontext bei,[33] stellt sich Lukas einen Strafprozeß vor, dessen Bedeutung und dessen Ergebnis nicht durch den Kontext der Endzeit vorgegeben ist, sondern durch die ihn konstituierende Rechtsprechung und deren Elemente. Nach Lk 12,11f lohnt es, sich zu verteidigen.[34]

III Die lukanische Apokalypse Lk 21,5-36

Die Thematik von Lk 12,11f wird in der lukanischen Apokalypse, Lk 21, 5-36, wieder aufgenommen. Für die Diskussion der Verrechtlichung in Lk 21 ist die literar- und formkritische Einschätzung von Mk 13, der dem Lukastext zugrundeliegenden Quelle, von großer Bedeutung. Egon Brandenburger hat in seiner Monographie zu Mk 13 gezeigt,[35] daß Mk 13 als esoterische Jüngerunterweisung in testamentarischer Form komponiert ist, in die wiederum ältere Traditionen eingearbeitet sind. So liegt in Mk 13,9b-13 vormarkinische Tradition vor, die unter dem Stichwort Verfolgung zusammengestellt worden ist. Die Verfolgungssituation wird dort als eine sich

---

[33] Heinz Schürmann, *a.a.O.*, S.83f.

[34] Aufgrund dieser Beobachtung stellt sich die Frage, ob in der Diskussion um "Verfolgung" der christlichen Gemeinden, speziell der lukanischen Gemeinde, deutlicher unterschieden werden sollte zwischen a) gerichtlichen Verfahren im eigentlichen Sinne, b) Konflikten mit dem Koerzitionsrecht von Amtsträgern, c) nicht rechtlich vorgegebenen Formen der Verfolgung und d) den in all diesen Vorgängen wirksamen Aversionen gegen die frühen Christen in ihren jeweiligen religions- und sozialgeschichtlichen Kontexten. Diese Differenzierung fehlt bei Dennis M. Sweetland (Discipleship and Persecution: A Study of Luke 12,1-12, *Biblica* 65 [1984] S.61-79), der die Situation der lukanischen Christen zwischen Verfolgung, Martyrium und Apostasie einordnet, ohne zu erkennen, daß in lukanischer Zeit die Bandbreite der Handlungs- und Verstehensmöglichkeiten größer war. Auch Horn (a.a.O., S.349) provoziert Mißverständnisse, wenn er eine Reihe von Formulierungen aus unterschiedlichen sozialen und juristischen Kontexten zusammenfassend als "jüdische(n) Bestrafungsmaßnahmen" bezeichnet. Ansätze zur Differenzierung bei Stegemann, *a.a.O.*, S.268f. Für die Situation im römischen Kontext: Antonie Wlosok, Die Rechtsgrundlagen der Christenverfolgungen der ersten zwei Jahrhunderte, *Gymnasium* 66 (1959) S.14-32; T.D.Barnes, Legislation angainst the Christians, *JRS* LVIII (1968) S.50: "It is in the minds of men, not in the demands of Roman law, that the roots of the persecution of the Christians in the Roman Empire are to be sought."

[35] Brandenburger, *Markus 13 und die Apokalyptik.*

wiederholende Bewährungssituation vorgestellt, die immer wieder neu zu bewältigen ist.[36]

Im Kontext von Mk 13 wird die in den Versen 9b-13 gebündelte Verfolgungserfahrung durch die redaktionelle und kompositorische Arbeit des Markus auf die Gegenwart der markinischen Gemeinde bezogen.[37] Sie antwortet als erinnerndes Ermuntern auf Zweifel der Jünger angesichts der unheilvollen Gegenwart an der sich endzeitlich durchsetzendenen Grundordnung Gottes und interpretiert das Verfolgungsgeschehen als Zeit der Bewährung, in der "der besorgt nach der Einlösung des Königtums Gottes in der Zeit fragende Mensch in der ihm zugemessenen Zeit *selbst* auf dem Spiel steht."[38] In dieser Zeit geht es um die Bewährung der Zugehörigkeit zu den ἐκλεκτοί, die im Vernichtungsgericht ausgespart bleiben. Vor den gerichtlichen Instanzen (συνέδρια, συναγωγαί) und in Verfolgungen (V.12f.) kommt es darauf an, an diesem Status festzuhalten, um am "Ende" gerettet zu werden.

Lukas kannte die Konzeption des Mk und verstand durchaus ihre besondere apokalyptisch-paränetische Intention.[39] Er greift sie allerdings nicht auf,[40] sondern rückt Paränese und Endzeiterwartung auseinander, indem er die Paränese auf irdisches Verhalten und Ergehen beschränkt und das endzeitliche Gericht deutlich von der Bewährung im Leben trennt. Einzig die Aufforderung zur Wachsamkeit gegenüber dem plötzlich hereinbrechenden Ende sichert noch einen gewissen Zusammenhang zwischen Ethik und endzeitlichem Gericht. Lukas scheidet die Elemente der esoterischen Tradition fast vollständig aus.[41] Er unterscheidet zwischen "Dingen, die

---

[36] *A.a.O.*, S.151.

[37] *A.a.O.*, S.153.

[38] *A.a.O.*, S.155.

[39] So kann er in der kleinen Apokalypse (Lk 17,20-37) das Motiv der esoterischen Jüngerbelehrung aufnehmen, das er in Lk 21 bewußt gegenüber der Mk-Vorlage eliminiert. Vgl. Conzelmann, *a.a.O.*, S.114. Zum Verhältnis von Apokalyptik und Paränese s. Brandenburger, *a.a.O.*, S.125-147. Eine sorgfältige literarkritische Analyse von Lk 21 findet sich bei W.Nicol, Tradition and Redaction in Luke 21, *Neotestamentica* 7 (1973) S.61-71. Vgl. auch Fridolin Keck, *Die öffentliche Abschiedsrede Jesu in Lk 20,45-21,36: Eine redaktions- und motivgeschichtliche Untersuchung*, Stuttgart 1976 (fzb 25).

[40] Anders Josef Zmijewski, Die Eschatologiereden Lk 21 und Lk 17: Überlegungen zum Verständnis und zur Einordnung der lukanischen Eschatologie, *BiLe* 14 (1973) S.30-40, hier S.34.

[41] Markus wählt als Ort den Ölberg (Mk 13,3 κατέναντι τοῦ ἱεροῦ) und

sofort geschehen müssen" und dem eigentlichen "Ende" (V.9). Folgerichtig zieht er das in Mk angekündigte Gericht in zwei Vorgänge auseinander: in das aus seiner Persepktive schon ergangene Gericht über Jerusalem,[42] "den Tagen der Vergeltung" (22f), und den noch ausstehenden "Tag", das endzeitliche Gericht (V.25-28.34f).[43] Zwischen diese beiden Gerichtsereignisse tritt in V.24 "die Zeit der Heiden" (καιροὶ ἐθνῶν).[44] Es entsteht eine Zeitspanne zwischen dem schon ergangenen Gericht Gottes über Jerusalem und dem noch ausstehenden Endgericht. Beiden Ereignissen gehen "Zeichen" voran, die sie jeweils als *göttliches* Gericht qualifizieren. Vor dem Gericht über Jerusalem geschehen die in V.8f. beschriebenen Ereignisse (Auftreten der Irrlehrer, Kriege und Aufruhr), aber diese sind nicht endzeitlich. Um dies zu unterstreichen, werden ihnen in V.10f die großen endzeitlichen Zeichen (ἀπ' οὐρανοῦ σημεῖα μεγάλα) gegenübergestellt. Darauf folgt in V.12 das retardierende Element πρὸ δὲ τούτων πάντων. Vor den endzeitlichen Zeichen wird der Gemeinde das in V.12-19 Beschriebene widerfahren.

---

schafft so eine "eschatologische Symbolik der Szenerie" (Conzelmann, *a.a.O.*, S.72). Ist bei Mk nur der engste Kreis der vier Jünger (κατ' ἰδίαν) gegenwärtig, spricht Lukas von τινές (Lk 21,5), die noch nicht einmal eindeutig auf den Jüngerkreis einzuschränken sind. "Lc 21 endlich richtet sich bei Lukas an *alle.*" (Conzelmann, *a.a.O.*, S.112) So wird aus dem esoterischen Lehrgespräch auf dem Ölberg eine öffentliche Tempelrede. Gegenüber der markinischen Gerichtsvorstellung, die die ἐκλεκτοί (Mk 13,20.27) vor dem Vernichtungsgericht gerettet sieht, spricht Lukas stärker alttestamentlich orientiert vom Tag des Zornes, der keine Gruppe von Auserwählten vor dem Gericht kennt, sondern an dem alle einem richtenden Handeln unterworfen und in dem dann Gerechte und Ungerechte getrennt werden. So fehlt seiner Gerichtsvorstellung das Motiv von der dem Gericht entzogenen Gruppe, zu deren Mitgliedschaft allein das Bekenntnis und nicht in erster Linie eine bestimmte Ethik berechtigt. Vgl. Brandenburger, *a.a.O.*, S.144; Keck, *a.a.O.*, S.279-282 u. S.316. Conzelmann, *a.a.O.*, S.72. 112. 144f.

[42] Conzelmann, *a.a.O.*, S.104.

[43] Brandenburger (Gericht Gottes, S.479) sieht richtig, daß die Vorstellung vom Gericht Gottes sich bei Lukas in zwei Richtungen verändert. Es ist schon in der Zeit ergangen, namentlich in der Zerstörung Jerusalems, und steht noch für die Parusie aus.

[44] Anders Zmijewski *(a.a.O.)*. Er spricht von einem sachlichen Zusammenhang der Zerstörung Jerusalems mit dem Weltenende (S.33) und benutzt diese Überlegung zu einer dem Lukas fremden antijudaistischen Polemik, indem er die Zerstörung Jerusalems mit einem "vorweggenomme(n) Endgericht über das sein Heilsangebot ablehnende(n) Judentum damals" gleichsetzt (S.34).

V.20 setzt erneut bei dem Gericht über Jerusalem ein, ohne es als den Zeitpunkt für den Beginn oder das Ende der in V.12-19 beschriebenen Situationen zu bezeichnen. Das Ergehen der Gemeinde und ihr Verhalten steht seit ihren Anfängen unter dieser Ansage Jesu. Sie werden nicht zeitlich präzisiert im Gegensatz zu den sorgfältig differenzierten Gerichtsereignissen, die Lukas in Polemik gegen die Irrlehrer, die behaupten "die Zeit ist nahegekommen", deutlich in die Vergangenheit (Zerstörung Jerusalems) und in die Zukunft verweist (Endgericht). Die Geschichte und die Gegenwart der Gemeinde erhält demgegenüber ein eigenes Profil. Sie bleibt unbeeinflußt von der Zerstörung Jerusalems, wird aber davon geprägt, daß die "Zeit der Heiden"[45] angebrochen ist. Die gedankliche Struktur der endzeitlichen Rede bei Lukas stellt sich so dar:

V.7 Frage nach dem Zeitpunkt der Tempelzerstörung und dem sie ankündigenden Zeichen.
V.8 Warnung vor Irrlehrern, die das Ende ankündigen.
V.9 Kriege und Aufruhr sind Zeichen für die Tempelzerstörung, die nicht das Ende ist.
V.10f Die Zeichen für das Ende.
V.12-19 Die Zeit der Bewährung in der Verfolgung beginnt schon vor der Tempelzerstörung und dauert bis zum endzeitlichen Gericht.
V.20-24 Dann kommt das Zorngericht über Jerusalem durch die Heiden.
V.24 Dem folgt "die Zeit der Heiden".
V.25-28 Wenn diese "Zeit der Heiden" vollendet ist, kommt das endzeitliche Gericht des Menschensohnes, das die Erlösung bringt.
V.29-33 Gleichnis vom Feigenbaum und Trostworte.
V.34-36 Aufforderung zur Wachsamkeit.

Das πρὸ δὲ τούτων πάντων (V.12) ist für die sachliche Gliederung des gesamten Abschnittes von zentraler Bedeutung. Mit diesen Worten weist Lukas den dann (12-19) berichteten Ereignissen der Bedrängnis einen eigenen Raum zu, der von

[45] Diesen Begriff greift Conzelmann (*a.a.O.*) erstaunlicherweise kaum auf, nur S.176, Anm. 1.

den endzeitlichen Wehen zeitlich wie sachlich unterschieden wird. Seit dieser Prophezeiung Jesu im Tempel war die Jüngerschaft in Bedrängnis und sie wird es bis zum Ende der Zeiten sein. Lukas bleibt in 21,12 der Mk-Vorlage (Mk 13,9) weitgehend treu, baut deren Aussagen allerdings aus. Verfolgung, Gefangennahme und Vorführung werden ebenso detailiert benannt wie die Instanzen und Institutionen, denen die Jünger gegenüber zu treten haben, nämlich Synagogen, Gefängnisse, Könige und Provinzstatthalter.[46] Dort werden sie sich wegen des Namens Jesu (ἕνεκεν τοῦ ὀνόματός μου) zu verantworten haben. Während das Zeugnis in Mk 13,9 und Mt 24,18 an die Verfolger gerichtet ist (εἰς μαρτύριον αὐτοῖς), bevorzugt Lukas (21,13) nicht zufällig den absoluten Gebrauch. Die markinische Intention, das Zeugnis – sei es belastend, sei es verkündigend gemeint –[47] an die Prozeßgegner zu richten, nimmt Lukas nicht auf. Das lukanische μαρτύριον ergeht nicht an die Richter.[48]

Lukas läßt Mk 13,10 aus.[49] Dort wird die Evangeliumsverkündigung als ein dem Ende des Äons notwendig vorausgehendes Geschehen (πρῶτον δεῖ κηρυχθῆναι τὸ εὐαγγέλιον) geschildert. Diese apokalyptisch motivierte Verknüpfung von Mission und Weltende lehnt Lukas ab.[50] In Lk 21,14 fordert der lukanische Jesus den Verzicht auf die Vorbereitung einer Verteidigungsrede. Lukas verstärkt durch den Gebrauch technischer Termini (μὴ προμελετᾶν ἀπολογηθῆναι) den schon bei Mk vorhandenen prozessualen Assoziationshintergrund erheblich,[51] bleibt aber der markinischen Aussage zunächst treu, daß auf eine Vorbereitung für diese Situationen zu verzichten sei. Mit den Ausführungen von V.15 geht er aber wieder in eine andere Richtung als die Mk-Vorlage. Er verzichtet auf die in den Worten ἐν ἐκείνῃ τῇ ὥρᾳ (Mt 24,19 und Mk 13,11) zum Ausdruck gebrachte eschatologische Dimension und spricht

[46] Auch hier fallen die Synhedrien weg. Vgl. o. S.290.

[47] Vgl. die Diskussion bei Brandenburger, *Markus 13 und die Apokalyptik*, S.31.

[48] Johannes Beutler, Art. μαρτύριον, *EWNT*² 2 (1992) Sp.964-968, hier 967f.

[49] Mt 24,18 (καὶ τοῖς ἔθνεσιν) transformiert den Gedanken von Mk 13,10, nimmt ihn aber auf.

[50] Brandenburger, *a.a.O.*, S.30-32.

[51] Gerhard Schneider, *Das Evangelium nach Lukas*, S.421. Walter Bauer, *Wörterbuch zu den Schriften des Neuen Testaments*, Berlin-New York 5.Aufl. 1971, Sp.1405.

von erfolgreicher Verteidigung, zu der zwar nicht das Memorieren einer Verteidigungsrede befähige, aber in der den Angeklagten Mund und Weisheit gegeben werde, so daß die Widersacher – und das sind hier die Prozeßgegner – nicht mehr überzeugend gegenreden können. Wie in Eph 6,10-20 und in Act 4,1-22 wird die juristische Auseinandersetzung gleichzeitig als Bewährung und Bewahrheitung des Glaubens gegenüber der Öffentlichkeit verstanden.

Lukas konzentriert seine Ausführungen auf die forensische Situation, indem er kompendienartig ergänzt und zwei bei Mk mit der Verfolgung verknüpfte Probleme ausscheidet: die eschatologische Relevanz der Vorgänge und die Verkündigung.[52] Der Abschied von der eschatologischen Dimension führt ihn dazu, auch die apokalyptische Tradition vom endzeitlichen Verrat und Morden[53] in die historische Erfahrung der Jesusgemeinden zu übersetzen[54]: die Jesusanhänger werden von Familienangehörigen und Freunden den Behörden übergeben und *einige* von ihnen werden getötet werden.[55] Lukas 21,16 ergänzt φίλοι gemäß der in IV Esr 5,9 und 6,24 überlieferten Tradition vom endzeitlichen Zerwürfnis zwischen den Freunden.[56] Wir haben hier ein weiteres Indiz für

---

[52] Acta ist gegenüber einer Verkündigungsdimension juristischer Verwicklungen vollends skeptisch. Act 13,12 berichtet zwar davon, daß der Statthalter Zyperns, Sergius Paulus, aufgrund der überlegenen Wunderkraft des Paulus "gläubig" geworden sei (ἐπίστευσεν), aber in juristischen Zusammenhängen berichtet Acta nie von der Bekehrung der Prozeßbeteiligten; sie ironisiert sie in Act 26,28 sogar. Natürlich haben die Erzählungen als solche für die Leser Verkündigungsdimension, auch wenn sie nicht von Bekehrungen innerhalb prozessualer Verfahren berichten.

[53] Schon Mi 7,6 entwirft mit dem Bild vom Morden in der Familie eine "wahrhaft eschatologische Situation" (Hans Walter Wolff, *Dodekapropheton 4: Micha* (BKAT XIV/4) 1982, S.183), die zur Tradition wird (Esra Apok. III,12f; Jub 23,18-20; äthHen 100,1f; vgl. auch IV Esr 5,9; 6,24 und syrBar 70,3).

[54] Brandenburger (*Markus 13 und die Apokalyptik*, S.24) meint, schon Mk 13,12 setze "die Verarbeitung längerer Konflikt- und Martyriumserfahrungen voraus." Aber kann man das dort beschriebene Morden innerhalb von Familien als Gemeindeerfahrung voraussetzen oder wie Dieter Lührmann (*Das Markusevangelium*, Tübingen 1987 (HNT 3) S.221) darin die "Formulierung des Risses durch Familien" mit Bezug zu Mk 3,31-35 sehen?

[55] Hier klingt Dan 11,35 an.

[56] 5,9: "Und im Süßwasser findet man Salziges. Freunde bekämpfen einander plötzlich; dann wird sich die Weisheit verbergen, und die Einsicht in ihre Kammer zurückziehen." 6,24: "In jener Zeit werden Freunde ihre Freunde wie Feinde bekämpfen." Übersetzung nach Josef Schreiner, *Das 4.Buch Esra*, Gütersloh 1981 (JSHRZ V/4).

den Umgang des Lukas mit Traditionen. Nicht nur die Mk-Vorlage, sondern auch Motive der zwischentestamentlichen Literatur werden von Lukas zwar aufgenommen, aber uminterpretiert. Lukas bricht mit der apokalyptischen Tradition der Mk-Vorlage, die dem Morden in der Familie das Endgericht folgen läßt,[57] und mit der in den Texten aus IV Esr angesprochenen endzeitlichen Perspektive, die die Feindschaft unter Freunden als Ereignis der letzten Tage versteht. Lukas kennt einige, die sterben werden, andere aber, so muß man ergänzen, werden überleben und das Endgericht wird so nicht angekündigt.

V.17 entspricht wörtlich der Markus-Vorlage in 13,13 und bringt den Haß zur Sprache, der der Gemeinde entgegenschlagen wird, bei Lukas aber wieder nicht im Horizont des τέλος wie Mk 13,13 und Mt 24,13, sondern durch die Zusage des göttlichen Schutzes (Lk 21,18) gemildert. Die "Standhaftigkeit" (ὑπομονή) der Jünger führt nicht zur Rettung im Endgericht (Mk 13,13), sondern zur Bewahrung ihres Lebens (Lk 21,18f).

Der Abschnitt 12-19 zielt auf das imperativische Futur in V. 19: ἐν τῇ ὑπομονῇ ὑμῶν κτήσασθε τὰς ψυχὰς ὑμῶν. Eine Interpretation von ψυχή als "ewiges Leben" wäre für Lukas singulär.[58] Schweizer möchte dieser Schwierigkeit mit einer von Mk 13,13 und Lk 21,16b bestimmten Interpretation entgehen.[59] Es ist aber methodisch angemessener, den eindeutig lukanischen Vers 19 auf der Ebene lukanischer Redaktion zu verstehen, als auf die markinische Vorlage selbst oder auf den stark an der markinischen Vorlage orientierten Versteil 16b zu reflektieren. Lukas tritt mit V.19 konsequent aus dem eschatologischen Horizont von Mk 13,13b heraus. Die Gerichtsvorstellung, die Mk 13 prägt und die dort bruchlos auf das Ergehen und Verhalten der Jünger bezogen ist, lehnt Lukas ab. Weder τέλος noch σῴζειν (Mk 13,13) finden bei Lukas Aufnahme. Er spricht mit der Einschaltung von V.18 die Hoffnung auf das physische Überleben direkt aus. Ebenso

[57] Vgl. den Kontext der in Anm.53 genannten Stellen.

[58] Eduard Schweizer, Art. ψυχή D. NT, *ThWNT* 9 (1973) S.635-657. Die Kommentare lassen diese Entscheidung gerne offen: Schneider, *a.a.O.*, S.419-422; Walter Grundmann, *Das Evangelium nach Lukas*, Berlin 1971 (ThHK III) S.380-382.

[59] Schweizer, *a.a.O.*, S.647.

lebenspraktisch denkt sich Lukas die geforderte ὑπομονή, die den Grundzug in der *Vita Christiana* bildet.[60] Zieht man zur Interpretation von V.19 noch den in V.15 dargestellten prozessualen Vorgang heran, wird der angemessene Kontext von V.19 deutlich. Die lukanischen Jesusanhänger sollen mit Klugheit und Geistesgegenwart ihr Recht verteidigen (ἀπολογεῖσθαι). Lukas hat dabei weniger an ein selbstmörderisches Bekenntnis als an eine erfolgreiche Verteidigung gedacht.[61] In V.19 ist ψυχή wie an allen anderen Stellen bei Lukas mit "Leben" zu übersetzen: "durch eure Standhaftigkeit werdet ihr eure Leben erwerben".

Die Verse 12-19 können entweder als Vorausschau auf die in der Acta berichteten Ereignisse gelesen[62] oder als die Darstellung der Realität der lukanischen Christen interpretiert werden.[63] Conzelmann verknüpft diese beiden Möglichkeiten, indem er davon ausgeht, daß die in Acta vorgestellte Situation die der lukanischen Christen oder die ihrer jüngsten Vergangenheit sei, und somit die beiden oben unterschiedenen Möglichkeiten zusammenfallen.[64] Die sprachliche und sachliche Weite von V.12-19 spricht eher dafür, daß Lukas eine große Anzahl verschiedener Konfliktsituationen unter die Ansage Jesu stellen wollte. So werden bei ihm differenziert, realistisch und gleichzeitig umfassend konkrete Verfolgungserfahrungen benannt. In dieser Zusammenfassung sind die Erfahrungen der Christen seit dem Auftreten Jesu bis zur Gegenwart und damit auch die in Acta berichteten Ereignisse angesprochen. Im Wissen um die unterschiedlichen Folgen der gerichtlichen und nichtgerichtlichen Verfolgungen stellt Lukas alle diese Begebenheiten unter die Ansage Jesu, daß dies so kommen wird, und unter die Zusage seines inspirierenden Beistandes.

---

[60] Conzelmann, *a.a.O.*, S.217-19.

[61] Vgl. a. Dennis M. Sweetland, Discipleship and Persecution: A Study of Luke 12,1-12, *Biblica* 65 (1984) S.61-79.

[62] Schneider, *a.a.O.*, S.420.

[63] Stegemann, *a.a.O.*, S.90.

[64] Conzelmann, *a.a.O.*, S.119.

IV Verrechtlichung im lukanischen Schrifttum

Lukas nimmt in Lk 21,12-19 und Lk 12,11f die Traditionen aus Q, Mk und das in IV Esr belegte Motiv des endzeitlichen Zerwürfnisses unter Freunden auf, arbeitet sie aber um. Er teilt nicht den apokalyptischen Horizont des Mk-Textes, der Mission, Verfolgung und Bewährung in engem Bezug zum Ende des Äons und dem sich dann ereignenden Endgericht sieht. Die Mk-Vorlage hat für Lukas dadurch entscheidende Defizite: sie interessiert sich nicht für die konkreten Umstände der Strafverfolgung und der gerichtlichen Instanzen und entwickelt keine Perspektive für eine rechtspolitische oder auch nur rechtspragmatische Auseinandersetzung.

Q interpretiert Verfolgung und Bewährung eher pragmatisch im Rahmen seines Nachfolgeverständnisses.[65] Dabei bleiben die Überlegungen auf den konkreten Beistand in der Verfolgungssituation beschränkt und verstehen sich nicht wie Mk 13 (und IV Esr 5,9 und 6,24) als Teil einer umfassenden endzeitlichen Konzeption. Lukas möchte es aber bei dem radikalen Nachfolgekonzept von Q (Mt 10,19) nicht bewenden lassen, da es dem irdischen Ergehen wenig Aufmerksamkeit entgegenbringt. Er interpretiert die Tradition neu, indem er sie in den Kontext konkreter prozessualer Abläufe stellt. Die Erfahrungen der Gemeinde mit polizeilichen und gerichtlichen Auseinandersetzungen möchte er in seinen Schriften über die Entstehung und Ausbreitung der Jesusanhängerschaft konstruktiv bearbeiten. Er entlastet die juristischen Vorgänge von einem ihnen unangemessenen Interpretationsrahmen, indem er sie aus dem Bezug zum Endgericht und zur Parusie löst, und schafft so Raum für das Interesse am Bestehen in der konkreten rechtlichen Situation. Die Jesusanhäger sollen sich vor Synagogen, Versammlungen, Behörden und Gerichten so verhalten können, daß sie auch nach den dort geltenden Regeln freigesprochen werden können.

Die beiden hier behandelten lukanischen Texte belegen die Tendenz des Lukas zur Anreicherung der Überlieferung mit rechtlichen Themen und Details. Die dort gewonnenen Erkenntnisse führen zu weiteren Beobachtungen im *Lukasevangelium*, insbesondere im Passionsbericht.

---

[65] Lührmann (*a.a.O.*, S.175f u. 221) spricht von einer eschatologischen Überhöhung der Q-Nachfolgetradition bei Mk.

Lk 22,33 verändert gegenüber Mk 14,29 die Versicherung des Petrus, er nehme keinen Anstoß an Jesus, zu einem Gelöbnis seiner Bereitschaft, die polizeiliche Verfolgung und gerichtliche Bestrafung mitzutragen.[66]

Lk 23,2 als Einleitung des Verhörs durch Pilatus ergänzt Mk 15,1f um die Anklage der Aufhetzung des Volkes, die in Lk 23,5 verschärft wiederholt wird und bei Mk ebenso fehlt wie die dreifache Feststellung des Pilatus, Jesus sei unschuldig (Lk 23,4 und 23,14-16.22).

Das juristische Interesse des Lukas führt zur Aufnahme der Sonderüberlieferung in Lk 23,4-16, die ein korrektes polizeiliches Verhör, die Einschaltung der zuständigen Instanzen (Herodes, weil Jesus Galiläer ist) und als Ergebnis dieser Untersuchung die Unschuldsvermutung des Pilatus bringt (V.14-16). Auch die von Pilatus vorgeschlagene Prügelstrafe (V.16.22) entspricht einer korrekten Amtsführung. Sie ist durch die Koerzitionsgewalt des Statthalters legitimiert.[67]

In Lk 23,[17]18-25 wird die Mk-Vorlage durch zwei Motive neu interpretiert: die ausführliche Darstellung des Barabbas als Verbrecher (V.19.25), die weit über die Andeutung in Mk 15,7 hinausgeht,[68] und die schon erwähnte Unschuldsvermutung des Pilatus (Lk 23,22).

Die Hervorhebung der Unschuld Jesu durch den Vergleich mit echten Verbrechern wird auch benutzt, um die Überlieferung von den zwei mit Jesus gekreuzigten Verbrechern anzureichern. Lk 23,32f nennt sie ausdrücklich κακοῦργοι gegenüber dem ungenaueren λῃστής in Mk 15,27.[69] Der Einsichtige der beiden Verbrecher formuliert das juristische

[66] Lk 22,31-33 gehen auf eine um Mk 14,30 (=Lk 22,34) ergänzte Sonderüberlieferung zurück. Mk 14,29 ist also kaum die von Lukas bearbeitete Vorlage zu Lk 22,33. Dennoch zeigt Lk 22,34, daß Lukas Mk 14,26-31 gekannt hat.

[67] Kaser, *a.a.O.*, S.127.

[68] Es wird in Mk 15,7 nicht deutlich, ob Barrabas einer der Aufrührer und Mörder ist oder ob er nur mit ihnen im Gefängnis sitzt. Bei Lukas ist er dann nicht mehr nur Teil einer Gruppe, sondern individuell als Aufrührer und Totschläger verhaftet worden. Die Wiederholung (Lk 23,19 und 25) hebt das zusätzlich hervor.

[69] K.H. Rengstorf (Art. λῃστής, *ThWNT* 4 (1942) S.262-7) und Martin Hengel (*Die Zeloten*, Leiden-Köln 1961, S.25-47) betonen die Nähe des Begriffes zum politischen Banditentum, auch wenn Hengel die Behauptung Rengstorfs von λῃσταί als Selbstbezeichnung der Zeloten widerlegt (Hengel, *a.a.O.*, S.36f.). Dagegen hat κακοῦργος eindeutig kriminellen Sinn, so Michael Lattke, Art. κακοῦργος, *EWNT* 2 (1981) Sp.590.

Resümee der vorher berichteten Ereignisse (Lk 23,41): "Wir sind nämlich gerechterweise (verurteilt), denn wir erhalten gemäß dessen, was wir getan haben. Dieser aber hat nichts Unrechtes getan."

Zum gleichen Ergebnis kommt der Zenturio unter dem Kreuz (Lk 23,47). Während ihm in Mk 15,39 das Bekenntnis der wahren Gottessohnschaft Jesu in den Mund gelegt wird,[70] interessiert sich Lukas viel stärker für einen weiteren Zeugen der jesuanischen Unschuld im juristischen Sinne. Der Zenturio ruft aus: "Dieser Mensch war wirklich gerecht."[71] Hier tritt wie in Lk 12,11f und 21,12-19 das Bekenntnis hinter dem juristischen Gehalt des Geschehens zurück.[72]

Die *Apostelgeschichte* erfordert unter dem Gesichtspunkt der Quellenbearbeitung eine völlig andere Beurteilung als das Lukasevangelium.[73] Man bewegt sich hier auf unsichererem Grund als im Falle des Lk und sollte dies auch beachten. Deswegen sollen hier nur einige Hinweise auf die Grundlinie der Verrechtlichung innerhalb der Apostelgeschichte gegeben werden.

1. Erzählungen, die von rechtlich relevanten Situationen (Gefangennahmen, Gefängnisaufenthalten, Verhören und Bestrafungen) berichten, nehmen einen quantitativ bedeutenden Teil der Acta ein (4,1-23; 5,17-41; 6,12-7,60; 12,1-19; 16,19-39; 17,6-9; 18,12-17; 19,35-40; 21,27-40; 22,24-23,11; 24-26; 28,16). Es begegnen entsprechend häufig juristische Termini.[74]

2. Rechtliche Umstände bestimmen viel stärker als im Evangelium den konkreten Ablauf der Ereignisse. Sie sind nicht nur als Details hinzugefügt, sondern prägen ganze Erzählabschnitte und deren Handlungsabläufe. So bringt der Verweis des Paulus auf sein römisches Bürgerrecht in Jerusalem (22,25; vgl. 23,27) eine entscheidende Wende in der Behandlung durch die Behörden. Da das Appellationsrecht (25,10f) an den Kaiser Folge seines Bürgerrechtes ist, kann man sagen,

---

[70] Mk 15,39: ἀληθῶς οὗτος ὁ ἄνθρωπος υἱὸς θεοῦ ἦν.

[71] Lk 23,47: ὄντως ὁ ἄνθρωπος οὗτος δίκαιος ἦν.

[72] Grundmann (*Das Evangelium nach Lukas,* S.435 Anm.25) sieht zwar das Problem, stellt aber fest: "ein Grund zur Änderung des bekenntnismäßig stärkeren Markus-Wortes durch Lukas (ist) nicht erkennbar."

[73] Eckard Plümacher, Acta-Forschung 1974-1982, *ThRNF* 49 (1984) S.120-138. Vgl. dazu o. Anm.6.

[74] Vgl.o.S. 290.

daß der Ablauf der berichteten Ereignisse von 22,25 an durch das Rechtsinstitut des Bürgerrechtes strukturiert wird.

3. Die rechtlichen Elemente werden in einen bewußt gestalteten erzählerischen Spannungsbogen eingefügt. So werden z.B. die Beziehungen des Paulus zu Tarsus[75] und Rom[76] zunächst nur angedeutet, um später als tarsisches und römisches Bürgerrecht den Ablauf der Ereignisse und das Ergehen des Paulus entscheidend mitzubestimmen. Die Beobachtungen an den lukanischen Texten machen es wahrscheinlich, daß Lukas zunächst nur von einem Beinamen des Paulus wußte[77] und zu dieser Überlieferung das tarsische Bürgerrecht hinzufügte. Ebenso wird er das römische Bürgerrecht des Paulus nicht einfach frei erfunden haben, sondern aus einer Einzelinformation einen den Fortgang des paulinischen Prozesses prägenden Rechtshintergrund geschaffen haben.

4. Neben der unklaren Quellensituation stehen einer präziseren Beurteilung der Verrechtlichung in Acta auch andere Einflüsse im Wege, die sich der Kreativität des Erzählers Lukas verdanken.[78] Am wichtigsten erscheint mir dabei die Berücksichtigung der von Richard I. Pervo gemachten Beobachtungen zum Unterhaltungswert der Gerichtsepisoden der Acta zu sein.[79] Gerichtsszenen sind ein im antiken Roman häufig eingesetztes erzählerisches Mittel zur Erzeugung von Spannung.[80] Innerhalb von Acta bleibt die Freude des Lesers an diesem Erzählmotiv zunehmend ungetrübt, da nach dem Stephanusmartyrium keiner der Jesusanhänger mehr den Tod findet und nach der Philippiepisode auch keine polizeiliche

---

[75] Act 9,11; vgl. 9,30; 11,25.

[76] In der Philippiepisode verweist Paulus zum erstenmal auf sein römisches Bürgerrecht (Act 16,37). Der berichtete Geschehensablauf bleibt davon aber unberührt, denn seine Freilassung ist schon längst beschlossene Sache. Schon Ferdinand Christian Baur (*Paulus, der Apostel Jesu Christi*, Stuttgart 1845, S.153) wunderte sich über die merkwürdige Tatsache, daß Paulus in der eigentlichen Verhandlung sein römisches Bürgerrecht verschwieg.

[77] Act 9,11: Σαῦλον ὀνόματι Ταρσέα.

[78] Vgl. Robert C. Tannehill, *The narrative unity of Luke-Acts*, 2 Bde, Philadelphia 1986 u. 1990. Dort sind die rechtlichen Elemente in ihrer Bedeutung für die erzählerische Gesamtkonzeption leider unabeachtet geblieben.

[79] *Profit with Delight: The literary genre of the Acts of the Apostles*, Philadelphia 1987, S.42-48

[80] Vgl. außer den Belegen bei Pervo, *Profit with Delight*, S.47, noch *Ach.Tat.* 7.7.1-7.14.1.

Bestrafung mehr durchgeführt wird.[81] Insgesamt ist festzustellen, daß Lukas mit zunehmender Quellenunabhängigkeit auch literarisch freier gestaltet.

V Der traditions- und sozialgeschichtliche Hintergrund

Abschließend soll der historische Kontext und der traditionsgeschichtliche Hintergrund der Verrechtlichungstendenz im lukanischen Schrifttum näher bestimmt werden. Es handelt sich dabei um eine vorläufige Skizze, die einigen Anregungen Dieter Georgis aus dem Epilog zur englischen Übersetzung seines Buches *Die Gegner des Paulus im 2. Korintherbrief: Studien zur religiösen Propaganda* nachgeht.[82]

Eine wesentliche Hilfe zum Verstehen leistet der Vergleich des lukanischen Schrifttums mit den Traditionen der jüdisch-hellenistischen Apologetik. Georgi meint, ein wesentliches und bisher wenig beachtetes Element der jüdischen Apologetik sei ihr Engagement in politischen Fragen über den Weg der diplomatischen und juristischen Auseinandersetzung mit ihrer jeweiligen Umwelt. Auch die dabei erzielten diplomatischen Erfolge seien als die praktischen Aspekte der jüdischen Missionstheologie zu interpretieren. Die Archivierung der von der jeweiligen Obrigkeit gewährten Privilegien, wie wir sie bei Philo und Josephus finden, diene der weiteren propagandistischen Verwertung innerhalb des missionarischen Konzepts des hellenistischen Judentums.[83] Diese Kombination von politisch-juristischem Interesse und religiösem Selbstbewußtsein finde sich nicht nur bei Philo und Josephus, sondern sei ein Wesenselement der hellenistisch-jüdischen Mission:

---

[81] *Ebd.*, S.43 zu den gerichtlichen Szenen: "If the accounts do little to illuminate the legal situations of early Christians, they do make for pleasant diversion." Die Einführung dieses erzählerischen Gestaltungselementes in die neutestamentliche Überlieferung spiegelt auch den politischen Wandel wieder. Die antike Rhetorik, die zu Zeiten Ciceros noch von eminenter politischer und juristischer Bedeutung war, wird im frühen Prinzipat zu einem Bildungsgut. So Peter Garnsey und Richard Saller, *The Early Principate: Augustus to Trajan*, Oxford 1982 (Greece & Rome. New Surveys in the Classics No.15) S.36f.

[82] Dieter Georgi, *The Opponents of Paul in Second Corinthians*, Philadelphia 1986, S.333-450.

[83] Georgi, *Opponents*, S.404-6.

"They demonstrated juridical and political competence combined with diplomatic skills among the gifts and demonstrations of the Jewish θεῖος ἄνθρωπος."[84]

Georgi benennt die geistesgeschichtlichen Zusammenhänge, in denen Recht und Religion zueinander stehen, untersucht aber nicht den Vorgang der Verrechtlichung von Traditionen als literarisches sozusagen schriftstellerisch technisches Phänomen. Sowohl Philos *Legatio ad Gaium*, seine Schrift *In Flaccum* als auch die *Antiquitates Judaicae* des Josephus ließen sich unter diesem Gesichtspunkt in einer anregenden Perspektive neu lesen und verstehen. Diese an der jüdisch-hellenistischen Literatur gewonnenen Beobachtungen Georgis[85] lassen sich durch einen Blick auf die historische Entwicklung der rechtlichen und politischen Situation des Judentums, besonders in Hinsicht auf das Verhältnis zu Rom, präzisieren.

Die Aufnahme *diplomatischer Beziehungen* zwischen Rom und der jüdischen Elite Palästinas seit der Makkabäerzeit[86] ist als wichtige Quelle von Erfahrungen des rechtlich und vertraglich gebundenen Umgangs der Juden mit Rom zu beachten.[87] Nicht nur die Juden Palästinas, sondern auch die organisierte Judenschaft der Diaspora hatte immer wieder Verhandlungen zu führen und Auseinandersetzungen zu bestehen, die den Bestand oder die Ausweitung rechtlicher Privilegien, oft aufgrund der Eigenart der jüdischen Religion, zum Gegenstand hatten.[88] Durch die sich im 2. Jh. v. Chr. anbahnende Alleinherrschaft Roms über den Mittelmeerraum bekamen die Vereinbarungen der palästinischen Juden mit Rom, besonders das Freundschaftsbündnis mit Rom (*amicitia*),[89] auch Bedeu-

[84] *Ebd.*, S.405.

[85] Vgl. dazu noch Erwin R. Goodenough, *The Politics of Philo Judaeus: Practice and Theory*, New Haven 1938; Reinhold Mayer und Christa Möller, Josephus: Politiker und Prophet, *Josephus-Studien*, hg. von Otto Betz, Klaus Haacker und Martin Hengel, Göttingen 1974, S.271-284.

[86] II Makk 11,34b-37; I Makk 8; 12,1-4.16; 14,16-19.40; 15,16-21; Jos *Bell* I 38 und 48; Jos *Ant* XIII 259-266.

[87] Thomas Fischer, Zu den Beziehungen zwischen Rom und den Juden im 2. Jahrhundert v. Chr., *ZAW* 86 (1974) S.90-93; Jörg Dieter Gauger, *Beiträge zur jüdischen Apologetik*, Köln-Bonn 1977 (BBB 49); Uwe Baumann, *Rom und die Juden: die römisch-jüdischen Beziehungen von Pompeius bis zum Tode des Herodes*, Frankfurt, Bern u. New York 2.Aufl. 1986 (Studia Philosophica et Historica) S.17f.

[88] Z.B. Philo *LegGai* 117f.

[89] Gauger, *a.a.O.*, S.261-3.

tung für die Situation der Juden in den hellenistischen Städten.[90] Die hohe, zwischenstaatliche Diplomatie hatte durchaus Auswirkungen auf lokale Verhältnisse. Mit der Eroberung Jerusalems durch Pompejus (64 v.Chr.), der Bildung römischer Klientelstaaten in Palästina und schließlich der Umwandlung Judäas zur römischen Provinz (6 n.Chr.) endet die Phase der diplomatischen Vertragsbeziehung auch für Palästina und es beginnt die direkte Konfrontation mit römischer Rechtssprechung.

Daneben sind auch *Einzelkonflikte* in den Erfahrungsschatz der jüdischen Apologetik eingegangen, wie etwa, um auch nichtjüdische Quellen zu nennen, der Streit um den Sabazios Kult (ca. 139 v.Chr.) in Rom und die darauf erfolgte Ausweisung der Juden aus Rom wegen der Praktizierung ihrer Sitten und Gebräuche im öffentlichen Raum (*in publico*),[91] der Konflikt um die Berechtigung von Goldtransporten der Juden der Provinz Asia für den Tempel von Jerusalem (59 v.Chr.),[92] oder die bei Sueton genannte und auch in Acta erwähnte Ausweisung der Juden aus Rom (49 n.Chr.).[93]

Die in diesen Konflikten und ihren rechtlichen Implikationen erworbenen Kenntnisse im Umgang mit römischen Verhältnissen werden in ihrem Wert durch die räumliche Ausdehnung der Machtsphäre Roms und durch die kulturelle Durchdringung der neuen Gebiete erhöht. Die *Ausweitung des römischen Rechts* vollzieht sich auch als Verdichtungsprozeß nach innen. Dabei ging die Bedeutung lokaler Regelungen bis in die römische Kaiserzeit nicht völlig verloren, wie z.B. der Brief des Claudius an die Alexandriner zeigt, der die Aufrechterhaltung des status quo fordert.[94] Die Römer akzeptierten

---

[90] I Makk 15,16-23; Jos *Ant* XIV 185-267 bringt eine umfangreiche Sammlung von städtischen Beschlüssen, die auf ein *senatus consultum* antworten.

[91] Zum Sabbazios-Kult in Rom: Georgi, *Opponents*, S.189 n.124, S.197f n.237; W.C. van Unnik, Die Anklage gegen die Apostel in Philippi, in: *Mullus.* FS f. Theodor Klausner, Münster 1964 (JAC 1) S. 366-373; hier S.372f. Grundlage der Überlegungen ist ein Exzerpt aus *Val. Max.* 1,3,3; Texte auch in: *Greek and Latin authors on Jews and Judaism*, Bd. I: From Herodotus to Plutarch, hg.v. Menahem Stern, Jerusalem 1974, S. 357-360. Vgl. Emil Schürer, *The history of the Jewish people in the age of Jesus Christ*, New English edition, vol III.1 (1986) S.73-75.

[92] Cic. *Flacc.* 28, 66-69.

[93] Sueton *Claud.* 25,4; Act 18,2.

[94] H. Idris Bell, *Juden und Griechen im römischen Alexandria: eine historische Skizze des alexandrinischen Antisemitismus*, Leipzig 1926 (Beiheft zum Alten

die Rechtssprechung der Bewohner ihrer Provinzen gemäß dem schon in vorrömischer Zeit gebildeten Volksrecht,[95] wie sie auch innerhalb römischer Gebiete Teile der Rechtssprechung untergeordneten Instanzen wie den *collegia* und vor allem den *familiae* beließen. Mit dem Prinzipat beschleunigte sich allerdings die Entwicklung, die höhere Gerichtsbarkeit in die eigene Hand zu nehmen. Die römische Bürgerrechtspolitik forcierte die Zentralisierung und die Vereinheitlichung der Rechtssprechung zusätzlich.[96] Durch die Verbreitung des römischen Bürgerrechtes wurden immer mehr rechtliche Sachverhalte der lokalen Gerichtsbarkeit entzogen und vor der römischen Provinzialobrigkeit (Legaten, Prokuratoren und Praetoren) verhandelt.

Mit dieser Situation hatten sich auch die Missionsbewegungen in neutestamentlicher Zeit auseinanderzusetzen. Während aber die jüdischen Gruppen lange Erfahrung mit rechtlichen Auseinandersetzungen um Privilegien und Sicherheiten hatten und diese auch jeweils neu reflektierten, wie I-III Makk, die politischen Schriften Philos und die des Josephus zeigen, operierten andere expandierende religiöse Bewegungen vor einem völlig anderen Hintergrund und hatten für eine den politischen Gewalten gegenüber unabhängige Identitätswahrung ihrer Anhänger wesentlich schlechtere Voraussetzungen.[97] Es lag nahe, daß sich Teile der Jesusanhängerschaft

---

Orient 9); Maurits Engers, Der Brief des Kaisers Claudius an die Alexandriner, *Klio* 20 (1926) S.168-178. Richard Laquer, Der Brief des Kaisers Claudius an die Alexandriner, *Klio* 20 (1926) S.89-106. Diskussion der Probleme und weitere Literatur bei E. Mary Smallwood, *Philonis Alexandrini Legatio ad Gaium*, Leiden ²1970, S.6f.

[95] Kaser, *a.a.O.,*, S.155-159.

[96] Kaser, *a.a.O.*, S.116f; Friedrich Vittinghoff, *Römische Kolonisation und Bürgerrechtspolitik unter Caesar und Augustus*, AAWLM.G 14 (1951) S.1312-1315; Wolfgang Stegemann, War Paulus römischer Bürger?, *ZNW* 78 (1987) S.214f. Die Bemerkung Suetons (Suet. *Aug.* 40.) über eine Zurückhaltung des Augustus in der Bürgerrechtsverleihung kann nicht als Beleg für eine insgesamt restriktive Politik in dieser Sache dienen. Sie bezog sich im Grunde nur auf den außermilitärischen Bereich. Der von Cicero (Cic. *Balb.* 22f und 51) aufgestellte Grundsatz, daß derjenige, der für Rom Waffen in die Hand genommen und damit sein Leben eingesetzt habe, mit vollem Recht römischer Bürger heißen dürfe, war davon nie tangiert. Vgl. Hartmut Wolff, Die Entwicklung der Veteranenprivilegien vom Beginn des 1. Jahrhunderts v.Chr. bis auf Konstantin d.Gr., *Heer und Integrationspolitik*, hg. v. Werner Eck und Hartmut Wolff, Köln-Wien 1986 (Passauer Historische Forschungen 2), S. 44-115.

[97] Walter Burkert, *Antike Mysterien: Funktionen und Gehalt*, München 2.Aufl. 1991, S.53-55.

an den Vorbildern aus der jüdisch-hellenistischen Apologetik zu orientieren suchten.

Lukas versucht, an die Traditionen der jüdisch-hellenistischen Apologetik anzuknüpfen. Er hat dabei aber eine Reihe von wesentlichen Unterschieden zwischen der sich ausbreitenden Jesusanhängerschaft und dem Judentum zu beachten. Philo und Josephus handeln in ihren diplomatischen und militärischen Missionen als Repräsentanten einer bedeutenden Volksgruppe. Sie verkehren als Vertreter der jüdischen Oberschicht mit den jeweiligen römischen Statthaltern von Angesicht zu Angesicht und können ihre Anliegen bzw. die ihres Volkes persönlich vor den jeweiligen römischen Kaisern vertreten.[98] In ihren Schriften greifen sie auf bedeutendes dokumentarisches Material und auf rechtsverbindliche Urkunden zurück, die der höchsten diplomatischen und verfassungsrechtlichen Ebene angehören.[99]

Im Gegensatz dazu handelt es sich bei den von Lukas berichteten Vorgängen nicht um hohe Diplomatie zwischen Völkern, sondern um Konflikte einer marginalen religiösen Gruppierung, eben der Jesusanhängerschaft, mit ihrer Umwelt. Deswegen unterscheiden sich sowohl die Inhalte der Auseinandersetzung als auch die Perspektive, in der sie von Lukas gesehen werden. In Lk 12,10 und 21,10-19 thematisiert er die Konflikte mit der Obrigkeit noch ohne grundsätzliche rechtspolitische Perspektive. Dort geht es um die Loslösung von der apokalyptisch orientierten Überbewertung der Verfolgungssituationen. Lukas vertritt eine pragmatische Sicht: der oder die einzelne hat das Recht zur Verteidigung gegenüber polizeilichen und gerichtlichen Verfolgungen. Seine Überarbeitung der Passionsgeschichte betont juristische Gesichtspunkte, die zeigen sollen, daß Jesus gerade aus römischer Sicht unschuldig ist. In seinem Evangelium sind Lukas noch durch die Bindung an Quellen und durch die Vertrautheit sei-

---

[98] Philo *Flacc* 97-103; *LegGai* 174ff. Dort wechselt Philo in die autoptische Erzählpersepktive des Wir-Berichtes. Jos *Vita* 16; 361-64; 414-29; *Bell* 3.398f.

[99] I Makk 5,10b-13; 8,23-30; 10,18-20.25-45.52-54.70-73; 11,9f.30-37.42f.; 12,6-18.20-23; 13,15f.36-40; 14,20-24.27-45; 15,2-9.16-21.28-31; II Makk 1,1-10a.10b-2,18; 9,19-27; 11,16b-21.22b-26.27b-33.34b-38. Philo *LegGai* 243-253; 276-329; 334; dort auch Paraphrasierungen von Briefinhalten: 207; 248-253; 259f. Jos *Ant.* XIV 185-267.

ner Leser mit der Überlieferung Grenzen in der verrechtlichenden Überarbeitung gesetzt. In Acta aber ist die Orientierung an der jüdisch-hellenistischen Apologetik deutlich zu fassen. Lukas interessiert sich nun für den sozialen und personenrechtlichen Status seiner Protagonisten.[100] Er möchte damit einem Grundprinzip römischer Rechtssprechung und polizeilicher Verfolgung gerecht werden: der *condicio personae.*[101] Im römischen Recht (aber auch in der antiken Rechtssprechung überhaupt) ist das Ansehen der Person (*condicio personae*) von wesentlicher Bedeutung. Je geringer der soziale Status der Angeklagten, desto rücksichtsloser das polizeiliche und gerichtliche Vorgehen. Die Informationen über das Ansehen und den Status der ersten Jesusanhänger sind vor diesem Hintergrund als ein weiteres Element der Verrechtlichung zu verstehen. In Acta greift Lukas ein Stilmittel der jüdisch-apologetischen Literatur auf. Er versucht wie I und II Makk, Philo und Josephus mit dokumentarischen Material zu arbeiten und fügt Schriftstücke mit rechtlich relevanten Inhalten in seine Darstellung ein.[102] Er kann aber nicht auf rechtsverbindliche Beschlüsse von Körperschaften wie den Senat von Rom oder den Stadträten hellenistischer Städte zurückgreifen, auch die Briefe der jeweiligen Machthaber bleiben ihm verschlossen. Die Unterschiede in Sozialstatus und in der rechtlichen Absicherung sind nicht zu verwischen. Lukas sieht deutlich, daß dieser Mangel der Selbstbehauptung der neuen religiösen Bewegung in der römischen Welt im Wege steht. Er versucht diesen Nachteil auszugleichen durch die Verrechtlichung seiner Quellen, durch die erzählerische Bearbeitung rechtlich relevanter Themen und durch die Einordnung ihm bekannter Vorgänge in juristisch-prozessuale Ereignisfolgen.

Verrechtlichung im lukanischen Schrifttum ist als ein Element von Mission und Apologetik in der religiösen Konkurrenz des ersten Jahrhunderts zu verstehen. Der mit diesem Begriff erfaßte Vorgang der Neubestimmung von Traditionen

---

[100] Schon Act 4,13 reflektiert diese Problem. Deutlicher dann in 4,34; 6,7; 8,27; 9,1f; 10,1f; 13,1; 16,14.37f; 17,34; 21,39; 22,3-5; 22,25-28; 28,16.

[101] Géza Alföldy, *Römische Sozialgeschichte,* 2.Aufl. Wiesbaden 1979, S.97-102; Peter Garnsey, *Social Status and Legal Privilege in the Roman Empire,* Oxford 1970, S.76-79. 207-9. 234-280; Kaser, *a.a.O.*, S.128.

[102] Act 15,23b-29; 23,26-30.

angesichts neuer rechtlicher Kontexte ist eine Antwort auf die Ausbreitung und Festigung römischer Herrschaft und römischen Rechtes in der Mittelmeerwelt und greift auf Erfahrungen und Traditionen der jüdischen Apologetik in der hellenistisch-römischen Welt zurück.

PROPAGANDA UND GEGENPROPAGANDA IM FRÜHEN CHRISTENTUM: SIMON MAGUS ALS GESTALT DES SAMARITANISCHEN CHRISTENTUMS

Klaus Berger (Universität Heidelberg)

Es erscheint dringend geboten, die Gestalt des Simon, genannt Simon Magus, nicht von vornherein als exotischen Gnostiker oder als primitiven Simonisten (der Geist mit Geld kaufen will) zu sehen, sondern als Repräsentanten eines frühen samaritanischen Christentums. Es ist bekannt, daß der Verfasser von Act ("Lukas") diese Gestalt und ihre Ambitionen mißbilligt und daß sich spätere Gnostiker auf Simon berufen. Doch unter der lukanischen Polemik treten Züge hervor, die zwar nicht orthodox im Sinne des Lukas sind, aber die doch unser Bild vom frühen Christentum bereichern. Denn auch Lukas kann nicht verschweigen, daß Simon Christ ist, nach Lukas sogar getauft worden ist (Act 8,13). Wenn im folgenden der Versuch unternommen wird, Simon als Christ zu sehen, dann geschieht dieses aus der Erfahrung heraus, daß lukanische (und moderne) Kriterien für Orthodoxie nicht schon immer gegolten haben und daß sich in der Regel eine Nachfrage lohnt.

1. Simon wird als "Magie treibend" und die Leute "außer sich bringend" verstanden (Act 8,9). Dieses weist – insbesondere in Kombination – eindeutig auf einen Wundertäter. Denn "Magie" nennt man illegitimes charismatisch begründetes Wirken, und Menschen "außer sich bringen" (gr.: ἐξιστάνειν) können mit ihren Wundertaten auch Jesus, der Geist und die Jünger (Mk 2,12; 5,42; 6,51; Mt 12,23; Lk 2,47; 8,56; Act 2,7.12; 8,13; 10,45).

2. Besonders interessant ist, daß Simon seinerseits angesichts der Taten des Apostels Philippus "außer sich gerät" (Act 8,13). Damit wird Philippus als der überlegene Wundertäter dargestellt. – Überhaupt ist Simon als Magier in sehr ähnlicher Weise Gegenspieler des Philippus wie der Magier Bar-Jesus (!) nach Act 13 Gegenspieler des Paulus ist. Der Name Bar-Jesus könnte auch dort einen Christen bezeichnen.

3. Simon nennt sich "groß" bzw. er wird von seinen An-

hängern "die Große Kraft Gottes (gr.: δύναμις τοῦ θεοῦ)" genannt (Act 8,10). Nun ist "Kraft Gottes" auch ein Attribut Jesu Christi (1 Kor 1,24), so daß sich Simon nicht als Gott, sondern nur als seinen Repräsentanten bezeichnen muß. Das Attribut "groß" ist schließlich aus Aussagen über Mose bekannt, der in zeitgenössischen Texten der "Große Bote" genannt wird (lat.: *magnus nuntius*), so in AssMos 11,17. Theologisch gesehen liegt daher die Konzeption einer Repräsentation Gottes zugrunde, ähnlich der beim Kyrios- und beim Apostelbegriff. Wie dort äußert sich diese Repräsentation Gottes durch Wunderzeichen.[1]

Wenn sich Simon daher als "große Kraft" bezeichnen läßt, dann im Sinne des maßgeblichen göttlichen Gesandten. Will man Simon als einem Christen gerecht werden, dann ist dieser Anspruch ebensowenig eine Konkurrenz zu Jesus Christus wie der paulinische Apostolat. Denn auch von Paulus könnte man in bestimmter Hinsicht sagen, er sei ein "anderer" Christus. Schließlich ist auf die von Mk als Pseudochristen gebrandmarkten christlichen (!) Verkünder hinzuweisen, die nach Mk 13 für sich beanspruchen oder wenigstens dafür gehalten werden, daß in ihnen Christus wiedergekommen sei. Hier geht es um archaische Formen der Repräsentation. – Der Übergang von der Akklamation ("Groß ist die Kraft Gottes") zum Titel ("Die große Kraft Gottes") spielt in der Forschung auch immer

---

[1] Der Bezug zu Wundern legt sich sowohl inner- als auch außerchristlich nahe. - Im paganen Bereich gibt es Übergänge zwischen dem akklamatorischen und dem hypostatischen Gebrauch, wenn man sagt: "Ein Gott ist im Himmel, der große himmlische Men, die große Macht (gr.: μεγάλη δύναμις) des unsterblichen Gottes" (vgl. dazu: E.Peterson, Heis Theos, Göttingen 1926, 268f; H.G. Kippenberg, Garizim und Synagoge, Berlin 1971, 343f).- Der hypostatische Gebrauch legt sich vor allem aufgrund jüdischer Texte nahe: Die Weisheit ist "Hauch der δύναμις Gottes" (SapSal 7,25; der Bezug zur Weisheit ist wegen 1 Kor 1,24 wichtig), nach LXX ist Gott der "Herr der Mächte", bei Paulus und Lukas sind Geist (Gottes) und δύναμις immer wieder synonym. Ein Zusammenhang mit Aposteln besteht in Eph 3,7; Kol 1,29.- Zum Wortfeld gehört auch "wirkmächtig sein" (gr.: ενεργ-). Fazit: Wenn eine Einzelgestalt die δύναμις Gottes genannt wird, so handelt es sich um die einzige und maßgebliche Repräsentation Gottes. Die Attribute Gottes "Weisheit und Kraft" (vgl. Hiob 9,4; 12,13.16; Dan TH 2,23) werden auch sonst im Judentum hypostasiert. Im Blick auf 1 Kor 1,24 sind besonders die o.g. Stellen über das Wirken von Gottes Kraft im Apostel wichtig. In der christologischen Aussage wird die über den Apostel radikalisiert: Jesus Christus ist selbst in Person, was in den anderen nur wirkt. Ähnlich ist der Heilige Geist selbst die Kraft Gottes. Die Korrespondenz zwischen Christologie und Pneumatologie ist wichtig im Blick auf die spätere Dogmengeschichte.

wieder bei der Erörterung des Kyrios-Titels eine Rolle.

4. Der laut Act 8 ausgefochtene Streit mit Simon bezieht sich nicht auf die Wundervollmacht, sondern lediglich darauf, daß er wünscht, den heiligen Geist verleihen zu können. Diese Fähigkeit besitzt er nicht. Aber er ist darin ja nicht allein, denn auch die Hellenisten und auch Apollos vermögen dieses nicht, so sehr sie selbst laut Lukas vom heiligen Geist erfüllt sind. Denn es ist das eine, den heiligen Geist zu besitzen, und es ist etwas anderes, diesen dann auch noch mitteilen zu können. Simon leidet an der Unfähigkeit zu letzterem. Das heißt: Die Auffassung von Repräsentation Gottes, die Simon für sich in Anspruch nimmt, rivalisiert mit einer Pneumatologie.[2]

Für Lukas ist dieselbe pneumatologische Konzeption das die Zwölf und Paulus verbindende Element; die Gabe, den heiligen Geist weiterzugeben, macht erst den Apostel. Und Lukas konstatiert öfter, daß solches bei anderen christlichen Richtungen fehlt, z.B. bei den sog. Johannesjüngern in Ephesus und eben auch in Samarien. Doch war dieses Versäumnis laut Lukas durch Apostel bzw. Paulus nachholbar; anders bei Simon. Es gibt daher, und das reflektiert Act 8, ein frühes samaritanisches Schisma. Ein Teil der samaritanischen Christen ordnet sich den Jerusalemer Aposteln unter, ein anderer Teil nicht. Dieser andere Teil wird bei Lukas als Einzelfigur Simon dargestellt. Doch es steht zu vermuten, daß er nicht allein blieb.

Simon erkennt nun laut Lukas sehr wohl die Notwendigkeit, das Fehlende nachzuholen. D.h. Lukas notiert für Samarien Bestrebungen, sich der frühchristlichen apostolischen Gemeinde anzuschließen. Dieser Versuch ist mißglückt, da Simon von den Aposteln nicht mit Apostelwürde ausgestattet werden konnte – denn das kann nur Gott. Der Weg, auf dem Simon das versucht, ist nun keineswegs plump materialistisch zu nennen, sondern hat sein Analogon in der Kollekte der paulinischen Heidenmission. Auch dort versuchen ja bisher nicht-anerkannte, illegitime Christen durch finanzielle Auf-

[2] Entweder gibt Gott seinen Geist in das "Herz der Kinder Gottes", der Geist ist dann etwas von Gott in denen, die zu ihm gehören. Und diese Gabe ist unter Umständen (bei Lukas: wenn sie apostolisch ist; Zusammenhang mit Lk 24,47?) weitergebbar. Oder ein Mensch repräsentiert Gott - wie Simon; wer ihn tangiert, tangiert Gott. Es liegt ein magisch-juristischer Repräsentanzbegriff vor.

wendungen in Verbindung mit anderen Christen älteren Rechts zu kommen. Im Falle Samariens ist dieses Modell jedenfalls gescheitert.

Lukas berichtet die Taufe Simons erst spät, jedoch besagt das nichts über die Frage, ob Simon nicht auch vorher schon Christ war. Lukas schweigt darüber. Wahrscheinlich war die Taufe ein noch gelungener Versuch, die samaritanischen Christen an die christlichen Gemeinden anzubinden.

Lukas kennt auch an anderen Stellen der Act autochthone Christentümer, so in Act 9 in Damaskus und in Ephesus nach Act 18. Durch den Gang der Ereignisse, konkret durch Paulus, werden diese aber "apostolisiert". Besonders interessant ist in dieser Hinsicht Act 9, denn es handelt sich nicht nur um die "Einführung" des Paulus, sondern ebenso um die Legitimierung des vorpaulinischen Christentums in Damaskus.

Simon scheitert daran, daß er – den Aposteln gleichrangig – den heiligen Geist mitteilen können will. Er kann aber von den Aposteln nicht anerkannt werden. Und es scheitert der Versuch, eine Legitimität des samaritanischen Christentums durch finanzielle Anbindung zu erlangen.

Fazit: Was man bislang für eine exotische Häresie gehalten hat (die "Gnosis" des Simon Magus) ist seinem Ursprung nach ein Schisma unter samaritanischen Christen. Lukas konstatiert nur, daß es dort nicht-apostolische Christen gibt. Daß der weitere Weg der schismatischen samaritanischen Christen in die Gnosis führte, trifft nun nicht allein für die samaritanischen Christen zu, sondern war ein allgemeineres Phänomen. Hinter dem mißlungenen Kaufantrag des Simon verbirgt sich die historische Wirklichkeit, daß hier Christen ihre Selbständigkeit gegenüber Jerusalem auf finanziellem Wege zu erreichen suchten.

An der Art des Lukas, durch Apostel die "eine Christenheit" zu erstellen, werden ältere, davon verschiedene Verhältnisse sichtbar. Lukas reflektiert damit zwei Phasen frühchristlicher Missionsgeschichte:

a) frühchristliche Gruppen entstehen an verschiedenen Orten, so in Antiochien, in Samarien, in Ephesus, in Rom

b) die Gemeinde von Jerusalem entwickelt zentralistische Ambitionen; sie sendet ihre Vertreter nach Samarien (Act 8,14) oder nach Antiochien (Gal 2).

Diese folgenschwere Entwicklung beruht nicht auf Sachzwängen in Richtung Herrschaft, sondern ist darin begründet, daß in Phase a) Christen in der Regel noch mehr oder weniger im Verband des Judentums stehen und keine ausgrenzenden Organisationsformen entwickelt haben, und daß in Phase b) die Christen zu einer selbständigen Gruppe werden, die jüdische Organisationsformen nun nachahmt (z.B. in der finanziellen Ausrichtung nach Jerusalem per Kollekte). Daher wird gleichzeitig mit der langsam sich vollziehende Trennung von Christen und nichtchristlichen Juden paradoxerweise der Einfluß Jerusalems immer größer. Die Geschichte der paulinischen Mission zeugt davon. Die Kollekte des Paulus war ein Weg, im Rahmen dieses Modells wenigstens zu denken. Der Druck des nichtchristlichen Judentums bringt es mit sich, daß sich die Christen analog zum Judentum dann selbst mit Jerusalem als Zentrum organisieren.

Am Ende sind wohl beide Versuche der finanziellen Anbindung nichtjüdischer Christen an Jerusalem auf finanziellem Weg gescheitert. Für den samaritanischen Weg gibt Lukas das offen zu, für den paulinischen findet er eine andere Lösung (Verwendung der Kollektengelder für Nasiräer). Vielleicht lag es einfach daran: Im Unterschied zu Paulus war Simon Magus kein Jude. Der alte Gegensatz zwischen Samaritanern und Juden war es wohl letztlich, der eine Gleichstellung des Simon unmöglich machte.

PAUL

ΕΙΣ ΤΗΝ ΣΠΑΝΙΑΝ: THE FUTURE AND PAUL

Arthur J. Dewey
(Xavier University, Cincinnati, Ohio)

"Go West, young man."
Horace Greeley

"To boldly go where no one has gone before..."
Gene Roddenberry

"Hope imagined a land at the end of the world, but still of this world..."
Ervin Rohde

1. Introduction

For the most part biblical scholarship has treated Paul as a distant creature of the past. With his legendary death in Rome, Paul's hope for the future suffered a more inglorious fate. The institution of later Christianity not only has rewritten what remains of the Pauline fragments but also has redirected the fundamental utopian orientation of Paul. The domestication of Paul can be seen concretely in the way the Bible reader usually reads Paul—as ending his correspondence and career in Rome—just as the development of Christianity was to depict. Indeed, one can simply consult the typical maps in Bibles and New Testaments and note what is missing (namely the Western Mediterranean) and where the ancient world pictorially comes to an end. But that is to miss the future in Paul's thought and, I would maintain, to misunderstand completely the intent of Paul. For, if it is axiomatic that one only understands another by understanding the other's hope for the future, then, we have greatly misunderstood Paul insofar as we leave his imagination imprisoned in Rome. We confine ourselves to the text, whereas Paul has always seen beyond the margin; we are mesmerized by the powerbase while Paul remains enchanted by unchartered possibilities.

In attempting to return to the margin of Paul's thought, I

begin the investigation with a simple question: What is Paul getting at in wanting to go to Spain via Rome?[1] Such remarks in Rom 15:24, 28 seem simply to be indications of his travel plans. Apparently preparing for and justifying his intended presence in Rome, these remarks are, at first blush, incidental to the letter, adding only to the background information of this prospective visitor.

But is this really the case? What are we to do with the possibility that Paul well may have delivered a backhanded compliment to his audience? Why do the Roman communities serve as a transit connection for Paul? In contrast to the theological geography in Acts, Paul does not want to finish up in Rome. Rome is not the intended end of the journey. At best it is a departure point for a larger mission. In a period where everything led to Rome, Paul appears remarkably off-center. It would not be inappropriate to see in these brief lines a very significant act of displacment. For Paul's envisioned journey effectively displaces the centrality of Rome and moves to the geographical and ideological margins. Why would Paul imagine such a displacement? Once again, what is he getting at in wanting to journey to Spain in this fashion?

2. The Scope and Character of Romans

Ever since F. C. Baur broke up the dogmatic glacier over Romans, there has been constant debate about the historical situation and purpose of the last extant letter of Paul. Arguments have been waged over the make-up of the Roman Jesus-believers, as well as the relationship of the various contents to the possible historical situation. At least, the rhetorical question of preparing for an unknown audience had become a major part of the discussion. Günther Bornkamm[2] threw further light on the anticipatory imagination of Paul when he argued that Romans should be read on two fronts. In writing

[1] It will come as no surprise to my fellow contributors and readers of this volume to find out the origin of my paper. These reflections are a response to a question Dieter Georgi made to me some years ago. "What would Paul's letter to Spain be like?" His typically provocative question challenged me to extend my pursuit of Paul's utopian thinking, which I had explored in my Harvard doctoral thesis.

[2] "Der Römerbrief als Testament des Paulus," in *Geschichte und Glaube*, Teil 2, Gesammelte Aufsätze 4, (BEvTh 53; München: Chr. Kaiser, 1971) 201-39.

to Rome, Paul was envisioning his upcoming encounter in Jerusalem. One would need therefore to read Romans bifocally in order to catch the historical nuances. Ernst Käsemann[3] has pushed the location of the debate back to Rome because he has noted that Rome appears to play the mediating role of "springboard" for the Spanish mission. Paul needs to enlist those Jewish Jesus-believers left among the Roman communities to dispel any criticism that might emerge from Jerusalem and to prevent any obstruction for his future work. Dieter Georgi[4] has pointed out more recently that one needs to read Romans with an eye to Paul's indirect critique of the εὐαγγέλιον of the Empire. Paul anticipates not simply the confrontation in Jerusalem but the possible collision with the social consensus of the first century which culminated in the Caesar religion. Slowly the historical investigation of Romans has enlarged the scope of Paul's vision.

In this paper I underscore the third leg on Paul's journey: Spain. Käsemann has suggested this point already but did not follow up on the utopian possibilities which underlie this move. What I would suggest is that Paul's intention to travel to Spain is a significant intimation of his ever-widening missionary scope and theological vision. I would also like to argue that one needs to take this expanded scope into consideration when investigating the structure and contents of Romans. Indeed, I would suggest that this letter is neither a comprehensive resumé of his earlier thought nor a final testament. Rather, one might well adopt the metaphor of a roadmap. For Paul is presenting a new strategy of envisioning and maneuvering with the utopian forces of the world. We must remember that neither the ancients nor the medievals shied away from making maps which embody desire as well as location. Legend and rumor, haunting the borders of the world, are part of the very make-up of a map. In Romans Paul shows us that human hope, wishing, and dreams are part of the world map. Through extended engagement with major figures and types, as well as his exposing the forces at work and seeing their limits, Paul attempts to disclose lines of direction, inviting his audience to join in the trek. Hence, the matter of Spain will be seen as crucial to the entire letter and strategy,

[3] *Commentary on Romans* (Grand Rapids, MI: Eerdmans, 1980) 404.
[4] *Theocracy in Paul's Praxis and Theology* (Minneapolis: Fortress, 1991) 81.

for Paul's vision is not a closed circle but an ever-widening spiral.

3. The Jewish Presence in Spain

The question of why Paul would go to Spain is linked to the usual assumption that there were Jewish communities in Spain which Paul customarily would use for his initial base of operations. Indeed, Paul's being intent on visiting Spain becomes a primary piece of evidence in the case for Jewish settlement in Spain before the fall of the Temple (70 CE). As S. Safrai and M. Stern put it:

> "Paul, towards the end of his life, intended to preach the Christian gospel in Spain and Illyricum. Since it was his custom to go to countries where the ground had been prepared by the Jews, it may be assumed that there already was a Jewish settlement in Spain during the Julio-Claudian period, especially as later traditions frequently stress the ancient origins of the Jewish community in the Iberian peninsula."[5]

Michael Grant[6] also points to Paul's expressed wish for confirmation of Jewish presence in Spain. Käsemann adds without supporting evidence the following claim:

> "Spain was a common place of travel, as has often been shown. There were certainly some synagogues there."[7]

In attempting to make the strongest circumstantial case for Jewish settlement in Spain during the time of Paul, L. Garcia Iglesias finally comes back to the assumption about Paul's customary practice:

> "Dado que, según el Apóstol en otro lugar de la misma carta, era su costumbre e intención adoctrinar primero al judío y después al griego (Romanos 1.16), es normal que se admíta que el texto de Pablo presupone le existencia de communidades judias en nuestra Península..."[8]

Of course, the reason for so much dependence upon these verses in Romans for the settlement of Jews in Spain is that

---

[5] *The Jewish People in the First Century* (Philadelphia: Fortress, 1974) 169-70.

[6] *The Jews in the Roman World* (New York: Charles Scribner's, 1973) 168.

[7] *Commentary on Romans*, 398.

[8] *Los Judíos En La España Antigua* (Madrid: Ediciones Cristiandad, 1978) 48.

there is such meagre evidence, whether literary or non-literary, to support such an assumption. Many have attempted to identify Tarshish[9] with pre-Roman Spain. Yet, as Iglesias admits (33), such an attempt has had proponents for entirely different locales. The Book of Jubilees 9:12 is cited for mentioning the region "beyond the third tongue till it approaches the east of Gadir (Cadiz?)." Further, 1 Macc 8:3-4 indicates that the Jews know of the Roman conquest of Spain and the existence of ores of silver and gold in a place "far distant." In addition it can be noted that Herod Antipas was exiled to Spain according to Josephus (*Bell.* 2.183). Yet, in *Ant* 18.252 Herod is said to be exiled to France.[10] There is some indication of trade with Spain. In *m. Šabbat* 22.2 and m. Maširin 6.3 sea-food and tunny-fish from Spain are mentioned, while in m. Maširin 6.3 roes and fish-entrails in brine from Pelusium and Spain are noted. None of these provides us with evidence of Jewish settlement in Spain. At best one can say that there was some general knowledge of the area along with its Phoenician contacts and major exports. As for the possibility of Herod Antipas' presence in Spain, one could easily turn this around by pointing out that in the Empire exile meant separation from one's people and one's gods. So Herod's exile would argue precisely in the opposite direction.

A second line of argument comes from the variety of assertions that the Jewish people are found throughout the Mediterranean. *Sib. Or.* 3.271 declares: "The whole earth will be filled with you and every sea." Deut 28: 37, 64, 65 point to a universal diaspora as does Ezek 5:14-15. Acts 2:5 would make a similar point. Josephus (*Ant* 14.115) quotes Strabo to the effect that "this people has made its way into every city." This is reiterated in *Bell.* 2.398 and *Ap.* 2.282. Yet, as W. P. Bowers[11] has pointed out, there seems to be a marked discrepancy be-

---

[9] 1 Kg 10:22; 22:48; 1 Chr 1:7; 7:10; 2 Chr 9:21; 20:36, 37; Esth 1:14; Pss 48:7; 72:10; Isa 2:11; 23:1, 6, 10, 14; 60:9; 66:19; Jer 10:9; Ezek 27:12, 15; 38:13; Jonah 1:3; 4:2. The argument is made by linking the Phoenician traders (Tarshish) with their presence in pre-Roman Spain to the description of gold and silver. The indication of great distances sailed also is mentioned.

[10] The solution appears to be a place on the border of Gaul and Spain (Lugdunum Convenarum) according to O. Hirschfield (Safrai and Stern *The Jewish People in the First Century*, 287).

[11] "Jewish Communities in Spain in the Time of Paul the Apostle," *JTS* 26 (1975) 395-402, especially 401.

tween the citation of a general propagandistic claim and an actual listing of places (e.g., Acts 2:9-11; 6:9; 1 Macc 15:16-24; Philo, *Leg. Gai.* 281-284). He goes on to wonder whether this omission of various regions from the lists might well indicate that Rome itself may have been effectively the western limit to the Diaspora.[12] Safrai and Stern agree that there is:

> "...no concrete evidence of Jewish settlements during the Julio-Claudian period in the Latin provinces of the empire and in the African and Mauretanian provinces, which is particularly surprising in view of the ancient ties between Jews and Phoenicians which favor the assumption that Jews had settled in Carthage even before the Romans took over. For a later period we do in fact have such evidence both for Africa and Mauretania. That neither Philo nor the New Testament should allude to Jews living in these areas is therefore all the more astonishing."[13]

The material evidence for Jewish occupation in Spain is even less promising than the majority of non-literary evidence for anything before 70 CE. An amphora from Ibiza in the Balearic Islands, perhaps of Samaritan origin, bears the imprint of two Hebraic characters which can be dated to the first century CE or a little earlier.[14] But this may indicate only the result of trade, not settlement. Nothing else can be found before the second century, with the majority of non-literary evidence coming from the fourth century. Indeed, Jewish tradition traces the first Jewish settlement in Spain to a weaver of the Temple tapestries who fled after the fall of Jerusalem (*b. ʾArakin* 10b; *m. Yoma* 3.1; *b. Yoma* 38a). What one can conclude is that possibly there was some Jewish presence in Spain after 70 CE. It is more probable for the second century CE.

But how do such results square with what seems to have been Paul's *modus operandi*? Further, how can there have been such far-reaching claims regarding Jewish presence? First, the assumption that Paul would follow standard operating procedure ad infinitum becomes problematic when Rom 15:20 is read closely. Paul evidently intends to go to an unmarked region, "where the Anointed has not been named," and where he would not be building upon "another's foundation." This is consistent with 2 Cor 10:16. In other words, Paul himself dis-

[12] Ibid., 402.
[13] *The Jewish People in the First Century*, 169.
[14] See W. P. Bowers, "Jewish Communities in Spain," 396.

putes the assumption. A strategic change in his mission may well be underway. Such an assumption is a glaring example of the tendency in Pauline scholarship to think that one knows where Paul was going and how he is going about it. In fact, it displays an imagination that never reaches the front, never anticipates, but, instead, settles for past patterns.

Second, what one can derive from the universal claims of Jewish presence is not the sheer fact but the propagandistic direction. In other words, such statements are more indicative of the utopian drive of diaspora Judaism than a commonplace report. Such language needs to be interpreted from a forward-looking rather than a backward-looking angle of the hellenistic Jewish mission. Even here we are dealing with vistas and visionary landscapes.

4. Roman Spain

The Roman provinces of Σπανία were undergoing a significant economic upturn during the period of Paul's missionary activity. With Marcus Vipsanius Agrippa's suppression of the final major rebellion in 19 BCE, the nearly two hundred year war of Spanish pacification was completed. The Spanish provinces during this pacification process had figured in the sequence of conflicts of the Civil War which stretched from one end of the world to the other.[15] In 24 BCE Augustus returned to Rome to celebrate a triumphal campaign of northwestern Spain. The pacification of Spain was brought about not simply by Roman military success. With the armies came Roman culture and the construction of roads, ports, towns and cities. Army veterans were pensioned throughout the provinces, providing the basis of security and stability. Along with the increasing Italian colonization, came the eventual granting of Latin status.[16] In fact, by 73-4 CE Vespasian granted Latin status to every community in Spain. The spread of Roman culture was so successful that Strabo (3.2.15) pointed to the astonishing results:

"...the Turdetanians, however, and particularly those who live

[15] Caesar, *Bell. Civ.* 1.37-87; 2:17-21; *Bell. Hisp. passim.* Dio Cassius 41-43, 45.

[16] See M. Rostovzeff, *The Social and Economic History of the Roman Empire* (Oxford: Oxford University Press, 1926) 35.

> along the Baetis (Guadalquivir), have completely changed over to the Roman mode of life, not even remembering their own language any more."[17]

The traffic was not all one way. Even during the Republic many silver mines in southern Citerior and Ulterior Spain provided Rome's most immediate source of revenue. The need for precious metal certainly did not slacken during the Empire. In addition the agricultural potential of Spain, intitially realized during the late Republic, began to come into its own by the middle of the first century CE. Beyond silver, were gold, tin and lead, wheat, barley, flax, olives, olive oil, wine, fruits, nuts, lumber, dyes, drugs, horses, cattle, pottery, tunny-fish, mackerel, snails, oysters, and garum (a product of fish entrails) all featured exports.[18] Olive oil and grain were produced so abundantly that food shortages in Rome could be alleviated by the Spanish exports. By the end of the second century grain and olive oil exports had assumed a critical role in supplying the city of Rome and the army on the frontiers. The Spanish economic miracle represented a major turn-around in the ancient world, as S. J. Keay relates:

> "Between second century BC and second century AD, therefore, Hispania was transformed from being a net importer of luxury goods into a dynamic exporter of wine, olive oil, fish sauce and ceramics to an extensive but often select clientele at Rome and throughout the western empire."[19]

In effect Rome's success in taming Iberia meant that the immense natural resources of the provinces could underwrite the cost of further Roman imperial expansion throughout the known world. The extractive economic system of Rome depended vitally upon Spain for its maintenance. Unlike the modern Bible reader Pliny was quite aware of the place of Spain in the Roman scheme of things. He mentions that Augustus completed the Porticus Octaviae which contained a map of the world, that painstakingly measured the Spanish

---

[17] This excerpt and all subsequent citations from Greek and Latin sources are from the Loeb Classical Library series.

[18] See J. J. van Nostrand, "Roman Spain", in Tenney Frank ed., *An Economic Survey of Ancient Rome*, vol. 3 (Paterson, N.J.: Pageant Books, 1959) 184.

[19] *Roman Spain* (London: University of California Press/British Museum, 1988) 114.

province (*Hist. Nat.* 3.2.17). Moreover, as Keay[20] points out, a second-century floor mosaic found at Emerita in Spain in the Casa del Mitreo is, perhaps, most emblematic of Rome's desire for imperial stability:

> "Among the images are the celestial forces, namely the celestial triad (*Saeculum, Caelum* and *Chaos*), the family of Titans (*Polum*), the rising sun (*Oriens*) with bright gold rays emerging from his head, the clouds (*Nubes*) and the four winds (including *Boreas* and *Zephyrus*). Further down are personifications of terrestrial forces like the mountains (*Mons*), snow (*Nix*) and probably the Seasons. The bottom part of the mosaic is dominated by maritime forces, like the rivers (*Nilus* and *Euphrates*), and aspects of the sea (*Oceanus, Pharus,* and *Navigius*). The Greek conception of cosmic forces was embodied in these 'Romanised' figures executed with such a fine attention to detail. The whole ensemble reflected the ubiquity and stability of the Roman Empire, which, in turn, reflected the universe in one harmonious and eternal unity."

Finally, the most symbolic indicator of Roman dominance is seen in the appearance of Imperial worship. Coins issued at Tarraco depict an altar erected in 26 BCE to the worship of Augustus and the Empire. The coins display a copy of the ceremonial shield granted by the Senate to Augustus in 27 BCE. The inscription contains the telling politico-theological qualities of the Emperor: *virtus, iustitia, clementia,* and *pietas.* Tiberius granted the people of Tarraco permission to build a temple to the recently deceased Augustus. Another soon followed at Emerita. By 25 CE a hierarchy of priesthoods had been formally developed in the towns. The elite of the Spanish provinces manifested their loyalty to the Emperor through their public demonstrations of service and spectacles which, in turn, steered the goodwill of the poor towards the Imperial cult.[21]

In sum, Paul intended in Rom 15: 24, 28 to journey to what was an economic *miraculum.* Such a journey would appear to mimic the Roman advance begun centuries before. Does Paul's progress fit in with the contemporary advance of other competing religious movements[22] into this area of the Empire?

---

[20] Ibid., 134-35.

[21] Ibid., 155-59.

[22] As Keay (ibid., 164, 166) points out, the cult of Cybele reached Spain early in the first century, whereas that of Isis came in the latter part of the same century.

Moreover, it will be crucial to see how the extractive, centrist economic policy of Rome relates to Paul's plans. Georgi[23] has demonstrated already that Romans brings a counter-cultural theology into the debate over what constitutes the social basis of the οἰκουμένη. Does Paul's intent to come to Spain suggest a further counter-cultural move? Is this related to the possible displacement of Rome's centrality mentioned above?

5. The Myth of Eldorado

Surrounding and providing dramatic support for the concrete realization of Roman Imperial policy were the pre-existing mythic traditions regarding Iberia. The geographer Strabo provides an excellent example of these mythic dimensions in his account of Iberia. His descriptions easily move in a utopian direction:

> "(Baetica) takes pre-eminence in comparison with the entire inhabited world in respect to fertility and of the goodly products of land and sea." (3.1.7.)
>
> "Turdetania itself is marvellously blessed by nature; and while it produces all things, and likewise great quantities of them, these blessings are doubled by the facilities of exportations; for its surplus products are bartered off with ease because of the large number of merchant vessels." (3.2.4)
>
> "For the sea-routes all pass through a zone of fair weather, particularly if the sailor keeps to the high seas; and this fact is advantageous to the merchant-freighters." (3.2.5)
>
> "There are exported from Turdetania large quantities of grain and wine, and also olive oil, not only in large quantities, but also of the best quality." (3.2.6)
>
> "For the whole country of the Iberians is full of metals.... Up to the present moment, in fact, neither gold, nor silver, nor yet copper, nor iron, has been found anywhere in the world, in a natural state, either in such quantity or of such good quality....in the flooded districts gold-dust glitters." (3.2.8)

Citing Poseidonius' retelling of an extravagant story, Strabo does not at all discount it:

> "(Poseidonius) says that, when at a time the forests had been burned, the soil, since it was composed of silver and gold ores, melted and boiled out over the surface, because, as he says, every mountain and every hill is bullion heaped up there by

[23] *Theocracy*, 81-104.

> some prodigal fortune. And, in general, he says, anyone who has seen these regions would declare that they are everlasting storehouses of nature, or a never-failing treasury of an empire." (3.2.9)
>
> "But among the Artabrians, who live farthest on the north-west of Lusitania, the soil 'effloresces,' (Poseidonius) says, with silver, tin, and 'white gold.'" (3.2.9)

The magic mountains of myth turn real in Iberia:

> "Not very far from Castalo is also the mountain in which the Baetis is said to rise; it is called Silver Mountain on account of the silver-mines in it." (3.2.11)

Moreover, when Strabo enters into the mythic regions of the poets he can find some rational basis for such tradition. Even the poetical invention of Tartarus easily could refer to the regions about Tartessus. Strabo (3.2.12) can understand how through a slight alteration of letters Homer could mythically equate the place which is "farthermost in the west" (πρὸς δύσιν ἐσχάτη) with the region where the sun sets and night reigns (Hades). Real life serves as a model for his fantasy. Secondly, Strabo accepts the tales of the expeditions of Heracles, the Phoenicians, as well as those of Aeneas, Antenor, Diomedes, Menelaus et al. It appears evident to Strabo that the expedition of Odysseus was made to Iberia. This was the historical pretext for what happens poetically in the *Odyssey*. Indeed, Strabo exegetes *Od.* 4.563-568 in precisely such a fashion: "ἀλλά σ' ἐς Ἠλύσιον πεδίον καὶ πείρατα γαίης ἀθάνατοι πέμψουσιν, ὅθι ξανθὸς Ῥαδάμανθυς, τῇ περ ῥηίστη βιοτὴ πέλει ἀνθρώποισιν· οὐ νιφετὸς οὔτ' ἄρ χειμὼν πολὺς οὐδέ ποτ' ὄμβρος, ἀλλ' αἰεὶ Ζεφύροιο λιγὺ πνείοντος ἀήτας Ὠκεανὸς ἀνίησιν ἀναψύχειν ἀνθρώπους."

Strabo comments that the pure air and gentle breezes belong quite fittingly to Iberia, since it is both in the west and warm. The phrase "at the ends of the earth" also belongs to it, since this is where Homer has "mythically placed" Hades. The citation of Rhadamanthys additionally suggests to Strabo the association with Minos, "rendering decisions to the dead." He then goes on to support this by noting that later poets kept drilling these stories into peoples' ears with further tales of Heracles seeking the golden apples of the Hesperides (3.2.13).

Strabo continues his analysis of the sources of mythic material by pointing out that the informants of Homer were the Phoenicians. Since they occupied the best parts of Iberia before Homer and continued to do so until the Roman victory, they had ample time to spread the word concerning this fantastic territory. Strabo adds that some historians claimed that, when the Carthaginians began their campaign against Iberia, they found its people using "silver feeding-troughs and wine-jars" (3.2.14).

What is critical in this consideration of Strabo is that despite his rationalistic approach to the matter of Iberia he does not entirely lose the mythic dimension by suggesting explanations for the poetic "displacements." On the contrary, he actually builds a case for the reality of such utopian possibilities. If one follows his argument, one can see that he first prepares the reader with an extended exposition of the resources and riches of Iberia. It is only then that he introduces the mythic material, which he quickly alligns with the territory that he has just exposed. The conclusion that one reaches is hardly that the poets improved upon reality. Rather, one receives the distinct impression that reality, in this case, Iberia, is a three-dimensional utopia, or, better, a utopia-in-the-making. When one reads these pages through the eyes of Roman imperial policy, there is the exciting possiblity that Iberia is the place where the Roman experiment can prosper and provide the needed surplus for the *salus* of the world.

6. Israel and the "ends of the earth"

If we return to those passages mentioning "Tarshish" in the Hebrew Scriptures, we do not have to fall into an historicist trap. As noted above, scholars are divided over the actual locale referred to by "Tarshish." The point to be made here, however, is that the original locale may very well *not* have been the understanding of the first-century reader, including Paul. Just as Strabo contoured the text for his vision of the world, so also may have the Jewish reader of scripture. Indeed, when one considers how first century Jews read their sacred scrolls in light of their present experience and future hope (such as at Qumran), then it is quite unlikely that a mere historical reference would have been detected or desired. Rather, such exotic place names may well have led readers literally to the borders of their imagined worlds. At the same time this imaginative "displacement" would have been done in the hope of bringing about somehow that utopian vista.

Clearly "Tarshish" refers to the Phoenicia of Isa 23:1:

> "The oracle concerning Tyre. Wail, O ships of Tarshish, for Tyre is laid waste, without house or haven! From the land of Cyprus it is revealed to them."

Trito-Isaiah continues to play upon this Phoenician possibility. Yet in Isa 60:9 it is not clear that the term refers to Tyre itself. Perhaps the "silver and gold" mentioned already (Strabo 3.2.8) picks up an Iberian ring:

> "For the coastlands shall wait for me, the ships of Tarshish first, to bring your sons from far, their silver and gold with them, for the name of the LORD your God, and for the Holy One of Israel, because he has glorified you."

Jeremiah and Ezekial maintain the trade connection with Tarshish, featuring the exports of silver and gold. From our reading in Strabo 3.2.8 such descriptions sound quite familiar:

> "Beaten silver is brought from Tarshish, and gold from Uphaz. They are the work of the craftsman and of the hands of the goldsmith; their clothing is violet and purple; they are all the work of skilled men." (Jer 10:9)
>
> "Tarshish trafficked with you because of your great wealth of every kind; silver, iron, tin, and lead they exchanged for your wares." (Ezek 27:12)

But there is a further dimension to the prophetic writings. Such exotic places are mentioned in light of a new future. This future breaks in as a possibility for blessing or curse even to the non-Jews. In Ezek 38:13 the innocent foreigners threatened by the mythicized Gog (Babylon) cry out to their invaders who will be punished for doing evil:

> "Sheba and Dedan and the merchants of Tarshish and all its villages will say to you, 'Have you come to seize spoil? Have you assembled your hosts to carry off plunder, to carry away silver and gold, to take away cattle and goods, to seize great spoil?'"

Moreover, in Isa 66:19 we find a most interesting reversal of the diaspora effected by the Babylonian experience. The surviving expatriates will be a missionary source of Yahweh's glory among the goyyim:

> "I will set a sign among them. And from them I will send survivors to the nations, to Tarshish, Put, and Lud, who draw the bow, to Tubal and Javan, to the coastlands afar off, that have not

> heard my fame or seen my glory; and they shall declare my glory among the nations."

Isa 60 speaks of a reversal of fortunes as the foreign nations actually bring back to Israel not only the lost generations but sumptuous evidence of submission to the God of Israel:

> "For the coastlands shall wait for me, the ships of Tarshish first, to bring your sons from far, their silver and gold with them, for the name of the LORD your God, and for the Holy One of Israel, because he has glorified you. Foreigners shall build up your walls, and their kings shall minister to you; for in my wrath I smote you, but in my favor I have had mercy on you. Your gates shall be open continually; day and night they shall not be shut; that men may bring to you the wealth of the nations, with their kings led in procession." (9-11)

This vision of the *miraculum* does not end with the prophets. In *Praem. Poen.* 162 ff. Philo produces a most startling scenario of the conversion of those who had been scattered abroad "on the farthest boundaries of the earth" (ἐν ἐσχατιαῖς γῆς). In fact, he builds upon Deut 30:3-5:

> "...then the LORD your God will restore your fortunes, and have compassion upon you, and he will gather you again from all the peoples where the LORD your God has scattered you. If your outcasts are in the uttermost parts of heaven, from there the LORD your God will gather you, and from there he will fetch you; and the LORD your God will bring you into the land which your fathers possessed, that you may possess it; and he will make you more prosperous and numerous than your fathers."

Philo paraphrases Deut 30:3-5 thus:

> "For even though they dwell in the farthest ends of the earth, in slavery to those who led them away captive, one signal, as it were, one day will bring liberty to all. This conversion in a body to virtue will strike awe into their masters, who will set them free, ashamed to rule over better men than themselves." (164)

Philo has changed the "utmost parts of the heavens" to "the farthest ends of the earth." Ἐσχατιά also can be understood as "coastlands," suggesting thereby a possible linkage with Isa 60:9. In either case we can see that his utopian vision moves horizontally as well as vertically (as indicated later in *Praem. Poen.* 168). Continuing on a horizontal plane, this initial freedom is followed by a universal pilgrimage of those who had been scattered "in Greece and the outside world over the islands and continents (165)." From exile they come home guided by a "divine vision" and aided by the kindness of God, the intercessions of the "founders of the race," and the internal reformation within each person (166-167). Upon their return home, ruined cities will be restored, the barren will be fruitful, and desolate land inhabited. All this flows (vertically) from the gracious bounties of God, who gives to all a deep stream of wealth leaving no room for envy (168). A cosmic reversal occurs with miscarriages of justice finally being righted (170). Such a transformation, when seen rooted in the souls of individuals, serves as the basis for nations to grow into a teeming society (πολυανθρωπίαν, 172).

Philo has married the prophetic eschatology to the utopian dreams of the first-century world. His utopian prospect is inherently dramatic, with a major reversal and an enormous horizontal movement from the ends of the earth to "home." Significantly this startling pilgrimage leads to the benefactions desired by both the hellenistic Jewish mission and the imperial ideology.[24]

What we can say, then, is that by the first century the utopian resources were present in the Jewish prophetic tradition for anyone to use with an eye towards the transformation of the world. Distances in time as well as space seemingly could be overcome if the possibility presented itself. Even the mystic Philo indulges in a utopian exercise, an Alexandrian "New World Symphony." Despite the strong probability that there were no Jewish settlements in Spain prior to the last quarter of the first or early second century CE, the wherewithal to imagine the real was quite accessible and awaiting someone who would dare to touch those "farthest shores."

7. Paul's Pre-Roman Intimations

Paul's utopian stance was not born with the Letter to the Romans. We must look, first of all, into earlier Pauline material to catch glimpses of this developing trajectory. Thus, we find in 1 Thess 1:8 something more than just a rhetorical flourish. Within his thanksgiving Paul declares that the trust which the Thessalonians have towards God has become universally known (ἐν παντὶ τόπῳ). Although this most likely means the

[24] See Georgi, *Theocracy*, 81-85.

areas beyond Achaia and Macedonia, the hyperbole points to Paul's conviction that the energies unleashed through the preaching of the "Word of the Lord" are active, on the move into wider, unspecified regions. Already we have a grass-roots ground swell of the divine momentum. This forward movement is spurred on by the vision of the coming end in 1 Thess 4:13-18. It is the future itself which impels both the community and Paul. On the other hand, as Georgi[25] rightly sees, the revolution is underway where the people themselves are now equipped with what once belonged solely to the divine warrior. A realized eschatology, competing with that of the Empire, takes a clear stand.

In Galatians Paul takes on what were considered crucial forces in the constitution of the ancient world: law and tradition. Through parody, argument, and humor[26] Paul shakes up what would be the basic assumptions of that world. For the sake of brevity I quote from my earlier investigation:

> "Paul's letter to the Galatians thus paints in broad, mythic strokes the lifeworlds of those who would live either ἐξ ἔργων νόμου or ἐξ ἀκοῆς πίστεως. His subsequent argument continues to reinforce this double vision of tradition. Not only in temporal terms but even in spatial images does he seek to show the implications of each lifeworld for the Galatian communities. What appears, then, at first to be a matter of cultic or religious concern becomes very quickly an issue which determines how one interprets the very powers and forces of existence."[27]

With the Corinthian correspondence we find Paul continuing to develop his far-ranging vision. Already in 1 Cor 1:2 we find the possibilities of a universal appeal (cf. Rom 10:12-13) from every place to a counter-cultural sovereign. In 1 Cor 1:26-29 the fundamental cultural value of honor is overturned. V.28 is particularly significant, suggesting that even the "nothings of this world" have a place in the divine plan. Could this be the seed for the inverted argument of Romans 9:25-26?[28] Further, Georgi has pointed out the political potential in the participatory democracy of the body of the Anointed.[29]

---

[25] Ibid., 27-30.

[26] Ibid., 49-51.

[27] Arthur J. Dewey, *Spirit and Letter in Paul*, Harvard University Doctoral Dissertation, 1982 (forthcoming from Edwin Mellen Press) 86.

[28] Could Paul have followed this through in viewing his Spanish mission precisely as a call to those who are not?

[29] See his *Theocracy*, 59-61.

Now it is in the first fragment of Second Corinthians (2:14-6:13; 7:2-4) where Paul, under the influence of his opposition, presents an image of a universal triumphal procession of revelatory force:

> "But return the favor to God who always leads us in triumph in the sphere of the Anointed and reveals through us everywhere the scent of his knowledge" (2 Cor 2:14).

This sense of revelation comes home in 2 Cor 4:6, where Paul declares that what is being communicated is the very act of creation. Genesis 1:3 is happening now within the communication to and from the Corinthian community. Such a staggering vision continues to build in 2 Cor 5:17, where the foundation of a new world can be found in the reconciling actions of the community of the Anointed.[30]

In the second fragment of 2 Cor (10-13) we can detect further utopian reaches. In defending his relationship with the Corinthians, Paul argues that he has not overstepped the κανών of his labor. His confidence is based upon the economics of the eschatological missionary situation.[31] Recognizing that the missionary situation partakes of transcendent infusion (2 Cor 10:15), he hopes that his "field" will increase through this transcendent influence so that he might preach in "areas beyond," without having to compete with another missionary (2 Cor 10:15-17).

In regard to the utopian elements in 2 Cor 8 and 9 we need to recall Georgi's work on the collection for Jerusalem. As Georgi points out, the collection is seen by Paul within the sphere of divine activity:

> "[T]he Creator is allowing the eschatological miracle of the pilgrimage of the peoples to Jerusalem to coincide with the collection of Pauline congregations (consisting in the majority of Gentiles) taken up for the Jesus-believing congregations in Jerusalem. The collected assets (in fact a donation from God himself) will certainly increase under the hands of the Gentile believers and produce blessings of far-reaching results even for these Gentile believers. Those who had been heathens have in the collection revealed that they belong to God's sphere of salvation."[32]

---

[30] Here the competition with the claims of the tradition regarding Alexander the Great becomes evident (See Georgi, *Theocracy*, 65-66).

[31] See Dewey, *HTR* 78 (1985), 215.

[32] *Remembering the Poor: The History of Paul's Collection for Jerusalem* (Nashville: Abingdon, 1992) 101.

Finally, the utopian elements are quite clear in Phil 2:9-11. However, this universal exaltation is quite different from that of Alexander the Great or Augustus.[33] (Georgi, 1964, 1991). Jesus becomes "first among equals" by becoming subject to the limits of the human condition. Indeed, the very means of his death by a Roman cross throw an unsubtle challenge to the Imperial vision of the world. Moreover, as Georgi carefully observes,[34] the impact of this process is the democratization of the "stars" of this world. No longer is preeminence left to the elite; rather, those who find themselves in solidarity with the one who has given all have the possibility of exercising genuine human responsibility for the world.

8. The Roadmap of Romans

In Romans Paul not only maintains his utopian momentum but actually increases it to another level. The length of Romans suggests this. Unlike 1 Cor, Romans is not a letter written to a known community regarding particular problems upon which Paul gives specific advice. The fact that Paul is addressing unknown Jesus-believers has been addressed considerably since Baur. What interests us here is to see what the utopian signs are within this letter. Paul obviously is attempting to persuade his Roman audience not only to give him a hearing but to provide a base of operations for further missionary effort. Is it the case that Paul is delivering a resumé of his previous experiments, both theoretical and practical, for their inspection? In other words, does this letter function as a means of introduction and recommendation simultaneously? While this may seem to be the ostensible function of Romans since Paul does pick up many threads from previous correspondence, these threads, as we shall see, are woven upon a different, and larger, frame of thought. Perhaps the question might be better addressed by asking how and why Paul attempts to persuade his audience to join him on this new

---

[33] See Dieter Georgi, "Der vorpaulinische Hymnus Phil. 2,6-11," in Erich Dinkler and Hartwig Thyen, eds., *Zeit und Geschichte: Dankesgabe an Rudolf Bultmann zum 80. Geburtstag* (Tübingen: Mohr, 1964) 263-93; idem, *Theocracy*.

[34] *Theocracy*, 76.

extension of his trek. As mentioned at the outset, I consider the matter of Spain not something which is merely tossed in at the end of the letter to fill in the blanks for those at Rome who want to know Paul's itinerary. Rather, the entire letter is a renewed exercise of the utopian imagination of Paul, whose strategy is to win over not simply an audience but conspirators willing to participate in the longed-for *miraculum* coming to life right before their eyes and ears. The following reading of Romans comes from that enlargened perspective. Underlying this investigation will be the ever-lurking question: What happens to this material when we see it from the perspective of the West? What forces emerge, what impressions surface, what images take on a new shape, when a world-wide horizon, as suggested from the earlier argument, is assumed?

From the outset Paul's extremely formal salutation (1:1-6) announces a very specific challenge to the Imperial social gospel within a universal scope. Right from the start there is a motif of displacement. Here is a letter, received in the heart of the Empire, that throws down the gauntlet as to who is the genuine sovereign of the world. Georgi rightly puts it,

> "Paul's gospel enters into critical dialogue with the good news that universal peace has been achieved by the miracle at Actium"[35]

Indeed, Paul understands his role to be that of communicating this message to "all the nations" (1:5). In his attempt to win the Romans' attention, Paul declares in his thanksgiving to God that the trust of the Roman Jesus-believers is announced "in all the world" (1:8). It is also significant that he states somewhat ambiguously that he would share with them some χάρισμα to strengthen them so that they might be mutually encouraged by each other's trust (1:11-12). He then goes on to say that he wants to visit them in order finally to "get some yield out of them" and the rest of the "nations" (1:13). He is, in the typical terms of hellenistic propaganda for the unity of humanity, under obligation to "Greeks and barbarians" (1:14). His visit to Rome becomes, therefore, an instance of this universal responsibility.

Paul then points to the universality of the power of the gospel. While he does write "to the Jew first and also to the

---

[35] Ibid., 87.

Greek" (1:16), suggesting the probable pattern of his earlier mission work, it is not to be assumed that this pattern is going to continue, either in the letter itself or in the *modus operandi* of Paul.

The matter of universality continues to unfold in 1:18-3:20, where Paul produces a complex and extended diatribe to demonstrate that the usual assumptions concerning the power of the law to create and to determine what authentic humanity is about are subject to fundamental critique.[36] Two items emerge: first, the very force which both Roman and hellenistic Jew would assume could build and control the world, that is, the law, can beget only critical chaos; second, the impetus to name the primordial human comes directly into the discussion.

The momentum towards the universal continues with the conclusion Paul reaches in 3:29-30. The universality of the God of Israel touches even the Gentiles. This God is truly God of all. It is important to see that only here does the figure of Abraham enter the discussion. While bringing forward his reflections from Gal 3, Paul has prepared a much more universal base for his argument (1:18-3:31). Indeed, he expands on his Galatians material by introducing time (4:11) as well as the note of world inheritance (4:13) for all (4:16) into the picture. He then adds that Abraham is not called the "father of many nations" for no purpose (4:17); rather, he switches the question of a single offspring (Gal 3:16) to the promise of numerous descendants despite appearances to the contrary (4:18). Paul makes it quite clear that these words were written for contemporary ears (4:24). Utopia has a foothold.

In Rom 5:6-8 Paul understands the Anointed's act of solidarity as bringing about the deliverance of all human beings (since all are condemned, 3:10-18). This is then followed by pushing matters back in time, even before the giving of the Law (5:12ff.). The note of the primordial human, already articulated in 1:18-2:29, now recurs under the mythological motif of Adam. This liberation from a fated past (5:12-21) and for a life of genuine responsibility (6:1-23) finds a further exploration in chs.7-8. Here we see how the world of convention (ὁ νόμος), where the law serves apparently as the instru-

[36] See Dewey, *Spirit and Letter in Paul*, 230.

ment of highest human order and control, is exposed as inherently self-contradictory and lethal. Ironically, the forces of chaos and death, which rule over those who give themselves to this construction of the world, are unmasked in Paul's personified diatribe.[37] On the other hand, 8:2-39 presents the radically different possibility for those in the sphere of the Anointed. The "new creation" intimated in 2 Cor and Gal breaks through in communal and cosmic proportions. Under the impulse of this new universal vision, Paul explores the landscape of this utopia coming to life. Both communal or liturgical (e.g., 8:14-17) and apocalyptic language (8:18-25) meet in a revolutionary language-experiment that ends with a sweeping utopian tour de force (8:31-39). Nature itself becomes an expectant collaborator with the children of God as they wait patiently in hope. No forces, neither of time nor space, earthly or heavenly, can prove to be an obstacle to the utopian reach of this life together (8:37-39). In other words the deepest and longest hopes of humanity can no longer be ultimately thwarted.

This Pauline "Ode to Joy" is sobered considerably by the problem of Israel's non-acceptance of the gospel. The question of the Jewish rejection becomes critical for Paul, not simply because he is going shortly to Jerusalem with the collection for the poor, but because this experience of rejection itself needs to be located within his emerging utopian vision (which includes his theology of the collection). How can such a magnificent picture in Rom 8 find connection with the problems in Rom 9-11? What Paul does is to work through the inherent social ambiguity in which he finds himself. He refuses to accept exclusivistic solutions, including the time-honored theory of the remnant. In fact, the universal access to the Lord (the very heart of Deut 30:11-14), experienced in actual worship, allows Paul to discern that there is no distinction between Jew and Gentile. Alexander the Great's dream of founding a civilized world, where distinctions are no longer obstacles to human life,[38] becomes real on the lips of anyone who appeals to the Lord (10:12-13). Paul resolutely and creatively focuses upon the negative elements and turns

[37] Ibid., 241-259.

[38] See Arthur J. Dewey, "A Re-hearing of Romans 10:1-15," *SBLSP* (Atlanta: Scholars Press, 1990) 273-282, especially 277.

them into possible utopian fulcrums. The rejection by the Jews becomes an opportunity for the Gentiles, which, in turn, will provoke his fellow Jews to jealousy.[39] The very basis for missionary competition in the ancient world, grounded in the lethal self-comparisons Paul decries (2 Cor 10:12), may well disclose a further possibility, namely, the salvation of all of Israel (11:25). These points have even more force if we consider that Paul is anticipating going into what is most probably a non-Jewish area—Spain. Just as the "nobodies" have already begun to listen and trust his message (9:25-26), so now he intends to go "to the ends of the earth (10:8b)" to "non-people" who did not even ask for God (10:20). The missionary intention of Paul is so provocative that it may well startle his fellow Jews into enlightenment (10:2; 11:13-15). Furthermore, this entire speculation by Paul falls under the mystery of God's merciful intent for all humanity. Although Paul does not discern any "final solution," he does sketch out a possible itinerary for the stumbling steps of humanity. His primary negative experiences become the basis for an experimental re-mapping of human relationships.

In Rom 12-14 we find how Paul weds praxis to his utopian vision. In other words, the communal possibilities disclosed in Rom 8 come home in the day-to-day building up of the community. In fact, genuine worship (12:1) occurs in critical and responsible service to one another (12). Even the Empire falls under this practical vision (13:1-7). As Georgi[40] observes, this is a throwback to Jewish tradition of the republican period. What seems to so many interpreters as a simple justification of the state is actually a subtle criticism which undermines the centralist ideology of Caesarism.

When we turn to the final chapter of Romans, we see Paul moving from his practical exhortation (15:1-2) to a further elaboration of the solidarity of the Anointed with those who are under reproach. Rom 15:3 puts the words of Ps 69:9 on the lips of the Anointed. Thereupon Paul makes an interesting comment. Whatever was literally "fore-written" was written for the present (Cf. Gal 3:1, 8). In other words, the present reader

---

[39] See idem, "Outlaw/In-Law: Social-Historical Observations on Romans 9-11," Proceedings, *EGLBS* 8 (1988) 101-15.

[40] *Theocracy*, 102.

of scripture discovers the future in the past traditions. This was done so that people might have hope through the "encouragement of the scriptures" (15:4). Such reasoning would permit the interpretation of Ps 69:9 but it would not necessarily end there. As we shall see there is an "unfinished" capacity to such material which can be further mined. Indeed, in v.5 we see that the divine supplies the energy for being in harmony (to be understood with its musical connotation) with the Anointed (cf. Phil 2:5) so that people can sing in worship, glorifying God, their Patron, and the Anointed Lord Jesus (v.6). The words of Ps 69:9 thus could be heard on the lips of all.

Vv.7-13 are crucial for understanding the remaining part of chapter 15, for here Paul gives us a most extraordinary reading of scripture. His understanding of the implications of justification in Christ leads to a re-envisioning of scripture. First, he exhorts his listeners to become partners (προσλαμβάνω) with one another, inasmuch as the Anointed has brought them aboard with him. No discrimination or distinction is possible any longer. The Anointed has become, as Georgi puts it so well, "the archetype of solidarity."[41] But this action is interpreted by Paul in vv.8-9a. The Anointed becomes a servant to those of the circumcision on behalf of the truth of God for a double purpose: to confirm the promises of the fathers and (to allow) the Gentiles to glorify God for his mercy. This formulation is not far from what we have seen in Gal 3: 13-14. Obviously what is missing in Romans is the concern from Gal for the "curse." Here Paul is interested in going in another direction, which is made quite apparent in his citation of a series of scriptural verses. Abraham is no longer important. As we have seen before in Romans, the more primordial human figure anticipates, displaces, or revises the specific type, such as Abraham. At the moment Paul is interested in moving into the widest possible human direction.

At this point Paul gives his listeners four scriptural citations (Ps 18:49; Deut 32:43; Ps 117:1; Isa 11:10). Here we have, in Paul's understanding of scripture (15:4), four promises of the fathers (15:8b). The first citation is curiously ambiguous. Who is the "I" giving praise among the Gentiles (v.9b)? One

[41] Ibid., 103.

possibility is that this refers immediately back to the experience of the Romans in v.6. They would be praising the Lord in the midst of the Gentile world. But it could also suggest, in a more indirect fashion, Paul. What Paul probably means is that such distinctions do not really matter. Such a verse could be sung by one and all in the midst of the nations. The second quotation is most interesting since it combines the Gentiles with the people of Israel. Here a most hopeful situation is intimated, far beyond the jealousy spoken of in 9-11. The third citation, taken from a remarkably brief psalm, focuses upon the universal praise of God by all the nations. The repeated "all" should not be overlooked. Finally, the Isaianic citation is quite pregnant with possibilities. First of all, we have a direct reference to a utopian royal figure, thereby continuing Romans counter-theology. Second, his "rising" to rule may hearken back to Rom 1:4, where Jesus is enthroned as Son of God by his resurrection. Third, this royal figure becomes an embodiment of the hope of the Gentiles. If we put all these quotations together, if we allow them to make their rounds in our ears, we have a variety of voices propelling those who hear them into ever-widening directions. Certainly not all the Gentiles are in Rome, nor can one sing praise to the Lord only in Rome among the Gentiles. In effect, there is by the very momentum of these verses an unfinished quality which demands confirmation. If the Anointed has already become a servant to confirm these promises, and if these words are not totally fulfilled, then what does this mean? It means that there is a surplus of intent within the scriptures, which will continue to work upon and impel those who will mine them. Indeed, the concluding prayer of Paul for his listeners is precisely that the God of hope may grant them a surplus of hope.

Paul continues to think in terms of this divine surplus in v.14, where the Jesus-believers can function in solidarity with one another directly from that output. However, in vv.15-16 Paul makes a rather surprising statement. First, he says that he has written rather boldly to remind them of his appointed function as λειτουργός to the Gentiles. The language of v.16 makes it unmistakable that Paul is using cultic terminology. What is remarkable is that he would describe his service to the Gentiles in such priestly terms. From what we could have gathered in Rom 9-11, such service would have had a distasteful or taboo aspect to it from a Jewish perspective. Indeed, in taking over such service, Paul is risking being considered socially impure. Thus, to use such cultic language upsets the normal Jewish assumptions. For Paul it is indeed a matter of honor (v.17). But for many it would seem to be a fool's mission. Of course, that would be exactly how Paul understands the way in which the Anointed has entered into solidarity with sinful humanity (5:6-8). As we shall see, Paul is joining company with those who are not, who are at the very end of the earth, the farthest in distance from the center of the Jewish world — Jerusalem. This sense of solidarity with the Anointed restrains Paul from mentioning anything but that which the Anointed works through him (v.18), thereby keeping Paul from boasting. Yet, he does touch on the "signs and wonders" (v.19) that have occurred during his mission in the eastern Mediterranean. This successfully enlargening mission brings him to desire to spread the message where the name of the Anointed has not been uttered. As he has already stated in 2 Cor 10:15-16, he is not wont to poach in another's territory. Rather, he would go where no Jesus-missionary has gone before (v.20; cf. Isa 52:15). Thus, even before he mentions Spain directly, the Roman listeners are led to see that his line of vision extends far beyond them. In fact, the citation of Isa 52:15 would suggest a further unfinished promise that demands some human realization.

Paul then suggests that because of such enormous labors he has not had the opportunity of visiting the Roman communities (v.22), but now he recognizes the fact that he no longer has any τόπος in those regions. Such a statement can be read on two levels. Certainly it refers to the fact that Paul considers his field of operations "worked out" and that it is time to move on. But is that all? Could the τόπος also provide us with another clue to Paul's utopian character? It would seem so since the τόπος he chooses to work is not simply Rome but Spain itself (v.24). Furthermore, there is a decided relationship between his intended journey via Rome to Spain and the collection for the poor in Jerusalem. Not only is there the cycle of χάρις, where the interdependence of the Gentiles and the Jewish Jesus believers will be played out. The successful completion of this mission will continue to increase the divine surplus of χάρις, such that Paul can be confident of journeying to Spain through Rome in the fulness of the blessing of the Anointed. This most likely is the χάρισμα alluded to in 1:11.

But it is not simply an uninterpreted cycle of divine energy. This χάρις will allow for the mutual encouragement of one another, such that the Romans can "send him off" (v.24) to Spain. This well may refer to material support. However, it becomes abundantly clear from what Paul has written to the Romans that he would want their understanding in his missionary effort (15:15). For Paul would invite them to come with him, perhaps even provide company for him, in this utopian venture (cf. *Od* 4.563-568). He is asking them to support him as he enters territory basically unknown to Jewish missionaries and other other religious competitors from the eastern Mediterranean. Do they understand that, in Paul's estimation, they are all part of an ever-widening arena of triumph? Would they catch the utopian clues that he has been leaving throughout the letter? Were they excited by his re-mapping of the fundamental images of being human in the first century? Would they have accepted his surprising revision of Jewish missionary thinking as well as his indirect critique of the Imperial gospel? Would they follow him through all the ins and outs of his ever-widening roadmap for humanity?

Such questions facing the Roman communities lead to further considerations. Paul's envisioned journey to Spain displaces the centrality of Rome on the geographical and political plane. Here we have a move to the "margins." This is quite in keeping with Paul's understanding of a God who enters into the conditions of human life, especially a God who descends to the depths. Now the movement is a lateral one. This imagines the collapse of the existing social pyramid, not only from the top to the bottom but now from the center to the edge. Further, Georgi has argued that Paul is taking on the Roman state religion, that is, the utopian hopes of Rome. If we now add Spain, we see that Paul's breadth of vision extends to the very borders of the Roman dream. With Spain comes the possibility of collision, where Roman economic dreams of an extractive economy would come directly up against the revision of Paul's sense of God's solidarity (δικαιοσύνη) with humanity (and with the creation). One easily can envision a war of utopian proportions in the making.

9. Paul's Letter to Spain

In a profound sense Paul's letter to Spain already exists; it can be found, as I have been suggesting, in the intimations of Paul's extant letters. In fact, one can continue to play Paul's game of unfinished or surplus meaning with the very texts he used. For example, if we were to examine more carefully Isa 11:10 within its own surrounding verses, we could see some interesting possibilities of where Paul would go with his mission to Spain. First of all Isa 11:11 would reinforce the return from the "coastlands." Second, the royal figure would raise a "sign" for the "nations" and gather the outcasts (11:12). Third, jealousy would cease to exist within Israel (11:13). Fourth, both the peoples of the east and the west would be "plundered" (11:14). Fifth, there would be a miraculous act, whereby people would cross the waters dryshod and a highway for the people would appear. In other words, the Exodus would come alive in universal and novel fashion. Likewise, in Isa 52 (which Paul cites in Rom 2:24; 10:15; 15:21) we also could see the note that "all the earth" would see the salvation of the Lord (52:10); that this work could be considered cultic, that is, holy (52:11); and that this action would be part of a surprising event (52:15).

With these texts in mind one could continue to speculate as to the way in which the hoped-for Gentiles' acceptance of the message would provoke a Jewish reconsideration. Both Paul and Philo (*Praem. Poen.* 162 ff.) can imagine a stupendous reversal of cosmic proportions. However, in contrast to Philo, Paul sees himself already on the path of the eschatological momentum; he is, in fact, carrying forward the *surplus* of χάρις and allowing it through his missionary effort to have greater and greater effect. Already in Romans Paul suggests that nothing less than the salvation of Israel is expected. To anticipate a positive response from the "ends of the earth" would play upon the prophetic possibilities (especially Isa 60) mentioned above. Nothing less than the final consummation (the *Totum*) is desired. In addition Paul consistently introduces the negative aspects of experience into the utopian drive for meaning in order to continue to ride the wave of divine benefaction, while God continues to remain in faithful solidarity with humanity throughout this mission. Thus, Paul would be open to the questions what sort of contact he would have made with Spain and what did he learn from that initial experience. It would seem that Paul would permit himself to be surprised enough even to re-imagine his utopian roadmap.

Furthermore, what would have happened if Paul had brought such a counter-cultural gospel to a land that staggered many ancient imaginations? Would the Roman Spaniards have appreciated a world map that no longer had a center which could claim domination? Moreover, Paul did not intend to settle down in Rome. But neither was Spain his final destination. Paul sought total restoration. How comfortable would the Roman Spaniards have been with this utopian topos? Ironically this appreciation of what amounts to be no permanent center is part and parcel of the modern cosmological dilemma. Yet, unlike Paul's understanding, there is little utopian resolve today to correspond to such physical theory.

But that is not it exactly, for the letter to Spain is a communication to the New World, to those who would join with Paul in the conspiracy of creation over against dead-end economic grab bags. Perhaps the letter is best left unwritten in this sense: it prevents us from thinking that the letters of Paul contain the momentum and we simply look up the meaning. For the letter to be sent and received there must be engagement at a primordial level, where dreams and hopes meet, collide, and compete for human space. The letter to Spain is heard every time we engage in this co-operative life together, every time someone can re-create the givens of a culture, which promise everything but deliver death. The letter to Spain is understood every time fundamental human hopes emerge, are articulated, and acted upon.

Paul's letter to Spain is his unfinished symphony. This is better than a completed letter since that may well suggest a note of individual success, of personal righteousness. Paul would have distanced himself greatly from that position. For it would have short-circuited the divine current of χάρις. Ironically it may be better for us that Paul was cut off in the midst of his dream—not killing the dream but provoking others to discover how the dream can continue to come alive for humanity and, thus, through such very human means, demonstrate the provocative power of the resurrection.

Paul's letter to Spain is still underway whenever we catch the impetus of his missionary imagination, his utopian sense, whenever we can learn to press to the margin, to see that the action of transcendence occurs beyond the presumed centers of power. This essay has not been an attempt to conjure the ghost of Paul, to construct a museumpiece for our admiration and wonder, but an attempt to participate in envisioning the future that he was endeavoring to open up. This is what Dieter Georgi has been doing throughout his career, sensing the background, detecting the intimations that either go off the page or have never been concretely captured on the page. As the "first student of his classes," he has taught again and again that continuing the conversation with Paul does not mean imitating what he did but discerning the direction of his imagination.

Although one does not really know another unless one knows the other's future, many theologians traditionally have stopped asking Paul about his future. In so doing the academy has kept him "cribbed, cabined and confined" (Shakespeare, *Macbeth* III.IV.24) in Rome. This essay attempts to rewire the short-circuiting of Paul's hope by challenging his would-be readers to discern his future as well as their own. For I would suspect that from his unfinished "remains" Paul refuses to join in the lifeless stockpiling of the past or in the self-defensive construction of success at another's expense. Instead, he remains trusting and hopeful, a suggestive part of the unknown, the human incognito at the edge of our imagination, until the promises of utopia have been confirmed.

PAUL AND OPPONENTS IN 2 COR 10-13 – *THEIOI ANDRES* AND SPIRITUAL GUIDES[1]

Anitra Bingham Kolenkow
(Dominican School of Philosophy and Theology,
Graduate Theological Union, Berkeley, California)

In some New Testament scholarship Paul is a symbol of those early Christians who followed the model of a suffering Christ. In contrast Paul's opponents in 2 Cor 10-13 are seen as θεῖοι ἄνδρες,[2] who seek a power based exclusively on miracles and visions. At most, it is said, Paul's boasting in 2 Corinthians is done as an ironic contrast to that of his opponents. Further, it is argued that there is no picture of suffering apostleship which would be agreed upon by Paul and his opponents in 2 Cor 10-13.[3]

The catalogue of 2 Cor 11-12 is a *crux interpretum* for this argument – a passage often considered the particular result of a conflict between two disparate forces. However, 2 Cor 11-12 (and particularly 11:23-29) also may be used to argue that both Paul and his opponents agree upon a general standard of

---

[1] In appreciation of Dieter Georgi, especially of his fostering diversity and questions. This is a characteristic of true teaching and responsible scholarship. He encouraged and allowed us to be the "grains of sand in the mandarin's eye" (according to the story he once told us). His Frankfurt students tell me he continues in this way.

[2] This term (used by Georgi) is useful even if controversial because scholarship sees it as uncommon in the ancient world.

[3] The presentation of Dieter Georgi (*Die Gegner des Paulus im 2 Korintherbrief: Studien zur religiösen Propaganda in der Spätantike* [WMANT 11; Neukirchen-Vluyn: Neukirchener, 1964]), which provided both a consideration of Jewish missionary ethos and a viable dichotomy between Paul and his opponents, for a while drowned out the work of those who felt that the differences between Paul and his opponents were not that irreconcilable. Cf. Adolf von Schlatter (*Die Korinthische Theologie* [BFCTh 18:2; Gütersloh: C. Bertelsmann, 1914] 110, 107), Ernst Käsemann ("Die Legitimatät des Apostels," *ZNW* 41 [1942] 42, 54) and Walter Schmithals (*The Office of the Apostle in the Early Church* [Nashville: Abingdon, 1969] 224). I disagree with Schmithals (ibid., 221) that Paul's opponents accept no money (cf. 2 Cor 11:20-21), although he is correct about 1 Cor. 9:4ff (222) with respect to making a living by the gospel as a "non compulsory-personal decision" (1 Cor 9:15). For the history of research see John Fitzgerald, *Cracks in an Earthen Vessel* (SBLDS 95; Atlanta: Scholars' Press, 1988) 7-31.

"suffering apostleship." In order to confirm this point the characteristic virtues of such a catalogue should be found either (or both) in Paul's other discussions of apostleship, or (and) in the presentations of apostleship coupled with περιστάσις catalogues which occur outside of the Pauline corpus. In fact, this tradition of suffering often is tied to the performance of miracles. The critic must discuss, therefore, both the common structures of Pauline boasts in suffering as well as the tradition of Christian περιστάσις literature particularly as it is related to miracle working.[4] The paper then will employ this study to illumine the peculiarities of 2 Cor 10-13 and their anthropological history-of-religions situation. This especially concerns the anthropology of spiritual guidance which includes many of the characteristics argued about by Paul and his opponents.

I. The Boasting Catalogue of 2 Cor 11:22-12:10 – What Picture Does It Give of Paul and His Opponents?

2 Cor 11-12 is used to support the position that the opponents of 2 Cor 10-13 were θεῖοι ἄνδρες who lacked a standard of apostolic suffering – and thus may be contrasted to Paul whose apostolic virtue *is* suffering. In this argument it is assumed that the opponents would not agree with Paul about the importance of suffering *and* that, in 2 Cor 12:1-9 and 12, Paul merely is making a boast in miracles like that which his opponents had made. Dieter Georgi's argument in *Die Gegner des Paulus im 2 Korintherbrief* often serves as the basis of this picture. However, the problem with positing such a dichotomy (at least in relation to suffering) becomes evident in the discussion of 2 Cor 11:23, where Paul compares himself to his opponents saying: "Are they servants of Christ? I am a better one with far greater labors...." In his analysis of this passage, Georgi says Paul is not claiming, "I am, even more than the opponents, a representative of Christ because I suffer more than they do." Rather, Georgi says Paul is asserting, "I am an apostle of Christ because I, in contrast to them, can boast in suffering."[5] However, this contrast is itself problematic. When

[4] Signs of a true apostle (2 Cor 12:12-13) have been done (even if not rewarded). Miracles are the normal basis of exchange for support.

[5] See Georgi, *Die Gegner*, 295.

Paul claims that he suffers more than the opponents do (and admits at the same time that he is talking like a madman) Paul actually does say what some exegetes assert that he is not saying. There is no "in contrast" implied between Paul and his opponents. The use of "far greater, far more" (περισσότερος) shows (as Schlatter, Käsemann, and others have noted)[6] that Paul is taking up a common boast or theme which also is used by his opponents. Paul claims that he, Paul, is superior in the labors and sufferings required of all apostles.

The understanding that the opponents of Paul in 2 Cor 10-13 have a concept of "suffering apostleship" similar to Paul's own is strengthened further both by Paul's general presentation of the opponents in 2 Cor 10-13 and by the structure of his own boasting in 2 Cor 11-12. In 2 Cor 10:12, Paul speaks of his opponents as ones who measure themselves by one another. In 11:12, part of the beginning of Paul's "boasting," the rival apostles are presented as saying that they work on the *same* terms as Paul does. They disguise themselves as apostles of Christ (11:13). Paul then says he will boast in a worldly way as they do, and he makes the claim, "Whatever anyone dares boast of, I also will boast of." This comparison is the context of his boasting; accordingly, one would expect that what Paul emphasizes, when he is boasting and speaking like a madman, is that which his opponents likewise emphasize. What has been called "irony" is actually (as Paul says in 2 Cor 10:12) defense on the same terms.

In his boast Paul makes a short introductory vaunt about his Jewishness. He then makes an extended boast (11:23 – 12:10), which begins and ends with περιστάσις catalogues of boasting in suffering. Included in this long boast is a rather short defensive claim of weakness ("who is weak and I am not weak..."; cf. also 1 Cor 9:22, 2 Cor 8:9),[7] together with a description of someone's vision of the Lord (12:2-4) and an account of a revelation to Paul (which is brought in under the *topos* of a description of weakness). The boasting, as noted, is completed by another περιστάσις catalogue (12:10).[8] The boasting

---

[6] Cf. n. 3 above.

[7] Identification is a typical feature of apostles (cf. 1 Cor 9:22) and a characteristic of Christ (2 Cor 8:9). The one who is sent must resemble those to whom he is sent – and yet have possess power (e.g., 2 Cor 4:10-11).

[8] See Rudolf Bultmann (*Der Stil der paulinischen Predigt und die kynisch-stoische Diatribe* [FRLANT 13; Göttingen: Vandenhoeck & Ruprecht, 1910] 78). Bultmann also notes the section 11:16 -12:10.

completed, Paul makes a small apology for having done so, saying he had been compelled to it. In fact, the note about "the signs of the true apostle" as well as the note about not burdening the community are parts of the apology and not the boast. Moreover, it is not even clear that the opponents particularly boast in "signs" except for revelations, since Paul's boast in "signs" is placed outside of the "boast" pattern. Thus, if one seeks the basic form of boasting common to both Paul and his opponents, the structure of 2 Cor 11:22 – 12:10 provides the material for which one should seek parallels.

II. Boasting and ΠΕΡΙΣΤΑΣΙς Catalogues

If Paul is drawing on general structures and materials of apostolic boasting in suffering, one might expect to find the pattern of such descriptions of suffering apostleship elsewhere. That is, they would not be confined exclusively to the opponents in 2 Cor 10-13. Although the structures might differ in detail, the types of material and categories should be sufficiently similar to show that in 2 Cor 10-12 Paul is not producing a unique structure of "boasting in suffering" for the purpose of speaking to apostles who did not emphasize suffering. Ideally, one also would find varieties of descriptions of suffering, as in 2 Corinthians, such that one might see a standard form emerging together with certain other characteristic methods of description, grouped together and used for a generally similar purpose although in different contexts.

A. The Structure in Phil 3

The structure of boasting in 2 Cor 11-12 seems to be a pattern of boast in "being a Hebrew" followed by a boast in "being a servant of Christ in suffering" – which brings with it a possibility of a boast in "the revelation or power of Christ." One finds this type of pattern in Philippians as well,[9] a letter with different addressees and different concerns than in 2

[9] See Hans Windisch, *Der 2. Korintherbrief* (MeyerK 6; Göttingen: Vandenhoeck & Ruprecht, 1924) 78.

Corinthians. In Philippians, Paul first boasts in being a Hebrew, both in the flesh (3:4-6; cf. 2 Cor 11:18) and in actions, a lengthier boast than he makes in 2 Corinthians. Then (3:7-11), Paul says he suffered loss of all things, considering them "refuse" (σκύβαλα, vs 8) so that he, Paul, may gain and know the power of Christ's resurrection (3:8-11). Here we see a sequence: high (a Hebrew), made low (suffering loss), high (knowing Christ).[10] The components of the sequence are similar to those listed above for 2 Cor 11-12, although "knowledge of Christ" comes from revelation in 2 Cor 12:9. In Philippians, Paul speaks out against those who glory in their Jewishness, and this would explain the extra emphasis on their Jewishness. However, since in Phil 3 Paul uses a boast pattern resembling that of 2 Cor 11-12, one might say that the boasting in 2 Cor 11-12 (including that in suffering) is not merely a reaction to the boasting of particular 2 Cor 10-13 opponents. Philippians as well may provide us with an inkling of the rationale behind the lowliness or suffering motif: the suffering person hopes to know Christ and be raised up with him.

B. The περιστάσις Catalogues of 2 Cor 4 and 6

2 Cor 4:8-9 and 6:4-10 resemble the catalogue in 2 Cor 11 in that they are associated with the term "service" or "servant."[11] The parallel between 2 Cor 11 and 6:4-5 is especially unambiguous because 2 Cor 6:4-5 is a boasting catalogue, commending a person as a servant of God. However, the descriptions of suffering in 2 Cor 4 and 6 show that although the catalogues have similar components and patterns they are not identical in composition. This means the existence of catalogues with similar component-patterns combined in different configurations. Thus, the catalogues display the possibility of a rhetorical change of structure by contrast of pattern, as well as show that it is possible to combine patterns. 2 Cor 4:8-9 and

---

[10] Is this sequence likewise influenced by hymns like Phil 2:5-9, where Christ becomes a servant and subsequently is highly exalted? One encounters the use of the imitation motif here in Philippians as well as in 1 Corinthians 4.

[11] This point was emphasized by Georgi, *Die Gegner*, 244. See 2 Cor 4:5 "your servant" for Jesus Christ, 4:14 "raised up," and cf. 2 Cor 5:1-4.

6:8-10 are not merely catalogues of suffering.[12] 2 Cor 4:8-9 uses what may be called "Joseph" sequences, that is, a formal pattern of suffering followed by a description of God's help. These combine a serial description of difficulties with exemplifications of endurance or success because the power is God's – a description whose closest parallel is the various descriptions of Joseph.[13] The righteous person is afflicted but not crushed, perplexed but not in despair, persecuted but not forsaken. In the story of Wisdom's servants[14] in the Wisdom of Solomon, the story of Joseph emphasizes that Wisdom is with Joseph even in suffering:

> 10:9 "Wisdom rescued from trouble those who served her..."
> Σοφία δὲ τοὺς θεραπεύσαντας αὐτὴν ἐκ πόνων ἐῤῥύσατο.
>
> 10:13 "When a righteous man was sold, wisdom did not desert him."
> Αὕτη πραθέντα δίκαιον οὐκ ἐγκατέλιπεν, ἀλλὰ ἐξ ἁμαρτίας ἐῤῥύσατο αὐτόν.

To these one should add the (undoubtedly Christianized) *T.Jos.* 2:4, 7, which gives Joseph's account of how God sustained him in adversity:

> "For God doth not forsake them that fear him, Neither in darkness, nor in bonds, nor in tribulations or necessities... In ten temptations He showed me approved, And in all of them I endured."
> Οὐ γὰρ ἐγκαταλείπει Κύριος τοὺς φοβουμένους αὐτόν,
> Οὐκ ἐν σκότει, ἢ δεσμοῖς, ἢ θλίψεσιν, ἢ ἀνάγκαις...
> Ἐν δέκα πειρασμοῖς δόκιμον ἀπέδειξέ με
> καὶ ἐν πᾶσιν αὐτοῖς ἐμακροθύμησα.

Such catalogues portray and promise succor to the suffering righteous.[15]

---

[12] On περιστάσις catalogues, see the useful bibliography of Hans Dieter Betz (*Der Apostel Paulus und die sokratische Tradition* [BHT 45; Tübingen; J.C.B. Mohr, 1972] 98).

[13] See Peter Stuhlmacher ("Erwägungen zum ontologischen Charakter der καινη κτισις bei Paulus" [*EvTh* 27 1967] 34), who cites 2 Cor 6:3-10 as related to the Joseph tradition of suffering and God assisting the righteous. This is a motif in Dan 2:19, 3:25, 6:22.

[14] Second Isaiah would seem to have influenced Wisdom of Solomon here (in the use of the servant motif) as elsewhere.

[15] See also *T.Jos.* 1:4-7, which combines Joseph motifs with the apostolic motifs of sickness, imprisonment, and persecution, and illustrates God's salvation and support.

The characteristics of Paul's schedule of suffering occur elsewhere. The use of this "continuing power of God" (like Joseph) type περιστάσις catalogue in 2 Cor 6:8-10 is particularly important because it is utilized to *supplement* both a "boasting" catalogue of afflictions and a catalogue of virtues that commend a person as a servant of God (6:4-5). In 2 Cor 6:4-10, one *first* encounters boasting ("We commend ourselves as servants of God") followed by a list of sufferings and virtues (4-7), *next* a contrast of repute, and *then* a catalogue of contrasting changes and realities which climax in an affirmation that the discrepancies actually prove to be a testimony of honor (e.g., poor oneself, yet making many rich). This catalogue resembles somewhat that of 2 Cor 4:8-9, but because it is consists of "servant-charge" dichotomies it builds a still greater sense of contrast and triumphant synthesis based directly on the requirements of poverty for the person of power.[16]

C. The περιστάσις Catalogue in 1 Cor 4

1 Cor 4, like 2 Cor 11-12 and 6, employs a catalogue of sufferings as a criterion for servants of Christ or of God. If the opponents faced in the two letters are different, the presence of terms for servant (though not identical)[17] in association with arguments about apostolicity in both letters would seem to indicate that "servant" was a common term for "apostle" and not only the characteristic title of the opponents in 2 Corinthians.

[16] In 2 Cor 6 the "Joseph" motif may be used as a lead-in to Paul's argument that he is open to the Corinthians and is not simply a sufferer who reacts in anger.

[17] For "servant of Christ," see 2 Cor 11:23, 1 Cor 4:1; for "servant of God," see 2 Cor 6:4. 1 Cor 4 uses the term ὑπηρέτης and not διάκονος. Nevertheless, the common syndrome of description would seem to describe the same personage. May the general equivalence of terms for servant and apostle also be argued on the basis of the comparable usages of 1 Cor 12 and Romans 12 and 15? 1 Cor 12:28 enumerates the three leading posts as being apostles, prophets, and teachers. Rom 12:7 places "service" between "prophecy" and "teaching" in its list of the first three "gifts" and lacks a term for apostleship altogether. Rom 15:8 likewise speaks of Christ as servant to the circumcized. Cf. δοῦλος Χριστοῦ in Gal 1:10. On Pauline criteria, see J. Cambier on "ἀσθένεια," in "Le critère paulinien de l'apostolat en 2 Cor 12,6s.," *Bib* 43 (1962) 488-98.

1 Cor 4 emphasizes the point that apostles are those chosen to suffer. Paul introduces the catalogue of 1 Cor 4:11-13 saying: "God has exhibited us apostles last of all, as sentenced to death" (4:9).

In order to define his picture of apostles here, Paul uses several types of catalogues. In a "contrast" catalogue apostles are called fools, weak (ἀσθενεῖς) and in disrepute in contrast to the wise, honorable, and strong Corinthians. Then (4:11-12), Paul uses a straightforward catalogue of poverty and suffering followed by a catalogue of the "Joseph" type constructed of components like those found in the persecution beatitude of Matt 5:11 (cf. Luke 6:22): reviled, persecuted, spoken evil against (λοιδορούμενοι, διωκόμενοι, δυσφημούμενοι). Finally, there is a "refuse" statement. 1 Cor 4 thus contains a series of four different patterns for "boasting in suffering" material (cf. the emphasis on boasting in 1 Cor 3:21 and 4:7). The shared components of the series in 1 Cor 4 and 2 Cor 6 and 11 point to a widespread understanding of the demand for, or boasting in, apostolic suffering and lowliness. This understanding is expressed by lists of toil and afflictions. The lists take a variety of forms – each of which expresses a different type of emphasis on suffering. 1 Cor 4 uses a "contrast" catalogue, a straightforward list of lowliness characteristics, a catalogue resembling Matt 5:11 (which also presents the apostle making a positive response to evil), and a "refuse" motif. In 1 Cor 4 (as in Matt 5), lowliness motifs precede and outnumber persecution-suffering motifs.

Hence, the structures of 2 Cor 11-12 rightly are regarded as not unique to 2 Cor 11-12, but are used elsewhere in Pauline literature and would seem to be set forms for describing suffering apostleship: a high(Jew)-low-high-(knowing Christ) structure and περιστάσις catalogues (lists of "servant" sufferings containing standardized motifs). Paul's writings show that it is common practice to use one type of "suffering presentation" to modify or complement another. In 2 Cor 11-12 περιστάσις catalogues are employed as parts of a high-low-high structure. Paul has availed himself of two standard descriptions of the suffering apostle *for the purpose* of defending himself.

III. THE "Q" CATALOGUE OF SUFFERINGS – THE BEATITUDES AND OTHER CATALOGUES AS REQUIREMENTS FOR APOSTLES

1 Cor 4 reminds the exegete of what may be forgotten in the discussion of περιστάσις catalogues and 2 Corinthians. 1 Cor 4 reminds one that the tie between apostleship and requisite suffering is not unique to Paul among early Jesus-believers. The material in 1 Cor 4 is parallel in emphasis and even in wording and order to what are known as the "beatitudes" in "Q." These sayings in "Q" would come from a period at least as early, or earlier than, the Pauline Corinthian writings. That Paul does know this type of material is evident from Rom 12:14. In "Q" the material is particularly addressed to disciples: "He lifted his eyes to the disciples and said" (Luke 6:20); "His disciples came to him and he taught them" (Matt 5:1-2). It seems also to be characteristic of "Q" that some disciples were called apostles (see Luke 6:13; cf. Matt 10:12 which may draw upon Mark 3:14-15 and "Q"): "And when it was day, he called his disciples and chose from them twelve whom he named apostles" (Luke 6:13); "And he called to him his twelve disciples...and the names of the twelve apostles are these..." (Matt 10:1-2).

Originally, "Q" would seem to have contained the call of the disciples (who are called apostles) and a special teaching for them, the "beatitudes." "Q" also places this material within a context of Jesus' miracleworking activities (Matt 4:23-25, Luke 6:17-19). Accordingly, the virtues of the beatitudes are criteria for apostleship (given by a miracle worker), which is the form in which Paul seems to be acquainted with such materials. The beatitudes also have a strong "reward in the future" orientation, that is, if one is poor, meek, hungry, reviled and persecuted, one will have recompense in heaven. (Cf. Phil 2.)[18] Initially, apostles are told of blessings as return for lowliness and hunger. Thereafter follows a "blessing for suffering-persecution" list (cf. Matt 5:3-10, 11).

As later literature makes evident, the beatitudes are a positive way of saying that meekness and suffering are criteria for the righteousness of those who possess powers: *Herm. Man.* 11:7-16 tests prophets by their lives; those approved are meek

[18] Thus, one could propose that the gospel and "Q" are proceeding along a similar line of thought to that of the Philippians' structure, which stresses that one is lowly now – to be raised hereafter in the flesh.

(ταπεινόφρων), refrain from evil, and make themselves lower than other persons (cf. *Herm. Vis.* 3:2:1). *Did.* 3:9 contrasts people who consort with the lofty *versus* the righteous and ταπεινος. This is associated with a command for meekness similar to that of the beatitudes, "Be thou meek, for the meek shall inherit the earth." (ἴσθι δὲ πραυΰς, ἐπεὶ οἱ πραεῖς κληρονομήσουσι τὴν γῆν. *Did.* 3:7). The *Acts of Thomas* (which portrays Thomas performing miracles) also notes the demand for meekness and association with the meek (85-6, 94). Indeed the *Acts of Thomas* also could be an exposition of the various features of apostolic boasting. It is emphasized that Thomas is a Hebrew (and therefore considers himself almost too good to go to India). Nonetheless, he is sold as a slave to an Indian (1-2). Thomas (107) not only emphasizes his meekness and performs miracles, but also goes to prison rejoicing:

> "to endure much for thy sake.... I thank thee, Lord, that for thy sake I am called a sorcerer and wizard.[19] Receive thou me therefore with the blessing of the poor... and the blessings of them whom men hate and persecute and revile and speak evil words of them. [Note that there are two separate sets of blessings here.] For lo, for thy sake I am hated" (107).

As Thomas is about to die he speaks of a vision in which riches are full of loss and bring injury to those who gain them.
He then continues with a picture of his own life:

> "I have therefore fulfilled thy commandments... and become poor and needy and a stranger and a bondman and set at naught and a prisoner and hungry and thirsty and naked and unshod, and I have toiled for thy sake, that my confidence might not perish.... and my much labor might not be in vain and my weariness not be counted for nought" (145).[20]

Thus, Thomas shows the double demand that one become poor and be persecuted, lest one's work and weariness be counted for naught. One sees that perhaps there was a tendency on the part of apostles and prophets to claim power. Indeed they did do miracles, have visions, and demonstrate their sincerity by suffering. One further criterion had to be met, i.e., that they be lowly, needy, and outsiders. In short, the

[19] Cf. the accounts of Jewish accusations against Jesus and cf. Acts 6:8.

[20] Montague James, *The Apocryphal New Testament* (London/Oxford 1953) 424.

Acts of Thomas features activities resembling those which we saw Paul doing in 2 Cor 12, namely, adding wonderous signs and "no reward" to catalogues of suffering. Afflictions are tied to miracles.

The apostolic categories of the *Acts of Thomas* 145 should remind the exegete of another list of categories, those of the last judgment in Matt 25 – particularly in view of Dieter Georgi's observation that "the representative of God should be treated as God."[21] The demands upon the apostle in the *Acts of Thomas* indicate that the list of characteristics in Matt 25:35-6 originally was a list of apostolic characteristics: hungry, thirsty, alien, naked, sick, imprisoned.[22] Matthew's story may well at first have been about treatment of apostles. Matthew has made

---

[21] Dieter Georgi, *Die Gegner*, 199.

[22] The *Acts of Thomas*' use of an apostolic list also found in Matt 25 shows that a list of apostolic characteristics existed and that these did not come from Matt 25 since *Acts of Thomas* would not find the apostolic image in Matt 25. The same argument is fostered by the usage of *T. Jos.* 1, which also provides no general picture of those to be helped, but does have a specific image of the righteous man whom God succors. (Cf. Ps 41 for the motif that God heals the righteous when they are sick.) The usages of *Acts Th.* 145 and *T. Jos.* 1 speak against the assertions of M.D. Goulder (*Midrash und Lection in Matthew* [London: SPCK, 1974] 444) and Jindřich Mánek ("Mit wem identifiziert sich Jesus? Eine exegetische Rekonstruktion ad Matt 25,31-46," in Barnabas Linders et al., eds., *Christ and Spirit in the New Testament* [Cambridge: Cambridge University Press, 1973] 19) who use Pauline materials to explain Matt 25, claiming that it is dependent on Paul. However, *Acts of Thomas* gives evidence of a common Christian apostolic catalogue of a type upon which both Paul and Matthew based their respective catalogues. In a study of Matt 25, J. Ramsey Michaels ("Apostolic Hardships and Righteous Gentiles: A Study of Matthew 25:31-46," *JBL* 84 [1965] 27-37) cites Matt 25 as referring to apostles because of its relation to Matt 10:40-42. He argues, as do those whom he follows, that Matthew meant chapter 25 to speak to those going forth (disciples, apostles). According to Michaels, the *Acts of Thomas* and *Apostolic Constitutions* are dependent on a post-Pauline and post-Matthean combination of Matt 25 and Paul. The differences between Matt 25 (which seems to universalize the command about apostles) and *Acts of Thomas* (which acknowledges the commands as related to apostles specifically) can speak against the point that the material employed by Thomas was taken over from Matthew. These materials would argue instead that Matthew himself is drawing on materials which list sufferings of apostles like those upon which Paul also draws. The *Acts of Thomas* and the *Apostolic Constitutions* do indeed have lists of apostolic sufferings, but Matt 25 shows, that the lists were like those which Matthew uses and alters (and not that they were dependent on him). Michaels follows A. Wilkenhauser ("Die Liebeswerke in dem Gerichtsgemaelde Mt 5:31-46," *BZ* 20 [1932] 366-77) with an extensive group of parallels to Matt 25. Cf. also the list of Fitzgerald (*Cracks in an Earthen Vessel*, 207) including 4 Macc 16:20-21 and Heb 11:35-38.

the demand general because he does not make the apostolic connection explicit (a characteristic which would seem to be typical of Matthew). Thus, one has one more instance of an apostolic catalogue of weaknesses or sufferings.

Such studies show that the suffering-weakness catalogues of 2 Corinthians are not unique to 2 Corinthians in early Christian literature. Such catalogues describe (or require) these characteristics of apostles or other church leaders. The "extra-Pauline" catalogues show that the image of weakness-sickness, which Paul employs in his catalogues in both 1 and 2 Corinthians, also plays a role in the catalogues of *T.Jos.* 1:6 (cited in part II above) and Matt 25, together with the parallel material from the *Acts of Thomas*. Thus Paul did not add "weakness-sickness" to a catalogue of suffering, but rather appropriated a standard category used in catalogues of suffering for his own purposes.

IV. The Role of Catalogues of Suffering – and Miracles

Critics generally would agree that early Christian literature shows criteria of (or demand for) miracles[23] and visions for apostles. However, study of Christian περιστάσις catalogues makes clear that miracles and visions are not the sole recognized requirements for apostleship. Apostles also must undergo anguish unto death or endure lowliness (hunger, thirst, association with the meek, sickness). In particular, the beatitudes and the *Acts of Thomas* (cited above) show that one who performs miracles is required, or requires his followers as well as himself, to undergo suffering or deprivation and powerlessness.

Indeed it should be recognized as a commonplace that Jewish and Hellenistic persons of power must demonstrate their righteousness or the validity of their vocation by being poor.[24] In addition to poverty, a death of witness also may be

[23] Paul claims he has done "signs" (2 Cor 12:12; cf. Rom 15:19, Wis 10:16, Heb 2:4 as well as the gospels and Acts).

[24] It is a popular motif that wonder-working rabbis are poverty-stricken and should not use their power to gain the things of this world. Cf. the story of the golden table leg, in which the wife of R. Hanina complains about being destitute and requests that R. Hanina pray for relief. He prays and a hand bearing a table leg of gold appears. Thereafter he has a dream

required as in the case of Jesus or Socrates (cf. Plato *Rep.* 361e regarding crucifixion). 1 Cor 13:1-3 provides the most comprehensive list of attributes of persons of power[25] ranging from eloquence (cf. 2 Cor 10:6), prophecy, and miracle-doing to being poor and giving one's body to be burned on the model of Hercules and Lucian's mockery of the Cynic Peregrinus the Prophet (24-27). These are θεῖοι ἄνδρες and they are expected to endure suffering (although opponents may mock "they cannot save themelves"). The tie between miracle-doing or experiencing visions and persecution is commonplace in stories related to the Christian tradition as well. In both Mark and John, the Jews seek Jesus' death after he performs miracles (Mark 3:6; John 5:18, 11:53).[26] "Q" emphasizes both miracles and the demand for following in suffering. The *Ascension of Isaiah* 3 shows Isaiah persecuted and killed because he claims visions; Isaiah even has a vision at the very moment of his death.[27] Stephen (Acts 6:8, 7:55-60) performs miracles, undergoes martyrdom, and sees a vision as he is dying.

---

that the pious would eat on a three-legged golden table, but he would eat on a two-legged table (i.e., reward taken now means no reward in heaven). R. Hanina prays that the table leg be taken away – an even greater miracle (*b. Ta'anit* 25a). The apologetic motif of poverty appears also in Apuleius *Apology* 18 and Apollonius of Tyana *Vit.Ap.* 8.7.3. Aelius Aristides makes illness an integral part of his call and mission. Cf. the lover of virtue in Philo *Det. Pot. Ins.* 34 and, as among the Cynics, the centrality of lowliness for the philosophic life.

[25] The parallel argument of Oda Wischmeyer (*Der höchste Weg* [SNT 13; Gütersloh: Gerd Mohn, 1981] 80-86) came to my attention through the recent history of scholarship in J. Fitzgerald, *Cracks in an Earthern Vessel*, 25. Wischmeyer uses chiefly Jewish martyrdoms. Fitzgerald, who does not treat 2 Cor 10-13, works basically from Stoic sage materials without emphasizing the relation of extraordinary signs to suffering.

[26] See Anitra Bingham Kolenkow, "A Problem of Power: How Miracle Doers Counter Charges of Magic in the Hellenistic World," *SBLASP* (1976) 105-10; idem, "Healing Controversy as a Tie Between Miracle and Passion Material for a Proto-Gospel," *JBL* 95 (1976) 623-38. Miracles and visions are proof of power that is not subject to regulation. The powers of the world often oppose it by means of their powers of death (cf. Deut 13:5), thus giving the divinity behind the miracle a time and place for negative action and/or conversion (cf. *Life of Aesop*).

[27] In fact, this may be part of the argument (as shown later in Origen *Cel.*). Miracle-doers were not acting for their own benefit or they would have averted their own suffering. The combination of miracles and suffering which occurs in the gospels also characterizes Paul and his opponents and is not merely a late Markan combination, although Gnostics or others may have used angelic epiphany models to tell of Jesus' appearences, and these accounts, in turn, may have circulated separately.

In summary: There was a common expectation (and pattern) that Christian apostles not only perform miracles but suffer deprivation as well, and there are various verbal structures with which these demands are conveyed. These latter serve as the common ground between Paul and his opponents – the basis upon which Paul attempts to justify himself in 2 Cor 10-13.

V. What are the Issues in 2 Cor 10-13 (if not Suffering, Visions, and Miracles)?

What, then, are the issues in 2 Cor 10-13 after one recognizes that Paul and his opponents are unanimous that being a Hebrew, deprivation (including a catalogue of sufferings), visionary experiences, and miracles are characteristics shared by genuine apostles?[28]

In 11:27 he moves into a typical "hunger, thirst, cold" group. However, in 11:28 Paul breaks the structure with a χωρίς note about the affairs of the churches. In 11:29, although he is still speaking of a matter (being sick or weak) which is common to περιστάσις catalogues, Paul alters his mode of speech, and this alerts the critic to an increased stridency in Paul's tone. The focal points of 11:29 seem to be that Paul indeed is associating with the weak and that he is concerned with those who are being caused to stumble. The context of boasting in 2 Cor 10 evidences several problems for Paul. His opponents have said, "His letters are weighty and strong but his bodily presence is weak" (10:10). As H.D. Betz has pointed out, Paul seems to have been accused of being a γόης.[29] For the opponents, Paul acts in a worldly way, claiming power when absent but not actually wielding it when he is in a concrete situation (10:1-2, 10).

In Paul's presentation of the opponents, they are strong, they accept money (11:20, cf. 12:13-15; hence, they are γοήτες),

[28] The catalogues analyzed in this study provide a new basis for studying the differences between Paul and his opponents. Although the catalogues cited often place "lowliness" demands or boasts first, in 2 Cor 11-12 Paul gives priority to suffering, using several separate listing structures such as "far more," "10 times." Either the opponents consider suffering all-important or Paul feels his suffering is beyond question – and hence useful in introducing the argument of 2 Cor 11:23-27.

[29] *Der Apostel Paulus*, 41, 132.

and they are willing to apply force and authority. They have moved into Paul's mission territory and seized power. Paul knows that they consider him weak (yet strong *in absentia*). Paul maintains a consistency in weakness: he is weak with the churches, he was weak at the time of his commissioning, and, indeed, he was ordained to weakness. On the very issues of money and judgment (as well as the bad behavior of followers), he himself uses terms related to ταπεινός, a term used in the lowliness catalogues of 11:7, 12:21. In 11:30-12:12, Paul resumes his defensive stance (weakness and signs). Two more issues enter here, each heightened by Paul's announcement of a "third coming" after having raised issues of burdening (12:14-18) and behavior (13:1-11); he is accused of not keeping order and not having power. The central issues of 2 Cor 10-13, then, pertain to church government.

Paul justifies his apparent weakness in church government on the grounds that his type of "weakness"-government is a part of the received list of apostolic requirements (e.g., that he associates with the weak-sick). He uses the familiar criterion of association with the weak – part of his form of judgment, cf. 2 Cor 12:21 – and says he is concerned with those who are offended (11:29). He then uses the "high-low-high" structure (see page 355 above) as a bridge to the question of visions, and concludes this section on weakness by a vision intended to show that it is a part of his mandate from God that he (Paul) be perennially weak. This speaks to the opponents' claim that he is goetically "double-faced." Paul claims that he is the same always in his weakness-infirmity. However, when Paul promises at the end of the letter to return and be strong in judgment, he effectively admits that his opponents were correct about his "not taking authority." Both the defensive attitude of the catalogue (especially 11:29) and the catalogue's context show that Paul had been attacked on the issue of "government by weakness." Paul utilizes apostolic catalogues of suffering to defend himself but then acknowledges the validity of the attack and indicates that he will return to meet the opponents on their own terms.[30]

[30] Paul's defensive use of standard catalogues suggests two things: First that the catalogues were commonplace. (One does not use an unfamiliar argument in a quarrel.) Second, both his strident (or at least upset) use of catalogue terms in 2 Cor 11:29 as well as his reversal of argument at the end of the letter show that he is not merely availing himself of the catalogue to mock his opponents.

Thus, the issue is not that there exist no differences between Paul and his opponents, but that the differences are not based on suffering even to the point of death. Legitimate uses of power and methods relating to discipleship are the issues.

VI. The θειος ανηρ and the Spiritual Leader – Anthropology

In fact, the 2 Cor 10-13 interplay alerts us that what we ought to have recognized is not only the model of θεῖος ἀνήρ-γόης but also that of the spiritual guide-leader.[31] There (and in the anthropology of both ancient and modern worlds) the powers of the θεῖος ἀνήρ are tied to the formation of disciples and spiritual guidance. The θεῖος ἀνήρ characteristics (lineage, miracles, eloquence, suffering – as in 1 Cor 13)[32] are what attract and reinforce willingness to become a disciple. Tradition:lineage, power:miracles, and trials:suffering are elements Paul and his opponents have in common. Strength (authority and its characteristics), money, and the behavior of one's followers are the contact points at which they confront each other. The characteristics of θεῖος ἀνήρ and the methods of spiritual formation and spiritual guidance converge.

Typical θεῖος ἀνήρ characteristics frequently are tied to conversion or to the payment of living expenses. For example, Apollonius of Tyana (Philostratus *Vit. Ap.* 4.20) exorcizes and converts a person who subsquently transforms his life style.[33] The Jewish person who is the disciple-*hasid* expects miracles from his guide-*rebbe* and likewise reckons with having to support the guide and his family (see note 41).

---

[31] 2 Cor 11 effectively lists the characteristics. Specifically, Paul would say opponent-spiritual guides enslave, strike, prey upon his spiritual charges (v.20); they possess lineage (v.22); are suffering servants of Christ (vv.23-28); they have revelations (12:1) and do signs (12:12). Paul counters by pointing out that he has done the required signs; cf. Rom 15:19 as well as Heb 2:4 with the gospels and Acts).

[32] Cf. Lucian *Peregrinus* 24-33.

[33] Note: the conversion itself may be a miracle; cf. "immediately" in Mark as characteristic not only of miracle stories but of conversions. A conversion-exorcism of Apollonius precipitates a change of lifestyle marked by austerity and the donning of the philosopher's (worn) cloak in Philostratus *Vit.Ap.* 4.20. Philostratus portrays the "falling in love" with austerity (and with the spiritual guide) which may occur in the conversion experience. Cf. Plato *Symposion*. People may require "divine" impetus from teachers. Miracle-doers like Apollonius can give salvation. The gospels portray Jesus reinforcing "humbleness" and his sayings by means of miracles in the presence of "fearing" disciples. Would Paul's gospel be different?

Nonetheless, the powers to which the θεῖος ἀνήρ has access are subject to abuse (e.g., the ethics of a righteous θεῖος ἀνήρ *versus* the unethical γόης). Persons possessing unethical powers should not demand payment or do miracles for their own benefit;[34] yet, the spiritual guide requires financial and material support (unless s/he is self-supporting like Paul), and it is the disciple who provides this support. Of course, persuasion against a person's will is the mark of a γόης-rhetor; according to Plato's *Gorgias* the rhetorical art of his day urgently required a professional ethics.[35]

A typical pedagogical method is the hitting of face and/or hands heavily or lightly. This may demonstrate the teacher's authority, test obedience or endurance (as among the Cynics and Tibetans), enable the disciple "to perceive and break the cycle," or simply "wake up" (as in Buddhism). Another method is the injunction to do the irrational (i.e., to relinquish one's own will as well as interrupt a cycle). A major problem arises when the disciple does not change lifestyles regardless what a teacher does.[36]

These *spectra* of characteristics are important for understanding Paul's dialogue with his opponents. Paul is saying, "I have done what θεῖοι ἄνδρες do (signs, the endurance of tribulations). My opponents (not I) have performed the half-dubious actions of the θεῖος ἀνήρ or the spiritual guide (coercive measures, asking for material support). I do not wield power for destruction."

The opponents could say, "But you have collected money, and your disciples do not behave well (i.e., you have not struck or disciplined them). You simply write tough." And the reader does realize that Paul not only stresses his own power over strongholds at the beginning of 2 Cor 10-13. The reader also hears the reiterated "three times" of 12:14 concerning burdens

---

[34] See Bingham Kolenkow, "A Problem of Power," 105-10.

[35] Speaking ability (as in the Pauline situation) was important. This might have been the normal eloquence (as of fluent rabbis) or attributable to the power of God (tied to healing, as in the case of Hanina ben Dosa, *b. Ber.* 34b).

[36] See especially Hasani bin Ismail, *The Medicine Man* (London/Oxford, 1968) 187, n.383, on whether the disciples prove to be good or evil. Cf. also the miracle-doing disciples of Rabbi Jochanan ben Zakkai as effectual vindicators of his teaching.

(money?) and the "three times" of 13:1 concerning sin. Indeed, the question is whether the disciples (and/or Paul) will be reckoned ἀδόκιμοι.[37]

Considered anthropologically, Paul's letters display a spectrum of characteristics typical in modern Egypt or Jewish Hasidic communities. A *murshid* ("spiritual guide," either Coptic or Muslim) may strike the face of the pupil (either as a "joking" uncle, demonstrating rank, or in order to punish harshly).[38] Moreover, it is commonplace that a *murshid* train a son in obedience by asking the son to do the irrational or foolish. Each is part of a possible "guide" style; each differs from one guide-leader to another. Lineage (one's own or that of one's *murshid*) is often important. The expectation, at least in minority (or alternative philosophic) communities, is that the leader suffer on behalf of the group.[39] The *murshid* is expected to perform miracles for the disciple. In the words of an Egyptian monk in more recent times: "The beginning of your relationship will be one of miracles. Keep them in your memory. It will be more difficult later." Sons tell of revelations and other holy powers on the part of their *murshid*; the son is the preeminent propagandist for his *murshid*.[40]

[37] Sociologically, Paul is in a situation where money and power are valued by leaders and followers alike. If other leaders routinely demand perks from a congregation, a leader-parental figure who has not done so, and whose power seems weak (2 Cor 12:12-17), might unwittingly make his congregation "fair game" for other leaders. Paul does speak of recompense (2 Cor 8:2-9) and authority (2 Cor 10:8) but in a different way (1 Cor 9:1). See n. 52 below. If the opponents query, "Why are you not acting as we do?" and some reply, "We have a right to a wife and support" (1 Cor 9:4-14), Paul is vulnerable. Peter examplifies in part the opposite spectrum of attributes (i.e., in contrast to Paul's not having a wife and not demonstrating strength and authority when present). Paul's letters may reflect Peter's request of support for a wife; in Acts, Peter bids God strike a liar. Clement of Alexandria relates how Peter exhorted his wife to a martyrdom which occurs before his own (*Strom.* 7.11.46-51).

[38] Cf. 2 Cor 11:20, 1 Cor 4:22, or Pachomius *Life* G 103 for a spectrum including "severity" (τὸ ἀπότομον) and "goodness" (ἡ χρηστότης). For the text of Pachomius, see *The Life of Pachomius*, trans. Apostolos Athanassakis, Missoula, MT.: Scholars Press, 1975; English translation of both Greek and Bohairic in *Pachomian Koinonia*, trans. Armand Veilleux (3 vols.; Kalamazoo, MI.: Cistercian, 1980).

[39] Such suffering is proof of belief and its foreknowledge is expected (see nn. 28 and 53). See also Plato *Resp.* 361e.

[40] The present author is aware of the role of *murshid* both from her undergraduate concentration in Islamic History and her firsthand work in

Jewish *rebbes*/guides also claim to do miracles for their *hasiodim*/disciples. The *rebbe*'s power with God is used for the benefit of the *hasid*, who is expected to make repayment by supporting the *rebbe* and his family.[41] At the same time the *hasid* is expected to accept any mistreatment and rejoice in crumbs from the *rebbe*'s table. For modern Copts as well as Jews the greatest power is salvation-forgiveness which brings the soul to heaven. The alternative, if one opposes the leader is the expectation of a negative use of power.[42] In fact, we have moved beyond the "lineage and suffering" materials which would not be controversial (though perhaps mockable) to an area which is particularly controversial: How does one attract and deal with one's students? How to "convert" by "miracle" or rhetoric, how to demonstrate power (or prepare them for suffering), how to receive money, how to discipline and induce obedience (i.e., over against bad behavior)? Methods are highly controversial, whether Paul's, Apollonius of Tyana's or those of the present.[43]

Coptic Orthodox monasteries since 1982. Not every *murshid* possesses all of the above-mentioned qualities. One monk once said to me, "The intellectual person does not need miracles." Yet this informant admired visions and miracles as befitting the description of his *murshid*. He also said that his *murshid*'s willingness to work among the poor and disabled was a sign of the *murshid*'s true stature.

[41] See Zalmon Schachter-Shalomi, *Spiritual Intimacy* (Northvale, NJ.: Aronson, 1991) 118-19 and *passim* on *pidyon* ("contribution"). Note also stories about the Copt who was requested by an intermediary that the money he *did not* pay for an operation (he had experienced a miraculous recovery) be donated to the *murshid*'s community. On Weberean analysis, see Bengt Holmberg, *Paul and Power* (Lund: CWK Gleerup, 1978), especially 10-11.

[42] See also the stories of R. Eliezer ben Hyrcanus's miracles against his opponents (*b B.Me.* 59b) and Paul's warning about judgment and not sparing (2 Cor 13) as well as handing over to Satan (1 Cor 5:5) those followers who have sinned. See also Pachomius *Life* G 103 and Symeon the New Theologian in H.J.M. Turner, *Symeon the New Theologian and Spiritual Fatherhood* (Leiden: Brill, 1990) 120-151.

[43] The γόης does actually possess imitative-acting powers (see Walter Burkert, "*ΓΟΗΣ*. Zum Griechischen 'Schamanismus,'" *RhMusPh* 105 [1962] 41-42. See also Dieter Georgi on the Serapis community where the personal god entices/allows his followers to become (and be treated as) his representatives (*Die Gegner*, 197-200), and my "The Magician's God, the Personal-Support God, The Universal God" (unpublished paper) in: Conference on Themes in Magic. Berkeley, 1993. On Weber's further analysis of such persons, see Holmberg, *Paul and Power*, 138-39.

VII. Ancient Contexts and Conflicts – Government and Sharing

The ancient world gives particular contexts and labels to certain characteristics. The ancient world also would have understood that a teacher who struck disciples might resemble those "Cynic-Stoic" philosophers and merely be training disciples.[44] It was familiar with the language of philosophical conflict.[45] Furthermore, the Greco-Roman world knew of groups (e.g., Pythagoreans such as Apollonius and his rivals) which had internal divisions: Some did miracles, for instance, and had special means for obtaining forgiveness.[46] Paul resembles Apollonius' opponents, but he is less in conflict with his opponents over powers of θεῖοι ἄνδρες than are Apollonius and his rivals. Whereas Paul claims to do miracles, Apollonius' opponents demur, although they are capable of performing them. Apollonius' opponents permit sinners to live/suffer in proximity to them[47] but do no more

---

[44] See Musonius Rufus 10 (76.17-7.8 Lutz); Epictetus *Diss.* 2.21.10, 3.22.81-4, 3.24.113. See also Schmithals (*Office of the Apostle*, 111) and, regarding Cynic Epicurean sages, Heracles, Lucian's *Peregrinus* and 1 Cor 13, Schmithals, *Office of the Apostle*, 223. See Fitzgerald (*Cracks in an Earthern Vessel*, 64; I. Hadot, "The Spiritual Guide," in A.H. Armstrong, ed., *Classical Mediterranean Spirituality* (New York: Crossroad, 1986) 445, 457, n. 42 on Epicurean Spiritual Guides; and Paul Rabbow, *Seelenführung* (München: Kösel, 1954) 269-70. Georgi himself notes Pythagorean-Cynic parallels (*Die Gegner*, 193-97), but he has reduced them to mere miraculous traits. On obedience and severity, see also John Climacus' "shepherd" and Symeon in Turner, *Symeon the New Theologian*, 148-49. "Christianity, let your face-smiting enemy be your teacher" (Matt 5:34) as Celsus knew (Origen *Cel.* 7.58). See also Lucian's *Peregrinus* 17 concerning training in Egyptian asceticism.

[45] See Betz, *Der Apostel Paulus*, 104, 116 *passim*.

[46] See *Vit. Ap.* 6.5 (cf. also Plato *Resp.* 363a-65a on Orphics who grant absolution in return for money), whereas Apollonius' opponents did few miracles and allowed persons condemned by society to lead a life of abstinence in their vicinity until the proper time had expired or a sign of forgiveness had occurred. The opponent-philosophers lived near the Memnon statues. In fact, "living with statues" (i.e., living in the temples where the statues were, e.g., Chaeremon in Porphyry *Abst.* 4.6) was viewed positively. Similarly, people sought to be buried near the scattered remains of Osiris and sought residence in temples for protection from demons. See especially Erich Luddekens, "Gottesdienstlichen Gemeindschaften im Pharaonischen, Hellenistischen und Christlichen Aegypten," *ZRG* 20 (1968) 202.

[47] Both groups (Apollonius and his opponents) are Pythagoreans who would take upon themselves a "burden" (πόνος). All are θεῖοι ἄνδρες. The ancient world was the spectator of a debate in which one group was more prone to resort to miracles. Such differences were important for the many

than that, in contrast to Apollonius, who heals/forgives (or exorcizes/converts at another time). Lucian's[48] stories of Peregrinus and Menippus the Cynic remind one of such conflicts within the Cynic camp. Peregrinus was a Cynic prophet and martyr (negatively caricatured), and Menippus is Lucian's Cynic teacher whom Lucian portrays as journeying to the Underworld. Lucian participates in a kind of mockery-recognition of the characteristics and tendencies which were part of the Cynic ascetical heritage.

How do we define the differences between Paul and his opponents? Theirs would be an inner group conflict, all the more because the respective leaders each believed themselves to be endowed with powers or to enjoy a relationship to divine power. We have said that Paul is less in conflict with his opponents regarding the powers of θεῖος ἀνήρ; rather he argues in terms of method and role. Betz has observed correctly that Paul employs θεῖος ἀνήρ arguments to plead for "weakness." In addition, Paul uses the typical argument of the righteous θεῖος ἀνήρ to the effect that he is not exercizing power for his own benefit.

Paul "moves back in order to move forward" again by use of an oracle in response to his request for healing. Paul says he was told by the Lord that power was made perfect in weakness. This legitimates Paul's stand with the poor and proves divine authorization for not being healed.[49] Paul's use of a "refusal" oracle moves towards the greatest of all prophetic powers, namely the forecast of harm or adversities and one's own death – the ultimate proof that the prophet was not seeking his own benefit.[50] There is, of course, ambiguity here, for Paul neither forecasts anything new, nor does he heal himself.

Paul not only uses θεῖος ἀνήρ arguments, he also uses the

---

groups whose members believed in divine powers and which needed to regulate their members' use of power (as, for instance, Judaism at the time of Jesus or Eliezer ben Hyrcanus later).

[48] An admirer and student of the Cynics; see especially his *Dem.* 21-23 (LCL *Lucian* vol. 1, Cambridge, MA.: Harvard University Press, 1921) where Demonax and Peregrinus confront each other. See *Dem.* 23 for Demonax as a mock *magus.*

[49] Cf. Origen *Cel.* 2.17 on why Jesus did not escape death, as well as Aesop *Fab.* 161.

[50] See Anitra Bingham Kolenkow, "Forecasts of One's Own Death in the Greco-Roman World and the New Testament," *ANRW* II 26:2 (forthcoming).

arguments of good government and perhaps those advocated by intercessory spiritual guides. From the outset of 2 Cor 10-13, Paul has been building on the model of the virtuous ruler. Paul commences his argument by speaking about the πραΰτητος and ἐπιεικίας, "meekness" and "gentleness" (sc. the "government") of Christ, together with Paul's own role in applying God-given powers to bring about obedience[51] to Christ. Paul is using known philosophic wording to describe good rulers.[52] He finishes in 13:10 by speaking of the ἐξουσία which the Lord has bestowed on him.

There is also real role-modeling on Jesus as participant and redeemer-figure in 2 Cor 10-13. Additionally, the role of the spiritual guide-leader as mediator before God (as well as judge) is at issue here: Paul may be reduced to a role of humility and mourning before God *because* sinners have not repented (2 Cor 12:21; cf. 9:2-4). Paul's care is the church. Its members' weaknesses are a cause for identification (2 Cor 11:28-29). Paul sees both himself and Christ as having abased themselves in order that the Corinthians may be made rich (2 Cor 8:9, 11:7). The leader-redeemer participates in both the

[51] In 2 Cor 10, not only are obedience and ἐξουσία emphasized but the κανών which God has given Paul. Thus Paul's authority is given him by that which God requires of him. The term κανών is still used by Egyptian monks to speak of the rule of daily life and obligations laid down by spiritual fathers.

[52] Paul emphasizes the issue of government-guidance by weakness – meekness, lowliness – which many rightly have compared to Matt 11:29, even if the Greek is not identical; cf. also φορτίον "burden"). Paul in fact uses the same wording (πραΰτητος, ἐπιεικίας) as the philosopher Plutarch in the latter's description of rulers (*Per.* 39.1, *Ser.* 25.4; cf. *Caes.* 57.3 [Barrett, et al.]). The term ἡγεμών is used to connote "leader" and Epicurean or Neo-Platonist "spiritual guide." Teacher and ruler are basic spiritual guides. See I. Hadot, "The Spiritual Guide," 437-44. (Later the term is used of an abbot who unites leadership and spiritual direction roles.) Although Paul does not use the term, he indeed is in the world of the ἡγεμών-ἡγούμενος. The latter was used in Heb 13:7, 17 of those who spoke the word of God and whom one obeyed, as well as in Luke 22:26 of the leader as one who serves. The use of "philosophy of rulership" language (minus the ἡγούμενος wording but with the word διάκονος) suggests (along with the Lukan language) that this vocabulary was familiar to both Paul and his opponents. Precisely because Paul and his opponents do share this common heritage, it is even more important that the Corinthians' behavior improve – hence the importance of Paul's use of "shaming" language in 2 Cor 12:20. Cf. Josephus' parallel in Robert Hodgson, "Paul and First-Century Tribulation Lists," *ZNW* 74 (1983) 69. In 1 Cor 4:14-15, Paul tries to lower the language to "father" and παιδαγωγός.

life and the actual punishment of sinners while interceding on their behalf. Humility and mourning are the forecasted fate and role-reward of the failed guide as well as of the sinner.[53] In combination with repentance these qualities may induce the mercy of God. Paul verbalizes his role in terms of God's humbling him and his mourning with sinners (2 Cor 12:21). Paul's situation resembles that of the Apostle John at the close of Clement of Alexandria's *Can the Rich Man Be Saved*: John, having left a person who then falls into a life of robbery and sin, returns and shares the fasting and struggling required of repentant sinners until they are considered saved.[54] If Paul returns to sinners, he will share their mourning.

Thus, the issues between Paul and his opponents reach beyond miracles and suffering. The issues are tied to methods of spiritual leadership and to how intermediaries or leaders and sinning followers relate to each other. Indeed, the virtues of the θεῖος ἀνήϱ and leader-guide (ἡγούμενος-ἡγεμών) are expected to be united in one and the same person, if a leader

[53] The failings of the disciples and the sufferings of the leader-guide become part of the prophecy (as in the life of Jesus) and part of the beatitudes' expectation for disciples (as above); cf. Rom 12:15. There is reward for the successful spiritual guide who brings disciples to God, and Paul emphasizes that he obtains reward if he brings someone to Christ. Cf. 1 Thess 2:6-7, 9-11 (not glory but gentleness, not burden but encouragement of each). Clearly, the argument is not restricted to the Corinthian community. In later spiritual fathers such as Pachomius, his disciple Horsiesios (*Test.* 11) and Symeon the New Theologian (*Hymns* 41:157ff.), the spiritual father-guide is held responsible for disciples' sins or rewarded for bringing souls to heaven. Paul participates in a spectrum (or trajectory) of materials that includes Ex 32:30-32; Isa 53:4-10; 4 Macc 6:28-29; "beatitude"-sufferers who mourn with others; and Col 1:22-24, where the διάκονος of a reconciler (i.e., Paul as servant of Jesus) completes what is lacking. Paul understands himself (and other apostles) as ones who act as Jesus acted not only in performing miracles but also as participating in redemption and intercession through suffering on behalf of sinners. They suffer with sinners in order to insure the redemption of sinners. That they do this is God's recompense and a means of redemption for their failed service. God thus places them in a situation of humility.

[54] This "sharing the life and punishment of sinners" continues in the church where the father assigns and divides the punishment with the sinner as in the story of the Apostle John. Cf. Pachomius and others in Anitra Bingham Kolenkow, "Sharing the Pain," *Acts of the Fifth International Congress of Coptic Studies; Washington, D.C. 12-15 August 1992* (Rome: C.I.M., 1993) 2:1:247-61, over against Rudolf Bultmann ("Exegetische Probleme des Zweiten Korintherbriefs," *SymBU* 9 [1947] 30-31) on the incredibility of Paul's being humiliated by God.

would legitimately exercise power in the ancient or modern world.[55]

---

[55] See Bingham Kolenkow, "Forecasts," regarding rulers who seek to gain powers of astrological forecasting and bishops in modern Egypt expected to heal.

KOINΩNIA BEI PAULUS

Josef Hainz (Universität Frankfurt a.M.)

In seiner Habilitationsschrift von 1962 ist Dieter Georgi der außerordentlich bewegten "Geschichte der Kollekte des Paulus für Jerusalem" nachgegangen[1], in der er die ganze "Geschichte der selbständigen Mission des Paulus"[2] sich spiegeln sah. Die Studie hat bis heute nichts an Wert verloren, und man wird sie nicht nur zum Thema "Kollekte", sondern immer, wenn es um das Wirken des Paulus geht, zu Rate ziehen müssen.

Ich selber[3] konnte in meiner Habilitationsschrift von 1974 dankbar auf diese gründlich informierende und überaus anregende Untersuchung zurückgreifen, mit deren Ergebnissen ich weitgehend[4] übereinstimme. Die Übereinstimmung betrifft nicht zuletzt "den Aspekt der inneren Beziehung von Kollekte und Kirchenverständnis"[5], der mich in meiner Arbeit vor allem interessierte.

Georgi konnte als Konvergenz der neueren Paulusforschung feststellen, "daß Kollekte und Kirchenverständnis aufs engste miteinander verknüpft sind", und dies dahingehend erläutern, "daß die Kollekte die heilsgeschichtliche Begründung der

---

[1] D. Georgi, *Die Geschichte der Kollekte des Paulus für Jerusalem*, Hamburg-Bergstedt 1965 (ThF 38). Im Druck befindet sich eine 2. Auflage, die unter dem Titel "Der Armen zu gedenken: Die Geschichte der Kollekte des Paulus für Jerusalem" 1993 im Neukirchener Verlag erscheinen wird; sie war mir leider noch nicht zugänglich, entspricht aber der Übersetzung ins Englische: *Remembering the Poor: The History of Paul's Collection for Jerusalem*, Nashville 1992 (English translation with a Preface, new Appendices and an Afterword).

[2] *Ebd.*, S.9.

[3] J. Hainz, *Koinonia. "Kirche" als Gemeinschaft bei Paulus*, Regensburg 1982 (BU 16).

[4] Probleme sah ich v.a. in einer Reihe von Hypothesen, "die fast alle mit der Chronologie des Lebens und der Briefe des Paulus zusammenhängen" (*Koinonia*, S.151); diese Probleme scheinen mir durch die zwischenzeitlich vermehrten Teilungshypothesen zu den Paulusbriefen noch erheblich zugenommen zu haben. Ansonsten teile ich die Bedenken von K. Berger, Almosen für Israel. Zum historischen Kontext der paulinischen Kollekte, in: *NTS 23* (1977) S.180-204, v.a. S.181, gegenüber Georgis These von der Erfüllung der Verheißung der Völkerwallfahrt in der Durchführung der Kollekte.

[5] *Koinonia*, S.151.

Gemeinde Jesu Christi wie auch die geschichtliche Bindung der Einzelgemeinden an die Jerusalemer Gemeinde und die Bedeutung Jerusalems als Zentrum der Gesamtgemeinde unterstreicht"[6].

Umso erstaunlicher fand ich, daß Georgi in diesem Zusammenhang dem Begriff κοινωνία kaum Aufmerksamkeit schenkte, obwohl er mehrfach in Verbindung mit der Kollekte begegnet,[7] ja sogar für die Kollekte selbst stehen kann[8] bzw. sich geradezu als Schlüssel zum Verständnis der Kollekte aufdrängt.[9]

Der Grund für diese Nichtbeachtung dürfte sein, daß seinerzeit die Untersuchung von H. Seesemann[10] den wissenschaftlichen Konsens bestimmte, wonach κοινωνία lediglich als Formalbegriff zu betrachten und mit "Teilhabe" etc. wiederzugeben sei. Zwar spielte auch Seesemann – und das gerade im Zusammenhang mit den Kollektentexten – mit der Übersetzung "Gemeinschaft", doch wirklich ernst gemacht hat er mit seinen diesbezüglichen Beobachtungen nicht.[11] Den inneren Zusammenhang von "Gemeinschaft durch (gemeinsame) Teilhabe", der den paulinischen Sprachgebrauch von κοινωνία etc. erst verständlich macht, hat er nicht wahrgenommen.

Ähnlich unverbunden begegnen nun "Gemeinschaft" und "Teilhabe" aber auch bei Georgi. In Gal 2,9f übersetzt er die Wendung δεξιὰς ἔδωκαν ... κοινωνίας mit "Vertragshand zur Teilhaberschaft" und erläutert dies mit H. Schlier als "Vertragsabschluß" durch "Teilhaberhandschlag"[12] – was immer das bedeuten soll. Gleichzeitig spielt auch er mit den Begriffen "Gemeinschaft" und "Gemeinsamkeit",[13] so daß sich in der Sache auch hier viele Übereinstimmungen zwischen

---

[6] *Kollekte*, S.10.

[7] Vgl. Gal 2,9f; 2 Kor 8,4; 8,23; 9,13; Röm 15,26f.

[8] Röm 15,26.

[9] Gal 2,9f.

[10] H. Seesemann, *Der Begriff KOINΩNIA im Neuen Testament*, Gießen 1933 (BZNW 14).

[11] So kann er S. 32 zu den Stellen mit κοινωνεῖν resümieren: "An allen diesen Stellen geht die Bedeutung von κοινωνέω über 'teilhaben' zwar hinaus und kann vielleicht am besten mit 'verbunden sein, Gemeinschaft haben' wiedergegeben werden", aber er zieht daraus keine Konsequenzen für die theologische Bedeutung des Begriffsfeldes κοινωνία.

[12] *Kollekte*, S.21 mit Anm. 45.

[13] *Ebd.*, S.22: Unter der Überschrift "Bekundung der Gemeinsamkeit durch Respektierung der Jerusalemer Gemeinde" ist die Rede von

Georgi und mir ergeben: Etwa wenn Georgi die Kollekte als "Klammer zwischen Juden- und Heidenchristenheit" bezeichnet; oder wenn er verdeutlicht, daß es bei der Kollektenvereinbarung "um die Würde der christlichen Gemeinde in Jerusalem" ging, in deren Selbstbezeichnung als "die Armen" (und man könnte hinzufügen: "die Erwählten", "die Berufenen", "die Heiligen", "die ekklesia = endzeitliche Sammlung Gottes") ihr Anspruch Ausdruck fand, "die wahren Frommen, das wahre Israel, der heilige Rest zu sein"; oder wenn er das "Gedenken" von Gal 2,10 auslegt im Sinne von "anerkennend an jemand denken", wobei "die Anerkennung auch eine innere Bindung ... und eine entsprechende Verpflichtung" impliziere.[14] Vor allem aber gehe ich völlig einig mit Georgi, daß für Paulus

> "die wirtschaftliche Fürsorge ... dem sachlich theologischen Sinn des 'Gedenkens' ein- und untergeordnet" ist, so daß "primär also an eine innere Haltung" zu denken ist, "doch an eine, die sich zugleich äußert in Anerkennung, Dankbarkeit und Fürbitte und dann auch in wirtschaftlicher Hilfe".[15]

Ergo: Daß die Kollekte bei ihrer Vereinbarung auf dem Apostelkonzil (48/49) "als äußerer Ausdruck des *Willens zur Gemeinschaft* verstanden worden" ist und dabei der Gedanke "einer geschichtlichen *Dankesschuld*" im Hintergrund steht,[16] würde ich ebenso unterstreichen wie Georgis Resümee, wenn er von den heidenchristlichen Gemeinden sagt:

> "Sie wissen darum, daß sie durch die kirchengründende Predigt von der Auferstehung Jesu von den Toten einer weltweiten Gemeinschaft mit einer bestimmten Geschichte zugeführt und eingeordnet sind: dem Gottesvolk der neuen Schöpfung. Sie

---

"Gemeinschaft kirchlicher Verantwortung" oder davon, daß "die kirchliche Gemeinschaft" gerade durch eine gewisse Trennung gewahrt werden sollte.

[14] Zitate *ebd.*, S.22f.27.

[15] *Ebd.*, S.29. Weil es sich aber zum einen um ein ständiges Gedenken, zum anderen um ein einmaliges, längere Zeit beanspruchendes Unternehmen handelte, kommt – zumindest für Paulus – eine Interpretation der Kollekte als "Steuer" etc. nicht in Frage. Ob man das in Jerusalem bei der Abmachung anders sah, ist seit A. Holl, Der Kirchenbegriff des Paulus in seinem Verhältnis zu dem der Urgemeinde, in: *SAB*, Berlin 1921, 2. Halbband, S.920-947, jetzt auch in: *Das Paulusbild in der neueren deutschen Forschung*, hrsg.v. K.H. Rengstorf, Darmstadt 1964, S.144-178, eine viel diskutierte Frage.

[16] *Ebd.*, S.39f (Hervorhebungen von mir).

> erfüllen die Verpflichtung, die daraus für sie entspringt. Ihre Spende ist ein Erweis ihres Willens zur Partnerschaft. Sie ist 'Zeichen der Gemeinschaft' mit den Armen unter den Heiligen in Jerusalem."[17]

"Zeichen der Gemeinschaft": Im Ergebnis herrscht also keinerlei Dissens; auch ich verstehe die Kollekte "als eine Konkretion bzw. als Ausdruck und Beweis der zwischen Jerusalem und den heidenchristlichen Kirchen bestehenden 'Gemeinschaft'".[18] Nur scheint mir diese unmittelbar mit κοινωνία, dem "Schlüsselbegriff" der Jerusalemer Vereinbarung nach Gal 2,9f, angesprochen zu sein. Nicht ohne Grund operiert H. Seesemann gerade hier mit der Bedeutung κοινωνία = "die 'Gemeinschaft' im Sinne von 'Einigkeit, gemeinsames Anteilhaben'".[19]

"Gemeinschaft" – das hat Seesemann durchaus richtig empfunden – umschließt zum einen den "Willen zur Gemeinschaft" und damit den "Willen zur Einheit", und zum anderen geht es bei "Gemeinschaft" um "gemeinsames Anteilhaben"; letzterem ist Seesemann aber nicht weiter nachgegangen. Es kann sich vom Kontext her nur auf "die gemeinsame Teilhabe am Evangelium bzw. seiner Verkündigung" beziehen. Ich habe daher in meiner Auslegung die Tendenz von Gal 2,9f so zusammengefaßt:

> "Die durch Handschlag bekräftigte Gemeinschaft wird *dahingehend näher bestimmt, daß* sie auf gegenseitiger Anerkennung der verschiedenen Ausprägungen des einen Evangeliums beruht *und daß* sie durch die vereinbarte Kollekte ihren Ausdruck findet."[20]

Bezieht man alle übrigen von mir untersuchten κοινωνία-Texte bei Paulus mit ein, ergibt sich folgendes Ergebnis im Überblick:

1. Der κοινωνία kommt ein hoher Rang zu im ekklesiologischen Denken des Paulus; immer sind es *Gemeinschaftsver-*

---

[17] *Ebd.*, S.84. Auf die Wandlungen im Verständnis der Kollekte bzw. ihre paulinischen Uminterpretationen (etwa in der einschränkenden Wendung "für die Armen unter den Heiligen" in Röm 15,26) muß hier nicht eingegangen werden; vgl. *Koinonia*, S.145-148.

[18] *Koinonia*, S.152.

[19] *KOINΩNIA*, S.99.

[20] *Koinonia*, S.134. Vgl. dazu jetzt meinen Beitrag "Gemeinschaft (κοινωνία) zwischen Paulus und Jerusalem (Gal 2,9f). Zum paulinischen Verständnis von der Einheit der Kirche", in: *Kontinuität und Einheit* (FS F. Mußner), hrsg.v. P.-G. Müller und W. Stenger, Freiburg-Basel-Wien 1981, S.30-42.

hältnisse, die da entstehen zwischen solchen, die "die geistigen Güter" mitteilen bzw. "vermitteln", und denen, die sie "empfangen" (vgl. zu 1 Kor 9,11 und Röm 15,27 v.a. Gal 6,6).

2. Für Paulus haben die Empfänger grundsätzlich eine *Dankesschuld* zu erbringen; das gilt zuerst und vor allem für das Verhältnis neu entstehender Gemeinden im Verhältnis zu Jerusalem als "Ur- bzw. Muttergemeinde aller Christengemeinden", von der das Evangelium seinen Ausgang nahm (vgl. Röm 15,27: ὀφειλέται εἰσιν/ ὀφείλουσιν).

3. Paulus anerkennt diesen Anspruch und betrachtet die in Jerusalem vereinbarte *Kollekte als Ausdruck des "Willens zur Gemeinschaft"* (vgl. Gal 2,9f).

4. Wenn er Röm 15,26 einschränkend von einem κοινωνίαν τινὰ ποιήσασθαι spricht, so ist damit gesagt: Die Kollekte ist eine *"partielle Konkretion" der zwischen den paulinischen Missionsgemeinden und Jerusalem bestehenden Gemeinschaft; sie ist ebenso freiwillig wie prinzipiell geschuldet* (vgl. V 27), keine Auflage oder Steuer etc., sondern Zeichen von Solidarität und Erweis des Willens zur Gemeinschaft.

5. Die Akzentuierungen des Paulus in Röm 15,25-28.31, die jeden rechtlichen Aspekt abwehren und darin vermutlich einer Uminterpretation der Jerusalemer Vereinbarungen gleichkommen, sind wohl der Grund, warum Paulus besorgt sein muß im Blick auf die Ablieferung der Kollekte in Jerusalem und deren Aufnahme.

6. Für Paulus geht es also zwar um Anerkennung des Vorrangs Jerusalems, sofern alle Heilsgüter in der dortigen Muttergemeinde ihren Ursprung haben; aber die darin begründete Verpflichtung zur κοινωνία legitimiert keinen Jerusalemer Rechtsanspruch; sie ist eine Sache der Freiheit, der Dankbarkeit, der Verbundenheit.

7. Prinzipiell also versteht Paulus die κοινωνία durchaus als umfassende *"Gemeinschaft des Anteil-Gebens und Anteil-Nehmens zum Zwecke des gemeinsamen Anteil-Habens"*; aber konkret verlangt das nur gewisse Zeichen der Anerkennung bestehender Gemeinschaftsverhältnisse und des Willens zur Gemeinschaft.

8. Das gilt nicht nur für das Verhältnis der Gemeinden zu Jerusalem (vgl. Röm 15,25ff), sondern ebenso für das der Gemeinden zu ihrem Gründerapostel (vgl. 1 Kor 9,4ff.11), wie für das der im Glauben Unterwiesenen zu ihren Katecheten (vgl. Gal 6,6).

9. Es geht dabei immer um einen *Austausch von Gütern;* nur in

diesem Sinne könnte man von einer "Art" von Gütergemeinschaft sprechen. Die Güter selbst können gänzlich unterschiedlich sein: So werden z.B. "geistliche" Güter mitgeteilt, mit "fleischlich-irdischen" kann und soll geantwortet werden (Röm 15,27).

10. Finanzielle Unterstützungen, Kollekten etc., werden also von Paulus im Rahmen seines κοινωνία-Verständnisses interpretiert als *Zeichen eines lebendigen Gemeinschaftsbewußtseins.* Als solche sind sie geradezu "gottesdienstliche Akte" (vgl. das λειτουργῆσαι in Röm 15,27).[21]

11. Im Hintergrund des paulinischen κοινωνία-Verständnisses steht dabei jene im Herrenmahl grundgelegte "Gemeinschaft" unter den Gliedern des "Leibes Christi", die durch deren (gemeinsame) "Teilhabe" am "Leib des Χριστός" entsteht, durch die sie erst zum "Leib Christi" einer Gemeinde werden (1 Kor 10,16f). Die so durch den erhöhten Kyrios gestiftete "Gemeinschaft" ist das "Grundmodell" jener in den christlichen Gemeinden erfahrbaren "Gemeinschaftsverhältnisse", die letztendlich der (gemeinsamen) "Teilhabe" am göttlichen Pneuma entstammen (Phil 2,1).[22] *Immer wird "Gemeinschaft" durch "Anteilgabe" gestiftet, die zur "Anteilnahme" verpflichtet und sich daher konkret erweisen muß.*

Insofern ist der Philipperbrief geradezu ein Musterbeispiel dafür, wie sich Paulus diese κοινωνία gelebt vorstellt. Zwar scheint es auch in Philippi Gefährdungen gegeben zu haben, die Paulus besorgt machen (vgl. 3,1 oder 2 – 4,1 oder 3); aber das "Gemeinschaftsverhältnis" zwischen ihm und den Philippern blieb davon unberührt; und es war immer von besonderer Art. Mit keiner anderen Gemeinde stand Paulus von Anfang an in einem so unbelasteten Verhältnis von "Geben und Nehmen" (4,15), daß er mehr als nur einmal Unterstützung seitens dieser Gemeinde anzunehmen bereit war (4,16).

Daß Dieter Georgi hervorhebt, Paulus nehme in Phil 4,10-20 (bei ihm: 23) "Gedanken auf, die auch im Zusammenhang mit der Jerusalemer Kollekte auftauchen",[23] ist m.E. völlig zutreffend, wenn auch erläuterungsbedürftig; denn mit "Verhält-

---

[21] Vgl. *Koinonia,* S.148-151.
[22] Vgl. *ebd.*, S.15-61.
[23] *Kollekte,* S.47.

nis gegenseitiger Abrechnung"[24] ist die Analogie (vgl. V 15) nicht zu bestimmen.

Unstrittig hingegen ist die Beobachtung, daß Paulus bemüht ist, "den Blick von dem materiellen Wert der philippischen Spende wegzulenken und auf ihre geistliche Bedeutung zu richten". So ist sie zum einen für die Philipper eine Gelegenheit, "ihre fürsorgliche Gesinnung zu beweisen" (zu V 10), und zwar durch die "Teilnahme an seiner bedrängten Situation" (zu V 14). Zum anderen sieht Paulus in der Spende einen "Gewinn, der den Philippern selbst durch ihr Geben zukomme" (zu V 17). Begründung:

> "Eigentlich gilt die Gabe ja gar nicht ihm, sondern Gott. Sie ist 'ein lieblicher Opferduft, ein angenehmes, Gott wohlgefälliges Opfer'"

(zu V 18).[25] Nach Georgi schließt sich in diesem Geschehen ein "Kreislauf", den er zusammenfassend so beschreibt:

> "Gott ist durch sein Gnadenhandeln, durch die eschatologische Heilstat (das Christusgeschehen ...) Urheber dieses Geschehens. Einbezogen in dieses Geschehen und abhängig von seiner Bewegung sind alle Glieder am Leibe Christi, auch der Apostel. Paulus ist davon überzeugt, daß der von den Jerusalemern zuerst empfangene und weitergegebene Strom des Gnadenhandelns und der Gnadengaben Gottes in Gestalt der Kollekte und des darin bekundeten Dankes wieder zu den Jerusalemern zurückfließt, sie wieder zum Danken und erneutem Geben bewegt, so daß der Kreislauf in Gang bleibt."

Wieder ist es eigentlich nur der "κοινωνία-Gedanke", der mir bei Georgi unterbewertet zu sein scheint, so daß die Vermittlerrolle des Paulus so wenig deutlich wird wie das ihr korrespondierende Gemeinschaftverhalten der Philipper. Darauf ist zurückzukommen. Festzuhalten ist hingegen, daß Georgi Phil 4,10-20 "als exegetisches Modell für die weitere Interpretation der Kollektentexte" verstehen möchte.[26] Das Dankschreiben der Philipper gehöre

---

[24] Übernommen von M. Dibelius; vgl. *ebd.*, Anm. 161.

[25] *Ebd.*, S.47f; freilich ist es irreführend zu sagen, die Gabe gelte nicht "eigentlich" Paulus. Im übrigen sammelt Georgi hier wertvolles Material zu Phil 4,18 und deutet S.49 erstmals an, was er im folgenden (S.53.67.77) des öfteren aufnimmt und S.86 abschließend zusammenfaßt als "Kreislauf" (s.o.).

[26] *Ebd.*, S.50.

> "zeitlich sehr eng mit den Texten zusammen, die von der Sammlung für Jerusalem reden", behandle "ein ähnliches Thema" und zeige "mancherlei stilistische, begriffliche, sachliche und religionsgeschichtliche Berührungspunkte".

Diesen religionsgeschichtlichen Berührungspunkten geht nun Georgis Schüler Lukas Bormann mit seiner Dissertation "*Philippi: Stadt und Christengemeinde zur Zeit des Paulus*" nach.[27] Ihn interessiert allerdings nicht die Nähe der philippischen Unterstützung für Paulus zur Kollekte der paulinischen Gemeinden für Jerusalem, sondern "die Beziehung zwischen Paulus und den Philippern im Spiegel römisch-hellenistischer sozialer Konventionen" – so der bilanzierende Teil II.C) seiner Arbeit. Bormann versucht sich bewußt freizuhalten von Interpretationsmöglichkeiten aufgrund anderer Paulustexte; er will den Phil so offen wie möglich auslegen, mit keinem vorgegebenen Auslegungskonzept Möglichkeiten des Verstehens verbauen, sondern im Gegenteil neu nach solchen suchen. Und er glaubt, sie in römisch-hellenistischen Konventionen finden zu können.

Er untersucht zu diesem Zwecke a) die "φιλία-Konzeption", b) das "Beneficialwesen", c) die "konsensuale societas" und v.a. d) das "Patronats- bzw. Klientelwesen". Als römische Kolonie läßt Philippi erwarten, daß die in der Stadt lebende Christengemeinde nicht unbeeinflußt blieb von deren Denken und Konventionen. Und daß dem so war, versucht Bormann am "Dankesbrief 4,10-20" aufzuweisen; er dient ihm "als Schlüssel zum Verständnis der Beziehung zwischen Paulus und der Philippergemeinde".[28]

In diesem Zusammenhang kann Bormann zu den Intentionen des Paulus in 4,14f schreiben:

> "Jetzt schildert er im scharfen Kontrast zu den Versen 11-13 sein Verhältnis zu den Philippern *als Gemeinschaft* (συγκοινωνέω; κοινωνέω), *die auf einem ganz anderen Prinzip beruht* als das Modell der religiös-ethisch herausragenden Persönlichkeit, nämlich auf einem echten Austausch des Gebens und Nehmens."[29]

Das hier abgewiesene Prinzip hat Georgi vertreten, der in seiner Arbeit mehrmals auf das Modell des Pneumatikers verwies,

---

[27] Die Dissertation wurde im SS 1993 in Frankfurt eingereicht.

[28] *Ebd.*, S.170ff.

[29] *Ebd.*, S.187 (Hervorhebung von mir), wo er in Anm. 54 auf W. Bauers Wörterbuch, Sp. 1533, hinweist, wonach συγκοινωνέω meint: "zusammen Anteil haben" – ein Hinweis, dem Bormann leider nicht weiter nachgeht.

der für seine pneumatischen Leistungen materielle Unterstützung von der Gemeinde verlangen durfte;[30] aber das von Bormann favorisierte "Gemeinschaftsverhältnis", das auf einem "Austausch des Gebens und Nehmens" beruhe, wird bei ihm leider nicht vom paulinischen κοινωνία-Konzept her entwickelt. Ihn interessiert lediglich "der Ausgleich im Sinne angemessener Reziprozität der Beziehungen"[31].

Die von P. Marshall vertretene "φιλία-Konzeption"[32] kommt dafür nach Bormann[33] als Erklärungsmodell nicht in Frage:

> "Die Unterstützung der Philipper für Paulus und die sozialen Beziehungen in den paulinischen Gemeinden beruhen nicht auf dem hellenistischen Freundschaftsideal. Ihre ethische und theologische Reflexion greift ebensowenig auf den hellenistischen Tugendbegriff zurück."

Anders steht es mit dem "Benefizialwesen". Hierzu kann Bormann als Ergebnis festhalten:

> "Paulus bewegt sich in seinem Umgang mit der philippischen Spende im Rahmen der Möglichkeiten, die die hellenistische Ethik in der Institution des beneficium zur Verfügung stellt".

Freilich muß er einschränkend hinzufügen:

> "Seine theologische Interpretation verläßt sowohl den Boden zeitgenössischer praktischer Philosophie als auch den sozialer Konventionen, indem sie die Geldspende der Philipper einem über ihre Nützlichkeit hinausgehenden oder besser in ihrer Nützlichkeit enthaltenen theologischen Sinn gibt."[34]

Insofern gibt es natürliche Gemeinsamkeiten; denn gewiß ist die Spende der Philipper ein *beneficium*, wenn man dieses definiert als eine

> "Wohltat, die der Geber aus innerer Freiheit leistet und die einzig auf das Wohl des Empfängers gerichtet ist".[35]

Weder an der Freiwilligkeit der Philipper noch an ihrem Wunsch, Paulus in seinen Bedrängnissen zu helfen, besteht

---

[30] *Kollekte*, S.47 und 83.

[31] *Philippi*, S.188.

[32] P. Marshall, *Enmity at Corinth: Social Conventions in Paul's Relations with the Corinthians*, Tübingen 1987 (WUNT II/23).

[33] *Philippi*, S.203-211, hier S.211 als Zusammenfassung.

[34] *Ebd.*, S.211-226 in Auseinandersetzung mit Senecas Schrift *De beneficiis*, hier S.225f.

[35] *Ebd.*, S.218 zu "a) Die Gabe und ihre Gewährung" (S.218-220).

ein Zweifel. Auch "Reziprozität" kann man feststellen; Paulus spricht ja ausdrücklich von einem Austausch des "Gebens und Nehmens" (4,15).

Freilich benutzt Paulus hier geradezu Kaufmannssprache; er redet von einer "Rechnung" , vom "Konto" und will offensichtlich "quittieren" (4,15-18). Damit ist aber das *beneficium* in Gefahr, seinen Charakter als "freiwillige Wohltat" zu verlieren. Für Bormann hat sich Paulus hier nur der Kritik Senecas *angenähert,* ohne ihr zu unterliegen. Hätte er analoge Texte aus anderen Paulusbriefen herangezogen – wie z.B. 1 Kor 9,11; Gal 6,6; Röm 15,27 – , hätte er den Charakter solcher Spenden als "geschuldeter", aber nur in Freiheit zu leistender Dankbarkeitserweise nicht übersehen können. Solche Ausblicke auf andere Paulusbriefe hatte Bormann aber in seiner Untersuchung von 4,10-20 eigens ausgeschlossen.

> "Die Gegenüberstellung von sarkischer und pneumatischer Leistung und ihre Zuordnung zum Apostel (pneumatisch) bzw. zu der ihm verbundenen Gemeinde (sarkisch) kommt im Dankesbrief nicht zur Sprache. Der Austausch auf zwei qualitativ unterschiedlichen Ebenen klingt nicht an. ... Der Austausch zwischen Paulus und der Gemeinde wird weder auf der Ebene sarkisch/pneumatisch noch unter Zuhilfenahme eschatologischer Schuldkonten zum Ausgleich gebracht. Die materielle Leistung der Gemeinde wird als ethische verstanden, der Paulus zunächst nichts als *Gegenleistung* entgegenzusetzen hat." [36]

Hier klingt an, was bei Bormann unter dem Stichwort "Annahme" behandelt wird und in seiner ganzen Arbeit die Perspektive verzeichnet: Paulus nehme die Gaben der Philipper eher widerwillig an. Der Widerwille rühre v.a. daher, daß Paulus in seiner prekären Lage als aktuell Gefangener keine Gegenleistung erbringen könne. "Die Philipper haben Rechte an ihn, die er ausdrücklich anerkennt und hervorhebt", und zwar "aufgrund ihres materiellen Engagements". Ja, Paulus sehe sich "in einem Schuldverhältnis zu den Philippern".[37] Damit dürften die Dinge auf den Kopf gestellt sein; denn nach paulinischem Verständnis ist ja gerade das Verhalten der Philipper Ausdruck ihrer geschuldeten Dankbarkeit. Eine

---

[36] *Ebd.,* S.196f (Hervorhebung von mir); Bormann sieht hier "die so wichtige Parität der Beziehung gefährdet". Zu "c) Die Reziprozität" (S.222-226).

[37] *Ebd.,* S.189.192, vgl. auch S.258ff.

Verzeichnung dürfte auch vorliegen, wenn Bormann meint, die Gabe der Philipper rufe bei Paulus "nicht nur freudigen Dank hervor", sondern bringe ihn "in eine Situation, die er als Bewährung versteht". Bormann denkt an die "Verführung durch materielle Güter", spricht daher von einer "Herausforderung", die Paulus "nur mit einer bestimmten Interpretation" akzeptieren könne, was ihn einem von Seneca scharf getadelten Verhalten annähere: der "widerwillige(n) Annahme einer Wohltat"[38]. Das ist eine Deutung der VV 11-13, die dem Gesamtduktus der paulinischen Ausführungen nicht entspricht.

Daß es also Gemeinsamkeiten mit dem "Benefizialwesen" gibt, macht dieses doch keineswegs zur Erklärung der philippischen Gaben für Paulus. Dessen "theologische Deutung" des Handelns der Philipper, in der dieses "in den Rang einer religiösen Leistung" erhoben wird, läßt die "Gegensätze" ... "unüberbrückbar" erscheinen, wie Bormann selber festzustellen gezwungen ist: "Eine solche Interpretation steht dem strikt innerweltlich denkenden Seneca nicht zur Verfügung."[39]

Den 3. Weg, nämlich mit Hilfe des Modells der "konsensualen *societas*" die "Formen der christlichen Gemeinschaft, wie sie sich in den Paulusbriefen widerspiegeln, in den Horizont römischer Rechtstraditionen einzuordnen", wie das Paul Sampley versuchte, hält Bormann selbst für ungangbar, so daß ich mich damit nicht weiter auseinandersetzen muß.[40]

> "Die konsensuale *societas* ist eindeutig auf die Verfolgung gemeinsamer Interessen im wirtschaftlichen Bereich beschränkt und mit der Interpretation als bruderschaftliche Gemeinschaft, wie sie Sampley intendiert, überfordert."[41]

Dagegen sympathisiert Bormann stark mit dem "Patronats- bzw. Klientelverhältnis", um die Beziehung der Philipper zu Paulus und umgekehrt zu deuten.[42] Anknüpfen kann er v.a. an der Situation des gefangenen Paulus; denn "der Prozeß ist

---

[38] *Ebd.*, S.220-222 zu "b) Die Annahme"; vgl. auch Anm. 29.

[39] *Ebd.*, S.224.

[40] *Ebd.*, S.226-232, hier S.226 zu J.P. Sampley, *Pauline Partnership in Christ*, Philadelphia 1980; ders., "Societas Christi. Roman Law and Paul's Conception of the Christian Community", in: *God's Christ and His People. Studies in Honour of N.A. Dahl*, hrsg. v. W. Meeks and J. Jervell, Oslo 1977, S.158-174.

[41] *Ebd.*, S.257.

[42] *Ebd.*, S.232-275.

die klassische Situation des Zusammenwirkens von Patron und Klientel."...

> "Das Verhältnis der Philipper zu Paulus entspricht strukturell der Klientelbeziehung. Der Apostel in der Rolle des Patrons vertritt die gemeinsame Sache (das Evangelium) nach außen. ... Die Klientel kann sich nun nicht um ihn scharen, da der Prozeß in einer fremden Stadt stattfindet. Sie nutzt aber die ihr gegebenen Möglichkeiten zur Unterstützung und Einflußnahme."[43]

Das Beispiel macht deutlich, in welchen Grenzen das Patronats- bzw. Klientelverhältnis auf Paulus und die Philipper anwendbar ist: Wo es um Rechtsstreitigkeiten ging, um Rechtsvertretung, Rechtsschutz und Rechtsberatung, da war der Patron in die Pflicht genommen; er hatte im weitesten Sinne für das Wohl der Klienten zur sorgen. Die Klientel hatte ihrerseits den Patron in allen Belangen zu unterstützen und ihm Dienste zu erweisen. Aber im Kern ist das Patronats- bzw. Klientelverhältnis doch ein Arrangement zwischen Mächtigen und Untergebenen, auch wenn man in Rechnung stellt,

> "daß das Klientelverhältnis sich von seinen Anfängen als Rechtsbeziehung zu einer Sozialbeziehung in der späten römischen Republik gewandelt hat".[44]

Es gilt:

> "Nicht Zuneigung oder gar Liebe sind ihr inneres Band, sondern Humanität und staatsbürgerliche Einsicht."[45]

Nun muß man nicht bestreiten, daß das Verhältnis zwischen Paulus und den Philippern Züge aufweist, die sich dem beschriebenen Patronats- bzw. Klientelverhältnis einordnen lassen und gerade in der Außenperspektive von seiten der römischen Kolonie Philippi und ihren amtlichen Vetretern so gedeutet werden konnten, "daß hier Konkurrenz zum religiöspolitischen Programm des Prinzipats im Entstehen" war, woraus sich manche Unannehmlichkeiten der philippischen Christen erklären mögen.[46] Aber insgesamt ist die Basis des sogenannten Dankbriefleins von Phil 4,10-20 und sein Sujet der philippischen Gaben für den gefangenen Paulus doch zu

---

[43] *Ebd.*, S.265.
[44] *Ebd.*, S.233.
[45] So Bormann, *ebd.*, S.256, mit Bezug auf Dionysios von Halikarnaß, *Antquitates Romanae*, Buch II, 9-11, hier 11.2, seinen Hauptgewährsmann.
[46] *Ebd.*, S.272-275, hier S.273.

schmal, um das Erklärungsmodell Bormanns überzeugend zu machen.

Problematisch scheint mir vor allem, wenn Bormann dem Text entnimmt, Paulus sei "durch Erwartungen und Vorstellungen, die die Philipper mit ihrer Gabe verbinden, verunsichert", und daraus schlußfolgert, diese Vorstellungen seien "stärker von sozialen Konventionen der römisch-hellenistischen Welt geprägt als von theologischen Gesichtspunkten".[47] Ich kann die von Bormann behaupteten "Unsicherheiten und Brüche" in Phil 4,10-20, v.a. in der Einordnung der VV 11-13, nicht erkennen. Paulus freut sich, daß die Philipper wieder einmal in der Lage waren, ihn zu unterstützen; aber er freut sich nicht seinetwegen – er wäre nicht von solcher Unterstützung abhängig; er freut sich ihretwegen (vgl. V 17). Sie erwiesen sich als "Mitteilhabende an seiner Bedrängnis" (V 14) und haben ihr Verhältnis von κοινωνία zu Paulus neuerdings bestätigt (V 15). Es ist dies – wenn man den geschäftsmäßig klingenden Ausdruck "auf Rechnung von" nicht unnötig gewichtet – eine "Gemeinschaft des Gebens und Nehmens".

Hätte Bormann die zweimalige Erwähnung des κοινωνία-Verhältnisses zwischen Paulus und seiner Gemeinde nicht gänzlich außer Betrachtung gelassen, hätten ihn die VV 14 und 15 aufmerksam machen müssen, daß Paulus in fast allen seinen Briefen in ähnlicher Weise sein Verhältnis zu seinen Gemeinden als "Gemeinschaftsverhältnis" deutet. Bormann übersieht den Widerspruch in seinen eigenen Aussagen. Einmal argumentiert er mit der aktuellen Notsituation, die das Klientelverhalten herausfordert, zum anderen betont er aber:

> "Die materielle Unterstützung, die Paulus nach Phil 2,25-30 erhält und auch schon früher erhalten hat, wird nicht ad hoc aufgrund der besonderen Notsituation zusammengestellt, sondern ist Teil der auf die Initiative der Gemeinde zurückgehenden, schon länger währenden Unterstützung, mit der Paulus fest rechnet."[48]

Letzteres freilich tut Paulus gerade nicht; er ist nicht abhängig von solcher Unterstützung und wartet nicht darauf. Genau

[47] *Ebd.*, S.256f.

[48] Zum Zitat S.262 vgl. die Ausführungen S.263: "Die Philipper interpretieren diese Situation im Rahmen des Klientelverhältnisses als eine Solidarität herausfordernde gemeinsame Notsituation."

das betont er in den VV 11-13. Aber er freut sich, daß die Philipper wieder einmal Gelegenheit hatten, ihrer Gemeinschaft mit ihrem Gründerapostel Ausdruck zu geben (4,10). Zwar ist es eine Sache von Freiwilligkeit, ein solches "Gemeinschaftswerk" zu veranstalten (vgl. Röm 15,26), aber im Grunde eben doch geschuldet (vgl. Röm 15,27; Gal 6,6).

Dieser Gedanke fehlt auch im Phil keineswegs. In 2,30 erinnert Paulus die Philipper, Epaphroditos, den er einen 'Gesandten der Gemeinde und Diener seines Bedarfs' nennt (2,25), habe 'ihren Mangel des Dienstes für ihn auffüllen' sollen. Epaphroditos tat, wozu im Grunde die Gemeinde ihrem Gründerapostel gegenüber verpflichtet war. Von solcher "Verpflichtung" spricht auch Bormann,[49] obwohl er Phil 2,30 nicht näher untersucht. Freilich ist es ihm eine Verpflichtung im Rahmen des Klientelverhältnisses, nicht eine aufgrund der "gemeinsamen Teilhabe am Evangelium" zustandegekommenen κοινωνία.

Bezieht man alle κοινωνία-Texte des Phil mit ein, ergibt sich ein geschlossenes Bild. Schon zu 1,5 zeigt die Auslegungsgeschichte,[50] daß ein Schlüssel zum Verständnis, der die verschiedenen, von den Auslegern jeweils für sich betonten Aspekte zusammenschauen läßt, erst gefunden ist, wenn man das paulinische κοινωνία-Konzept zugrundelegt – jenes "Gemeinschaftsverhältnis", das durch wechselseitiges Anteil-Geben und Anteil-Nehmen entsteht und sich so auch immer neu realisiert. Ich habe es so verdeutlicht:

> "Das Gemeinschaftsverhältnis entsteht dadurch, daß jemand gemeinsam mit einem anderen Anteil empfängt an einer Sache; geschieht dies durch den andern, wird er zu dessen Schuldner und ist verpflichtet, ihm auch seinerseits Anteil zu geben an seinen Gütern. Im Einzelfall kann jeweils das 'Gemeinschaft haben' oder das 'Gemeinschaft halten' akzentuiert sein; also im ersten Fall die gemeinsame Teilhabe mit jemandem an etwas, im zweiten Fall das (bei Paulus häufig antwortende) jemandem Anteil geben an etwas. Immer bleibt das Ergebnis wechselseitiger Anteilnahme und Anteilgabe das Gemeinschaftsverhältnis zwischen Personen. κοινωνοί sind deshalb 'Personen, die in einem Gemeinschaftsverhältnis zueinander stehen, weil sie gemeinsam Anteil haben an etwas'; und mit κοινωνεῖν werden vornehmlich die Akte des Anteilgebens und Anteilnehmens selbst ausgedrückt."

---

[49] *Ebd.*, S.264.

[50] Vgl. *Koinonia*, S.89-95, v.a. S.90.

Bezogen auf Phil 1,5 heißt das: Das Gemeinschaftsverhältnis zwischen Paulus und den Philippern

> "entstand durch die gemeinsame, durch Paulus vermittelte Teilhabe am Evangelium. In V 7 wird Paulus in ganz ähnlicher Weise von den Mitteilhabern an der durch ihn vermittelten Gnade reden. Der Sinn dürfte nicht allzu sehr differieren; denn in beiden Fällen ist an 'Heilsbotschaft und Heil' zugleich zu denken, woran die Philipper Anteil bekamen und wodurch zwischen ihnen und dem Apostel als deren Vermittler 'ein wechselseitiges Verhältnis des Gebens und Empfangens' entstand."[51]

Phil 1,5 zeigt dann, daß ein solches Gemeinschaftsverhältnis wirksam werden muß und daß die Unterstützung des Apostels ein solches Wirksamwerden bedeutet. Daß dabei "diese Dienste seitens der Gemeinde vorwiegend dem Paulus (als 'ihrem' Apostel) persönlich geleistete Dienste, also eigentlich nur mittelbar Dienste am Evangelium sind, macht für Paulus keinen Unterschied." Die Gemeinschaft ist "durch das Evangelium gestiftet, an dem sie gemeinsam Anteil haben, und auf das Evangelium bezogen, dem sie je auf ihre Weise dienen".[52]

Phil 1,7 nennt Paulus die Philipper "Mitteilhaber meiner Gnade" bzw. "meine Mitteilhaber an der Gnade". Hier ist der Dienst des Apostels als "Vermittler" der Gnade angesprochen, sofern er "von Gott her jenes Gnadengeschehen in Gang bringt bzw. jene Gnade vermittelt, woran teilzuhaben Paulus an den Philippern rühmt". Apostel und Gemeinde stehen also "miteinander in einem Gemeinschaftsverhältnis, dadurch, daß die Gemeinde durch ihn Anteil erhielt an der Gnade – 'seiner' Gnade, weil durch ihn vermittelt".[53]

Phil 3,10 spricht von der "Gemeinschaft zwischen Apostel und Gemeinde durch gemeinsame Teilhabe an den Leiden Christi". Ich habe die Auslegung der Stelle so zusammengefaßt:

> "Christus gibt Anteil an der Kraft seiner Auferstehung, aber auch Anteil an seinen Leiden. Die darin gründende Gemeinschaft mit ihm hat die völlige Gleichgestaltung der Gläubigen zum Ziel in Tod und Auferstehung."

Ein Vergleich mit 2 Kor 1,5-7 ergibt:

---

[51] *Koinonia*, S.92-93.
[52] *Ebd.*, S.94-95.
[53] *Ebd.*, S.119-120.

> "Die Leiden Christi sind überreich auf den Apostel übergegangen; ebenso aber auch die Ermutigung durch Christus. Beides soll er weitervermitteln an die Gemeinden, die mit ihm in einem Gemeinschaftsverhältnis stehen als Teilhaber an den Leiden wie an der Ermutigung (d.h. seinen Leiden und seiner Ermutigung, die zugleich Leiden und Ermutigung Christi sind)."[54]

Von hier aus versteht sich jetzt auch Phil 4,14: "Paulus dankt den Philippern, daß sie Gemeinschaft hielten mit ihm durch gemeinsame Teilhabe an seiner Bedrängnis." Das Gemeinsame wird hier durch die Präposition συν verstärkt zum Ausdruck gebracht. Wichtig war mir bei meiner Auslegung,[55] folgendes zu verdeutlichen:

> "Versteht man diese Anteilnahme als 'tätige', denkt man allzu ausschließlich an die materiellen (und personellen) Hilfeleistungen selbst, während es Paulus gerade darauf ankommt, diese auszulegen als Zeichen der realen Anteilnahme an seiner Bedrängnis und darin als Ausdruck der Gemeinschaft, die zwischen ihnen besteht."

So lebt "Gemeinschaft", wie sie Paulus versteht, vom gegenseitigen Geben und Nehmen: Phil 4,15. Verlangt wird keine völlige "Gütergemeinschaft": "die auszutauschenden Güter bleiben verschiedenartig".[56]

> "Die Totalität gilt wohl prinzipiell und der Intention nach, aber Paulus wird nirgends zum Schwärmer. Was er erstrebt – und doch nur annehmen kann, wenn sie in Freiheit geleistet wird – , ist die Gemeinschaft, in der Geben und Nehmen einander korrespondieren, wie es bei den Philippern von Anfang an der Fall war. Die Unterstützungen, die sie Paulus angedeihen ließen, waren Ausdruck der Dankbarkeit, die sie ihrem Apostel schuldeten, und der Gemeinschaft, die sie mit ihm hielten, halten wollten und auch als einzige in dieser Form halten durften."

Bormanns Untersuchungen bleiben trotz meiner Einwendungen hilfreich und anregend. Auch nach meinem anderen, von Paulus selbst her gewonnenen Auffassungen basiert das Verhältnis zwischen dem Apostel und den Philippern nicht auf φιλία oder *consensus*, so daß diese beiden von Bormann untersuchten Verstehensmöglichkeiten auch aus meiner Sicht ausscheiden müssen. Aber auch um *beneficia* handelt es sich bei

---

[54] *Ebd.*, S.95-99, hier S.99.
[55] *Ebd.*, S.117f.
[56] *Ebd.*, S.112-115, hier S.114f.

den Unterstützungen, die Paulus durch die Philipper erfährt, nicht, sondern um Zeichen der Philipper, daß sie das besondere Gemeinschaftsverhältnis zum Apostel begriffen haben, dessen Verkündigung sie sich in ihrer Existenz als Christen verdanken – wie Kinder sich ihrem Vater verdanken: Dieser Vergleich, den Paulus selbst gern auf sein Verhältnis zu seinen Gemeinden und zu Menschen, die durch ihn zum Glauben kamen, anwendet (vgl. 1 Thess 2,11; 1 Kor 4,15; Phil 2,22), bringt besser zum Ausdruck, wie Paulus dieses Verhältnis versteht – nicht als Patronats- und Klientel-, sondern als Gemeinschaftsverhältnis. So sympathisch ich daher den Ansatz Bormanns und sein Bemühen finde, bislang unbeachtet gebliebene Möglichkeiten in Betracht zu ziehen und fruchtbar zu machen, sollte man doch wohl zuerst die Eigenaussagen des Paulus ausschöpfen, bevor man nach außertextlichen Analogien und Erklärungsmöglichkeiten sucht. Bormanns Beschränkung auf den "Schlüsseltext" 4,10-20 verhinderte die Einbeziehung der übrigen κοινωνία-Aussagen des Philipperbriefs. Dabei hätten die VV 14 und 15 ihre Berücksichtigung eigentlich erzwungen.

Hier stimme ich in der Sache mehr mit seinem Lehrer überein:[57] Die Unterstützungen, die Paulus durch die Philipper erfährt, entsprechen dem gleichen Grundsatz wie die Kollekte der paulinischen Gemeinden für Jerusalem. Solches Anteilgeben an eigenen Gütern ist Ausdruck jenes Gemeinschaftsverhaltens, das nach paulinischer Auffassung gefordert ist, wo jemand durch einen anderen Anteil empfängt an den Heilsgütern des Evangeliums. Zwischen ihnen entsteht ein "Gemeinschaftsverhältnis von Geben und Nehmen".

---

[57] Vgl. Georgi, *Kollekte*, S.47.50.

ARCHÄOLOGIE UND PAULUS IN THESSALONIKE

Helmut Koester (Harvard Universität)

Archäologie, die sich mit den Stätten der paulinischen Mission befaßt, scheint mehr zu versprechen als der Versuch, den Fußtritten Jesu im Heiligen Lande Schritt für Schritt archäologisch zu folgen. Letzteres kann kaum dem Odium entrinnen, Biblische Archäologie im traditionellen Sinne zu sein oder das, was mein Lehrer Ernst Fuchs einmal als "Archäologie des leeren Grabes" bezeichnete. Aber auch in der Beschäftigung mit archäologischem Material aus den Wirkungsstätten des großen Heidenapostels ist die Versuchung groß, nach Funden zu suchen, die unmittelbar die Umwelt des Paulus und eventuelle Angaben über die Orte seiner Wirksamkeit, etwa aus der Apostelgeschichte, illustrieren.

So tauchen dann immer wieder archäologische Funde auf wie die armselige Inschrift [ΣΥΝΑ]ΓΩΓΗ ΕΒΡ[ΑΙΩΝ] ("Synagoge der Hebräer"),[1] die in Korinth gefunden wurde, aber gar nichts über die jüdische Gemeinde in Korinth zur Zeit des Paulus sagt, da sie aus einer viel späteren Zeit stammt. Vielleicht trägt es schon etwas mehr aus, wenn man auf die Inschrift des Hohenpriesters Iouventianos[2] aus Isthmia hinweist, der sich im 2.Jh. n.Chr. rühmt, daß er zum ersten Male feste Quartiere für die Athleten der Isthmischen Spiele errichtet habe. Also wohnten die Athleten sowie auch die Besucher der Spiele zur Zeit des Paulus noch in Zelten, was Paulus als Zeltmacher eine gute Arbeitsgrundlage gegeben haben mag. Doch auch aus solchen Angaben lernt man wohl mehr über die beachtliche Bautätigkeit des 2.Jh.s n.Chr. als über die Mission des Paulus.

Mit dem archäologischen Material aus Thessalonike steht es noch schlechter. Die vielberufene Inschrift über die Politarchen von Thessalonike[3] beweist zwar, daß der Verfasser der

---

[1] Vgl. Hans Conzelmann, *Der erste Brief an die Korinther* (MeyerK 5; Göttingen 1969) 26.

[2] *IG* IV, 203. Siehe dazu Helmut Koester und Eric Sorensen, "Isthmia," in Helmut Koester, *Archaeological Resources for New Testament Studies* Bd. 2 (Philadelphia: Trinity Press International, 1994) Nr. 39-40.

[3] Charles Edson, *Inscriptiones graecae Epiri, Macedoniae, Thraciae, Scythiae,* 1. Teil: *Inscriptiones Macedoniae,* 1. Heft: *Inscriptiones Thessalonicae et viciniae*

Apostelgeschichte eine recht gute Lokalkenntnis besaß,[4] aber besagt nichts über die Mission des Paulus. Der früheste archäologische Nachweis für die Anwesenheit einer Religionsgemeinschaft aus Israel ist eine griechische Inschrift mit zwei Zeilen in hebräischer Schrift.[5] Sie stammt frühestens aus dem 4.Jh. n.Chr., und ist nicht jüdisch sondern samaritanisch.[6] Diese Inschrift ist wichtig als Anzeichen für das Fortbestehen einer samaritanischen Diaspora in der frühchristlichen Zeit, läßt sich aber wohl kaum als Beweis für die Hypothese verwenden, daß Paulus seinerzeit in einer samaritanischen Synagoge gepredigt hat.

Mit unserer Kenntnis der heidnischen Religionen zur Zeit des Paulus steht es nicht viel besser. Natürlich kann man annehmen, daß die traditionellen griechischen Religionen vertreten waren, wenn auch archäologische Funde recht spärlich sind. Daß Dionysos verehrt wurde, ist aus einer Reihe von Inschriften evident.[7] Aber aus der kleinen Dionysos-Herme mit einem eingesetzten Phallus kann man weder schließen, daß es einen Ritus gab, bei dem dieser Phallus feierlich eingesetzt wurde, noch läßt sich daraus der schwierige und umstrittene Satz τὸ ἑαυτοῦ σκεῦος κτᾶσθαι ἐν ἁγιασμῷ καὶ τιμῇ aus 1 Thess 4,4 erklären,[8] noch ergibt sich aus der Existenz der Verehrung dieses Gottes des Weines der Grund für Paulus' Warnung vor der Trunkenheit und seine Mahnung zur Nüchternheit in 1 Thess 5,7.[9]

(Berlin: De Gruyter, 1972) 126. Das Datum der Inschrift ist umstritten (1.Jh. v.Chr. bis 2.Jh. n.Chr.).

[4] Politarchen als höchste Beamte einer Stadtverwaltung gab es nur in Thessalonike und einigen anderen makedonischen Städten; cf. die Kommentare zu Acta 17,6 z.B. Ernst Haenchen, *Die Apostelgeschichte* (MeyerK 3; Göttingen [7]1977) 488.

[5] *Inscriptiones Thessalonicae et viciniae* 789. Die Inschrift zitiert den Text von Num 6:22-27 in einer griechischen Übersetzung, die sich von der Septuaginta unterscheidet und dem hebräischen Text der Samaritaner nahe steht.

[6] Cf. B. Lifshitz und J. Schiby, "Une synagogue samaritaine a Thessalonique," *RB* 75 (1968) 368-78; E. Tob, "Une inscription grecque d'origene samaritaine trouve a Thessalonique," *RB* 81 (1974) 394-99; J. Purvis, "Paleography of the Samaritan Inscription from Thessalonica," *BASOR* 221 (1976) 121-23.

[7] *Inscriptiones Thessalonicae et viciniae* 28, 59, 259, 503, 506.

[8] K. P. Donfried, "The Cults of Thessalonica and the Thessalonian Correspondence," *NTS* 31 (1985) 338.

[9] Donfried, ebenda; R. Jewett, *The Thessalonian Correspondence; Pauline Rhetoric and Millenarian Piety* (Foundations and Facets; Philadelphia: For-

Ebensowenig überzeugend ist der Versuch von Robert Jewett,[10] aus der Kombination verschiedener Angaben über die Kabiroi das Vorhandensein einer chiliastischen Bewegung in Thessalonike zur Zeit des Paulus zu erschließen. Ein Trinkgefäß aus dem 5.Jh. v.Chr. aus Theben mit tanzenden ithiphallischen Satyren und der Inschrift ΚΑΒΙΡΟΣ ist zeitlich und räumlich viel zu weit entfernt, um etwas über den Enthusiasmus des Kabiroskultes im paulinischen Thessalonike aussagen zu können. Und daß ein Priester aus Thessalonike zum Kabirenheiligtum auf Samothrake reiste und im 3.Jh. n.Chr. ein Mitglied der Aristokratie und Politarch Aufseher des Kabirenkultes in Thessalonike war,[11] heißt ja noch lange nicht, daß zur Zeit des Paulus (oder zu irgendeiner anderen Zeit) der Kult des Kabiros der breiten Schicht der arbeitenden Bevölkerung entfremdet worden war. Niemand bezweifelt indes die große Bedeutung des Kabiroskultes für Thessalonike und für seine Bevölkerung, obgleich wenig über den Kultus selbst und sein Ritual bekannt ist.[12] Der Kabiros war neben der Tyche der Beschützer der Sadt und ihrer Mauern. Mit der Tyche zusammen erscheint er oft auf Bronzemünzen von Thessalonike. Es ist auch wahrscheinlich, daß später der Heilige Demetrios die Funktion des Kabiros als Beschützer der Stadt übernommen hat.[13] Aber vergebens sucht man im archäologischen Material aus Thessalonike nach Beweisen für den religiösen Enthusiasmus und Fanatismus dieses Kultus, so daß Jewetts Hypothese über Paulus' Reaktion gegen eine solche Bewegung in den Thessalonicherbriefen[14] reine Spekulation bleiben muß.

---

tress, 1986) 127. Zur Auseinandersetzung mit Donfried und Jewett hier und im folgenden cf. auch Helmut Koester, "From Paul's Eschatology to the Apocalyptic Schemata of 2 Thessalonians," in Raymond F. Collins, ed., *BETL* 87 (Leuven: Leuven University Press, 1990) 442-45.

[10] Jewett, *Thessalonian Correspondence*, 161-78.

[11] Zu den entsprechenden Inschriften siehe L. Robert, "Inscriptions de Thessalonique," *Revue Philologique* 48 (1974) 180-246.

[12] Cf. Holland L. Hendrix, "Thessalonica," in idem und Helmut Koester, *Archaeological Resources for New Testament Studies 1* (Philadelphia: Fortress, 1987) Nr. 25-26.

[13] Vgl. das entsprechende frühbyzantinische Mosaik in der Basilika des Heiligen Demetrios; siehe Hendrix, ebenda, Nr. 46; Ernst Kitzinger, *Byzantine Art in the Making* (Cambridge, MA: Cambridge University Press, 1977) 105-6 und Tafel 189.

[14] Jewett hält beide Thessalonicherbriefe für paulinisch und sieht auch in den Warnungen des 2.Thess vor einer Naherwartung eine paulinische Reaktion gegen den enthusiastischen Chiliasmus des Kabiroskultes.

Sämtliche Versuche, direkte Linien von archäologischen Materialien zu neutestamentlichen oder anderen frühchristlichen Texten zu ziehen, leiden unter drei grundsätzlichen und fatalen methodischen Fehlern: 1. Sie wollen faktische Angaben, die sich aus der Archäologie ergeben, dazu benutzen, um neutestamentliche Texte in einer bestimmten historischen Situation und einer begrenzten Lokalität zu verankern; sie sind somit nichts weiter als eine Fortsezung der alten "biblischen Archäologie". 2. Solche Versuche übersehen die Notwendigkeit, archäologisches Material zunächst einmal in Bezug auf den Gesamtrahmen der Kultur- und Religionsgeschichte der griechisch-römischen Welt zu verstehen. 3. Es bleibt ungeklärt, aus welcher Fragestellung heraus denn nun sowohl die frühchristlichen Texte als auch die archäologischen Funde interpretiert werden sollen.

Soweit die neutestamentliche Forschung viele Jahrzehnte lang von der neutestamentlichen Theologie beherrscht wurde, dienten Erkenntnisse über die nichtchristlichen Religionen jener Zeit oft als negative Folie für die Ausarbeitung der Überlegenheit frühchristlicher theologischer Einsichten. Überhaupt war dann oft "Theologie" das Schlagwort, das in sich selbst die Überlegenheit des frühen Christentums über das Heidentum implizierte, denn dort handelte es sich *nur* um "Religionen". Das Christentum wurde als "das Ende der Religion" dargestellt. Man könnte Abhilfe schaffen, indem man auch das Heidentum und das Judentum jener Zeit theologisch interpretierte, um so die Basis für einen unvoreingenommen Vergleich zu schaffen. Dabei würden aber weiterhin die nichtliterarischen Materialien zu kurz kommen. Auch geht es nicht an, die theologische Fragestellung einfach durch eine soziologische Fragestellung zu ersetzen. Gewiß gäbe das die Möglichkeit, archäologisches Material besser in die Betrachtung einzubeziehen. Aber entweder ist man dann versucht, Sachen und Personen hinsichtlich ihrer sozialen Herkunft und Stellung zu charakterisieren, ohne daß deutlich wird, wie sich diese soziologische Einordnung zur Geschichte der Religion und Theologie verhält. Oder man abstrahiert wieder eine Ideologie aus einer soziologischen Interpretation nichtliterarischer Materialien und stellt sie einer christlichen Ideologie gegenüber, wie das etwa bei Jewett der Fall ist.

Es scheint mir ratsamer, die Begriffe "Religion" und "Religionsgeschichte" wieder zu ihrem Recht kommen zu lassen und sowohl für die christliche als auch für die nichtchristliche Welt geltend zu machen. Auf diese Weise wird es möglich sein, religionsgeschichtliche Phänomene einschließlich der aus dem nichtliterarischen Bereich stammenden Materialien in den Griff zu bekommen. Kulturelle und soziale Phänomene werden so in die religionsgeschichtliche Fragestellung einbegriffen. Die Religionsgeschichte wird sich gerade auch um solche Phänomene kümmern müssen, die nur in der archäologischen Forschung sichtbar werden und in der Literatur nicht ohne weiteres greifbar sind.

Die religionsgeschichtliche Fragestellung kann auch die grundsätzliche Unterscheidung zwischen christlicher Theologie, Judentum und heidnischen Kulten nicht akzeptieren. Als religionsgeschichtliche Erscheinungen gehören Christentum, Heidentum und Judentum zunächst einmal zusammen als Phänomene des religiösen Lebens der Antike und Spätantike. Einzelheiten der Organisationsformen, der religiösen Rituale und der literarischen und architektonischen Ausdrucksformen mögen in manchen Fällen verschieden sein. Aber es ist ein und dieselbe griechisch-römische Welt und ein und dieselbe religions- und kulturgeschichtliche Entwicklung, der alle diese Religionen angehören. Für die Arbeit an archäologischen Materialien heißt das vor allem, das es nicht angeht, primär heidnische archäologische Funde als Illustration für die Umwelt des frühen Christentums zu verwenden. Sowohl christliche als auch nichtchristliche Materialien, seien sie nun literarisch oder nicht-literarisch, müssen in gleicher Weise interpretiert werden für ein besseres Verständnis des Gesamtphänomens der Religionsgeschichte der griechisch-römischen Welt. Erst dann kann man über die Besonderheiten der christlichen Texte sprechen.

Eine Reihe von Schwierigkeiten müssen bewältigt werden. Vor allem ist es wichtig, die Zusammenarbeit der verschiedenen Disziplinen zu intensivieren. Unter uns Neutestamentlern, die an der Archäologie der paulinischen Städte interessiert sind, finden sich kaum Facharchäologen oder Kunsthistoriker und Epigraphiker. Gelehrte in diesen Disziplinen stellen oft auch ganz andere Fragen als die unseren. Es ist deshalb nötig, daß Neutestamentler lernen, auf ihre Fragen zu hören. Aber es ist ebenso erforderlich, daß wir unsere eigenen Fragen in die Diskussion einbringen, um so gemeinsam zu einer Interpretation archäologischer Materialien zu gelangen.

Eine weitere Schwierigkeit läßt sich unmittelbar an der Frage der Archäologie und der paulinischen Gemeinde in Thessalonike erläutern. Auf der einen Seite ist es wichtig, regionale Unterschiede ernst zu nehmen; auf der anderen Seite darf man solche Unterschiede nicht zu hoch veranschlagen. Es steht außer Frage, daß die Entwicklung des frühen Christentums in Palästina sich unter sozialen und kulturellen Bedingungen vollzog, die keineswegs mit denen des ägäischen Raumes identisch waren. Archäologische Funde aus den verschiedenen Bereichen der römischen Welt beweisen genugsam die erheblichen Unterschiede in gesellschaftlicher Struktur, politischer Organisation, Wirtschaft und Handel. Doch bestanden auch viele Gemeinsamkeiten, durch die die Einwohner des Ostens und des Westens verbunden waren. Wohin immer die Griechen kamen, bauten sie Theater; wohin immer die Römer gelangten, errichteten sie Bäder und Aquädukte. Auf dem Gebiet der Religionsgeschichte läßt sich beobachten, daß zum Beispiel Statuen des Sarapis immer dem gleichen Kanon folgen, ob sie nun aus Köln oder Rom oder Ephesos stammen. Und im Christentum, jedenfalls bis zur Zeit des Marcion, benutzten alle Gemeinden die Bibel Israels als Heilige Schrift.

In Bezug auf archäologische Funde muß man daher fragen, ob sie einem spezifischen regionalen Phänomen angehören oder sich auf allgemein gültige Erscheinungen beziehen. Aber selbst wenn sich aus archäologischen Funden auffallende Besonderheiten der Religion der Thessalonier zur Zeit des Paulus ergeben sollten, bleibt doch die Frage offen, ob Paulus sich in seinem Brief an die Thessalonier darauf bezieht oder ob er nicht vielmehr in einer Sprache spricht, die damit gar nichts zu tun hat, sondern in allgemein gültigen Vorstellungen verankert ist, wie zum Beispiel in der Heiligen Schrift und in der politischen Propaganda Roms.

Im Fall von Thessalonike ist diese Frage besonders wichtig; denn die archäologischen Funde sind hier so zufällig und unzusammenhängend, daß sie nur sehr begrenzte Urteile für irgendeinen bestimmten Zeitraum zulassen und nur in wenigen Fällen hinreichen, eine kontinuierliche religionsgeschichtliche Entwicklung nachzuzeichnen. Für die ersten beiden Jahrhunderte v.Chr. läßt sich eine Verehrung der römischen Wohltäter rekonstruieren, die ganz deutliche Züge einer Lokaltradition trägt.[15] Aber auf diese Zeit folgt hinsichtlich des Kultes der römischen Kaiser eine Lücke von fast 300 Jahren bis zu den Monumenten aus der Zeit des Galerius. Jedoch handelt es sich dann nicht mehr, wie in der vorchristlichen Zeit, um einen für Thessalonike spezifischen Lokalkult, sondern um das Auftauchen allgemein gebräuchlicher Symbole des Kaiserkultes.

Der Übergang vom Lokalkult Thessalonikes für die römischen Wohltäter zur allgemeingültigen Spätform des Kaiserkultes ist an den in Thessalonike geprägten Bronzemünzen des 3.Jh.s n.Chr. erkennbar. Auf Bronzemünzen der frühen Kaiserzeit erscheint wohl das Porträt des göttlichen Caesars (*divus Iulius*) mit der Beischrift ΘΕΟΣ, aber weder Augustus noch einer seiner Nachfolger (mit der Ausnahme Neros) wird auf den Münzen jemals so bezeichnet.[16] Der normative Münztypus war die Prägung, in der die Tyche der Stadt mit Mauerkrone auf der Vorderseite und der Kabiros auf der Rückseite der Münze erschien. Am Anfang des 3.Jh.s n.Chr. wird die Tyche auf diesen Münzen durch das Portait der Julia Domna Augusta, der Frau des Kaisers Septimius Severus, ersetzt. Etwas später erscheint auf der Rückseite dieser Münzen an Stelle des Kabiros der Kopf römischer Kaiser mit dem Strahlenkranz der Sonne, während auf der Vorderseite die Tyche wieder ihren traditionellen Platz erhält. Auf dem Marmorbogen, der im Palast des Galerius gefunden wurde, ist wiederum Tyche mit Mauerkrone auf ihren gewohnten Platz, während ihr gegenüber der Kopf des Kaisers Galerius an Stelle des Kabiros dargestellt ist.[17] Hier hat also der Kaiser die Funktion des Kabiros als Beschützer der Stadt übernommen. Soweit schließt sich die Propaganda für den Kaiserkult noch an die traditionellen lokalen Schemata an.

Das ist aber in den Reliefs des Triumphbogens des Galerius in Thessalonike nicht mehr der Fall. Hier wird auf religöse und politische Themen angespielt, die zur Lokaltradition der

---

[15] Das hat Holland Hendrix in seiner Arbeit *Thessalonicans Honor Romans* (Harvard Univ. Diss. 1984) gezeigt.

[16] Hendrix, *Thessalonicans Honor Romans,* 170-77; idem, "Thessalonica," Nr. 21-22; Charles Edson, "Macedonia: State Cults of Thessaloniki," *HSCP* 51 (1940) 125-36.

[17] Hendrix, "Thessalonica," Nr. 38.

Stadt keinerlei Beziehung haben. Sie stehen vielmehr ganz im Dienste der Propaganda der universalen Ideologie der Tetrarchen. Das Relief des dritten Registers auf der Nordseite des Südpfeilers[18] zeigt in der Mitte die Tetrarchen inthronisiert in der himmlischen Welt (ἐν τοῖς ἐπουρανίοις): Diokletian, Augustus des Ostens, sitzend zur Linken, also auf der östlichen Seite; sein Caesar Galerius steht links neben ihm; rechts neben Diokletian, also auf der westlichen Seite, ebenfalls sitzend, der Augustus des Westens Maximian; neben ihm steht sein Caesar Konstantius Chlorus. Knieende weibliche Figuren neben den beiden Caesaren repäsentieren die beiden befriedeten Provinzen Mesopotamia und Britannia. Auf beiden Seiten sind die Tetrarchen umgeben von Göttern. Auf der östlichen Seite zunächst Sarapis, klar an seinem Kalathos erkennbar. Von Isis, der äußeren linken Figur, ist nur noch das Sistrum erkennbar. Auf der westlichen Seite sind die entsprechenden Götter wahrscheinlich Jupiter und Fortuna. Oceanus und Tellus in den beiden unteren Ecken betonen, daß die Tetrarchen in der Tat als göttliche Weltherrscher dargestellt sind.[19] So sehr hier die religiöse Propaganda der Tetrarchen zum Ausdruck kommt, so wenig läßt sich aus diesem Relief etwas über die spezifische Form des Kaiserkultes der Thessalonier erschließen.

Der wißbegierige Neutestamentler möchte natürlich auch gern Orte und Plätze finden, an denen Paulus gepredigt haben mag, vor allem die Agora der alten Stadt. Jedoch stammt das große Forum, ein rechteckiger römischer Markt, erst aus dem 2.Jh. n.Chr. Soweit ist erst der größere Teil des oberen, höher gelegenen Bezirks ausgegraben.[20] Im Süden schloß sich offenbar ein etwas tiefer gelegener Bezirk an. Die Säulenreihe des Süd-Portikus des oberen Marktes stand auf einem Kryptoportikus, der gleichzeitig die obere, nördliche Grenze des unteren Bezirks bildete, der aber noch nicht

---

[18] Zur Interpretation dieses Registers siehe Hendrix, "Thessalonica," Nr. 33.

[19] Weitere Figuren, die zwischen den Göttern stehen, sind wahrscheinlich die Dioskuren und Virtus und Honos; siehe Hendrix, "Thessalonica," Nr. 32-33; ders., "Imperial *Apotheosis* on the Arch of Galerius at Thessalonike," *Numina Aegea* 3 (1980) 25-33; Margaret Rothman, "The Panel of the Emperors Enthroned," *GRBS* 2 (1975) 19-40.

[20] Charalambos Bakirtzis, "Der Thessalonische Agora Komplex," *Ancient Macedonia II* (Thessaloniki: Institute for Balkan Studies, 1977) 257-69 [auf Griechisch].

ausgegraben ist. Die hier zu beobachtende Umwandlung eines älteren Marktes in zwei ganz von Säulenreihen umgebenen Fora ist wiederum keine für Thessalonike typische Erscheinung. Vielmehr spiegelt sich hier die allgemein verbreitete Tendenz der römischen Kaiserzeit wieder, die älteren offenen Plätze der griechischen Stadt durch umschlossene Fora zu ersetzen. Auch sonst ist bei den Ausgrabungen in Thessalonike fast nichts gefunden, das sich mit Sicherheit dem 1.Jh. n.Chr. zuweisen läßt.

Was die Religionen von Thessalonike betrifft, so ist die Verehrung der ägyptischen Götter die einzige Religion, deren Existenz durch Monumente aus verschiedenen Jahrhunderten nachgewiesen werden kann.[21] Die älteste von insgesamt 69 Inschriften,[22] die sich auf den Kult der ägyptischen Götter beziehen, läßt sich in das Jahr 187 v.Chr. datieren.[23] Von Gebäuden der ägyptischen Religion ist bisher nur ein kleiner Tempel (11 mal 8 m) gefunden worden, dessen Konstruktion sich ungefähr auf das 2.Jh. n.Chr. datieren läßt.[24] Das Modell dieses Tempels im Archäologischen Museum von Thessalonike (da er unter einer modernen Straße liegt, ist der Tempel nicht mehr zugänglich) zeigt, daß es sich hier nicht um einen typisch griechischen Tempel handelte, sondern um einen Versammlungsraum. Die Tempelstatue stand wahrscheinlich in der Nische der Apsis, während der gesamte Innenraum Platz für die gottesdienstliche Gemeinde bot. Ungewöhnlich und interessant ist die Tatsache, daß sich unter dem westlichen Vorraum des Tempels eine Krypta befand, die durch einen zehn Meter langen gewölbten Gang zugänglich war, der von außen durch eine kurze Treppe neben der Apsis des Tempels erreicht wurde. In der Krypta befand sich ein Altar, auf dem die oben erwähnte Dionysos-Herme stand. Es ist anzunehmen, daß die Krypta eine Funktion in den geheimen Initiationsriten des ägyptischen Kultes hatte.

---

[21] Mehrere dieser Funde sind im einzelnen diskutiert in Hendrix, "Thessalonica," Nr. 6-15.

[22] *Inscriptiones Thessalonicae et viciniae* Nr. 3, 15, 16, 37, 51, 53, 59, 75-123, 221, 222, 254-259.

[23] *Inscriptiones Thessalonicae et viciniae* 3. Es handelt sich hier um die Veröffentlichung eines Briefes von Philipp V, in dem dieser makedonische König verbietet, Einkünfte des Sarapeions für nicht-kultische Zwecke zu verwenden.

[24] Charalambos Makaronas, "Excavations at the Serapeion," *Makedonika* 1 (1940) 464-65; Daniel Fraikin, "Note on the Sanctuary of the Egyptian Gods in Thessaloniki," *Numina Aegea* 1 (1974).

Ein Relief mit einer Inschrift bezieht sich auf solche Initiationsriten. Die Inschrift[25] ist dem "Mysten Osiris" (᾿Οσείριδι μύστει) gewidmet, was möglicherweise besagt, daß der Stifter des Reliefs sich als Eingeweihter mit Osiris identifizierte. Ein anderer Stein bringt unter dem Relief des ägyptischen Gottes Anubis eine Inschrift,[26] die sich in das 2.Jh. n.Chr. datieren läßt, mit den Namen der Mitglieder einer kultischen Tischgesellschaft (ἱεραφόροι συγκλίται) des Gottes Anubis. Die Namen dieser Inschrift zeigen, daß es sich um einen Verein von Freigelassenen handelte. Also waren wohl religiöse Vereine, die zum ägyptischen Kult gehörten, nach der sozialen Stellung der Mitglieder organisiert.

Höchst interessant ist eine im ägyptischen Heiligtum gefundene Inschrift, die von der Einführung des Sarapis-Kultus in der lokrischen Stadt Opus berichtet.[27] Es ist wahrscheinlich eine Kopie aus dem 1.Jh. n.Chr. eines älteren Dokumentes aus Opus aus dem 2.Jh. v.Chr. Die Inschrift berichtet, daß Xenainetos aus Opus während seines Aufenthaltes in Thessalonike im Traum von Sarapis den Befehl erhielt, dem Euronymos in Opus zu befehlen, den Gott und seine Schwester (d.h. Isis) in Opus einzuführen. Xenainetos wacht auf und erinnert sich daran, daß dieser Euronymos sein politischer Gegner ist, schläft wieder ein und findet, als er zum zweiten Mal aufwacht, den von Sarapis angekündigten Brief unter seinem Kissen. Er überbringt den Brief, und Euronymos, nachdem er den Brief gelesen und die Erzählung des Xenainetos gehört hat, beschließt, Sarapis und Isis in Opus einzuführen. Dieser Bericht hat eine enge Paralelle in der Erzählung von Apostelgeschichte 10, gehört also zu den für die Ausbreitung der hellenistischen Missionsreligionen typischen Propagandaerzählungen. Die Inschrift ist am Ende nur fragmentarisch erhalten. Aus den wenigen noch lesbaren Worten kann man

[25] *Inscriptiones Thessalonicae et viciniae* 107.

[26] *Inscriptiones Thessalonicae et viciniae* 58.

[27] *Inscriptiones Thessalonicae et viciniae* 255; Daniel Fraikin, "Introduction of Sarapis and Isis in Opus," *Numina Aegea* 1 (1974); Philip Sellew, "Religious Propaganda in Antiquity: A Case from the Sarapeum at Thessaloniki," *Numina Aegea* 3 (1980); R. Merkelbach, "Zwei Texte aus dem Sarapeum zu Thessalonike," *Zeitschrift für Papyrologie und Epigraphik* 10 (1973) 45-54; F. Sokolowski, "Propagation of the Cult of Sarapis and Isis in Greece," *GRBS* 15 (1974) 441-48.

schließen, daß ursprünglich eine weitere Geschichte, offenbar einer wunderbaren Heilung, folgte.[28] Dann handelt es sich bei dieser Inschrift also um eine Aretalogie, in der die großen Taten des Gottes Sarapis erzählt wurden.

Andere Funde, die Zeugen für die Religionen der Thessalonier in der hellenistischen und römischen Zeit sind, wie etwa eine Bronzehand des Sabazios, zwei Inschriften für Zeus Hypsistos und eine Gußform für eine Terrakotta der Kybele, beweisen zwar die Existenz einer Reihe von typisch hellenistischen Religionen, lassen aber sonst keine Schlüsse hinsichtlich der Rituale und der Popularität dieser Religionen zu. Sicher spielte auch die Verehrung des Dionysos eine Rolle, wie bereits die im ägyptischen Tempel gefundene Dionysos-Herme zeigte. Doch stammen die meisten dieser Funde aus der vorchristlichen Zeit.[29]

In allen Fällen können Rückschlüsse auf typische lokale Besonderheiten dieser Religionen nur sehr begrenzt sein. In den meisten Fällen müssen diese Funde im Zusammenhang mit weiterem Material aus Makedonien, Griechenland, Kleinasien und aus anderen Bereichen der griechisch-römischen Welt interpretiert werden. Dieses Urteil muß aber überhaupt für die Suche nach archäologischen Funden aus der Umwelt des frühen Christentums gelten. Geographisch sowie chronologisch gilt für ihre Interpretation, sie in einen größeren Zusammenhang einzuordnen. Gewiß können gelegentlich Besonderheiten aus einem begrenzten geographischen Raum wichtige Informationen über die religiösen Verhältnisse einer bestimmten Zeit und eines bestimmten Ortes Auskunft geben. Eine sorgfältige Durchsicht des Materials muß deshalb zunächst die Besonderheiten einer bestimmten Stadt oder eines enger begrenzten Bereiches in Rechnung stellen. Aber der Zusammenhang mit der Kultur und Religion der größeren Bereiche (Palästina/Syrien, Länder der Ägäis, Rom und der Westen, Ägypten) sowie des römischen Reiches sollte dabei immer in Betracht gezogen werden. Zudem ist auch bei den

[28] Daß der ägyptische Kult in Thessalonike ein Heilkult war, ergibt sich auch aus mehreren Votivgaben; vgl. *Inscriptiones Thessalonicae et viciniae* 100.

[29] Berühmt ist die vergoldete bronzene Begräbnisurne mit Szenen aus dem Dionysoskult aus Derveni bei Thessalonike; sie stammt aus dem 4.Jh. v.Chr.

frühchristlichen Schriften damit zu rechnen, daß sie nicht auf spezifisch lokale Situationen ausgerichtet sind, sondern universal gültigen Konventionen, Ideologien und Sprachzusammenhängen verpflichtet sind, wie zum Beispiel der Apokalyptik und der politischen Propaganda des römischen Imperiums.

DER GLAUBE AUS DEM HÖREN
ÜBER DAS GESPROCHENE UND DAS GESCHRIEBENE WORT BEI PAULUS

Peter Müller (Pädagogische Hochschule Karlsruhe)

Wie das Verhältnis von gesprochenem und geschriebenem Wort bestimmt werden kann, ist ein altes Problem und zugleich eine Gegenwartsfrage. Platon ist, wo immer das Gespräch darüber geführt wird, Quelle und philosophischer Gewährsmann; Luther ist als theologischer Gesprächspartner überall zu finden; die Literaturwissenschaft schöpft aus beiden Traditionen und fügt eigene Zugänge und eigenes Vermögen hinzu, dem Sinn von Texten nachzuspüren. Genau dies steht heute aber zunehmend in Frage: daß einem Text *ein* Sinn innewohne, der durch geeignete Mittel der Interpretation geborgen werden könne.

In meinem Beitrag zur Festschrift für Dieter Georgi soll es im wesentlichen um diese Frage gehen – und zwar, dem Exegeten angemessen, unter Rückbezug auf Paulus und seinen bekannten Satz, daß der Glaube aus dem Hören komme (Röm 10,17). Weil aber Dieter Georgi die neutestamentliche Exegese immer sowohl in den größeren Rahmen der antiken Welt als auch in den Zusammenhang gegenwärtiger Diskurse und gesellschaftlicher Entwicklungen stellt, ist es wohl angemessen, nicht nur Paulus selbst und die Bedingungen des gesprochenen und geschriebenen Wortes in der Antike, sondern auch die aktuelle Diskussion mitzuberücksichtigen.

I

Das gegenwärtige Interesse am Verhältnis von gesprochenem und geschriebenem Wort verdankt sich verschiedenen Impulsen. Die *Grammatologie* von Jaques Derrida[1] ist ein wichtiger literarischer Bezugspunkt, an den sich zunächst in der Philosophie, dann aber weit darüber hinaus eine lebhafte Diskussion angeschlossen hat. Innerhalb der Literaturwissenschaft hat die Entwicklung von der Werkästhetik zur Rezep-

[1] Frankfurt 1974 (Paris 1967).

tionsästhetik und weiter zu den Fragen von Dekonstruktion und Intertextualität auch den Blick für das grundlegende Verhältnis von Stimme und Schrift geschärft. Die neuen Medien und das in Zusammenhang damit oft vorausgesagte Ende der Lese- und Buchkultur, des Gutenberg'schen Zeitalters, rücken praktische Fragen des Buchmarktes ins Zentrum des Interesses, ebenso aber auch theoretische Überlegungen zur Rolle des Buches. Daß diese verschiedenen Fragestellungen die Theologie nicht unberührt lassen können, liegt auf der Hand. Denn das Buch ist für die Theologie mehr als nur vorteilhafte Form zur Aufbewahrung von Geschriebenem. Von den Anfängen christlicher Überlieferung an ist die wesentliche Bezugsgröße christlichen Glaubens und Denkens ein Buch. Die Bezeichnung der Bibel als "Buch der Bücher" ist augenfälliger Beleg dafür, daß das Buch als "ureigenste(s) Medium des Glaubens"[2] gilt. Die angesichts der Veränderungen in der Medienlandschaft verstärkt vorgetragene Forderung nach einer neuen "christlichen Lesekultur"[3] und einer "Theologie des Lesens" verwundert auf diesem Hintergrund nicht.

1) Bei diesem theologischen Lob des Buches[4] und des Lesens fällt allerdings eine deutliche Ambivalenz auf. Das Lob gilt nämlich gar nicht in erster Linie dem Buch als solchem, als Geschriebenem, sondern der Stimme, dem mündlichen Wort, das in den Buchstaben und durch sie hindurch zum Sprechen kommt. Das Buch ist ein "zum Stehen gekommenes Sprechen", schreibt Guardini,[5] und das Lesen dementsprechend ein "Erwachenlassen des ursprünglichen Sprechens". Diese Auffassung reiht sich ein in eine lange Tradition, deren Kronzeuge Platon ist. Seine bekannteste Aussage zum geschriebenen und gesprochenen Wort findet sich im Phaidros:

> "Denn dieses Schlimme hat doch die Schrift, Phaidros, und ist darum ganz eigentlich der Malerei ähnlich: Denn auch diese

[2] Muth, L.: *Lesen – ein Heilsweg. Vom religiösen Sinn des Buches,* Freiburg 1987, S.46; vgl. auch ders.: *Glück, das sich entziffern läßt. Vom Urmedium des Glaubens,* Freiburg/Basel/Wien 1992.

[3] Vgl. Khoury, Th. (Hrsg): *Glauben durch Lesen? Für eine christliche Lesekultur,* Freiburg/Basel/Wien 1990.

[4] Rödszus-Hecker, M.: *Der buchstäbliche Zungensinn. Stimme und Schrift als Paradigmen der theologischen Hermeneutik,* Waltrop 1992, S.134ff.

[5] Guardini, R.: Lob des Buches. Ein Vortrag, in: *Börsenblatt des Deutschen Buchhandels,* 22 (1952), S.99-104, hier S.102.

> stellt ihre Ausgeburten hin als lebend, wenn man sie aber etwas fragt, so schweigen sie gar ehrwürdig still. Ebenso auch die Schriften. Du könntest glauben, sie sprächen, als verstünden sie etwas, fragst du sie aber lernbegierig über das Gesagte, so enthalten sie doch nur ein und dasselbe stets. Ist sie aber einmal geschrieben, so schweift auch überall jede Rede gleichermaßen unter denen umher, die sie verstehen, und unter denen, für die sie sich nicht gehört, und versteht nicht, zu wem sie reden soll und zu wem nicht. Und wird sie beleidigt oder unverdienterweise beschimpft, so bedarf sie immer ihres Vaters Hilfe, denn selbst ist sie weder imstande, sich zu schützen und sich zu helfen" (275d-e).

Phaidros stimmt zu (276a) und kommt antwortend zu der Unterscheidung

> "der lebenden und beseelten Rede des wahrhaft Wissenden, von der man die geschriebene mit Recht wie ein Schattenbild ansehen könnte".[6]

Dem Sprechen kommt ein Vorrang gegenüber dem Schreiben zu, weil es im Gegensatz zu jenem lebendig ist. Die Schrift dagegen wird als sekundär angesehen, als Aufbewahrungsort des Gesprochenen, aber als unzureichender; denn weder kann die Schrift im Austausch mit anderen weiterkommen noch ist sie in der Lage, sich gegen Anwürfe zu verteidigen. Und daß jeder sie lesen kann, gibt sie dem Mißverstehen preis. Mangelnde Direktheit und sekundäre Künstlichkeit kennzeichnen die geschriebene Sprache. Natürlich darf man Platon auf Grund dieser Äußerung nicht zum reinen Verfechter des gesprochenen Wortes stilisieren. Im Politikos (278, auch in Theait. 201-206) kann er das Lesenlernen anhand einzelner Buchstaben und Silben als Beispiel für den philosophischen Erkenntnisvorgang verwenden, und die Tatsache, daß er an-

---

[6] Übersetzung nach Schleiermacher/Kurz, Darmstadt 1990². Vgl. auch den 7. Brief Platons (341b-344d). Kurz vor der Phaidros-Stelle geht Platon auf die Sage von der Herkunft der Schrift von dem Gott Theuth ein. Den Hinweis, daß die Schrift das Gedächtnis fördere, weist er zurück (Phaidr. 274c-275b). Sie führe umgekehrt gerade zur Vernachlässigung des Gedächtnisses, weil die Lernenden sich nunmehr nur mit Hilfe der Schrift erinnerten. Überhaupt könne man aus schriftlichen Aufzeichnungen nichts Sicheres entnehmen. Interessanterweise greift Neil Postman in seinem neuen kulturkritischen Buch (*Das Technopol. Die Macht der Technologien und die Entmündigung der Gesellschaft*, Frankfurt 1992³, S.11ff) genau diese Legende von Thamus und Theuth als grundlegendes Beispiel dafür auf, daß wir "heutzutage von ganzen Scharen eifernder Theuths umgeben" seien, "die nur sehen, was die neuen Technologien zu leisten vermögen, und sich nicht vorstellen wollen, was sie zerstören" (ebd., S.12).

ders als Sokrates in Dialogform *schreibt*, belegt ebenfalls, daß er sich des Übergangs vom gesprochenen zum geschriebenen Wort und des Mediums der Schrift bewußt ist.[7] Dennoch bleibt ein Vorrang des Sprechens gegenüber dem Schreiben, des Hörens gegenüber dem Lesen bestehen und die Forderung, daß das Lesen wieder zum Hören werde, zieht sich im Anschluß an Platon durch die gesamte abendländische Geistesgeschichte hindurch. Daß dabei in der Antike und zum großen Teil auch im Mittelalter das Lesen im Sinne des Vorlesens auf Grund der äußeren Gegebenheiten tatsächlich zum Sprechen und Vortragen wird, ist allerdings wichtig und wird uns noch beschäftigen.

Das Zeitalter der Reformation hat in der neuen Technik des Buchdrucks eine wichtige Voraussetzung. Buchbesitz wird für breitere Bevölkerungsschichten erschwinglich, für viele wird Lesen möglich, mit Flugschriften werden neue Ideen propagiert. Schon von diesen äußeren Voraussetzungen her verwundert es deshalb nicht, daß wir bei Luther eine ganze Reihe von Bemerkungen zum Verhältnis von gesprochenem und geschriebenem Wort finden. Insgesamt bleibt bei ihm die Vorrangstellung des gesprochenen Wortes in Kraft. Besonders für Luthers Verständnis des Evangeliums ist die Mündlichkeit konstitutiv: "Nur in mündlicher Gestalt vermag das Evangelium im strengen Sinn als Wort Gottes laut zu werden".[8] Das Evangelium ist

> "ain gut geschray, ain gutt gerucht, das nit auff bapir geschriben, sonder in der welt, in lebendiger stimm berufft und bekent wirt".[9]

Als "gut gerucht, rede, geschrey von Christo" soll es in alle Welt hinausgerufen werden.[10] Urbild dieser mündlichen Gestalt des Evangeliums ist Christus selbst, der nichts aufgeschrieben hat; auch die Apostel haben das Evangelium überwiegend durch die mündliche Verkündigung weitergetra-

---

[7] Vgl. hierzu Goody, I./Watt, I.: Konsequenzen der Literalität, in: Goody, I. (Hrsg): *Literalität in traditionalen Gesellschaften*, Frankfurt 1981, S.45-104, besonders S.77-85.

[8] Beutel, A.: Erfahrene Bibel. Verständnis und Gebrauch des verbum dei scriptum bei Luther, in: *ZThK 89* (1992) S.302-339, hier S.310.

[9] *WA* 10,3; 305, 2-4.

[10] *WA* 17,2; 73,34f; weitere, vergleichbare Aussagen bei Beutel, *Bibel*, S.309f.

gen.[11] Demnach ist es die Aufgabe der Kirche, "ein mundhawß, nit ein fedderhawß" zu sein.[12]

Nun hat Luther zur Kirche als "fedderhawß" allerdings selbst nicht unwesentlich beigetragen, und seine Hervorhebung des gesprochenen Wortes ist denn auch keineswegs so eindeutig, wie es oft dargestellt wird.[13] Angesichts um sich greifender Irrlehren erweist sich die Verschriftlichung des Evangeliums sogar geradezu als notwendig. Und aus dieser Notwendigkeit erwächst zugleich die Möglichkeit, den Glauben am nunmehr geschriebenen Wort zu identifizieren und zu verifizieren:

> "Lieber Bapsts, lieber keiser, und wer ihr mehr seit ... Dieses wort hab ich nicht erdacht, ich habs auch nicht geschrieben, nemet Brillen in die hand und thut die heilige schriefft auff, darinnen werdet ihrs also finden".[14]

Von hier aus können Lektüre und Studium der Schrift von Luther geradezu empfohlen werden. So reicht der Modus der Schriftlichkeit zwar nicht an die Lebendigkeit des gesprochenen Wortes heran, ist aber in der Lage, den dem gesprochenen Wort innewohnenden Mangel des Unkontrollierbaren und Willkürlichen zumindest teilweise auszugleichen. Wichtig ist in diesem Zusammenhang auch die Feststellung, daß das Wort als solches, sei es schriftlich oder mündlich, nicht ins Herz dringen kann, sondern der Wirkung des heiligen Geistes bedarf, der das Wort "in das Herz webt".[15] So ist das geschriebene Wort wohl notwendig, gerade auch als Mittel der Auseinandersetzung und Klärung, es drängt aber zur Verkündigung und dient der Wirkung des Geistes als Vehikel. Auf diese Weise wird der Text zum ansprechenden und bewegenden Wort, die Schrift wird erneut zur Stimme.[16] Im Anschluß an Luther gewinnt die Metapher von der "Stimme der Schrift" in der evangelischen Theologie allgemeine Geltung in einem Maß, "daß sie den Stellenwert einer Er-

---

[11] Vgl. *WA* 7; 526, 16f; *WA* 10,1,1; 626,15ff.

[12] Vgl. hierzu *WA* 10,1,2; 48,1-15.

[13] Vgl. hierzu insgesamt Rödszus-Hecker, *Zungensinn*, S.19ff; Beutel, Bibel, S.311f.

[14] *WA 47*; 405,21-24.

[15] *WA TR 1*; 174; Rödszus-Hecker, *Zungensinn*, S.40ff.

[16] Zur Metapher von der "Stimme des Textes" vgl. Rödszus-Hecker, *Zungensinn*, S.49ff.

klärung annimmt und selbst gar nicht mehr erklärungsbedürftig erscheint".[17]

Neben das philosophische und das theologische Beispiel für die Vorrangstellung des gesprochenen Wortes sei noch eines aus der literarischen Hermeneutik gestellt. Es belegt den Einfluß dieser Auffassung auch in der Literaturwissenschaft und reicht zudem bis an die Gegenwart heran. Es handelt sich um eine Beschreibunng des Lesens im Rahmen des sogenannten "Sinnentnahme-Konzeptes":

> "Lesen ist ... Inhalt-Entnahme, Sinnerfassung ... Aus der bis zur Kümmerlichkeit genial vereinfachten Schriftzeichenfolge muß der eingebrachte Sinn in allen seinen Nuancen, Schichtungen, Ober- und Untertönen nachschöpferisch entbunden werden, damit die intendierte geistige Kommunikation überhaupt statthabe. Sinnverkörperung geschieht jedoch in vollem Umfange allein im lebendigen gesprochenen Wort mit seinen verschiedenen Dimensionen. Schrift ist sinnerfüllte Form also in dem Maße, in dem der Adressat den vom Schreibenden intendierten 'Inhalt' kraft seiner Sprachmächtigkeit nachgestaltend zu heben, aus der Einsargung in graphische Zeichen zu befreien vermag".[18]

"Einsargung in graphische Zeichen" – ein starker Ausdruck, der allerdings dem häufiger zu findenden "toten Buchstaben" entspricht[19] und der Stimme vor der Schrift den Vorrang einräumt. Die Schrift ist wohl in der Lage dazu, das mündliche Wort aufzubewahren, ihr Ziel aber ist es, dieses Wort wieder hörbar zu machen.

2) Gegenüber dieser großen Koalition zugunsten des gesprochenen Wortes hat Jaques Derrida eine Neubewertung des Verhältnisses von Stimme und Schrift vorgenommen und damit in der Philosophie und der Literaturwissenschaft, mit einiger Verzögerung auch in der Theologie, eine intensive Diskussion angeregt. Ihm geht es darum, den Phonozentrismus, die Vorrangstellung des gesprochenen Wortes, auf

[17] *Ebd.*, 67.

[18] Beinlich, A.: Das grundlegende Lesenlernen heute, in: Baumgärtner, A. (Hrsg): *Lesen – Ein Handbuch*, 1973, S.391.

[19] Vgl. in der Theologie beispielsweise Schleiermacher, F.D.E.: *Über die Religion. Reden an die Gebildeten unter ihren Verächtern*, in: Kritische Gesamtausgabe, hrsg. von H.-J. Birkner u.a., Erste Abteilung, Band 2, Berlin/New York 1984, S.242, Z.9ff. Schleiermacher spricht dort von der "todten Schrift" als dem "Mausoleum der Religion".

seine Grundlagen hin zu untersuchen und seine beherrschende Stellung zu hinterfragen. Wenn nämlich üblicherweise dem Wort die Unmittelbarkeit zum Bezeichneten zugestanden, der Schrift aber die Differenz, der Abfall des Wortes von der Sache durch das künstliche Zeichen, angelastet wird,[20] so greift diese Divergenz nach Derrida zu kurz; denn auch das gesprochene Wort hat im Verhältnis zu dem Gedanken und Eindruck, die es hervorrufen, etwas Nachträgliches und reicht nicht unmittelbar an das heran, was es benennen will. Wenn die Schrift durch Nachträglichkeit und Distanz zum Bezeichneten charakterisiert ist, dann gilt dies folglich auch für die Stimme, die dementsprechend ebenfalls als "Schrift" charakterisiert werden kann.[21] Insofern es nämlich die Sprache in einem ursprünglichen Sinn, als Unmittelbarkeit von Signifikant und Signifikat, von Zeichen und Sache, nie gegeben hat, trägt auch die gesprochene Sprache nach Derrida immer schon das Merkmal der Schrift an sich. Genau genommen gibt es kein Signifikat,

> "das dem Spiel aufeinander verweisender Signifikanten entkäme, welches die Sprache konstituiert, und sei es nur, um ihm letzten Endes wieder anheimzufallen. Die Heraufkunft der Schrift ist die Heraufkunft des Spiels".[22]

Wenn sich jedes Signifikat immer schon in der Position des Signifikanten befindet,[23] dann ist Sprache von Anfang an Schrift, eine "Ur-Schrift" gewissermaßen. Einen absoluten Ursprung des Sinns gibt es demgegenüber nicht. Er kann nur in der Metapher der "Spur" benannt werden[24]:

> "In Wirklichkeit ist die Spur der absolute Ursprung des Sinns im allgemeinen; was aber bedeutet ..., daß es einen absoluten Ursprung des Sinns im allgemeinen nicht gibt. Die Spur ist die Differenz, in welcher das Erscheinen und die Bedeutung ihren Anfang nehmen ... Kein Begriff der Metaphysik kann sie beschreiben. Und da sie a fortiori der Unterscheidung zwischen den Sinnesorganen, dem Laut und dem Licht vorgängig ist, wie könnte es dann noch sinnvoll sein, eine 'natürliche' Hierarchie

---

[20] Vgl. *Grammatologie*, S.24 (unter Hinweis auf Aristoteles), und die ausführliche Diskussion der Linguistik von Ferdinand de Saussure, *ebd.*, S.49ff.

[21] *Ebd.*, S.99.

[22] *Ebd.*, S.17.

[23] *Ebd.*, S.129.

[24] Vgl. *ebd.*, S.99ff, besonders S.109f.114; das folgende Zitat S.114.

> zwischen dem akustischen Eindruck und dem visuellen (graphischen) Eindruck zu errichten? Das graphische Abbild wird nicht gesehen und das akustische Abbild wird nicht gehört".

Auf diesem Hintergrund wird der Unterschied verständlich, den Derrida zwischen Buch und Text erkennt. Das Buch repräsentiert den Gedanken einer Totalität von Signifikanten und eine bereits davor gedachte Totalität des Signifikats, ist also gekennzeichnet durch Geschlossenheit und Kohärenz:

> "Die Idee des Buches, die immer auf eine natürliche Totalität verweist, ist dem Sinn der Schrift zutiefst fremd. Sie schirmt die Theologie und den Logozentrismus enzyklopädisch gegen den sprengenden Einbruch der Schrift ab, gegen ihre aphoristische Enge und ... gegen die Differenz im allgemeinen".[25]

Der Text dagegen steht für Unabgeschlossenheit und Offenheit; Schreiben, Schrift und Text sind gekennzeichnet durch eine dezentrierende, unendlich verweisende Kraft, die Schrift ist andauerndes Spiel. Das Buch lebt aus dem "Trugbild des Ursprungs, des Endes, der Linie, der Schleife, des Bandes, des Zentrums",[26] die Schrift dagegen lebt vom und im Spiel von Text und Kontext, im Spiel der Intertextualität.[27]

So weit einmal in aller Kürze Derrida. Andere haben diesen Denkansatz aufgegriffen und weiter ausgeführt, beispielsweise Foucault, der den Autor eines Textes nicht mehr als Subjekt mit einer bestimmten Intention verstehen will, sondern als Funktion zu bestimmen sucht.[28] Daß solche Positionen eine Herausforderung an die Theologie darstellen, liegt auf der Hand. Denn mit dem Konzept des Buches steht das "Buch der Bücher" in Frage, zugleich das "Trugbild des Ursprungs", der göttliche Logos, und im fortschreitenden Spiel von Text und Intertext bekommen Autorintention, Anspruch und Sinn des Geschriebenen den Charakter der steten Veränderung.

---

[25] Ebd., S.35. Vgl. hierzu auch die Ausführungen von Timm, H.: *Das ästhetische Jahrzehnt. Zur Postmodernisierung der Religion,* Gütersloh 1990, besonders S.172-175.

[26] Derrida, J.: *Die Schrift und die Differenz,* Frankfurt 1992^5, S.444.

[27] Zu den Konsequenzen für das Verhältnis von Autor und Rezipient vgl. Rödszus-Hecker, *Zungensinn,* S.133.

[28] Foucault, M.: Was ist ein Autor?, in: ders.: *Schriften zur Literatur,* Frankfurt 1988, S.7-31.

II

Ist damit der Horizont der gegenwärtigen Frage abgesteckt, so wende ich mich nun, grob gesprochen, der Zeit des Paulus zu, von Horaz angefangen bis zum Ende des 1.Jahrhunderts n.Chr. Was Schrift und Buch bedeuten, ist nämlich keineswegs eindeutig, sondern dem Wandel unterworfen, und gerade in der bezeichneten Epoche deutet sich ein Wandel an. Ihm gehe ich mit einigen Hinweisen nach, nehme etwas ausführlicher zu dem 20.Brief im ersten Brief-Buch des Horaz Stellung und greife einige weitere, charakteristische Äusserungen anderer Autoren des 1.Jahrhunderts n.Chr. auf.

1) Die Briefe sind ein Teil des Alterswerkes von Horaz. Er verbindet in ihnen tiefe philosophische Gedanken mit leichter Heiterkeit (vgl. etwa epist. I 4,13f und 15f). Ausgehend von eigenen Erfahrungen und in gepflegtem Alltagston formuliert er Erkenntnisse, die über das Alltägliche doch weit hinausgehen. Der 20.Brief, den ich hier vorstelle, schließt die erste Sammlung der Briefe ab. An das Buch selbst gerichtet beschreibt er mit launischen Worten dessen künftiges Ergehen bis zum ziemlich düsteren Ende, kommt aber gleichwohl zu einem versöhnlichen Schluß. Der Brief ist mit einem Augenzwinkern geschrieben und will wohl auch so verstanden werden. Die autobiographischen Details im Schlußabschnitt (Z.19-28) stimmen mit anderen Bemerkungen bei Horaz selbst, aber auch bei Vergil, überein und die Altersangabe weist die Abfassung des Briefes in das Jahr 21 v.Chr. Mit seinen Schlußbemerkungen lehnt Horaz sich an die Tradition der Sphragis an, einer Siegelung, mit der ein Dichter seinen Namen in seinen Text einfügt und ihn damit gewissermaßen als geistiges Eigentum reklamiert.[29] Allerdings gestaltet er die Sphragis in eine ausführlichere Charakterisierung des Autors um, läßt aber die typische Namensnennung beiseite. Das bestätigt die Eigenständigkeit dieses "kleinen Meisterwerkes sui generis".[30]

---

[29] Vgl. hierzu ausführlich Kranz, W.: Sphragis. Ichform und Namenssiegel als Eingangs- und Schlußmotiv antiker Dichtung, in: ders.: *Studien zur antiken Literatur und ihrem Fortwirken. Kleine Schriften* (hrsg. v. E.Vogt), Heidelberg 1967, S.27-78; zu Horaz besonders S.72ff.

[30] Fraenkel, E.: *Horaz*, Darmstadt 1963, S.425.

Daß das Buch unter milderer Sonne den *Zuhörern* von seinem Verfasser erzählen soll (Z.19), ist für das Verhältnis von gesprochenem und geschriebenem Wort von Bedeutung, weil hier die dem modernen Betrachter selbstverständliche Unterscheidung zwischen (leisem) Lesen und Sprechen relativiert wird. Das Buch hat offensichtlich Zuhörer (*pluris admoverit auris*, Z.20), denen es vorgelesen wird. Daß das Lesen in der gesamten Antike ganz überwiegend lautes Lesen war, ist vielfach belegt. Ich begnüge mich deshalb mit einigen Hinweisen. Bei Platon (Phaid. 97b) "hört man aus einem Buch" und in gleicher Weise läßt Plinius der Jüngere (ca 62-113 n.Chr.) "aus einem Buch lesen" (*liber legitur*, epist. IX,36; III,5). An anderer Stelle (epist. VIII,1) klagt Plinius:[31]

> "Mein Vorleser Encolpius, mein guter Geist in Ernst und Scherz, hat sich durch den Staub eine Halsentzündung zugezogen und Blut ausgeworfen. Wie traurig für ihn selbst, wie bitter für mich, wenn er, der seine ganze Beliebtheit meinen Studien verdankt, für die Studien untauglich wird! Wer wird alsdann meine Arbeiten so vortragen, so lieben? Wen werden meine Ohren so gerne hören?"

Und wenn Augustin rund 300 Jahre später in Conf IV,3 das leise Lesen des Ambrosius mit verschiedenen Gründen zu erklären versucht, dann zeigt sich daran, daß es auch in dieser Zeit keineswegs die Regel, sondern die Ausnahme war.

Lesen gehört also als Vorlesen in einen Kreis von Zuhörern hinein. Der soziale Rahmen für solches Vortragen ist in der griechisch-römischen Antike der kleinere, halböffentliche Kreis von Freunden und Klienten oder das größere Publikum bei der öffentlichen Darbietung. Daß das Publikum allerdings bisweilen aus angeheuerten Claqueuren bestand, kann man in bissigen Bemerkungen bei Iuvenal (Iuv. VII,37-41), Tacitus (Dial 9,3) oder wiederum Plinius (epist. IIII,13 u.ö.) nachlesen. Plinius, der von vielen Lesungen berichtet, hat offenbar den kleineren Kreis bevorzugt. Und Horaz selbst sieht das große Publikum ebenfalls mit kritischer Distanz, wie epist. I,19,34ff zeigt:[32]

---

[31] Übersetzung nach H.Kasten, Darmstadt 1990[6].

[32] Daß der kleinere Kreis von Freunden und Klienten eine bestimmte Gesellschaftsschicht voraussetzt, habe ich an anderer Stelle ausführlicher beschrieben (Müller, P.: *In der Mitte der Gemeinde. Kinder im Neuen Testament*, Neukirchen-Vluyn 1992, S.134ff).

> "Ich bin der Mann nicht, des wetterwendischen Pöbels Stimmen zu ködern mit dem Aufwand von Mählern und mit der Gabe abgetragener Kleidung".

Ein kleinerer Kreis ist nun offensichtlich auch am Ende des 20. Briefes vorausgesetzt. Was diesem Kreis vorgelesen werden soll, finden wir im Hauptteil des Briefes auf burleske Weise beschrieben:

> "Es scheint, mein Buch, du schaust nach Ianus und Vertumnus aus, wohl um dich zum Verkauf zu stellen, schön glatt gemacht durch Bimsstein von den Sosii. Du haßt die Schlüssel und die Siegel auch, die dem Anständigen doch teuer sind. Daß wenige dich sehn, das nimmst du schwer und preist die öffentlichen Orte – so freilich zog ich dich nicht auf! So renn denn fort, wohin du strebst hinabzusteigen! Bist du erst draußen, wird es keine Wiederkehr mehr für dich geben" (Z.1-6).[33]

Offenbar ist das Buch mit dem Vorgelesenwerden im kleinen Kreis nicht zufrieden und strebt in die Öffentlichkeit, auf den Marktplatz mit den Götterstatuen. Es fühlt sich eingesperrt und haßt Schlüssel und Siegel. Ihren besonderen Reiz bekommen die Zeilen dadurch, daß mit dem *liber* nicht nur das Buch angesprochen ist, sondern, ermöglicht durch das Maskulinum, auch ein junger Mann, ein Sklavenjunge, im Hause seines Herrn genährt (*nutritus*, Z.5) und erzogen (vgl. etwa epist. II 2,5ff). Wie das Buch strebt dieser *liber* nach draußen, in die Öffentlichkeit, die vermeintliche Freiheit, und bietet sich dort an. *Prostes* (Z.2) ist in diesem Zusammenhang ein zweideutiger Begriff[34] und auch im weiteren Verlauf finden sich solche Assoziationen: Die Papyrusrolle wird mit Bimsstein geglättet, aber auch die Haut des Jungen, der auf dem Markt seine erotischen Dienste anbietet; Schlüssel und Siegel sind beiden verhaßt; der *amator* in Z.8 bezeichnet den Liebhaber, und zwar sowohl des Buches als auch des jungen Sklaven; und daß schließlich der Erfolg zurückgeht, wenn der Reiz des Neuen oder der Jugend nachläßt (Z.9f), trifft ebenfalls auf beide zu. Aber ich habe vorgegriffen. Der Text lautet folgendermaßen:

> "'Was hab ich Armer nur getan? Was hab ich denn gewünscht?' So wirst du sprechen dann, hat etwas dich verletzt. Du weißt ja

[33] Übersetzung von B.Kytzler, Stuttgart 1986.
[34] Vgl. hierzu und zum folgenden Fraenkel, *Horaz*, S.419.

> auch, in welchen engen Winkel eingerollt du dich dann finden wirst, ist satt dein Liebhaber geworden und hat genug von dir. Doch wenn der Wahrsager sich nicht aus Ärger über deinen Fehltritt täuscht, wirst du in Rom wohl teuer sein – zumindest bis die Jugend dich verläßt. Fängst du erst an, von Pöbelhänden abgegriffen auszusehen, so wirst entweder still du nichtsnutzige Motten nähren oder wirst entweichen bis nach Utica oder in Banden nach Ilerda gehen müssen. Dann wird der Warner, dem du dein Gehör nicht schenken wolltest, lachen – jedoch wie jener Mann, der seinen Esel, der so schlecht im folgte, im Zorn die Felsen abwärts stieß: Wer wollte sich die Mühe machen, den noch zu retten, und gegen seinen Willen noch dazu? Und auch das steht dir schließlich noch bevor: Das Alphabet wirst du den Kindern beizubringen haben, wenn in entlegenen Vororten des Alters Stottern dich ergreift".

Das Schicksal, das dem Buch bevorsteht, ist mit einigen markanten Strichen gezeichnet. Von vielen Händen wird es abgegriffen,[35] von Ungeziefer angefressen oder aber in die ferne Provinz gebracht, nach Nordafrika (Utica) oder Spanien (Ilerda), als Ladenhüter allerdings. Und selbst dort hält der Abstieg des Buches noch an: in der Provinz muß es schließlich für den Elementarrunterricht der Kinder herhalten.[36]

Damit ist deutlich: Eine Rückkehr in den kleinen Kreis der Zuhörer gibt es für das Buch nicht. Indem es sich als Buch der Öffentlichkeit anbietet, gibt es sich ihr preis. Es geht ihm wie dem hübschen Jungen mit seinen erotischen Diensten. Die düstere Aussicht wird allerdings im Schlußabschnitt doch noch umgestimmt: wenn das Buch einmal mehr Zuhörer haben sollte, dann kann es von seinem Verfasser erzählen.

2) Horaz formuliert seinen Brief mit augenzwinkernder Leichtigkeit. Daß er den zeitgenössischen Literaturbetrieb und Buchhandel gut kennt, ihm zugleich aber mit kritischer Distanz gegenübersteht, ist allerdings nicht zu übersehen. Sie hat ihren Grund zum Teil in dem Gefühl des Abschieds, den das Buch von seinem Autor nimmt,[37] wenn es in die Öffentlichkeit hinausgeht. Zugleich deutet sich hier aber ein grundlegender

---

[35] *contrectare* (Z.11) ist wiederum ein Wort aus dem erotischen Bereich: betasten, befühlen, berühren.

[36] Vgl. beispielsweise Quint. *inst.* I 4,8. Geübt wurde vorzugsweise an Klassikertexten; waren diese nicht vorhanden, wurden auch andere Schriften verwendet.

[37] In überraschend ähnlicher Weise ist dieses Gefühl aufgenommen bei Sarah Kirsch, *Erlkönigs Tochter. Gedichte,* Stuttgart 1992, S.68.

Wandel im Verständnis des Geschriebenen an, der über einen längeren Zeitraum hinweg stattfindet, in der augusteischen Epoche aber besonders hervortritt. Dies läßt sich anhand verschiedener Beobachtungen zeigen.

Ich bleibe zunächst bei Horaz. Daß Bücher vorgelesen werden, findet sich auch sonst bei ihm, beispielsweise in der 10. Satire des ersten Buches, wo er auf unterschiedliche Könnerschaft beim Versemachen eingeht. Possen allein sind noch keine Dichtung, meint er, und "also genügt es nicht, mit Gelächter das Maul deines Hörers aufzureißen (Sat. I 10,15f).[38] Nur ein paar Zeilen weiter spricht Horaz vom "Vortrag" (sermo, Sat. I 10,31), auch dies ein Hinweis auf das laute Vorlesen des Geschriebenen, und wenn in Z.82 von den Lesern die Rede ist, so sind faktisch Vorleser und Hörer gemeint. Im übrigen grenzt Horaz sich in dieser Satire von Lucilius, dem literarischen Vorbild, ab. Dieser schrieb für gewöhnlich zweihundert Verse vor dem Essen und ebensoviele danach (Z.68f), wobei deren Qualität aber nicht immer überzeugt (Z.64ff). Würde Lucilius (ca 180-102 v.Chr.) in der Zeit des Horaz leben,

> "würd' von sich vieles er abreiben, alles, was über Vollendung nachschleppt hinaus, das würd er stutzen, und würde beim Dichten oftmals den Kopf sich kratzen und nagen am blutigen Nagel. Oftmals verkehre den Griffel, willst schreiben du zweimal zu lesen Würdiges, mühe dich nicht, daß der Haufe dich anstaunt, zufrieden mit nur wenigen Lesern! Oder möchtest verrückt du lieber, daß deine Gedichte diktiert in der Klippschule werden?" (Z.77-83)

Dem Vielschreiber Lucilius wird hier das Bild des Dichters gegenübergestellt, der seine Worte wägt, überdenkt und immer wieder korrigiert, bevor er sie entläßt, der also an seinem *geschriebenen* Text feilt und ihn überarbeitet. Das Schreiben wird zur intensiv betriebenen Arbeit[39] und nur durch diese Arbeit am geschriebenen Text ist vollendete Dichtung möglich. So wird der Dichter zum Philologen und Schreiber.[40] Ver-

---

[38] Übersetzung nach K.Büchner, Stuttgart 1986.

[39] Vgl. Fuhrmann, M.: *Dichtungstheorie der Antike. Aristoteles – Horaz – 'Longin'. Eine Einführung*, Darmstadt 1992², S.159-161.

[40] Vgl. auch Horaz, *Ars poetica*, Z.445ff: "Der gute und sachverständige Mann wird kunstwidrige Verse tadeln, plumpe mißbilligen, zu schmucklosen ein schwarzes Zeichen mit schrägem Federstrich setzen, üppigen Zierat beschneiden, den Stellen, die nicht hell genug sind, mehr Licht zu geben erzwingen, mißverständlich Gesagtes verklagen, was zu ändern ist,

gil schreibt zehn Jahre an seiner Aeneis und schafft ein Werk, das in seiner Fülle für den Vortrag kaum geeignet ist.[41] Und Sueton bezeichnet den Vergil in einer Notiz (vita Verg. 90-94) deutlich als Schreiber: Am Nachmittag redigiert er die Verse, die er während der Vormittagsstunden diktiert hat, und reduziert so das Material auf die Verse, die ihm geglückt erscheinen. Durch die Arbeit, die in den Text investiert wird, bekommt das geschriebene Wort ein eigenes und besonderes Gewicht. Zugleich rückt dadurch die Produktion des Textes, seine genaue Fixierung und Weitergabe, ebenso auch die Überarbeitung (bis hin zur zweiten Auflage) in den Blick. Auf der Seite der Rezeption entspricht dem ein genaueres Textstudium. Das private Studieren gewinnt an Boden.[42] In der 4. Satire des ersten Horaz'schen Buches ist diese Änderung bei der Produktion und Rezeption von Literatur deutlich zu fassen.

Sie tritt umso deutlicher hervor, wenn man kurz noch einmal auf die Vorstellung vom auf Grund göttlicher Inspiration schaffenden Dichter bei Platon zurückblickt:

> "Denn nicht durch Kunst oder Wissenschaft sagst du, was du vom Homeros sagst, sondern durch göttliche Schickung und Besitzung, so wie die Korybanten nur auf jenen Gesang recht hören, der von dem Gotte herrührt, welcher sie besitzt, und auf dessen Weise einen Reichtum an Gebärden und Worten haben, um andere sich aber gar nicht bekümmern" (Ion 536c).

Dementsprechend sind nach 534a die Liederdichter beim Schaffen ihrer Lieder nicht bei vernünftigem Bewußtsein, sondern bringen ihre Schöpfungen durch göttliche Kraft hervor, so daß diese "nicht Menschliches sind und von Menschen, sondern Göttliches und von Göttern, die Dichter aber nichts sind als Sprecher der Götter" (534e), die vortragenden Rhapsoden wiederum "Sprecher der Sprecher". Beide, sowohl der Rhapsode als auch der Dichter, können deshalb als "göttliche Menschen" bezeichnet werden (542a.b). Die göttliche Einwirkung wirkt sich schließlich im Sinne konzentrischer Kreise bis zum Zusehen und Zuhören aus (535e). Daß das

---

wird er bezeichnen, er wird zum Aristarch" (Übersetzung nach E.Schäfer, Stuttgart 1989).

[41] Vgl. hierzu ausführlicher Quinn, K.: The Poet and his Audience in the Augustan Age (*ANRW II 30,1*), S.76-180, hier S.86f.144.

[42] *Ebd.*, S.88.

geschriebene Wort gegenüber dem gesprochenen nur als Schattenbild anzusehen sei (Phaidr. 276a), ist mit diesen Bemerkungen anschaulich ausgeführt.

Horaz nimmt nun in der *Ars poetica* zu dieser alten Auffassung kritisch Stellung:

> "Ob durch Naturtalent eine Dichtung Beifall erringt oder durch Kunstverstand, hat man gefragt. Ich kann nicht erkennen, was ein Bemühen ohne fündige Ader oder was eine unausgebildete Begabung nützt; so fordert das eine die Hilfe des andren und verschwört sich mit ihm in Freundschaft." (Z.408-411)

Wer unausgebildet nur auf sein Talent pocht, gerät leicht zum Marktschreier (*merces*, Z.419), der Sonderangebote macht, deren Qualität aber zu wünschen übrig läßt (Z.419-433). Solche kritischen Bemerkungen konnten die Hochschätzung des gesprochenen Wortes beim deklamierenden Vortrag insgesamt zwar nur wenig erschüttern, wie die vielen Hinweise auf öffentliche und halböffentliche Lesungen belegen, die am Ende des 1.Jahrhunderts in den Pliniusbriefen zu finden sind. Aber auch bei Plinius tritt gegenüber der alten Auffassung vom gesprochenen als dem wahrhaft lebendigen Wort eine Verschiebung in der Argumentation ein. Ein kleiner Abschnitt aus epist. II 3 kann dies verdeutlichen:

> "Zum Lesen hast du stets Gelegenheit, zum Hören nicht immer; überdies packt, wie man gemeinhin sagt, das lebendige Wort viel mehr. Denn mag treffender sein, was man liest, tiefer in der Seele haftet doch, was Vortrag, Mienenspiel, Haltung und Gebärde des Redenden in sie senkt".

Die Nüchternheit gegenüber der platonischen Argumentation fällt deutlich ins Auge: Man hat nicht immer Gelegenheit zum Hören, also soll man sie nutzen, wenn man sie hat. Mienenspiel und Gebärden lassen das Gehörte besser in der Seele haften und geben so trotz der größeren Genauigkeit beim (privaten) Lesen dem Vortrag den Vorzug. Dennoch ist deutlich: Das geschriebene Wort hat eine eigene Wertigkeit bekommen. Es ist immer zur Hand und gewährleistet eine größere Genauigkeit beim Verfassen wie bei der Rezeption. Daß diese Entwicklung ambivalent beurteilt wurde, belegt der 20.Brief des Horaz auf plastische Weise. Aufhalten ließ sich die Entwicklung aber offensichtlich nicht.

3) Dabei ist auch nicht zu übersehen, daß eine gewisse

Inflation des vorgetragenen Wortes die Wertschätzung des Geschriebenen verstärkte. Bei Horaz zeigt sich das bereits in der Einschätzung des Vielschreibers Lucilius. Nun schrieb dieser seine Verse nicht selbst, sondern diktierte sie einem Schreiber. Daß er dabei viele und zum Teil unwürdige Nachahmer gefunden habe, hält Horaz in epist. II 1,10ff fest. Im Gegensatz zu den hergebrachten Sitten des römischen Hausherrn habe sich des Volkes Sinn nun leichtfertig gewandelt:

> "Es glüht jetzt nur noch vor Gier, was zu schreiben: Knaben wie strenge Väter speisen, geschmückt ihr Haar mit Laub, und diktieren Gedichte dabei".[43]

Und daß der Drang, das so Geschaffene zu Gehör zu bringen, auch aufdringliche Züge annehmen konnte, hält einige Jahrzehnte später Martial in einem Epigramm spöttisch fest:

> "Du liest mir vor im Stehen und im Sitzen; ich laufe – du liest mir vor; ich sitz am Lokus – auch dort liest du mir vor; ich flieh ins Schwitzbad – dort bist du auch und dröhnst mir in die Ohren ... Soll ich dir sagen, was du angerichtet hast? Du bist ein braver Kerl, bist hochanständig – und man hat Angst vor dir" (epigr. III 44).[44]

So ist es denn kein Wunder, daß die Begeisterung, Vorträgen zu lauschen, angesichts einer zunehmenden Zahl solcher Deklamationen abnahm. Plinius kommt nicht umhin festzustellen, daß zwar die Studien blühen und fast kein Tag vergehe, an dem nicht jemand vortrage.

> "Freilich kommt man nur verdrossen zusammen, um sie zu hören. Die meisten sitzen in ihren Lokalen und vertun die Zeit des Vortrags mit Schnurrpfeifereien, lassen sich von Zeit zu Zeit melden, ob der Vortragende schon eingetreten ist, ob er die Vorrede gesprochen hat, ob er sein Manuskript schon zum größeren Teil abgerollt hat, dann erst kommen sie herein und auch jetzt noch zögernd und bedächtig, halten aber nicht durch, sondern verdrücken sich vor dem Ende, die einen heimlich und verstohlen, einige offen und ungeniert" (epist. I 13).

Dieser Abschnitt zeigt mit der deutlich zutage tretenden Unlust am Vorgetragenen selbst, daß das literarische Interesse gegenüber der sozialen Funktion der Lesungen in den Hin-

---

[43] Zum deklamierenden Charakter des Diktierens vgl. Quinn, Poet, S.84f.167-169.

[44] Nach der Übersetzung von H.C.Schnur, Stuttgart 1991. Vergleichbar ist wiederum Horaz, *Ars poetica*, Z.472-476.

tergrund tritt.[45] Die Bedeutung von Texten kann nun nicht mehr in der Hauptsache am gesprochenen Wort festgemacht werden. Ohne daß die Lesung ihre soziale Funktion verlieren würde, gewinnt das geschriebene Wort zunehmend an Bedeutung. Die Veröffentlichung des geschriebenen Textes in Form des vervielfältigten Buches und das Studieren des Textes gewinnen zunehmend Einfluß als Form der literarischen Kommunikation.

Mit am deutlichsten ist diese Wandlung gegen Ende des ersten Jahrhunderts bei Martial festzustellen. Nicht nur, daß er sich, wie es dem Epigrammatiker gebührt, spöttisch über das deklamierende Lesen ausläßt, etwa so:

> "Sollte mein Büchlein ich bringen und ans Deklamieren mich machen, möge dies Halstuch dir dann dienen als Ohrenverband" (epigr. III 44; vgl. auch IV 41).

Es wird bei ihm auch deutlich, daß er beim Schreiben zunehmend den einzelnen Leser und die Leserin im Auge hat. Im ersten Buch rät er ausdrücklich zu der (vermutlich in Kodexform herausgegebenen) "Taschenausgabe", die handlich ist und gut geeignet für unterwegs (I 1). Die Dame, die sein Buch schon aus der Hand legen wollte, bringt er durch einige Hinweise auf die folgenden galanteren Teile zum gründlichen Studieren derselben (III 68; vgl. XI 17). Und im übrigen belegt die Neuausgabe des 10.Buches der Epigramme auch bei Martial, daß das Schreiben, das Verändern und Verbessern, nun zum Merkmal des Dichters geworden ist (X 2).

Damit in Zusammenhang wird verstärkt der Abschied des Autors von seiner Schrift thematisiert. "Das Wort, das du von dir gabst, kennt keine Rückkehr" (*nescit vox missa reverti*), schreibt Horaz in der *Ars poetica* (390). Gewiß stehen hinter diesem Satz die Unwägbarkeiten, die in der Antike mit der Veröffentlichung eines Buches gegeben waren, die Unsicherheit des Textes beim Kopieren ebenso wie das fehlende Autoren- und Verlagsrecht. So betrachtet stellte die Publikation eines Werkes immer ein Risiko dar. Zugleich stecken jedoch die öffentlichen und halböffentlichen Lesungen in einer Krise und das geschriebene Wort erfährt eine Aufwertung. Zwar drängt es nach wie vor zum mündlichen Vortrag, zur lebhaften Darbietung. Zugleich aber tritt es verstärkt mit dem Anspruch

---

[45] Vgl. hierzu ausführlicher Quinn, Poet, S.163ff.

auf, bearbeitetes und ausgefeiltes Wort zu sein, Literatur also, die nun auch gelesen und studiert werden und damit als geschriebenes Wort wirken will.

III

Ich komme zu Paulus. Daß er in den Lese-Traditionen und -Gepflogenheiten seiner Zeit steht, ist offensichtlich. Er diktiert seine Briefe und legt Wert darauf, daß sie in der Gemeindeversammlung (vor-) gelesen werden (I Thess 5,27). Und inhaltlich scheint er dem gesprochenen Wort den Vorrang vor dem geschriebenen zu geben. Jedenfalls hält er in dem ersten uns bekannten Brief fest:

> "Als ihr das Gotteswort unserer Predigt empfangen habt, habt ihr es aufgenommen nicht als Wort von Menschen, sondern als Wort Gottes, was es auch tatsächlich ist" (I Thess 2,13).

In dem unserer Kenntnis nach letzten Paulusbrief ist dieser Gedanke in einer bekannten Passage prägnant formuliert: "Der Glaube (kommmt) aus dem Hören" (Röm 10,17), und zwar, wie der Zusammenhang ab V.14 zeigt, aus dem Hören des verkündeten Wortes, also der Predigt. Und in Gal 4,20 bringt Paulus seine Ratlosigkeit angesichts der Situation in den galatischen Gemeinden zum Ausdruck: Lieber wäre er selbst dort und könnte unmittelbar zu ihnen sprechen. Angesichts solcher Stellen hat es den Anschein, daß das gesprochene Wort bei Paulus dem geschriebenen durchgängig vorgeordnet sei. Ich halte diesen Schluß jedoch für voreilig und bin vielmehr der Meinung, daß Paulus sich bei aller Wertschätzung des gesprochenen Wortes der Schriftlichkeit als Mittel der Kommunikation sehr wohl bewußt ist und sie mit seinen Briefen in den Austausch mit den Gemeinden einbringt. Dies will ich mit verschiedenen Beobachtungen belegen. Ich gehe dabei zunächst etwas ausführlicher auf Röm 10,14ff ein, wende mich dann einigen Stellen zu, die das Verhältnis einerseits von Glauben und Hören, andererseits von Buchstabe und Geist thematisieren und komme dann auf die Auseinandersetzung des Apostels mit seinen korinthischen Gegnern über Sprache und Schrift zu sprechen. Schließlich ist auch die allgemeine Tatsache zu bedenken, daß Paulus das Medium des Briefes als Mittel der Kommunikation mit seinen Gemeinden verwendet.

1) Röm 10,14-21 gehört in den gesamten Kontext des 10. Kapitels hinein.[46] Zwischen den einzelnen Argumentationsgängen (V.1-4.5-13.14-21) bestehen intensive Querverbindungen. Die These von Christus als Ziel und Ende des Gesetzes (V.4) wird in V.5-8 aus der Schrift begründet. Daß Mose dabei *schreibt* (V.5), die Glaubensgerechtigkeit dagegen *spricht* (V.6), fällt im Zusammenhang des hier behandelten Themas natürlich auf. Nun darf man diesen Unterschied gewiß nicht überbewerten; denn nach V.11 spricht auch die Schrift, in V.16.20f spricht Jesaja und nach V.19 Mose selbst. Der Sprachgebrauch ist also nicht einheitlich. Dennoch ist ein unterschiedlicher Akzent beim Schreiben und Sprechen nicht zu übersehen. Dies zeigt sich besonders am Zitat aus Dtn 30,14 in V.8: "Nah ist dir das Wort, in deinem Mund und in deinem Herzen", wobei die Abschlußwendung vom "Wort des Glaubens, das wir verkündigen" dies noch unterstreicht.[47] Die Glaubensgerechtigkeit hat es also mit dem Verkündigen des Wortes zu tun. Das "Bekennen mit dem Mund" (V.9) ist die dem verkündigten Wort entsprechende Reaktion der Glaubenden. Dies wird durch inhaltliche Beobachtungen unterstrichen: Wenn die Schrift "spricht" (V.11), dann spricht sie vom Glauben; und wenn Mose "spricht", dann wendet er sich gegen die Juden, die er mit dem Hinweis auf die Heiden eifersüchtig machen und zum Heil reizen will (V.19 im Anschluß an Dtn 32,21). Auch sie sollen dahin kommen, "den Herrn anzurufen" (V.12f; Joel 3,5). Wenn Mose dagegen "schreibt", schreibt er von der Gerechtigkeit, die aus den Werken kommt. Von Mose kann also sowohl im Modus des Schreibens als auch des Sprechens die Rede sein. Schrift ist dementsprechend nicht ganz und gar Schrift und gesprochenes Wort nicht ausschließlich gesprochen. Das ist eine erste wichtige Beobachtung.

Das Stichwort des Anrufens ist der Ausgangspunkt für den in V.14ff folgenden Gedankengang. In einem Kettenschluß wird das Anrufen des Herrn zurückbezogen auf das Gläubig-

---

[46] Die Stichworte ἐπικαλέω, κηρύσσω und πιστεύω belegen den Zusammenhang mit 10,1ff. Ich verweise hierzu auf Wilckens, U: *Der Brief an die Römer* (EKK VI/2), Zürich/Einsiedeln/Köln und Neukirchen-Vluyn 1980, S.218ff. Anders Käsemann, E.: *An die Römer* (HNT 8a), Tübingen 1973, S.283.

[47] Daß Paulus hier bewußt einen Gegensatz zu V.5 formuliert, wird besonders daran deutlich, daß er die Schlußwendung aus Dtn 30,14 ("daß du es – das Wort – tust") wegläßt.

werden, dies auf das Hören und die Verkündigung, diese wiederum auf die Sendung der Verkündiger. Die rhetorisch ausgefeilte Form des Rückschlusses zeigt dabei, daß es sich nicht um eine zufällige, sondern eine notwendige Abfolge handelt, sodaß also auch dem Hören Notwendigkeit zukommt. V.15b rundet den Kettenschluß mit einem Zitat ab, das sich an Jes 52,7 LXX anlehnt. Der von dort stammende Hinweis auf die Füße der Verkündiger nimmt natürlich direkt deren Sendung in V.15a auf. Dennoch sollte man im letzten Glied der Kette nicht ihre alleinige Pointe sehen.[48] In V.16 werden jedenfalls auch andere Glieder hervorgehoben, besonders das Hören. Der Kettenschluß ist insgesamt wichtig und verweist darauf, daß wirklich alles geschehen ist, was die Anrufung Christi als des Herrn möglich macht. Allerdings haben nicht alle der Botschaft des Evangeliums gehorcht, wie Paulus in einem Wortspiel von ἀκούω und ὑπακούω formuliert. Die Retrospektive vom Anrufen bis zur Sendung ist offenbar nicht einfach umzukehren; wohl kann man vom Glauben auf das Hören zurückschließen, es führt aber nicht jedes Hören notwendig zum Glauben. Daß es Paulus hier aber um die glaubende Annahme der Botschaft geht und daß er von ihr aus argumentiert, macht das Jesaja-Zitat deutlich. Damit ist wieder eine gedankliche Periode (V.14-16) abgeschlossen.

V.17 hebt nun das glaubende Hören der Botschaft, das aus dem Wort Christi kommt, besonders hervor. Die Aussage ist in dem Kettenschluß bereits angelegt. Die Annahme, daß es sich hierbei um eine spätere Glosse handele,[49] ist wegen dieser engen Verbindung nicht notwendig. Vielmehr wird der zentrale Gedanke von V.14f, daß die rettende Botschaft verkündet, gehört und glaubend angenommen werden will, noch einmal aufgegriffen und in V.18 auf die Möglichkeit des Hörens bezogen. Deutlich nimmt nämlich ἤκουσαν (V.18) die ἀκοή (V.17) auf: Was in der ganzen Welt verkündigt wird, kann Israel nicht verborgen geblieben sein (Ps 18,5 LXX), zumal die Botschaft ja von Israel ihren Ausgang nahm. Es ist also nicht so, daß Israel nicht gehört und nicht verstanden hätte,

---

[48] Gegen Käsemann, *ebd.*, S.284. Anders mit Recht Siegert, F.: *Argumentation bei Paulus gezeigt an Röm 9-11* (WUNT 34), Tübingen 1985, S.152ff.

[49] So Bultmann, R.: Glossen im Römerbrief, in: *ThLZ 72* (1947) S.197-202.

worum es geht. Es war vielmehr voll Widerspruch gegen die Botschaft (V.16.21), hat ihr nicht gehorcht und sie deshalb auch nicht begriffen (V.19). Will man diesen Abschnitt noch näher unterteilen, kann man V.17f und V.19-21 jeweils für sich nehmen. Aber es handelt sich dabei nur um Akzentuierungen der grundlegenden Frage nach dem Hören, sodaß V.14-21 einen größeren Zusammenhang bilden und wiederum eng mit V.1-13 verbunden sind.

Aber noch einmal zurück zu V.17! Was die ἀκοή bezeichnet, ist nicht eindeutig festgelegt. Sie nimmt aus V.14 das Verkündigen, das Hören und das Gläubig-Werden auf und bezieht sich deshalb sowohl auf das Gehörte, also die verkündete Botschaft, als auch auf den Vorgang des Hörens.[50] Beides geschieht διὰ ῥήματος Χριστοῦ. Diese Wendung ist im Anschluß an 10,8 zu verstehen, wo sich "das Wort des Glaubens" auf die apostolische Verkündigung bezieht. ῥῆμα ist dort vom Zitat aus Dtn 30,14 übernommen. Röm 10,17 greift diese Wendung auf, geht aber zugleich darüber hinaus: im verkündigten und gehörten Wort des Glaubens kommt der erhöhte Christus selbst zur Sprache.[51] Das "Wort Christi" ist also lebendiges, ansprechendes Wort, Botschaft der Verkündiger, in ihr und durch sie hindurch aber zugleich Christi Wort.

Wenn nun auch beim Verkündigen und Hören zunächst an das mündliche Wort der Predigt gedacht ist, so ist die Schrift doch nicht einfach ausgeschlossen. Die Zitate in Röm 10,16-21 belegen dies mit ihren Einleitungswendungen. Auch Jesaja und Mose "sprechen" zu Israel; auch das geschriebene Wort kann zur "Anrede" werden, wo man bereit ist, sich ihm auszusetzen. Und das Zitat in V.15 ist als "Schrift" eingeführt, inhaltlich aber eine Bestätigung der Verkündigung und Sendung in V.15a. Die Lebendigkeit des Wortes ist also nicht notwendig an den Modus der Mündlichkeit gebunden; und umgekehrt führt nicht jedes verkündete und gehörte Wort zum Glauben. Hören und Gehorchen sind vielmehr als *Akt der Verlebendigung* verstanden und können sich sowohl auf Geschriebenes als auch auf Gesprochenes beziehen.

2) In Gal 3,2.5 spricht Paulus von der ἀκοὴ πίστεως. Auch hier

---

[50] Louw, J.P./Nida, E.A: *Greek-English Lexicon of the New Testament Based on Semantic Domains*, Vol.1, New York 1989², S.283.

[51] Käsemann, *a.a.O.*, S.262.

sind im Stichwort ἀκοή beide Aspekte miteinander verbunden, die Predigt des Glaubens und das annehmende Hören. Die Galater haben nach 3,2 den Geist ja empfangen, dies aber nicht nur dadurch, daß das Wort vom Glauben verkündet wurde, sondern ebenso dadurch, daß sie es angenommen haben. Nach V.5 handelt es sich dabei nicht um einen einmaligen Vorgang, sondern um ein fortdauerndes Geschehen. Das Darreichen des Geistes und das Wirken von Krafttaten (Präsens!), auch dies geschieht aus dem Hören des Glaubens. Ähnlich wie in Röm 10,16ff schließt Paulus auch hier in V.6 an die Frage, ob die Galater den Geist aus den Werken des Gesetzes oder aus dem Hören der Glaubenspredigt empfangen haben, ein Zitat (aus Gen 15,6) an, mit dessen Hilfe er den Glaubensgehorsam untermauert. Überhaupt dient in Gal 3f die Schrift als ständiger Beleg der paulinischen Botschaft. Eine Korrespondenz zwischen dem gesprochenen und gehörten Wort auf der einen, dem geschriebenen und angenommenen Wort auf der anderen Seite ist auch hier zu erkennen.

In einem anderen Zusammenhang geht es in II Kor 3,4-18 um einen vergleichbaren Gedanken. V.7-11 sind durch eine Reihe von Gegensatzpaaren gegliedert, von denen hier vor allem die Gegenüberstellung des tötenden Buchstabens und des lebendig machenden Geistes hervorzuheben ist (V.6f). Sie ist in V.12ff verbunden mit dem "Lesen des Mose" (V.14b.15), also mit dem Vorlesen der Tora im Synagogengottesdienst. Nun wird die Tora aber auch in christlichen Gottesdiensten gelesen und von Paulus selbst, besonders auch in diesem Abschnitt, herangezogen. Dies zeigt, daß γράμμα hier nicht der geschriebene Buchstabe als solcher (und zwar im Gegensatz zum gesprochenen Wort) ist. Es geht Paulus vielmehr um die Perspektive, unter der die Schrift betrachtet wird und für die der Begriff γράμμα kennzeichnend ist: "Buchstabe" ist das Gesetz, und zwar betrachtet unter der Voraussetzung, daß es die einzige Willensbekundung Gottes sei. Unter der Leitung des Geistes gelesen weist dasselbe Gesetz aber auf Christus hin, führt damit in die Freiheit (V.17) und ist so keineswegs tötender Buchstabe, sondern bezeugende Schrift. Bei dem Gegensatz von γράμμα und πνεῦμα geht es Paulus deshalb nicht um das geschriebene Wort im Gegensatz zum gesprochenen, sondern um die jeweilige Perspektive, unter der das Wort der Tora gelesen wird.

Der Gegensatz von Buchstabe und Geist findet sich auch in Röm 2,25-29, und zwar verbunden mit der Thematik von Beschneidung und Unbeschnittensein. Der Buchstabe als solcher, das "Haben der Tora", macht nach Paulus den Juden noch nicht aus, ebensowenig wie das äußere Zeichen der Beschneidung. Der "Jude im Verborgenen", der im eigentlichen Sinn Jude ist und dessen Lob von Gott kommt (V.29), zeichnet sich durch die Beschneidung des Herzens aus. Diese Vorstellung findet sich nicht erst bei Paulus. Sie ist aus Dtn 10,16; Jer 4,4 bekannt und in einer etwas anderen Akzentuierung auch aus Jer 38 (vgl. Hes 11,19f; 36,26). In Jer 31,33 zeichnet sich die Vorstellung von dem "ins Herz geschriebenen Gesetz" ab, und dieser Akzent ist nun auch bei Paulus aufgegriffen.[52] γράμμα in V.29 bezeichnet denn auch hier nicht einfach das Geschriebene als solches; es handelt sich vielmehr um die Schrift, wenn und solange sie ohne die Führung des Geistes gelesen wird. Unter dieser Voraussetzung bleibt der Buchstabe nämlich Forderung und Anspruch von außen her; der Geist dagegen macht als wirksames Wort Gottes den Buchstaben lebendig und bewegt dadurch den Menschen von innen heraus.

In Röm 7,6 ist der Gegensatz von γράμμα und πνεῦμα[53] verbunden mit der aus 6,4-6 aufgegriffenen Opposition des Alten und des Neuen. In der Neuheit des Geistes zu wandeln ist möglich im Glauben an den auferstandenen Herrn. Ohne den Geist bleibt die Schrift Buchstabe, in der Führung des Geistes aber ist sie ansprechendes Wort, das auf Christus hinweist.

3) Eine weitere, wichtige Beobachtung ergibt sich aus II Kor 3,1ff und 1,13. Hier geht es nicht um das Lesen der Schrift, sondern der Briefe des Apostels. Die Gegner in Korinth verweisen auf Empfehlungsschreiben, die ihre besonderen Fähigkeiten belegen sollen. Anders als sie will der Apostel seine Autorisierung nicht mit solchen Schreiben bekräftigen. Er

[52] Vgl. zur Lebendigkeit dieser Vorstellung in der jüdischen Tradition 1QpHab 11,13; 1QS 5,5; Jub 1,23; OdSal 11,1-3. In Kol 2,11 ist diese Traditionslinie ebenfalls aufgenommen.

[53] Daß Palus hier auf II Kor 3,6 zurückgreift, zeigt sich eben an dem Begriff γράμμα, der vom Kontext nicht vorgegeben ist; zu erwarten wäre eher νόμος. Georgi, D.: *Die Gegner des Paulus im 2.Korintherbrief* (WMANT 11), Neukirchen 1964, S.257.272, hält es für wahrscheinlich, daß die Formel am Ende von Röm 7,6 aus der Auseinandersetzung mit den korinthischen Irrlehrern stammt.

beruft sich auf einen Brief anderer Art, der von seinem Dienst Zeugnis ablegt (3,2f):

> "Unser Brief seid ihr, eingeschrieben in unsere[54] Herzen, verstanden und gelesen von allen Menschen, offenbar gemacht, daß ihr ein Brief Christi seid, der von uns besorgt wurde, geschrieben nicht mit Tinte, sondern mit dem Geist des lebendigen Gottes, nicht auf steinerne Tafeln, sondern auf Tafeln, die fleischerne Herzen sind".

Natürlich legt sich mit der Vorstellung des Briefes das Lesen nahe und soll es auch in der Auseinandersetzung mit den Gegnern. Auch den Brief des Paulus kann man lesen und verstehen (vgl. ohne Bild I Thess 1,8). Wie die Gegner kann er diesen Brief vorweisen, wenn auch nicht als Papyrusblatt, dafür aber eingegraben in sein Herz und öffentlich bekannt als lebendige Gemeinde. Es ist deutlich, daß Paulus hier nicht auf einen in gleicher Weise wie Papier und Tinte objektivierbaren Sachverhalt hinweist, sondern auf eine Beziehung, die sich auf ihn selbst und auf die Gemeinde auswirkt. Auf Paulus, weil er diesen "Brief" immer bei sich tragen kann, auf die Gemeinde, weil sie von dem Apostel, dem sie ihre Existenz verdankt, keine zusätzlichen Empfehlungen braucht. "Ihr seid unser Brief" ist Ausdruck dieser Beziehung.[55] Die Empfehlungsschreiben der Gegner sollen deren besondere Fähigkeiten *unabhängig* von der Gemeinde hervorheben. Die Legitimation des Paulus liegt dagegen gerade in der Beziehung zur Gemeinde, von der sowohl seine Verkündigung als auch seine Briefe getragen sind. Was nun aber von dieser Beziehung gilt, wird in einem weiteren Gedanken auf die Gemeinde als "Brief Christi" bezogen. Auch mit dieser Wendung kommt eine Beziehung zum Ausdruck, und zwar zwischen der Gemeinde und Christus, eine Beziehung, deren Diener Paulus ist (dadurch, daß er die Gemeinde gegründet hat und sie nun begleitet). In diesem ganzen Vorgang ist der Geist Gottes lebendig gewesen und noch wirksam (V.17, vgl. 4,5f).

In diesem Zusammenhang ist nun die Aussage in 1,13 von

---

[54] Im Zusammenhang des Themas der Bestätigung und Empfehlung durch Briefe hat die Lesart ἡμῶν ein sachliches Übergewicht (vgl. Wolff, C.: *Der zweite Brief des Paulus an die Korinther*, ThHK 8, Berlin 1989, S.58).

[55] Zu den Beziehungen zwischen Paulus, den Gemeinden und Christus verweise ich auf Reck, R: *Kommunikation und Gemeindeaufbau. Eine Studie zu Entstehung, Leben und Wachstum paulinischer Gemeinden in den Kommunikationsstrukturen der Antike* (SBB 22), Stuttgart 1991, S.199-228.

Bedeutung, daß die Korinther lesen und verstehen können, was Paulus ihnen schreibt. Paulus verbindet dies mit dem Wunsch, die Korinther möchten, was er ihnen schreibt, durch und durch verstehen. Paulus setzt hier Vorwürfe voraus, die ihm gemacht wurden: den Vorwurf der Unaufrichtigkeit, Unlauterkeit (1,17; 2,17; 10,2) und Unzuverlässigkeit, gerade auch im Hinblick auf seine Reisepläne. Demgegenüber erhebt der Apostel den Anspruch, daß für ihn ganz allgemein und besonders im Hinblick auf die Korinther Einfachheit, Echtheit und Ehrlichkeit Kriterien seines Handelns sind. Diese Kriterien ergeben sich von seiner Botschaft und letztlich von Gott her: Das Auftreten des Apostels gründet in der Gnade und Lauterkeit Gottes und muß ihm deshalb auch entsprechen. Deshalb gibt es Ruhm (vgl. V.12.14) angesichts des Gerichts Gottes nicht im Blick auf sich selbst, sondern immer nur auf den Partner. Das Wortspiel von "lesen, verstehen und völlig verstehen" in V.13 bezieht sich auf diese Ausführungen. Lesen bewirkt nämlich nicht automatisch das Verstehen, es gibt auch teilweises und die Bitte zu völligem Verstehen. Das völlige Verstehen aber läßt sich offenbar nicht trennen von der bisherigen Kommunikation zwischen dem Apostel und der Gemeinde[56] und von ihren Lebensäußerungen, von der Aufrichtigkeit des Verhaltens, vom Sich-Rühmen und vom Getragen-Sein durch Gottes Gnade. Deshalb geht es bei dem Verstehen nicht in erster Linie darum, wie bestimmte Äußerungen von der Gemeinde *richtig* zu interpretieren seien; es geht auch nicht um die Hervorhebung bestimmter apostolischer Fähigkeiten pneumatischer oder rhetorischer Art. Es geht Paulus vielmehr um die Frage, ob die Korinther in der Beziehung zu Christus bleiben und ob sie das, was Paulus ihnen schreibt, aus dieser Beziehung heraus verstehen. Die Bitte zum völligen Verstehen in 1,13 ist also die Bitte darum, das Verhältnis des Apostels zur Gemeinde und damit auch sein aktuelles Schreiben von Christus her zu verstehen. Die Bedeutung der Wendung "Ihr seid mein Brief" in 3,2 liegt somit nicht allein im Ausdruck selbst; sie geht auch über die Auseinandersetzung um die Empfehlungsschreiben der Gegner hinaus. Die Wendung spricht die Korinther darauf an, daß

---

[56] Probst, H.: *Paulus und der Brief. Die Rhetorik des antiken Briefes als Form der paulinischen Korintherkorrespondenz (I Kor 8-10)* (WUNT 2.Reihe, 45), Tübingen 1991, S.102.

sie ihre Beziehungen zum Apostel und zu Christus, daß sie also ihre eigenen, bisher gemachten Erfahrungen beim Lesen mit hineinlegen. Phil 1,27 und 2,12 lassen sich ebenfalls in dieser Perspektive lesen. Unter dem Blickwinkel der Rezeptionsästhetik kann man die Metaphern "Brief des Apostels" bzw. "Brief Christi" geradezu als Leerstelle bezeichnen,[57] die die Korinther mit ihren eigenen Erfahrungen füllen können. Die Empfänger des Briefes wirken auf diese Weise an der Konstituierung seines Sinnes mit.

Im übrigen ist der Kontext von II Kor 1,13 noch in einer anderen Hinsicht interessant. Paulus geht ja in 1,15ff.23f; 2,1-4 näher auf den Vorwurf der Unzuverlässigkeit bei seinen Reiseplänen ein und begründet sein Fernbleiben damit, daß er die Spannungen nicht durch einen neuerlichen Besuch habe verschärfen wollen (vgl. 2,1). Um so wichtiger wird unter dieser Voraussetzung die Bitte des Paulus, die Korinther möchten völlig verstehen, was er ihnen schreibt. Offensichtlich hat der Brief in der angespannten Situation einen eigenen Stellenwert, ist also nicht bloßer Ersatz des mündlichen Wortes, sondern kann möglicherweise sogar mehr bewirken als die Anwesenheit des Apostels selbst.[58] Und II Kor 13,2.10 belegt, daß dem gesprochenen Wort keine höhere Autorität zukommt als dem Wort im Brief (vgl. auch I Kor 5,3f). Gerade im Vergleich mit Gal 4,20 verdient dieser Aspekt Berücksichtigung.

4) Die Auseinandersetzung mit den Gegnern in Korinth ist noch in einer weiteren Hinsicht für den Zusammenhang von Schriftlichkeit und Mündlichkeit von Bedeutung. In II Kor 10-13 wird mehrfach das Problem der persönlichen An- und Abwesenheit des Apostels angesprochen. In 10,1.10f nimmt Paulus einen Vorwurf der Gegner auf, aus dem Erkenntnisse sowohl über die Gegner als auch über Paulus zu gewinnen sind. In seinen Briefen, so lautet der Vorwurf, sei der Apostel zwar kraftvoll und mutig, während seiner persönlichen Anwesenheit aber verhalte er sich "demütig" (ταπεινός 10,1); seine Briefe seien von Gewicht, das persönliche Auftreten

[57] Iser, W.: *Der Akt des Lesens. Theorie ästhetischer Wirkung* (UTB 636), München 1990³, S.284ff.

[58] Vgl. Reck, *Kommunikation*, S.208.

dagegen schwächlich und die Rede armselig (10,10).[59] Paulus wird weiterhin vorgeworfen, er sei ἰδιώτης τῷ λόγῳ (11,6), also in der Rede ungeübt und laienhaft. Für die Gegner folgt daraus offensichtlich, daß er deshalb auch keine Weisheit und Erkenntnis für sich beanspruchen kann, sondern nur aus sich selbst redet, eine Konsequenz, die Paulus deutlich abweist, deren Evidenz für die Gegner aber auf der Hand liegt. Ihr Anspruch geistvoller Verkündigung und Sendung (vgl. 11,13.23) begründet sich gerade durch das geistgewirkte Reden, ebenso durch Wundertaten (12,12) und ekstatische Phänomene (12,1ff). Sie können auf Empfehlungsschreiben hinweisen (II Kor 3,1; vgl. 12,11), die den Geistbesitz der Überbringer und ihre pneumatischen Krafttaten dokumentieren.[60] Der aktuelle Ausweis pneumatisch bewirkter Rede wird so durch andere Zeugnisse bestätigt, wesentlich aber bleibt die im persönlichen Auftreten erkennbare, pneumatisch geprägte Bevollmächtigung. Bei den Empfehlungsschreiben geht es deshalb nicht um Autorisierung durch eine entsendende Stelle, sondern um eine Dokumentation der "pneumatischen Tüchtigkeit".[61] Die "Narrenrede" in 11,16ff weist als paulinische Persiflage auf das Selbstverständnis der Gegner dieselben Züge auf.

Nun ist der Vorwurf des armseligen persönlichen Eindrucks trotz kraftvoller Briefe in doppelter Hinsicht interessant. Zum einen belegt er das Gewicht des Paulusbriefes, das anzuerkennen sogar die Gegner nicht umhin können. Dem geschriebenen Wort wird ganz offensichtlich Wirkung zugestanden. Aus der Perspektive der Gegner wird diese Wirkung des geschriebenen Wortes aber geradezu konterkariert durch das schwächliche Auftreten des Paulus und seine mangelnde Gewandtheit in der Rede. Denn für sie steht das frei gesprochene, lebendige, rhetorisch ausgefeilte und auf Wirkung zielende Wort so sehr im Vordergrund, daß es den noch so gewichtigen schriftlichen Text in den Schatten stellt. Diese Hochschätzung des gesprochenen Wortes ist bei den Gegnern

---

[59] Daß hier ein Vorwurf aufgenommen ist, zeigt besonders das φησίν in V.10 und der unpaulinische Gebrauch von ταπεινός in V.1 (anders Phil 2,1-11). Vgl. Betz, H.D.: *Der Apostel Paulus und die sokratische Tradition* (BhTh 45), Tübingen 1972, S.54ff.60ff.

[60] Vgl. zu den Empfehlungsschreiben besonders Georgi, *Gegner*, S.241ff.

[61] Georgi, *ebd.*, S.220ff.

eindeutig festzustellen, wie die Argumentation des Paulus in 11,6 und I Kor 2,1f.13 ebenfalls erkennen läßt. Wenn man mit Georgi die Gegner im 2. Korintherbrief auf dem Hintergrund des hellenistischen Judenchristentums versteht,[62] läßt sich diese Hochschätzung der machtvollen Rede leicht nachvollziehen: Beeindruckendes Auftreten und große Redegabe gehören innerhalb dieses Rahmens zum Ausweis des Predigers, der mit göttlicher Vollmacht auftritt.

Für Paulus ergibt sich dagegen eine andere Einschätzung. Sie weist zunächst einen theologischen Aspekt auf, der sich aus II Kor 10,1 ergibt. Der Hinweis auf die Sanftmut und Milde Christi macht dort deutlich, daß der gegnerische Vorwurf nicht nur die möglicherweise mangelnde rhetorische Begabung des Apostels, sondern Christus selbst trifft.[63] Dessen Kennzeichen ist nach Phil 2,1-11 ja gerade, daß er sich erniedrigte. Wenn der Apostel bei seiner persönlichen Anwesenheit in Demut auftritt, dann entspricht er dem Verhalten Christi. In ähnlicher Weise kommt dies in II Kor 1,12 zum Ausdruck: In Einfachheit[64] und Lauterkeit ist Paulus bei den Korinthern aufgetreten, und zwar auf Grund von Gottes Gnade, nicht etwa aus Schläue oder Berechnung. I Kor 2,1 bringt diesen Gedanken ausdrücklich mit der Rede in Verbindung. Paulus ist eben nicht mit außerordentlicher Beredtsamkeit nach Korinth gekommen, sondern in Schwachheit, in Furcht und Zittern. Gerade dadurch jedoch ist die Verkündigung des Paulus als geistgewirkte Kraft zum Vorschein gekommen (V.4). Und wenn sich Paulus selbst rhetorischer Mittel gegen die Rhetorik der Gegner bedient,[65] so will er sie nicht eingesetzt sehen, damit sie Menschen ergötzt (Gal 1,10) und eigene Fähigkeiten herausstreicht, sondern die Lauterkeit Gottes (II Kor 1,12; 2,17) und die Führung des Geistes (I Kor 2,13) erkennen läßt. Im übrigen macht das Stichwort ὑπεροχή mit der Vorstellung des Maßes auch hier deutlich, daß die Verkündigung der Botschaft entsprechen muß.[66]

[62] *Gegner*, zusammenfassend S.301ff.

[63] Daß Paulus am Verhalten der Gegner gerade "das rechte Verhältnis des Verkündigers zu der von ihm vertretenen Sache" einfordert, hält Georgi, *ebd.*, S.227, fest.

[64] Ich bevorzuge mit dem Nestle-Text die Lesart ἐν ἁπλότητι.

[65] Vgl. Siegert, *Argumentation*, S.248ff.

[66] Vgl. hierzu Schrage, W.: *Der erste Brief an die Korinther* (EKK VII/1), Zürich/Braunschweig und Neukirchen-Vluyn 1991, S.225.

5) Das Auftreten des Paulus und seine Einschätzung der Rhetorik hat aber auch einen literarischen Aspekt. In diesem Zusammenhang ist auf die Rolle der Paulusbriefe im Rahmen des Austausches mit den Gemeinden einzugehen. Anders als bei den Gegnern läßt sich eine eindeutig unterschiedliche Bewertung des gesprochenen und des geschriebenen Wortes bei Paulus nicht erkennen. Zwar wäre er nach Gal 4,20 lieber in der Gemeinde anwesend, um angesichts ihrer Bedrohung persönlicher und eindringlicher sprechen zu können als im Brief. Der ratlose Apostel befürchtet offenbar, daß die innere Distanz zur Gemeinde aus der äußeren Distanz heraus mit dem Mittel des Briefes allein nicht überwunden werden kann. Das geschriebene Wort ohne den persönlichen Kontakt scheint ihm in der Konfliktsituation defizitär zu sein. Auf der anderen Seite traut er nach II Kor 1,15ff; 2,1ff ebenfalls in einem Konfliktfall dem Brief offenbar mehr zu als der persönlichen Anwesenheit. In I Kor 5,3 erhebt Paulus (wiederum in einem Konfliktfall) mit dem geschriebenen Wort den Anspruch Recht setzender Autorität. Wenn er in 11,34 ankündigt, "das Weitere" bei seiner Anwesenheit zu regeln, läßt diese Formulierung darauf schließen, daß er die Anweisungen im Brief keineswegs als Nebensachen ansieht.[67] Und was Paulus der Gemeinde in I Kor 14,37 schreibt, ist Gebot des Herrn. Offensichtlich greift Paulus mit dem geschriebenen Wort werbend und leitend in die Lebensvollzüge der Gemeinden ein. Insofern sind der Brief und die persönliche Anwesenheit des Apostels miteinander vergleichbar (vgl. II Kor 10,11). Aber der Brief ist nicht lediglich *Ersatz* für die Anwesenheit, er ist auch nicht nur "halbierter Dialog", wie der Brief im Rückgriff auf Demetrius oft bezeichnet wurde.[68] Das "Sprechen" im Brief ist vielmehr wesentlich gekennzeichnet durch die Schriftlichkeit der Sprache.[69] Die unterschiedliche Wirkung, die die

---

[67] Schrage, *ebd.*, S.82.

[68] Vgl. Demetrius, *Eloc* 223f. Im Parusia-Motiv wird diese Auffassung noch gesteigert im Sinne des *quasi adesse* (Cicero, *Fam* 15,16,1) und sogar des *te totus in litteris vidi* (*Fam* 16,16,2). Allerdings wird bereits in der antiken Diskussion darauf hingewiesen, daß der Brief nicht einfach Reproduktion des Gespräches ist, sondern sich diesem gegenüber durch eindeutigere und sorgfältigere Gestaltung wie durch größere Klarheit auszeichnet (vgl. Demetrius, *Eloc.* 228.231.234).

[69] Vgl. Thraede, K.: *Grundzüge griechisch-römischer Brieftopik*, München 1970, S.22f.

Briefe einerseits, das persönliche Auftreten des Paulus andererseits hervorrufen (II Kor 10,1.10; 11,16), belegen dies ebenso wie der Umfang der Korintherbriefe und des Röm.[70] Und die dringende Mahnung in I Thess 5,27, den Brief der ganzen Gemeinde vorzulesen, ist gerade durch die Schriftlichkeit ermöglicht und unterstützt. Die Aufforderung zum Austausch von Briefen in Kol 4,16 ist demgegenüber zwar nachpaulinisch, liegt aber direkt in der Konsequenz der Mahnung aus I Thess.[71] Eine Abwertung des Geschriebenen ist jedenfalls nicht zu erkennen. Der Brief ist nicht Kommunikation minderer Qualität, sondern dient Paulus als eigenständiges Medium, dessen Nachteile er ebenso kennt wie die Vorteile.

Dies gilt, um noch einmal auf Gal zurückzukommen, trotz Gal 4,20 insgesamt auch für diesen Brief. Wenn Hans Dieter Betz das Schreiben auf dem Hintergrund der griechisch-römischen Rhetorik interpretiert,[72] so hat dieser Versuch natürlich sein Recht, zumal Querverbindungen zwischen Rhetorik und Epistolographie nicht gut bestritten werden können. Es ist in keiner Weise fraglich, daß sich rhetorische Elemente sowohl in Gal als auch in den anderen Paulusbriefen nachweisen lassen. Ob Gal als schriftliches Dokument aber *insgesamt*, wie Betz meint, mit Hilfe der *rhetorischen* dispositio gegliedert und erklärt werden kann, bleibt mir durchaus fraglich. Auch halte ich das (von der traditionellen Höherbewertung der Rede beeinflußte) Urteil von Betz für keineswegs eindeutig, daß der Brief "von reduzierter Wirkung" sei und als "Ersatz (sc. der Rhetorik) in der Tat kläglich."[73] Denn einerseits hat die minutiöse, ganz der rhetorischen Disposition

[70] Wenn denn I Kor ein einziger Brief ist und nicht, wie II Kor, in verschiedene Briefe aufgeteilt werden muß; vgl. hierzu neuerdings Probst, *Paulus*, S.361ff.

[71] Vgl. hierzu Müller, P.: *Anfänge der Paulusschule. Dargestellt am 2.Thessalonicherbrief und am Kolosserbrief* (AThANT 74), Zürich 1988, S.335f.

[72] *Der Galaterbrief. Ein Kommentar zum Brief des Apostels Paulus an die Gemeinden in Galatien*, München 1988, S.54ff. Zum Vergleich von Paulustexten mit der antiken Rhetorik weise ich hin auf Probst, *Paulus*, S.30-54.

[73] Betz, *ebd.*, S.69: "Der Brief vertritt seinen Verfasser, kann jedoch nicht so agieren und reagieren, wie es sein Verfasser in persona könnte. So drückt sich der Absender in absentia und ohne den vollen Umfang der kommunikativen Mittel aus, die mit einer mündlichen Unterhaltung verbunden sind ... Da es sich um nichts weiter als ein lebloses Stück Papier handelt, ist eine der wichtigsten Waffen des Rhetorikers, der mündliche Vortrag, ausgeschaltet".

verpflichtete Gliederung des gesamten Briefes bei Betz[74] einen übertrieben künstlichen Charakter und das Stichwort einer "theologia rhetorica"[75] kann einem schon dabei einfallen; andererseits wird nicht genügend bedacht, daß Briefe für die antiken Theoretiker durchweg etwas Anderes sind als die Rede[76] und daß die Beobachtung rhetorischer Elemente noch nicht rechtfertigt, einen Brief insgesamt im Rahmen einer bestimmten Redeform zu interpretieren. Ein Brief ist nicht einfach eine "Rede im Briefumschlag".[77] Das verstärkte Interesse an der antiken Epistolographie[78] hat zudem gezeigt, daß der antike Brief keine einheitliche Grundstruktur aufweist, sondern sich einer Gestaltungs- und Formenfülle bedienen kann, die man bei der Gattungsbestimmung berücksichtigen muß.[79] Für den Gal muß man dabei sicher sowohl die angespannte Situation in Galatien als auch die den ganzen Brief tragende Absicht des Paulus bedenken, die Galater bei seinem Evangelium zu halten. Mahnung und Zurechtweisung, Tadel und Kritik bestimmen ebenso wie werbendes Bemühen weite Passagen des Briefes und sind für seine Bestimmung wichtig.[80] Ich kann hierauf im Rahmen dieses Aufsatzes nicht im einzelnen eingehen. Es kommt mir ja mehr auf die Frage nach dem Modus der Sprache an. Deshalb will ich hervorheben, daß auch Gal als Brief, d.h. als Kommunikation im Modus der Schriftlichkeit, gewürdigt werden muß.[81] Denn obwohl Paulus lieber eindringlich und überzeugend zu den Galatern sprechen möchte, ist sein Brief nicht lediglich Ersatz des

---

[74] *Ebd.*, S.54ff. Zur Kritik an Betz vgl. Classen, C.J.: Paulus und die antike Rhetorik, in: *ZNW 82* (1991) S.1-33.

[75] Schrage, ebd, S.81.

[76] Vgl. Koskenniemi, H.: *Studien zur Idee und Phraseologie des griechischen Briefes bis 400 n.Chr.* (AASF.B 102/2), Helsinki 1956, S.43.

[77] So Jegher-Bucher, V.: *Der Galaterbrief auf dem Hintergrund antiker Epistolographie und Rhetorik. Ein anderes Paulusbild* (AThANT 78), Zürich 1991, S.204.

[78] Einen knappen Forschungsüberblick gibt Taatz, I.: *Frühjüdische Briefe. Die paulinischen Briefe im Rahmen der offiziellen religiösen Briefe des Frühjudentums* (NTOA 16), Freiburg/Schweiz und Göttingen 1991, S.9-12.

[79] Ich verweise etwa auf Probst, *Paulus*, S.61ff; Aune, D.E.: *The New Testament in Its Literary Environment*, Philadelphia 1987; Stowers, S. K.: *Letter Writing in Greco-Roman Antiquity*, Philadelphia 1986; Strecker, G.: *Literaturgeschichte des Neuen Testaments* (UTB 1682), Göttingen 1992, S.89-95.

[80] Vgl. hierzu Demetrius, *Typoi* 3.6ff.

[81] Vgl. hierzu bereits Güttgemanns, E.: *Offene Fragen zur Formgeschichte des Evangeliums* (BevTh 54), München 1977, S.110-115.

gesprochenen Wortes, sondern eigenständige Kommunikation im Rahmen eines über die Anfangsverkündigung hinausgehenden, weiteren Austausches mit den Gemeinden, bei der es um grundlegende paulinische Themen und um ihre offensichtlich planvolle Verknüpfung geht: das Apostelamt, das Evangelium von der Gerechtigkeit durch den Glauben und die Frage, wie die Glaubensgerechtigkeit im Leben Gestalt gewinnt. Diese Themen stellt Paulus den Galatern keineswegs im Sinne einer Gerichtsrede vor, über die die Empfänger als "Jury" ein Urteil zu fällen hätten,[82] und auch die Interpretation des Briefes im Sinne deliberativer, also zu einer Entscheidung über die zur Diskussion stehende Thematik führender Rede,[83] trifft m.E. das Selbstverständnis des Schreibens nicht. Bereits die Wendung "Paulus, Apostel, nicht von Menschen und nicht durch einen Menschen ..." in 1,1 setzt einen anderen Akzent (vgl. auch 6,17). Sowohl aus äußerer Veranlassung wie aus innerer Notwendigkeit[84] kommt Paulus zu theologischen Äußerungen grundsätzlicher Art, die er nicht etwa zur Debatte stellt, sondern mit höchster Autorität (1,8f) und nun auch in schriftlicher Form stützt. Der eigenhändige Schluß (6,11ff) hebt denn auch die Schriftlichkeit ausdrücklich hervor. Daß die Schrift auf Anfragen nicht antworten kann (als Teil der "reduzierten Wirkung" bei Betz und längst zuvor bei Platon), ist ja nur solange ein Manko, solange man sie mit der Rede vergleicht. Wenn Paulus sich aber zum Brief entschließt und damit das "Ritual einer Schreibweise" akzeptiert,[85] ist das Produkt des Schreibens mit eigenem Maß und mit eigenem Anspruch an Kohärenz zu messen. Das zeigt sich bereits darin, daß Paulus sich im Brief an die verschiedenen (Haus-) Gemeinden Galatiens wenden kann, ein Sachverhalt, der sich erst aus der Schrift ergibt (vgl. II Kor 1,1).

Sehr deutlich tritt die Eigenständigkeit des geschriebenen Wortes in dem ausführlichen und durchkomponierten Brief an die Römer hervor, also an eine dem Paulus bis dahin unbekannte Gemeinde. Auch wenn man "in der ganzen Welt" vom

---

[82] So Betz, *Galaterbrief*, S.69.

[83] In diesem Sinn interpretieren u.a. Smit, J.: The Letter of Paul to the Galatians: A Deliberative Speech, in: *NTS 35* (1989) S.1-26; Vouga, F.: Zur rhetorischen Gattung des Galaterbriefes, in: *ZNW 79* (1988) S.291f.

[84] Vielhauer, P.: *Geschichte der urchristlichen Literatur*, Berlin/New York 1975, S.113.

[85] Japp, U.: *Hermeneutik*, München 1977, S.98f.

Glauben der römischen Gemeinde spricht (1,8), sieht Paulus sich als "Diener Jesu Christi für die Völker" (15,16) verpflichtet, auch dieser Gemeinde das Evangelium zu verkündigen, zwar nicht als Anfangsverkündigung, aber als ein entfaltendes, werbendes und verkündigendes Erinnern, das Paulus als dem Apostel der Heiden zukommt.[86] Das Medium des Briefes ist für diese Aufgabe wegen der Unbekanntheit mit der Gemeinde geradezu konstitutiv. So erweist sich denn das Schreiben als ein "außerordentlich reflektierter Text",[87] dessen Schriftlichkeit sein wesentliches Merkmal ist. Verschiedene Themen aus vorangegangenen Briefen sind hier wieder aufgenommen und neu durchdacht.[88] Diese neue Stufe der Reflexion seines Evangeliums dient Paulus nicht nur als Vorstellung und Werbung in Rom, sondern zugleich als Rechenschaft für die bevorstehende Auseinandersetzung in Jerusalem. Im Vergleich mit dem Galaterbrief, bei dem nicht nur die Thematik, sondern streckenweise auch der Aufbau vergleichbar ist, tritt der Text-Charakter des Röm nun noch deutlicher in den Vordergrund. Offenbar hat Paulus an den einzelnen Themen weiter gearbeitet und sie auf eine neue Stufe der gedanklichen Durchdringung und Darstellung gebracht. Was ihm die Gegner nach II Kor konzedieren, daß nämlich seine Briefe von Gewicht sind, gilt in noch höherem Maß für den Römerbrief als schriftliches Dokument.

IV

Im Schlußabschnitt will ich versuchen, die einzelnen Ergebnisse zusammenzufassen und auf die gegenwärtige Frage nach Wort und Schrift zurückzuführen.

1) Daß der Glaube nach Röm 10,17 aus dem Hören kommt, ist zunächst auf dem Hintergrund der antiken Lesegewohnheiten zu verstehen. Lesen, auch das private, ist dabei in erster Linie lautes Lesen; es wird weiterhin überwiegend als öffentliche oder halböffentliche Angelegenheit verstanden. Den gedanklichen Hintergrund hierfür bildet die platonische Auffassung vom geschriebenen Wort als einem Schattenbild

[86] Müller, P.: Grundlinien paulinischer Theologie (Röm 15,14-33), in: *KuD 35* (1989) S.212-235, hier besonders S.224f.

[87] Wilckens, *Röm I*, S.VI.

[88] Bornkamm, G.: Der Römerbrief als Testament des Paulus (*GA IV*), München 1971, S.120-139, hier S.130f.

des gesprochenen. Um Lebendigkeit wiederzugewinnen, drängt deshalb das geschriebene Wort zum Vortrag. So ist die Verlautlichung dem Lesen in der Antike wesenhaft eigen. Dieser Sachverhalt ist auch für eine Aussage wie Röm 10,17 von grundlegender Bedeutung. Er verbietet es nämlich, zwischen dem gelesenen und dem (gesprochenen und) gehörten Wort in gleicher Weise zu unterscheiden, wie dies im Rahmen moderner Kommunikationsbedingungen üblich geworden ist. Gehörtes und gelesenes Wort gehören in der Antike vielmehr unmittelbar zusammen – und wenn der Glaube aus dem Hören kommt, so heißt dies durchaus nicht, daß er nicht *auch* aus dem (Vor-)Lesen kommen könne.

Nun läßt sich aber für die Zeit etwa von Horaz an bis zum Ende des 1.Jahrhunderts n.Chr. eine Entwicklung feststellen, die zu einer veränderten Bewertung des geschriebenen Wortes führt. Horaz selbst thematisiert in epist. I,20 zwar eindrücklich die Gefährdungen, denen ein geschriebener Text beim Abschied von seinem Autor ausgesetzt ist. Auf der anderen Seite hebt er aber das eigene Gewicht des Geschriebenen deutlich hervor. Am Text zu arbeiten und zu feilen wird ihm zum Kennzeichen des Dichters. Der Modus der Schriftlichkeit wird prägend für die Literatur und dementsprechend nimmt auch das genaue Lesen und Studieren von Texten zu. Der geschriebene Text ist nicht mehr nur gewissermaßen eine Partitur für den Vortrag, sondern gewinnt ein eigenständiges Gewicht. Hinzu kommt die Beobachtung, daß die Lesungen trotz lebhaften Interesses und offenbar großer Zahl in einer Krise stecken. Bemerkungen bei verschiedenen Schriftstellern, vor allem bei Plinius, belegen dies deutlich. Und Martial macht sich in der ihm eigenen, zupackenden Sprache darüber lustig. Diese Krise des öffentlichen Lese-Betriebes macht von einer anderen Seite aus noch einmal die veränderte Bedeutung des geschriebenen Wortes deutlich.

2) Paulus hat Anteil an den Lese-Gewohnheiten und -Voraussetzungen seiner Zeit. Auch für ihn ist Lesen lautes Lesen und es gehört in einen bestimmten Rahmen hinein (vgl. I Thess 5,27; II Kor 3,15). Dieser Rahmen ist für ihn allerdings nicht die Sozialgemeinschaft von Freunden und Klienten, auch nicht der öffentliche Vortrag, sondern die Gemeinde und dabei in besonderem Maß die gottesdienstliche Feier. Gelesen wird dort in erster Linie die Sammlung

der Schriften und damit nicht Literatur, über die zu befinden wäre, sondern heilige Schrift. Sowohl der gottesdienstliche Rahmen als auch diese Qualität des Geschriebenen geben dem Lesen eine eigene Bedeutung. Allerdings gehören auch in diesem Rahmen gelesenes und gehörtes Wort eng zusammen. Wenn nach Röm 10 die Schrift spricht (V.11), Jesaja spricht (V.16.20), wenn selbst Mose spricht (V.19), dann *sprechen* sie ja in der Tat, insofern nämlich, als Geschriebenes laut wird. Offenbar geht es Paulus beim Hören des gelesenen Wortes nicht nur um ein Wahrnehmen, sondern ein Aufnehmen im Sinne der Verlebendigung im Lebensvollzug. Deutlicher Beleg hierfür ist das Wortspiel von ἀκούω und ὑπακούω in Röm 10,16f, ebenso auch das "nahe" Wort im Mund *und* im Herzen (V.8). Von hier aus erklärt sich nicht nur der Unterschied zwischen dem Verstehen (V.19) und dem Gehorchen (V.17) gegenüber dem verkündeten Wort, sondern auch der zwischen γράμμα und γραφή. Wenn Geschriebenes gelesen, aber nicht im Herzen verlebendigt wird, bleibt es γράμμα. Dasselbe geschriebene Wort kann aber – gelesen unter der Leitung des Geistes – als γραφή die Menschen anstoßen und bewegen. Der Modus der Sprache tritt gegenüber dieser Unterscheidung in den Hintergrund.

Nun geht Paulus davon aus, daß in den gottesdienstlichen Versammlungen auch seine eigenen Briefe vorgelesen werden (I Thess 5,27; vgl. Kol 4,16). Sie entstehen aus den Beziehungen zu den Gemeinden und wirken selbst wiederum auf diese Beziehungen ein. Insofern haben sie *Dialog*-Charakter. Als halbiertes Gespräch sind sie jedoch noch nicht hinreichend bestimmt, und auch ihre Einordnung in bekannte Redeformen wird, so viel Richtiges dabei im einzelnen zu beobachten ist, ihrem Schrift-Charakter und ihrer materialen Präsenz nicht wirklich gerecht. Wohl ist der Brief das, was hätte gesagt werden können; indem er aber die Rede umgeht, läßt er sich auf das Medium der Schriftlichkeit mit den ihm eigenen Kohärenzbedingungen ein. Zwar tritt der Schrift-Charakter in den einzelnen Briefen mit unterschiedlicher Deutlichkeit hervor, am deutlichsten ohne Zweifel im Römerbrief, er muß aber generell berücksichtigt werden. Dies gilt unbeschadet der Tatsache, daß eine genaue epistolographische Einordnung der paulinischen Schreiben wegen der Formenvielfalt antiker Briefe schwierig ist. Allerdings muß bereits diese Variationsbreite des antiken Briefes vor einer minutiösen Gliederung von Paulusbriefen anhand eines bestimmten rhetorischen Schemas warnen. Auf jeden Fall zeigt sich, daß die Briefe für Paulus nicht lediglich Ersatz für das Gespräch oder die mündliche Verkündigung sind, sondern eigenständiges Mittel in der Kommunikation mit den Gemeinden.

Eine unterschiedliche Bewertung des gesprochenen und geschriebenen Wortes tritt in der Auseinandersetzung mit den korinthischen Gegnern deutlich hervor. In ihren Augen sind die Briefe trotz kraftvoller Wirkung kein Ausgleich für das mangelnde rhetorische Vermögen des Apostels. Briefe können dieser Auffassung nach zwar als Bestätigung und Beleg dienen, ersetzen aber keinesfalls die Unmittelbarkeit der Rede. In diesem Punkt wird bei den Gegnern die traditionelle Vorordnung des gesprochenen Wortes vor dem geschriebenen erkennbar – die von Paulus aber gerade nicht geteilt wird. Was er den Korinthern *schreibt*, können sie lesen und verstehen (II Kor 1,13), und zwar auf dem Hintergrund der Beziehung, die sie zum Apostel und darüber hinaus zu Christus haben; sie sind ja ein "Brief" des Apostels und Christi selbst (3,1ff). Auf diesem Hintergrund spielt einerseits die Frage von An- oder Abwesenheit des Apostels und damit zugleich nach dem Modus der Sprache eine eher untergeordnete Rolle; andererseits bekommt der Brief als Mittel der Kommunikation ein eigenes, nicht vom gesprochenen Wort abgeleitetes Gewicht. Die Aussage vom Glauben aus dem Hören bezeichnet deshalb bei Paulus keine Defizienz der Schriftlichkeit, sondern hebt die Verlebendigung sowohl des geschriebenen als auch des gesprochenenn Wortes im eigenen Lebensvollzug hervor.

3) Von hier aus nun noch einmal zurück zur gegenwärtigen Diskussion um Schrift und Wort. Die Sprache in einem ursprünglichen Sinn, schreibt Derrida, die Sprache als Unmittelbarkeit von Signifikant und Signifikat gebe es nicht, ebensowenig das Buch als Repräsentant einer Totalität von Signifikanten und einer bereits davor gedachten Totalität des damit Bezeichneten. Der Weg von der Schrift über das gesprochene Wort zum dahinter liegenden Sinn sei versperrt. Neben Platon und der an ihn sich anschließenden langen Tradition bezieht sich Derrida mit diesen Äußerungen in besonderem Maß auch auf das "Buch der Bücher" und konsequenterweise auch auf den darin festgehaltenen Satz, der Glaube komme aus dem

Hören. Nun zeigt sich aber auf der einen Seite gerade bei Paulus (jedoch andeutungsweise bereits bei Platon und deutlicher bei Luther) eine viel differenziertere Auffassung zu Wort und Schrift als Derrida erkennen läßt. Im Grunde trifft nämlich Derridas Kritik viel eher das Verständnis des gesprochenen Wortes bei den Gegnern des Paulus in Korinth, wogegen Paulus selbst Stimme und Schrift in gleicher Weise als Kommunikationsmittel achtet und sich der Vorzüge und der Nachteile von beiden offenbar bewußt ist (vgl. etwa Gal 4,20 mit II Kor 2,12-14.15ff). Auf dem Hintergrund einer umfassenderen Diskussion zum Thema und einer verschiedentlich feststellbaren Aufwertung des Geschriebenen werden die Chancen und die Grenzen beider Kommunikationsmittel vom Apostel mehrfach reflektiert. Zudem ist für Paulus wie für die gesamte Antike der Unterschied zwischen gehörtem und gelesenem Wort nicht gleichermaßen zentral wie für die Buchkultur in der Nachfolge der Gutenberg'schen Erfindung. Der Glaube aus dem Hören schließt für Paulus den Glauben aus der Schrift eben nicht aus. Derridas Kritik am Phonozentrismus erweist sich deshalb im Blick auf Paulus als unangemessen und pauschal.

Die Wechselbeziehung des gesprochenen und des geschriebenen Wortes findet zudem bei Paulus eine Begründung, die für die gegenwärtige Diskussion um "Schrift und Differenz" von Bedeutung ist. Sowohl das gesprochene als auch das geschriebene Wort erweist sich als "Wort in Beziehungen". Die Metapher vom "Brief des Apostels" und darüber hinaus vom "Brief Christi" unterstreicht die Beziehung der Gemeinde zu Paulus und beider zu Christus. Was Paulus den Korinthern schreibt, will er auf dem Hintergrund dieser Beziehung verstanden wissen. Innerhalb der Beziehung bleibt er als Autor wichtig und die Korinther, darunter selbst die Gegner des Apostels, kümmert es schon, wer da spricht.[89] Zur Bedeutung kommt der Brief des Paulus aber nicht nur durch seine Autorintention, sondern auch durch das, was die Empfänger an Eigenem hineinlegen. Es geht deshalb in II Kor 1,13 weniger um ein "richtiges" Verstehen des einen "ursprünglichen" Sinnes, sondern um ein Verstehen, dessen Grundlage die angesprochenen Beziehungen sind; es geht also nicht um "Ursprungs-Sinn" des Textes, sondern um "Be-

[89] Diese Formulierung entnehme ich Foucault, Autor.

ziehungs-Sinn", in den die Korinther ihre eigenen Erfahrungen (oder, wenn man im Sinne der Intertextualität unbedingt so formulieren will: ihren "Text") mit einbringen und auf diese Weise den Text entfalten. Wenn Paulus in I Kor 3,10 von dem Fundament spricht, das nicht verändert werden kann, so wird im Bild des Weiterbauens ja deutlich, daß sich dieses Fundament auf eine aktuelle Beziehung hin auswirkt. Und wenn der Apostel in Gal 1,6-9 auf ein "ursprüngliches" Evangelium zurückgreift, so ist der Beziehungs-Sinn doch bereits in 1,1-5 angesprochen; der Zusammenhang von beiden Abschnitten zeigt ja, daß der Rückgriff auf einen ursprünglichen Sinn obsolet wird, wenn die weitergehende Beziehung in Frage steht. Da nun aber Beziehung immer beides ist, trennend und einigend,[90] kann mit diesem Begriff sowohl die Differenz als auch das Verstehen als Suche nach dem Beziehungs-Sinn bezeichnet werden. Von hier aus betrachtet sind Derridas Konzept von Schrift und Differenz und die ihm folgenden Diskussionsbeiträge um Verstehen und Sinn unvollständig und einseitig. Bei Paulus finde ich jedenfalls, daß "Graphismus statt Phonismus"[91] die Alternative nicht ist, die man heute gerne daraus macht.

---

[90] Vgl. Japp, U.: *Beziehungssinn. Ein Konzept der Literaturgeschichte,* Frankfurt 1980, S.224. Zur "Hermeneutik der Entfaltung" vgl. auch Japp, *Hermeneutik,* S.85ff.

[91] Vgl. Timm, *Jahrzehnt,* S.173.

THE RHETORICITY OF HISTORICAL KNOWLEDGE: PAULINE DISCOURSE AND ITS CONTEXTUALIZATIONS

Elisabeth Schüssler Fiorenza
(Harvard Divinity School, Cambridge, Massachusetts)

Almost twenty years ago I had the opportunity to choose a topic for a graduate level seminar on Jewish and Christian traditions sponsored by the Rosenstiel foundation. I long had been an admirer of professor Georgi's book on the opponents of Paul,[1] which was translated into English only much later.[2] Hence, I welcomed the opportunity to explore further the area of "religious propaganda," which his book had constructed as an explanatory frame of meaning for interpreting Paul's correspondence and theology. Therefore, I invited him together with other Jewish and Christian scholars to address the problem of Greco-Roman, Jewish and Christian religious propaganda in the first century CE. Although during the early decades of this century considerable research had been done on the topic of religious propaganda in antiquity,[3] such research interests almost had disappeared in the intervening years, probably because of the negative political connotations of the term "propaganda." So I hoped that the subsequent publication of the invited papers would engender renewed discussion of religious propaganda among Jewish and Christian scholars.[4]

---

[1] Dieter Georgi, *Die Gegner des Paulus im 2. Korintherbrief: Studien zur religiösen Propaganda in der Spätantike* (Neukirchen-Vluyn: Neukirchener Verlag, 1964).

[2] *The Opponents of Paul in Second Corinthians* (Philadelphia: Fortress, 1986).

[3] See, e.g., M. Friedländer, *Geschichte der jüdischen Apologetik als Vorgeschichte des Christentums* (Zürich: Verlag Caesar Schmitt, 1903); K. Axenfeld, "Die jüdische Propaganda als Vorläuferin der urchristlichen Mission," *Missionswissenschaftliche Studien. Festschrift Warneck* (Berlin: Evangelische Missionsgesellschaft, 1904) 1-80; Paul Wendland, *Die hellenistisch-römische Kultur in ihren Beziehungen zu Judentum und Urchristentum* (Tübingen: J.C.B. Mohr, 1907); P. Derwacter, *Preparing the Way for Paul: The Proselyte Movement in Later Judaism* (New York: Macmillan, 1930). See also the discussion of missionary activity in Dieter Georgi, *The Opponents*, 83-228, 358-89, 422-45.

[4] Elisabeth Schüssler Fiorenza, ed., *Aspects of Religious Propaganda in*

Judaism as well as Christianity had a period of great expansion at the beginning of our era. The spread of Hellenistic culture had torn down many ethnic barriers separating peoples from peoples, cultures from cultures and religions from religions. The imperial imposition of the *Pax Romana*[5] made religious exchange, extensive travel, and cultural alliances easy. In appealing to audiences of the Greco-Roman world, Jews and Christians could utilize the means and methods of Greco-Roman rhetoric. The appropriation of such missionary propagandistic forms was indispensable if Jews and Christians were to succeed in competing with other religious associations or philosophical movements.

Centuries earlier Judaism already had confronted the task of communicating its ethos to a wider public, since over an extended period of time Jewish faith-communities had been spreading throughout the Greco-Roman world. Still, this success of Jewish expansion provoked also anti-Semitic reactions and slanderous attacks. In order to counter such defamation Jewish thinkers had produced a body of sophisticated apologetic literature in Greek. This literature sought to convince both members of the Jewish community and Gentile readers that such vilifying criticism of Judaism was not justified. Positively, Jewish writers wanted to persuade their diverse audiences of the truth, antiquity, and high moral standing of their own religion and community. In a similar fashion early Christian writers intended to strengthen the identity of Christian audiences who shared the pluralistic ethos of the Greco-Roman world, although in many instances they were still members of Jewish communities.

In my introduction to *Aspects of Religious Propaganda*, I attempted to highlight that early Christian writers engaged in rhetorical, persuasive discourses which were at home in the public political sphere.[6] Working within the methodological framework of redaction criticism, I sought to show how the author of Acts shapes his narrative in such a way that it functions as a persuasive argument within the contesting dis-

Judaism and Early Christianity (Notre Dame: University of Notre Dame Press, 1976).

[5] Cf. Klaus Wengst, *Pax Romana. Anspruch und Wirklichkeit* (München: Chr. Kaiser Verlag, 1986).

[6] Elisabeth Schüssler Fiorenza, "Miracles, Mission and Apologetics: An Introduction," in *Aspects of Religious Propaganda*, 1-26.

courses of Greco-Roman and Jewish religious propaganda. Other contributions to this volume did not concentrate on the function and form of rhetorical discourse. Instead they circled around another concern of Georgi's work: the Hellenistic figure of the "divine man" – a figure which was very much debated in the 1970s.[7]

In the intervening years scholarly interest in both rhetoric as a literary device and rhetoric as a cultural-religious discourse and public political practice has increased steadily in biblical studies.[8] This is due for the most part both to epistemological discourses, which have rediscovered the significance of rhetoric in general, and to the theoretical discussions of historiography[9] which have underscored the rhetoricity of historical texts and interpretations in particular. These theoretical explorations have shown that the choice of explanatory models, organizing images, or reconstructive paradigms depends on the socio-political location and communicative interests of those who produce historical knowledge.[10]

The understanding of rhetoric/rhetorical as a communicative practice that involves interests, values, and visions must be

---

[7] Cf. Dieter Georgi, "Socioeconomic Reasons for the 'Divine Man as a Propagandistic Pattern," in *Aspects of Religious Propaganda*, 27-42, and the discussion in his epilogue to the American edition of *The Opponents*, 390-415.

[8] See, e.g., George Kennedy, *Classical Rhetoric and its Christian and Secular Tradition from Ancient to Modern Times* (Chapel Hill: University of North Carolina Press, 1980); idem, *New Testament Interpretation through Rhetorical Criticism* (Chapel Hill: University of North Carolina Press, 1984); Elisabeth Schüssler Fiorenza, *Bread Not Stone: The Challenge of Feminist Biblical Interpretation* (Boston: Beacon, 1984); Duane F. Watson, "The New Testament and Greco-Roman Rhetoric: A Bibliography," *Journal of the Evangelical Theological Society* 31/4 (1988) 465-72; Wilhelm Wüllner, "Hermeneutics and Rhetorics: From 'Truth and Method' to 'Truth and Power'," *Scriptura* 3 (1989) 1 54; Burton L. Mack, *Rhetoric and the New Testament* (Minneapolis: Augsburg Fortress, 1990).

[9] Cf. Dominick Lacapra, *Rethinking Intellectual History: Texts, Contexts, Language* (Ithaca: Cornell University Press, 1983); Daniel Stempel, "History and Postmodern Literary Theory," in Joseph Natoli, ed., *Tracing Literary Theory* (Urbana: University of Illinois Press, 1987) 80-104; Pietro Rossi, ed., *Theorie der modernen Geschichtsschreibung* (Frankfurt: Suhrkamp, 1987); H. Aram Veeser, ed., *The New Historicism* (New York: Routledge, 1989).

[10] See my SBL presidential address "The Ethics of Biblical Interpretation: Decentering Biblical Scholarship," *Journal of Biblical Literature* 107/1 (1988) 3-17; William A. Beardslee, "Ethics and Hermeneutics," in T.W. Jennings, ed., *Text and Logos: The Humanistic Interpretation of the New Testament* (Atlanta: Scholars Press, 1990) 15-32; D.J. Smit, "The Ethos of Interpretation – New Voices from the USA," *Scriptura* 3 (1990) 16-28.

distinguished carefully from its negative popular use. Generally, the label rhetoric/rhetorical masks persuasive speech as stylistic ornament, technical means or linguistic manipulation, as discourse utilizing irrational, emotional devices that are contrary to critical thinking and reasoning. Academic and popular parlance continues to label those statements as "rhetoric/rhetorical" which it wants to mark as "mere talk," stylistic figure, or deceptive propaganda. In short, popular public discourse continues the Enlightenment's negative understanding of rhetoric as a clever form of speech that is not true or honest, but rather lacking in substance.

The revival of the understanding of "rhetoric" not merely as stylistic means but as persuasive discourse during the past decade or so[11] aims at overcoming the modern academic and colloquial notion of rhetoric as deceitful and negative. Consequently, it seeks to revalorize rhetoric as a public form of discourse for the sake of liberating intellectual discourses from their captivity to so-called value free objective "science." Since the construction of a political framework of interpretation and socio-historical contextualization has been a focal point of Professor Georgi's work,[12] I hope that this essay in his honor will foster the recognition of the rhetoricity of biblical writings and contemporary interpretations as well as the articulation of a political ethos for our common discipline.

Dieter Georgi's work is exceptional in that he consistently has situated Paul's letters to the Corinthian community within the context of Greco-Roman political history and public discourse. His studies on religious propaganda in antiquity and early Christianity have been significant for the development of my own historical framework and interpretive method, although I have tended to read the Pauline letters differently. With the majority of critical scholars Georgi has constructed Paul's theology as "normative" over and against that of Paul's gnostic (1 Cor) or propagandistic (2 Cor) *opponents*. In this

---

[11] For discussion of this development and relevant literature, cf. Brian Vickers, ed., *Rhetoric Revalued* (Binghampton: New York University Press, 1982); idem, *In Defence of Rhetoric* (Oxford: Clarendon Press, 1988); William A. Beardslee, "Theology and Rhetoric in the University," in David R. Griffin and Josef C. Hough, eds., *Theology and the University* (Albany: SUNY, 1991) 185-200.

[12] See especially his book *Theocracy in Paul's Praxis and Theology* (Minneapolis: Augsburg Fortress, 1991).

reading, Paul's remains the dominant "Christian" voice. In contrast, a reading that privileges the theological voices and visions of Paul's audience reconstructs his theological voice as one among many. In order to bring such alternative submerged voices to the fore, I have argued, historical interpretations of Paul must differentiate between the textually inscribed *rhetorical situation*, on the one hand, and the possible *historical situation* that must be reconstructed from all available sources on the other.[13] Rather than to engage these differences in interpreting Paul directly, I seek here to negotiate the difference in historical-theological rhetoricity on an epistemological theoretical level.

In addition to the recovery of rhetoric as a critical discipline of inquiry, a second epistemological debate has been decisive for my own theological reading and historical reconstruction which moves within a critical feminist framework of liberation.[14] In preparing the Rosenstiel seminar I became fascinated with the discovery – mentioned in primary as well as secondary sources – that in antiquity Judaism was attacked as a "religion of women" because it was believed to attract especially elite women as converts. The same charge is levied later also against the Christian mission. Yet, at the time I did not quite know how to engage this observation and its theoretical importance for the reconstruction of early Judaism and Christianity. Since in 1973/74 feminist historical and biblical discourses were not yet available or only in the beginning stages, I lacked a theoretical framework to do so.[15] Hence, I was not surprised that my colleagues also would or could not engage my question as to the participation and contribution of women to missionary propaganda.

---

[13] Elisabeth Schüssler Fiorenza, "Rhetorical Situation and Historical Reconstruction in 1 Corinthians," *New Testament Studies* 33 (1987) 386-403; and my book *Revelation: Vision of a Just World* (Minneapolis: Fortress, 1991).

[14] For the development of such a critical feminist liberationist framework, see my book *Discipleship of Equals: A Feminist Ekklesialogy of Liberation* (New York: Crossroad, 1993).

[15] See Judith P. Zinsser, *History and Feminism: A Glass Half Full* (New York: Twayne, 1993) for a discussion of the historical development of feminist historiography in the USA; Cheryl Johnson-Odim and Margaret Strobel, eds., *Expanding the Boundaries of Women's History* (Bloomington: Indiana University Press, 1992) for the history of feminism in the Third World; and Michelle Perrot, ed., *Writing Women's History* (Cambridge: Blackwell, 1992) for the development of women's history in France.

In subsequent years the problem of how to write women back into history – to use an expression of the feminist historian Joan Kelly[16] – has become groundbreaking for my own work. The question as to how one can reconstruct responsibly the participation and contribution of women to early Jewish and Christian history continues to raise far-reaching methodological and hermeneutical issues. The privileging of "women" in historical reading and scholarly discourse does not only demand a different model for the socio-political reconstruction of women's history in particular but also requires a critical reflection on historical scholarship and exegetical knowledge in general. It seeks to engender a theoretical paradigm shift in the self-understanding of biblical studies – a shift from a neopositivist "scientific" conceptualization to a rhetorical conceptualization of textual interpretation and historical reconstruction.[17]

I. Scientific Objectivist Frameworks

The twin epistemological problem of how to read the politics and rhetorics of ancient texts such as Paul's and of how to reconstruct Pauline history as that of the communities of the women and men to whom he writes, remains one of the foremost methodological problems in biblical studies. Since this problem is crucial for the theoretical debates and relations of malestream and feminist biblical scholarship, I will try to sketch its perimeters and ramifications.

1. Historical scientific criticism[18] generally considers texts as archives, sources, and transcripts of historical facts. It reads texts in general and Pauline texts in particular as windows on the world which give us accurate information and "data" about Pauline Christianity. "Scientific" descriptions of Pauline communities seek to create "realistic" historical accounts as though

[16] Joan Kelly,"The Doubled Vision of Feminist Theory," in eadem, *Women, History, and Theory* (Chicago: University of Chicago Press, 1984) 51-64.

[17] For a more fully developed argument and documentation, see my book *But She Said: Feminist Practices of Biblical Interpretation* (Boston: Beacon, 1992).

[18] For literature and discussion of this problem, see Archie L. Nations, "Historical Criticism and the Current Methodological Crisis," *Scottish Journal of Theology* 36 (1983) 59-71; W.S. Vorster, "The Historical Paradigm – Its Possibilities and Limitations," *Neotestamentica* 18 (1984) 104-23.

their historical narrative were an accurate transcription of how things actually were. Disinterested and dispassionate scholarship is believed to enable biblical critics to enter the minds and worlds of Paul's texts, to step out of their own times, and to study Pauline history or literature on its own terms, unencumbered by contemporary experiences, values and interests.

In this research paradigm variant scholarly accounts of the same historical information are contested with reference to *facts* rather than with reference to the rhetorical arguments that have transformed textual sources and historical events *into* data and facts. Positivist science does not require that the historian's narrative show *how* history is plotted, since it is supposed to be a faithful narration of what actually has happened. By asserting that a given interpretation of a Pauline text represents its objective "true" reading, scientific exegesis claims to comprehend the definitive meaning intended by the author, Paul. In privileging and legitimating one particular interpretation over other possible readings, one not only closures the text's multivalent meanings but also rules out alternative readings as illegitimate. If, and when, scholars admit that exegetical commentary is not free from rhetorical argument, they immediately assert that such argument must be restricted to demonstrating how competing interpretations have misread the Pauline text.

Social scientific studies,[19] in turn, map Paul's rhetorical argument and symbolic universe unto sociological or anthropological models of "Paul's" community and society. They maintain that their investigative research, critical methods, and explanatory models have scientific status because these are derived from the social sciences, in particular from theoretical sociology and cultural anthropology. Hence, anthropological and sociological biblical studies also understand their reconstructive work as an exercise in objective, social scientific criticism with universal truth claims. Consequently,

---

[19] See, e.g., John H. Elliott, "Social-Scientific Criticism of the New Testament: More on Methods and Models," *Semeia* 35 (1986) 1-34; Thomas Schmeller, *Brechungen. Urchristliche Wundercharismatiker im Prisma soziologisch orientierter Exegese* (Stuttgart: Verlag Katholisches Bibelwerk, 1989) 16-49; P.F. Craffert, "Towards an Interdisciplinary Definition of the Social-Scientific Interpretation of the New Testament," *Neotestamentica* 25 (1991) 123-44.

they tend to appropriate sociological or cultural reconstructive models without problematizing their underlying theoretical frames and political implications.[20]

For instance, scholars have taken over Weber's and Troeltsch's concept of patriarchalism for describing Pauline Christianity without taking its feminist, sociological, political, or theological critiques into account. By adopting a Weberian or Durkheimian analysis,[21] scholars not only separate ideology or theology from political and social struggles in the Roman empire but also treat the patriarchal institutionalization of some segments of early Christianity as a sociological given. Others adopt social science models such as Mary Douglas' group-grid construction, Wilson's typology of sects, or the system of honor and shame as scientific-objective givens and normative theoretical prescriptions.

Since social science models allegedly have been "tested" by the scientific disciplines of anthropology and sociology, biblical scholars claim that such scientific models enable them not only to avoid androcentrism and ethnocentrism but also to understand the cultures and peoples of the ancient Mediterranean world as they would have seen themselves. However, such a scientific reification or "naturalization" of sociological or anthropological theory overlooks that the disciplines of sociology, political theory and cultural anthropology also have begun to reshape their "scientific" objectivist self-understandings into a rhetorical ethos.[22] Above all, feminist theories have underlined the gendered character of theoretical concepts and scientific modes of investigation.[23]

---

[20] For a similar critique from a different hermeneutical perspective, see Itumeleng J. Mosala, *Biblical Hermeneutics of Black Theology in South Africa* (Grand Rapids, MI: Eerdmans, 1989) 55 ff.

[21] See Victoria Lee Erickson, *Where Silence Speaks: Feminism, Social Theory, and Religion* (Minneapolis: Augsburg Fortress, 1992), for a feminist critique of Durkheim's and Weber's understanding of religion.

[22] Cf., e.g., Renato Rosaldo, *Culture & Truth: The Remaking of Social Analysis* (Boston: Beacon, 1989); Terrence Ball, *Transforming Political Discourse: Political Theory and Critical Conceptual History* (New York: Blackwells, 1988).

[23] Cf. Sandra Harding, *The Science Question in Feminism* (Ithaca: Cornell University Press, 1986); Terry R. Kendal, *The Woman Question in Classical Sociological Theory* (Miami: Florida University Press, 1988); Mary Lyndon Shanley and Carole Pateman, eds., *Feminist Interpretations and Political Theory* (University Park: The Pennsylvania State University Press, 1991); Christine Farnham, ed., *The Impact of Feminist Research in the Academy* (Bloomington:

The posture of scientific objectivism masks the extent to which the concept of objective science is itself a theoretical construct.[24] This rhetoric of so-called disinterested science and presupposition-free exegesis silences reflection on the political interests and functions of biblical scholarship. Its claim to public scientific status suppresses the rhetorical character of Paul's texts and their interpretations as well as obscures the power-relations which constitute and shape Paul's rhetoric. Hence, biblical scholarship that continues to subscribe to ostensibly value-neutral "scientific" theories not only surreptitiously advocates an apolitical reading of canonical texts. It also fails to articulate its theoretical assumptions and to stand accountable for its political interests. Only if biblical studies begin to acknowledge their own social locations and interests, whether of confession, race, gender, nation or class, will they become accountable to a wider audience.

Positivist "scientific" interpretation is conceptualized in *kyriarchal* (Herr-schafts) terms insofar as readers are compelled to submit and relinquish their own readings in favor of the seemingly unequivocal meaning of the "scientific" reading of Pauline texts. This objectivist politics of meaning obscures both the rhetoricity of the text and that of its own interpretation in its assertion to provide a definitive objective account of Paul's meaning. Such a reifying politics of meaning also reinscribes patriarchal relations by inviting identification with Paul and his arguments. In such a readerly identification with Paul's rhetoric, his insistence on his fatherly authority, for instance, allows ecclesial and academic "fathers" to claim Paul's authority for themselves.

By emphasizing a total chasm between the past and the present, between Paul and himself, the exegete obscures the fact that Paul's meanings are present only in and through the words of his interpreters. Insofar as historical critical studies identify Pauline texts with Pauline reality, they obscure the *difference* between Paul's theological rhetoric and that of the

---

Indiana University Press, 1987); Ruth A. Wallace, ed., *Feminism and Social Theory* (Newbury Park: Sage Publications, 1989).

[24] Sandra Harding and Merill B. Hintikka, eds., *Discovering Reality: Feminist Perspectives on Epistemology, Metaphysics, Methodology, and Philosophy* (Dordrecht: D. Reidel, 1983); Louise M. Antony and Charlotte Witt, eds., *A Mind of One's Own: Feminist Essays on Reason & Objectivity* (Boulder: Westview, 1993).

early Christian communities which Paul's text may misrepresent or silence. The scholarly rhetoric of radical differences between past and present accordingly serves to construct *sameness* between Paul, "his" communities, and his interpreters.[25] It does so, either by identifying Paul's discourses with those of the communities to whom he writes and thereby suppressing and eradicating the historical voices and multiplex visions that are different from Paul's. Or it achieves its aim by claiming scientific authority for its own interpretations and by disqualifying those of others as biased, ideological, or as reading their own interests into the text. Finally, by understanding the "first" meaning of the Pauline text as a deposit of the definitive meaning of the author, historical biblical interpretation runs the risk of "shutting up" the "meaning" of the text in the past and turning it into an artifact of antiquity that is accessible only to the expert of biblical philology and history.

While serious scholars for the most part have abandoned extreme historical positivism, it is still widespread in popular culture. In popular discourses such "scientific" rhetoric serves the function of disqualifying alternative critical voices as "unscientific." A sample from an article on *Women and the Bible* which recently appeared in the popular American magazine *The Atlantic Monthly* may illustrate my point:

> "Scholarly work on women and the Bible faces certain inherent problems, certain inherent risks. In my talks with people in the field, the same worries were voiced by one scholar after another. A fundamental one has to do with the distinction between deriving an interpretation *from* a text and reading an interpretation *into* a text. It is one thing for a contemporary personal agenda – a desire, say to see women enjoy a position of full equality in religious institutions – to direct one's research focus. Agendas of one sort or another frequently drive scholarship. But can't they also get out of hand?"[26]

Neither the scholars who "one after another" voiced their "worries," nor the writer who previously had published a

---

[25] For an exploration of sameness and difference in Pauline interpretation, see the intriguing work of Elizabeth Castelli, *Imitating Paul: A Discourse of Power* (Louisville: Westminster/J. Knox, 1991), who utilizes Michel Foucault's theoretical framework for her analysis.

[26] Cullen Murphy, "Women and the Bible," *The Atlantic Monthly* 272/2 (August 1993) 64.

similar article on Jesus in the same journal, mention here that not only feminist work but all interpretive historical scholarship face the same risks. "Scientific" reconstructions of the Jesus of history, who is the central figure in early Christian writings, serve as a case in point. Claiming scientific accurateness and status for their own interpretations permits scholars and journalists both to remain silent about the ethico-political premises and interests of their own work and to remain oblivious to the ideological and disciplinary pressures of those scholarly or popular interpretive communities for whom they write.

2. *Postmodern literary and cultural criticism,*[27] in contrast to historical positivist criticism, underscores the impossibility of attaining objective historical knowledge from reading Paul's letters. Language and texts shape reality insofar as they not only transmit but also promote the values woven through the fabric of socio-historical discourses and patriarchal societies. As texts, the Pauline writings are not windows to the world but "doubled" mirrors that reflect back the image of Paul and his readers. Social scientific language and texts of scholars are no exceptions. Social science texts and models are not one-dimensional and self-evident, but rather perspectival, metaphorical and constructive. If one gives a definitive interpretation of a Pauline text or objective description – let's say – of Mediterranean society, one forcefully closures its meaning, insofar as texts are multi-layered and engender endless possibilities of interpretation. If one gives a "definitive" reading of a Pauline text, one not only cuts off other possible meanings but also privileges one's own framework and model of reading as "true" over and against other interpretations.

Literary critics further argue that one commits the "referential fallacy"[28] if one assumes, for instance, that Paul's letters to the Corinthians reflect historical circumstances, events or arguments as they actually took place. Formalist, decon-

---

[27] For feminist studies see Carolyn J. Allen, "Feminist Criticism and Postmodernism," in Joseph Natoli, ed., *Tracing Literary Theory* (Urbana: University of Illinois Press, 1987) 278-305. For biblical studies see especially Fred W. Burnett, "Postmodern Biblical Exegesis: The Eve of Historical Criticism," *Semeia* 51 (1990) 51-80 and Gary Phillips, "Exegesis as a Critical Praxis: Reclaiming History and Text from a Postmodern Perspective," *Semeia* 51 (1990) 7-50.

[28] For feminist biblical studies see, e.g., Janice Capel Anderson, "Matthew: Gender and Reading," *Semeia* 28 (1983) 3-28; Elizabeth Struthers

structivist, and rhetorical literary criticism insist that one cannot move beyond the Pauline text to the historical reality of Paul or of early Christian communities. Scientific literary analysis only can decipher and reconstruct the symbolic narrative world or the rhetorical strategies of the Pauline text, but not the intention of its author and the arguments of its historical audience. Hence, formalist literary or poststructuralist cultural theories contend that the past is *only* textual. History is available solely in and through narratives and texts.

Historiography remains caught up in the undecidability of text and the multivoicity of language. All that one can investigate is the rhetoricity of biblical texts and their interpretations. Historical reality no longer is accessible except as textual reality. In this view, the past is constituted as a domain of representation. "Facts" are created by the narrative acts of coding history and by the choice of narrative strategy, interpretive models, selection, plot and closure.[29] Historians construct "scientific" historical discourse by choosing from a multiplicity of traces left by past events and by turning these symbolic remnantss into historical facts.

Postmodern critical theory also challenges the modern progressivist dichotomy between historical reality and text, past and present. It insists that while ostensibly stressing the alien character of the text's world, historical narrative tells the story of ancient Greece or early Christianity by refracting the historical traces inscribed in the text into our own language and world. In the process of such a refracting, historians shape their materials by choosing a narrative frame, by selecting "data," by creating and valorizing time periods, and by ascribing significance to certain texts and methods of reading over and against others.[30] In short, historical reconstruction is linguistic re-presentation.

History is not only narrative-laden; it is also rhetorical.

Malbon, "Fallible Followers: Women and Men in the Gospel of Mark," *Semeia* 28 (1983) 29-48; Lone Fatum, "Women, Symbolic Universe and Structures of Silence: Challenges and Possibilities in Androcentric Texts," *Studia Theologica* 43 (1989) 61-80.

[29] Hayden White, *Tropics of Discourse: Essays in Cultural Criticism* (Baltimore: Johns Hopkins University Press, 1978).

[30] Feminist historians have specifically questioned the valuations of periodization. See, e.g., Joan Kelly, "Did Women Have a Renaissance?," reprinted in eadem, *Women, History, and Theory* (Chicago: University of Chicago Press, 1984) 19-50.

Scholars not only select their topics and materials but also utilize theoretical metaphors or models to organize them into a coherent argument. Models for historical reconstructions are metaphoric in the sense that metaphor is a way of describing something in terms of something else. For instance, the conception of history as seeking causal laws to explain objective facts has a mechanistic root-metaphor, whereas that of the evolution of history is based on an organic biological metaphor.[31] Moreover, historians create time-periods which reflect these root-metaphors and their politics of meaning. As a result historical periods such as Hellenism or early Christianity[32] actually are retrospective symbolic constructions which have been unavailable to those historical persons living at the time.

Over and against the modern self-understanding of biblical scholarship as "scientific, objective, and disinterested" a critical postmodern paradigm of interpretation recognizes that all historical narrative is informed by our own historical-cultural position, interwoven with the values and practices of our own time, and shaped by our historical-cultural location as well as by the ways we are implicated in power-relations. By underscoring the fact that all cultural forms of representation are ideologically grounded and that access to reality is always mediated through language, one can problematize and denaturalize the rhetorical assertions of what is real.

To sum up: malestream as well as some feminist discourses theorize the relationship between text and reality, between historical representation and history as event, between past

---

[31] See Richard Harvey Brown, *Society as Text: Essays on Rhetoric, Reason, and Reality* (Chicago: University of Chicago Press, 1987) 97-112.

[32] Georgi's arguments against using the marker "Christian" for the emerging communities of the Jesus-movement in the Mediterranean world have their place here. I concur with him that one should abandon the exclusivist differentiation between the Jesus-movement in rural Palestine and the early Christian missionary movement in the Greco-Roman urban centers, a distinction which I had taken over from Social World Studies in my book *In Memory of Her: A Feminist Theological Reconstruction of Christian Origins* (New York: Crossroad, 1983). Nevertheless, insofar as scholarly discourses have the function to classify and to order, they cannot but re-inscribe such classifications and distinctions from the perspective of their location in the present. The replacement of "Christian community" with Jesus- community does not overcome the historical split, acrimony, and violence of Christianity toward Judaism since the name of Jesus has authorized Christian anti-Jewish practices.

and present, and between the ancient and the contemporary reader either in terms of radical difference or in terms of radical identity. Those Pauline scholars who subscribe to historical criticism tend to emphasize the radical difference between contemporary interpreter and text, between our own and Paul's world. Those who adopt literary formalism, stylistic rhetorical analysis, or poststructuralist criticism emphasize the impossibility of moving from text to reality, underscore the linguisticality of all knowledge, and maintain the inextricable entanglement of present interpretation and knowledge of the past.

II. Kyriocentric Rhetoricity and Historical Reality

A feminist socio-critical rhetoric concurs with postmodern discourse analysis that all texts, interpretations, and historical reconstructions are relative and perspectival. If what one sees depends on where one stands, social-ideological location and rhetorical context are as decisive as text for how one reconstructs historical reality or interprets biblical texts. The socio-political locations and interests of interpreters determine historical knowledge production. Historical reconstructions are not value-free, objective descriptions of what actually happened, but are rhetorical insofar as they rest on the theoretical models and metaphors of reality that they employ. Historical writings such as the Pauline letters do not reflect historical reality; rather, as prescriptive and persuasive texts they construct it. Paul's texts do not merely respond to the rhetorical situation but also create it.

This insight into the rhetoricity of historical knowledge, however, does not persuade a critical feminist liberationist theory either to succumb to nihilism or to advocate a value-free relativist pluralism. Rather, it compels liberationist feminists to produce a *different* knowledge and history from their perspective as insider/outsiders or as resident aliens in a kyriocentric culture and academy.[33] In difference to "ludic" postmodern[34] textualism and relativism a critical feminist

[33] For the notion of *insider/outsider*, see P. Hill Collins, *Black Feminist Thought: Knowledge, Consciousness and the Politics of Empowerment* (Boston: Unwin Hyman, 1990), and for that of *resident alien* see my book *But She Said.*

[34] Rosemary Hennessy, *Materialist Feminism and the Politics of Discourse*

rhetoric of liberation does not abandon the modern critical interest in reconstructing the "history of freedom" as the history of those who have struggled for freedom, human dignity, and equality. Although we can know the past today only in and through texts and discourses, persons and events of the past are not simply fictions of historical imagination.

All women and subjected men shape and have shaped culture and religion, even though classic androcentric records do not mention our existence and work.[35] Recognition that the past is only known to us in and through textual traces is not "the same as saying that the past is only textual as the semiotic idealism of some forms of poststructuralism seems to assert."[36] Rather, the experience and analysis of patriarchal colonization tells us that all women and subjugated men are today – and always have been – historical subjects and agents. Historical narrative representation does not give *existence* but only *meaning* to the past. Therefore, feminist liberationist scholars claim the hermeneutical privilege of the oppressed for their theoretical work:

> "The 'master position' in any set of dominating social relations tends to produce distorted visions of the real regularities and causal tendencies in social relations... The feminist standpoint epistemologies argue that because men are in the 'master position' vis-à-vis women, women's social experience – conceptualized through the lenses of feminist theory – can provide the

(New York: Routledge, 1993) 3, proposes this distinction: "Whereas ludic postmodernism signals an emphasis on the mechanics of signification, with language understood as a formal system of differences, resistance postmodernism is concerned with the politics of the production and maintenance of subjectivities, that is with language as a social practice."

[35] For instance, neither Jürgen Becker, ed., *Die Anfänge des Christentums: Alte Welt und Neue Hoffnung* (Stuttgart: Kohlhammer, 1987), nor Howard C. Kee, "Sociology of the New Testament," *Harper's Bible Dictionary* (San Francisco: Harper & Row) 961-68 mention my book *In Memory of Her* or other feminist historical works alongside with those, e.g., of Judge, Meeks, or Theissen. According to such hegemonic "scientific" historical records, feminist historical work still does not exist! Yet, the eclipse of feminist work by androcentric scholarly records does not mean that in actuality such work does not exist. It only means that historians of the 22nd century will have to consult other sources to reconstruct the history of feminist biblical scholarship.

[36] Linda Hutcheon, *The Politics of Postmodernism* (London: Routledge, 1989) 81. See also Chris Weedon, *Feminist Practice and Poststructuralist Theory* (Oxford: Blackwell, 1987).

> grounds for a less distorted understanding of the world around us."[37]

A postmodern symbolic criticism, that eschews all historical diachronic reconstruction and rejects any attempt to give a "truer," more adequate account of the historical world[38] in which Paul and his audience lived, cannot but remain ensconced in the rhetorical world projected by the kyriocentric text which seeks to maintain the status quo. If there is no possibility of reconstructing a historical world *different* from the kyriocentric world construction of the text, or if it is impossible to take a reading position different from that engineered by the text, then historical interpretation is doomed to reinscribe the kyriarchal reality constructed by the grammatically masculine text. Consequently, a critical liberationist rhetoric seeks to show that one can break the hold of the androcentric text over the religious and historical imagination of its readers provided one recognizes the agency of interpreters in reading texts as well as in reconstructing their socio-historical contexts.

1. Feminist socio-critical deconstructive readings[39] investigate and display how, for instance, Paul's textual strategies and their subsequent interpretations are political and religious discursive practices. Communicative aims, point of view, narrative strategies, persuasive means, and authorial closure as well as audience perceptions and constructions are rhetorical practices which have determined not only the production of the bible but its subsequent interpretations as well. By interpreting the Pauline text from a particular socio-theological location, readers engage not only in a hermeneutical but also in a rhetorical practice. By carefully examining the rhetorical strategies of the androcentric Pauline text and its symbolic universes, readers are able to explore not only *what* the text

---

[37] Sandra Harding, *The Science Question in Feminism,* 191. For a similar position but different accentuation see Nancy C.M. Hartsock, *Money, Sex and Power: Toward A Feminist Historical Materialism* (New York: Longman, 1983).

[38] For the discussion of this position, see Judith Newton, "History as Usual?: Feminism and the New Historicism" *Cultural Critique* 9 (1988) 98.

[39] Irene Harvey, "The Wellsprings of Deconstruction," in Joseph Natoli, ed., *Tracing Literary Theory* (Urbana: University of Illinois Press, 1987) 127-47, and Mary Poovey, "Feminism and Deconstruction," *Feminist Studies* 14 (1988) 51-66, give an excellent introduction to the strengths and limits of deconstructive reading.

excludes, but also to investigate *how* the text constructs what it includes.[40]

Although feminist theory has underscored the ideological rhetoricity of grammar and language, biblical studies have not yet theorized sufficiently the far-reaching implications of a pragmatic understanding of language for reading historical source-texts. On the contrary, literary biblical studies have tended to adopt a framework of linguistic and symbolic determinism.[41] However, only a pragmatic understanding of language can break through the ideological strategies of androcentric language and grammar. Androcentric texts marginalize all women and subordinated men, subsume them under generic elite male terms, and through kyriocentric inscriptions eradicate altogether the historical presence of those marginalized. Thus, androcentric, grammatically masculine texts are not simply descriptive reflections of reality. Rather, as kyriocentric texts they produce linguistically the marginality and absence of all women and all subordinated men from public historical consciousness. How one reads the "silences" of the unmarked grammatically masculine Pauline text and how one fills in its "blank spaces" depend on how one contextualizes one's reading in specific historical political experience.[42]

If readers understand language not as a closed linguistic system but as a social convention and communicative tool, they can become accountable for their own readings which they negotiate and create in specific contexts and situations. For instance, in their interaction with a Pauline textual convention such as the masculine address "brothers," readers must decide how to read this androcentric appellation. Whether they read this expression in a generic or in a gender specific way, depends both on their judgment of Paul's specific linguistic and social contexts and on their own social experience and ideological interests. If language is not a straitjacket

---

[40]Adrienne Munich, "Notorious Signs: Feminist Criticism and Literary Tradition," in G. Greene and C. Kaplan, eds., *Making a Difference: Feminist Literary Criticism* (New York: Methuen, 1985) 256.

[41] For such a distinction see Deborah Cameron, *Feminism and Linguistic Theory* (London: MacMillan, 1985).

[42] Karen Dugger, "Social Location and Gender Role Attitudes: A Comparison of Black and White Women," *Gender & Society* 2 (1988) 425-48; Carole Ann Taylor, "Positioning Subjects and Objects: Agency, Narration, Rationality," *Hypatia* 8 (1993) 55-80.

into which our thoughts must be forced, that is, if it is not a naturalized closed system but rather a medium which is affected by social conditions and which changes in response to social changes, then writing, translation, and interpretation become the sites of the struggle for change.[43]

"Scientific" interpretation that does not undermine critically but continues to "naturalize" the rhetorical strategies of the kyriocentric text cannot but reproduce its historical perspective and symbolic universe. It is bound to deepen the historical silence about women and all those whom patriarchal and kyriarchal historical texts marginalize or have erased from historical consciousness. Only if one reads the kyriocentric text against its androcentric grain and makes those whom the text marginalizes or fails to mention at all central to historical reconstruction, is one able to break the text's ideological hold over its readers. If Pauline texts construct at one and the same time both the reality which brought them forth and the reality to which they respond, then this reality is accessible to us not only in the world which they display but also in all that they repress or marginalize. Hence, one cannot simply follow the directives for reading that are inscribed in the surface of the Pauline text; rather, one must interrogate the power/knowledge relations structuring both Pauline texts and the discourses of Pauline studies.

One can do so because androcentric language and male-authored texts presuppose all women's and subjected men's historical presence and agency, although for the most part they do not articulate it. True, the relationship between kyriocentric text and historical reality can not be construed as a window or a mirror-image. Nevertheless, it can be decoded as a complex ideological construction.[44] Consequently, the kyriocentric text's rhetorical silences, contradictions, argu-

[43] For a similar emphasis on the readers agency and the possibility of change, see, for instance, Robert M. Fowler, "Postmodern Biblical Criticism," *Foundations and Facets Forum* 5 (1989) 3-30.

[44] Rosemary Hennessey, "Women's Lives/Feminist Knowledge: Feminist Standpoint as Ideology Critique," *Hypatia* 8 (1993) 14-34. Hence, it is inappropriate either to restrict ideological criticism to feminist and sociohistorical readings or to assume that social science interpretation provides "intertextual data" about the Mediterranean world for a socio-rhetorical reading as though social-scientific readings were not also perspectival and ideological. For such an argument see Vernon K. Robbins, "Using a Socio-Rhetorical Poetics to Develop a Unified Method: The Woman who

ments, prescriptions and projections, its discourses on gender, race, class, culture, or religion can be exposed as the ideological inscriptions that they are.

2. *A critical feminist historiography* seeks both to break the hold of the kyriocentric Pauline text over historical imagination and to explore the textual exclusions and "scientific" choices which constitute the historical knowledge of early Jewish and Christian discourses in the Greco-Roman world. In so doing, it aims to make present the different voices inscribed both in the text and in its ancient and contemporary con-texts. To that end it exploits the contradictions and silences inscribed in the text for reconstructing not only the symbolic "world of the biblical text," but also the socio-historical worlds which have made possible the particular world-construction of the text.

As a rhetorical communicative practice a socio-critical feminist historiography does not seek to sunder text and reality, whether in an antiquarian or in a formalist fashion. Rather, its "texts" seek to re-construct and to construct a *different* socio-historical reality. By analyzing the socio-political functions of Pauline texts as well by articulating adequate models for historical reconstruction, it seeks to displace the dualistic inscriptions of the andro- and kyriocentric text. It does not deny but recognize that Pauline texts are rhetorical texts, produced in and by particular historical debates and struggles. Andro- and kyriocentric texts tell communal stories, narrate social worlds, and construct symbolic universes which mythologize, absolutize and idealize patriarchal differences. In so doing such texts obliterate or marginalize the historical presence of the devalued "others." For instance, if scholars read the *prescriptive* texts of the Pauline tradition which advocate patriarchal submission as *descriptive* of the patriarchal institutionalization process in early Christianity, they valorize this kyriarchal rhetorics by re-inscribing it as early Christian history.

A feminist socio-critical rhetoric argues that an emancipatory reconstruction of early Judaism and Christianity in the Greco-Roman world becomes possible when one interfaces the kyriocentric text with a reconstructive historical model that

Anointed Jesus as a Test Case," in Eugene H. Lovering, ed., *Society of Biblical Literature 1992 Seminar Papers* (Atlanta: Scholars Press, 1992) 302-19.

can bring to the fore the contributions of those marginalized or silenced by the classical or sacred text. Pauline rhetorical discourses create a world in which those whose arguments they oppose either become the "deviant" Others or are no longer heard from at all. On the one hand, an inclusive reconstructive historical model allows one to interrogate the persuasive strategies of the canonical or classical text and its author, as well as to focus on the subjugated knowledges and submerged voices inscribed in their discourses. On the other hand, such a model enables one to dislodge texts from their androcentric or kyriocentric frame of reference (Herr-schaftsdenkrahmen) and to reassemble and recontextualize them in a different frame of meaning.

Such a "doubled" process of historical interpretation could be likened to quilting a patchwork or to creating a mosaic. The image of quilting[45] rather than that of reporting or transcribing is an apt metaphor for a postmodern liberationist understanding of the historian's task. The process of the displacement of androcentric source-texts, which have generated the politics of submission and rhetorics of otherness, and of their reorganization together with all other available information in an emancipatory historical model, reconstructs historical-social "reality" not as a "given fact" but as a plausible "subtext" to the kyriocentric text. Such a reconstructive historical model of early Jewish and Christian struggles and arguments about the "politics and rhetorics of patriarchal submission" allows one to understand the cultural dependencies and effects generated by these debates and struggles. The validity and adequacy of this (as of all) historical reconstruction must be judged on whether it can make centrally present as historical agents and speaking subjects those whom the kyriocentric text marginalizes or excludes.[46]

---

[45] A fuller elaboration of this organizing metaphor can be found in my article, "'Quilting' Women's History: Phoebe of Cenchreae," in Judith Long, ed., *Lessons From Women's Lives* (Syracuse: Syracuse University Maxwell School of Citizenship and Public Affairs, 1984) 22-29.

[46] See also my article, "Text and Reality – Reality as Text:The Problem of a Feminist Historical and Social Reconstruction Based on Texts," *Studia Theologica* 40 (1989) 19-34, and the proposal of Joan W. Scott, "Deconstructing Equality-Versus-Difference: On the Uses of Poststructuralist Theory for Feminism," *Feminist Studies* 14 (1988) 33-50.

III. "Religious Propaganda" in a "Doubled" Process of Interpretation

Such a "doubled" mode of socio-critical rhetorical analysis can shed light on the debate of religious propganda in antiquity. If one contextualizes both the interpretations of Paul's correspondence to the Corinthians and the discussions on early Jewish and early Christian propaganda in the ancient world within a reconstructive emancipatory framework, one is struck by the dualistic conceptualizations of both. Exegetical discourses continue to understand the writings of the Christian Testament[47] either theologically as documents of inner-Christian struggles between different parties, groups, and theologies. Or they read them sociologically as records of opposing sectarian groups that are defined in contrast to the institutionalized church. In both instances, scholars understand early Christian canonical writings as products of doctrinal, especially christological controversy and sectarian strife, rather than as cultural religious rhetorical practices.

Moreover, scholars tend to conceptualize not only the literature but also the history of early Christianity in terms of dualistic oppositions and exclusivist dichotomies. Thus, they fail to reconstruct the history of early Christian literatures and communities as the history of communicative persuasion, emancipatory struggles, and common visions. This failure is compounded by the inclination to sunder early Christianity from early Judaism, to sever mission from apologetics, and to delineate strict boundaries between inside and outside, between Mediterranean culture and ours. In so doing scholars disregard that the self-understanding of religious communities is intertwined with their cultural-religious environment, and they overlook that communication or historical reconstruction

[47] Since the designations "Old Testament" and "New Testament" as parts of the Christian Bible suggest anti-Jewish supersessionism, I generally attempt to replace the appellation New Testament with "Christian Testament," a designation that points to the Christian authorship and ownership of first- century canonical writings. Other scholars use "First and Second Testament" to underscore the secondary character of the New Testament. Yet, a widely accepted solution is not likely to emerge as long as popular and academic Christian discourses maintain the kind of theological supersessionist anti-Jewish rhetorics that are associated with the appellation "New Testament."

is only possible if and when one can assume some kind of common language and shared symbolic universe.

As I have argued above, this research situation invites a "doubled" critical strategy of exploration. It invites a deconstructive reading that interrogates the pervasive kyriocentric dualisms, on the one hand, and on the other a historical-political reconstructive rhetoric that reassembles available information and retells ancient history within the framework of an emancipatory democratic paradigm.

1. A deconstructive reading has three key moments: first, it investigates key organizing models and structuring images of scholarship.[48] Second, it scrutinizes tacit assumptions and unconscious premises, and third, it suspects the historical critical discourses' interestedness in coherence, univoicity and symbolic totality.

First, as we have seen, the discourses on Paul's theology and ancient propaganda construct a series of dualistic religious, cultural, and political oppositions such as orthodoxy – heresy, community – market, honor – shame, mission – propaganda, and apologetics – rhetorics, rather than underscore democratic values such as differences, pluriformity, equality and deliberation. This series of dualisms privileges the first term of the opposition by claiming it either for Paul, Orthodoxy, Christianity, Judaism, or hegemonic patriarchal culture, and constructs the second term as "other" by attributing it to, e.g., the opponents, Hellenistic propagandists, Jewish legalists and so on. Such interpretive dualistic oppositions obfuscate the third series of linking terms such as "audience," "community," "assembly" by subsuming it under either pole of the opposition. The most telling dualistic construct is that of patriarchal gender, which already is inscribed in the Pauline letters insofar as Paul understands himself as the "father" of the Corinthian community who presents the community "as a pure bride to her one husband," Christ (2 Cor 11:2-3). This genderization of the community possesses negative overtones since it is connected with a reference to the seduction of Eve. The symbolic construct of gender dualism at once coheres in and undermines the other oppositions to the degree that it

[48] See my early article "Women in the Pre-Pauline and Pauline Churches," *Union Seminary Quarterly Review* 33 (1978) 153-66.

casts all speaking subjects (Paul, the serpent, the opponents, the interpreters) as *masculine* and construes their audience (the Corinthian community, early Judaism, the Greco-Roman world, the readers) as passive, immature, and gullible in *feminine* terms.

Second, the tacit assumption underlying such dualistic constructions is the supposition that the actual rhetorical situation and its historical power relations are identical to and correspond with the rhetorical situation inscribed in the Pauline correspondence[49] or in other textual sources. In other words, such dualistic oppositions presuppose the "scientific" theoretical understanding of texts either as windows or as mirrors and thereby mystify the rhetoricity of text and language. Such a premise privileges the "masculine" hegemonic voice inscribed in kyriarchal Pauline or in other ancient source-texts rather than particularize and relativize this voice by reconstructing a varied chorus of voices.[50] Yet, the *reconstruction* of a pluriform congregation of fully responsible "adult" voices who have equal standing becomes possible only if one *deconstructs* the gendered conceptualization of dualistic oppositions. It would require that one re-construct a radical democratic historical model which can comprehend the disputes in the Corinthian *ekklēsia* in terms of *parrēsia* – the free speech of citizens – rather than cast them in terms of confessional internecine altercations or imperial market competition.

Third, a postmodern deconstructive reading must name the impetus to coherence, unity, and identity as the motivating ideological force in Pauline studies, a drive that engenders the oppositional models and rhetorical assumptions of the prevalent gendered discourses on Pauline theology and religious propaganda. This impetus comes to the fore, for instance, in the attempts of Pauline scholarship to declare texts such as 1 Cor 11:2-16 and 14:34-36 as later interpolations

---

[49] Cf. Elizabeth Castelli, "Interpretations of Power in 1 Corinthians," *Semeia* 54 (1992) 159-96.

[50] Cf., e.g., my article "Missionaries, Coworkers, and Apostles: Rom 16 and the Reconstruction of Women's Early Christian History," *Word and World* 6/4 (1986) 420-33; Antoinette Clark Wire, *The Corinthian Women Prophets: A Reconstruction through Paul's Rhetoric* (Minneapolis: Augsburg Fortress, 1990).

because they do not cohere with the reigning scholarly appreciation of Paul's theology. Or, scholars rearrange the extant text and reconstruct the rhetorical situation of the diverse fragments of Paul's Corinthian correspondence in such a way that the symbolic coherence of Paul's theological argument is safeguarded. Feminist theorists have unmasked this drive to coherent reading, univoicity, and symbolic totality as the western "logic of identity" and "politics of otherness."[51] This "politics and rhetorics of othering" establishes identity either by declaring the difference of the other to be the same or by vilifying and idealizing difference as otherness.[52] It justifies relationships of ruling[53] by obfuscating structures of domination and subordination as "naturalized" differences. Ancient and modern philosophy have developed the ideological "politics and rhetorics of otherness" in the attempt to legitimate a situation whereby not all but only certain people can claim the rights of citizen, participate in democratic government, or deliberate in public debate.[54]

2. *A postmodern emancipatory historiography*, however, does not cease with a deconstructive reading. Rather, it seeks to displace the politics and rhetorics of subordination and otherness by means of a politics and rhetorics of equality and multivoicity. My interpretive work has sought to develop such a reconstructive historical model that valorizes difference, plurivoicity, and democratic participation. It conceives of early Christian writings as "taking sides" in the emancipatory struggles of antiquity and it conceptualizes early Christian community as a

[51] For discussion and literature on the "politics of otherness," see Elisabeth Schüssler Fiorenza, "The Politics of Otherness: Biblical Interpretation as a Critical Praxis for Liberation," in Mark Ellis and Otto Maduro, eds., *The Future of Liberation Theology: Essays in Honor of Gustavo Gutiérrez* (Maryknoll: Orbis, 1989) 311-25.

[52] Cf. Sandra Lee Bartky, *Femininity and Domination: Studies in the Phenomenology of Oppression* (New York: Routledge, 1990).

[53] For this expression see Dorothy E. Smith, *The Conceptual Practices of Power: A Feminist Sociology of Knowledge* (Boston: Northeastern University Press, 1990).

[54] For the development of the "political philosophy of otherness" as legitimizing patriarchal societal structures of domination in antiquity, cf. Susan Moller Okin, *Women in Western Political Thought* (Princeton: University Press, 1979) 15-98; Elizabeth V. Spelman, *Inessential Woman: Problems of Exclusion in Feminist Thought* (Boston: Beacon, 1988) 19-56; and especially Page duBois, *Centaurs & Amazons: Women and the Pre History of the Great Chain of Being* (Ann Arbor: University of Michigan Press, 1982).

democratic assembly (*ekklēsia*) of differing voices and socio-rhetorical practices. The differences and contradictions in the rhetoric of early Christian sources point to socio-political conflicts and religio-cultural tensions among Hellenistic, Jewish, or early Christian "egalitarian" movements and their dominant patriarchal Greco-Roman, Jewish and emerging Christian socio-political contexts.

These differing and contradictory socio-rhetorical practices likewise point to socio-political conflicts *within* early Christian communities. Such rhetorical tensions can be traced between those who advocate both the ethos of the *ekklēsia* as a "*basileia* discipleship of equals" and as "a community of freedom in the Spirit," on the one hand, and those reemerging hegemonic discourses within segments of the Christian community advocating patriarchal leadership and organization on the other. The latter arguments of a politics and rhetorics of submission seek to reintroduce the patriarchal division between the public and private spheres, between those who speak and those who are silent, between women and men, between slaves and free, between Jews and Greeks within the *ekklēsia*. They argue for relegating (elite) married women to the private sphere, for restricting their activity to properly "feminine" behavior, and for limiting women's leadership to women. Their arguments for the "ethics and politics of submission" engender not only restrictions against women's leadership but promote acceptance of slave women's sufferings as well and advocate the adaptation of the whole community to hegemonic kyriarchal structures.[55]

Pluralistic reconstructive historical models like the one delineated here enable readers to displace the "scientific" dualistic paradigm of sectarian conflicts and exclusions and to recontextualize early Christian debates within Greco-Roman and Jewish public democratic discourses. In such a new contextualization, early Christian writings can be read as public arguments seeking to persuade and convince "citizens" who share similar religious and cultural worlds. Rather than map-

---

[55] For the fuller development of such an emancipatory reconstructive argument, see my article "A Discipleship of Equals: Ekklesial Democracy and Patriarchy in Biblical Perspective," in Eugene C. Bianch and Rosemary Radford Ruether, eds., *A Democratic Catholic Church* (New York: Crossroad, 1992).

ping religious propaganda in a negative dualistic way and dividing it into two discrete areas, mission and apologetics, a rhetorical democratic model of analysis can understand missionary and apologetic discourses as the two sides of one and the same rhetorical "coin."

A socio-critical rhetorical model of historical reconstruction must distinguish, however, between "imperial" kyriarchal and emancipatory "egalitarian" forms of propagandistic functions, aspirations, and institutions and may not consolidate them as oppositional discrete formations. Instead, it should seek to reconceptualize "religious propaganda" as a site of interacting rhetorical-political and cultural-religious practices. In so doing it may not privilege the authorial voice of the canonical or classical text but must position itself on the side of the historical victims and their subjugated knowledges. Such a socio-critical rhetorical model could be likened to a nestling doll. Like Russian dolls within which smaller dolls fit inside ever larger ones, so a feminist liberationist reconstruction of the historical tensions and struggles between imperial patriarchy and self-determining *ekklēsia* in Greco-Roman society, early Judaism, and early Christianity seeks to situate the religious history of women within early Christian history, within Jewish history, within Greco-Roman history, and within the history of Western society, rather than playing one of these against the other. Such a conflictive model of historical reconstruction would be misapprehended, however, if it were read either in terms of an uninterrupted linear development or in terms of a rapid and uncontested decline from *ekklēsia* as the discipleship of equals to *ekklēsia* as the patriarchal household of God.

This model seeks, instead, to conceptualize early Christianities and their struggles as pluriform movements of women and men engaged in ongoing debates over equality and full "citizenship." If the exegetical reconstruction of Pauline debates is interfaced with an inter-cultural and inter-religious reconstructive historical model, one can show that such emancipatory rhetorical practices and socio-political religious struggles for freedom[56] as well as the right of "citizenship" had

[56] Orlando Patterson, *Freedom*, vol. 1: *Freedom in the Making of Western Culture* (New York: Harper Collins, 1991), claims to be the first such emancipatory history of freedom. It seems not accidental that his historical reconstruction of the struggles for freedom in antiquity recognizes women's crucial participation and contribution to these struggles.

begun long before the Christian movements emerged on the scene. These have continued throughout Western history and are still going on today. The recognition of the rhetoricity of Pauline discourses encourages and challengess scholars to position their research within the ongoing history of such struggles. Dieter Georgi's work is an important step in this direction.

IS BELIEF THE CENTER OF RELIGION?[1]

Bernadette J. Brooten
(Brandeis University, Waltham, Massachusetts)

In the increasingly religiously pluralistic society of the United States, the U.S. Supreme Court faces the challenge of how to define religion. I believe that, while the Court has taken steps to conceptualize religion in a manner appropriate to this nation's religious diversity, a Christian understanding of religion shapes the Court's thinking. A number of U.S. Supreme Court decisions concerning free exercise of religion illustrate that the U.S. legal system distinguishes between religious belief and religious practice, and implicitly characterizes belief as the essence or core of religion. While the view that practice derives from belief may be well suited for conceptualizing Christianity, especially Protestant Christianity, it has not helped the Court to understand the religiosity of Native Americans or Orthodox Jews. In antiquity pagan judges, who held practice, rather than belief, as central to religion, tested early Christians, for whom belief was central, by demanding that they perform certain cultic acts to prove their loyalty to the Roman Empire. Thus, I am struck by the irony of the Supreme Court's testing of religions that do not hold belief central by means of the category of belief.

In what follows, I will give a brief historical sketch of several Supreme Court cases that illustrate the Court's focus on belief as central for religion and will argue that this focus does not do justice to the self-understanding and self-definition of several non-Christian religions. I then will discuss how the

[1] Dieter Georgi always has urged his fellow New Testament scholars, whether students or colleagues, to go beyond the narrow confines of scholarship on antiquity and to speak to the world. In this essay I take up his challenge by addressing a troubling aspect of U.S. legal discourse concerning religion. In suggesting ways in which a study of the New Testament in its cultural context can improve that understanding, I write out of gratitude to Dieter Georgi for challenging his students and colleagues to cross boundaries from which other scholars shy away.

I express gratitude to Denise Kimber Buell, Caroline Johnson, and Melanie Johnson-DeBaufre for their assistance with this article, as well as to Ronald Thiemann and Preston Williams for their helpful comments.

apostle Paul, as an influential representative of early Christianity, focused on belief in a way that changed religious history and redefined what it means to be religious.

In addition, the Supreme Court's focus on belief fosters an individualistic and privatistic understanding of religion, since belief is generally understood as a highly personal, private matter.[2] Theologians and New Testament interpreters also sometimes have taken Paul's concept of belief as personal, private, and centered on the individual, but the more careful analysis undertaken by several recent scholars reveals the communitarian aspects of Paul's concept of belief.

Both historical situations, namely, that of the religiously pluralistic contemporary U.S. and that of the religiously pluralistic Roman world – including Paul and other early Christians – require conceptualizations of religion sufficiently complex to describe these religions and their communities. New Testament scholars have a responsibility to join the effort to define religion in a culturally appropriate way, since it is in the New Testament where we can investigate and clarify the earliest Christians' emphases on belief and from the New Testament that modern Christianity, especially Protestant Christianity, claims to draw its self-definition. Interpreters of early Christianity and of other Graeco-Roman religions, who have made great strides in conceptualizations, can give historical depth to the discussion of contemporary religion by illustrating that current definitions are culture-bound and historically relative.

The U.S. Supreme Court on Religion as Belief

In 1879 the U.S. Supreme Court based its holding that religiously allowed bigamy is a criminal act on Thomas Jefferson's distinction between religious opinions and religious actions; this applied to Mormons, despite their permitting bigamy on religious grounds. Jefferson held that "the legislative powers of the government reach actions only, and not opinions."[3] The

[2] For a far-ranging critique of the Supreme Court's treatment of religion see Stephen L. Carter, *The Culture of Disbelief: How American Law and Politics Trivialize Religious Devotion* (New York: Basic Books, 1993), especially 23-43 ("God as a Hobby").

[3] *Reynolds v. United States*, 98 U.S. at 164 (1879).

Court emphasized its guarantee of freedom of religious opinion, but insisted that this freedom did not extend to religious practice in the case of bigamy, which it classified as a threat to the social order. In a 1940 landmark decision, the Court slightly expanded the scope of the Free Exercise Clause to include some religious acts when it stated that the Free Exercise Clause of the First Amendment embraces

> "two concepts, – freedom to believe and freedom to act. The first is absolute but, in the nature of things, the second cannot be."[4]

This debate concerning opinion or belief and practice also has continued in several recent free exercise cases. In 1988 the Court held that the Free Exercise Clause does not prohibit the government from constructing a road or harvesting timber on a piece of federal land historically used by the Yurok, Karok and Tolowa tribes for Native American religious ceremonies requiring "privacy, silence and an undisturbed natural setting."[5] The Court conceded that the road construction and timber harvest "could have devastating effects on traditional Indian religious practices,"[6] but determined that the government was not thereby coercing the Yurok, Karok and Tolowa tribes "into violating their religious beliefs."[7] The Court assumed the existence of Native American religious beliefs that exist independently of religious ceremonies and that could continue even if the geographically-specific religious ceremonies ceased. Justice Brennan, however, recognized the problem of forcing "Indian concepts into non-Indian categories."[8] In his dissenting opinion Justice Brennan attempted to make clear that land, sacred space, is central to Native American religion, rather than "dogma" or "[e]stablished or universal truths."[9]

In another case concerning Native American religious practices, the Court held in 1988 that employers at a drug and alcohol abuse prevention agency may dismiss Native American

---

[4] *Cantwell v. Connecticut,* 310 U.S. at 303-4 (1940).

[5] *Lyng v. Northwest Indian Cemetery Protective Association et al.*, 485 U.S. at 442 (1988).

[6] *Lyng v. Northwest Indian Cemetery Protective Association et al.*, *supra,* at 451.

[7] *Lyng v. Northwest Indian Cemetery Protective Association et al.*, *supra,* at 449.

[8] *Lyng v. Northwest Indian Cemetery Protective Association et al.*, *supra,* at 459.

[9] *Lyng v. Northwest Indian Cemetery Protective Association et al.*, *supra,* at 460.

rehabilitation counselors for the use of peyote in religious ceremonies.[10] Here once more the Court viewed religious action, in this case the ceremonial ingestion of peyote, as protected to a lesser degree than religious belief. In its argument the Court implied that religious groups can rest assured that, at the minimum, it will protect their religious beliefs, if not all of their religious practices. However, this belief/practice *schema* may not apply to Native American religion at all.

A 1986 case of an Orthodox Jewish man, in which the Court upheld an Air Force order prohibiting him from wearing his yarmulke while on duty, poses somewhat similar problems.[11] The Court defined as evenhanded the Air Force's prohibition of visible religious apparel and acceptance of religious apparel that is not visible. In his concurring opinion Justice Stevens emphasized the military's need for the "uniform treatment for the members of all religious faiths."[12] In contrast, in his dissenting opinion, Justice Brennan rejected the implied division of religions into "two categories – those with visible dress and grooming requirements and those without," a categorization that Brennan recognized as favoring majority religions over minority ones.[13]

While I cannot address the full complexity of these cases,[14] the problem I have outlined here needs to be addressed. Since a conceptual framework that distinguishes between belief and practice and grants privilege to the former over the latter will not lead to the fair treatment of religions that call for special clothing, sacred space, or the ingestion of particular substances, I propose that scholars of religion assist the Court in developing a better understanding of religion for adjudicating Free Exercise of Religion challenges. I recognize that a society may need to impose limits on religious practices, such as when it deems these practices as damaging to society. But the view of belief as religiously more central than practice does not

[10] *Employment Division, Department of Human Resources of the State of Oregon, et al. v. Smith,* 485 U.S. 660 (1988).

[11] *Goldman v. Weinberger,* 475 U.S. 503 (1986).

[12] *Goldman v. Weinberger, supra,* at 512.

[13] *Goldman v. Weinberger, supra,* at 521.

[14] I am aware that factors other than the belief/action distinction also play a role in these cases and that, in some cases, the Court has protected religious actions under the Free Exercise Clause, e.g., *Wisconsin v. Yoder* 406 U.S. 205 (1972). Moreover, Christian thinking is certainly not the only influence on the Supreme Court's view of religion.

correspond with the self-understanding of many of our society's religious traditions.

Paul and Belief: The Individual and the Community

A better understanding of the history of religions can assist us to recognize the Court's focus on belief as culture-specific and Christian-centered. The apostle Paul exemplifies the early Christian paradigm shift in conceptualizing religion as belief. An examination of his views within the context of the Roman world will enable us to understand better the extent and limits of that shift within Western religious history.

In placing belief[15] in Christ at the center of human existence, Paul altered the Judaism into which he had been born, which had law as its center. Paul's move was an unusual one since in his world few, if any, would have thought of belief as the central characteristic of religion. To be sure, πίστις had been a term of religious piety since Plato,[16] but nevertheless, sacred space, blood sacrifice, drink offerings, veneration of one's ancestors, rituals concerning the dead, festivals, cultic objects, commandments concerning gifts to the poor, tithing, cultic purity, and a host of other concerns were more likely than belief to come to the mind of a person in the Roman world at the mention of religion.[17] Thus, Paul's theology signals a paradigm shift within ancient religious history in its placement of faith as central and sacred space, seasonal religious festivals, and many other religious practices as peripheral.

Paul's shift to faith as central for salvation created a theo-

---

[15] Although I translate πίστις here as belief, I am fully cognizant of the translation difficulties inherent in Paul's usage of the term. See, e.g., E.P. Sanders, *Paul* (Oxford: Oxford University Press, 1991) 45-49; Dieter Georgi, *Theocracy in Paul's Praxis and Theology*, trans. David E. Green (Minneapolis: Fortress, 1991) 43, 83-84.

[16] See, e.g., Plato, *Laws* 966 D. Plato defines an ἄθεος person as one who questions the existence of the gods (*Apology* 26 C). A hypostatized πίστις also enjoyed status as a deity. E.g., Hesiod refers to πίστις as a deity, while under Augustus the worship of *Fides* as a deity was revived and a temple built to her in Rome. (See *Der Kleine Pauly*, s.v. *Fides* and *Pistis*.) See Dieter Georgi, *Theocracy in Paul's Praxis and Theology*, 84.

[17] See, e.g., Helmut Koester, who states, "But *religio* was and remained for the Romans the exact observation of established rites on behalf of the whole political community" (*Introduction to the New Testament*, vol. 1: *History, Culture and Religion of the Hellenistic Age* [New York: De Gruyter, 1982] 363).

logical conflict for him, namely: What is the relationship between God's revelation in Christ and God's earlier revelations to the people of Israel?[18] Was the believer in Christ to follow the ancestral customs of Israel? Some of Paul's earliest opponents apparently feared that his focus on belief meant that Paul understood πίστις as purely personal and private and unconcerned with behavior (e.g., Rom 3:8, 31). Accordingly, Paul had to answer, first, whether faith in Christ meant that good deeds were no longer necessary; second, whether such faith meant that God's revelations to Israel had run their course and no longer were valid; and third, whether people who did not follow the ancestral customs of Israel could be saved. In response to these questions Paul argued that life in the spirit bears the fruit of good works, and that life in the spirit is not life under the law (e.g., Gal 5:16-24); that God has not rejected Israel (e.g., Rom 11:1); and that people are saved by faith and not the works of the law (e.g., Rom 3:21-2). Paul's answers differ greatly from the ways in which other Jews of his time addressed the religious function and meaning of behavior.

For Jews in this period (and subsequently), proper behavior rather than proper belief characterized a righteous Jew. Thus, Josephus defines an apostate from Judaism as a person "who hates the customs of the Jews" or "who does not abide by the ancestral customs."[19] Similarly, the divisions between the Jewish sects arose to a far greater extent over disputes about law than over disputes about belief.[20] Jews in antiquity did, of course, have beliefs. Ephraim Urbach, for example, has attempted to systematize the concepts and beliefs of the Tanna'im and Amora'im.[21] But Urbach recognizes that the implicit concepts that he systematizes do not form the basis of

[18] See E.P. Sanders, *Paul* (Oxford: Oxford University Press, 1991) 44.

[19] Josephus *Bell.* 7.3.3. § 50; *Ant.* 20.5.2 § 100. See Shaye J.D. Cohen, *From the Maccabees to the Mishnah* (Philadelphia: Westminster, 1987) 61.

[20] Shaye J.D. Cohen points out that ancient Judaism lacked the organization necessary to impose dogma on Jewish communities scattered throughout the Mediterranean basin. The Roman Catholic Church, for example, has the pope and the teaching magisterium of the world's bishops to ensure that Catholics throughout the world will receive the same dogma (*From the Maccabees to the Mishnah* [Philadelphia: Westminster, 1987] 61, 124-73).

[21] Ephraim E. Urbach, *The Sages: Their Concepts and Beliefs*, trans. Israel Abrahams (2 vols.; Jerusalem: Magnes Press, 1975).

the organization of the rabbinic *corpus*, which is organized around questions of practice.[22]

Practice as the observance of ancestral customs not only conveyed a special relationship to God, but also shaped Jewish group-identity. In fact, observance of the Torah required economic and social cooperation in such matters as dietary laws and sabbath observance.[23] Ancient Jewish practice, therefore, even though carried out by private individuals, had certain public and group aspects that aided in the preservation of the Jewish community.

Paul's Jewish contemporaries, for whom the preservation of the Jewish community and of Jewish group-identity were central, apparently viewed his response to the Jewish law with considerable skepticism. According to Acts 28:17, Paul defended himself vis-à-vis the Jewish leaders of Rome, claiming he "had done nothing against our people or the customs of our ancestors."[24] According to his own correspondence, however, he was quite willing to depart from such ancestral customs as circumcision and dietary laws (Gal 2:11-14; 5:2-12; Rom 14).[25]

If Paul's response to the Jewish law raised questions about his commitment to Jewish ancestral customs and the preservation of the Jewish community, does that mean that he understood πίστις as a purely individual phenomenon? Traditionally, theologians have interpreted Paul's concept of πίστις as deeply personal and focused on the individual.[26] But more recently, interpreters coming from different positions, such as

---

[22] Similarly, the collection of texts compiled by George W.E. Nicklesburg and Michael E. Stone, *Faith and Piety in Early Judaism: Texts and Documents* (Philadelphia: Fortress, 1983; reprinted Philadelphia: Trinity Press International, 1991), derives from a variety of unrelated contexts.

[23] E.g., the availablilty of ritually slaughtered meat and of wine from which no libation to pagan deities had been made or the creation of multiple-unit dwellings through external boundaries in order to facilitate sabbath observance required an extensive Jewish infra-structure.

[24] Cf. Acts 6:14.

[25] To be sure, Paul drew upon the law at certain points; see Bernadette J. Brooten, "Paul and the Law: How Complete Was the Departure?" *The Princeton Seminary Bulletin* Supplementary Issue, No. 1 (1990) 71-89, and Peter J. Tomson, *Paul and the Jewish Law: Halakha in the Letters of the Apostle to the Gentiles* (Compendia Rerum Iudaicarum ad Novum Testamentum 3.1; Assen/Maastricht: Van Gorcum; Minneapolis: Fortress, 1990).

[26] Rudolf Bultmann exemplifies an understanding of πίστις as affecting mainly the individual and the individual's salvation (*Theologie des Neuen Testaments* [6th ed.; Tübingen: Mohr-Siebeck, 1968] 191-353).

Krister Stendahl,[27] Robert Jewett,[28] and Dieter Georgi[29] have recognized Paul's communitarian concern with the salvation and well-being of groups of people and not simply of the individual believer. In other words, the current individualistic understanding of belief implied in recent Supreme Court decisions may not correspond to that of Paul, one of the most fundamental shapers of Christian concepts of faith.

If we look beyond the debate between Paul and his fellow Jews, we find that in other Graeco-Roman religions, practice rather than belief shaped self-understanding and identity.[30] Pagans did, however, presuppose the presence of awe or intentionality in one's religious activity,[31] although the precise relationship between acts and awe or intentionality in Greek and Roman religion has posed difficulties for interpreters. Perhaps the difficulty lies not in the unclarity of the relationship between belief and practice in antiquity so much as in modern scholars' tendency to see these religions as wholly other and as consisting of cultic acts devoid of anything resembling the depths of Christian faith.[32] Some scholars, in contrast, go to great lengths to defend pagan religions as incorporating the same depths of piety as Christianity, thereby placing these religions within a Christian interpretive framework.[33] Current inter-religious dialogue, which often concep-

---

[27] Krister Stendahl, *Paul Among Jews and Gentiles and Other Essays* (Philadelphia: Fortress, 1976), especially "Paul and the Introspective Conscience of the West," 78-96.

[28] Robert Jewett, "Following the Argument of Romans," in *The Romans Debate*, ed. Karl P. Donfried (revised and expanded edition; Peabody MA: Hendrickson, 1991) 265-77.

[29] See especially Dieter Georgi, *Theocracy in Paul's Praxis and Theology*.

[30] While atheism (ἀθεότης) in the Roman world could refer to people not believing in the existence of the deities, it also connoted not participating in the cults of the deities.

[31] Robin Lane Fox, *Pagans and Christians* (New York: Knopf, 1987) 31-32.

[32] In addition, scholars often have viewed ancient pagan religions through the lens of Protestant/Catholic debates. See, e.g., Jonathan Z. Smith, *Drudgery Divine: On the Comparison of Early Christianities and the Religions of Late Antiquity* (Chicago: University of Chicago Press, 1990), who argues this point for modern research on the Greek mystery religions.

[33] André-Jean Festugière seems to employ an overly Christian framework for describing Greek religion. He is at pains to describe the Greeks as having a depth of personal piety, a thirst for closeness with God, and "belief in a fourth dimension," which is his definition of religion (*Personal Religion among the Greeks* [Berkeley: University of California Press, 1954] 1 and passim).

tualizes religion as faith, compounds the historical problem of understanding Greek and Roman religions adequately because this dialogue often shapes the categories we employ for studying and assessing historical religions.[34]

An examination of the Roman world illustrates decisively that not all cultures and historical periods define religion in the manner of the current U.S. Supreme Court. In the time of the early church, most people defined religion differently. In fact, the early Christian focus on belief as central was something of a novelty, a departure from culturally-accepted understandings of religion. A definition of religion that accounts for the diversity of religious self-understanding in contemporary American society may, in fact, resemble a scholarly definition of religion in the Roman world. If we theologians, New Testament interpreters, and historians of religion can build upon the best research in our respective fields, we will be more capable of providing the Court with sufficiently nuanced definitions of religion and of challenging it to guarantee the "free exercise of religion," not the "free exercise of faith," to all inhabitants of the United States.[35]

---

[34] Wilfred Cantwell Smith has attempted to delineate comparatively the contours of religion, but he too sees faith as central. For example, he states that "Christians have seldom appreciated the significance of a tradition such as the Jewish or Islamic where law has been faith's primary and controlling expression" (*The Meaning and End of Religion* [New York: Macmillan, 1962; reprinted Minneapolis: Fortress, 1991] 179). The view of faith as central and law as its expression is a Christian mode of conceptualization.

[35] Since completion of this article, Congress passed the Religious Freedom Restoration Act of 1993, which addresses the problem of the peyote case, but not of the yarmulke or sacred land cases. The problem of the conceptualization of religion also remains.

ON BECOMING AN ANGEL: RIVAL BAPTISMAL THEOLOGIES AT COLOSSAE

Harold W. Attridge
(University of Notre Dame, Notre Dame, Indiana)

The religio-historical problem of the Epistle to the Colossians has long intrigued students of the New Testament. In the words of the distinguished recipient of this Festschrift, it is an example of "Torah-related Gnosticism,"[1] but the precise meaning of that designation has proved to be somewhat elusive. We may now be in a position to make that designation more specific.

One of the most puzzling aspects of the phenomenon to which the author of Colossians reacts has been the role of angels in the piety of the community. That they do play a role is clear from the warnings of Col 2:16-19 (I cite the RSV):

> "Therefore let no one pass judgment on you in questions of food and drink or with regard to a festival or a new moon or a sabbath. These are only a shadow of what is to come; but the substance belongs to Christ. Let no one disqualify you, insisting *on self-abasement and worship of angels, taking his stand on visions,* puffed up without reason by his sensuous mind, and not holding fast to the Head, from whom the whole body, nourished and knit together through its joints and ligaments, grows with a growth that is from God."

Colossians is not the only early Christian text to treat angels. Their cameo appearances in the Gospels and Acts, in the annunciation stories, in the temptation and Gethsemane accounts, at the empty tomb, all portray them in a positive light, as obedient servants, messengers of God on high. Similarly, Revelation has a large contingent of angels. There, too, they serve as obedient messengers, as well as heavenly choirsters, acolytes and subdeacons. One place where there is a jarring note about angels is, of course, Colossians. A similar attitude

---

[1] See Dieter Georgi, *Remebering the Poor: The History of Paul's Collection for Jerusalem* (Nashville: Abingdon, 1992; ET, revised, of *Geschichte der Kollekte des Paulus für Jerusalem* (Hamburg-Bergstedt: Reich, 1965). Georgi acknowledges his indebtedness to Gunther Bornkamm, "Die Häresie des Kolosserbriefes," in *Gesammelte Aufsätze* I (Munich: Kaiser, 1966) 139–56.

toward angels is occasionally detected in the Epistle to the Hebrews, although there angels function primarily as part of a rhetorical synkrisis to exalt the status of the Son, as I have argued elsewhere.[2]

What, then, is going on at Colossae and why is there some form of disparaging reference to angels? Numerous options have been suggested, from Hellenistic syncretism,[3] to Gnosticism, to Jewish merkavah piety.[4] Most are handily surveyed some time ago in the monograph *Conflict at Colossae* by Francis and Meeks[5] or more recently in the dissertation by Thomas J. Sappington, *Revelation and Redemption at Colossae.*[6] What I would like to do is to reflect on some relatively new data and to suggest a model for understanding what might have been at stake. The model may be construed as a variation on themes proposed by Francis and refined by Sappington, but I believe that it avoids some of the overly neat religio-historical categorizations that have affected discussions of the problem. It in turn has some implications for understanding the origins of Gnosticism.

The raw material for constructing a model for what is going on at Colossae are the polemical epithets and remarks that the author uses:

1. a "philosophy" (2:8), which I take to be a self-descriptor of the problematic group which the author of Colossians polemically labels "vain deceit" and "human tradition."
2. criteria of authenticity having to do with observances in regard to food, drink and a cultic calendar with sabbaths and new moons (2:16). These surely point in the direction of a practice with Jewish roots.

---

[2] See Harold W. Attridge, *Hebrews: A Commentary on the Epistle to the Hebrews* (Hermeneia Commentaries; Philadelphia: Fortress, 1989) 9–11, 51–52.

[3] See Eduard Lohse, *Colossians and Philemon: A Commentary on the Epistles to the Colossians and to Philemon* (Hermeneia Commentaries: Philadelphia: Fortress, 1971; ET of *Die Briefe an die Kolosser und an Philemon* [MeyerK 14; Göttingen: Vandenhoeck & Ruprecht, 1968).

[4] See Jarl Fossum, "Colossians 1.15-18a in the Light of Jewish Mysticism and Gnosticism," *NTS* 35 (1989) 183-01.

[5] Wayne Meeks and Fred O. Francis, *Conflict at Colossae*(Sources for Biblical Study 4; Missoula, MT: Scholars Press, 1973), especially pp. 163-96; Fred O. Francis, "Humility and Angelic Worship in Col 2:18," reprinted from *Studia Theologica* 16 (1963) 109-34.

[6] Thomas J. Sappington, *Revelation and Redemption at Colossae* (*JSNT* 53; *JSOT*: Sheffield, 1991).

3. criteria of authenticity having to do with a visionary experience somehow involving angels (2:18).
4. ascetical practice that flows from the visionary experience and works in conformity with the cultic calendar, an asceticism described as "rigor of devotion and self-abasement and severity to the body" (2:23).
5. the much-studied Christ hymn of chapter 1 is very often taken as further, though oblique, evidence of what is going on at Colossae. It may be, and it would be possible to integrate it into the model that I will propose, but I would prefer to leave it aside at present.

To these factors I would add a sixth, somewhat neglected, factor that I think is crucial for understanding the problem, the practice of baptism. It is clear enough that the author of Colossians opposes to the objectionable "philosophy" (Col 2:8) a bit of baptismal theology found at Col 2:9:

> "See to it, that no one makes a prey of you by philosophy and empty deceit, according to human tradition, according to the elemental spirits of the universe, and not according to Christ. For in him the whole fulness of deity dwells bodily, and you have come to fulness of life in him, who is the head of all rule and authority. In him also you were circumcised with a circumcision made without hands, by putting off the body of flesh in the circumcision of Christ; and you were buried with him in baptism, in which you were also raised with him through faith in the working of God, who raised him from the dead. And you, who were dead in trespasses and the uncircumcision of your flesh, God made alive together with him, having forgiven us all our trespasses, having canceled the bond which stood against us with its legal demands."

I suggest that Colossians makes this appeal to baptism precisely because all of the other objectionable elements cohere within a certain kind of baptismal theory and consequent practice. Some of the texts from Nag Hammadi provide interesting evidence for the phenomenon in question. Whether that means that the problem at Colossae is a form of Gnosticism remains to be seen. First, it is necessary to review what I take to be the relevant parallel material.

The pattern features most prominently in the tractate *Zostrianos* (NHC VIII, 1), recently made available in an excellent edition by John H. Sieber.[7] The tractate is an apocalypse, or account of heavenly journey, in which the ascetical, philosophically-minded seer, Zostrianos, reports how he was instructed in the mysteries of cosmogony and cosmology. At various stages of the mystical journey, the seer, guided by an angelic interpreter, is baptized and transformed into a heavenly or angelic state. So transformed, Zostrianos receives a revelation about the subjects of his inquiry. Upon his return from the mystical journey, he preaches a homily which calls for renunciation of the physical world.

The "baptismal" experiences of the seer are prominent. The journey begins when Zostrianos encounters an angel. He had been despondent, unable to resolve basic metaphysical questions. The "angel of the knowledge of eternal light" (3,29) invites Zostrianos to join him. Zostrianos leaves his body behind (4,24 > Col. 2:23?) and takes off. Somewhere in the clouds of light (4,31) he is baptized (5,14; [ⲁ]ⲉⲓϫⲓ ⲱⲙⲥ) and transformed: "I received the image of the glories there. I became like one of them." (5,15-17; ⲁⲉⲓϫⲓ ⲡⲓⲛⲉ ⲛⲛⲓⲉⲟⲟⲩ ⲉⲧϩⲙ ⲡⲙⲁ ⲉⲧⲙⲙⲁⲩ. ⲁⲉⲓϣⲱⲡⲉ ⲙⲡⲣⲏⲧⲉ ⲛⲟⲩⲁ ⲙⲙⲟⲟⲩ).

This transformation is only the initial step. The seer immediately ascends higher, to the archetypical "repentence which really exists," and he is baptized four more times. Nothing is noted of a transformational experience at this stage.

Zostrianos then ascends to the aeon of Autogenes, the self-begotten one who is the "root" of all things, obviously an important figure in the metaphysics of the tractate. There Zostrianos is baptized in the name of Autogenes by the "powers that are upon the living waters," Michar and Micheus (6,7-10).[8] The initiation ritual has another step as Zostrianos is sealed (6,13-14; ⲁⲩⲣⲥⲫⲣⲁⲅⲓⲍⲉ ⲙⲙⲟⲉⲓ) by certain other heavenly powers. This dipping and sealing effect a decisive transformation of the seer. He becomes a "root-seeing angel," and he "takes his stand upon the first aeon, that is the fourth" (6,17-19; ⲁⲩⲱ ⲁⲉⲓϣ[ⲱⲡⲉ] ⲛⲟⲩⲁⲅⲅⲉⲗⲟⲥ ⲛⲣⲉϥⲛⲁⲩ ⲉⲛⲟⲩ-[ⲛⲉ] ⲁⲩⲱ ⲁⲓⲁϩⲉⲣⲁⲧ ϩⲓϫⲛ ⲡⲓϩⲟⲩⲉ[ⲓⲧ] ⲉⲧⲉ ⲡⲓⲙⲉϩϥⲧⲟⲟⲩ ⲛⲛⲉⲱⲛ ⲡ[ⲉ])The verse requires some comment. The epithet "root-seeing" clearly refers to one who is enabled to gaze on the generative spiritual principle or "root," Autogenes. The

---

[7] John H. Sieber, ed., *Nag Hammadi Codex VIII* (NHS 31; Leiden: Brill, 1991).

[8] Mikhar and Mikheus appear in the list of beings that preside over baptism in the Sethian *Gospel of the Egyptians* (NHC IV,1:76,4-10) and the *Trimorphic Protennoia* (NHC XIII,1:48,19).

two different ordinal numbers refer to the position of the "aeon" upon which the visionary takes his stand reckoned in two ways, from the bottom of the heavenly hierarchy (first) or from the top (fourth).

When Zostrianos proceeds a step higher, the same sequence of events occurs. He is baptized a second time, (7,1-2; ⲁⲉⲓ[ϫⲓ] ⲱ[ⲙⲥ ⲙⲡⲓ]ⲙⲉϩⲥⲟ[ⲡ ⲥ]ⲛⲁⲩ), becomes an "angel of the male race" (7,4-5; ⲁⲉⲓϣⲱⲡⲉ ⲛⲟⲩⲁⲅⲅⲉⲗⲟⲥ ⲛⲅⲉⲛⲟⲥ ⟨ⲛ ⲅⲉⲛⲟⲥ⟩ ⲛ ϩⲟⲟⲩⲧ), and "took his stand on the second aeon ... with the children of Seth"(7,6-9; ⲁⲉⲓⲁϩⲉⲣⲁⲧ ϩⲓϫⲛ ⲡⲓⲙⲉϩⲥⲛⲁⲩ ⲛⲛⲉⲱⲛ ⲉⲧⲉ ⲡⲓⲙ[ⲉϩ]ϣⲟⲙⲧ ⲡⲉ ⲙⲛ ⲛϣⲏⲣⲉ ⲛⲧⲉ [ⲥ]ⲏⲑ).

The third and fourth baptisms in the name of Autogenes follow immediately, with the by now expected result: becoming a visionary angel and standing upon an aeon (7,9-21). All of this baptizing and angelification enable Zostrianos to learn from an angel, named Authrounis (7,22–13,6), about the basic structure of the heavenly world, which is organized, on good Platonic lines, into strata in which the inferior replicate less perfectly those that are superior. Another lengthy set of revelations by an angel, Ephesech (13,7–57,12), introduces some new philosophical jargon, the triad Being, Mind, and Life. These principles, particularly at home in Platonic circles of the third and fourth centuries, mediate between the more transcendent to the less transcendent spheres of being.

Zostrianos requires a new set of baptisms before the third set of revelations, delivered by an angel Youel (57,13–63,17). Precisely what goes on in these baptisms is difficult to determine, given the damaged state of the text. Yet it is clear that the power to perceive spiritual truth is a result of the transformational experience (61,14–20).

In Zostrianos, then, we find a portrait of baptism as an important part of a revelatory experience. It is understood to create the conditions necessary to "see" the realm of the spirit. It does so by transforming the baptized into an angelic state, thereby allowing revelatory commerce with the angels.

Two other points about the tractate *Zostrianos* are worth noting. First, the explicit content of the revelation that Zostrianos receives is philosophical. It responds to the metaphysical questions which he poses and uses technical terminology of the Platonic tradition. The details of the philosophical system cannot be explored now. Others have treated them already, although without sufficient attention to the layers of philosophical speculation and theurgic practice contained in the text, a fact that may be relevant to the assessment of the age of the traditions in the text.[9]

Finally, the practical implications of the revelation that Zostrianos receives are decidedly ascetical. The text closes with a homily (130,16–132,5) that the seer, returned to earth, delivers to the race of Seth. Much of this homily consists of generic exhortations. Two items, however, are worth noting. For one, Zostrianos urges his addressees not to "baptize yourselves with death nor entrust yourselves to those who are inferior to you" (131,2–5). This sounds like polemic against the baptismal theology of the Pauline or later orthodox Christian variety and against those who administer it. The remarks bespeak a sectarian stance. The seer also apparently advocates celibacy saying, "flee from the madness and the bondage of femaleness, and choose for yourselves the salvation of maleness." The language, which is hardly politically correct, is conventional in encratite circles of the second and third century.[10]

Zostrianos is a fairly clear example of a particular pattern of piety. The text posits, in an idealized literary form to be sure, a baptismal ritual with a transformative function, enabling vision on an angelic plane, leading to receipt of a philosophical revelation which issues in ascetical practice. It explicitly rejects a notion of baptism that involves "death." Two questions emerge. Is there evidence of this pattern elsewhere and is it of relevance to the problem of Colossians?

Other Evidence of the Baptismal Tradition of Zostrianos

Space does not permit complete review of texts with baptismal implications from the Nag Hammadi corpus and related literature. Such texts appear in both Valentinian and Sethian gnostic sources. The former are not of interest here, being generally much closer to the baptismal traditions of the great

[9] For discussion of some of the issues raised by the text, see Harold W. Attridge, "Gnostic Platonism," *Boston Area Colloquium on Ancient Philosophy 1991* (Washington, DC: University Press of America, 1992).

[10] See Harold W. Attridge, "Masculine Fellowship in the Acts of Thomas," in Birger Pearson, ed., *The Future of Early Christianity* (Helmut Koester Festschrift; Minneapolis: Augsburg-Fortress, 1991) 406–13.

church, whether or not those traditions are accepted. The latter are more interesting, but also more diverse and diffuse.[11] None has quite the same array of elements noted in *Zostrianos*, although many parts of the pattern are in evidence.

In the complex *Gospel of the Egyptians*, also entitled the *Holy Book of the Great Invisible Spirit* (NHC III,2; IV,2),[12] we find an account of the establishment of baptism by Seth, with some supplementary references to Jesus (IV,2:75,15). Baptism, as in *Zostrianos*, is something "higher than the heavens" (75,14; III,2:65,23) and here, too, it involves the presence of heavenly powers and principalities. The understanding that the ritual is designed to transform the initiand into a heavenly state, bringing transforming knowledge, is expressed in a hymn in which the initiand responds to the reception of baptism:

> "This great name of yours is upon me, o self-originate that lacks nothing and is free,
> O invisible unto all but [me]!
> O invisible unto all!
> For what being can comprehend you by speech or praise?
> Having myself become acquainted with you, I have now mixed with your unchangeableness;
> And I have girded myself and come to dwell in an armor of loveliness and light, and I have become luminous" (IV,2:79,3-16).

A second striking example related to the familiar baptismal pattern may be found in the *Trimorphoric Protennoia* (NHC XIII,1), a lengthy tractate largely in the form of a first-person revelation discourse.[13] The revealer figure, described as the Thought, Voice, and Word of the Transcendent One, describes her missions to harrow the hell of ignorance that is this world. To save those within it she brought a baptismal ritual, described as the Five Seals, which effects transformation into a heavenly state. The tractate is divided into three subsections. Near the end of the second the revealer declares:

---

[11] See Jean Marie Sevrin, *Le dossier baptismal séthien: Études sur la sacramentaire gnostique* (Bibliothèque copte de Nag Hammadi, Section "Études" 2; Québec: Les presses de l'université Laval, 1986).

[12] Alexander Böhlig, and Frederik Wisse, *Nag Hammadi Codices III,2 and IV,2: The Gospel of the Egyptians (The Holy Book of the Great Invisible Spirit)* (NHS 4; Leiden: Brill, 1975). I cite primarily from Codex IV. For a translation, see Bentley Layton, *The Gnostic Scriptures* (New York: Doubleday, 1987) 101–20.

[13] See the edition by John Turner in Charles W. Hedrick, ed., *Nag Hammadi Codices XI, XII, XIII* (NHS 28; Leiden: Brill, 1990) 371–454.

> "And I am inviting you into the exalted, perfect Light. Moreover (as for) this (Light), when you enter it you will be glorified by those [who] give glory, and those who enthrone will enthrone you. You will accept robes from those who give robes and the Baptists will baptize you and you will become gloriously glorious, the way you first were when you were Light" (45,12-20).

In the third section of the text, the revealer offers an even more detailed description of the baptismal process by which an unnamed initiand is transformed:

> "And I delivered him to those who give robes – Yammon, Elasso, Amenai – and they [covered] him with a robe from the robes of the Light; and I delivered him to the Baptists and they baptized him – Micheus, Michar, Mnesinous – and they immersed him in the spring of the [Water] of Life. And I delivered him to those who enthrone – Bariel, Nouthan, Sabenai – and they enthroned him from the throne of glory. And I delivered him to those who glorify – Ariom, Elien, Phariel – and they glorified him with the glory of the Fatherhood. And those who snatch away snatched away – Kamaliel, [...]anen, Samblo, the servants of the great holy Luminaries – and they took him into the light-[place] of his Fatherhood. And [he received] the Five Seals from [the Light] of the Mother, Protennoia, and it was [granted] him to partake of [the mystery] of knowledge, and [he became a Light] in Light" (48,15-35).

Finally the revealer summarizes the results of the process:

> "These are the glories that are higher than every glory, that is [the Five] Seals complete by virtue of Intellect. He who possesses the Five Seals of these particular names has stripped off the garments of ignorance and put on a shining Light" (49,26-32).

John Turner, editor of the text in the Coptic Gnostic Library edition, summarizes the evidence of baptism in the *Trimorphic Protennoia* thus:

> "The baptismal rite of the Five Seals is a mystery of celestial ascent which strips off the psychic and somatic garments of ignorance (cf. Col 2:11-15), transforming and purifying Protennoia's members and clothing them with radiant light. The author's reference to the recipients of this rite in the first-person plural (36,33b-37,3a; cf. 42,22-23) and as 'brethren' suggests a (Sethian) community with a well-established tradition of water baptism which has been spiritualized into a mystery of celestial ascent" (p. 379).

I would want to nuance that summary in a slightly different way, particularly on the point about the rite becoming "spiritualized." The key point to note is that celestial baptism is something performed by and in the company of angels. Its effect is to transform the baptizand into a being like the angelic liturgists, a being of Light, perfect in intellect and therefore capable of receiving revelation.

This brief survey of some of the Nag Hammadi evidence should be sufficient to indicate that the portrait of baptismal experience found in Zostrianos is but the tip of a significant iceberg.

Orthodox Remnants of the Tradition

The baptismal theology of some of the Nag Hammadi texts, with its portrait of a ritual of transformation that brings the recipient into an angelic state, is unparalleled in orthodox literary sources. Yet there is a related theme in ascetical traditions, the notion that the celibate life of the ascetic, the monk, is "angelic."[14] This understanding of the ἀγγελικὸς βίος is absolutely commonplace in the monastic literature of the fourth and fifth centuries. It is ultimately based, of course, on the response attributed to Jesus that in the resurrected state there will be no giving or taking in marriage, but all will be like the angels (Matt 22:30; Mark 12:25; Luke 20:35-36). The explicit development of the notion as a way of conceptualizing the ascetical life can be traced into the second century in Clement of Alexandria in his portrait of the ideal gnostic (*Strom.* 7.12.57.1; 7.14.84.1):

> "So is he [the Gnostic] always pure for prayer. He also prays in the society of angels, as being already of angelic rank, and he is never out of their holy keeping; and though he pray alone, he has the choir of the saints standing with him" (7.12.57.1).
> "Now, of what I may call the passionlessness which we attribute to the Gnostic (in which the perfection of the believer, 'advancing by love, comes to a perfect man, to the measure of full stature' [Eph 4:13] by being assimilated to God, and by becoming truly angelic), many other testimonies from Scripture occur to me to adduce"(7.14.84.1). [Clement then cites 1 Cor 6:1].

---

[14] P. Suso Frank, O.F.M., *AGGELIKOS BIOS: Begriffsanalytische und Begriffsgeschichtliche Untersuchung zum "engelgleichen Leben" im frühen Mönchtum* (Beiträge zur Geschichte des alten Mönchtums und des Benediktinerordens 26; Münster: Aschendorff, 1964) and Peter Nagel, *Die Motivierung der Askese in der alten Kirche und der Ursprung des Mönchtums* (TU 95; Berlin: Akademie, 1966).

Origen, in Clement's footsteps, picks up the theme and notes that those who have become perfect are made like angels (*Contra Celsum* 4.29): "We know too that angels are so far superior to men that when men are made perfect they become equal to angels. 'For in the resurrection of the dead they neither marry nor are given in marriage, but the righteous are as the angels of heaven' [Matt 22:30] and they become 'equal to angels'" [Luke 20:36].

Whether the tradition represented in these Alexandrian sources is related to the unusual baptismal tradition that I have been exploring is unclear. The Alexandrian sources may, in any case, illumine one element of our baptismal tradition. One specific point of similarity that seems to be distinctive particularly of Clement, differentiating him both from the obvious scriptural referent of the imagery and from the later monastic topos, is the notion that the ascetical perfection of the angelic state has to do not simply with ascetical practice but with cognition, with gnosis. Clement emphasizes the purely ethical dimensions of the life of a gnostic, but that he is trying thereby to deconstruct a problematic category is highly likely. Such an Alexandrian connection of philosophical gnosis and the angelic life seems to be a feature of the Alexandrian piety from which Clement emerges, and such Alexandrian piety probably lies behind *Zostrianos.*

Relevance of the Tradition to Colossians

In considering the relevance to the problems of Colossians of the baptismal tradition that I have been exploring, two large questions arise. First, are these texts in any way evidence of religious practice and piety? Secondly, how far back into the history of early Christianity and its environment can any possible practices be traced?

The first, rather interesting methodological question arises because the Nag Hammadi texts are not descriptions of or prescriptions for baptismal rituals. They are not, for instance, the Gnostic equivalent of the *Apostolic Tradition* of Hippolytus, – although I suggest parenthetically that it may have been such texts that in part called forth the explicit regulations of the Church Order literature. What we have in *Zostrianos* and its cousins are, for the most part, literary descriptions of heavenly journeys, the literary epigones of ancient apocalypses. This fact has led some scholars to view the baptismal language as purely metaphorical or symbolic.[15] Two general considerations, however, lead me to suspect that beneath the literary fictions lies some ritual experience. First, the survey by Sevrin[16] of baptismal elements in the so-called Sethian texts from Nag Hammadi has uncovered enough references to or treatments of dippings and sealings in settings that have some reference to communities, to suggest that some such rituals were indeed practiced in the circles that trasmitted these texts. Secondly, the metaphysics of virtually all the literature from Nag Hammadi, whether Valentinian, Sethian or other, involves a rigorous exemplarism, probably derived, in most instances, from contemporary Platonism. By exemplarism I simply mean that all that is found here below somehow replicates a purer model, an ideal form, in the world of spirit. Therefore, what a visionary in a text such as *Zostrianos* is portrayed as seeing in the course of a fictional heavenly journey is not simply an abstract metaphor, but the essential, ideal reality that makes sense of something in the phenomenal world. In short, what we find in the descriptions of heavenly baptisms in several of the Nag Hammadi texts is a theology of or rationale for baptism, a rationale that conceives baptism as a transformation of the baptizand into a heavenly state that enables "vision" of the divine such as that accorded to angels. Thus, to view the Nag Hammadi portraits of heavenly baptism as "spiritualizations" in the fashion of Turner is simply not adequate.

Was, therefore, this understanding of baptismal practice available when Colossians was written? The question is raised because of the date of the Nag Hammadi materials that we have surveyed. For *Zostrianos*, at least, we have a *terminus ante* of 250 at the latest.[17] The text is one of the group of philosophizing gnostic works referred to by Plotinus and his disciples in Rome in the mid-third century.[18] How much earlier it was composed remains unclear, but given the state of philosophical categories deployed in the text, it is unlikely to

---

[15] So Layton, *The Gnostic Scriptures*, 19–20.

[16] See my note 11 above.

[17] Layton (*The Gnostic Scriptures*, 122) sets the *terminus* at 268. Sieber locates it somewhat earlier.

[18] See Porphyry *Life of Plotinus* 16 for an explicit reference to *Zostrianos*.

have been written much before the beginning of the third century. The other Nag Hammadi texts with related baptismal traditions are to be dated without certainty between the second and fourth centuries.

To trace a clear line of tradition from early third-century Rome to late first-century Asia Minor is impossible. Hence, the proposal that *Zostrianos* is relevant to Colossians remains somewhat speculative, but the connection can be shown to be at least plausible since all of the elements found in the baptismal theology of *Zostrianos* were available in the first century, and available to the sort of people who may well been active at Colossae.

Before reviewing those elements it is important to note one preliminary fact, the multiplicity of baptismal traditions and theologies in the earliest Christian communities. We may tend to forget that fact, given the importance in the Western tradition of the Pauline baptismal theology with its notion of the ritual as a participation in the death and resurrection of Christ. Readers of Acts 18:25-26 and 19:1-7 know of Apollos and the unnamed disciples at Ephesus and their mysteriously defective baptismal theology.[19] Liturgists have made some suggestions about what alternatives might have been available. They have long noted[20] that Pauline theology only came to dominate the baptismal scene in the fourth century. The existence of alternative traditions, particularly preserved in the

[19] On the possible baptist group see Joseph Thomas, *Le mouvement baptiste en Palestine et Syrie (150 av. J.-C.–300 ap. J.-C.)* (Gembloux: Duculot, 1935) 89-139. See also Ernst Haenchen, *The Acts of the Apostles* (Philadelphia: Westminster, 1971) 549-57.

[20] For eastern sources, see Sebastian Brock, "The Syrian Baptismal Ordines (with special reference to the Anointings)," *Studia Liturgica* 12 (1977) 177–83, and idem, *The Holy Spirit in the Syrian Baptismal Tradition* (The Syrian Churches Series 9; Poona: Anita, 1979); Gabriele Winkler, *Das Armenische Initiationsrituale: Entwicklungsgeschichte und liturgievergleichende Untersuchung der Quellen des 3. bis 10. Jahrhunderts* (Or. Chr. Anal. 217; Rome: Institutum Studiorum Orientalium, 1982); and Paul Bradshaw, ed., *Essays in Early Eastern Initiation* (Alcuin/GROW Liturgical Study 8; Bramcote: Grove, 1988). For collections of baptismal materials, see E. C. Whitaker, *Documents of the Baptismal Liturgy* (London: SPCK, 1970) and, most recently, Thomas M. Finn, *Early Christian Baptism and the Catechumenate: West and East Syria* (Message of the Fathers of the Church 5; Collegeville, MN: Liturgical Press [Michael Glazier], 1992), and idem, *Early Christian Baptism and the Catechumenate: Italy, North Africa, and Egypt* (Message of the Fathers of the Church 6; Collegeville, MN: Liturgical Press [Michael Glazier], 1992).

Syrian east, is well documented. One such tradition viewed baptism, with an emphasis on the baptismal anointing, as a means for the baptizand to participate in the messianic status of Christ. Another viewed the rite as a transformation of the baptizand into the primordial paradisical condition where male and female were not separated.[21] What I am in effect suggesting is the existence of another tradition that from very early on competed with what we know as the Pauline one.

The roots of the phenomenon which finally emerges in *Zostrianos* are certainly to be found in Jewish apocalyptic sources, the sort of traditions to which many analysts of the problem in Colossae have been pointing in recent years. I would, however, put the center of gravity in such comparisons at a slightly different point and suggest that by the time of Colossians an important religious mutation has taken place. Of the many parallels that have been adduced for the "vision upon entry" and the "worship of angels" (understood subjectively) the most interesting are in the Enochic tradition. There we find figures who have been exalted to a heavenly status and, in one way or another, transformed into angelic beings in order to participate fully in the heavenly liturgy and to receive the fulness of revelation. The literary tradition recounting such experiences starts with the *Parables of Enoch* and its account of the translation of Enoch. As the visionary relates (*1 Enoch* 71:1-17):

> "And it came to pass after this that my spirit was translated
> and it ascended into the heavens and I saw the holy sons of God.
> ... (3) and the angel Michael seized me by my right hand,

[21] So Wayne Meeks, "The Myth of the Androgyne: Some Uses of a Symbol in Earliest Christianity," *HR* 13 (1974) 165–208, and Dennis R. MacDonald, *There Is No Male and Female* (HDR 20; Philadelphia: Fortress, 1987). It would, of course, be a short step to move from the notions that the celibate state is angelic and that baptism restores a state where celibacy is possible and required, to the conclusion that baptism transforms one into an angelic state. I suggest that precisely that move was made by the forebears of *Zostrianos*. Furthermore, I suggest that those forebears operated in the kind of environment in which there was one more vitally important characteristic of the angelic state, namely the access to gnosis on which Clement lays such emphasis. I suggest, in other words, that the origins of the baptismal tradition of *Zostrianos* are to be found in Alexandria and that what we have in *Zostrianos* is the remnant of a very early kind of baptismal theology.

and lifted me up and led me forth into all the secrets,
and he showed me all the secrets of righteousness.
... (5) and he translated my spirit into the heaven of heavens,
and I saw there as it were a structure built of crystals,
and between those crystals tongues of living fire.
... (7) and round about were Seraphin, Cherubin, and Ophaninin:
And these are they who sleep not and guard the throne of His glory.
... (11) and I fell on my face, and my whole body became relaxed,
and my spirit was transfigured and I cried with a loud voice,
with the spirit of power, and blessed and glorified and extolled.
... (14) And he (i.e., the angel) came to me and greeted me with His voice, and said unto me:
'You are the human being who is born unto righteousness,
and righteousness abides over you
and the righteousness of the Head of Days forsakes you not.'
And he said unto me:
'He proclaims unto thee peace in the name of the world to come;
for from hence has proceeded peace since the creation of the world,
and so shall it be unto thee for ever and for ever and ever.
And all shall walk in your ways since righteousness never forsakes you.
With you will be their dwelling-places, and with you their heritage,
and they shall not be separated from you for ever and ever and ever.
And so there shall be length of days with that human being,
and the righteous shall have peace and an upright way
In the name of the Lord of Spirits for ever and ever'" (Charles *APOT* 2.235-36).

Here the seer, with his spirit transfigured, is effectively installed as a member of the order of angels, capable of seeing what they can see. This is, of course, a literary fiction, a way of describing what happened to the biblical Enoch, but it may at the same time be paradigmatic of what happens to any visionary.

A similar bit of evidence is found further in the Enochic tradition in *2 Enoch* 22.4-7, the *Book of the Secrets of Enoch*.[22] This

---

[22] The significance of these passages for understanding the roots of *Zostrianos* was pointed out by Madeleine Scopello, "The Apocalypse of *Zostrianos* (Nag Hammadi VIII.1) and the Book of the Secrets of Enoch," *VC* 34 (1980) 376-85.

apocalypse, like *Zostrianos*, also involves a heavenly journey in which Enoch is led on an ascent through the heavens. The process involves a transformation of Enoch that has decidedly ritual elements. In the tenth heaven, in God's own presence, Enoch is installed as a member of the angelic host:

> (Charles, version B): "and I fell prone and could not see the Lord God and I bowed down to the Lord, and the Lord God spoke to Michael, 'Take Enoch, and take him out from his earthly (sc. garments), and anoint him with sweet oil, and clothe him in garments of glory,' and Michael took me out from my garments and anointed me with sweet oil; and the appearance of that oil is better than great light, and its ointment like sweet dew, and its smell like myrrh, and shining like the rays of the sun.
>
> And I looked down looking at myself, and I was as one of the glorious ones, and there was no difference. And the terror and trembling went away from me, and the Lord with his mouth summoned me and said: 'Have courage Enoch, fear not, stand before my face into eternity.'[23]
>
> And the Lord's commander in chief (*archistrategos*) Michael brought me before the face of God. The Lord tempted his servants, and said to them: 'Let Enoch step up to stand before my face into eternity.' And the Lord's glorious ones bowed down, and said: 'Let him step up'" (*APOT* 2.443).

Perhaps the most famous of the exaltation scenes in the Enochic tradition is even more graphic in its description of the transformation of a human being into an angelic state. *3* (or Hebrew) *Enoch* recounts the process by which Enoch was transformed into an angel, Metatron, who bears God's own name. Enoch-Metatron reports to R. Ishmael in chapter 7:

> "When the Holy One, blessed be he, removed me from the generation of the Flood, he bore me up on the stormy wings of the Shekinah to the highest heaven and brought me into the great palaces in the height of the heaven of Arabot, where the glorious throne of the Shekinah is found, and the chariot, the cohorts of wrath, the hosts of fury, the fiery shinanim, the blazing cherubim, the smoldering ophanim, the ministers of flame, the lightning hashmallim and the flashing seraphim. He stationed

[23] (In version A): "And the Lord said to Michael: 'Go and take Enoch from out his earthly garments, and anoint him with my sweet ointment, and put him into the garments of My glory.'

And Michael did thus, as the Lord told him. He anointed me, and dressed me, and the appearance of that ointment is more than the great light, and his ointment is like sweet dew, and its smell mild, shining like the sun's ray, and I looked at myself, and was like one of his glorious ones."

> me there to serve the throne of glory day by day" (Charlesworth *OTP* 1.262).

Enthroned on high, Enoch is given a robe, crown, and new name, "the lesser Yahweh" (*3 Enoch* 13). All of these elements are reminiscent of the ritual features associated with the exaltation of Enoch in *2 Enoch.* They are an important part of the tradition. Once installed in this state, the visionary in *3 Enoch* 11 has access to revelation:

> "The Holy One, blessed be he, revealed to me from that time onward all the mysteries of wisdom, all the depths of the perfect Torah and all the thoughts of men's hearts. All the mysteries of the world and all the orders of nature stand revealed before me as they stand revealed before the Creator. From that time onward I looked and beheld deep secrets and wonderful mysteries. Before a man thinks in secret, I see his thought; before he acts, I see his act. There is nothing in heaven above or deep within the earth concealed from me" (Charlesworth *OTP* 1.264-265).

The Enochic tradition of visionary transformation into an angelic state is certainly related to the piety present in *Zostrianos* and the other Nag Hammadi texts that we have surveyed. *2* and *3 Enoch* provide the information that the transformation, a literary image to be sure, involved a ritual component comprised of elements (anointing, change of clothing) that played a significant role in Christian initiation rituals. Yet there is a further development in the Nag Hammadi texts on three points: (1) The transforming ritual is clearly labelled baptism and involves a (perhaps metaphorical) water immersion; (2) the transformation involves not simply glorification and reception of revelation, but explicitly the empowerment for philosophical insight; (3) the ascetical implications of the transformation are made explicit.

Two of these items shared by Colossians and *Zostrianos*, the concern for revelation defined in philosophical terms and rigorous ascetical practice, are abundantly present in certain first-century contexts, particularly in Hellenized Jewish circles known to us from Philo. These well-known themes in Philo hardly need extensive documentation here. Merely recall that for the Alexandrian, to be an Israelite is to follow in the footstepts of the "Man who sees God." Recall, too, his insistence on a rational ascesis for all as well as his exaltation of the ascetical lifestyle of the contemplative specialists, the Therapeutae.

The following line of development leading to *Zostrianos* appears likely. Traditions about the transformation of legendary seers into an angelic state were ritualized, already prior to the formation of Christianity. An initiation ritual involving anointing and re-clothing provided people access to the angelic world. Such traditions probably developed in Palestinian Jewish circles in the second temple period. They were given at some juncture a more Hellenistic veneer as the revelation provided by the initiation ritual was given a more philosophical cast. At some juncture, the initiation ritual was understood to involve baptism. The relationship between these two developments is unclear. For neither development is it necessary to posit a Christian environment, although Jewish Christians, in evidence at least at Colossae, appropriated this whole schema as a way of understanding their baptismal practices.

In sum, the combination of ingredients that accounts for most of the features of *Zostrianos* and, by the way, of Colossians, were blended by some Hellenistic Jewish (or Jewish-Christian) group that revered the traditions of visionary transformation and attempted to provide access to that experience sacramentally.

Were the Colossian Baptists Gnostic?

Much, of course, depends on how we define the term. If we take an approach to the Gnostic phenomenon that highlights the myth of the fall of Sophia, then there is no evidence for Gnosticism at Colossae. The kind of baptismal theology and practice that lies in the background of *Zostrianos* and in the environment of Colossae is independent of the myth of origins and cosmological speculation that are at the heart of Gnostic thought in the strictest sense. Yet, those who developed such conceptual schemes probably did so in the context of a community that sought after visionary experience and tried to prepare for it ritually. Tracing the development of the baptismal traditions culminating in *Zostrianos* provides a useful way of understanding a category "proto-Gnostic" that has often been used of the Colossian problem. It also confirms the rootedness of one important element of the Gnostic phenomenon in Jewish apocalyptic piety of the second temple period.

Why Paul (or Pseudo-Paul) Objected

Let me conclude with a few reflections on what it was about the problematic piety to which Paul or Pseudo-Paul objected, for I believe that my hypothesis about the structure of the piety at issue helps to clarify the rhetorical and pastoral strategy of the author of Colossians. Given the force of the arguments in chapters 3 and 4 of Colossians, it would appear that the primary concern is not with the lack of a Christocentric focus among the opposition. The opponents may well have had it, if they understood Christ to be the foremost of the angelic world to which their baptism had given them access. The author's emphasis is clearly on maintenance of the social order. I suspect that the baptismal piety under criticism was a threat to that order precisely because it offered the alternative of "living like the angels" as a result of the visionary initiation.

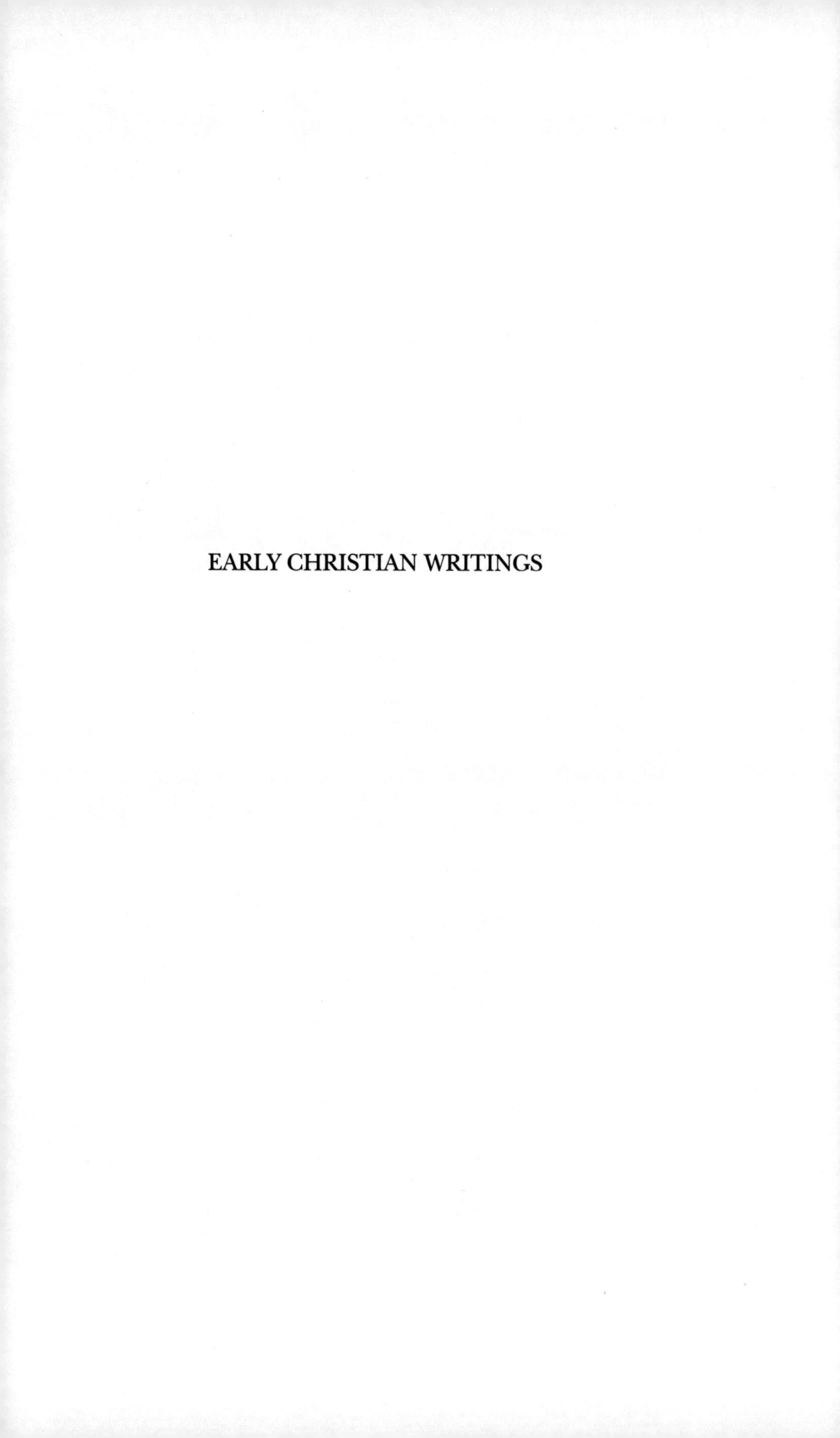

EARLY CHRISTIAN WRITINGS

ALTERNATE BEGINNINGS – DIFFERENT ENDS: EUSEBIUS, THOMAS, AND THE CONSTRUCTION OF CHRISTIAN ORIGINS

Ron Cameron
(Wesleyan University, Middletown, Connecticut)

"In the Church conformity with the origins is evidence of truth."
Arnaldo Momigliano, *The Classical Foundations of Modern Historiography*

I

It must surely go down as one of the most significant events in the formative history of Christianity. In the last decade of the third century or, more likely, the first decade of the fourth, in the coastal city of Caesarea Palestinae, Eusebius wrote the first edition of his monumental *Church History*: a work comprising seven original books that eventually would be issued in four full-fledged editions and ten complete books before Eusebius finished his task in 325/326 CE.[1] We moderns are not the first to recognize the *Church History* as "the first full-length continuous narrative history written by a Christian."[2] Eusebius himself knows that he is "a pioneer in the field."[3] He acknowl-

[1] See Robert M. Grant, *Eusebius as Church Historian* (Oxford: Clarendon Press, 1980) 10-21; Glenn F. Chesnut, "Eusebius of Caesarea," *ABD* 2:675. Timothy D. Barnes (*Constantine and Eusebius* [Cambridge/London: Harvard University Press, 1981] 128, 277-78) argues that Eusebius "originally wrote"the first seven books of the *Church History* "before the end of the third century." Arnaldo Momigliano ("Pagan and Christian Historiography in the Fourth Century A.D.," in idem, *The Conflict between Paganism and Christianity in the Fourth Century* [Oxford: Clarendon Press, 1963] 80) dates the first edition to the year 312 CE. Major studies of the various editions of the text were published by Eduard Schwartz, ed., *Eusebius Werke: Die Kirchengeschichte* (2 vols. in 3 parts; GCS; Leipzig: Hinrichs, 1903-9) 2/3:xlvii-lxi; Richard Laqueur, *Eusebius als Historiker seiner Zeit* (Arbeiten zur Kirchengeschichte 11; Berlin/Leipzig: De Gruyter, 1929). The most recent discussion is found in Harold W. Attridge and Gohei Hata, "Introduction," in idem, eds., *Eusebius, Christianity, and Judaism* (Detroit: Wayne State University Press, 1992) 37-39.

[2] Chesnut, "Eusebius of Caesarea," 675.

[3] Grant, *Eusebius as Church Historian*, 16. Momigliano ("Pagan and Christian Historiography," 89) states that Eusebius "was not vainly boasting when

edges at the outset of his work that he is "the first to venture on such an undertaking" (*Hist. eccl.* 1.1.3), and he describes in his preface the following literary method by which he constructed a narrative, composite though consistent in its themes, that is given coherence through careful placement within an historical framework:

> "Thus from the scattered hints (τῶν μνημονευθέντων) dropped by my predecessors I have picked out whatever seems relevant to the task I have undertaken, plucking like flowers in literary pastures the helpful contributions of earlier writers, to be embodied in the continuous narrative (δι' ὑφηγήσεως ἱστορικῆς ... σωματοποιῆσαι) I have in mind" (*Hist. eccl.* 1.1.4).[4]

"It is," he states,

> "especially necessary that I should devote myself to this undertaking, for, so far as I am aware, no previous Christian author has been concerned with this kind of writing" (*Hist. eccl.* 1.1.5).

For Eusebius, therefore, the time was ripe for discrete Christian traditions to be converted into a grand church history through the dual processes of collecting "useful [anthological] materials out of what earlier authors [had] mentioned sporadically," and then "unifying . . . these materials by means of [a narrative] 'historical arrangement.'"[5]
Eusebius recognized the composite character of his work. Indeed, he cites almost 250 passages from ancient Christian sources, "many of which would otherwise be lost to us."[6] Although "the fabric" of the *Church History* "is woven from a number of quite disparate strands or themes," the "sentence which opens the work" identifies six principal subjects that will be dealt with in detail:[7]

---

he asserted that he was the 'first to enter on the undertaking, as travellers do on some desolate and untrodden way.'"

[4] *Eusebius: The History of the Church from Christ to Constantine* (Penguin Classics; trans. G.A. Williamson; rev. ed. Andrew Louth; Harmondsworth, Middlesex: Penguin, 1989) 2.

[5] Grant, *Eusebius as Church Historian,* 22. Barnes (*Constantine and Eusebius,* 132) remarks that, since Eusebius was "hampered . . . by his inability to contemplate theological development," his "account of the internal history of the Church and of Christian literature is less a coherent narrative than a series of disconnected notes."

[6] Chesnut, "Eusebius of Caesarea," 675.

[7] Barnes, *Constantine and Eusebius,* 129 with n. 11, omitting the final reference to the Great Persecution, initiated by Diocletian, of 303-313 CE.

1. a chronology of apostolic succession
2. events in the internal history of the church
3. leading Christian writers and teachers
4. the innovation of heresy
5. the fate of the Jews
6. the persecution of Christians (*Hist. eccl.* 1.1.1-2).[8]

Parenthetically, we might note that a seventh main topic, which forms "a recurrent theme"[9] throughout the *Church History*, is mentioned later in the text: "Eusebius provides what is in effect a history of the text and canon of the Bible in the early Church."[10]

The overarching theme of the entire work, of course, is the apologetic scheme of God's plan through Christ in human history. This conception undergirds Eusebius's presentation of each of the items listed above. Thus, the Incarnation (τῆς παρουσίας, *Hist. eccl.* 1.4.2; τῆς ἐπιφανείας, *Hist. eccl.* 1.5.1; 2.pref.1) "became the nodal point of all human history."[11] By situating the "dispensation and divinity" (*Hist. eccl.* 1.1.7) of God in Christ at a particular juncture in history, a theology of the Incarnation actually made it possible for Eusebius to imagine a way to construct a purposeful narrative of the formative centuries of Christianity. A divine economy both willed and worked it. Accordingly, the first sentence of the preface concludes with the words:

> "Therefore, I shall begin my writing with the divine plan first directed toward our Savior and Lord, Jesus, the Christ of God" (*Hist. eccl.* 1.1.2).

Grant (*Eusebius as Church Historian*, 10, 14, 34, 44) argues that "Eusebius' whole preface, as it now stands, was produced for his edition of 315 and does not exactly correspond with what he had written earlier" (p. 14). Thus, when one begins an analysis of the *Church History* with its opening sentence, that is "not because the preface is early and shows what Eusebius had in mind at the beginning but because it is late and shows what he thought he had done" (p. 10).

[8] See Ferdinand Christian Baur, "The Epochs of Church Historiography," in idem, *On the Writing of Church History* (A Library of Protestant Thought; ed. and trans. Peter C. Hodgson; New York: Oxford University Press, 1968) 53-66.

[9] Grant, *Eusebius as Church Historian*, 126.

[10] Barnes, *Constantine and Eusebius*, 129 (cf. *Hist. eccl.* 3.3.3; 5.8.1). A.C. Sundberg, Jr. ("Canon of the NT," *IDBSup* 136-40) has argued cogently that Eusebius was the first to compile a list of "canonical" texts (cf. *Hist. eccl.* 3.25.1-7).

[11] Barnes, *Constantine and Eusebius*, 131.

"For," he adds at the very end of the preface,

> "whoever intends to commit to writing the history of Christian origins is obliged to start at the very beginning, with the divine plan first directed toward Christ himself" (*Hist. eccl.* 1.1.8).

This means that, though organized historically, Eusebius's *Church History* is inspired and driven by a theological agenda. On the one hand, there is the claim that

> "the origins of the church are divine because the church has its beginnings in the dispensation given by the divine Christ."[12]

On the other hand, divine truth serves not only as the premise but also as the standard used to construct the beginnings, and thereby design the ends, of the *Church History*. As Robert L. Wilken has observed:

> "In the history of the Christian church, in so far as it is founded on the teaching of the apostles, [people] see the divine truth as it exists in time. . . . [Accordingly,] Eusebius' critical [historical] principle comes from a theological idea of the truth of Christianity and the church. . . . Christianity was not [just] another religion among religions. Clearly it was the only true religion given by God."[13]

Pioneer that he was, Eusebius still had precursors. In the late second and early third centuries, Hegesippus wrote his *Memoirs* (completed between 175 and 189 CE), Clement of Alexandria his *Outlines* (ca. 180-200 CE), and Sextus Julius Africanus his *Chronographies* (completed ca. 221 CE). None of these writings is extant in its entirety; what remain are fragments of all three texts, preserved primarily in the *Church History* of Eusebius. Each author was a Christian who reported traditions that Eusebius found useful to paraphrase or quote, but none provided a continuous narrative history. Hegesippus, for example, also dealt with the themes of continuity and succession,[14] important events and notable teachers in the Christian church,[15] the development of heresy,[16] the fate of the Jews,[17] the contest between Christians and the Roman em-

[12] Robert L. Wilken, *The Myth of Christian Beginnings: History's Impact on Belief* (Garden City, NY: Doubleday, 1971) 61.

[13] Ibid., 62, 64, 65; cf. 74.

[14] *Hist. eccl.* 3.11.1-12.1; 4.22.3.

[15] *Hist. eccl.* 2.23.4-18; 3.5.2-3; 3.16.1; 4.22.1-2, 4.

[16] *Hist. eccl.* 3.32.7; 4.22.5-6, 9.

[17] *Hist. eccl.* 2.23.4-18; 4.22.7.

pire,[18] and he was even interested in other gospels and "the so-called Apocrypha."[19] Nevertheless, his *Memoirs* fundamentally differed from the *Church History*. Eusebius himself notes this, stating that, when he used Hegesippus's work, he had to "rearrange the narratives chronologically" (*Hist. eccl.* 4.22.8). "Hegesippus was [simply] no historian";[20] he "wrote apologetic, not history."[21] His work and others' were thus "a source but not a model for the *Church History*."[22]

There were, however, two late antique models to which Eusebius could and did appeal.[23] The first was Josephus, whom Eusebius calls "the most famous of the historians among the Hebrews" (*Hist. eccl.* 1.5.3). It was Josephus's "apologetic tone," presentation of supporting documents, and, especially, the conviction that he was writing the history of a nation set apart by God that distinguished Josephus's work and influenced Eusebius so decisively.[24] The second was Luke, the author of the third Gospel and the Acts of the Apostles. Even though Eusebius refers to Luke-Acts as "divine scripture,"[25] he "views Luke as a historian" and "uses Acts as history,"[26] which he supplements frequently with corroborative

---

[18] *Hist. eccl.* 2.23.4-18; 3.20.1-6; 3.32.1-8; 4.8.2.

[19] *Hist. eccl.* 4.22.8-9.

[20] Grant, *Eusebius as Church Historian*, 38.

[21] Momigliano, "Pagan and Christian Historiography," 89, adding: "Apart from [Hegesippus], there is no other name that can seriously compete with Eusebius' for the invention of ecclesiastical history."

[22] Grant, *Eusebius as Church Historian*, 38. See Glenn F. Chesnut, "Hegesippus," *ABD* 3:110-11.

[23] See Grant, *Eusebius as Church Historian*, 41.

[24] Momigliano, "Pagan and Christian Historiography," 91.

[25] *Hist. eccl.* 1.10.2; 2.1.8; 2.9.4; 2.10.10; cf. 2.18.9.

[26] Grant, *Eusebius as Church Historian*, 39-40. Eckhard Plümacher ("Luke as Historian," *ABD* 4:401) maintains that, "because Luke had no successors, Eusebius has received the title 'Father of Church History.' Yet the honor of having been the first Christian historian belongs to the unknown author of this twofold opus [Luke-Acts], . . . even if he has only been (re)discovered as a historian in modern biblical studies." Recent summaries of a rich scholarly discussion of the historiography of Acts can be found in idem, "Apostelgeschichte," *ThRE* 3 (1978) 513-15; David E. Aune, *The New Testament in Its Literary Environment* (Library of Early Christianity; Philadelphia: Westminster, 1987) 77-157; Hans Conzelmann, *Acts of the Apostles* (Hermeneia; Philadelphia: Fortress, 1987) xl-xlviii; Richard I. Pervo, *Profit with Delight: The Literary Genre of the Acts of the Apostles* (Philadelphia: Fortress, 1987) 1-11; Gerd Lüdemann, *Early Christianity according to the Traditions in Acts: A Commentary* (Minneapolis: Fortress, 1989) 1-18; W. Ward Gasque, *A History of the Interpretation of the Acts of the Apostles* (1975; reprinted, Peabody, MA: Hendrickson, 1989) 251-305, 345-59.

"tradition" gleaned from such sources as the *Outlines* of Clement of Alexandria.[27] The *Jewish Antiquities* and *Jewish War* of Josephus, for their part, are repeatedly quoted in the *Church History*[28] – but cited to "confirm the historical truth of the scriptures" and, especially, "the reliability of Acts."[29] This means that Eusebius employed Josephus's works as proof texts in the service of Luke, whose Book of Acts formed the cornerstone, became the epic standard, and so bore noble, apostolic witness[30] to the historicity and truth of the Christian gospel.

Even though "Eusebius would not have been able to invent Ecclesiastical History" without Josephus,[31] we still may agree with Arnaldo Momigliano that "Eusebius appears . . . to have been the first full-fledged historian of a specific religion."[32] "A new chapter of historiography begins with Eusebius," Momigliano argues,

> "not only because he invented ecclesiastical history, but because he wrote it with a documentation which is utterly different from that of the pagan historians."[33]

For this reason, "one may doubt whether any other ancient historian made such an impact on successive generations as [Eusebius] did."[34] The anthological character of the *Church*

---

[27] *Hist. eccl.* 1.12.1-3; 2.1.2-5; 2.9.1-2; cf. 2.22.1-2; 3.4.4-5.

[28] *Hist. eccl.* 1.5.3-6; 2.10.2-10; 2.11.1-3; 2.11.3-12.2; 2.21.3.

[29] Grant, *Eusebius as Church Historian*, 39-40.

[30] On the importance of bearing "witness" (μάρτυς) in the theological program of Luke, cf. Luke 24:48; Acts 1:8, 22; 2:32; 3:15; 5:32; 10:39, 41; 13:31; 22:15, 20 (cf. 7:58); 26:16.

[31] Arnaldo Momigliano, *The Classical Foundations of Modern Historiography* (Sather Classical Lectures 54; Berkeley/Los Angeles/Oxford: University of California Press, 1990) 27.

[32] Arnaldo Momigliano, "Historiography of Religion: Western Views," in idem, *On Pagans, Jews, and Christians* (Middletown, CT: Wesleyan University Press, 1987) 19. See idem, "Popular Religious Beliefs and the Late Roman Historians," in idem, *Essays in Ancient and Modern Historiography* (Middletown, CT: Wesleyan University Press, 1977) 145; idem, *Classical Foundations of Modern Historiography*, 138.

[33] Momigliano, "Pagan and Christian Historiography," 92, noting that Eusebius "introduced a new type of historical exposition," one "which was characterized by the importance attributed to the more remote past, by the central position of doctrinal controversies and by the lavish use of documents" (ibid., 91). Eusebius's form of documentation means, in Wilken's (*Myth of Christian Beginnings*, 74) words, that "history in the Eusebian model will always be history from within, history by Christians about Christianity, history from the perspective of Christian faith."

[34] Momigliano, *Classical Foundations of Modern Historiography*, 138. See

History, thematically unified by the designs of divine providence, gives the narrative its lovely, lasting quality.[35] But Eusebius's decision to base his history on Luke's Acts of the Apostles was a fateful one.[36] Biblical scholarship is still living with that legacy.[37]

II

It is not coincidental that Eusebius begins his discussion of the history of the church (which really starts with Book 2) with a rehearsal of the story of the Book of Acts. Underlying his entire construction of Christian origins is the understanding that "the apostolic age is the definitive period in the history of Christianity."[38] Accordingly, Eusebius accepted as established fact the beliefs that Christianity is unchanging and the past is normative,[39] writing both of these theological views into his

---

Chesnut, "Eusebius of Caesarea," 675. According to Wilken (*Myth of Christian Beginnings*, 57), "Eusebius' vision of a Christian history, the diligence with which he executed his task, his singularity among his fellow Christian authors, and the sheer usefulness of his work for later historians set him apart, whatever his bias, as one of the boldest innovators in the history of Christianity."

[35] See Momigliano, *Classical Foundations of Modern Historiography*, 141: "In the simplicity of its structure and in the manner of its documentation the Ecclesiastical History of Eusebius was one of the most authoritative prototypes ever created by ancient thought: indeed it was the last model elaborated by ancient historians for the benefit of later generations." Wilken (*Myth of Christian Beginnings*, 53) maintains that the *Church History* is "the most important historical work ever written on Christianity and one of the three or four most important books to survive from the early church."

[36] Momigliano ("Pagan and Christian Historiography," 91; idem, *Classical Foundations of Modern Historiography*, 139-40) notes several important differences between Acts and Eusebius, in particular, the latter's treatment of the emergence of heresy and the persecution of the church.

[37] Baur ("Epochs of Church Historiography," 65-66) recognizes that "it is of high significance for ancient church historiography that no one after Eusebius made the era first described by him the object of a new presentation. . . . This indicates the degree to which he is the classic historian of the ancient period and, as the first who undertook to write the history of the Christian church over a longer period of time, the father of church history."

[38] Wilken, *Myth of Christian Beginnings*, 20, adding: "By idealizing the apostolic period, i.e., a particular historical epoch in the past, Christians have prized as values tradition, antiquity, apostolicity, uniformity, and permanence, and they have spurned change, innovation, novelty, and diversity" (ibid., 21).

narrative history of the church. In this respect Eusebius reproduced that mythic "pattern of thinking" which Wilken has identified as "characteristic of most of the ecclesiastical writers of the period":

> "1. The apostolic age is wholly unique. It is not simply the first period in the history of Christianity, but the foundation of all later history and the standard by which all other ages are judged.
> "2. From this it follows that what is older in the tradition is generally thought to be closer to the apostolic age and therefore closer to the truth.
> "3. Uniformity is preferred to diversity, since the apostles handed on one system of truth.
> "4. The only sure access to this apostolic tradition is the succession of right-thinking bishops who handed on the apostolic tradition from generation to generation until it reached the present.
> "5. The responsibility of later generations is to preserve, guard, and keep the ancient tradition, not to introduce new ideas, add to the tradition, or alter it in any way."[40]

Following the example of Luke who, two centuries earlier, "began to forge, for the first time, a Christian construction of the past,"[41] Eusebius presents his own version of this basic Christian myth. Extending Luke's creative efforts, Eusebius provides a narrative of opposition and resistance to the eternal truth of the gospel, which would triumph, uncorrupted and unchanged, by faithful adherence to the apostolic witness enshrined in privileged accounts of pristine origins.[42] Two features of this argument are noteworthy.

First, Eusebius understands the beginnings of the church to be primitive in two fundamental senses. Christianity, he con-

---

[39] Ibid., 22-25.

[40] Ibid., 44-45.

[41] Ibid., 33. Aune (*New Testament in Its Literary Environment,* 139) argues that "from Christianity's beginnings until ca. A.D. 325, when Eusebius of Caesarea supposedly created the 'new' genre of church history (*Church History* 1.1.3), no literary work had appeared that attempted to narrate the origins and development of early Christianity, with the exception of Luke-Acts. . . . [Therefore,] Luke, rather than Eusebius, should be credited with creating the 'new' genre of church history."

[42] Wilken (*Myth of Christian Beginnings,* 43-44, 71-73) notes that Eusebius followed Hegesippus in invoking, as an historical category, the "beguiling metaphor" of the church as an unsullied "virgin," to refer to that primitive period of Christian history when the church was unmolested, perfect, and pure (cf. *Hist. eccl.* 3.32.7-8; 4.22.4-6).

tends, is both universal and true: (a) universal, in that it is primeval, the world's original religion; (b) true, in that its origins in church history were uniformly orthodox. For Eusebius, God's revelation in Jesus Christ attests to the "antiquity and divine character of Christianity" (*Hist. eccl.* 1.2.1). Therefore, the "ancient history" and "antiquity" of the "Christian way of life" (*Hist. eccl.* 2.pref.1) mean that Christianity

> "was not a new religion but [is, in fact,] the primeval religion from which the traditional religions of mankind were mere offshoots or declensions."

Moreover, Christianity "is not novel or strange, even though the Christian church . . . [had] existed for less than three centuries" by Eusebius's day. Although "Christianity acquired its name when Jesus appeared on earth," its

> "way of life and the religious beliefs manifested in [it] are [actually] much older. Christianity is identical with the religion of the [ancient Hebrew] patriarchs, and the worshipers of God from Adam to Abraham were Christians in all but name."[43]

Accordingly, as T.D. Barnes has shown, Eusebius considers Christianity:

> "the most ancient and most venerable of all religions: accepted of old by Abraham and the patriarchs, now proclaimed to all [people] through the teaching of [Jesus] Christ, Christianity is the original, the only, the true way to worship God."[44]

"Let this suffice at the beginning of my narrative" (*Hist. eccl.* 1.4.1), readers of the *Church History* are told:

> "The practice of religion imparted by Christ's teaching is primitive, unique, and true" (*πρώτην ὑπάρχειν καὶ μόνην καὶ ἀληθῆ κατόρθωσιν εὐσεβείας ... παραδοθεῖσαν*, *Hist. eccl.* 1.4.15).

Second, Eusebius understands primitive Christianity to be unique in that the history of the church is continuous with the normative truth of its origins: attested by trustworthy witnesses,

---

[43] Barnes, *Constantine and Eusebius*, 126-27.

[44] Ibid., 127. See Jaroslav Pelikan, "Eusebius: Finality and Universality in History," in idem, *The Finality of Jesus Christ in an Age of Universal History: A Dilemma of the Third Century* (Ecumenical Studies in History 3; Richmond, VA: Knox, 1966) 48-57, 68-71; Wilken, *Myth of Christian Beginnings*, 60-65; Michael J. Hollerich, "Eusebius as a Polemical Interpreter of Scripture," in Attridge and Hata, eds., *Eusebius, Christianity, and Judaism*, 596 (cf. *Hist. eccl.* 1.2.1-4.15; *Dem. ev.* 1.5; *Praep. ev.* 7.1, 6-8).

guaranteed by apostolic succession, and established in opposition to the heretical innovations of gnosticism. In making such an argument, Eusebius is an heir to the tradition that originated with Luke, who claims to predicate his construction of the early church on the historiographic model of the accurate testimony of eyewitnesses.[45] It is significant, therefore, that Eusebius prefaces his own account of the *Church History* proper by referring "particularly," at the outset, to "the details of [Jesus'] recent Advent, the events leading up to the Passion, and the choice of the apostles" to continue his work "after the Ascension" (*Hist. eccl.* 2.pref.1-2).[46] This choice of topics is not innocent. Jesus' death and resurrection are considered the essential core of a momentous drama inaugurated by Jesus and continued through the church. Moreover, by invoking both the Ascension (*Hist. eccl.* 2.pref.2; cf. Acts 1:2, 11, 22) and the accompanying selection of Matthias to join the apostles (*Hist. eccl.* 2.1.1; cf. Acts 1:25-26) in succession to Jesus (cf. *Hist. eccl.* 1.1.1; 1.10.7; 1.12.3), Eusebius simply reproduces the Lukan construction of the beginnings of Christianity drawn from the opening chapters of Acts.

In the final analysis, Eusebius bases his entire history of early Christianity on Luke's account of its alleged origins in the Jerusalem church. The Book of Acts is taken as documentation

---

[45] Luke's appeal to eyewitnesses as the guarantors of the truth, who were present at the beginning and continuously ever since, from the baptism of Jesus to the establishment of the church (cf. Luke 1:2; Acts 1:8, 21-22, 25-26), is a curious way to authenticate the historicity of the Book of Acts. Not only does this privilege the very notion of eyewitnesses. The inclusion of Matthias among the apostles overloads the notion of originating events as well, by maintaining the fiction of constant testimony by authoritative figures at momentous occasions and over time.

[46] The reference to Jesus' Passion refers back to *Hist. eccl.* 1.11.7-8 (the *Testimonium Flavianum* in Josephus *Ant.* 18.3.3 §§ 63-64; on which see Emil Schürer, *The History of the Jewish People in the Age of Jesus Christ [175 B.C.-A.D. 135]* [3 vols.: in 4 parts; rev. Geza Vermes and Fergus Miller; ed. Matthew Black; Edinburgh: T. & T. Clark, 1973] 1.428-41; Geza Vermes, "The Jesus Notice of Josephus Re-Examined," *JJS* 38 [1987] 1-10; John P. Meier, "Jesus in Josephus: A Modest Proposal," *CBQ* 52 [1990] 76-103; Wolfgang A. Bienert, "The Witness of Josephus [*Testimonium Flavianum*]," in Wilhelm Schneemelcher, ed., *New Testament Apocrypha* [2 vols.; rev. ed.; trans. ed. R. McL. Wilson; Cambridge: James Clarke; Louisville KY: Westminster/Knox, 1991] 1.489-91; Louis H. Feldman, "Josephus," *ABD* 3:990-91); cf. *Hist. eccl.* 1.10.6; 1.12.4-5 (citing 1 Cor 15:5-7). Grant (*Eusebius as Church Historian*, 39-40) argues that Eusebius's preface to Book 2 contains "an echo of the preface to Acts [1:1-2]."

of a pristine era, whose unique beginnings evoke nostalgia,[47] whose eschatological ends inspire confidence, and whose faithful recounting would establish "precedent and tradition"[48] for "a new kind of history."[49] However, the *Church History* that

> "Eusebius wrote [is] a history of Christianity in which there is no *real history*, for there is no place for change in his portrait"

of the church. Given the logic of his argument, therefore, "Christianity [ultimately] is and remains forever what it was at its beginning."[50] And so, in "writing national history" for Christians,[51] Eusebius attributes "transcendental significance . . . to the period of the origins."[52] Such a conviction, constructed in accordance with Luke's theological enterprise,[53] remains definitional in virtually every scholarly reconstruction of the formative history of early Christianity. For "in the Church" – no less than in its historiography – "conformity with the origins is evidence of truth."[54]

---

[47] Compare the assessment of Wilken, *Myth of Christian Beginnings*, 36: "In the hands of later writers [than Luke], the first generation [of Christianity] will become a unique and unparalleled epoch, the springtime of the church's history, the model for all later generations."

[48] See Momigliano, *Classical Foundations of Modern Historiography*, 137.

[49] Momigliano, "Pagan and Christian Historiography," 90.

[50] Wilken, *Myth of Christian Beginnings*, 73, adding: "Eusebius' history tells no story; it reports on an eternal conflict taking place over and over [again]. . . . His history reads like a set of one-act dramas strung together without plot, movement, or development. . . . There is no genuine history [here], for there *can be* no history. . . . In Eusebius' history, nothing really happens – or, more accurately, nothing *new* happens. The history of the church is a history of an eternal conflict between the truth of God and its opponents. . . . In the end, Eusebius' history is uncritical. . . . The patrimony of Eusebius is [thus] a theological conception of church history formed by a theological idea of Christian truth" (ibid., 66, 73, 74; emphasis his).

[51] Momigliano, "Pagan and Christian Historiography," 90.

[52] Momigliano, *Classical Foundations of Modern Historiography*, 138. Jonathan Z. Smith (*Drudgery Divine: On the Comparison of Early Christianities and the Religions of Late Antiquity* [Jordan Lectures in Comparative Religion 14; London: School of Oriental and African Studies, University of London, 1990] 40) observes that the scholarly quest for Christian origins evokes, typically, "a nostalgia for the 'specialness' conceded to early Christianity" as incomparably "unique."

[53] See Dieter Georgi (*The Opponents of Paul in Second Corinthians* [Philadelphia: Fortress, 1986] 441 n. 182), who argues that Luke-Acts is "the oldest 'Christian' apologetic work."

[54] Momigliano, *Classical Foundations of Modern Historiography*, 136. See Mark Pattison, *Isaac Casaubon: 1559-1614* (2d ed.; Oxford: Clarendon

III

Biblical scholars continue to follow the example of Eusebius in "using the Acts of the Apostles as the main source" and model for writing "the history of early Christianity"[55] – even though they admit that Acts is tendentious. This scholarly proclivity is clear no matter what perspective a person has or methods are employed to determine the origins of Christianity, whether one is engaged in biblical theology,[56] social description,[57] historical criticism,[58] feminist analysis,[59] apologetic historio-

Press, 1892) 322: "The German reformation is imperfectly described as an appeal to scripture *versus* tradition. It was rather an appeal to history. The discovery had been made that the church, as it existed, was an institution which no longer corresponded to its original, that it was a corrupted, degraded, perverted institution. . . . As the doctrine of the fall of man [sic] was the key of human, so the doctrine of the corruption of the church was the key of ecclesiastical history." (I owe this reference to Jonathan Z. Smith, who also cites it in idem, *Drudgery Divine*, 13.)

[55] Jacob Jervell, "The History of Early Christianity and the Acts of the Apostles," in idem, *The Unknown Paul: Essays on Luke-Acts and Early Christian History* (Minneapolis: Augsburg, 1984) 13.

[56] E.g., Rudolf Bultmann, *Theology of the New Testament* (2 vols.; London: SCM, 1952-55) 1.37, 42-43, 58, 60-61: "*That the earliest Church regarded itself as the Congregation of the end of days*, is attested both by Paul and the synoptic tradition . . . [as well as by] the fact that Jesus' disciples after the Easter experiences in Galilee soon betook themselves to *Jerusalem* as the focus of the coming Reign of God. . . . The earliest Church presents itself as an eschatological sect within Judaism, distinguished . . . especially by the fact that it is conscious of being already the called and chosen Congregation of the end of days. . . . All that went before [now] appears in a new light – new since the *Easter faith in Jesus' resurrection* and founded upon this faith. . . . *The direction of the Church* was at first in the hands of 'the twelve' . . . as a symbol of the eschatological Congregation as the true Israel. [But] tradition requires continuity, i.e., *succession*, . . . [and] the idea of tradition and succession finds characteristic expression in the fact that *Jerusalem is regarded as the center of the whole Church* – and obviously is so regarded not merely in the consciousness of the Jerusalem Church. Paul and the author of Acts also bear witness to that fact" (emphasis his).

[57] E.g., E.A. Judge, *The Social Patterns of Christian Groups in the First Century* (London: Tyndale, 1960) 11, 12, 50, 54, 56, 57, 77: "The eschatological fervour that motivated the disciples was of course not unparalleled [at the time, though] . . . the original Christian group at Jerusalem . . . is [still] to be sharply marked off from other Palestinian religious movements. . . . The Christian preachers worked from the assumption that they had a universal obligation. . . . The literary form of the book of Acts suggests an apologetic intention along these lines. It begins by showing that the Pentecostal gift was designed to carry the testimony 'unto the uttermost part of the earth.' . . . The initial group at Jerusalem centred on the following of Jesus still resident in that city. . . . [As a result of the persecution of the Jerusalem church,] the many foreign converts had to be hurriedly evacuated. . . .

graphy,[60] experiential hermeneutics,[61] literary studies,[62] or

It was out of the action of these persons that the organized expansion of Christianity proceeded, and particularly its vigorous propagation among non-Jews. . . . The belief which originally marked [Christians] out from Israel [is] that Jesus is the Messiah. His Messiahship was vindicated by the resurrection, which in turn anticipated the imminent judgment. It is in terms of these two events, which were deemed to be . . . epoch-making, that the New Testament writers consistently evaluated their social relationships."

[58] E.g., Helmut Koester, *Introduction to the New Testament* (2 vols.; Hermeneia: Foundations and Facets; Philadelphia: Fortress; Berlin/New York: De Gruyter, 1982) 2:83, 84, 87: "The proclamation of Jesus did not result directly in the founding of Christian communities. . . . But even where the churches explicitly referred to Jesus' words and deeds, in the situation after Easter they appeared in a completely new light. . . . We are on much firmer ground with respect to the appearances of the risen Jesus and their effect. . . . The content and effect of the appearances were decisive. . . . The resurrection and appearances of Jesus are best explained as a catalyst which prompted reactions that resulted in the missionary activity and founding of the churches, [as well as] in the crystallization of the tradition about Jesus and his ministry. . . . The Christians in Jerusalem . . . were radically different . . . from other Jews in Jerusalem because of their enthusiastic consciousness of the possession of the spirit. . . . The overwhelming experience of the spirit's being poured out and its interpretation as an eschatological event must have persuaded these first Christians to organize themselves through preliminary structures . . . which corresponded to this eschatological experience."

[59] E.g., Elisabeth Schüssler Fiorenza, *In Memory of Her: A Feminist Theological Reconstruction of Christian Origins* (New York: Crossroad, 1983) 160, 162, 164-65, 184, 185: "The beginnings of the early Christian missionary movement are shrouded in historical darkness. . . . [Nevertheless,] it appears that very soon after the execution and resurrection of Jesus the community of so-called Hellenists gathered alongside the Aramaic-speaking community of Jerusalem. . . . Although Acts claims that the believers were 'one heart and one soul' in the Jerusalem church, a conflict between the so-called Hebrews and Hellenists [arose]. . . . Although no women are mentioned among the seven Hellenists appointed to devote themselves to the *diakonia* at table, . . . women [were nevertheless] involved in the original conflict which, according to Acts, . . . resulted in the expulsion from Jerusalem of the Hellenists, who then initiated the Christian missionary movement to the gentiles. . . . The experience of the power of the Spirit is basic for [the theological self-understanding] of the Christian missionary movement. . . . 'Equality' in the Spirit is summed up by the early Christian movement in the words of the prophet Joel [cf. Acts 2:17-18]."

[60] E.g., Martin Hengel, "Acts and the History of Earliest Christianity," in idem, *Earliest Christianity* (London: SCM, 1986) 35, 37, 41, 42: "Our particular interest [here] will be not so much in the gospels as in Luke's Acts of the Apostles and the course taken by the message about Jesus *after* his ministry, his death and the events of the resurrection which gave rise to the Christian community. . . . The earliest Christian faith created an eschatological (and at the same time religious and missionary) awareness which was a revolutionary new development in antiquity. . . . We owe our thorough knowledge of the origins of Christianity above all to the fact that

church history.[63] All of the studies that I have cited here,

Luke and similarly the authors of the other two synoptic gospels . . . were not simply preachers of an abstract message. . . . In their accounts of the activity and suffering of Jesus of Nazareth they were concerned above all to relate the story of God's eschatological revelation of himself. . . . Luke then took this narration further . . . [and] developed first beginnings. . . . The earliest Christian history writers narrated this account of the eschatological consummation as a unique event which, though now past, determined both present and future, and embraced both time and eternity" (emphasis his).

[61] E.g., Luke Timothy Johnson, *The Writings of the New Testament: An Interpretation* (Philadelphia: Fortress, 1986) 98, 101, 106: "Some sort of powerful experience generated the [early Christian] movement. . . . Christianity . . . begins with Jesus' followers experiencing Jesus after his death in an entirely new way. . . . The primitive Christian experience consisted in encountering the Other in the risen Jesus. *The resurrection faith is the birth of Christianity*. . . . The resurrection experience that gave birth to the Christian movement was the experience of the continuing presence of a personal, transcendent, and transforming power within the community. This understanding of the resurrection is given expression in . . . John 20:20-23, . . . [which] clearly states that the empowerment of the disciples, which enables them to carry on the mission of Jesus in the world, derives from a Holy Spirit, which comes directly from Jesus himself [cf. Luke 24:47-49]. . . . In Acts 2:1-4, Luke provides a narrative symbolization of this empowerment, on the day of Pentecost, . . . followed by the first proclamation of Jesus as risen Lord, in Peter's speech" (emphasis his).

[62] E.g., Aune, *New Testament in Its Literary Environment*, 11, 137, 138-39: "Christianity began as a Jewish religious reform movement launched by Jesus of Nazareth. . . . His followers believed that God had delivered him from death and exalted him to heaven and regarded him as the Messiah whom Judaism expected to appear in the last days. Christianity spread rapidly. . . . By ca. A.D. 50, Christianity was a religious movement needing definition, identity, and legitimation. . . . [Luke met all these needs, in part,] by demonstrating the Jewish origins of Christianity and by emphasizing the divine providence which was reflected in every aspect of the development and expansion of the early church. Luke-Acts [thus] provided historical definition and identity as well as theological legitimation for the author's conception of normative Christianity. . . . Luke was an eclectic Hellenistic Christian historian who narrated the early history of Christianity from its origins in Judaism with Jesus of Nazareth through its emergence as a relatively independent religious movement open to all ethnic groups. . . . His achievement is remarkable in view of the early date of his work (ca. A.D. 90) and the long period that elapsed before he found an imitator and continuator in Eusebius."

[63] E.g., Henry Chadwick, "The Early Christian Community," in John McManners, ed., *The Oxford Illustrated History of Christianity* (Oxford/New York: Oxford University Press, 1992) 21-22: "For the community of [Jesus'] disciples the crucifixion was not the end. . . . As an act of God, Easter is not accessible to the methods of historical investigation. The historian knows that something important occurred to transform the disciples from a huddle of frightened men [sic] into bold missionaries risking their lives for their faith. But resurrection is not resuscitation . . . but a mysterious 'going to God.' The apostolic community experienced his presence in their worship. . . . Faith that Jesus was God's anointed prophet and king (Messiah)

which collectively represent the range of critical disciplines devoted to investigating the history and literature of early Christianity, presuppose at the inauguration of the Christian era a dramatic event, a kerygmatic conviction, and a linear development, based primarily on the narrative construct of the Book of Acts. A comparison of the categories used in reconstructing the beginnings of Christianity indicates that its origins universally are regarded as "eschatological": set in motion by Jesus' death, necessitating the resurrection, which gave rise to the primitive church established in Jerusalem, that served as the center for the early Christian mission, addressed first to the Jews and then, finally, to the Gentiles.

This picture of Christian origins needs to be revised, for it takes for granted, as self-evident history, an acceptance of Luke-Acts as gospel truth. Even though scholars recognize that "the reports in the first chapters of the Acts of the Apostles about the early church in Jerusalem are dominated by legendary and idealizing tendencies," they still begin their discussion of "the earliest Christian communities" with "the early community in Jerusalem," arguing that "there is enough information to reconstruct an approximate picture" of the founding of the church in Jerusalem.[64] The problem with such a reconstruction, however, is not primarily historical. The fundamental issue is conceptual: How should we imagine the beginnings of Christianity? How should we undertake the critical task of describing the formative history of the Christian religion? Are we tacitly to assume that there was a common message of Christian proclamation that differed merely in its forms and applications? Are we really to presume that the origins of Christianity can be understood only on the basis of an entrenched frame of reference, constructed from texts of epic imagination, as dramatized in Acts and canonized by Eusebius?

The reason Christian origins have been conceived of "eschatologically" is that some dramatic event or moment apparently is believed to be essential to account for the uniqueness of the

was basic to self-definition for the first church. [But] the Christians did not initially think of themselves as separate from the Jewish people. . . . God's call was to the Jew first."

[64] So, e.g., Koester, *Introduction to the New Testament,* 2:86; cf. 2:199.

early Christian experience. This sentiment has been described, and given an incisive critique, by Burton L. Mack:

> "Some event, it is thought, or moment, or impulse, needs to be discovered as the source for the novelty Christianity introduced into the world. . . . The fundamental persuasion is that Christianity appeared unexpectedly in human history, that it was (is) at core a brand new vision of human existence, and that, since this is so, only a startling moment could account for its emergence. The code word serving as sign for the novelty that appeared is the term unique (meaning singular, incomparable, without analogue). For the originary event the word is transformation (rupture, breakthrough, inversion, reversal, eschatological). For the cognitive effect of this moment the language of paradox is preferred (irony, parable, enigma, the irrational). It is this startling moment that seems to have mesmerized the discipline [of New Testament scholarship] and determined the applications of its critical methods."[65]

The concerns of contemporary biblical scholarship, therefore, may be regarded as an elaboration of the myth of origins that Eusebius put forth in his *Church History*. Whereas Eusebius proclaimed that the Christian religion was "primitive, unique, and true" (*Hist. eccl.* 1.4.15), modern scholars endeavor to explain the origins of Christianity by appealing to the transcendent character of the death of Jesus and the Easter appearances of the risen Christ. The adjective "eschatological" is the term that is currently being employed almost exclusively in a theological sense, in a way that stands for the basic incomparability of Christianity. Rather than describing an actual historical situation in the life and thought of early Christian groups, the term "eschatological" has been "transformed into an indicator of absolute (ontological) uniqueness." In such a displaced usage, eschatology has come to be understood as "a locus of uniqueness": the "'unique' becomes an ontological rather than a taxonomic category; an assertion of a radical difference so absolute that it becomes 'Wholly Other,' and the act of comparison is perceived as both an impossibility and an impiety."[66]

Here we should recall the perceptive remarks of Dieter Georgi:

---

[65] Burton L. Mack, *A Myth of Innocence: Mark and Christian Origins* (Philadelphia: Fortress, 1988) 3-4.

[66] Smith, *Drudgery Divine*, 41, 38.

> "[Rudolf Bultmann] opposes what he calls the relativism of the history-of-religions school. [In this context one] need[s] to mention the term 'eschatological.' It works for Bultmann and for many New Testament scholars and systematic theologians ever since as a magic wand. Whereas for the history-of-religions school the term 'eschatological' described the foreignness of Jesus and of the early church – together with Jewish apocalypticism and other comparable ancient eschatologies – for Bultmann and many contemporary New Testament scholars and Christian theologians the term 'eschatological' stands for the novelty of Christianity, its incomparable superiority, the uniqueness of the victorious religion, deservedly victorious. Wherever a comparison is ventured, wherever analogies lift their head, wherever challenges are heard from other religious options but the canonical ones, the invocation of the 'eschatological' is made, and the demons, the shadows have to disappear. Historical criticism thus turns into exorcism."[67]

Accordingly, the language of the "eschatological," used to refer euphemistically to Jesus' death, resurrection, and the experience of the spirit, must be abandoned as the starting point of scholarly discourse about the beginnings of Christianity. Eschatological language does not express a hard-won category of critical scholarship, but is a self-evident, mystifying notion which serves to maintain a theological claim that "guarantees the uniqueness of early Christianity by locating its novelty beyond data and debate."[68]

We desperately need a critical review of the relationship of the conventional picture of Christian origins (traditionally accepted as authoritative history) to the myths of Christian origins that the biblical texts provide. Such a review is urgent: to continue to imagine the origins of Christianity the same way as Eusebius, governed by Luke's fiction of the genesis and growth of the church, is no longer constructive. If progress is to be made in reconstructing the formative history of Christianity, alternative explanations will have to be given, based on sophisticated theories, supported by detailed descriptions, not

---

[67] Dieter Georgi, "Rudolf Bultmann's *Theology of the New Testament* Revisited," in Edward C. Hobbs, ed., *Bultmann, Retrospect and Prospect: The Centenary Symposium at Wellesley* (HTS 35; Philadelphia: Fortress, 1985) 82.

[68] Mack, *Myth of Innocence*, 7-8 n. 3, adding: "By allowing the mystery of Easter and the appearances to mark the point from which the Spirit effected the new age of Christian experience and mission, everything else can be examined rigorously without threatening the notion of originary uniqueness."

restricted to alleged originating moments, and advanced for different academic ends.

IV

A single shift in perspective can launch a new beginning in early Christian studies, by replacing the age-old preoccupation with the dramatic quest for a singular genesis with a fresh, disciplined focus upon the social history and imaginative labor documented by the texts. Such a shift would not only afford scholars the opportunity to produce "thicker" descriptions[69] of the various movements that make up the Christian tradition. It would also enable them to introduce into the discussion other, "apocryphal" texts often rejected and long neglected by scholarship, from the rich archives of ancient Christian literature. But the focus of this initiative would be to understand, not the supposed generative experiences, but the social and intellectual occasions for imagining such beginnings. To investigate the reasons for constructing Christian myths, and to position early Christian texts and traditions at the intersection of complex literary and social histories, would be to explore the activities of late antique religious groups as human achievements of cultural significance appropriate for the times. In this respect, a reorientation of early Christian studies as a discipline cannot be accomplished by accumulating more data and then reducing it all to variations of habituated patterns of thought. No. "What is required" are theoretical advances that take seriously "the development of a [descriptive] discourse of 'difference,' a complex term" which, Jonathan Z. Smith has taught us, "invites negotiation, classification and comparison, and, at the same time, avoids too easy a discourse of the 'same.'"[70] For in the study of religion, as in any historical discipline, "the greatest impediment to scientific innovation is usually a conceptual lock, not a factual lack."[71]

---

[69] The term is adopted from Clifford Geertz, "Thick Description: Toward an Interpretive Theory of Culture," in idem, *The Interpretation of Cultures: Selected Essays* (New York: Basic Books, 1973) 3-30.

[70] Smith, *Drudgery Divine*, 42.

[71] Stephen Jay Gould, *Wonderful Life: The Burgess Shale and the Nature of History* (New York/London: Norton, 1989) 276. Smith (*Drudgery Divine*, vii, viii) describes the "urgent . . . task of rethinking" the comparative study of

If alternative origins for Christianity are to be reconstructed, we will have to conceive of a different way to describe the rationales of identifiable communities who documented their beginnings by appealing to Jesus, but who did not necessarily imagine his death (and resurrection) as the decisive moment in the founding of the Christian church. The *Gospel of Thomas* raises the critical issue of the historical construction of Christianity, for it is a document from the early period that has been either treated in isolation or simply ignored by most biblical scholars because its account of Christian beginnings does not square with the conventional picture gathered from the writings of the New Testament. The effects of subordinating the *Gospel of Thomas* to the canonical gospels are especially pernicious, in that *Thomas* is not taken seriously as a gospel worthy of study in its own right, but is reduced to the status of a textual variant in the history of the synoptic tradition. Whenever *Thomas* has been discussed, moreover, it invariably has been interpreted according to the prevailing model of Christian origins, even though it recognizes other factors at work in the social formation of its community. Accordingly, *Thomas* presents a direct challenge to the established construction of the formation of the church.

The *Gospel of Thomas* is a venerable document. Fragments of three different manuscripts of the Greek text were discovered among the Oxyrhynchus papyri (*P. Oxy.* 1, 654, 655) and published in 1897 and 1904.[72] In addition, a Coptic translation of the entire gospel was unearthed at Nag Hammadi in 1945, first published in a facsimile edition in 1956,[73] then in German in 1958,[74] English in 1959,[75] and now in a critical edition in

religion as "an area of scholarly inquiry, not unlike others within the human sciences, where progress is made not so much by the uncovering of new facts or documents as by looking again with new perspectives on familiar materials. For this reason, matters of methods and models ought to be central." On the centrality of theory to argumentation, see idem, "Connections," *JAAR* 58 (1990) 9-11.

[72] Bernard P. Grenfell and Arthur S. Hunt, eds., *LOGIA JESOU: Sayings of Our Lord* (New York: Frowde, 1897); idem, *New Sayings of Jesus and Fragment of a Lost Gospel from Oxyrhynchus* (London: Frowde, 1904).

[73] Pahor Labib, ed., *Coptic Gnostic Papyri in the Coptic Museum at Old Cairo*, vol. 1 (Cairo: Government Press, 1956). This initial publication of the photographic plates has been superseded by *The Facsimile Edition of the Nag Hammadi Codices: Codex II* (Leiden: Brill, 1974).

[74] Johannes Leipoldt, "Ein neues Evangelium? Das koptische Thomasevangelium übersetzt und besprochen," *ThLZ* 83 (1958) 481-96.

1989.[76] Although the text was discovered this century, the *Gospel of Thomas* was read widely in antiquity: the existence of "three different copies of the Greek text made at different times . . . in the third century"[77] is proof of the regard that early Christians accorded this gospel. Indeed, Eusebius himself seems to have known it, for he identifies a *Gospel of Thomas* by name in his list of writings rejected by the church (*Hist. eccl.* 3.25.6), and he appears to allude to a variant of *Gos.Thom.* 2, which is referred to as a "written oracle" allegedly used by the "Simonians" (*Hist. eccl.* 2.13.7).[78]

Whereas Eusebius's synthetic reconstruction of early Christianity is based on Luke's account of the eschatological drama of Jesus' saving mission, the *Gospel of Thomas* is acquainted with traditions that characterized Jesus' speech, destiny, and consequence differently from what became the gospel story. This means that any apparent references in *Thomas* to the traditional view of Christian origins will have to be assessed on their own terms, without recourse to a kerygmatic imagination, and independently of the dramatic events thought to be essential to the construction of Christian origins. Accordingly, let us look again at the prevailing view of the beginnings of Christianity in order to see what, if anything, *Thomas* has to say about those momentous occasions that scholars have assumed at the outset of the church: the indispensability of the cross and resurrection, and the inauguration of the Christian mission in Jerusalem. I shall discuss these briefly in reverse order.

---

[75] A. Guillaumont, H.-Ch. Puech, G. Quispel, W. Till, and Yassah ʿAbd al Masîḥ, eds., *The Gospel According to Thomas* (Leiden: Brill; New York: Harper & Brothers, 1959).

[76] Bentley Layton, ed., *Nag Hammadi Codex II,2-7 together with XIII,2*, Brit. Lib. Or.4926(1), and P. Oxy. 1, 654, 655* (2 vols.; NHS 20-21; Leiden: Brill, 1989) 1:37-128. For an introduction to the text with special attention to the history of scholarship, see Francis T. Fallon and Ron Cameron, "The Gospel of Thomas: A Forschungsbericht and Analysis," *ANRW* 2.25.6:4195-4251. An updated discussion can be found in Ron Cameron, "Thomas, Gospel of," *ABD* 6:535-40.

[77] Joseph A. Fitzmyer, "The Oxyrhynchus Logoi of Jesus and the Coptic Gospel According to Thomas," in idem, *Essays on the Semitic Background of the New Testament* (SBLSBS 5; Missoula, MT: Scholars Press, 1974) 362.

[78] See Grant, *Eusebius as Church Historian*, 137, who notes that "Eusebius speaks of the greater secrets of the Simonians and says that he who first hears of them will be astonished and 'according to a written oracle of theirs will marvel'" (τὸν πρῶτον ἐπακούσαντα ἐκπλαγήσεσθαι καὶ κατά τι παρ' αὐτοῖς λόγιον ἔγγραφον θαμβωθήσεσθαι, *Hist. eccl.* 2.13.7; cf. *Gos.Heb.* frg. 4).

First, the *Gospel of Thomas* is aware of instructions for the Jesus-movement, though it does not present them as imperatives for a Christian mission. A request for laborers for the harvest (saying 73//Q 10:2)[79] neither initiates missionary activity nor is related to the following directives about the appropriate behavior of community members when they are welcomed in houses of hospitality (saying 14.2//Q 10:8-9; cf. Mark 6:10; 1 Cor 10:27):

> "Jesus said to them, 'If you fast, you will bring sin upon yourselves; and if you pray, you will be condemned; and if you give alms, you will do harm to your spirits.'
> "And if you go into any land and walk through the countryside, should people receive you, eat whatever is set before you and attend to (ⲉⲣⲓⲑⲉⲣⲁⲡⲉⲩⲉ) the sick among them.'
> "For what goes into your mouth will not defile you; rather, what comes out of your mouth – that will defile you'" (*Gos.Thom.* 14).

Here, *Thomas* presents a critical assessment of traditional codes of religious etiquette (fasting, prayer, and almsgiving; cf. saying 6; Matt 6:1-8, 16-18), in which the social context of being entertained in another's house is used to reflect upon what ("whatever"), and with whom ("the sick"), one may eat. In marking the differences that define group membership, an "etiquette of cordial relations"[80] is elaborated in *Thomas* to introduce a contrast, and thus issue a challenge, to the clean/unclean conventions of early Judaism (cf. Mark 7:15, 18, 20).

Second, the *Gospel of Thomas* does not interpret Jesus' death by means of a theology of the cross or the resurrection, but advances a set of characterizations in which such a rationale was not necessary. Cognizant that he would pass away, Jesus' followers reflect upon the implications of his departure in terms of group leadership (saying 12.1):

> "The disciples said to Jesus, 'We are aware that you will pass away from us (ⲕⲛⲁⲃⲱⲕ ⲛⲧⲟⲟⲧⲛ). Who will be our leader?' Jesus said to them, 'No matter where you are, you are to go to James

[79] In keeping with current scholarly practice, I shall designate the chapters and verses of the Sayings Gospel Q according to their placement in Luke. Thus, Q 10:2 = that Q text which is found at Luke 10:2//Matt 9:37-38. See John S. Kloppenborg, ed., *Q Parallels: Synopsis, Critical Notes, and Concordance* (Foundations and Facets: Reference Series; Sonoma, CA: Polebridge, 1988).

[80] So Burton L. Mack, *The Lost Gospel: The Book of Q and Christian Origins* (San Francisco: HarperCollins, 1993) 129.

> the righteous, for whose sake heaven and earth came into being'" (*Gos.Thom.* 12).

The irony of the fact that, in other early Christian traditions, James was regarded as a witness to the resurrection, and thus, as a prominent figure of the Jerusalem church, should not go unnoticed.[81] This suggests that the *Gospel of Thomas* was familiar with other Christian groups and was distinguishing itself from them by means of leading questions broached by the "disciples." In this respect it is striking that *Thomas* addresses the question of Jesus' departure concretely in terms of discipleship rather than by notions of the possession of the spirit,[82] which other texts employed to give the origins of Christianity the protective aura of uniqueness. Nevertheless, in sayings gospels such as *Thomas,* Jesus' death is

> "not considered to be an insuperable [theological] obstacle, requiring a special moment of divine vindication. . . . Rather than invoking the apocalyptic metaphor of resurrection"[83]

to affirm that Jesus and his followers were justified by God, the *Gospel of Thomas* links Jesus' death conceptually to the lives of his followers, who bear their own crosses in imitation of Jesus' stance of endurance (saying 55//101.1//Q 14:26-27; cf. Mark 8:34-35):

> "Jesus said, 'Whoever does not show disregard for (ⲡⲉⲧⲁⲙⲉⲥⲧⲉ … ⲁⲛ) his father and his mother cannot be my disciple. And whoever does not show disregard for (ⲛϥⲙⲉⲥⲧⲉ) his brothers and his sisters and take up his cross like me (ⲛϥϥⲉⲓ ⲙⲡⲉϥⲥⲧⲁⲩⲣⲟⲥ ⲛⲧⲁϩⲉ) will not become worthy of me'" (*Gos.Thom.* 55).

So, then, there is no need to appeal to the crucified and risen Christ in order to imagine the origins of Christianity, for *Thomas* documents an alternate rationale sufficient to account for its beginnings. Methodologically, therefore, any claim to a single point of origination for Christianity, based on Eusebius,

---

[81] Cf. Gal 1:19; 2:9, 12; 1 Cor 15:7; Acts 12:17; 15:13; 21:18; *Gos.Heb.* frg. 7; *Ap.Jas.* 16.8-11; *1 Apoc.Jas.* 25.15; *2 Apoc.Jas.* 44.13-15; *Ep.Petri* 1.1; Eusebius *Hist. eccl.* 1.12.4-5; 2.1.2-5; 2.23.1-25; 3.7.8; 4.22.4; 7.19.1; cf. Josephus *Ant.* 20.9.1 § 200.

[82] Cf. John 7:39; 14:16-17, 26; 15:26; 16:13; 20:22; Acts 1:2, 5, 8; 2:4, 33; 5:32; 10:38, 44-45; 11:15-16.

[83] John S. Kloppenborg, "'Easter Faith' and the Sayings Gospel Q," *Semeia* 49 (1990) 92, 90.

Luke-Acts, or some other textual tradition, will have to be rejected. Were we to adopt another perspective, however, and investigate the ways in which early Christians expressed their social thought and experience through the reflective activity of mythmaking, a new beginning might be imagined for the study of early Christianity. Initially, the objective would be to concentrate on the particular forms of social formation among early Christian groups, and then to consider how ideologies and symbols were constructed and honed to rationalize and replicate the occasions for solidarity. To advocate such a proposal is not to replace one form of origination with another, equally "originary" moment, but to call for a different approach to the demanding task of describing the formative history of Christianity. The challenge is to understand mythmaking as a correlate to social formation.

Take *Thomas*, for example. In late antiquity, collecting the sayings of a sage became an authoritative vehicle for characterizing distinguished individuals, cultivating distinctive lifestyles, transmitting traditional cultures, exploring religious alternatives, and marking social differences.[84] The *Gospel of Thomas* is such a collection, fundamentally concerned with issues of social self-definition. As the guiding religious statement of autonomous scribal origins, *Thomas* took Jesus seriously as a teacher who spoke with authority. It celebrated his memory by preserving sayings in his name that sanctioned the formation of a distinctive community. Those sayings that assess the significance of baptism (*Gos.Thom.* 21.1-2, 22, 37),[85] table fellowship (*Gos.Thom.* 61.1-2, 64.2), and the codes of religious etiquette (*Gos.Thom.* 6, 14, 27, 53, 104) were constructed to address whether there were standards for admission into the community, and what conduct was proper to designate belonging in that community.

---

[84] See Mack, *Lost Gospel*, 194-201.

[85] See Jonathan Z. Smith, "The Garments of Shame," *HR* 5 (1965-66) 217-38, reprinted in idem, *Map is Not Territory: Studies in the History of Religions* (SJLA 23; Leiden: Brill, 1978) 1-23; Wayne A. Meeks, "The Image of the Androgyne: Some Uses of a Symbol in Earliest Christianity," *HR* 13 (1973-74) 165-208; Dennis Ronald MacDonald, *There Is No Male and Female: The Fate of a Dominical Saying in Paul and Gnosticism* (HDR 20; Philadelphia: Fortress, 1987). Against April D. de Conick and Jarl Fossum, "Stripped Before God: A New Interpretation of Logion 37 in the Gospel of Thomas," *VC* 45 (1991) 123-50.

What does all this mean for the founder-figure of the group? Ascribing of the *Gospel of Thomas* to Jesus, who is characterized as a sage with a distinguished reputation, presupposes that his counsel is endowed with special wisdom. By identifying him as the "living Jesus," moreover, the claim is made that his wisdom is invested with divine authority. Jesus' sayings are thus understood to be those of the voice of divine Wisdom manifesting herself. His authority neither resides in the mythology of the cross of Christ, nor is

> "grounded in an ['Easter'] event at the end of his life, but instead arise[s] out of the character of his words as words of, and ultimately guaranteed by, [the figure of Wisdom]."[86]

Accordingly, the *Gospel of Thomas* has not "de-eschatologized" the Jesus tradition,[87] but presents a wisdom paradigm as a mythic precedent for purposes of reflecting upon its social history. *Thomas* exhibits the typicalities characteristic of its genre as a sayings gospel. Questions of definition, identity, experimentation, and legitimation are alternately entertained and explored. Thus, the sayings offer their own account of the significance of Jesus and the Jesus-movement that is not authorized by an apocalyptic vision, established as a kerygmatic cult, or sustained as a missionary movement. This means that the *Gospel of Thomas* actually functions as a myth of origins, providing the rationale for an identifiable group that locates its position within the early Christian tradition as an independent Jesus-movement.

The *Gospel of Thomas* cannot be explained as a variation of the Christian myth constructed by Luke and canonized by Eusebius. Its challenge to the conventional view of Christian origins is therefore clear. Rather than resurrecting illusory origins or awaiting apocalyptic ends, we are invited to enter into a different world of imaginative discourse, in which an independent group of Jesus people invested its energies in

---

[86] Kloppenborg, "'Easter Faith' and the Sayings Gospel Q," 92.

[87] Against Michael Fieger, *Das Thomasevangelium: Einleitung, Kommentar und Systematik* (NTAbh NS 22; Münster: Aschendorff, 1991) 284-85, who uses the term *enteschatologisieren* to characterize the "parables of the kingdom" in *Gos.Thom.* 20, 57, 76, 96, 97, 98, 107, 109. See Ron Cameron, "Parable and Interpretation in the Gospel of Thomas," *Foundations and Facets Forum* 2/2 (1986) 3-39; idem, "The *Gospel of Thomas* and Christian Origins," in Birger A. Pearson, ed., *The Future of Early Christianity: Essays in Honor of Helmut Koester* (Minneapolis: Fortress, 1991) 389-92.

building an interesting, alternate social formation. *Thomas* challenges the habituated assumptions and patterns of privilege granted the writings of the New Testament. They have no claim to special historical status. With texts like the *Gospel of Thomas* finally coming into view, our construction of the beginnings of Christianity will now have to be revised.[88]

[88] An earlier draft of this paper was presented at Brandeis University. I am especially grateful to Peggy Hutaff, John Kloppenborg, Burton Mack, Chris Matthews, Merrill Miller, Dennis Smith, and Jonathan Z. Smith for providing me with helpful comments and critical suggestions.

ΛΟΓΟΣ ΑΓΩΝΙΣΤΙΚΟΣ: HIPPOLYTUS' COMMENTARY ON DANIEL

Metropolitan Demetrios Trakatellis
(Holy Cross Greek Orthodox School of Theology,
Brookline, Massachusetts)

1. Introduction

From around the year 204 CE comes a very interesting exegetical work. Written by Hippolytus of Rome, it constitutes one of the earliest, if not the earliest, commentaries on a biblical book composed by an ancient ecclesiastical author.[1] This is Hippolytus' *Commentary on Daniel*.[2]

We are in the advantageous position of possessing most of this ancient biblical commentary preserved in its original language, i.e., Greek, while its full text has been preserved in an Old Slavonic translation. The work is divided into four subdivisions or books (Λόγοι) under the following headings: a) "On Susanna and Daniel," b) "On the image which Nebuchadnezzar the King made," c) "On Nebuchadnezzar and on Daniel when he was cast into the den of lions," and d) "On the vision of the prophet Daniel." In effect, what we encounter under the four headings is a running commentary on the entire book of Daniel, commencing with Daniel 1 and ending with Daniel 12, including *Susanna* and the *Hymn of the Three Youths*, which were parts of Hippolytus' text.

---

[1] Johannes Quasten, in his *Patrology*, Vol. 2 (Utrecht: Spectrum, 1964) 171, notes about this work that, "composed about the year 204, it represents the earliest known exegetical treatise of the Christian Church that we possess." See Gustave Bardy and Maurice Lefèvre, *Hippolyte, Commentaire sur Daniel* (SC 14; Paris: Cerf, 1947) 10, where the suggested date of composition is 202-204 CE.

[2] Hippolytus' commentary on Daniel under the title *Τοῦ Ἁγίου Ἱππολύτου εἰς τὸν Δανιήλ*, has been published in the critical edition of G. Nathanael Bonwetsch, *Hippolyts Kommentar zum Buche Daniel* (GCS 1.1; Leipzig, 1897). The same text, with the addition of newly discovered fragments, has been published by G. Bardy and M. Lefèvre in the series Sources Chrétiennes (see note 1 above). In the present paper, I use the Bardy-Lefèvre edition of the text under the abbreviation Hippolytus *Daniel*, supplying in parentheses the page of this edition where the quoted passages can be found.

Hippolytus' *Commentary on Daniel* offers a kind of exegesis which has similarities to that which John Chrysostom, speaking two centuries later of some of his own exegesis, calls λόγος ἀγωνιστικός, i.e., debating word, agonistic speech.[3] In this instance, the term λόγος ἀγωνιστικός implies an attitude of ἀγών, competition and dispute in dealing with theological or religious issues encountered in a biblical text. It clearly means a full awareness of opponents who must be answered, contradicted and confuted. It also indicates an evangelistic mentality, an impetus for a positive proclamation of the Gospel which aims beyond the refutation of the opponent's ideas.

All of these characteristics seem to be present, in one way or another, in Hippolytus' exegesis of Daniel. More specifically, his *Commentary on Daniel* easily could be viewed as λόγος ἀγωνιστικός inasmuch as a) it deals with the book of Daniel which in itself is a text filled with conflicts, with battles related to faith, and with competitive religious ideas and practices; b) the exegesis it offers focuses on the agonistic character of faith, on the constant danger of persecution, and on the deadly challenge issued by hostile political, social or religious powers; and c) it takes the essential data which result from the exegesis of Daniel and consistently applies them to the current conditions of the Church, urging the believers to be vigilant, to fight and struggle for the faith, and to persevere in persecution.

As λόγος ἀγωνιστικός, Hippolytus' *Commentary on Daniel* becomes one of the earliest exegetical works of the ancient Christian literature that witnesses to the phenomena of evangelization, religious propagandas and conflicts of competitive theologies, and therefore it is worth studying. In the present paper I shall make an effort to highlight and study some of the most prominent features that show Hippolytus' exegesis of Daniel as λόγος ἀγωνιστικός. Such a study brings us close to issues with which Professor Dieter Georgi has been dealing ingeniously for years. Hence, this paper is appropriately dedicated to him.

---

[3] John Chrysostom in his *Exegesis on the Psalms* (*Ἑρμηνεῖαι εἰς τοὺς Ψαλμούς*, On Psalm 8, PG 55, 119), uses the term λόγος ἀγωνιστικός in order to indicate a fighting exegesis which deals with opposing views advanced by opponents, especially heretics, pagans, and Jews.

2. The Scriptural Basis

Hippolytus, as we know him from his polemical works such as the *Refutation of all Heresies* and *On Christ and on the Antichrist*, is fully aware of the imperative to depend upon a solid biblical basis for any serious religious ἀγών or theological debate. This is likewise the case with his *Commentary on Daniel*. Throughout his exegesis, Hippolytus is consistently and tirelessly declaring the absolute authority of the Scripture and its identity with the ultimate truth[4] while attempting to demonstrate that his arguments are based exclusively on the biblical text. In this instance I can enumerate a few characteristic examples which are indicative of Hippolytus' method of using and presenting the Scripture as an indispensable weapon in any faith-related ἀγών.

a) Hippolytus' commentary is inundated with biblical quotations: lengthy biblical pericopes or short passages constantly are interwoven with his own comments, while on the other hand brief scriptural phrases or terms are so fully and subtly integrated into his own sentences that only a specialist's eye can detect them. One could argue plausibly that the biblical texts cited verbatim by him cover more space than his own analysis of them.[5]

b) Hippolytus is not dealing with textual or literary problems related to the book of Daniel. He uses the prevailing Greek translation for Daniel[6] which is a Theodotion version, and begins with the story of Susanna which appears at the outset of that version. He makes, however, one observation of a textual nature, and this is polemical. He claims that the Jewish leaders eliminated the story of Susanna from the Bible because they were ashamed of the outrage perpetrated by the two Jewish elders of the story.[7]

---

[4] See, for instance, Hippolytus *Daniel* 1.29.1 (Bardy 122), 1.30.1 (ibid.), 2.28.6 (Bardy 170) 3.12.1-4 (idem 220-22), 4.1.2 (idem 260), 4.6.2 (idem 272), 4.22.1-2 (idem 300), 4.41.1 (idem 344).

[5] In a number of pages taken at random from Hippolytus' commentary, the distribution was three-fifths of biblical texts *verbatim* cited *versus* two-fifths of Hippolytus' own text.

[6] For the characteristics and the theological tendencies of this translation, see Sharon P. Jeansonne, *The Old Greek Translation of Daniel 7-12* (Washington: Catholic Biblical Association of America, 1988).

[7] Hippolytus *Daniel* 1.14.2 (Bardy 96).

c) He strongly insists on the need to pay the highest attention to the content and meaning of the biblical text. Even pious and devoted leaders of the Church, says Hippolytus, if they neglect to study the divine Scriptures intensely (ἐμπόνως)[8] and with an unerring and unshaken attention (προσέχειν ἀσφαλῶς),[9] may go astray and may lead others astray as well. He supports his claim with two concrete cases and adds:

> "These things happen to people who are uneducated and unintelligent, who do not pay serious attention to the Scriptures, but rather follow human traditions, and their own errors, and their own dreams and mythologies and silly words."[10]

One can easily detect here the polemical attitude of Hippolytus related to the tremendous importance of the dedicated study of the Scripture *versus* paying attention to "human traditions" and "mythologies."

d) Although the authority of the book of Daniel is undisputed because it is canonical, Hippolytus frequently offers comments about Daniel both as a person and as a prophet, perhaps with the intention of enhancing and emphasizing even more the authority of the book. Accordingly, Daniel is portrayed as a person of unmatched virtue, piety, and wisdom, proved to be a true prophet of God, and a man having the holy spirit of God.[11] It is not accidental, for instance, that in his exegetical comments on Dan 4:18-19 Hippolytus presents Daniel as being transformed almost into a heavenly being as he was about to interpret Nebuchadnezzar's dream ("he took upon himself the face of an angel," "he had a fiery face," "his eyes were shining like the flame of the fire," "sometimes he appeared like a human being whereas sometimes he showed

---

[8] Ibid. 4.18.2 (Bardy 296).

[9] Ibid. 4.19.1 (Bardy 298).

[10] Ibid. 4.20.1 (Bardy 298): Ταῦτα συμβαίνει τοῖς ἰδιώταις καὶ ἐλαφροῖς ἀνθρώποις, ὅσοι ταῖς μὲν γραφαῖς ἀκριβῶς οὐ προσέχουσιν, ταῖς δὲ ἀνθρωπίναις παραδόσεσιν καὶ ταῖς ἑαυτῶν πλάναις καὶ τοῖς ἑαυτῶν ἐνυπνίοις καὶ μυθολογίαις καὶ λόγοις γραώδεσι μᾶλλον πείθονται.

[11] Hippolytus *Daniel* 2.2.5 (Bardy 130), 2.6.9 (idem 136), 2.8.1-3 (idem 138-40), 3.1.1 (idem 194), 3.2.6 (idem 196), 3.7.5-7 (idem 210), 3.16.2 (idem 230), 4.11.1 (idem 282). Hippolytus did not need to use a hyperbolic language in order to establish Daniel's eminence and authority. As André LaCoque (*Daniel and His Time* [Columbia, SC: University of South Carolina Press, 1988] 182-96) has shown, the figure of Daniel is so complex and semantically rich that it offers itself as a model of more than one type of human perfection.

himself like an angel of God").[12] These kinds of exegetical comments subtly suggest Daniel's eminence as a prophet and as a person of God, and lend more weight to the authority and the veracity of his words, which in turn constitute Hippolytus' basis for nearly all of his arguments. A basis not merely presupposed and applied, but uncompromisingly advocated by Hippolytus as a condition *sine qua non* for any responsible theological debate.

3. The Jews, the Pagans, and the Heretics

Hippolytus' exegesis appears as λόγος ἀγωνιστικός whenever he makes references to the Jews, the pagans, and heretics as opponents. His main assertion in these instances is that the above-mentioned groups attack the Church and Christians whenever the opportunity arises. Hippolytus' relevant references and comments are always part of his interpretation of the text, and, although phrased in controlled language, they undoubtedly are expressions of a λόγος ἀγωνιστικός, of a combative mode of exegesis.

a) One encounters the first comments of this kind in Hippolytus' exegesis of the story of Susanna, with which he begins his *Commentary on Daniel.* His exegesis here has a strong allegorical tone, and it is through allegory that he is able to advance his ideas.[13] According to Hippolytus, Susanna is a prefiguration of the Church, Joakim her husband is a prefiguration of Christ, and the two elders who assaulted Susanna "are shown as a type (εἰς τύπον δείκνυνται) of the two peoples who plot against the Church, the one from the circumcision and the one from the Gentiles."[14] When the narrative speaks about the two evil elders who "parted from each other at mealtime" (Daniel, Susanna 13):

> "it metaphorically signifies that in matters of material food the Jews do not agree with the gentiles, but in matters of public spectacles (θεωρίαι) and in every mundane thing (παντί πράγματι

[12] Ibid. 3.7.5-7 (Bardy 210).

[13] It should be noted, however, that allegory is not the prevailing characteristic of Hippolytus' exegesis on Daniel. In his commentary, for instance, we do not encounter the degree and the type of allegorical exegesis found in the works of a strong allegorist like Origen.

[14] Hippolytus *Daniel* 1.14.5 (Bardy 96).

> κοσμικῷ) they go with them and join them (τούτοις συνερχόμενοι κοινωνοῦσιν)."[15]

Hippolytus goes even further and, by allegorically interpreting what the two elders did to Susanna, says that this is precisely what is happening now to the Church:

> "Whenever the two peoples (i.e., the Jews and the gentiles) agree to destroy some of the saints, they look for the appropriate day, and having entered the house of God, while all are praying and singing hymns to God, they take hold of some, drug and keep them, saying, 'come, agree with us and worship the gods or else we will testify against you.' And if they (i.e., the Christians) are unwilling, they (i.e., the Jews and the gentiles) bring them to the tribunal (βῆμα), accuse them of acting against the decree of Caesar, and they are sentenced to death."[16]

In the above instances Hippolytus does not leave out even details of the biblical narrative, if they can be applied allegorically in order to bolster his argument. Thus he takes the phrase from the text, "the two elders shouted against her (i.e., Susanna)," and adapts it allegorically to events of his own time:

> "The lawless (ἄνομοι) do not stop shouting against us and saying 'eliminate those (i.e., the Christians) from the earth, because they should not live.'" [17]

Hippolytus returns to the same negative characterization of the Jews and the Gentiles as lawless (ἄνομοι) in another passage related to Dan 7:13 which also suggests persecution:

> "All the prophets and the apostles witness him (i.e., Christ) but the lawless being disobedient blaspheme him and with contempt reject his words and oppress (καταπονοῦσιν) his servants by persecuting them (διώκοντες)."[18]

The language in all of the above cases is sharp and the exegesis is loaded with polemical overtones.

---

[15] Ibid. 1.15.5 (Bardy 98).

[16] Ibid. 1.20.2-3 (Bardy 108-10).

[17] The phrase used here, αἶρε ἐκ τῆς γῆς τοὺς τοιούτους (Hippolytus *Daniel* 1.22-23.3), is reminiscent of the phrase αἶρε τοὺς ἀθέους encountered in the *Martyrdom of Polycarp* (9.2). This might be an indication of Hippolytus' connection with Irenaeus, who probably had a copy of the *Martyrdom of Polycarp*.

[18] Hippolytus *Daniel* 4.12.1 (Bardy 284). The characterization of the Jews and the Gentiles as ἄνομοι (lawless), might have to do with their opposition to Christ, who according to Hippolytus wrote the Law on the tablets at Sinai (Hippolytus *Daniel* 3.14.7) and who was proclaimed in advance by the Law and the Prophets (ibid. 4.57.2-4).

b) For Hippolytus' fighting exegesis against the heretics, one could mention two characteristic examples. The first is encountered in his exegesis of Dan 3:26-27, where it is reported that the three youths who were thrown into the fiery furnace came out of it unharmed such that even their clothing and their sandals were not touched by the fire. Commenting on this incident, Hippolytus says:

> "Let the leaders of the heresies (αἱρεσιάρχαι) who deny their own resurrection, tell how they can claim that there is no resurrection of the flesh. Perishable clothing and sandals made from dead animals were not destroyed by the fire because they were wrapped around a holy body. The flesh then which is mortal but wrapped around a holy soul will not be sanctified with this soul and transposed to imperishability? If things which were by nature perishable (τὰ φύσει φθαρτὰ ὄντα) did not suffer corruption (φθορά), how come that the thing which was not by nature corruptible (i.e., the human flesh) but became dead through disobedience will not be resurrected after being vivified again by the power of God?"[19]

The heresiarchs here could be any religious teachers who deny the resurrection of the flesh.

The second characteristic example occurs in Hippolytus' exegesis of the *Hymn of the Three Youths*, which in his text was incorporated into the narrative immediately following Dan 3:22. Hippolytus emphasizes that the three youths in their hymn embrace the whole creation (πᾶσαν κτίσιν), showing that everything in heaven and on earth and under the earth is subjugated to God, who has created all through the Logos (τοῦ τὰ πάντα διὰ λόγου κτίσαντος). Consequently, no one could boast that any of the created entities (κτίσματα) is ungenerated (ἀγέννητον) or beginningless (ἄναρχον):

> "Let, therefore, the heresiarchs cease laying down doctrines, these heresiarchs who by naming powers and aeons and emanations (δυνάμεις καὶ αἰῶνας καὶ προβολάς) invent empty, absurd and fantastic stories (κενὰ τερατολογήματα), so that having easily deceived the people through strange words, [they] kill them and force them to worship the non-beings as beings."[20]

The leaders of the heretics mentioned in this instance are Gnostics, as becomes increasinly evident from the terminology

---

[19] Ibid. 2.28.4-5 (Bardy 170).
[20] Ibid. 2.30.5 (Bardy 176).

used. The unusual element here is the information that these heretics not only deceive but kill people. Is this a specimen of a hyperbolic polemical language or is it a report of a fact related to the likely involvement of the Gnostics in the persecution of the Christians? We do not know with certainty. One thing, however, is sure: the exegesis here is a λόγος ἀγωνιστικός, targeting very real opponents.

4. The State as Opponent

a) The polemical character of Hippolytus' exegesis is displayed fully in his dealing with the problem of the conflict between the state and believers in matters of religious faith and practice. This is not unexpected inasmuch as the central theme of the book of Daniel is precisely that conflict.[21] Hippolytus is not disputing the authority of the state in general, and he presupposes that the king, who is the embodiment of the power of the state, be it Nebuchadnezzar, Belshazzar or Darius, governs by the authorization, permission, or tolerance of the true king who is God. But, warns Hippolytus, when the king arrogantly elevates himself above human limits, and not only forgets God but demands that the people do things against God, then he cannot be obeyed and cannot expect to remain unpunished or to endure as a ruler. This precisely was the case with Nebuchadnezzar, argues Hippolytus in his exegesis of Dan 4, who, because he haughtily lifted himself up, received his due punishment from God. Thus he became an example for all human rulers and monarchs, so that they should not be presumptuous nor have a mindset which is above the human level, nor boast by lifting themselves up against God. The same thing happened to Antiochus Epiphanes, whom Hippolytus cites from 2 Macc 9:12 as uttering the confession, "It is right to be subject to God, and no mortal should think that he is equal to God,"[22] to Sennacherib and to Belshazzar.[23]

[21] Cf. Danna N. Fewell, *Circle of Sovereignty: Plotting Politics in the Book of Daniel* (Nashville,: Abingdon, 1991) 12: "The central political issue in Daniel is that of sovereignty. Who is sovereign in the human world? The question is, of course, also a theological one because the principal conflict in the book is between God and human monarchs over the very question: Who rules?"

[22] Hippolytus *Daniel* 3.4.4-6 (Bardy 200).

[23] Ibid. 3.17.6 (Bardy 234).

There is a spirit of confrontation and defiance discernible here vis-à-vis the sovereigns and the powers of the state. This attitude is expressed in stronger terms in other instances. In his exegesis on Dan 3:16, for instance, Hippolytus praises the three youths as model human beings who:

> "did not fear the mob of the satraps (ὄχλος σατραπῶν), nor did they lose courage on account of the words of the king."[24]

In another case, he urges believers not to pay attention to the human kings nor to flatter sovereigns since they too are mortals and move under the ruling authority of the One who created them. And he adds:

> "the glory of those who have ruling authority is similar to dry leaves, which having bloomed for a while immediately faded away."[25]

b) There are, of course, passages in Hippolytus' *Commentary on Daniel*, where his critique against the state authority becomes biting and his attitude overtly polemical. In dealing, for example, with Dan 2:14, he notes that Arioch the chief butcher[26] (or chief cook, ἀρχιμάγειρος) of the king was dispatched to kill Daniel and his friends together with the wise men of Babylon. Then he sarcastically adds:

> "As the butcher kills and butchers (ἀναιρεῖ καὶ μαγειρεύει) all the animals, the same way the rulers of the world kill the human beings butchering them as if they were unreasonable animals."[27]

Subsequently, in his interpretation of Dan 4, Hippolytus makes the observation that the wild beasts of Nebuchadnezzar's dream symbolically signify thc military forces which accompanied the king:

> "ready to fight and to destroy, and like the wild beasts ready to tear to pieces the human beings."[28]

---

[24] Ibid. 2.18.1 (Bardy 150).

[25] Ibid. 3.6.2-9 (Bardy 206-8).

[26] The Greek text of Daniel in this passage, uses the term ἀρχιμάγειρος, translated either as chief butcher or as chief cook. The Aramaic original uses the term rab-ṭabbāḥayyâ, which means "chief of the slaughterers," i.e., "high executioner," "chief of the bodyguards," or "chief of the police." See more in James Montgomery, *The Book of Daniel* (3rd ed.; Edinburgh: Clark, 1959) 155; Louis Hartman and Alexander DiLella, *The Book of Daniel* (Garden City: Doubleday, 1978) 139.

[27] Hippolytus *Daniel* 2.4.2 (Bardy 132).

[28] Ibid. 3.8.9 (Bardy 212-14).

Hippolytus returns to the same idea when he offers his exegesis on Dan 7:2-12, the pericope describing Daniel's vision of the four beasts. This passage, argues Hippolytus, is not about four wild beasts, but about the four kingdoms symbolized by them:

> "The beasts show in a type and in an image the kingdoms that rose up in this world like wild beasts destroying humanity."[29]

c) It is not without significance that Hippolytus includes in his sharp criticism the Roman state, which he regards as the fourth beast of the vision in Dan 7:2-12. Hippolytus does not mention the Roman emperor by name as previously was the case with the kings of the Babylonians, the Persians, and the Greeks. But he overtly states that the fourth beast is "the kingdom which is now in power" (ἡ νῦν ἐνεστῶσα βασιλεία), namely, "the kingdom of the Romans" (ἡ τῶν Ῥωμαίων βασιλεία).[30] Hippolytus has a particular explanation for the fact that the fourth wild beast of Daniel's vision bears no name, and this is the multi-national character of the Roman state.[31]

At this juncture, Hippolytus introduces a statement which presents an intriguing comparison between the nation of the faithful Christians (ἔθνος πιστῶν χριστιανῶν) created by Christ and the kingdom of the Romans. The comparison is based on the coincidence of the time of Christ's birth with the time of the census under Augustus Caesar:

> "Through the Apostles the Lord called all the nations and all the languages and made a nation of faithful Christians who hold in their hearts the new and dominical name. The kingdom that now rules 'by the activity of Satan' (2 Thess 2:9) has counter-imitated (ἀντεμιμήσατο) this fact, and similarly collecting from all nations the bravest, trains and prepares them for war, calling them Romans. This is why the first census occurred under Augustus when the Lord was born in Bethlehem, so that the men of this world being registered under the earthly king would

[29] Ibid. 4.2.1 (Bardy 262): ἐν τύπω καὶ εἰκόνι δείκνυσι τὰς ἐν τῷ κόσμῳ τούτῳ ἐπαναστάσας βασιλείας ὥσπερ θηρία διαφθείροντα τὴν ἀνθρωπότητα.

[30] Ibid. 4.8.1-2 (Bardy 274).

[31] Ibid. 4.8.7 (Bardy 276): "The wild beast that rules now is not one nation, but from all languages and from all races of people gathers to itself and prepares military power ready for war (παρασκευάζει δύναμιν εἰς παράταξιν πολέμου). They all are called Romans, but all are not from one country."

> be called Romans, whereas the ones who believe in the heavenly King would be called Christians, holding on their forehead the sign of the victory against death (τὸ τρόπαιον τό κατὰ τοῦ θανάτου ἐπὶ μετώπῳ βαστάζοντες)."[32]

Hippolytus' interpretation is indicative of tensions, hostility, and conditions of conflict and struggle: The Roman state, as we have seen, is identified with the fourth beast, an identification unmistakably negative; it rules by the activity of Satan, prepares people for war, and gathers them into a seemingly unified entity which actually is a counterfeit of the truly one nation of faithful Christians. Hippolytus flatly states that this fourth kingdom, the Roman state, will share the destiny of the three kingdoms which preceded it, i.e., it will be torn asunder, and like them it will be abolished and totally eliminated:[33] "Then the kingship will be handed over to the saints of the most high and they will keep it for ever and ever" (ἕως αἰῶνος τῶν αἰώνων).[34] Such harsh statements are perhaps justified by the text of Daniel as general statements, but when applied to the mighty Roman state, they reveal a fearless fighting attitude on the part of the exegete. Here again, Hippolytus' interpretation manifests itself as λόγος ἀγωνιστικός.

5. The Issue of Martyrdom

The story of the three youths thrown into the fiery furnace by King Nebuchadnezzar (Dan 3), a major narrative in the book of Daniel, provides Hippolytus with the opportunity to introduce distinctive martyrological motifs in his exegesis. The introduction of such motifs automatically endows his exegesis with the characteristics of a fighting speech, of a λόγος ἀγωνιστικός.

The story in itself is not a complete martyrological story inasmuch as the three youths did not die a martyr's death; in fact, they were not harmed at all. On the other hand, it is strongly martyrological because it presents a deadly conflict involving faith, and projects the three youths as superb models of a heroic and full witness to the true God and God's com-

[32] Ibid. 4.9.1-3 (Bardy 278).
[33] Ibid. 4.6.4 (Bardy 272), 4.10.2-3 (idem 280), 4.21.3 (idem 302).
[34] Ibid. 4.10.1-3 (Bardy 280).

mandments under conditions of persecution.

In this case Hippolytus' agonistic disposition is immediately discernible in the fact that he dedicates to the story of the three youths the major part of one of the four sections of his commentary (section or book 2). He appears as if he is captivated by the story to such a degree that he cannot let it go before he exhausts everything in it. Length of exposition, however, is not the most important indicator here. There are other features in this case which reveal Hippolytus' exegesis as an agonistic exegesis related to matters of persecution and martyrdom. The following represent some of the most characteristic.

a) First of all, Hippolytus makes the story of the three youths immediate and actual for his readers, as well as directly related to them, by giving it a strong christological interpretation. He does so by recognizing the pre-existent Christ in the person of the fourth figure who suddenly appeared with the three youths in the fiery furnace (Dan 3:24-25). Speaking in amazement about him, king Nebuchadnezzar describes him as "a son of the gods" (Dan 3:25). The Theodotion version of Daniel used by Hippolytus, does not have here "son of the gods" but rather "son of God" (καὶ ἡ ὅρασις αὐτοῦ ὁμοία υἱῷ θεοῦ). Hippolytus did not require additional evidence to declare that in this case one sees the son of God, the Logos, Christ. In a rhetorical fashion Hippolytus addresses the three youths with these revealing words:

> "Tell me, you the three youths,...who was the fourth person walking with you in the middle of the furnace and in one voice with you singing hymns to God? Describe to us his form and his beauty so that we also know him having seen him incarnate...Because it was the Logos who was with you and speaking through you..."[35]

Elsewhere, when interpreting Dan 3:25, he addresses Nebuchadnezzar in a similar fashion:

> "Tell me, Nebuchardnezzar, when have you seen the son of God so that you would confess this (i.e., the fourth man in the furnace) son of God? Who is the one, who cut you to the heart (ὁ τὴν καρδίαν σου κατανύξας), so that you would utter such words?...It was the hand of God, which was the Logos, that cut

[35] Hippolytus *Daniel* 2.30.1-3 (Bardy 176), 2.32.1-8 (idem 180-82).

> him [Nebuchadnezzar] to the heart so that recognizing him in the furnace he gave glory to him."[36]

b) Secondly, Hippolytus in his exegesis of the story of the three youths uses an impressive number of words and phrases related to athletic competition and to martyrological struggles. Thus, the three youths are called "athletes full of vitality" (ἔμψυχοι ἀθληταί), "good athletes" (καλοὶ ἀθληταί), "faithful martyrs" (πιστοί μάρτυρες). "They have remained faithful unto death" (ἔμειναν πιστοὶ ἄχρι θανάτου), "they have defeated the whole power of the Babylonians," "they did not let the mob of the Babylonians defeat their faith," "they have been fighting against the myriads of the unbelievers," "they were not afraid," "they were not cowards," "they did not let themselves be enslaved," and "they have shown that faith is something unsurpassed" (τὸ τῆς πίστεως ἀνυπέρβλητον).[37] Therefore, "Daniel admiring them as good athletes of the faith, crowned them as victors" (ὥς καλοὺς ἀθλητὰς τῇ πίστει ἐστεφάνωσεν).[38] This unmistakable athletic and martyrological vocabulary shows Hippolytus' exegesis as a agonistic exegesis.

c) Thirdly, Hippolytus hastens to make the three youths of Daniel's story a model for his contemporary Christians and for future believers everywhere.[39] He is eager to project through them the martyrological motif, and to make it strongly operative in the lives of the faithful. By projecting such a motif, he is promoting a spirit of resoluteness and combativeness within his community and among his readers. In order to enhance his effort, Hippolytus, in addition to his extensive presentation of the three youths as exemplary martyrs and athletes, brings into the discussion the example of the heroic seven brothers and their mother from 2 Macc 7:1ff.[40]

Having presented this second martyrological example,

[36] Ibid., 2.33.2-4 (Bardy, 182). It is interesting to note that in this case Hippolytus employs the appellation Logos for the son of God or theophanic agent who appeared in the furnace of fire in Dan 3. The fact that the Logos is related to the Old Testament theophanies presented by Hippolytus in 2.32.1-9, perhaps suggests a certain dependence on Justin Martyr.

[37] Ibid. 2.19.4-8 (Bardy 152-54), 2.18.1-3 (idem 150-52), 2.22.4-5 (idem 156-58).

[38] Ibid. 2.22.5 (Bardy 158).

[39] Ibid. 2.18.1 (Bardy 150-52): Ἰδέ, τρεῖς παῖδες ὑπόδειγμα πᾶσιν ἀνθρώποις πιστοῖς γενάμενοι.

[40] Ibid. 2.20.1-4 (Bardy 154-56).

Hippolytus turns to his readers and urges them "to study the martyrs" (τοὺς μάρτυρας μελετᾶν) because this is exactly what the spirit of the Father teaches them to do, exhorting them to defy death and to hasten towards the heavenly things. If someone is without the holy spirit,[41] argues Hippolytus, he becomes fearful and ridden by anxiety, he is scared and hides himself (φοβούμενος κρύβεται), he is afraid of an impermanent death (πρόσκαιρος θάνατος), and he crouches in fear of the sword because he is attached to the material and earthly things of this world.[42] The description seems to point to actual conditions of persecution and to imminent dangers. Hence, Hippolytus feels the need to intensify his language and to close his argument with two special sayings of Christ from Matt 10:38 and Luke 14:33, indicative of a spirit of struggle and sacrifice:

> "Therefore everyone who comes to the Logos must hear what the heavenly King and master commands: "he who does not take his cross and follow me is not worthy of me" and "whoever does not renounce all that he has cannot be my disciple."[43]

d) In his martyrologically-oriented exegesis of Dan 3, Hippolytus touches upon a specific question related to martyrdom, a question that appears to have been important for his readers: why God saved the ancient martyrs like the three youths and Daniel, whereas with the martyrs of the present time this does not happen.[44]

He answers the question by means of a lengthy argument in which he uses simple logic: If God saved all who were threatened with a martyr's death, who then would have become a real martyr? If, on the other hand, all the prospective martyrs died, then the unbelievers would have claimed that the God of martyrs is unable to rescue his faithful. In the case of Nebuchadnezzar, argues Hippolytus, Daniel and the three youths were saved so that the insolent king would recognize the power of God. In the case of Antiochus Epiphanes the seven heroic youths of 2 Macc 7 died so that they could become a model for believers.[45]

---

[41] The text at this point (Hippolytus *Daniel* 2.21.1-2) is damaged and has some *lacunae.*

[42] Hippolytus *Daniel* 2.21.1-2 (Bardy 156).

[43] Ibid. 2.21.3 (Bardy 156).

[44] Ibid. 2.35.1 (Bardy 184).

[45] Ibid. 2.35.1-9 (Bardy 184-86).

Hippolytus corroborates his thesis with various examples from the Old and New Testaments,[46] and insists that survival or destruction in a case of martyrdom should not weigh heavily on true Christians. He urges his readers:

> "Let us come to the example of Christ the King of glory, let us talk about the Son of God. Could not God save his Christ so that he would not be handed over to the Jews? Yes! He could. But he let him suffer, so that we may live through his death on the cross."[47]

So, the important point is:

> "to be firm and steadfast, not stammering in matters of faith (μήποτε τῇ πίστει βαμβαίνων), and when you receive a call to become a martyr promptly obey so that your faith will shine forth."[48]

Hippolytus' commentary on Dan 3 offers an exegesis which is agonistic *qua* martyrological with continuous interjections of admonitions and exhortations, and with obvious references to current conditions prevailing in his church. It is not accidental that the final part of his exegesis of Dan 3 is in essence an exhortatory speech, a veritable λόγος ἀγωνιστικός, culminating in a scene of an apparent victory celebration, whereby the faithful who are worthy of God receive the crown of imperishability like the blessed martyrs, singing together with them hymns to God.[49]

6. The Eschatological Front

The second part of the book of Daniel (chapters 7 to 12) contains abundant eschatological material. The visions of Daniel about the four beasts (Dan 7:1-28), about the ram and the he-goat (Dan 8:1-27), the prophecy about the seventy weeks (Dan 9:1-27), the vision of the last days (Dan 10:1-21), and the interpretation of the vision of history unfolding (11:1-12:13) give Hippolytus the opportunity to speak elaborately on eschatological issues. His exegesis in this instance, owing, of

---

[46] Ibid. 2.36.1-8 (Bardy 186-88).

[47] Ibid. 2.36.8 (Bardy 188).

[48] Ibid. 2.37.5 (Bardy 190).

[49] Ibid. 2.38.2-5 (Bardy 190-92):... ἵνα τὸν τῆς ἀφθαρσίας στέφανον καὶ ἡμεῖς λαβόντες ἅμα τοῖς μακαρίοις μάρτυσιν σὺν αὐτοῖς τὸν θεὸν ὑμνήσωμεν.

course, also to the nature of the Danielic text, is again marked by the agonistic spirit which we already have encountered in the preceding pages. From the copious amount of the pertinent materials, I have selected two major representative cases to be discussed briefly here.

a) The first is Hippolytus' interpretation of the vision of the four beasts (Dan 7:1-28). In this interpretation he offers two basic eschatological ideas which are very different from the ideas usually associated with this vision. According to the prevailing exegesis, the fourth beast of the vision symbolizes the Hellenistic Kingdom of the Seleucids, and the little horn of the same vision symbolizes king Antiochus IV Epiphanes (175-164 BCE), who persecuted the Jews.[50] Hippolytus, however, knows that such an identification of the beast and the little horn imposes limitations on the applicability of the vision to current eschatological questions that he and his church are facing. Therefore, he chooses to identify the fourth beast with the Roman empire, which is the fourth kingdom that succeeded the third, namely, the kingdom of the Greeks. The Romans are the now ruling kingdom (ἡ κρατοῦσα νῦν βασιλεία), "the beast presently being in place" or "the now ruling beast" (θηρίον ἀκμὴν ἐνεστώς, νῦν κρατοῦν θηρίον).[51] This interpretation is decisive because it contradicts the idea that the eschatological consummation already has begun and that the parousia is expected momentarily. In order for the end to come, Hippolytus argues, the time of the fourth beast must be completed (ὅταν ὁ χρόνος τοῦ θηρίου πληρωθῇ).[52] Only

> "when the now ruling iron beast will be divided into ten horns, and turbulences and disorders occur causing the kingdom to be broken into pieces, then will the end come upon them."[53]

It is obvious that in this interpretation Hippolytus places the Roman state under severe prophetic indictment and predicts its definitive downfall and annihilation as came to pass with

---

[50] See Hartman-DiLella 213-17; Montgomery 290-91; Robert Anderson, *Signs and Wonders: A Commentary on the Book of Daniel* (Grand Rapids: Eerdmans, 1984) 80-81; John J. Collins, *Daniel, with an Introduction to Apocalyptic Literature* (Grand Rapids: Eerdmans, 1984) 80-81.

[51] Hippolytus *Daniel* 4.5.1 (Bardy 270), 4.10.2 (idem 280), and 4.8.7 (idem 276).

[52] Ibid. 4.5.3 (Bardy 270).

[53] Ibid. 4.6.3-4 (Bardy 272).

each of the three preceding beasts-kingdoms. At the same time Hippolytus advances the idea that the eschatological end (συντέλεια) should not be expected momentarily since the Romans are still in power. Therefore, believers should not pay heed to the voices which try to convince them otherwise.

Hippolytus reinforces his exegesis with a second important eschatological idea-identification. He strongly suggests that the little horn of the vision in Dan 7:8 and 7:24-26 ought to be identified with the antichrist. Only when the Roman kingdom runs its time, and "all of a sudden the small horn which is the antichrist emerges...and justice is eliminated from the earth,"[54] only when the antichrist:

> "fights and persecutes the saints, then we should expect the epiphany of the Lord from heavens. Then the king of kings will be openly shown to all, and the judge of judges will be made known as coming with boldness and glory."[55]

Hippolytus' two characteristic interpretations of the fourth beast and the little horn of Dan 7 help him establish his ideas about the inescapable fate of the Roman state as the fourth kingdom,[56] and about the timing of the parousia.

The eschatological timing seems to have been a serious item of dispute for Hippolytus, as is evident from the energy he expends in addressing this issue and also from the two negative examples that he introduces into the discussion. These are the examples of two church leaders in Syria and in Pontus, presented by Hippolytus in full detail. The two leaders unleashed a very serious crisis among their people by preaching incorrect eschatological ideas and by persuading:

---

[54] Ibid. 4.5.3 (Bardy 270).

[55] In this passage (Hippolytus *Daniel* 4.24.7-8), Hippolytus speaking on the antichrist uses the phrase "about whom we spoke before" (περὶ οὗ ἔμπροσθεν λόγον ἐποιησάμεθα). The word "before" (ἔμπροσθεν), as Bardy-Lefèvre 311 observe, could be a reference to what Hippolytus had said in 4.5.3 or, more probably, to his special work *On Christ and on the Antichrist* (ed. H. Achelis [GCS 1.2; Leipzig, 1897]). Enrico Norelli (*Ippolito, L'Antichristo* [Florence: Nardini, 1987] 40), plausibly argues for the priority, by two years, of the *Antichrist* versus the *Commentary on Daniel*. This priority of the *Antichrist* is clearly implied in Hippolytus *Daniel* 4.5.1 (Bardy 272).

[56] As I noted earlier Hippolytus seems to have no doubt whatsoever about the downfall and dissolution of the Roman Empire, and even predicts it. See, e.g., Hippolytus *Daniel* 4.5.1-6 (Bardy 270), 4.6.4 (idem 272), 4.10.2-3 (idem 280), 4.21.3 (idem 302).

> "many of the brothers to go out into the wilderness with their wives and children in order to meet Christ" (εἰς συνάντησιν τῷ Χριστῷ).[57]

b) Hippolytus does not stop here. He knows that the people are anxious and curious, and that they are wondering when all these things will happen, when the antichrist will be revealed, and when the day of the appearance of the Lord will come. He replies that he truly does not know and that the Lord has hidden the day even from his disciples.[58] He then asks:

> "Why do you examine the times and search for the day, when the Savior has hidden it from us?... If the martyrs, the ones who shed their own blood for Christ, were requested to be patient and wait for a while (Rev 6:9-11), why cannot you too wait in patience, so that other people would be saved and the number of the called and the saints would be completed?"[59]

However, Hippolytus continues, in order not to leave anything unproven in this matter, and since we know that human beings are inquisitive and insatiable (λίχνοι), "we are pressed by the need and we are forced (ἀναγκαζόμενοι παρὰ βίαν) to say what ought not to be said" (ὅ μὴ ἔξεστιν εἰπεῖν).[60] With this expression of reluctance and discomfort, Hippolytus engages in an intensive, persistent, and lengthy presentation and analysis of passages from the Old and New Testaments in conjunction with his running exegesis of the Danielic text. He offers an expansive variety of data aiming at defining, as closely as possible, the *terminus ante quem* of the anticipated eschatological parousia. He marshals all of the numerical information provided by Daniel, engages in complicated time calculations, and presents various historical events, signs, and personages as characteristic and indispensable phenomena that must precede Christ's coming.[61] The final conclusion drawn by Hippolytus is that the time for the eschatological συντέλεια is not yet ripe, that the concrete pointers still are awaited, and that the only appropriate attitude is utter vigilance and alertness.

Hippolytus' exegesis of Daniel clearly reveals an author who

---

[57] Hippolytus *Daniel* 4.18.1-7 (Bardy 296-98) and 4.19.1-7 (idem 298-300).

[58] Ibid. 4.16.1-2 (Bardy 292).

[59] Ibid. 4.22.1-4 (Bardy 304-6).

[60] Ibid. 4.23.1 (Bardy 306): ἀναγκαζόμενοι ὅ μὴ ἔξεστιν εἰπεῖν παρὰ βίαν λέγομεν.

[61] Ibid. 4.23.1-4.60.3 (Bardy 306-86).

is fighting on the eschatological front and faces a variety of opposing ideas, but who is determined to protect and to promulgate what he considers to be the true biblical eschatology.

7. The Christocentric Aspect

Perhaps the strongest expression of Hippolytus' exegesis as λόγος ἀγωνιστικός is its christocentric focusing. At every step of his exegesis on Daniel, and regardless of the specific topic suggested by the pericope which he is interpreting, Hippolytus forcibly introduces Christ as a decisive hermeneutical key for the full and ultimate understanding of the text. This, however, does not mean that he ignores or suppresses the literary and historical facts contained in the text. Although he resorts to allegory in a number of instances, his exegesis follows the historical narrative even to the point that his commentary becomes a paraphrase of the text of Daniel. On the other hand, there is no doubt that he reads Daniel from a christocentric angle and that he regards such a reading not only as legitimate but also necessary for fully grasping the truth contained in the book of Daniel.

a) Hippolytus commences his christologically-oriented exegesis with the story of Susanna. He claims that the husband of Susanna, called Joakim, is no other than Joakim or Eliakim son of king Josiah, and that the offspring of Joakim and Susanna was king Jechonias, the one mentioned in Christ's genealogy in the Gospel of Matthew (Matt 1:12). As such, Susanna is directly involved in the ancestral line of Christ.[62]

She likewise is involved directly with Christ when, during her trial, she weeps and cries out to God for succor. According to Hippolytus:

> "through her tears she drew to her the Logos from heaven, the one who through tears would resurrect the dead Lazarus."[63]

---

[62] Hippolytus claims in this case (1.12.1-9) that Susanna was the daughter of Hilkiah, the high priest mentioned in 2 Kings 22:4, which means that she was from the tribe of Levi. Since her husband, Joakim, son of King Josiah, was from the tribe of Judah, their offspring and, ultimately, Christ would combine royal and priestly attributes. See more on this claim in Ludwig Bertsch, *Die Botshaft von Christus und unsere Erlösung bei Hippolyt von Rom* (Trier: Paulinus, 1966) 56-58.

[63] Hippolytus *Daniel* 1.24.6 (Bardy 116): διὰ γὰρ τῶν δακρύων ἐφείλκετο τὸν ἀπ' οὐρανῶν λόγον, τὸν μέλλοντα διὰ δακρύων ἐγείρειν τὸν Λάζαρον τεθνηκότα.

By interpreting the same story allegorically, then, Hippolytus sees the Church in the person of Susanna, Christ in the person of her husband, the Jews and the pagans in the persons of the two wicked elders, while Babylon symbolizes the world.[64] In so doing, he has transposed the story to the time and the realm of Christ and the Church.

b) Having shifted his attention to the narratives related to Nebuchadnezzar, Hippolytus continues to offer examples of a christologically-defined exegesis. Thus, the mysterious stone in Nebuchadnezzar's dream (Dan 2:34-35 and 2:44-45) is Christ and his kingdom:

> "We expect Christ coming from the heavens like a stone cut from a mountain (Dan 2:45), in order to remove the kingdoms of this world and to raise the heavenly kingdom of the saints, which will not ever perish (Dan 2:44), the very same Christ becoming mountain, and [the] city of the saints filling the whole earth (Dan 2:35). This is the reason why the blessed Daniel said that, after the end of the those days, the God of heaven will set up a kingdom which shall never be destroyed, nor shall its sovereignty be left to another people (Dan 2:44)."[65]

c) Another telling instance from the same cycle of narratives is the identification of the mysterious fourth person, appearing in the fiery furnace next to the three youths, with the Logos-Christ Son of God. As I pointed out earlier, Hippolytus speaks extensively about this identification;[66] in fact, he portrays Nebuchadnezzar himself as making the identification in the recognition-terminology which he utters (Dan 3:25). Hippolytus in this instance enlarges the cycle of the christological manifestations by declaring that the Son of God who appeared in the fiery furnace is the very same who defeated the Egyptians at the Red Sea, who rained fire and brimstone on Sodom, who holds the fire in his hands in Ezekiel's vision (Ezek 10:1ff.), and who is called by Isaiah "the Angel of the great will" (Μεγάλης βουλῆς ἄγγελος; LXX Isa 9:5).[67]

d) In the cycle of the narratives related to king Belshazzar,

---

[64] Ibid. 1.14.5-6 (Bardy 96).

[65] Ibid. 2.13.1-3 (Bardy 144-46).

[66] Ibid. 2.30.1-2.34.4 (Bardy 176-84).

[67] The idea of the Old Testament theophanies described here (Hippolytus *Daniel* 2.32.1-9) as theophanic appearances of the pre-existing Logos-Christ might have come to Hippolytus from Justin Martyr, whom Hippolytus knew (Hippolytus *Refutation of All Heresies* 8.16).

Hippolytus presents a new piece of christological exegesis in the incident of the mysteriously appearing hand which wrote on the wall (Dan 5:5 and 5:24-28). He claims that what is meant is the manifestation of the Logos, and that by the phrase "the fingers of a man's hand appeared" (Dan 5:5):

> "the Scripture means that the very same Logos ultimately will become incarnate (σωματοποιεῖσθαι) and take on human form (σχῆμα ἀνθρώπου ἀναλαμβάνειν), so that he would not be seen anymore as if in an image (ὡς δι' εἴδους) but in the flesh (σαρκικῶς), having become a human being and having associated himself with human beings."[68]

Hippolytus adds that, when the Scripture says "the hand wrote on the wall" (Dan 5:5), it signifies that it is the very same author who wrote the law of God on the tablets upon the mountain (i.e., Sinai).[69] Such an addition obviously is not accidental.

e) Hippolytus' christologically-oriented exegesis finds its fullest expression in his interpretation of the dreams and visions of Daniel in Dan 7:1-12:13. His focal point is, of course, the vision in Dan 7 about the son of man. Hippolytus urges all those who approach God with reverence and piety to recognize in the son of man (Dan 7:13) Christ, the:

> "incarnate God and man (ἔνσαρκος θεὸς καὶ ἄνθρωπος), the son of God and son of man coming from heaven to the world as judge, who will eliminate all the kingdoms of this world."[70] This "was the one who in the past manifested himself on the mountain, was shown by Moses to the people, was pre-announced by the prophets and was seen by the blessed Daniel as a man."[71]

Then, after describing the scene in Dan 7:2-10, Hippolytus continues:

> "No one should think that the kingdom given to him (i.e., to the son of man in Dan 7:13) by the Father is temporary. This is the reason why the prophet (i.e., Daniel) says, "his dominion is an everlasting dominion, which shall not pass away, and his kingdom is one that shall not be destroyed" (Dan 7:14). The Father, having then subjected everything in heaven and on earth and under the earth to his own son, has shown him through every-

68 Hippolytus *Daniel* 3.14.5-6 (Bardy 226).
69 Ibid. 3.14.7-9 (Bardy 226-28).
70 Ibid. 4.10.2 (Bardy 280).
71 Ibid. 4.11.1 (Bardy 282).

thing as a first-born in everything; a first-born from God, so that he would be demonstrated second after the Father[72] by being son of God; first-born before the angels, so that he would be lord also over the angels; first-born from a virgin so that he would be shown as refashioning in himself the first-created Adam; first-born also from the dead ones, so that he would become the beginning of our resurrection."[73]

Following such elaborate christological comments on Dan 7:13, Hippolytus presents a consistently christocentric exegesis of the remaining five chapters of Daniel. He deals very carefully with all of the data provided by the text, he examines and calculates the information related to chronological issues, he analyzes historical events and he evaluates the kings mentioned by Daniel. His concerted effort seems to be to connect the unfolding drama of prophetic-apocalyptic visions and history with Christ either in his first or in his second parousia. The exegesis offered is elaborate, complicated and intense, and Hippolytus is convinced that he presented everything possible to lead his readers to the genuine meaning of the visions of Daniel. Hence, as he reaches the end of his commentary, he poses a rhetorical question which reveals his confrontational attitude:

> "Why then, do you still hesitate, O man, about what was said, or how do you show disbelief to the words pronounced by the Lord, when his first parousia has already taken place, and the one who was standing on the water and was at that time seen by Daniel has now manifested himself to the world, and his passion has been declared to all?"[74]

8. Final Remarks

In his *Commentary on Daniel,* Hippolytus writes as a serious exegete who displays a noticeable respect and reverence for the biblical text which he is interpreting. He methodically proceeds in his exegesis from chapter to chapter throughout

---

[72] The terminology here, ἵνα δεύτερος μετὰ τὸν πατέρα υἱὸς θεοῦ ὢν ἀποδειχθῇ (Hippolytus *Daniel* 4.11.5) seems to imply a subordinationist Christology. The entire passage Hippolytus *Daniel* 4.11.1-5, however, is emphatic of Christ's absolute authority and power, and the word δεύτερος "second" probably aims at keeping in focus the hierarchical priority of the Father, a fact suggested by the very text of Dan 7:13-14.

[73] Hippolytus *Daniel* 4.11.4-5 (Bardy 282-84).

[74] Ibid. 4.58.2 (Bardy 380).

the book of Daniel, without achieving the critical, linguistic, and theological brilliance of his contemporary Origen, but, nonetheless, eager to abide within the realm of the truth revealed in this book which he considers fully and authoritatively prophetic. Hippolytus, to be sure, reads Daniel as a text addressed not only to the people of Daniel's time but to those of his own day, namely, his own community in Rome at the turn of the second and the beginning of the third centuries CE. He finds in Daniel messages of vital importance for his church as well as ideas directly applicable to current problems, difficulties, and afflictions. And he is attempting through the vehicle of his exegesis to evoke these ideas and messages, and to convey them to his readers. But this is not an easy task, for there are opponents of all kinds and there are opposing, or at least differing, views and standpoints militating against his interpretation. Hippolytus has to fight, therefore, in order to project and promulgate what he reads as authentic and God-inspired messages in Daniel. He must contend with hostile individuals, religious, ethnic, and socio-political entities, and against ideas espoused by these opponents or circulating independently. Under such circumstances, Hippolytus' exegesis naturally assumes polemical attributes and becomes a λόγος ἀγωνιστικός.

As we have seen, Hippolytus' *Commentary on Daniel* is a λόγος ἀγωνιστικός directed against those who do not heed the Scripture but rather "human traditions" and "mythologies," against Jews and pagans, especially when they seem to be involved in persecutions of loyal Christians, and, finally, against heretics, above all the Gnostics.

Hippolytus' fighting front extends itself chiefly along the lines of persecution and martyrdom, which plausibly were spheres of ongoing major confrontations. It also includes the domain of eschatology where competing ideas and popular misconceptions evidently had created a rather distressful and disruptive situation.

Hippolytus' exegesis as λόγος ἀγωνιστικός appears in its most forceful expression in his christocentric reading and interpretation of Daniel. In the body of this paper, I have examined several examples indicative of this kind of interpretation. What should be added here is that Hippolytus vividly presents Christ both as the powerful theophanic agent in the Old Testament and as the eschatological victor, ruler, judge, and monarch over everything visible and invisible, a sovereign whose kingdom will have no end.

Such an emphasis on the absolute authority, power, and sovereignty of Christ is not fortuitous. Hippolytus projects Christ's supreme and lasting sovereignty against the backdrop of the passing authority of the state, the Roman state in particular. As we have seen, an important target of Hippolytus' fighting exegesis is the Roman state. He predicts its demise and replacement by the heavenly kingdom of Christ. The projection of Christ as the ultimate and true king becomes a lethal blow to any kingdom or state – the Roman one included – which tends to forget its human and ephemeral nature, and assumes divine attributes.

Hippolytus' exegesis as λόγος ἀγωνιστικός is, of course, not a "neutral" or an "objective" exegesis. But, then, he did not live under circumstances fostering neutrality and encouraging objectivity. His exegesis, however, is particularly valuable precisely because it reflects these circumstances – because it is a λόγος ἀγωνιστικός.

BIBLIOGRAPHY OF DIETER GEORGI

Kelly Del Tredici and Angela Standhartinger

The abbreviations used here are those found in the Instructions for Contributors of the *Harvard Theological Review* 80:2 (1987) 243-60.

1956

1. "Blaise Pascal." *Die pädagogische Provinz* 10 (1956) 529-36.

1958

2. *Die Gegner des Paulus in 2. Kor. 2,14-7,4 und 10-13.* Dissertation. Heidelberg, 1958.
3. "Das Symbol und seine Bedeutung für evangelische Lehre und Unterweisung." *Die pädagogische Provinz* 12 (1958) 378-84.
4. "Ewiges Leben III A: Im Griechentum und Hellenismus." ^{3}RGG 2 (1958) 803-04.

1959

5. (with the Badische Sozietät) "Theologische Auseinandersetzung mit den Einwänden gegen die Thesen der Bruderschaften." In *Christusbekenntnis im Atomzeitalter?*, ed. Ernst Wolf, 109-38. Theologische Existenz heute NF 70; München: Kaiser, 1959.

1960

6. "Besprechung von Walter Schmithals: *Die Gnosis in Korinth.*" *VF* 9/10 (1960/62) 90-96.
7. "Leben-Jesu-Theologie." ^{3}*RGG* 4 (1960) 249-50.
8. "Macht II: Im Urchristentum." ^{3}*RGG* 4 (1960) 567.

1961/62

9. "*Die Geschichte der Kollekte des Paulus für Jerusalem.*" Habilitationsschrift. Heidelberg, 1961/62.

1963

10. "Das Christusverständnis des Neuen Testaments I." In *Wie denkt ihr über Christus? Tagungsbericht des 3. religionspädagogischen Lehrerkollegs in Tingleff (Dänemark) vom 30. September bis 8. Oktober 1963,*

ed. Lehrerkolleg der Kirchlichen Erziehungskammer für Berlin, 34-36. Tingleff (Dänemark), 1963.

11. "Das Christusverständnis des Neuen Testaments II (Exegese über Joh. 1,1-13)." In *Wie denkt ihr über Christus? Tagungsbericht des 3. religionspädagogischen Lehrerkollegs in Tingleff (Dänemark) vom 30. September bis 8. Oktober 1963*, ed. Lehrerkolleg der Kirchlichen Erziehungskammer für Berlin, 37-39. Tingleff (Dänemark), 1963.
12. "Das Entmythologisierungsproblem in der gegenwärtigen hermeneutischen Diskussion." In *Theologische Informationen für Naturwissenschaftler: Strömungen in der Theologie des 19. und 20. Jahrhundert*, ed. Evangelische Akademie in Hessen und Nassau, 19-39. Veröffentlichungen der Evangelischen Akademie in Hessen und Nassau 49; Frankfurt am Main, 1963.

1964

13. *Die Gegner des Paulus im 2. Korintherbrief: Studien zur religiösen Propaganda in der Spätantike.* WMANT 11; Neukirchen-Vluyn: Neukirchner Verlag, 1964. [English translation in 40.]
14. "Der vorpaulinische Hymnus Phil 2,6-11." In *Zeit und Geschichte: Dankesgabe an Rudolf Bultmann zum 80. Geburtstag*, eds. Erich Dinkler and Hartwig Thyen, 263-93. Tübingen: Mohr-Siebeck, 1964.
15. "Korrekturnachtrag zu Günther Bornkamm: Thomasakten." In *Neutestamentliche Apokryphen in deutscher Übersetzung II: Apostolisches, Apokalypsen und Verwandtes*, eds. Edgar Hennecke and Wilhelm Schneemelcher, 308. Tübingen: Mohr-Siebeck, 1964[3].

1965

16. *Die Geschichte der Kollekte des Paulus für Jerusalem. ThF* 38; Hamburg: Reich, 1965. [English translation in 52. Second German edition in 56.]

1966

17. "Formen religiöser Propaganda." In *Kontexte 3: Die Zeit Jesu*, ed. Hans Jürgen Schultz, 105-10. Stuttgart/Berlin: Kreuz, 1966. [English translation in 24.]
18. "Hoffnung auf einen Wundertäter." In *Alte Botschaft - Neue Wege: Wie erreicht die Kirche die Menschen von heute? Was verkündet die Kirche den Menschen von heute?*, ed. Hans-Joachim Girock, 109-16. Stuttgart: Quell, 1966.
19. "Günther Bornkamm." In *Tendenzen der Theologie im 20. Jahrhundert – eine Geschichte in Porträts*, ed. Hans Jürgen Schultz, 530-5. Stuttgart: Kreuz; Olten: Walter, 1966.

1967

20. "Der Kampf um die reine Lehre im Urchristentum als Auseinandersetzung um das rechte Verständnis der an Israel ergangenen Offenbarungen Gottes." In *Antijudaismus im Neuen Testament?*, eds. Willehad Paul Eckert, Nathan Peter Levinson, and Martin Stöhr, 82-94. Abhandlungen zum christlich-jüdischen Dialog 2; München: Kaiser, 1967.

1968

21. "Review of Joachim Jeremias: Rediscovering the Parables." *Action/Reaction* 1:3 Spring (1968) 14.
22. "Review of Neill Q. Hamilton: A Secular View of Jesus." *Action/Reaction* 2:1 Fall (1968) 4-5.

1971

23. (with John Strugnell) *Concordance to the Corpus Hermeticum Tractate One: The Poimandres.* Concordances to Patristic and Late Classical Texts: Preliminary Issue; Cambridge, Ma.: Boston Theological Institute, 1971.
24. "Forms of Religious Propaganda." In *Jesus in His Time*, ed. Hans Jürgen Schultz, 124-31. Philadelphia: Fortress, 1971. [English translation of 17.]
25. (with Peter Niederstein, Franz Peerlinck and Walter Schmithals) *Weiter aktuell, die Theologie Rudolf Bultmanns als Vermächtniss.* Evangelische Zeitstimmen 59/60; Hamburg: Reich, 1971.
26. "Bleibende Aufgaben, die uns Rudolf Bultmann stellt." In *Weiter aktuell, die Theologie Rudolf Bultmanns als Vermächtniss*, eds. Dieter Georgi, Peter Niederstein, Franz Peerlinck and Walter Schmithals, 65-76. Evangelische Zeitstimmen 59/60; Hamburg: Reich, 1971.

1972/1973

27. "The Records of Jesus in the Light of Ancient Accounts of Revered Men." *SBL Book of Seminar Papers* 2 (1972) 527-42. Published again, in *Protocol of the Fourth Colloquy of the Center for Hermeneutical Studies in Hellenistic and Modern Culture*, ed. Wilhelm Wuellner, 1-18. Berkeley: University of California Press, 1973.

1976

28. "Socioeconomic Reasons for the 'Divine Man' as a Propagandistic Pattern." In *Aspects of Religious Propaganda in Judaism and Early Christianity*, ed. Elisabeth Schüssler Fiorenza, 27-42. University of Notre Dame Center for the Study of Judaism and Christianity in Antiquity 2; Notre Dame: University of Notre Dame Press, 1976.

29. "First Letter to the Corinthians." *IDBSup* (1976) 180-3.
30. "Folly." *IDBSup* (1976) 340-1.
31. "Second Letter to the Corinthians." *IDBSup* (1976) 183-6.

1980

32. *Weisheit Salomos.* JSHRZ 3/4; Gütersloh: Gerd Mohn, 1980.
33. "Die Visionen vom himmlischen Jerusalem in Apk 21 und 22." In *Kirche: Festschrift für Günther Bornkamm zum 75. Geburtstag,* eds. Dieter Lührmann and Georg Strecker, 351-72. Tübingen: Mohr-Siebeck, 1980.

1984

34. "Das Wesen der Weisheit nach 'Weisheit Salomos.'" In *Religionstheorie und Politische Theologie 2: Gnosis und Politik,* ed. Jacob Taubes, 66-81. München/Paderborn/Wien/Zürich: Wilhelm Fink & Ferdinand Schöningh, 1984.
35. "Ergänzende Beobachtungen zum Thema Gnosis und Politik." In *Religionstheorie und Politische Theologie 2: Gnosis und Politik,* ed. Jacob Taubes, 90-91. München/Paderborn/Wien/Zürich: Wilhelm Fink & Ferdinand Schöningh, 1984.

1985

36. "Rudolf Bultmann's Theology of the New Testament Revisisted." In *Bultmann: Retrospect and Prospect: The Centenary Symposium at Wellesley,* ed. Edward C. Hobbs, 75-87. HTS 35; Philadelphia: Fortress, 1985.
37. "Das Unbehagen an dem Juden Paulus." In *Nicht Du trägst die Wurzel - die Wurzel trägt Dich: Hanna Wolff und die Frage nach einer christlichen Identität,* ed. Werner Licharz, 78-95. Arnoldshainer Texte 30; Frankfurt am Main: Haag & Herchen, 1985.
38. "Zu neuen Tendenzen gegenwärtiger Paulusforschung." *Der evangelische Erzieher* 37 (1985) 462-79.
39. "The Bombings of Dresden." *Harvard Magazine* March/April (1985) 56-64.

1986

40. *The Opponents of Paul in Second Corinthians.* Philadelphia: Fortress, 1986. [English translation of 13, but with an Epilogue.]
41. "Who Is the True Prophet?" In *Christians Among Jews and Gentiles: Essays in Honor of Krister Stendahl,* eds. George W.E. Nickelsburg and George W. MacRae, 100-26. Philadelphia: Fortress, 1986. Reprinted in *HTR* 79:1-3 (1986) 100-26.

1987

42. "Analyse des Liviusberichts über den Bakchanalienskandal." In *Unterwegs für die Volkskirche: Festschrift für Dieter Stoodt zum 60. Geburtstag*, eds. Wilhelm-Ludwig Federlin and Edmund Weber, 191-207. Frankfurt am Main/Bern/New York/Paris: Peter Lang, 1987.
43. "Demokratische Experimente englischer Flüchtlinge." In *Gott in Frankfurt?: Theologische Spuren in einer Metropole*, ed. Mathias Benad, 59-64. Frankfurt am Main: athenäum, 1987.
44. "Georg Wilhelm Friedrich Hegels Frankfurter Jahre (1797-1800)." In *Gott in Frankfurt?: Theologische Spuren in einer Metropole*, ed. Mathias Benad, 79-95. Frankfurt am Main: athenäum, 1987.
45. "Gott auf den Kopf stellen: Überlegungen zu Tendenz und Kontext des Theokratiegedankens in paulinischer Praxis und Theologie." In *Religionstheorie und Politische Theologie 3: Theokratie*, ed. Jacob Taubes, 148-205. München/Paderborn/Wien/Zürich: Wilhelm Fink & Ferdinand Schöningh, 1987. [English translation in 48.]

1988

46. "Frau Weisheit oder das Recht auf Freiheit als schöpferische Kraft." In *Verdrängte Vergangenheit, die uns bedrängt: Feministische Theologie in der Verantwortung für die Geschichte*, ed. Leonore Siegele-Wenschkewitz, 243-76. München: Kaiser, 1988.
47. "Dann werden die Steine schreien." In *Der Frankfurter Börneplatz: Zur Archäologie eines politischen Konflikts*, ed. Michael Best, 101-05. Frankfurt am Main: Fischer, 1988.

1990

48. *Theocracy in Paul's Praxis and Theology*. Minneapolis: Fortress, 1991. [English translation of 45, with a Preface.]
49. "Leben-Jesu-Theologie/Leben-Jesu-Forschung." *TRE* 20 (1990) 566-75.

1991

50. "Reflections of a New Testament Scholar on Plutarch's Tractates *De Alexandri Magni Fortuna aut Virtute*." In *The Future of Early Christianity: Essays in Honor of Helmut Koester*, eds. Birger A. Pearson, A. Thomas Kraabel, George W. E. Nickelsburg, Norman R. Peterson, 20-34. Minneapolis: Fortress, 1991.
51. "Auf dem Weg zu einer urbanen Theologie: Denkanstöße zur Funktion universitär verfaßter wissenschaftlicher Theologie in einer Metropole." In *Symposion: Protestantismus als integrative Kraft in der mulitikulturellen Gesellschaft?*, ed. Fachbereich Evangelische

[1] Exegetisch-homiletische Arbeitsgemeinschaft Heidelberg: Friedemann Merkel, Klaus Baltzer, Dieter Georgi.

Theologie der Johann Wolfgang Goethe-Universität Frankfurt. Frankfurt am Main, 1991.

1992

52. *Remembering The Poor: The History of Paul's Collection for Jerusalem.* Nashville: Abingdon, 1992. [English translation of 16, with a Preface, new Appendicies and an Afterword.]
53. "The Interest in Life of Jesus Theology as a Paradigm for the Social History of Biblical Criticism." *HTR* 85:1 (1992) 51-83.
54. "Verstehen als geschichtlicher Zugang: Geschichtliche Einordung und Beurteilung von Textzusammenhängen als Weg zum Bibelverständnis." In *Bis an die Enden der Erde: Ökumenische Erfahrungen mit der Bibel*, eds. Teresa Berger and Erich Geldbach, 132-44. Ökumene konkret; Neukirchen-Vluyn: Neukirchener Verlag, 1992.

1993

55. "Die Aristoteles- und Theophrastausgabe des Andronikus von Rhodus: Ein Beitrag zur Kanonsproblematik." In *Konsequente Traditionsgeschichte: Festschrift für Klaus Baltzer zum 65. Geburtstag*, eds. Rüdiger Bartelmus, Thomas Krüger, and Helmut Utzschneider, 45-69. OBO 126; Freiburg: Universitätsverlag; Göttingen: Vandenhoeck & Ruprecht, 1993.

1994

56. *Der Armen zu gedenken: Die Geschichte der Kollekte des Paulus für Jerusalem.* Neukirchen-Vluyn: Neukirchner Verlag, ^{2}1994. [Second edition of 16, with an Afterword and new Appendicies.]
57. (with Hans-Günther Heimbrock and Michael Moxter) *Religion und die Gestaltung der Zeit.* Kampen: Kok Pharos, 1994.
58. "Die Stunde des Evangeliums, Jesus und Caesar." In *Religion und die Gestaltung der Zeit*, eds. Dieter Georgi, Hans-Günther Heimbrock, and Michael Moxter, 52-68. Kampen: Kok Pharos, 1994.
59. "Das Problem des Martyriums bei Basilides: Vermeiden oder Verbergen?" In *Secrecy and Concealment in Ancient and Islamic History of Religion*, eds. Gedaliahu Stroumsa and Hans Gerhard Kippenberg. Supplement to *Numen* (forthcoming).
60. "Die Gnosis". *Religion heute* (forthcoming).

Sermons and Exegeses

The following are arranged according to the sequence of biblical books.

61. *Josh 24,1-2a; 13-25*[1], (9. Sonntag nach Trinitatis) Göttinger Predigtmeditationen (hereafter *GPM*) 20 (1965/66) 312-17.

---

[1] Exegetisch-homiletische Arbeitsgemeinschaft Heidelberg: Friedemann Merkel, Klaus Baltzer, Dieter Georgi.

62. *Isa 5,1-7*[1], (Buß und Bettag) *GPM* 18 (1963/64) 391-95.
63. *Isa 38,9-13 (14-16)17-20*[2], (12. Sonntag nach Trinitatis) *GPM* 17 (1962/63) 292-95.
64. *Isa 49,7-18*[1], (2. Advent) *GPM* 21 (1966/67) 23-27.
65. *Isa 52,13-53,12*[1], (Karfreitag) *GPM* 16 (1961/62) 154-59.
66. *Ezek 18,1-4; 21-24; 30-32*[1], (3. Sonntag nach Trinitatis) *GPM* 18 (1963/64) 233-38.
67. *Matt 10,16-20(22)*[3], (1. Sonntag nach Trinitatis) *GPM* 29 (1974/75) 290-97.
68. *Matt 13,10-17*[1], (Sexagesimae) *GPM* 17 (1962/63) 110-12.
69. *Matt 13,44-46,* (9. Sonntag nach Trinitatis). In *Gottesdienstpraxis*: 5. Perikopenreihe vol. 4, ed. Horst Nitschke, 119-22. Gütersloh: Gerd Mohn, 1988.
70. *Matt 24,1-14*[1], (2. Advent) *GPM* 19 (1964/65) 10-14.
71. *Luke 9,10-17,* (7. Sonntag nach Trinitatis). In *Gottesdienstpraxis*: 5. Perikopenreihe vol. 4, ed. Horst Nitschke, 115-17. Gütersloh: Gerd Mohn, 1988.
72. *Luke 10,25-37*[1], (13. Sonntag nach Trinitatis) *GPM* 15 (1960/61) 245-48.
73. *Luke 11,5-13*[2], (Rogate) *GPM* 17 (1962/63) 201-06.
74. *Luke 13,1-9*[1], (Buß und Bettag) *GPM* 15 (1960/61) 320-24.
75. *Luke 17,5-6,* (15. Sonntag nach Trinitatis). In *Gottesdienstpraxis*: 5. Perikopenreihe vol. 4, ed. Horst Nitschke, ed., 135-6. Gütersloh: Gerd Mohn, 1988.
76. *John 3,16-21*[1], (Pfingstmontag) *GPM* 15 (1960/61) 172-77.
77. *Acts 14,8-18*[1], (Erntedankfest) *GPM* 14 (1959/60) 281-85.
78. *Rom 7,14-25a,* (22. Sonntag nach Trinitatis) In *Gottesdienstpraxis*: 4. Perikopenreihe vol. 4, ed. Horst Nitschke, 137-40. Gütersloh: Gerd Mohn, 1987.
79. *Rom 9,1-5.31-10,4,* (10. Sonntag nach Trinitatis) ibid., 110-13.
80. *Rom 15,4-12,* (3. Advent) ibid., 11-13.
81. *2 Cor 5,14-21*[2], (Karfreitag) *GPM* 18 (1963/64) 143-50.
82. *Gal 4,1-7,* (Sonntag nach Weinachten) *GPM* 28 (1973/74) 54-62.
83. *Phil 2,5-11,* (Palmarum). In *Heidelberger Predigten: Neue Folge,* ed. Herbert Krimm, 41-45. Göttingen: Vandenhoek & Ruprecht, 1962/63.
84. *Heb 4,12-13,* (Sexagesimä) *GPM* 46 (1991/92) 126-132.
85. *Heb 11,(2.32b-38)39-40; 12,1-3*[4], (Palmarum) *GPM* 20 (1965/66) 158-66.
86. *Heb 12,4-11*[1], (21. Sonntag nach Trinitatis) *GPM* 20 (1965/66) 399-403.
87. *Eph 4,22-32*[1], (19. Sonntag nach Trinitatis) *GPM* 16 (1961/62) 307-14.
88. *Eph 5,9-14*[1], (6. Sonntag nach Trinitatis) *GPM* 14 (1959/60) 233-36.

[2] Exegetisch-homiletische Arbeitsgemeinschaft Heidelberg: Friedemann Merkel and Dieter Georgi.
[3] Dieter Georgi and Harvey Cox.
[4] Exegetisch-homiletische Arbeitsgemeinschaft Heidelberg: Dieter Georgi, Egon Brandenburger, Friedemann Merkel.

89. *Eph 5,15-21,* (18. Sonntag nach Trinitatis) *GPM* 38 (1983/84) 393-98.
90. *Col 3,12-17*[1], *GPM* 14 (1959/60) 167.
91. *1 Pet 3,8-15a (15b-17)*[1], (6. Sonntag nach Trinitatis) *GPM* 16 (1961/62) 244-49.
92. *1 Pet 3,18-22, EvTh* 31 (1971) 187-92.
93. *Rev 21,1-5(8)*[3], (Jubilate) *GPM* 26 (1971/72) 201-12.

INDEX

OLD TESTAMENT:

SUPPLEMENTS TO NOVUM TESTAMENTUM

ISSN 0167-9732

2. STROBEL, A. *Untersuchungen zum eschatologischen Verzögerungsproblem auf Grund der spätjüdische-urchristlichen Geschichte von Habakuk 2,2 ff.* 1961. ISBN 90 04 01582 5
6. *Neotestamentica et Patristica.* Eine Freundesgabe Herrn Professor Dr. Oscar Cullmann zu seinem 60. Geburtstag überreicht. 1962. ISBN 90 04 01586 8
8. DE MARCO, A.A. *The Tomb of Saint Peter.* A Representative and Annotated Bibliography of the Excavations. 1964. ISBN 90 04 01588 4
10. BORGEN, P. *Bread from Heaven.* An Exegetical Study of the Concept of Manna in the Gospel of John and the Writings of Philo. Photomech. Reprint of the first (1965) edition. 1981. ISBN 90 04 06419 2
13. MOORE, A.L. *The Parousia in the New Testament.* 1966. ISBN 90 04 01593 0
15. QUISPEL, G. *Makarius, das Thomasevangelium und das Lied von der Perle.* 1967. ISBN 90 04 01595 7
16. PFITZNER, V.C. *Paul and the Agon Motif.* 1967. ISBN 90 04 01596 5
17. BELLINZONI, A. *The Sayings of Jesus in the Writings of Justin Martyr.* 1967. ISBN 90 04 01597 3
18. GUNDRY, R.H. *The Use of the Old Testament in St. Matthew's Gospel.* With Special Reference to the Messianistic Hope. Reprint of the first (1967) edition. 1975. ISBN 90 04 04278 4
19. SEVENSTER, J.N. *Do You Know Greek?* How Much Greek Could the first Jewish Christians Have Known? 1968. ISBN 90 04 03090 5
20. BUCHANAN, G.W. *The Consequences of the Covenant.* 1970. ISBN 90 04 01600 7
21. KLIJN, A.F.J. *A Survey of the Researches into the Western Text of the Gospels and Acts.* Part 2: 1949-1969. 1969. ISBN 90 04 01601 5
22. GABOURY, A. *La Stucture des Évangiles synoptiques.* La structure-type à l'origine des synoptiques. 1970. ISBN 90 04 01602 3
23. GASTON, L. *No Stone on Another.* Studies in the Significance of the Fall of Jerusalem in the Synoptic Gospels. 1970. ISBN 90 04 01603 1
24. *Studies in John.* Presented to Professor Dr. J.N. Sevenster on the Occasion of His Seventieth Birthday. 1970. ISBN 90 04 03091 3
25. STORY, C.I.K. *The Nature of Truth in the 'Gospel of Truth', and in the Writings of Justin Martyr.* A Study of the Pattern of Orthodoxy in the Middle of the Second Christian Century. 1970. ISBN 90 04 01605 8
26. GIBBS, J.G. *Creation and Redemption.* A Study in Pauline Theology. 1971. ISBN 90 04 01606 6
27. MUSSIES, G. *The Morphology of Koine Greek As Used in the Apocalypse of St. John.* A Study in Bilingualism. 1971. ISBN 90 04 02656 8
28. AUNE, D.E. *The Cultic Setting of Realized Eschatology in Early Christianity.* 1972. ISBN 90 04 03341 6
29. UNNIK, W.C. VAN. *Sparsa Collecta.* The Collected Essays of W.C. van Unnik Part 1. Evangelia, Paulina, Acta. 1973. ISBN 90 04 03660 1
30. UNNIK, W.C. VAN. *Sparsa Collecta.* The Collected Essays of W.C. van Unnik Part 2. I Peter, Canon, Corpus Hellenisticum, Generalia. 1980. ISBN 90 04 06261 0
31. UNNIK, W.C. VAN. *Sparsa Collecta.* The Collected Essays of W.C. van Unnik Part 3. Patristica, Gnostica, Liturgica. 1983. ISBN 90 04 06262 9

33. AUNE D.E. (ed.) *Studies in New Testament and Early Christian Literature.* Essays in Honor of Allen P. Wikgren. 1972. ISBN 90 04 03504 4
34. HAGNER, D.A. *The Use of the Old and New Testaments in Clement of Rome.* 1973. ISBN 90 04 03636 9
35. GUNTHER, J.J. *St. Paul's Opponents and Their Background.* A Study of Apocalyptic and Jewish Sectarian Teachings. 1973. ISBN 90 04 03738 1
36. KLIJN, A.F.J. & G.J. REININK (eds.) *Patristic Evidence for Jewish-Christian Sects.* 1973. ISBN 90 04 03763 2
37. REILING, J. *Hermas and Christian Prophecy.* A Study of The Eleventh Mandate. 1973. ISBN 90 04 03771 3
38. DONFRIED, K.P. *The Setting of Second Clement in Early Christianity.* 1974. ISBN 90 04 03895 7
39. ROON, A. VAN. *The Authenticity of Ephesians.* 1974. ISBN 90 04 03971 6
40. KEMMLER, D.W. *Faith and Human Reason.* A Study of Paul's Method of Preaching as Illustrated by 1-2 Thessalonians and Acts 17, 2-4. 1975. ISBN 90 04 04209 1
42. PANCARO, S. *The Law in the Fourth Gospel.* The Torah and the Gospel, Moses and Jesus, Judaism and Christianity According to John. 1975. ISBN 90 04 04309 8
43. CLAVIER, H. *Les variétés de la pensée biblique et le problème de son unité.* Esquisse d'une théologie de la Bible sur les textes originaux et dans leur contexte historique. 1976. ISBN 90 04 04465 5
44. ELLIOTT, J.K.E. (ed.) *Studies in New Testament Language and Text.* Essays in Honour of George D. Kilpatrick on the Occasion of His Sixty-fifth Birthday. 1976. ISBN 90 04 04386 1
45. PANAGOPOULOS, J. (ed.) *Prophetic Vocation in the New Testament and Today.* 1977. ISBN 90 04 04923 1
46. KLIJN, A.F.J. *Seth in Jewish, Christian and Gnostic Literature.* 1977. ISBN 90 04 05245 3
47. BAARDA, T., A.F.J. KLIJN & W.C. VAN UNNIK (eds.) *Miscellanea Neotestamentica.* I. Studia ad Novum Testamentum Praesertim Pertinentia a Sociis Sodalicii Batavi c.n. Studiosorum Novi Testamenti Conventus Anno MCMLXXVI Quintum Lustrum Feliciter Complentis Suscepta. 1978. ISBN 90 04 05685 8
48. BAARDA, T. A.F.J. KLIJN & W.C. VAN UNNIK (eds.) *Miscellanea Neotestamentica.* II. 1978. ISBN 90 04 05686 6
49. O'BRIEN, P.T. *Introductory Thanksgivings in the Letters of Paul.* 1977. ISBN 90 04 05265 8
50. BOUSSET, D.W. *Religionsgeschichtliche Studien.* Aufsätze zur Religionsgeschichte des hellenistischen Zeitalters. Hrsg. von A.F. Verheule. 1979. ISBN 90 04 05845 1
51. COOK, M.J. *Mark's Treatment of the Jewish Leaders.* 1978. ISBN 90 04 05785 4
52. GARLAND, D.E. *The Intention of Matthew 23.* 1979. ISBN 90 04 05912 1
53. MOXNES, H. *Theology in Conflict.* Studies in Paul's Understanding of God in Romans. 1980. ISBN 90 04 06140 1
55. MENKEN, M.J.J. *Numerical Literary Techniques in John.* The Fourth Evangelist's Use of Numbers of Words and Syllables. 1985. ISBN 90 04 07427 9
56. SKARSAUNE, O. *The Proof From Prophecy.* A Study in Justin Martyr's Proof-Text Tradition: Text-type, Provenance, Theological Profile. 1987. ISBN 90 04 07468 6
59. WILKINS, M.J. *The Concept of Disciple in Matthew's Gospel, as Reflected in the Use of the Term 'Mathetes'.* 1988. ISBN 90 04 08689 7
60. MILLER, E.L. *Salvation-History in the Prologue of John.* The Significance of John 1: 3-4. 1989. ISBN 90 04 08692 7
61. THIELMAN, F. *From Plight to Solution.* A Jewish Framework for Understanding Paul's View of the Law in Galatians and Romans. 1989. ISBN 90 04 09176 9

64. STERLING, G.E. *Historiography and Self-Definition.* Josephos, Luke-Acts and Apologetic Historiography. 1992. ISBN 90 04 09501 2
65. BOTHA, J.E. *Jesus and the Samaritan Woman.* A Speech Act Reading of John 4:1-42. 1991. ISBN 90 04 09505 5
66. KUCK, D.W. *Judgment and Community Conflict.* Paul's Use of Apologetic Judgment Language in 1 Corinthians 3:5-4:5. 1992. ISBN 90 04 09510 1
67. SCHNEIDER, G. *Jesusüberlieferung und Christologie.* Neutestamentliche Aufsätze 1970-1990. 1992. ISBN 90 04 09555 1
68. SEIFRID, M.A. *Justification by Faith.* The Origin and Development of a Central Pauline Theme. 1992. ISBN 90 04 09521 7
69. NEWMAN, C.C. *Paul's Glory-Christology.* Tradition and Rhetoric. 1992. ISBN 90 04 09463 6
70. IRELAND, D.J. *Stewardship and the Kingdom of God.* An Historical, Exegetical, and Contextual Study of the Parable of the Unjust Steward in Luke 16: 1-13. 1992. ISBN 90 04 09600 0
71. ELLIOTT, J.K. *The Language and Style of the Gospel of Mark.* An Edition of C.H. Turner's "Notes on Marcan Usage" together with other comparable studies. 1993. ISBN 90 04 09767 8
72. CHILTON, B. *A Feast of Meanings.* Eucharistic Theologies from Jesus through Johannine Circles. 1994. ISBN 90 04 09949 2
73. GUTHRIE, G.H. *The Structure of Hebrews.* A Text-Linguistic Analysis. 1994. ISBN 90 04 09866 6
74. BORMANN, L., K. DEL TREDICI & A. STANDHARTINGER (eds.) *Religious Propaganda and Missionary Competition in the New Testament World.* Essays Honoring Dieter Georgi. 1994. ISBN 90 04 10049 0